NOVELL'S

GroupWise™ 5 Administrator's Guide

NOVELL'S

GroupWise™ 5 Administrator's Guide

SHAWN B. ROGERS AND RICHARD H. McTAGUE

Novell Press, San Jose

Novell's GroupWise™ 5 Administrator's Guide

Published by
Novell Press
2180 Fortune Drive
San Jose, CA 95131

Library of Congress Catalog Card No.: 97-70944

ISBN: 0-7645-4521-3

Printed in the United States of America

10 9 8 7 6 5 4 3 2 1

1A/QR/QY/ZX/FC

Distributed in the United States by IDG Books Worldwide, Inc.

Distributed by Macmillan Canada for Canada; by Transworld Publishers Limited in the United Kingdom; by IDG Norge Books for Norway; by IDG Sweden Books for Sweden; by Woodslane Pty. Ltd. for Australia; by Woodslane Enterprises Ltd. for New Zealand; by Longman Singapore Publishers Ltd. for Singapore, Malaysia, Thailand, and Indonesia; by Simron Pty. Ltd. for South Africa; by Toppan Company Ltd. for Japan; by Distribuidora Cuspide for Argentina; by Livraria Cultura for Brazil; by Ediciencia S.A. for Ecuador; by Addison-Wesley Publishing Company for Korea; by Ediciones ZETA S.C.R. Ltda. for Peru; by WS Computer Publishing Corporation, Inc., for the Philippines; by Unalis Corporation for Taiwan; by Contemporanea de Ediciones for Venezuela; by Computer Book & Magazine Store for Puerto Rico; by Express Computer Distributors for the Caribbean and West Indies. Authorized Sales Agent: Anthony Rudkin Associates for the Middle East and North Africa.

For general information on IDG Books Worldwide's books in the U.S., please call our Consumer Customer Service department at 800-762-2974. For reseller information, including discounts and premium sales, please call our Reseller Customer Service department at 800-434-3422.

For information on where to purchase IDG Books Worldwide's books outside the U.S., please contact our International Sales department at 415-655-3200 or fax 415-655-3295.

For information on foreign language translations, please contact our Foreign & Subsidiary Rights department at 415-655-3021 or fax 415-655-3281.

For sales inquiries and special prices for bulk quantities, please contact our Sales department at 415-655-3200 or write to the address above.

For information on using IDG Books Worldwide's books in the classroom or for ordering examination copies, please contact our Educational Sales department at 800-434-2086 or fax 817-251-8174.

For press review copies, author interviews, or other publicity information, please contact our Public Relations department at 415-655-3000 or fax 415-655-3299.

For authorization to photocopy items for corporate, personal, or educational use, please contact Copyright Clearance Center, 222 Rosewood Drive, Danvers, MA 01923, or fax 508-750-4470.

For general information on Novell Press books in the U.S., including information on discounts and premiums, contact IDG Books at 800-434-3422 or 415-655-3200. For information on where to purchase Novell Press books outside the U.S., contact IDG Books International at 415-655-3021 or fax 415-655-3295.

John Kilcullen, *CEO, IDG Books Worldwide, Inc.*
Steven Berkowitz, *President, IDG Books Worldwide, Inc.*
Brenda McLaughlin, *Senior Vice President and Group Publisher, IDG Books Worldwide, Inc.*

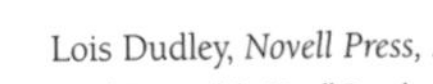

Lois Dudley, *Novell Press, Inc.*

Welcome to Novell Press

Novell Press, the world's leading provider of networking books, is the premier source for the most timely and useful information in the networking industry. Novell Press books cover fundamental networking issues as they emerge—from today's Novell and third-party products to the concepts and strategies that will guide the industry's future. The result is a broad spectrum of titles for the benefit of those involved in networking at any level: end-user, department administrator, developer, systems manager, or network architect.

Novell Press books are written by experts with the full participation of Novell's technical, managerial, and marketing staff. The books are exhaustively reviewed by Novell's own technicians and are published only on the basis of final released software, never on prereleased versions. Novell Press at IDG Books Worldwide is an exciting partnership between two companies at the forefront of the knowledge and communications revolution. The Press is implementing an ambitious publishing program to develop new networking titles centered on the current IntranetWare version of NetWare and on Novell's GroupWise and other popular groupware products.

Novell Press books are translated into 12 languages and are available at bookstores around the world.

Lois Dudley, Novell Press

Novell Press

Publisher
Lois Dudley

Project Specialist
Robin Wheatley

Acquisitions Editor
Jim Sumser

Development Editor
Ron Hull

Technical Editor
Cory Lindorff

Copy Editors
Nicole Fountain
Luann Rouff
Carolyn Welch

Project Coordinator
Katy German

Graphics and Production Specialists
Vincent F. Burns
Renée Dunn
Mark Schumann

Illustrators
Jessie Coleman
David Puckett

Proofreader
Christine Langin-Faris

Indexer
Ann Norcross

Cover Photographer
Kirsty McLaren

About the Authors

Shawn B. Rogers is the author of *Novell's GroupWise 4 Administrator's Guide* and the co-author of *Novell's GroupWise 4 User's Guide and Novell's GroupWise 5 User's Handbook* (all titles published by Novell Press and IDG Books Worldwide.) He is a Senior Instructional Designer for Novell Education. He has five years' teaching experience in GroupWise and other computing technologies. He is also a CNE and a Certified Novell Instructor (CNI) for Novell technologies. He lives in Spanish Fork, Utah.

Richard H. McTague is the co-author of *Novell's GroupWise 4 User's Guide* and *Novell's GroupWise 5 User's Handbook*, and served as technical editor for *Novell's GroupWise 4 Administrator's Guide* by Shawn Rogers (all titles published by Novell Press and IDG Books Worldwide). He is an instructor and message systems consultant for IKON Office Solutions Technology Services in Overland Park, Kansas. He is a Certified Novell Instructor (CNI) for all GroupWise courses and CNE. He lives in Overland Park, Kansas.

I dedicate this book to my sweetheart, Kellie, and my bestest buddy, Cameron, for everything they mean to me.

I also dedicate this book to my father, Burke W. Rogers, and in loving memory of Ja Neal Brailsford Rogers who brought much joy into his life.

Shawn B. Rogers

I dedicate this book to my parents, Dick and Dorothy McTague.

Rick McTague

Preface

In the years we have been teaching and writing about GroupWise, we have come to realize a couple of things about GroupWise systems.

First, no two GroupWise systems are identical. Because of the variety of computing platforms in use, the array of network operating systems, and the many different network topologies, the one constant in all GroupWise systems is that they are always unique. A configuration that works extremely well for one organization is not necessarily the best solution for another.

Second, no single person knows everything there is to know about GroupWise. However, two heads are better than one, and that's why we've teamed up on this project. Together we provide a balance of knowledge and resources that we think provides a powerful combination of development skills and real-world application and design.

As we analyzed the electronic messaging industry, we realized that there is a body of knowledge and a set of core skills that *every* GroupWise system administrator must have. Certain principles and techniques will help you get the most out of your GroupWise system, with the least amount of exasperation. These are the topics that we have addressed in this book.

Novell's GroupWise 5 Administrator's Guide is divided into six major parts. We urge you not to skip ahead to the chapters corresponding to your particular needs. If you do, you will miss important concepts in the earlier chapters. Most of the chapters are not designed to be read independently of the others.

Following is an overview of each part.

Part I: Introduction to GroupWise 5

Part I explains introductory concepts and terminology you need to understand before you begin installing and administering a GroupWise system. You should read this section before you break the seal on your GroupWise CD-ROM jacket. In Part I we explain the fundamental components of a GroupWise system, how GroupWise integrates with Novell Directory Services (NDS), and how to plan a GroupWise implementation.

Part II: Small GroupWise Systems

In Part II we explain how to install GroupWise as a small system that consists of only one domain and a single post office. The basic concepts presented in Part II apply to GroupWise systems of all sizes, however. This part covers essential

GroupWise skills, such as how to install the GroupWise system, how to install and configure the GroupWise client, how to administer a GroupWise post office, and how to manage GroupWise objects in the NDS tree.

Part III: Complex GroupWise Systems

Part III deals with more complex GroupWise systems that consist of multiple post offices in a single domain, and multiple-domain systems. Major topics in Part III include the GroupWise message transfer system, primary and secondary domains, directory synchronization, linking GroupWise components, setting up communication with external GroupWise systems, customizing the GroupWise agents, and maintaining GroupWise databases. As we explain the various GroupWise messaging configurations, we provide detailed message flow diagrams that will help you understand how messages move from point-to-point within the system. These diagrams are also extremely valuable for troubleshooting and identifying message delivery bottlenecks.

Part IV: Advanced Administration

Part IV delves into the more complex GroupWise administrative tasks. Most of these tasks are not performed on a regular basis, but when you need to know this information it is vital that you have a reference source. In Part IV we explain how to do such things as combine separate GroupWise systems into a single system, configure directory synchronization with scheduled ADA events, configure GroupWise to operate in Client/Server mode, migrate from GroupWise 4.1 to GroupWise 5, and implement GroupWise document management.

Part V: Connectivity and Mobile Computing

Part V focuses on GroupWise connectivity. We explain how to install and configure GroupWise gateways, how to support remote GroupWise users, and how to connect GroupWise to the Internet.

Part VI: Additional GroupWise Technologies

In Part VI we cover some tools and products that enhance your GroupWise system. We explain how to install and configure GroupWise WebAccess, and also provide an overview of additional development technologies that can provide functionality to your GroupWise system.

Acknowledgments

I would first like to thank my wife, Kellie, and son, Cameron, for the sacrifices they have made throughout this project. Their patience has been endless throughout all four of my books.

I also want to thank my co-author and friend, Rick McTague, for his expertise, his humor, his integrity, and his spiritual strength. Rick gladly stepped in and carried part of my load during some very stressful times. Thanks, Rick, for helping me maintain a sense of balance and proper priorities throughout this seemingly endless project.

Shawn B. Rogers

Right off the bat, I must thank my wife, Alison, and our children Richard, Patrick, and "Jamers" McTague for all of their help, understanding, and patience while we worked through this project. I don't take the freedom they gave me to work on this for granted.

I'd also like to thank my parents. The astounding love, support, and guidance I've received (and continue to receive) from them cannot be measured or even put into words, so I'm not going to try. I just remember my dad staying up late at night reading through thick computer printouts of some COBOL program he wrote, and using a metal ruler with a mechanical pencil to get things right. I also remember the sweetness my mom has for every real estate and Avon customer, somehow making time for both them and our family, while thinking of herself last. Mom and Dad, thank you for being my examples.

I owe a huge "thanks pal" to Shawn Rogers. Like two soldiers, we leaned on each other and got through this huge project together. His insight, humor, and writing ability kept us on track and in tune.

We did it!

Richard H. McTague

We would like to jointly thank Cory Lindorff of Novell Technical Services for providing his immense technical knowledge on this project. His suggestions have made a huge contribution to the technical integrity of this book.

Thanks also to Roman Gonzales, Systems Engineer for Novell, for his extra effort and invaluable help in many deep technical issues.

We also want to thank Ron Hull at IDG Books Worldwide for his ability to cut through our techno-babble and make it into something that sounds like a book. Thanks, Ron, for sticking with us through all of our projects thus far. Thanks also for mentoring us and helping us develop our writing skills.

We would also like to jointly thank several members of the Novell GroupWare division for their contributions and support—Ed McGarr, Bill Mangum, Scott Duncan, Brad Brown, and Lynn Madsen. A special thanks to Jeff Stratford, also a member of Novell Technical Services, for the GroupWise utilities found on the accompanying CD-ROM. We would also like to thank Ken Anderson, Lucinda Dove, and Donn Berke of Novell IS&T for contributing their expertise to the migration chapter of this book. And finally, a special thanks to Mitchell Smith of Novell Education for continually making suggestions on how to improve the overall content and quality of this book.

We would also like to thank Lois Dudley and Robin Wheatley of Novell Press, and Colleen Bluhm (formerly of Novell Press) and Jim Sumser of IDG Books Worldwide for making this book possible.

Contents at a Glance

Part VI Additional GroupWise Technologies

Appendixes

Contents

Part III Complex GroupWise Systems 187

Appendixes

PART I

Introduction to GroupWise 5

CHAPTER 1

Fundamental GroupWise Components

Welcome to the exciting world of Novell GroupWise 5 administration. You are (or soon will be) administering the most powerful corporate electronic messaging system available today.

This chapter gives you a brief history of GroupWise, highlights some of the new features in version 5.x, and explains some ground-level concepts you need to understand. We'll also introduce you to the basic components of electronic messaging systems. Along the way, you'll learn some important GroupWise terms and general messaging terminology.

History of GroupWise

Novell GroupWise has evolved a great deal over the past several years. Initially, the software was part of WordPerfect Library. Our first introduction to the software came in 1990, when the program was called WordPerfect Office v. 3.0. Soon version 3.1 was released, and it was this product that grabbed the attention of the e-mail world. WordPerfect Office 3.1 was a revolutionary product because it was the first e-mail package designed for networked PCs that had an Out Box to track the status of outbound e-mail messages. It also pioneered cross-platform functionality between DOS, Windows, Macintosh, Unix, VAX, and DG platforms.

In 1993, WordPerfect Office 4.0 demonstrated even more powerful capabilities. Version 4.0 was no longer merely an e-mail system; it now provided a complete corporate messaging system. In addition to traditional electronic mail, version 4.0 offered powerful calendaring and workflow features, along with several new kinds of messages (such as Appointments, Tasks, and Notes). The system's administration program was also dramatically enhanced, allowing for enterprise-wide administration from a central location. At that time, the WordPerfect Office client software became available for DOS, Windows 3.x, Macintosh, and UNIX clients.

When WordPerfect Corporation merged with Novell in 1994, WordPerfect Office became Novell GroupWise version 4.1. Under Novell's ownership, and because of ever-increasing integration with Novell NetWare, GroupWise 4.1 became a major player in the electronic messaging industry, grabbing huge chunks of marketshare from some of the better-known e-mail packages and quickly gaining more than six million users worldwide. When Novell sold WordPerfect and other application products to Corel, Inc., Novell retained ownership of GroupWise and has continued its development.

Even though the product is now called Novell GroupWise, its heritage from WordPerfect Office is still apparent if you dig deeply into the GroupWise infrastructure. For example, some of the GroupWise system directories still have names that include the initials WP, such as WPCSIN and WPCSOUT. Knowing the origin of GroupWise filenames and directories will make the product much easier for you to understand. We'll give you some background on the origin of GroupWise filenames and directories whenever that information is useful.

GroupWise 5 has again made major technical strides, becoming the first electronic messaging system to integrate so completely with Novell NetWare as to allow administration of both a network and its resident electronic messaging system from a single program—*NetWare Administrator*. Version 5 has also added more message types than previous versions and facilitates greater integration with other messaging products. GroupWise 5 has also added document management and other powerful capabilities, such as client/server support. These new features receive extensive coverage later in this book. For now, here's a brief overview of some of those features.

What's New in GroupWise 5?

Here's a rundown of the new features GroupWise 5 offers. (If you have only recently been introduced to GroupWise, you can skip ahead to the next section, "GroupWise Fundamentals.")

- **Integration with Novell NetWare and IntranetWare.** GroupWise 5 uses Novell Directory Services (NDS) as its master directory. No longer do you have to maintain separate accounts for your NetWare users and messaging system users. Unlike previous versions, GroupWise 5 is administered from NetWare Administrator, enabling you to administer your network and your messaging system from a single point.

- **Client/server computing.** GroupWise 5 is a true client/server application. The GroupWise 5 client can communicate via the TCP/IP suite of protocols with the GroupWise agents (the back-end processes that handle message transport and delivery). Don't worry, GroupWise 5 still supports the file sharing methods you are used to in GroupWise 4.1. The client/server abilities make GroupWise more secure and scalable.

- **Internet integration.** GroupWise 5 has made communication through the Internet more intuitive and functional with new features such as WebAccess, which allows you to access your messages from an Internet browser. Several new Internet-related features have also been added. You can also enter World Wide Web addresses in any GroupWise message, and that address will be converted to a hyperlink to the Internet location. A recipient can simply click the Web address to launch his or her browser and go to that location. If you include an Internet e-mail address in a GroupWise message, it is also converted to a hyperlink that opens a preaddressed e-mail message to that user when activated. Chapter 20 covers GroupWise connectivity to the Internet.

- **New open standards.** GroupWise 5 supports the open standards from the Internet, such as MIME, SMTP, and LDAP. These APIs are built right into the GroupWise engine, so any application supporting these standards will run natively on GroupWise. Novell has also made the entire API set available to developers so they can take advantage of GroupWise features, such as calendaring, scheduling, document management, and workflow. Chapter 22 explains these industry standard APIs. The CD-ROM included with this book contains the GroupWise Software Developer's Kit.

- **Document management.** GroupWise 5 has incorporated document management into the messaging system. Now users can manage their messages and documents from a single interface—GroupWise. GroupWise document management controls concurrent document access. Multiple versions of a document can be maintained in a GroupWise library, and the document management services integrate automatically with ODMA-compliant applications, such as Corel WordPerfect 7.0 for Windows. We cover document management in Chapter 17.

GroupWise Fundamentals

GroupWise 5 is based on a concept called *store-and-forward messaging*. Messages are stored in directories and databases and then forwarded to locations that can be accessed by recipients of the messages. As a store-and-forward messaging system, GroupWise has five basic components:

- GroupWise client
- Information store
- Directory store
- Message transfer system
- Administration system

In addition to these basic components, other advanced components extend GroupWise's capabilities. For example, several *gateways* are available that let GroupWise connect to the Internet and to other e-mail systems. (See Chapter 18 for more information about gateways.) Other add-on products give users access to their messages in different ways, such as through a touch-tone telephone or through a pager. We explain these additional components in Chapter 22.

GroupWise Client

The *GroupWise client* is the part of GroupWise that the user sees. The user accesses the client to read incoming mail and to send messages. The client performs other functions as well, such as message management, calendaring, task management, and document management. The GroupWise client provides the interface for accessing the GroupWise *Universal Mailbox*.

Figure 1.1 shows the GroupWise 5 client interface for Windows 95.

FIGURE 1.1

GroupWise Client Interface

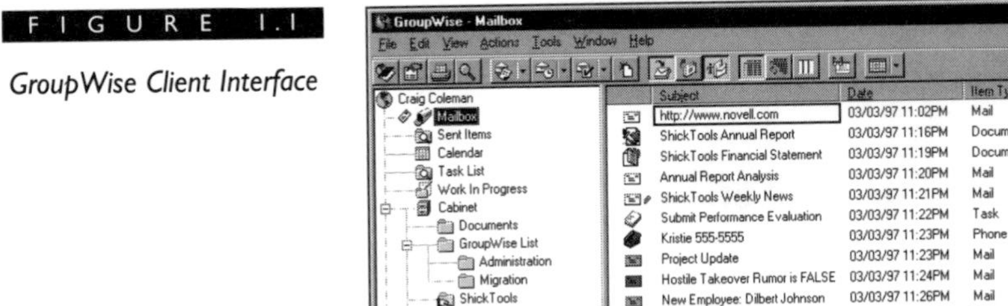

The GroupWise client is available for multiple computing platforms, including Windows 95, Windows 3.x, Macintosh, and UNIX. A special WebAccess client uses any Internet browser, such as Netscape Navigator, to view GroupWise messages.

The standard GroupWise clients can also be used in *Remote mode* so users can access their messages while not connected directly to the GroupWise system. Chapter 19 explains how Remote mode works.

This book focuses exclusively on GroupWise administration, and therefore does not explain how to use the GroupWise client programs. For a complete reference on the GroupWise Windows 95 client, see our previous book, *Novell's GroupWise 5 User's Handbook*, published by Novell Press and IDG Books Worldwide, Inc.

Information Store

The *information store* (formerly called the *message store*) is the place where messages are physically stored in an e-mail system. At its simplest level, the client software interacts with the information store to send and retrieve mail messages. We explain this interaction in much greater detail later in the book.

The information store has two fundamental components: the *message store* for message management and the *document store* for document management. We explain how the document store portion works in Chapter 17.

Figure 1.2 depicts the information store in action.

The GroupWise information store is actually a set of databases and directories stored on a shared network disk.

FIGURE 1.2

Simple Information Store Diagram

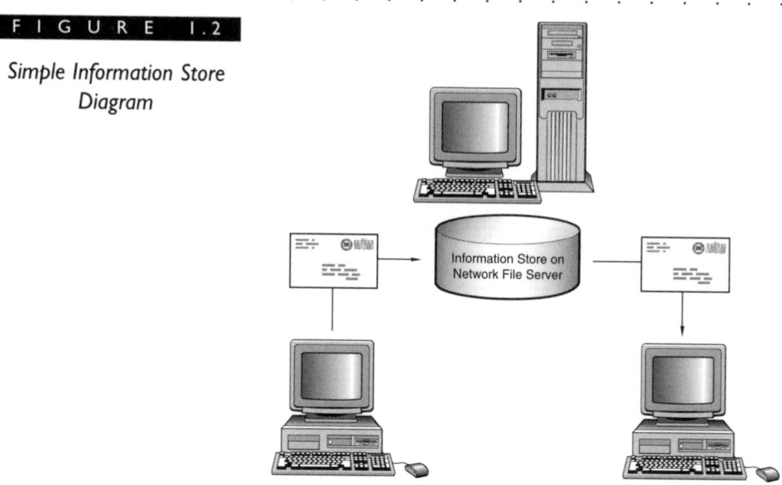

Because users need access to their personal messages, an information store must be accessible to every GroupWise user, either directly or through a client/server connection. It would not be practical for every user on the GroupWise system to access the same network disk that stores the messages. Consequently, multiple information stores exist in all but the simplest GroupWise systems.

The information store concept is key to the cross-platform functionality of GroupWise. Because the information store is not associated with any specific client platform, users can access messages from any client version (for example, Macintosh, UNIX, or Windows 95), assuming the appropriate network-level provisions have been made.

The GroupWise information store is completely encrypted with the GroupWise proprietary encryption scheme. GroupWise messages and documents are secure and cannot be read by intruders. The messages are encrypted during transit and storage. As long as users protect their mailboxes with passwords and practice smart network computing, their messages are completely private and secure.

NOTE

Security is available only inside of the GroupWise system. Outside messaging systems often are not as secure or encrypted as GroupWise. For example, once you send a message to the Internet, the message is converted from the GroupWise format to the Internet standard for e-mail (called *Simple Mail Transfer Protocol* or *SMTP*), which is much more easily compromised.

Directory Store

The *directory store* is the place where addressing information for users and objects in the GroupWise system is stored. When users access the GroupWise Address Book, they see information contained in the directory store.

Figure 1.3 shows the GroupWise client Address Book.

FIGURE 1.3

GroupWise Address Book Showing Data

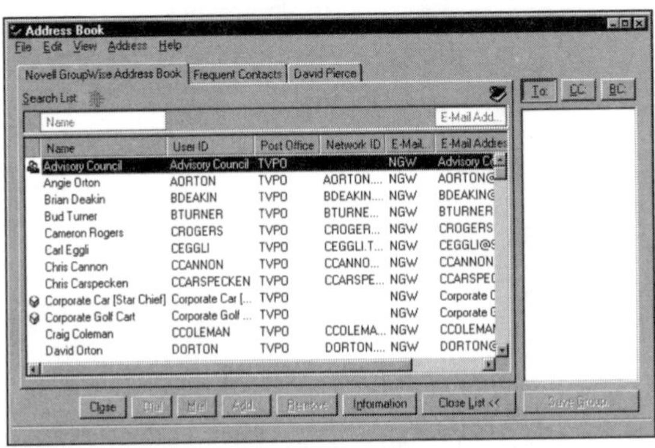

The GroupWise 5 directory store is tightly integrated with Novell Directory Services (NDS). When the network administrator makes a change to a User object in NetWare Administrator, such as changing the user's telephone number, the information is automatically synchronized with the GroupWise directory store and immediately reflected in the Address Book.

The GroupWise directory store is a set of databases that can be accessed by every GroupWise user. The databases are distributed throughout the GroupWise system and kept synchronized by GroupWise administration components working closely with NDS. Administration information, such as addressing instructions for the delivery of messages to other parts of the GroupWise system, is also stored and distributed along with Address Book information. We'll explain later on how this directory synchronization works.

Message Transfer System

The *message transfer system* handles the movement of messages between sender and receiver in the messaging system. The message transfer system is composed of two main components: the *message transfer agent* (MTA) and the *post office agent* (POA), both of which we explain later in the book.

For now, just remember that these agents work with the GroupWise information store and the network infrastructure to transfer messages from one point to another.

In Figure 1.4, User A sends a message to User B, but they do not share the same information store. When User A sends the message, the message transfer system moves the message from User A to User B's information store.

The message transfer system can run on NetWare as a set of NetWare Loadable Modules (NLMs) or it can run on Windows NT servers. As of this writing, Novell is planning to release several UNIX versions of the message transfer system.

(Later in this book, we'll explain message flow diagrams, which provide extensive detail about how messages move through GroupWise systems.)

Administration System

The *administration system* is the nerve center for GroupWise. It coordinates the activities of the users, the client, the information store, and the message transfer system. The GroupWise administration system has two main components. The first component is a set of "snap-in" management tools installed as part of the NetWare Administrator program. The second component is the ***administration agent***, or ADA, which performs back-end administrative tasks.

Figure 1.5 shows NetWare Administrator menus that contain options for administering GroupWise.

FIGURE 1.4

Message Transfer System

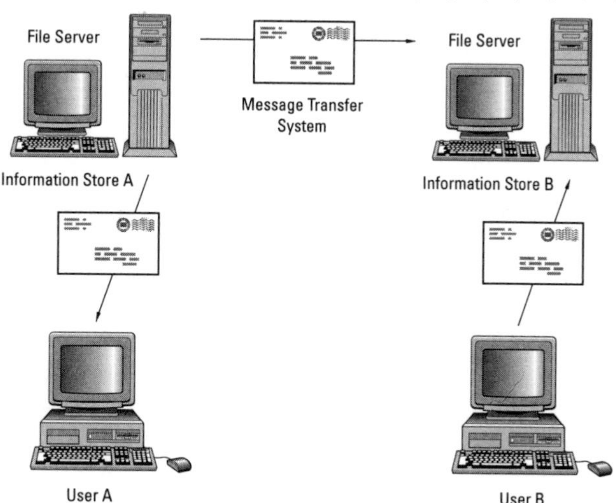

FIGURE 1.5

GroupWise Options in NetWare Administrator

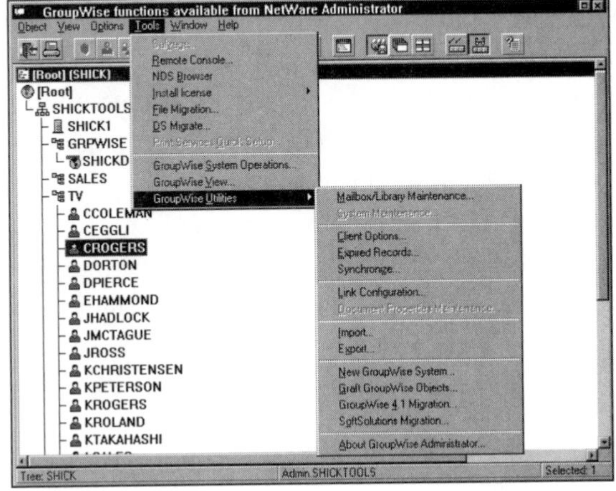

Some of the GroupWise administration tasks you perform using NetWare Administrator include the following:

- Creating user accounts
- Deleting user accounts
- Moving user accounts
- Setting user preferences
- Controlling GroupWise system security
- Troubleshooting the system
- Maintaining the information store
- Maintaining the directory store

The ADA works closely with Novell Directory Services (NDS) to maintain the directory store and the replication of GroupWise system information.

How the Pieces Fit Together

Figure 1.6 gives you an overview of how the basic GroupWise components work together to deliver a message.

FIGURE 1.6

Simple E-Mail Process

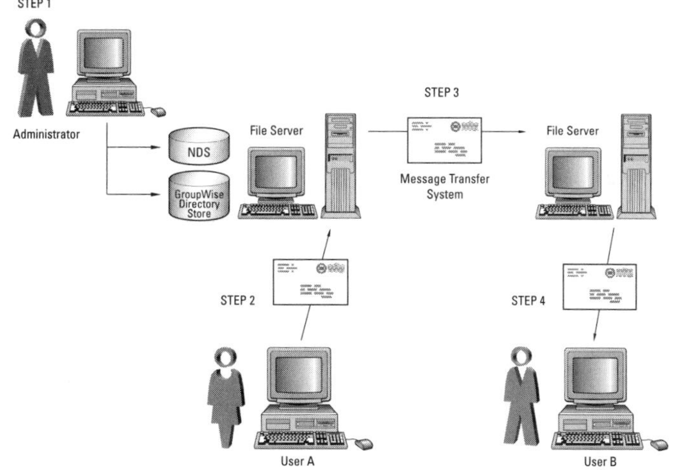

The steps illustrated in Figure 1.6 are as follows:

1 • The system administrator uses NetWare Administrator to configure the GroupWise system and give NetWare Users A and B GroupWise accounts. This information is written to both NDS and the GroupWise directory store.

2 • User A uses the GroupWise client to create and send a message, using the GroupWise Address book to access the directory store when addressing the message.

3 • The GroupWise message transfer system moves the message to an information store accessible by User B.

4 • User B runs the client program and reads the message located in that user's information store.

Summary

In this chapter we introduced you to the fundamental GroupWise components and explained in a very basic way how these components interact in a GroupWise system.

Chapter 2 explains the GroupWise architecture and details the role of each of the basic GroupWise system components introduced in this chapter.

CHAPTER 2

GroupWise 5 Architecture

GroupWise 5 is not an e-mail system; it is a "messaging platform." Unlike standard e-mail systems, which transfer only standard e-mail messages and file attachments, a *messaging platform* can provide an organization with an entire communications, scheduling, and document management infrastructure. The power of the GroupWise messaging platform derives from the strength and logic of its architecture.

What exactly do we mean by "architecture"? The term is often used loosely, but basically a system's *architecture* is its conceptual components—for example, domains, post offices, and so forth—and their relationship to the real-world features of the system, such as directories, databases, client software, and the like. The GroupWise architecture is Novell's own unique implementation of the basic messaging components discussed in Chapter 1.

GroupWise is a database-dependent messaging system. Earlier, rudimentary e-mail systems were file-based. By using databases to create, store, transfer, and deliver messages, the GroupWise architecture offers many benefits to system administrators. Because of its database-dependent architecture, GroupWise 5 is:

- *Portable.* The client and server processes are written using the same basic engine code, so the system can be installed on a wide variety of networks, such as IntranetWare and Windows NT.
- *Scalable.* The GroupWise "building blocks" are designed to be as flexible as possible, matching each organization's needs to the structure of the messaging system. GroupWise works on the network of a 15-person law office as well as on the network of an international enterprise with 15,000 users.
- *Modular.* Each component has a defined capacity in the overall delivery of each message. The server processes, for example, are divided into three individual roles that neither change nor overlap. Therefore, there is never a single point that can cause system-wide failure.
- *Robust.* This proven architecture can support many thousands of messages per hour, and the databases can swell to accommodate large numbers of messages while maintaining performance.

- *Reliable.* The indexing and tracking of messages is handled by the GroupWise server agent programs, *not* the network file system.

- *Secure.* The databases and messages in transit are encrypted and cannot be hacked into. Access to the information in mailboxes is secured by Novell Directory Services (NDS) authentication and rights protection.

- *Fault-tolerant.* The design of the databases and server processes allows for a measure of fault tolerance in the system. If network problems occur, GroupWise either continues to deliver messages or holds messages in message queues until the network problems are resolved. Fault tolerance is possible because many database files make up the entire GroupWise information store and if one fails, the message information is still safe.

The discussion of GroupWise architecture in this chapter is divided into two main sections: "Architectural Building Blocks" and "GroupWise Integration with NDS." If you're already familiar with an earlier version of GroupWise, you'll find the latter part of the chapter particularly helpful.

Architectural Building Blocks

This section covers the "logical" and "physical" definitions of the GroupWise system parts. As you will see later in this chapter, NDS defines the GroupWise components as logical objects in the NDS database. Each logical object in NDS has a physical counterpart. For example, Printer objects (which are logical objects) in NDS are used to represent physical printers that are attached to the network.

GroupWise systems can be scaled to accommodate organizations of all sizes. This flexibility means you can add more GroupWise "building blocks" to suit your enterprise. The following sections provide an overview of the different kinds of building blocks you'll find in a typical GroupWise system.

GroupWise Systems

What exactly is a *GroupWise system*? This rather broad term describes an organization's particular implementation of the GroupWise messaging platform and refers to all of the client workstations, post offices, domains, gateways, and so forth, that are administered by one organization (see Figure 2.1). You'll need to give your system a name during the installation procedure. The name of your system is important only when connecting to other GroupWise systems or managing the software directory. These procedures are explained in later chapters.

FIGURE 2.1

A GroupWise System

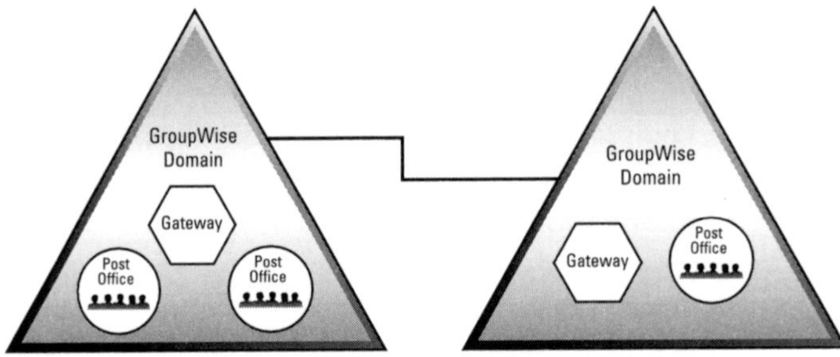

GroupWise Domains

Conceptually, a GroupWise *domain* consists of one or more post offices and gateways, as shown in Figure 2.2. The most basic GroupWise system consists of one domain and one post office.

The domain is an administration-level component of the GroupWise system. In other words, most users are unaware that they belong to a GroupWise domain because they need not concern themselves with its existence. Users are more likely to be aware of the GroupWise post office to which they belong. (Post offices are explained a little later in this chapter.)

IMPORTANT

Don't confuse the GroupWise domain with other kinds of domains in the computing industry, such as Windows NT domains or Internet domains. This distinction is important because it is possible to have a GroupWise domain within an NT domain. You may need to use the GroupWise domain name to connect your system to the Internet.

FIGURE 2.2

A GroupWise Domain

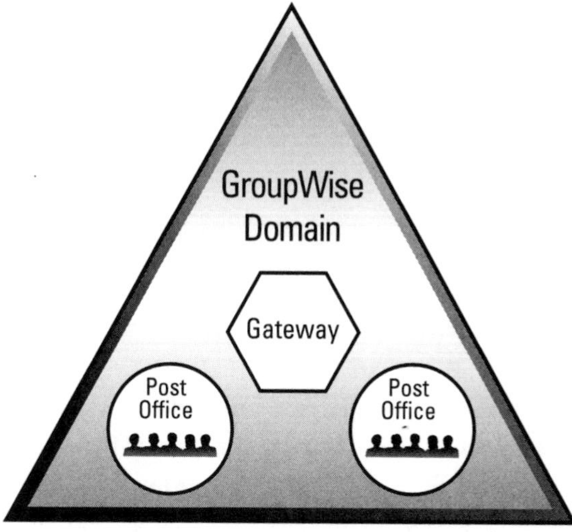

In terms of its physical characteristics, a domain exists as a directory on a file server. The *domain directory* is an administrative directory containing databases and other files used in system configuration. Users won't access this directory, and no messages will be stored here. The domain directory is used for administration and for routing messages between domains.

Components of the Domain Directory

Each domain directory has three main components:

- Domain database
- MTA queues
- Gateway directory

Domain Database This proprietary, encrypted database contains system information about the configuration of the domain itself and about certain domain-level programs. The filename of the domain database is WPDOMAIN.DB. You'll recall from Chapter 1 that GroupWise is a descendent of WordPerfect Office. As you may have guessed, the letters "WP" at the beginning of the filename stand for "WordPerfect" and have been retained to maintain interoperability and backward compatibility for each new version of the product's components (primarily the MTA and gateways). The extension .DB stands for "database."

The domain database is accessed by NetWare Administrator, which is the program used to perform all GroupWise administration. We discuss NetWare Administrator later in this chapter.

NetWare Administrator updates the domain database as certain changes are made. This is important to know, since changes in NDS can affect certain files on the network, and administrators must have rights to those files.

MTA Queues Each domain directory has two message transport agent (MTA) queues: WPCSIN and WPCSOUT.

NOTE

GroupWise 5 is the great-grandchild of a program called WordPerfect Office 4.0. WordPerfect Office used a program called "Connection Server" to move messages. The WPCSIN directory stands for "WordPerfect Connection Server Input" and the WPCSOUT directory refers to "WordPerfect Connection Server Output." These and other directories reflect this ancestry.

- *WPCSIN Directory.* This directory is known as the *message transfer agent (MTA) input queue*. This is where the message transfer agent transfers messages from another domain to post offices in your domain. Think of this directory as the entry into your domain.

- *WPCSOUT Directory.* This directory is the message server output queue. This is where the message transfer agent places messages for the next agent in line to take over and perform actions at the domain level.

These directories are discussed in more detail in Chapter 4.

WPGATE Directory This directory is where gateway software for the domain resides. Each gateway you install in a domain has its own directory with a unique name and its own set of databases and message transfer agent queues. The WPGATE directory is discussed in Chapter 18.

Types of Domains

The different types of GroupWise domains are listed in Table 2.1.

TABLE 2.1

Types of Domains

DOMAIN TYPE	DEFINITION	PURPOSE
Primary domain	The first GroupWise domain in a system	Serves as central administrative domain for entire GroupWise system
Secondary domains	Every other domain in a system after the primary domain	Used for grouping together post offices for administrative purposes
External GroupWise domains	GroupWise domains not part of the system	Used to represent GroupWise domains in other systems (for example, domains of other companies)
Foreign domains	Domains for connecting with non-GroupWise mail systems	Used to represent other systems (such as the Internet) for mail routing

NOTE

Within your GroupWise system, only the primary and secondary domains contain actual users with mailboxes. The other domain types represent mail recipients outside of your system. Those domains enable you to make outside users accessible through the GroupWise Address Book.

Directory Synchronization

When a change is made in GroupWise using NetWare Administrator, the change is written first to the domain database being currently accessed. (You'll learn how to gain access to different domain databases in Chapter 9.)

Changes need to be synchronized among the GroupWise databases so that Address Books are updated almost immediately. This is handled at the domain level, and the details of how this happens are covered later.

Directory synchronization is automatic between primary and secondary domains in your system. It is possible to configure synchronization with external GroupWise domains and even foreign domains if the gateway to the non-GroupWise mail system supports directory synchronization, such as the cc:Mail gateway.

Domain-Level Programs

Three programs operate at the domain level:

- Message transfer agent
- Administration agent
- NetWare Administrator

These programs are included on the GroupWise 5 CD-ROM, and they are installed on your server when the software is installed. Once they are installed, you need to configure and run the agent software. The GroupWise agents are available for NetWare Loadable Module (NLM), Windows NT, and UNIX platforms. Two agents are loaded for every domain: the message transfer agent and the administration agents. The post office agent is a post office-level program and is described later in this chapter.

Message Transfer Agent The main purpose of the *message transfer agent* (MTA) is to move messages between the post offices and gateways within the domain and to transport messages into and out of the domain. One MTA is required for each domain.

Administration Agent The *administration agent* (ADA) has two main functions: It synchronizes all of the GroupWise administrative databases with any changes that are made and pulls information from NDS into the domain database to update GroupWise Address Books.

NetWare Administrator *NetWare Administrator* reads and writes to the domain database. When you start NetWare Administrator, the domain database is read to obtain GroupWise information. Changes made to any GroupWise component or object are written into the domain database. NetWare Administrator accesses NDS in much the same way, as you will see later in this chapter.

GroupWise Post Offices

Conceptually, a *post office* is a grouping of users, distribution lists, and other GroupWise objects that can be recipients of GroupWise messages. These objects (described later) are said to "belong to a post office," as shown in Figure 2.3. As you will see in Chapter 3, you must consider many issues in deciding how many mailboxes a particular post office should hold and who its members will be. Generally, you group users who belong to the same department into a single post office.

FIGURE 2.3

A GroupWise Post Office

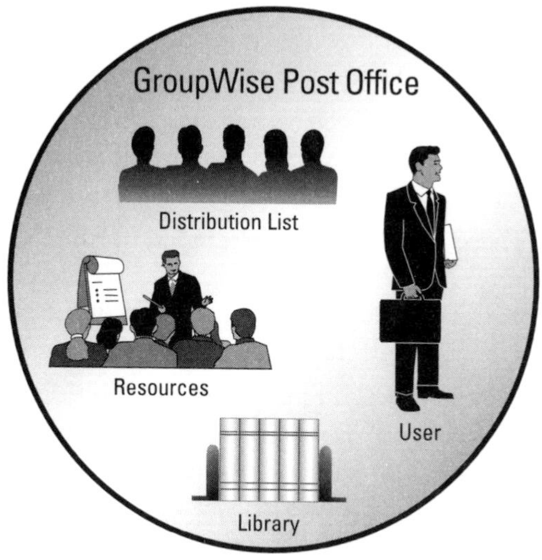

A post office consists of a post office directory on a file server and the corresponding post office-level programs. The post office directory is where users store all of their messages and where the GroupWise client program accesses those messages. The client program also uses the post office database (described later) to display the Address Book.

As you will see in Chapter 3, you need to count on the post office directory using a lot of disk space. As a general rule of thumb, you can plan on about 40MB of disk space per user for each post office.

Post Office Directory Structure

The post office directory is divided into two areas: the *administrative directories and files* and the *information store*. A complete diagram and description of a post office directory appears in Appendix E.

Administrative Directories and Files The administrative directories and files in a post office keep the Address Books current and allow messages to pass into and out of the post office.

- *Post Office Database.* This file, named WPHOST.DB, is the post office's administrative database, where the Address Book gets its information.
- *Message Server Input Queue.* This directory, named WPCSIN, is where the client places messages for the message transfer agent to transfer out of the sender's post office. This is discussed in more detail in Chapter 4.
- *Message Server Output Queue.* This directory, named WPCSOUT, is where the message transfer agent places messages coming into the post office. These directories are discussed in more detail in Chapter 4.

Information Store The information store is the most critical area of the entire GroupWise system. It contains every message created, along with any attachments. GroupWise has the ability to send and receive multiple message types, such as e-mail messages, Appointments, Tasks, Notes, and documents, to name a few. All of these message types are stored in the information store in the post office directory. The GroupWise client program is used to access the message store, to both send and receive messages.

The information store consists of two main database types: *message databases* and *user databases.*

Message databases hold all of the GroupWise messages. Message databases for a particular post office contain messages (as well as status and addressing information) that have been either sent by users in the post office or received by users in the post office. There can be up to twenty-five message databases. These databases are encrypted and use a unique database format (called "FLAIM" for all you trivia buffs) and can only be accessed by the GroupWise client program or the message delivery agents, which are discussed later in this chapter.

File attachments to messages are not usually stored in the message databases. They are kept in a set of subdirectories in the post office called OFFILES. The message record in the message database has a transparent pointer to these encrypted file attachments. This is discussed in much more detail in Chapter 6.

In addition to the message databases, the information store also contains user databases. Every recipient in a post office has an associated *user database.* Each user's database contains not messages, but pointers to messages located in the message databases.

Each user's database is unique to that user. Client settings, such as the password for the mailbox, the user's folder structure, rules, personal calendar items, and personal addresses are all contained in the individual user's database.

The user database is also referred to as the user's "mailbox," and is uniquely named with a *file ID* (for example, USER9GY.DB). A file ID (FID) is assigned to every recipient in the GroupWise system.

Post Office-Level Programs

The files and directories of a post office are accessed and managed with three main programs: the post office agent, the administration agent, and the GroupWise client.

Although we introduce these programs here, they are described in much more detail throughout this book.

Post Office Agent The *post office agent* (POA) has many duties and is the real workhorse of GroupWise. It is responsible for delivering messages into the information store for the post office. It also creates status messages for the messages it delivers. Chapter 6 discusses message delivery in detail.

In addition, the POA handles all client/server connections from the GroupWise client program to the information store. This feature of GroupWise allows TCP/IP to be used to connect the GroupWise client program to a user's mailbox in the information store. Chapter 15 discusses client/server connections.

The POA also handles information store database-maintenance tasks on a manual or scheduled basis (Chapter 13), GroupWise library indexing (Chapter 17), and remote requests from the GroupWise client in Remote mode (Chapter 19).

Administration Agent At the post office level, the *administration agent* (ADA) updates and maintains the post office database (WPHOST.DB) with changes from NDS. This keeps the Address Book accurate. The details about how ADA performs these updates is discussed in Chapter 12.

GroupWise Client The GroupWise *client program* accesses databases and files in the post office directory structure.

The GroupWise client program runs on each user's workstation, providing the interface to the information store for sending and receiving messages, managing the Calendar, and accessing documents. It is available for Windows 3.x, Windows 95, Windows NT Workstation 4.0, Macintosh, and UNIX.

The client uses three methods of accessing the information store: dedicated, client/server, and remote. When the GroupWise program in Dedicated mode (logged into the network with a drive mapping to the file server) is open on a user's workstation, the user has open files on the file server where the post office is located. Client/Server mode (accessing the mailbox via TCP/IP through the POA) is covered in Chapter 15, and Remote mode (accessing a remote version of the master mailbox) is covered in Chapter 19.

GroupWise Gateways

Gateways transfer messages between GroupWise and other systems. In the process they also translate those messages—including the message address information and attachments—between the GroupWise message format and the other system's message format.

Conceptually, gateways are like post offices in a GroupWise system. Each gateway is associated with one domain, and the MTA is responsible for moving messages to and from the gateway. The gateway has a directory structure (usually located in its domain's directory structure) complete with message transfer agent input and output queues, and there are several gateway-level programs.

Most gateways are available for the NetWare Loadable Module (NLM), Windows NT, or OS/2 platform, and are multithreaded processes. Some gateways require additional software for the connection, and possibly a dedicated workstation. The gateways were created for GroupWise 4.1 and are completely operational with GroupWise 5.

Chapter 18 explains the purpose and function of many different kinds of gateways. Details on installing, configuring, and running all gateways are found in white papers included on this book's companion CD-ROM. Chapter 19 covers one very important gateway, the Async gateway, in depth. The SMTP/MIME gateway to the Internet is explained in Chapter 20.

Up to this point, we have looked at the architectural building blocks of GroupWise 5. In the next section we describe the relationship between GroupWise and Novell Directory Services (NDS).

GroupWise Integration with NDS

Many companies don't see the need to hire e-mail administrators, and the job invariably falls on the LAN administrator. GroupWise 5 solves that problem. In the same window in which you set up a user's personal information, file rights, login script and print job configurations, you can establish 100 percent of the user's GroupWise information. Novell Directory Services (NDS) makes this all possible.

What is Novell Directory Services? It is a database containing information about all resources available on or through the network—users, file server, printers, to name a few. It is organized very much like the directory structure of a hard disk drive (root directory, subdirectories, and files). It consists of a root object (referred to as the [ROOT] object), container objects, and leaf objects (see Figure 2.4).

A Sample NDS Tree

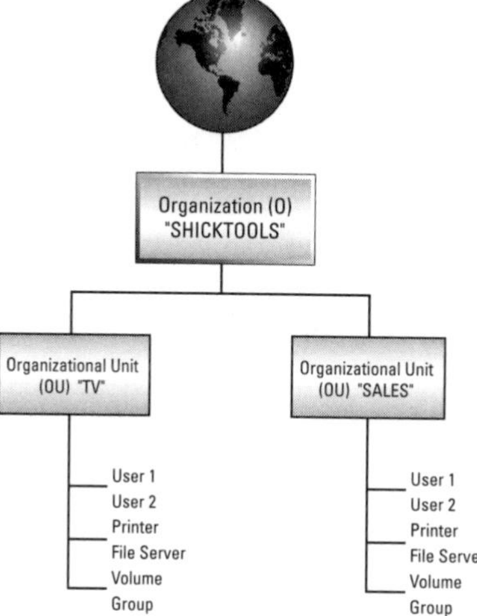

An exhaustive discussion of NDS is beyond the scope of this book. *Novell's Guide to IntranetWare Networks*, by Jeffrey F. Hughes and Blair W. Thomas (published by Novell Press and IDG Books Worldwide), is an excellent resource for more information on NDS and NDS security.

NDS can be structured in many ways, but the two most popular methods are by organization (Figure 2.4) or geography (Figure 2.5). The NDS tree in Figure 2.4

reflects the company's organizational layout, with the company name at the top, followed by the separate business units, departments, and employees.

FIGURE 2.5

NDS Structure Based on Geography

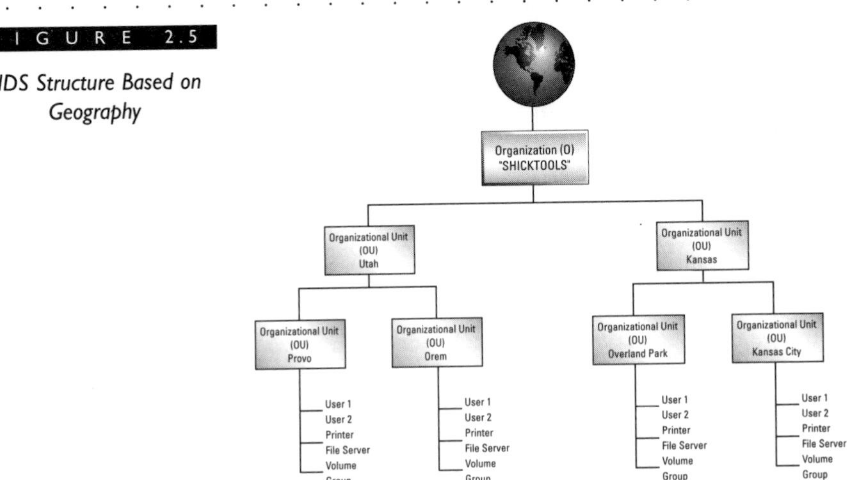

As you can see in Figure 2.5, an NDS structure based on geography has the main office at the top level, followed by cities, individual locations (represented as container objects), and the employees at those locations (represented as leaf objects).

With either of these structures, or a combination of both, the administrator has a clear definition of the network, the resources, and their working relationship to each other. As a matter of planning, the GroupWise components should fall into place under the containers to which they relate. For example, the Sales organizational unit should contain not only the Sales file server, the Sales employees, and the Sales printers, but also the Sales GroupWise post office.

NDS Basics

The NDS tree uses a system of *objects*, *properties*, and *values*. Think of NDS as a big table (see Table 2.2).

As you can see in Table 2.2, *objects* represent individual components of NDS, much like individual files in a directory on your hard drive.

TABLE 2.2

NDS Objects, Properties, and Values

OBJECT	PROPERTY	VALUE
User	Login Name	Bubba
GroupWise resource	Resource Name	MY_JUKEBOX
Printer	Printer Name	SALES_HP

Each object in NDS has a set of properties, and those properties have values assigned to them. Some object properties are mandatory; others are optional. A *property* is something that describes an object. For example, post offices can be described using post office names. Therefore, the Post Office Name is a property of a Post Office object.

The data associated with a particular property is that property's *value*. For example, the value of a Post Office Name property for a Post Office object might be "PO_1."

Objects are classified into three types: [ROOT], container, and leaf objects, as shown in Table 2.3.

TABLE 2.3

NDS Object Types and Purposes

OBJECT TYPE	PURPOSE	EXAMPLES
[ROOT]	Defines the top of the tree; there can be only one [ROOT] per NDS tree	[ROOT]
Container	Country (optional country designator)	c=US
	Organization (required designator of the company's or organization's name)	O=SHICKTOOLS
	Organizational Unit (defines subdivisions within a company)	OU=TV
Leaf	Individual objects in the tree	cn=CAMERA1 cn=son cn=era1

Note the abbreviations such as "O=" in Table 2.3. Abbreviations are used to help keep track of what type of object you are working with. They are optional in most cases.

NDS Schema

Although NDS is logically organized by objects, properties, and values, the actual databases comprising NDS have physical characteristics. The physical characteristics of NDS, the objects allowed in the tree, the kind of properties an object can have, and the rules that constrain the data for those properties are called the *NDS schema*.

As shown in Table 2.4, the NDS schema includes definitions of the properties an object can have. In keeping with our table analogy, the schema can be viewed as the number of columns or fields that describe details about an object.

TABLE 2.4

An NDS Schema

OBJECT TYPE	OBJECT NAME	OBJECT TITLE	OBJECT LOCATION	PRINT QUEUE	MEMBER LIST
User	Rick	Instructor	Kansas City	n/a	n/a
Printer	HP IV	n/a	Provo	HPIV_Q	n/a
Group	TVSALES	n/a	Kansas City	n/a	Jo, Gerry, Janet, Angie, Jaci, Brent

GroupWise NDS Schema Extensions

If you look at the list of properties in a freshly created NDS tree (created the first time you install NetWare 4.x or IntranetWare on a file server in your network), it includes only the properties defined by the programmers at Novell. The standard NDS schema includes network-specific information (such as node address), as well as organizational information about objects (such as mailing address or last name).

Installing GroupWise extends the NDS schema to add other information that can be specified for a given object, such as the GroupWise mailbox, the GroupWise FID, and the platform of the GroupWise agents (NLM, NT, and so on). This is covered in greater detail in Chapter 4.

In order to enable NDS to hold this extra information, the schema must be "extended." This means that the physical structure of the database must change to accommodate more properties, as shown in Table 2.5. Note that not all of the

GroupWise schema extensions (the additional properties and changes that installing GroupWise make to the NDS schema) are listed. This is done at the very beginning of the installation process, which is covered in Chapter 4.

TABLE 2.5

GroupWise NDS Schema Extensions

OBJECT TYPE	OBJECT NAME	OBJECT TITLE	OBJECT LOCATION	GROUPWISE DOMAIN	GROUPWISE POST OFFICE	GROUPWISE MAILBOX ID
User	Rick	Instructor	Kansas City	SHICKDOM	TVPO	rmctague
User	Shawn	Technical Writer	Provo	SHICKDOM	SALESPO	srogers

IMPORTANT

Make sure you have a good backup of the NDS database prior to installing GroupWise. Extending the schema is a one-way process. Once you've extended the schema, you can't go back.

Once you've extended the schema, the NDS database can now contain GroupWise objects (domains, post offices, users, distribution lists, and so forth), and NDS objects can have GroupWise properties (such as the post office to which a user belongs).

NetWare Administrator

NetWare Administrator is the program you use to administer a NetWare network and its resources (see Figure 2.6).

You can do many things with NetWare Administrator. You can create, modify, and delete containers and leaf objects, and you can perform file management tasks. This book discusses NetWare Administrator *only as it relates to GroupWise.*

NDS security controls what you are allowed to do with NetWare Administrator. This system of trustees, rights, inheritance, and effective rights determines, for example, whether you can add users to a GroupWise distribution list, modify the NDS schema, or use a printer.

FIGURE 2.6

NetWare Administrator

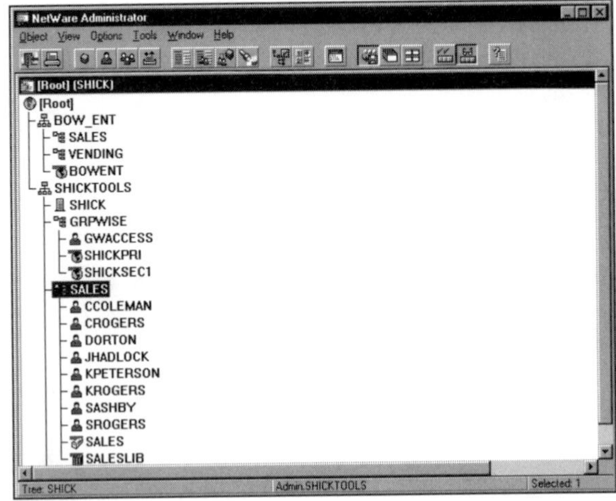

A thorough discussion of NDS security is beyond the scope of this book. Throughout this book, we will specify the NDS security rights (object and property rights) that are needed to perform common GroupWise tasks, such as using the client program, changing the properties of a gateway, or creating an Administration Agent object for a post office.

As you will see in Chapter 4, you must run a special setup program at each workstation from which you will perform GroupWise administration. This program will create a few files and allow the NetWare Administrator to see the extended schema and implement the GroupWise-related menu options. The network workstation where you initially install GroupWise is automatically enabled for GroupWise administration.

GroupWise Components and NDS

Container objects—namely, Country, Organization, and Organizational Unit—exist to hold other objects. Consequently, GroupWise objects must "fit in" with the other NDS objects. A clear understanding of your NDS structure is very important before you ever install GroupWise, because you'll need to know where the GroupWise objects are going to be located in the NDS tree. In Chapter 3 you'll learn how to plan a GroupWise system and see how GroupWise objects should be placed.

Note that the GroupWise domain and post office objects are themselves container objects. They hold the agent objects used to configure the operation of the message transfer agents. You'll see this in Chapter 4, after GroupWise is installed and the domains and post offices are created.

Table 2.6 summarizes the building blocks of GroupWise, their common use, and their relatives in the NDS database.

TABLE 2.6 *GroupWise Building Blocks*

GROUPWISE COMPONENTS	DESCRIPTION	NDS RELATIVE
System name	Defines the entire GroupWise Messaging system	NDS tree name
Domain name	Defines a major component of the organization	Organization name
Post office name	Defines departmental or business units in the company	Organizational unit name
Gateway Name	Defines connectivity options between messaging system components	None
GroupWise user IDs, resources, distribution lists, and nicknames	Defines individual users and addressable components	Leaf objects

NOTE

The table of GroupWise components and their potential counterparts in NDS is provided here to help you understand the purpose of the GroupWise components. It is not intended as a strict set of rules to follow when you place these GroupWise objects in your NDS tree.

User Object Properties

NDS users are able to achieve "GroupWise consciousness" only after they have been associated with a GroupWise post office. So, there is really no such thing as a GroupWise user; there are only NDS users with GroupWise properties.

If you need to create users who will use GroupWise but never log into NDS (such as a dedicated Remote mode user), you can create "external entities." They look and behave much like every other GroupWise user. Although they never log into NDS, they need GroupWise mailboxes just the same. External entities are described in Chapter 14.

The users and external entities are managed in NDS using NetWare Administrator and are displayed in the GroupWise Address Book.

The GroupWise-related NDS properties for users include the domain, post office, mailbox ID, and FID.

Other GroupWise Objects in NDS

In addition to NDS users with GroupWise properties, there are other GroupWise objects that belong to post offices. Distribution List objects enable users to send messages to a group of mailboxes at one time. Resources objects represent tangible things (such as conference rooms or company cars) that can be scheduled. GroupWise Library objects are created to enable document management.

All of these GroupWise-specific objects are created and managed in NDS through NetWare Administrator. The location of these objects in the NDS structure is not important, as they are accessed by the client program through the Address Book. Chapter 3 suggests strategies for the location of these and other GroupWise objects in NDS.

Distribution Lists

Configured and maintained by administrators, distribution lists are lists of users who receive messages as a group. Creating and managing distribution lists is covered in Chapter 7.

A typical example of a distribution list is "SYSOPS," which includes all of a company's system administrators. Mail sent to SYSOPS would be sent to the mailboxes of all the individual users on the list.

Resources

Resources are very handy objects. They have their own mailboxes and can represent a place (such as a conference room) or a thing (such as a limousine). Resources have an "owner" assigned to them. The owner has full access to the mailbox of the resource and is responsible for accepting and declining requests made on behalf of the resource.

Each resource is displayed in the Address Book. You can include resources in the list of recipients when you schedule a meeting.

Creating and managing resources is covered in Chapter 7.

Libraries

The integration of SoftSolutions technology into GroupWise 5 combines the power of document management with the Universal In Box. This means that documents can be treated as another message type and managed along with the GroupWise components in NDS using NetWare Administrator.

A GroupWise library is the NDS object through which documents are managed and accessed using the GroupWise Client and its integration with the most popular office productivity suites, such as Microsoft Office and Corel WordPerfect Suite. When this integration is enabled, the regular File/Open, File/Save interfaces are replaced with the GroupWise 5 document management interface (see Figure 2.7).

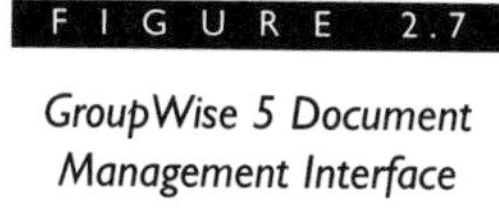

FIGURE 2.7

GroupWise 5 Document Management Interface

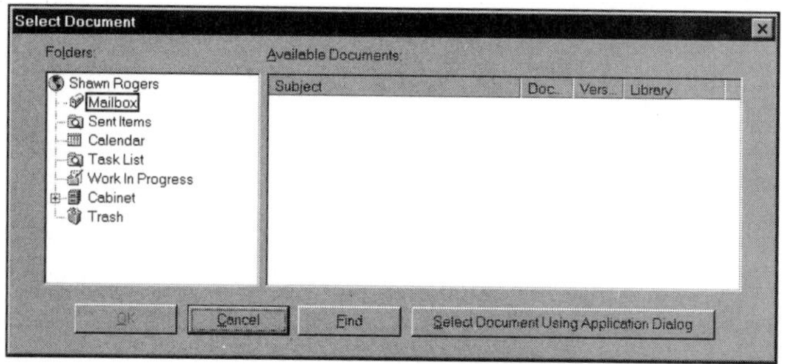

Documents are stored in GroupWise libraries and managed through a series of databases, which are a part of the GroupWise information store. Extensive document information, indexing, full-text search, check in/check out of documents, version control, and document locking are some of the features of GroupWise 5 document management. The Library object is associated with a post office, much like a Distribution List object or a Resource object. Chapter 17 covers document management in detail.

Summary

This chapter covered the GroupWise architecture on several different levels: NDS integration, NDS objects, and the GroupWise components. These concepts provide a solid background for understanding the next chapter on a GroupWise system.

CHAPTER 3

Planning a GroupWise System

This chapter covers techniques for planning the implementation of a GroupWise system. We will endeavor to make planning your GroupWise system not only understandable and workable, but as stress-relieving as possible.

These techniques have been successfully used at a number of organizations with very different messaging requirements. The first part of the chapter deals with planning the structure of your system—namely, how users, post offices, and domains are organized and connected. The second part of the chapter deals with the practical steps you need to take (such as NDS integration and hardware and software requirements) as you prepare to install the GroupWise system.

If you have some knowledge of networking, an understanding of what your company needs out of a messaging system, and a measure of courage, you can plan your GroupWise system with the methodology provided in this chapter.

Designing and Implementing Your System

In a general sense, you could say that GroupWise system design is done *from the ground up*. In other words, when you design a GroupWise system, you start out with the most fundamental pieces—users and the physical layer of the network (networking hardware and layout)—and work your way up to the post offices and the domain level.

As you can see in Figure 3.1, however, while design is done from the ground up, implementation of the GroupWise system is the exact opposite. You install GroupWise *from the top down*. When you create your GroupWise system, you create domains, then post offices, and then add users to the post offices.

When you design your domain and post office structure, you need to:

- Analyze the network substructure
- Group users into post offices
- Group post offices into domains

During the planning phase, try to be as thorough as possible. Be sure to document user names, site locations, administrators, and so forth.

FIGURE 3.1

Design Versus Implementation

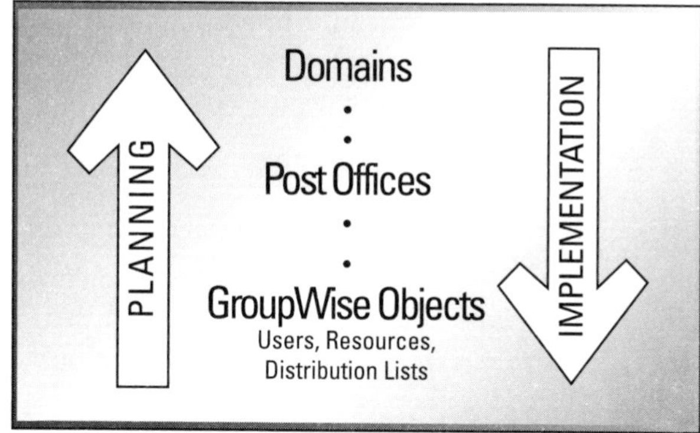

As you create the layout for the system, you need to settle on some naming conventions. The way you name the components of your GroupWise system is very important because once names are set, they are very difficult (and sometimes impossible) to change.

After you design the layout of the system and name the components, you need to plan the way you will connect the different parts of the system.

Analyzing the Network Substructure

The first step at this level is to gather information about the users. Things you're looking for include the following:

- *Workflow.* How do users communicate now? What communication patterns can you discern from the processes in place at the organization? Are there workgroups in place? Do workers in each group communicate primarily among themselves or with people outside the group?

- *Special messaging needs.* Do certain users frequently send large files (for example, graphics files) to one another? Are there mobile users or telecommuters from different departments who should be grouped into one post office for remote users?

- *Proxy.* Will some users need to access others' mailboxes? Although it's possible in GroupWise 5 to proxy across post offices, you'll generate less network traffic if you keep proxy users localized within one group rather than spread throughout your system.

- *Visibility.* Do some users want to be visible only in certain other users' Address Books?

Since messaging is such a vital component of today's business processes, now would be a good time to assess procedures to make sure they are efficient. This is called *business process re-engineering*. You can use GroupWise to eliminate redundancy in communications. And users will undoubtedly find new ways of doing old tasks.

IMPORTANT

When you're designing your system, remember to plan for growth.

The next step is to gather information about your organization's existing network. You'll need to analyze the following network-related issues:

- *Available bandwidth.* You may need to ask a network technician to analyze data traffic on your network and tell you how much "pipe" you have left for additional communications. This will help you decide whether the additional traffic created by GroupWise will cause too much strain on the network.

- *Protocols.* Identify which protocols are used on the various segments of your network. If you run IPX or TCP/IP, some of your GroupWise connectivity decisions will be easy to make, as you will find out later in this chapter.

- *Layout between sites.* Examine the layout of the physical connections between sites. The information you collect will help you decide on the links between the post offices and domains you set up.

- *Available servers/NOS.* You do not need to have NetWare 4.x installed at all of your sites in order to run GroupWise. However, GroupWise requires at least one NetWare 4.x or IntranetWare server for administration and NDS support.

In summary, assessing network issues will help you decide if, based on the hardware requirements, you are ready to install GroupWise. You need to assess what you have in place in terms of processor speed, RAM, and disk space. If you need to add hardware, your next step will be to determine exactly what you need (and how much you can afford). The specific hardware requirements for GroupWise 5 are discussed later in this chapter.

Grouping Users into Post Offices

Based on the information you learn about users' work habits and your network infrastructure, you need to combine users into post offices. Here are some common post office grouping strategies:

- *Users in the same department.* Perhaps the most common method of grouping users into post offices is to organize users by department. Usually, you can assume that users communicate most often with people in their own department.

- *Users who require a secure area for their messages.* Because messages for an entire post office are stored in a single directory on a file server, you should consider security when grouping people into post offices. If some messages are particularly sensitive, you might need to limit access to the file server where they are located.

- *Users who access the same file server.* If neither of the preceding conditions is relevant, you should look at the arrangement of file servers at your organization. It often makes sense to group users according to the file servers they access.

- *Users who share similar messaging habits.* You may want to create separate post offices for groups of users who have special messaging needs. For example, if certain members of an engineering department frequently send large CAD/CAM attachments to one another, they should be grouped together in their own post office. This helps to isolate heavy disk space usage to one location. You'll better understand the benefits of this type of arrangement after you read Chapter 6.

There's no right or wrong way to group users into post offices. However, if you can group together users who frequently correspond with one another, you'll have a system that operates more efficiently.

Grouping Post Offices into Domains

Once you have grouped users into post offices, you need to decide how to group the post offices into domains. You should consider several criteria when deciding how to group post offices into domains.

- Administration
- Interdepartmental communications
- Total number of post offices in your system
- MTA performance
- Political factors

The first thing to consider is how post offices will be administered. All of the post offices in a domain should fall under the same administrative umbrella. This means that all the users' networking and messaging needs are best handled as one logical grouping. Typical administrative duties include adding new users to the system, setting client program defaults, and managing the Information Store.

Next, look at the flow of interdepartmental communications. Messaging will be more efficient if you can group together the post offices that communicate the most frequently with one another. If certain post offices exchange messages frequently and you place them in different domains, message performance can suffer because two message transfer agents (MTAs) have to handle each message, as shown in Figure 3.2. If only one MTA is involved, the path a message takes from sender to recipient is much simpler.

FIGURE 3.2

Domain-to-Domain Messages

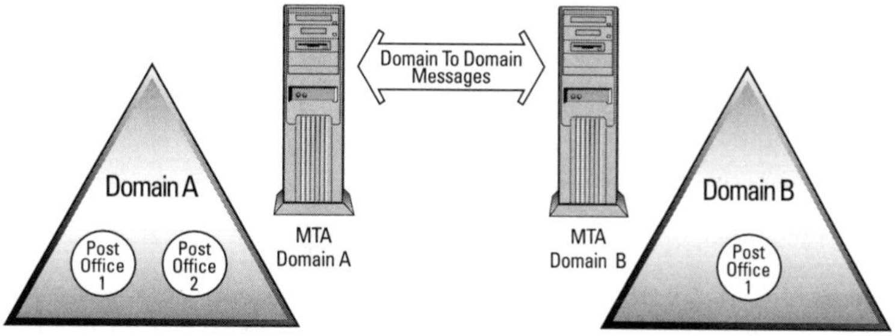

Another important factor to consider is the number of post offices in your system. As a general guideline, you should try to have no more than four to six post offices in a domain. Yes, we've heard of more, many more. But the new GroupWise licensing scheme doesn't force you to scrimp on your GroupWise message transfer system configuration. Trust us, four to six post offices in a domain is a manageable, highly functional configuration. If you have fewer than four post offices, you probably won't need more than one domain.

The critical factor here is the performance of the domain's MTA. The NLM, NT, and UNIX MTAs are about equal in terms of performance, so your choice of platform will be guided by available hardware and knowledge of the operating system.

If you are concerned about the speed of the links to post offices and the amount of time the MTA spends polling post office queues, you may consider creating a separate domain. This way, you have more MTAs involved, rather than overloading one MTA for many post offices.

Another factor in the performance of the MTA is its administrative synchronization role. If the MTA is moving a large number of administrative messages, it will be busy moving these instead of regular "production" messages. This is because administrative messages (Address Book updates and so on) are dealt with in the same priority directory as high-priority messages. You'll learn more about this in Chapter 9 when we explain directory synchronization.

Next, will there be a high volume of gateway traffic in this domain? If there will, the MTA will be less able to move messages between the post offices in that domain because it is so busy moving messages into and out of the gateway. Therefore, you might consider making a domain to hold only gateways.

Finally, there might be political reasons for grouping some post offices under a certain domain. For example, if a few departments make up a separate business unit within a company, it would probably make sense to group those departments in the same domain.

Deciding on Naming Conventions

Deciding on names for the different components of your GroupWise system is a crucial part of the planning process.

NOTE

Once you create a GroupWise system, domain, post office, or gateway, you cannot rename it without difficulty.

System Name

First of all, you need to decide on a name for your GroupWise system. It should represent your entire organization. The GroupWise system name is not used on a daily basis, or even seen by the end users. It is, however, used in two instances: when maintaining the software distribution directory and when setting up directory synchronization with other GroupWise domains.

The system name can be up to 32 characters long, but we recommend that you keep it short, like "SHICKSYS" for ShickTools, Inc.

Domain Names

Name Domain objects so that they correlate with the names of the post offices contained within them. You might decide to name your domains based on geography, business units, or divisions in your organization.

A domain name can also be up to 32 characters long, and you are restricted from using special characters. You can use numbers, letters, and even spaces. Remember, the domain will be an object in NDS, so if you have a naming convention established for NDS objects, you should use that for the GroupWise components.

Because the domain is a high-level GroupWise component, you name the domain based upon a geographic location, such as KCDOM, or after a major company division, such as SALESDOM. For example, if you have just one domain for your company, the domain will probably reflect the name of your company, like "SHICKDOM" for ShickTools, Inc. Don't name your domain something too generic, like GWDOMAIN. The domain name becomes part of the GroupWise address for every user in the domain.

It's a good idea to give the domain directory the same name as the domain. Consequently, you should try to come up with domain names that are eight characters (or fewer). You'll want to be able to tell from the directory name whether you're looking at a domain or post office directory.

Choose the domain name carefully. There's no easy way to change it once the domain is created.

Post Office Names

The post office name becomes part of the GroupWise address for every user in the post office. Consequently, post office names should somehow describe the corresponding users and objects. For example, in the Sales Department of our fictional company ShickTools, we might create a post office named "SALESPO." A post office name can be up to 32 characters long, but should be kept to eight characters or fewer. For administrative convenience, you should use the same name for the post office directory that you use for the post office itself.

Don't forget to use any established NDS conventions for the post office name.

Do not give your post office the same name as the server it resides on. This will cause a duplicate name conflict in NDS unless it is in a different container from the Server object. Also, be careful when choosing post office names. It's difficult to change names after post offices have been created.

Gateway Names

The naming of gateways is less crucial because they are system-level components. However, gateways should use intuitive names because users may specify the gateway name when they send mail through it.

The name of the gateway should reflect what type of gateway it is. For example, a good gateway name for your SMTP/MIME gateway would be "SMTP" or "INTERNET."

Object Names

If you already have a NetWare 4.x or IntranetWare network in place, the naming convention for NDS users will have been established when your NDS tree was developed. The GroupWise mailbox is a property of NDS user accounts. By default, the name of each user's mailbox is the same as the user's network login name. Nevertheless, when you create mailboxes, you have the option to give them different names.

GroupWise user names usually appear in the Address Book, and those names are the default names for Internet mail. Therefore, you should try to make every mailbox name in your system unique. This is particularly important for large organizations. If you are responsible for 3,500 users, you don't really want to set up user aliases for all of them. It is much easier if you can use the information you've already entered for the user names.

The mailbox name can be changed later on if your NDS naming convention changes (or if users' names change).

When naming GroupWise *resources*, you should select descriptive names. Users should be able to identify resources based on the names you choose. You should also try to keep resource names unique in order to simplify the Address Book listing. It is a good idea to develop a code to identify different kinds of resources: conference rooms, projectors, company cars, and so forth. This code might reflect the building the resources are in or the floor on which they're located.

Resources are associated with specific "owners." Resource owners must be GroupWise users that reside in the same post office as the resource. The owner automatically has full proxy rights to the resource's mailbox and is responsible for accepting or declining appointments made with the resource. Resources are discussed more in Chapter 7.

The last things to consider when deciding on naming conventions are distribution lists. Distribution lists are created by the system administrator in NDS and represent groups of mailboxes. These mailboxes could be actual users, resources, or both. The names of distribution lists need to be chosen early in the planning process so other administrators can follow established standards.

Planning System Connections

Once the GroupWise system has been laid out and naming conventions have been developed, you need to decide how you will link the system components. You'll need to determine the following:

- How the workstations will connect to each post office
- How the post offices will be connected within each domain

- How the domains in your system will be connected
- How to connect your system to other GroupWise systems
- How to connect your system to non-GroupWise e-mail systems and the Internet

NOTE

This section gives you an overview of various connection options. System connections are discussed in greater detail later in the book.

Workstation Connections

There are three ways of connecting the GroupWise 5 client to its post office information store and the post office agent:

- Direct with mapped connections
- Client/server with TCP/IP connections
- Remote connections

Your decision about which type of connections will be used is based largely upon the existing network protocols you are using. As a general rule of thumb, if you are using TCP/IP on your network, you should use client/server access.

If your network is exclusively IPX, you will probably decide to use direct IPX connections. If your network is exclusively TCP/IP, you will likely decide to use client/server connections. If you support multiple protocols in your network, pay close attention to the following descriptions of the connection types to decide how your users will connect to their post offices.

Direct with Mapped Using a suitable network connection software (network client) program, such as the NetWare 32-bit client for Windows 95, this type of connection uses a mapped drive to communicate with the post office directory. It requires that each user authenticate to the file server where the post office is located and, through NDS authentication, receive the necessary file system rights to access the information store.

When a user sends messages with a mapped connection, the message files are written to the information store; when a user receives a message, those messages are read from the information store. This type of configuration uses a licensed connection from the file server, and is generally used when you do not have TCP/IP implemented on your network.

Client Server with TCP/IP A client/server connection has three requirements (as you will see in Chapter 15): implementation of the TCP/IP protocol, a TCP/IP address for the workstation, and the TCP/IP address of the post office agent. A workstation using a client/server connection does not log in to the file server and use a connection; rather, it connects to the post office agent via a TCP/IP socket and sends the requests to the post office agent. Responses are then forwarded to the workstation. This type of connection requires no file system rights, thus enhancing file system security. Authentication is provided by NDS or at the mailbox with a GroupWise user ID and password.

Your primary concern when planning client/server connections has to do with the issues surrounding TCP/IP on your network. If you have other TCP/IP-based network applications (for example on an intranet), client/server would definitely be the preferred access method.

An excellent resource for TCP/IP networking is *Novell's Guide to TCP/IP and IntranetWare* by Drew Heywood (published by Novell Press and IDG Books Worldwide).

Remote Connections When users need to travel with their machines, GroupWise has the ability to run in Remote mode. In this mode, users do all GroupWise tasks (such as sending messages, managing appointments, etc.) offline and connect to the home system to upload changes.

During this remote connection, messages are uploaded to the post office, and incoming mail is downloaded. When planning for the use of GroupWise in Remote mode, you must plan on adding at least one GroupWise Async gateway to your system. The anticipated gateway traffic also needs to be taken into account.

For example, if one post office will have a relatively large number of mobile users, you should consider placing an Async gateway in the domain that houses that post office. If remote users are scattered throughout your system, you should place the Async gateway in a central domain. Chapter 19 covers remote connections.

Post Offices Connections The steps for creating the different kinds of post office links are covered in Chapter 8. For now, suffice it to say that the message transfer agent (MTA) is the process that moves messages between post offices within the same domain (see Figure 3.3).

FIGURE 3.3

Post Office Connections

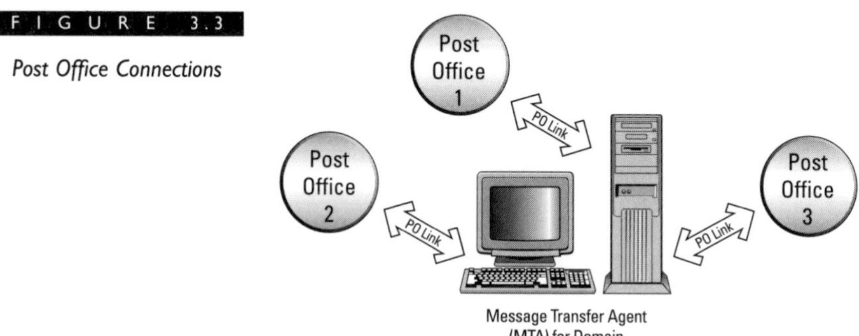

Again, based upon the protocols supported in your network, you will need to decide how post offices connect to other domains and post offices in the system. The same criteria apply here. If your network supports only IPX/SPX, you will likely use Universal Naming Convention (UNC), or mapped, connections. If your network supports only TCP/IP, you will likely use TCP/IP links between the post offices. If you support multiple protocols, review the link descriptions below to decide which types of post office connections you will use.

Generally, the TCP/IP method of connecting post offices is best used between physical locations connected by WAN links, such as Frame Relay, 56K, or T1. Within a single location over a LAN, UNC connections are best.

The different methods of connecting post offices determine how the MTA grabs messages from a sender's post office and transfers them to a recipient's post office.

A *UNC* or *mapped connection* is a direct connection between the machine running the MTA process and the file server that houses the post office you are configuring. A UNC or mapped connection requires authentication with a login ID and password, and it requires file system rights on the post office's file server. It also uses a network-licensed connection. This will add another license to your network operating system and require you to manage the assignment of adequate file system rights.

Alternatively, a GroupWise MTA can use a *TCP/IP link* to the target post office. Agents at both the domain and post office are defined in NDS as having a TCP/IP address, and these addresses use the TCP/IP networking protocol to send and receive messages. Chapter 10 covers this in much more detail.

The advantages of using a TCP/IP link to a post office are threefold: it does not require a login ID, file rights, or a connection. It is best used in a Windows NT environment or wide area network in which the MTA and the POA are located across a Frame Relay or 56K connection.

Domain Connections

When you link domains, you define the path messages take to get from one domain to another (see Figure 3.4). Messages between domains can be of any type—for example, e-mail, appointment requests, administration updates, error messages, or Internet messages.

FIGURE 3.4

Domain Links

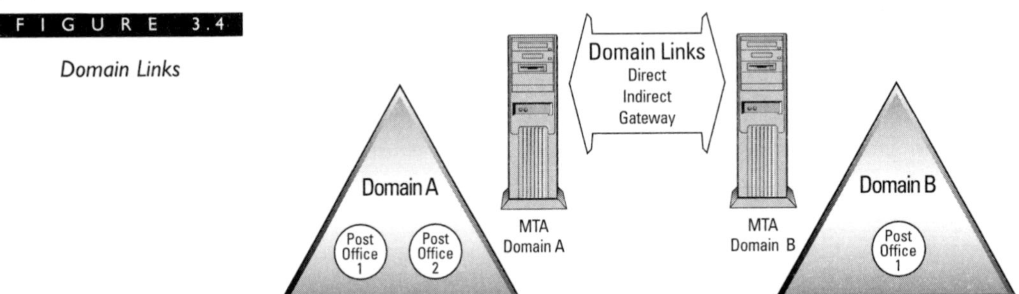

A direct UNC or mapped connection between two domains requires that one domain's MTA log in to the file server that houses the domain to which it's connected. This is accomplished by specifying a login ID and password for an "access account." The ID and password are used each time a connection is needed and give that account adequate file system rights to the target domain directory. In addition, the mapped connection takes up a network connection. We discuss GroupWise access accounts later in this chapter.

Use a mapped type of connection when the two domains are in the same building or on the same campus-type network with faster links.

A direct *TCP/IP connection* between domains is the preferred choice when the domain directories span many miles across slower connections, and where establishing a file system connection to the servers is not desirable or is even impossible. Another benefit of the TCP/IP link is that it allows communication between domains located on different network operating systems, such as NetWare and Windows NT or UNIX without needing unreliable or hard-to-configure connectivity software like NFS. A TCP/IP connection does not require a login ID, file system rights, or a connection. The only downside to it is the management of TCP/IP on your network.

When you have three or more domains, you might want to rely on *indirect links*, as shown in Figure 3.5. You can use your physical layer more effectively by routing messages through a common domain, instead of all domains sending messages directly to one another. Indirect links are discussed in more detail in Chapter 9, where we set up a multiple-domain system.

FIGURE 3.5

Indirect Domain Links

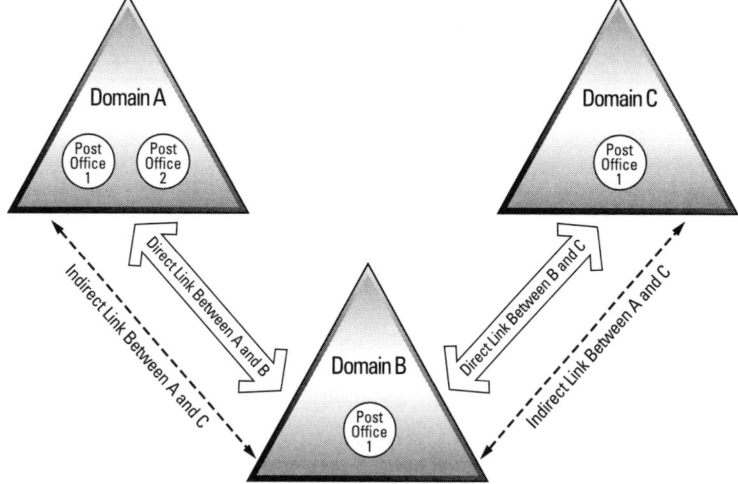

In some cases it may be necessary to set up *gateways* between two domains that are separated geographically. The system passes messages between the domains via the gateways. A multinational company with offices all over the world is a typical example of the need for this configuration. Physical connections that require a UNC, mapped, or TCP/IP connection may be very costly and difficult to maintain.

The Async gateway can be used to send messages between domains using two modems and a long-distance phone number. The benefits of using this configuration include the ability to maintain encrypted messages from point-to-point; security; and lower cost, since the connection is open only long enough to upload and download the messages, and is then broken. This is the preferred method of connecting two domains when a WAN connection to support either TCP/IP or mapped links would be costly or difficult to maintain.

Connections to Other GroupWise Systems

When it comes to making GroupWise interoperable with other messaging systems, Novell provides a wide array of gateways that give you extreme flexibility.

Whether you are connecting to another company that uses GroupWise or to another company that's never heard of GroupWise (perhaps somewhere in Redmond), gateways are most likely available that will provide an efficient solution.

When two separate companies both use GroupWise, you can implement gateways that ensure your messages are not being dissected and recompiled by some other type of messaging system, potentially losing formatting, message type, or status in the process.

When you need to communicate with other GroupWise systems, you represent their domains in your system as *external* GroupWise domains. Chapter 11 covers external domains in depth.

During the planning stages, you need to carefully evaluate the connectivity needs of your GroupWise system, finding out what other messaging systems GroupWise needs to connect with. This information will enable you to decide which gateways you need to implement, and where they will need to be located in the GroupWise system.

If your customers also use GroupWise, you can communicate with them using all of the GroupWise message types. If either your company or an outside company that you do business with has written an application to work with GroupWise, such as an order form, you can use this application within your client without needing to convert the message to some other e-mail system. You need to allow for this additional messaging overhead or potential gateways. Chapter 22 covers the technical "hooks" and programming interfaces into GroupWise.

GroupWise serves as an excellent platform for custom-written applications that can, for example, automatically send a message to reorder more carbide-tipped, 7" circular saw blades from your supplier. Their GroupWise system can then automatically forward the reorder message to the stock room, where the order would be fulfilled.

Even though you may create an external domain, post offices, and user records for the other GroupWise system, it is important to understand that from a security and planning perspective you remain completely independent from that system.

Within your organization, the domains, post offices, and mailboxes that you create physically exist as databases and directories on your network. The other GroupWise system's mailboxes, post offices, and domains are physically located on their file servers, while your GroupWise components are located "in house." The other system's administrators can't do anything to your actual user mailboxes or any other part of your GroupWise system.

In addition to keeping the GroupWise components separate, the naming conventions are independent as well. You import the other system's user names into your Address Book, but only as "external users," not actual users, on your system. The only requirement is that none of the other system's domain names are the same as yours.

Since you are remaining independent, you should populate your Address Books with the users on the other system, so they can be addressed easily. This is done initially by each system's administrator—exporting and importing the two lists of users. In other words, the other system's administrator will export its users to a file and send you the file. You will import them into your databases as belonging to the external domain and post office you have set up for them.

NOTE

When you add external users, you do not create any additional user databases. Consequently, you do not require any additional GroupWise licenses. You are *representing* the users from the other system.

GroupWise also has the ability to automatically synchronize Address Book changes between the two systems. This feature, along with Import and Export, is covered in detail in Chapter 11.

Just like any two domains in your system, you need to define the link between your domains and the domains in the other GroupWise system. You will define your link to them and they will define their link to you.

During the planning phase, the method of linking between the two systems will need to be established on both sides.

The use of *gateway links* to domains in other GroupWise systems is the most common method of linking between systems. The two most common gateways for this purpose are the GroupWise Async gateway and the SMTP gateway.

As we explain in Chapter 19, the Async gateway can be used with a modem at each domain. One gateway calls the other, and all messages are exchanged between the systems. The SMTP gateway is primarily used to send and receive Internet messages, but it can be used to link domains. Both domains must have the gateway up and running.

Since GroupWise will be used on both sides, there is an advantage with the SMTP gateway, called "passthrough messaging." This is very much like the large interoffice envelope that carries a smaller envelope. Once the receiving system gets the message, the outer SMTP envelope is removed and the original GroupWise message is delivered, unscathed by the gateway. Chapter 20 covers the SMTP/MIME gateway is much more detail.

A physical link between two separate companies is pretty rare, but it is an option. If there is a physical link between the two companies, depending on the protocol (IPX or TCP/IP) that it uses, you can set up a mapped or TCP/IP type of link. These links are covered in Chapter 10.

Connections to Non-GroupWise Systems and the Internet

The *external foreign domain* is used to define a non-GroupWise mail system. Chapter 20 explains in detail the steps for creating an external foreign domain.

Addressing Format Specifying your *addressing format* is a critical step in the plan for your GroupWise system, especially when you need to communicate with a non-GroupWise system. Inside the GroupWise system, your users use the Address Book to address messages, but there are many options for addressing messages to the outside world.

With the following features of GroupWise, you can manage how complicated (or not) the address for outside recipients will be:

- *Addressing Rules.* As you will see in Chapter 14, GroupWise lets you (the administrator) set up rules for addressing that can be applied to any domain. The Addressing Rules convert what the user types in the addressing fields in the client (To:, CC:, and BC:), into whatever form you set up as the resulting address. An example would be a long Internet address, i.e., `jack@sales.kansasuniversity.ks.edu`. With the appropriate rule set up, a GroupWise user could just type in `jack@ku.edu` and it would be converted to the actual address.

- *Explicit Addressing.* If you want to make your users work harder (and what administrator hasn't wanted to do that), you can spare yourself some system-level configuration and let the end user type in the necessary addressing components. This is discussed in more detail in Chapters 14 and 20. Explicit addressing can be used when only a few users need to communicate outside of GroupWise.

- *Aliases.* You can set up names for your users that don't have anything to do with the network (NDS login name or GroupWise mailbox name). These customized names let you use, for example, a registered domain name for the Internet as each user's Internet address. If you don't use aliases for either the user or the entire post office, the default Internet address for each GroupWise user will be used: `user@postoffice.domain.com`.

Planning your addressing format is important because—for security reasons—you usually don't want your GroupWise components to be published as part of your users' Internet addresses. In addition, if you use aliases, e-mail addresses to the outside world don't change when they are moved or renamed in the GroupWise system.

Legacy Systems If GroupWise is being installed alongside of a mainframe system that has a significant installed base, you will need to establish a connection to this system. This is done through a few gateways that Novell has for GroupWise: The SNADS gateway lets you talk to MVS- or AS/400-based systems (such as IMX, Memo, or Profs/Office Vision). The Profs/OV gateway for VM systems is available as well. If your legacy system is DEC, there is a DEC Message Router gateway for GroupWise. Chapter 18 covers these and other gateways.

Standards You need to decide what messaging standards you will support. Will you install five different gateways so you can talk to just about anyone, regardless of their system, or will you provide one or two of the more popular gateways? The answer really depends on how much your company is willing to spend in money and support to install and maintain these connectivity options. A few examples of the options you have include X.400, MHS, and SMTP/MIME.

Internet E-mail You can set up the SMTP/MIME gateway for anyone in your company who wishes to exchange mail with anyone on the Internet. You can put administrative controls on the use of this gateway—from getting a report of who uses it and where they send mail to limiting who has access to different levels of the gateway.

Getting Ready for Installation

This section discusses four practical aspects of preparing to install GroupWise in your company:

- Preparing NDS
- Checking Your Hardware
- Server-Level Implementation
- Client-Level Implementation

Preparing NDS

You'll recall from Chapter 2 that the basic structure of NDS includes container objects branching out from a [ROOT] object. Your NDS database is probably structured to match either your organization's structure or your organization's geographical layout. Consider the following NDS structure for our very own tool and dye company, ShickTools, Inc (see Figure 3.6).

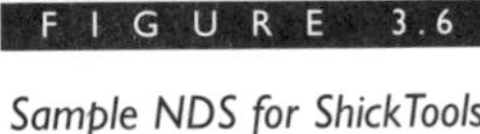

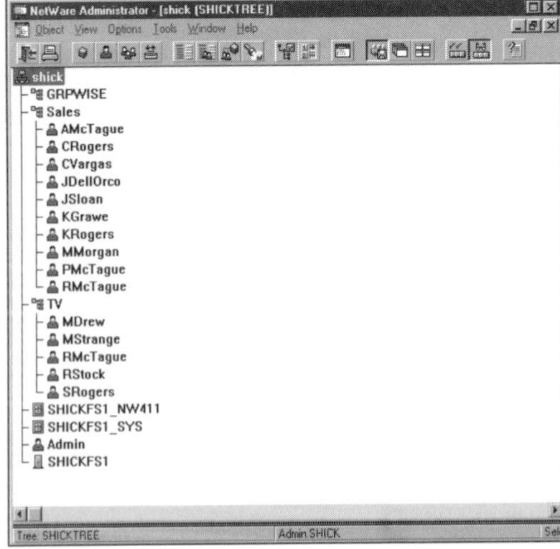

Sample NDS for ShickTools

Notice that the Organization (O) represents the entire company, while the Organizational Units (OUs) represent departments. Also notice the lack of any GroupWise objects in this tree. This condition is called *NDS B.G.* (before GroupWise). The GroupWise components must fit into this structure.

Creating GroupWise Component Containers

We suggest creating a separate organizational unit called "GRPWISE" for the system-level GroupWise components, and placing the user-level GroupWise components at the OUs where the users are located.

Consider the NDS tree in Figure 3.7, after we have added the GroupWise components.

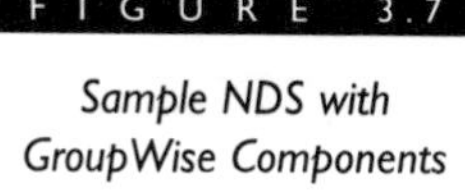

FIGURE 3.7

Sample NDS with GroupWise Components

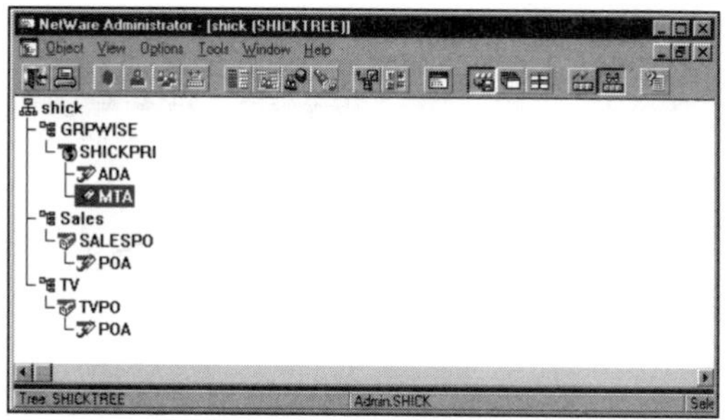

As you can see, we have created a "SALESPO" post office in OU=SALES, and a "TVPO" post office in OU=TV. OU=GRPWISE will hold the system-level GroupWise components: domain "SHICKPRI", user "GWACCESS," and the gateways that ShickTools will use. The benefits of having a separate container for the system components for GroupWise are twofold: it makes it easy to both grant and limit NDS rights for adding and denying access to change the properties of these components. It also makes it easy for administrators to find the domain they need to manage. This strategy is similar to some popular NDS tree designs in which Printer objects and other network resources have their own organizational unit.

Setting Up a GroupWise Access Account

You need an NDS user account that allows the GroupWise message transfer system to obtain access to the file system and NDS. This user account provides the login account required for the successful movement of messages and for the synchronization of NDS to the GroupWise Address Books. You won't use this user account on message transfer agents that use TCP/IP for all GroupWise communications in your system. However, you will use this for each administration agent (ADA) responsible for NDS user synchronization. This user account, which we like to call "GWACCESS," needs the NDS rights, as indicated in Table 3.1.

TABLE 3.1

NDS Rights for GWACCESS

OBJECT	NDS OBJECT RIGHTS	NDS PROPERTY RIGHTS
OU=GRPWISE	Supervisor	No Additional
Domain	Supervisor	No Additional
Post Office	Supervisor	No Additional

Table 3.2 shows the File System rights that GWACCESS needs.

TABLE 3.2

GWACCESS File System Rights

DIRECTORY	RIGHTS NEEDED
Domain Directory	R,W,C,E,M,F
Post Office Directory	R,W,C,E,M,F

In addition to these rights, the following properties need to be assigned for the user account GWACCESS:

- *Password.* You should set the password for the GWACCESS user and specify that it does not expire.
- *Login Restrictions.* Set the login restrictions for this user account to None.
- *Account Restrictions.* Configure the account with unlimited concurrent logins, and don't make any settings for workstation address limits.

In each STARTUP file for the agents that will use the GWACCESS account (the STARTUP file is a text file that includes the settings for each agent), you will use the GWACCESS username and password to gain access to the files and directories on other file servers. The STARTUP files are discussed in Chapter 4.

Designating NDS Rights for Administrators and Users

Table 3.3 shows the NDS object and property rights needed for GroupWise administrators and users:

TABLE 3.3

NDS Rights for Administrators and Users

NDS OBJECT	OBJECT RIGHTS (ADMIN)	OBJECT RIGHTS (USER)	PROPERTY	PROPERTY RIGHTS (ADMIN)	PROPERTY RIGHTS (USER)
Domain	Supervisor	None	N/A	No Additional	None
Post Office	Supervisor	Browse			
Distribution List	Supervisor	Browse	Name, Members	No Additional	Read
Resource	Supervisor	Browse	Name	No Additional	Read

Table 3.4 specifies the file system rights needed to administer and use GroupWise.

TABLE 3.4

File System Rights for Administrators and Users

	DOMAIN DIRECTORY	POST OFFICE DIRECTORY	SOFTWARE DIRECTORY
Administrator	R,W,C,E,M,F	R,W,C,E,M,F	R,W,C,E,M,F
Users	None	R,W,C,E,M,F	R,F

NOTE

To enhance the security of your post office directory, you can further assign rights to the individual subdirectories under the post office and limit the rights given to the "root" of the post office directory. See the online help files in NetWare Administrator.

NDS Version Patches

You will receive the latest version of NetWare 4.11 with GroupWise 5. This is a full-featured, two-user license version of NetWare. It is intended to be installed on at least one file server, for administration. This version already has the "latest and greatest" from Novell.

If you already have NetWare 4.1, you can use your existing version of NetWare without upgrading to 4.11. To do this, you must make sure you have the latest version of all of the patches for NetWare 4.x. These patches, current at the time of this writing, are available at `http://support.novell.com/search/patlst.htm`.

Instructions on how to update your operating system with these patches are included with each patch file. The self-extracting files will expand into several files, including a README.TXT file for installation instructions.

As with any operating system patch, make sure you have a good backup before applying the patches. We make these recommendations to patch your operating system based on many hours of lab time and also per instructions from Novell. Be advised that other software on your system might not like the newest versions of NLMs that these patches will install. We cannot be held responsible for lost data or other calamities that stem directly or indirectly from applying these patches. On the other hand, if you don't apply them, you are not guaranteed success.

Checking Your Hardware

Prior to the actual installation of GroupWise on a production network, we strongly recommend installing a test server (with its own NDS tree). This test system can be used to determine if there are any software conflicts, and how the patches will behave.

Use the following guidelines to help you set up the test system and to prepare your actual servers and workstations for GroupWise. These are the published requirements from Novell, plus some real-world requirements thrown in for good measure.

Server Requirements

These requirements apply equally to NetWare and Windows NT servers.

The domain directory will use about 30 MB of free disk space to house the domain directories and files. This estimate will grow as your system grows because the domain database holds information about your entire GroupWise system.

The server that will house the post office directories and information store will need about 30–40 MB of free disk space for every user in the post office. This allows for a fairly large number (500 or more) of messages per mailbox, plus calendar information and other message types. The amount of space required is greater if you implement GroupWise document management.

At a minimum, you should have at least 4MB of RAM for each GroupWise NLM that will run on the server. The total amount of memory on your server is relative to the software you are running and the size of the disk drives. On any Novell server, the amount of available memory (cache buffers) should be in the 75–85 percent range. See online help in the NetWare Administrator for more information on cache buffers.

NOTE

With regard to network operating system version requirements, GroupWise supports the NLM agents running on NetWare 3.x or later; and the NT agents running on Windows NT servers or Workstation 3.51 or later.

Workstation Requirements (Win32, Win 16)

On the workstation side, minimum hardware and software requirements must be met. Table 3.5 lists the workstation requirements for running the different versions of the GroupWise client.

TABLE 3.5

Workstation Requirements

PLATFORM	DISK SPACE	RAM	NETWORK CLIENT
Windows 95	8MB (Workstation) 24MB (Local)	20MB	NetWare Client 32 for Windows 95 Microsoft NetWare Client for Windows 95 (Requires patches—see online help)
Windows NT 4.0	8MB (Workstation) 24MB (Local)	32MB	NetWare Client 32 for Windows NT
Windows 3.1	2MB (Workstation) 20MB (Local)	16MB	Client 32 for DOS and Windows NetWare Client for DOS and Windows 3.x (VLMs)

NOTE

GroupWise Administration through NetWare Administrator can be performed on any Windows-based computer running a version of Novell's Client 32.

This section has outlined the hardware and software requirements of GroupWise on your network, from the file server to the workstation. Once you have met the requirements in this section and have a solid plan in place, you are ready to plan your rollout.

System-Level Implementation

The exact steps for installation of the GroupWise software are covered in Chapter 4. The purpose of this section is to give you the "big picture" so you can begin planning your project.

Administrator Training

Getting training is an excellent first step in implementation because you will be familiar with the screens and will have had your hands on the software before you install it on your live production system.

Certified training from Novell Education ensures that you receive the best training on this product. The courses cover all phases of installing, administering, and maintaining; the instructors are willing to answer your questions; and classroom training gives you a chance to break a system that you don't have to fix. For more information, see the Novell Education home page at `http://education.novell.com`.

Software Installation

The actual installation of the GroupWise software is pretty straightforward. With its Wizard-like interface, the Install program is easy to follow. It takes about one to two hours at the outside to complete installation. You will do two important things during the installation program: extend the NDS schema and copy software to the file server.

Creation of GroupWise Components

Immediately following the installation program, you will be able to launch right into NetWare Administrator. Here you are greeted by another Wizard. This one guides you through the creation of your first domain and post office, letting you add users, load agents, and install the client software on the workstation you are using.

Again, the installation routine is very well written, and it is easy to follow. For the simplest systems (single domain, single post office), you leave with a complete, functioning GroupWise system. You are ready to install the client on each workstation and GroupWise the day away.

For those with more complex systems, there is more work left. But never fear, your faithful co-authors are here to walk you through it.

Client-Level Implementation

When it comes time to implement the GroupWise client, you need to know the installation options so you can decide upon the most effective strategy for the client installation.

Installation Options

Decisions that need to be made with regard to the client software include where to install the executable files (on the local hard drive or the network), and which connection type you will use (connection types to the workstation were covered briefly earlier in this chapter).

A "standard" installation places the client on the user's local hard drive. This option provides the best GroupWise performance because it limits the amount of network traffic. However, this option is the most difficult to maintain because it requires a complete reinstallation each time the client software is updated.

A "workstation" installation only places a few GroupWise files on the local hard drive, and it modifies the Registry. This is a good option if network traffic is not an issue or when you need to upgrade the client software without touching each workstation.

We'll guide you through the installation of the client in Chapter 5.

Rollout

Usually, you start with a pilot project team that assesses how your company can best use GroupWise. The team can also help you make decisions about company e-mail policies regarding storage, privacy, and use of GroupWise. (Sample e-mail policies can be found in Appendix C.)

Following the pilot period, it makes sense most of the time to roll out the product one department at a time.

End User Training

There are many training options for users. Your local Novell Authorized Education Center probably has a solution for customized training of end users if they teach the GroupWise certification courses. Novell Press and IDG Books Worldwide have published our book *Novell's GroupWise 5 User's Handbook*, which covers all facets of the client.

Summary

In this chapter, we looked at the necessary steps for creating a design for your GroupWise system. We brought together the topics of designing the GroupWise components, naming conventions, connections, hardware and software requirements, and developing an implementation strategy for your system.

Chapter 4 explains GroupWise installation in more detail.

PART II

Small GroupWise Systems

CHAPTER 4

Installing and Configuring a GroupWise System

In Part I, you learned the background information you need before you can implement GroupWise. In Chapter 3, you learned how to plan your GroupWise implementation. Once you have developed an implementation plan, you are ready to begin the installation process. It's now time to get into the actual installation and configuration of a GroupWise system. In Part II, you'll learn how to install, configure, and manage a small system.

NOTE

If you are currently using a GroupWise 4 system, you can migrate to GroupWise 5 instead of starting over from scratch. See Chapter 16 for instructions on migration.

What You Need to Do Before Installation

The first thing you should do before running the installation program is go to the root of the GroupWise CD, retrieve README.TXT into a word processor, and print out a copy. This file is constantly updated with the latest "gotchas." While your installation may go perfectly and you won't need to refer to this file, it is your first line of defense if something does go wrong during the installation. This file also contains important information about preparing to install GroupWise, including details about patches and recommended network client versions and configuration settings.

If you are planning to upgrade your NetWare 4.1 system to IntranetWare or NetWare 4.11, you should perform the upgrade before installing GroupWise. This will ensure that you have the latest and greatest network operating system. Otherwise, make sure you have the latest NetWare patches on your 4.1 system, including the latest version of Directory Services (DS.NLM). (For information on the patches needed, see the README.TXT file.)

Here are the prerequisites for GroupWise 5 installation:

- You need at least one server running NDS. (At press time, NetWare 4.1 and IntranetWare are the only means of running NDS.)

- You need a workstation capable of running version 4.11 of NetWare Administrator. This requires Windows 95 or Windows NT 4.0 running NetWare Client 32, or a Windows 3.x machine running

Client 32 for DOS/Windows. (See the README.TXT on the GroupWise CD-ROM for the required versions and dates for your NetWare client.)

- You need to be logged in to NetWare as the Administrator (or equivalent) with Supervisor rights to the [ROOT] object of the NDS tree you are installing GroupWise in. These rights are needed to extend the NDS schema.

The Supervisor right to [ROOT] is only required for the schema extension operation. If the schema already has the GroupWise extensions, the Supervisor right to [ROOT] is not needed for GroupWise installation.

In addition to the preceding requirements, you should determine the following before you begin the installation process:

- The languages that you need to install to support your user base
- The gateway types that you need to use in your GroupWise system
- How you will distribute the GroupWise client software
- The client versions you will need to support
- The name for your GroupWise system
- The name for your GroupWise primary domain
- The NDS context that will contain your Domain object
- The name for your first GroupWise post office
- The NDS context that will contain your Post Office object
- The server platform (NetWare or Windows NT) that will hold the domain, post office, and software distribution directories

- The name of the server, volumes, and directories for the domain, post office, and software distribution directories
- Which NetWare users will be assigned to the first post office

This information should have been determined during system planning, explained in Chapter 3.

Finally, before you begin the installation process, you need to create the GroupWise access account, GWACCESS, and grant this user account the rights necessary to log in to NDS and access the servers on which the domain and post offices will be located. As explained in Chapter 3, this user account is necessary for the following reasons:

- The ADA needs this account to synchronize user information between NDS and the GroupWise system.
- The ADA, MTA, and POA need this account in order to write to the domain and post office directories on the servers on which the domain and post offices are located.

NOTE

The GWACCESS account is required anytime you are not using TCP/IP links between domains and post offices. We strongly recommend that you include a reference to this GWACCESS user account in each agent's startup file, whether it will be used by the agent or not. Agent configuration and links are discussed in Chapter 12.

As we recommended in the preceding chapter, create this user account in the GRPWISE container and grant the User object the following rights:

- Read and Compare property rights and Browse object rights to the Organizational Unit (OU) object containing the post office or to the Post Office object itself
- Read and Compare property rights and Browse object rights to any OUs containing users who will be added to the post office

- Read and Compare property rights and Browse object rights to the GRPWISE OU (where the GWACCESS User object resides and where you will place the Domain object)
- Read, Write, Create, Erase, Modify, and File Scan (R, W, C, E, M, F) file system rights to each domain and post office directory structure

Running the Installation Program

Before you begin installing GroupWise, we want to give you an advance warning: During the installation we will recommend two slight procedure deviations. First, toward the end of the installation, you are prompted to load the GroupWise agents from the installation program. We recommend that you skip this step and load the agents after the installation is complete. Second, the last step in the installation prompts you to install the client software. Again, we recommend that you skip this step, and in Chapter 5 we will teach you how to load the client in the normal way (i.e., not from within the GroupWise setup Advisor.)

We recommend these deviations because in most cases the installation routine is not very "real-world." The installation program is written to take you from D:INSTALL to sending GroupWise messages. While it is a nice goal (and will work well in a very small GroupWise system running on a single file server), in most cases it's not very practical.

One more note: In this section we'll assume you are running GroupWise in the traditional file access mode or "Direct Only mode" (that is, not in Client/Server mode). We explain how to configure GroupWise to run in Client/Server mode in Chapter 15.

Overview of Phase I

In Phase 1 of the installation program you extend the NDS schema and copy the GroupWise software to various places on the file server. In Phase 2, you will actually create the GroupWise components.

Starting the installation program is a simple process. From a Windows 95 machine on which you are logged in to the network with Administrator rights, click on Start, and then Run.

Browse to the root directory of the CD-ROM and double-click on INSTALL.EXE.

The Welcome to GroupWise Install window, shown in Figure 4.1, appears.

FIGURE 4.1

GroupWise Installation Window

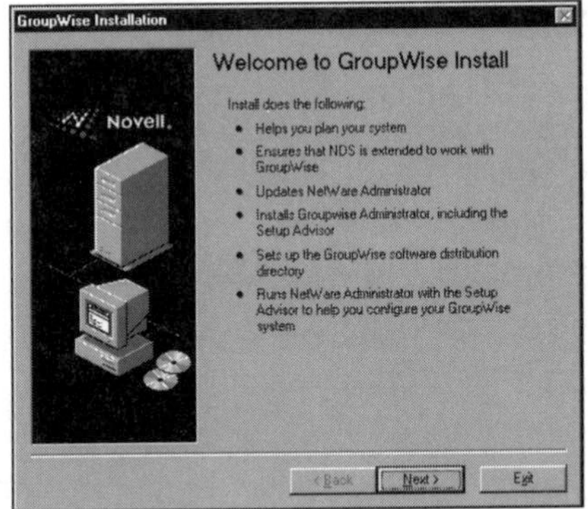

Click on Next to continue with the installation. The License Agreement dialog box appears. It contains important information that you should read very carefully, at least three times (yeah, right), and then click on Accept to proceed.

After you accept the license agreement, the Plan Your System dialog box appears. The Plan button launches GroupWise online help and gives you information about planning your system. But because you have already planned your system when you followed the procedure explained in Chapter 3, you can skip this and click on Next to jump into the installation. We think you should plan your system long before you start INSTALL.EXE.

The Check NDS dialog box, shown in Figure 4.2, appears.

IMPORTANT

If you have multiple trees in your NetWare or IntranetWare network, make sure that the NDS tree indicated in the Check NDS dialog box is the correct tree. If it is not correct, you should connect to the correct tree with the Network Neighborhood utility.

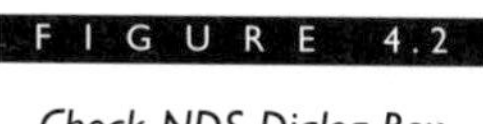
FIGURE 4.2

Check NDS Dialog Box

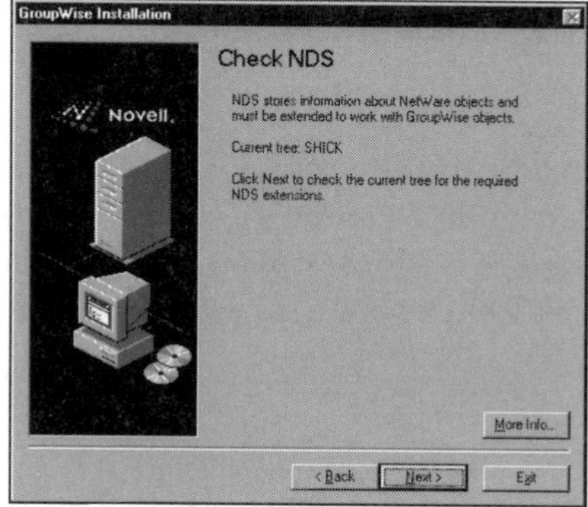

Extending the NDS Schema

Novell Directory Services (NDS) is the master directory database for NetWare 4.11 and IntranetWare. By default, NDS only contains fields for the NDS objects and their associated properties.

Because GroupWise needs to add information specific to the GroupWise system, the NDS schema must be extended to hold the GroupWise information. As you saw in Chapter 3, the NDS schema will be extended for the current NDS tree.

IMPORTANT

Make sure all servers in the replica ring of the root partition are up and running and in sync before you extend the schema. Also, make sure no one else is running a program that will extend the schema at the same time.

Note that extending the NDS schema is a universal change to the NDS database structure. We recommend that you make a backup of NDS before proceeding with the GroupWise installation.

To extend the schema:

1. From the Check NDS dialog box, click on Next. The installation program checks for the NetWare 4.1 base schema, the NetWare 4.11 base schema, schema extensions already made by the GroupWise 4.1 snap-in module, and GroupWise 5.0 schema extensions. A dialog box appears telling you if the NDS schema must be extended.

2. Choose Next to extend the NDS schema.

After the process completes, a dialog box appears indicating the success of the operation. When you click on Next, you will be prompted to select the language.

NOTE

Once the schema has been extended, Supervisor rights to [ROOT] are no longer necessary. The remainder of the GroupWise installation and configuration only requires file system rights to the locations of the software, post office, and domain directories; and NDS rights to the containers that will hold GroupWise objects.

Selecting the Software Languages

The languages you select in the dialog box (see Figure 4.3) determine the software languages that will be made available to you (as the administrator) and the GroupWise users.

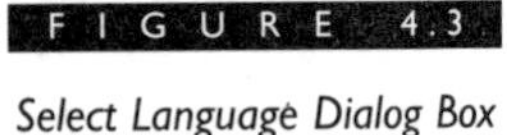
FIGURE 4.3

Select Language Dialog Box

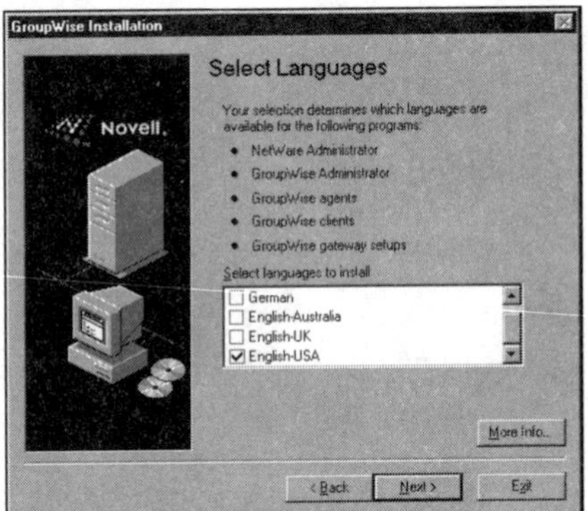

When users install the client at their workstations, only the languages you select in this dialog box will be available to them. Select one or more languages to install, and then choose Next.

The NetWare Administrator Path dialog box, shown in Figure 4.4, appears.

The NetWare Administrator Path dialog box prompts you for the path to the SYS:\PUBLIC directory on your NetWare server that will contain both the NetWare Administrator 4.11 program files and the GroupWise components that enable GroupWise administration from within NetWare Administrator.

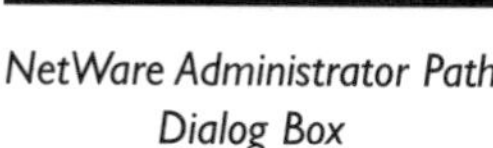

NetWare Administrator Path Dialog Box

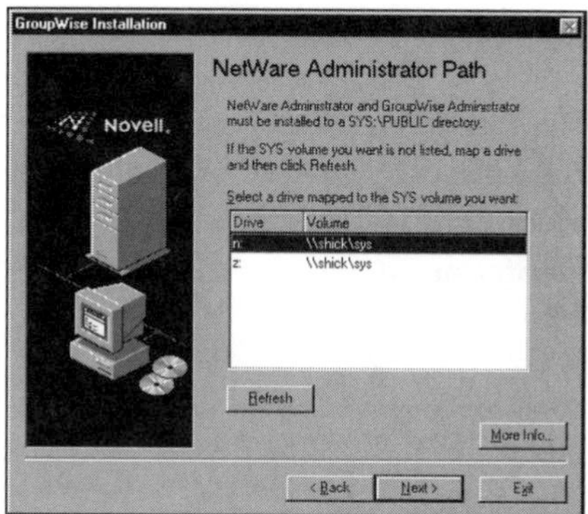

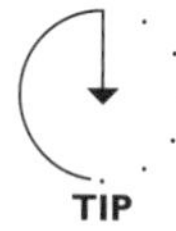

If you are not mapped to volume SYS:, click the desktop and use Network Neighborhood or Windows Explorer to map a drive to the SYS: volume. When you return to the GroupWise Installation window, click Refresh and the drive you mapped will appear.

Select a path and choose Next. The Select Gateway Setups dialog box appears (see Figure 4.5).

Selecting Gateways

In the Select Gateway Setups dialog box, shown in Figure 4.5, you must select the gateways that you will support in your GroupWise 5 system. This does not install the actual gateway software, but will install the supporting dynamic link library (DLL) files for supporting and administering the gateway from NetWare Administrator.

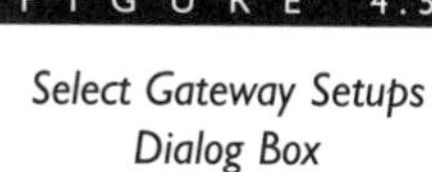

Select Gateway Setups Dialog Box

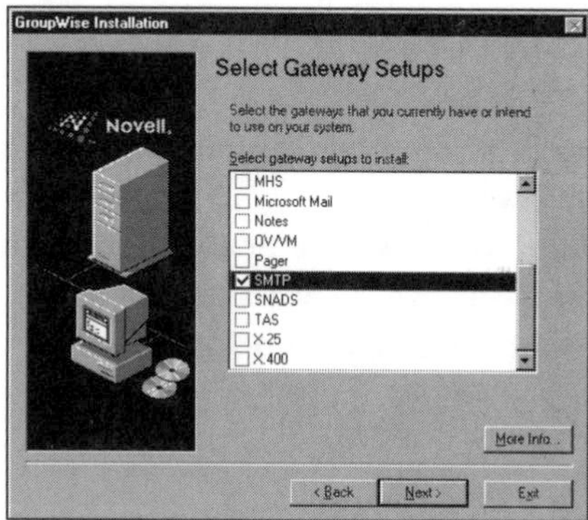

We recommend that you select any gateways you think you might eventually install. They don't take very much space, and might save you some additional steps later on. Otherwise, you will have to run this installation program again to enable new gateways for GroupWise. This is discussed in more detail in Chapter 18. We usually select all gateways for the installations we perform.

For each gateway you select, the gateway administration DLL files are copied to the SYS:\PUBLIC directory.

After you have made your gateway selections, click on Next.

Choosing a Software Distribution Method

When you choose Next in the Select Gateway Setups dialog box, the Software Distribution Method dialog box (see Figure 4.6) appears.

FIGURE 4.6

Software Distribution Method Dialog Box

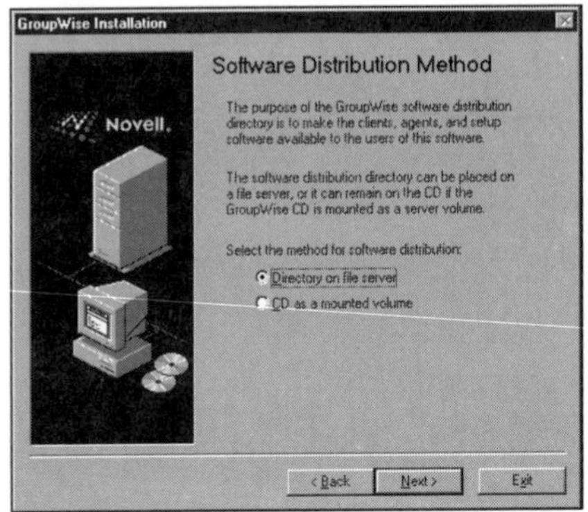

You have two options for the software distribution method. You can choose to place the GroupWise files on a directory on a file server (the most common choice), or you can choose to keep the GroupWise CD-ROM in a CD-ROM drive mounted as a NetWare volume.

NOTE

At this point you are only creating the initial software distribution directory. This software directory is going to be your primary software directory, which will be updated first with new versions of GroupWise. Later, you can create additional GroupWise software directories to meet the needs of other administrators and GroupWise users.

The advantages of placing the files on a NetWare directory are speed and efficiency of access, especially when multiple users are accessing the files simultaneously. It is most efficient to place the files in a NetWare directory if users will run the client from a network directory. The disadvantage of this method is that it is less convenient to update when newer GroupWise code is released.

The advantage of keeping the GroupWise files on a CD-ROM drive is ease of updating. You simply replace the CD when newer GroupWise code is released.

NOTE

If users will need to run GroupWise from the network, the CD-ROM drive will not provide satisfactory performance for loading the client software.

Select the option you want to use and click on Next. The Select Software dialog box appears, as shown in Figure 4.7.

FIGURE 4.7

Select Software Dialog Box

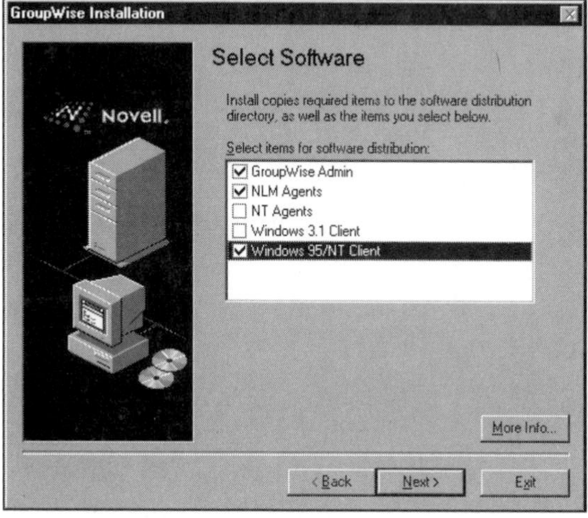

The Select Software dialog box presents you with the options for which versions of the client and agents you want to install. You should choose all of the versions you will use in your GroupWise implementation.

Use the following criteria to decide which options to mark in the Select Software dialog box:

- If you need to administer your GroupWise system from other administration workstations in the network, choose GroupWise Admin.

- If you will run the GroupWise Agents as NLMs on a NetWare server, select the NLM Agents option.
- If you will use the GroupWise Agents on a Windows NT Server, select the NT Agents option.
- If you have users running Windows 3.1, they will need the 16-bit GroupWise 5 client. Select the Windows 3.1 client option.
- If you have users who will be running GroupWise on Windows 95 or Windows NT 4.0, select the Windows 95/NT client option.

IMPORTANT

The options you choose in the Select Software dialog box are not mutually exclusive. You should select all software versions you need in your system.

Click on Next after making your selections. The Software Distribution Directory dialog box appears. Enter the directory for the software and click on Next.

At this point, you may get a warning dialog box stating that some of the files on your system are newer files or are flagged as read-only. If a warning dialog box appears, as shown in Figure 4.8, you should choose the default (replace the files that are read-only or do not replace newer files). Otherwise, GroupWise may not function properly. You can use the recommended choices made by the installation program with no problems. Remember, you should perform a complete backup before you install GroupWise.

If the dialog box shown in Figure 4.8 appears, select Replace Files and click on Next. The Ready to Install dialog box appears.

NOTE

Up to this point, only two things have been changed on your system: the schema extension and the creation of an empty software distribution directory. If you need to change any of the selections you have previously made, click on Back to cycle backward through the dialog boxes.

FIGURE 4.8

Existing Files Warning

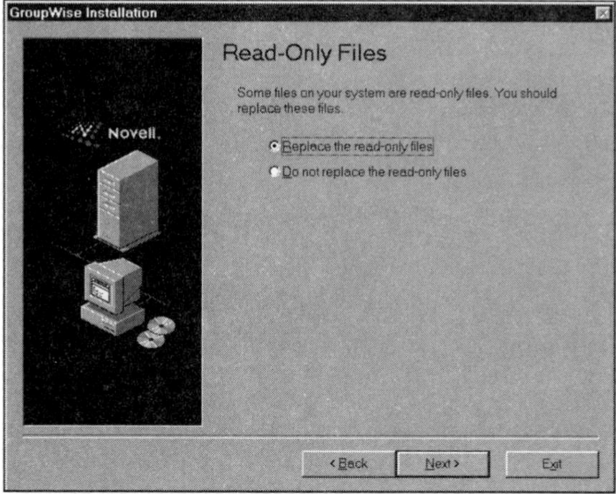

Installing the GroupWise Software

Now choose Install. The Installing GroupWise dialog box appears, showing the installation progress. This is a good time for a five- or ten-minute coffee break.

Several events occur behind the scenes during the installation. The NetWare 4.11 NetWare Administrator files, the GroupWise administration files, and the gateway DLL files are installed to the appropriate directories. In addition, the installation process creates the following software directories under the path defined for the software distribution directory (assuming that the CD-ROM option was not selected for software distribution):

- **ADMIN.** Contains the administration workstation setup program (explained later in this chapter) and the administration help files.
- **AGENTS.** Contains the agent files (MTA, ADA, POA, and supporting files)
- **CLIENT.** Contains the client files. It may contain WIN16 and WIN32 if you selected both versions to install.
- **DOMAIN.** Contains the domain database template files GWDOM.DC, WPDOMAIN.DC, and WPHOST.DC. (These files are needed when you perform maintenance on the GroupWise databases,

and to allow for backward compatibility with earlier versions of GroupWise. Database maintenance is explained in Chapter 13.)

- **PO.** Contains the post office database template files, NGWGUARD.DC and WPHOST.DC.

In addition to these files, a NetWare tools program group is created in Windows 95 with an icon for NetWare Administrator 4.11. A dialog box appears (see Figure 4.9), explaining the need to use NetWare Administrator 4.11 instead of earlier versions.

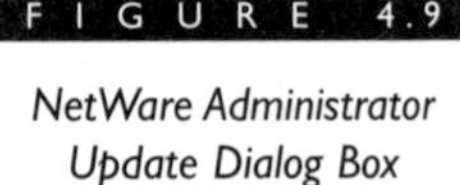

FIGURE 4.9

NetWare Administrator Update Dialog Box

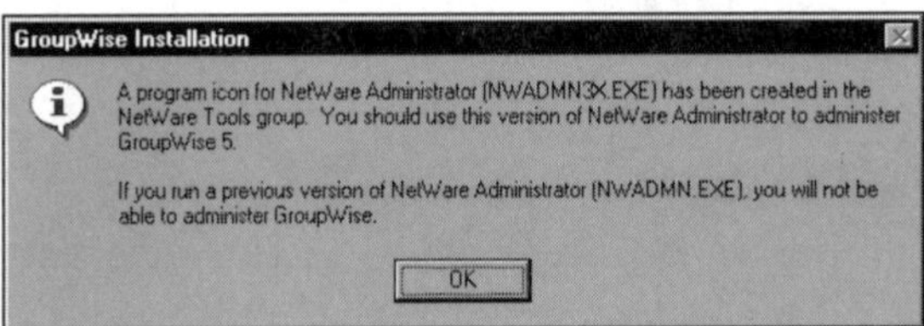

GroupWise Installation
A program icon for NetWare Administrator (NWADMN3X.EXE) has been created in the NetWare Tools group. You should use this version of NetWare Administrator to administer GroupWise 5.
If you run a previous version of NetWare Administrator (NWADMN.EXE), you will not be able to administer GroupWise.
OK

IMPORTANT

If you use a version of NetWare Administrator earlier than 4.11 (for example, the version in NetWare 4.1 called NWADMIN.EXE) you will still be able to administer your network, but the GroupWise objects will appear as question marks and will not be manageable. Note that it is possible to delete these objects. *Be careful not to delete them if they appear as question marks.*

Click on OK in the Update dialog box to continue.

Running NetWare Administrator

After the installation process is complete (and after you've finished your tall vanilla latte), the Run NetWare Administrator dialog box appears, as depicted in Figure 4.10.

When you click on Run in the Run NetWare Administrator dialog box, version 4.11 of NetWare Administrator launches. At this point you have installed the GroupWise software and are ready to begin creating your GroupWise system.

NetWare Administrator 4.11 uses an .INI file named NWADMN3X.INI. This file is located in the C:\WINDOWS directory and contains lines directing NetWare Administrator where to look to find a GroupWise domain. These lines are added to the .INI file when the primary domain is created.

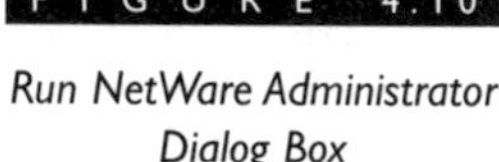

FIGURE 4.10

Run NetWare Administrator Dialog Box

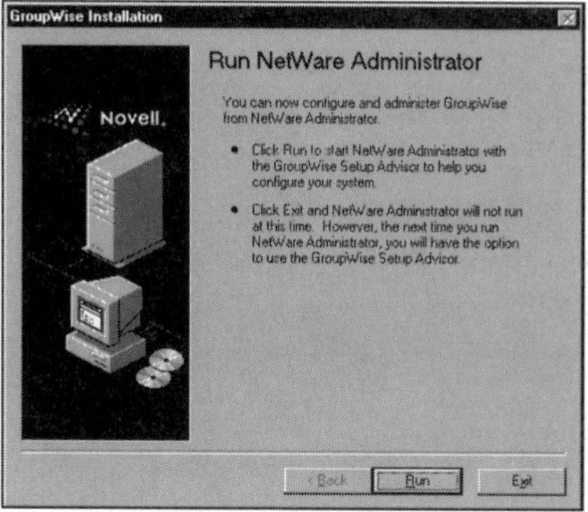

Because a GroupWise system has not been previously configured, NetWare Administrator detects no GroupWise system and launches the GroupWise 5 Setup Advisor.

NOTE

You may get a dialog box prompting you to update the NDS schema for NetWare Application Manager (NAM). If you get this dialog box, click Modify to add NAM fields to the schema and proceed. This is not related to the GroupWise installation, but to the upgraded version of NetWare Administrator.

The Setup Advisor first presents you with the Welcome to GroupWise Setup dialog box (see Figure 4.11) and asks you to specify if you are creating a new GroupWise system or migrating from GroupWise 4.1. (Migration is explained in Chapter 16.)

Choose Next to begin setting up a new GroupWise system.

And now for a word from our sponsors. At this point, you have created nothing. Doesn't that fill you with a sense of accomplishment? All you have done is prepare NDS for GroupWise and copied some software to a file server. In the next phase of the installation program, you will actually produce something—the first GroupWise domain and post offices—and then add users to the post office. We just wanted to stop and encourage you a little bit. And now, back to the show.

If you like, you can stop the installation at this point. The next time you run NetWare Administrator 4.11, you will again be prompted to start configuring GroupWise. Like that annoying battery-operated rabbit on TV, the prompt to create your GroupWise system will just keep popping up over and over until you do it.

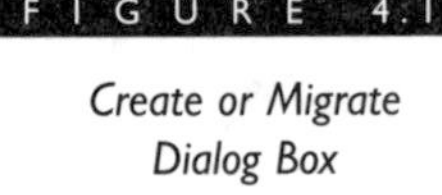
FIGURE 4.11

Create or Migrate Dialog Box

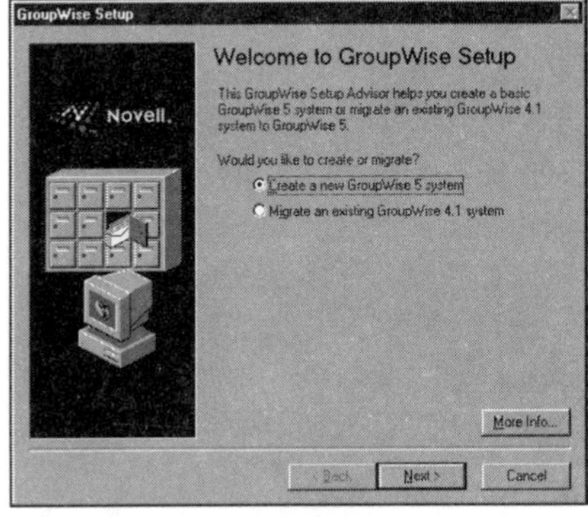

Overview of Phase 2

In Phase 2 of the installation, you will create the GroupWise components, install the agents, and be able to install the client. But, as we said at the beginning of this chapter, we cover the client installation in the next chapter. So we will be breaking out of the installation program at that point.

Naming Your GroupWise System and Creating the First Domain

The first dialog box you see when you begin setting up a GroupWise system is the GroupWise Setup Progress dialog box, shown in Figure 4.12. This dialog box will appear several times throughout the process, indicating the progress you are making with the system setup.

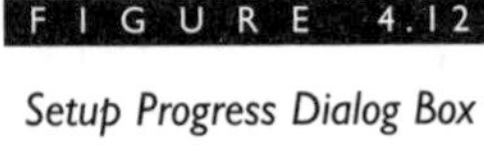
FIGURE 4.12

Setup Progress Dialog Box

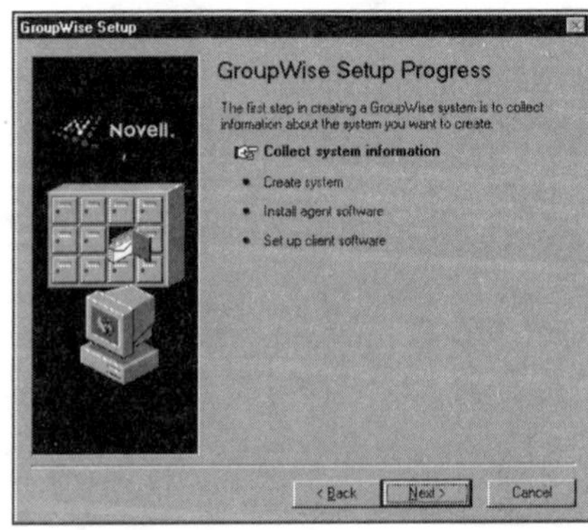

Choose Next to proceed. The Setup Advisor asks you to verify the location of the software distribution directory you created previously. Verify that the directory is correct and click on Next.

The Setup Advisor next asks if it has detected the correct NDS tree. The tree listed is where the GroupWise primary domain will be created. Verify that the correct tree is listed. If the correct tree is not listed, you can click outside of the Setup Advisor to get to NetWare Administrator. Then click on Tools, NDS Browser, and select the correct tree.

NOTE

In most systems, there will be only one NDS tree.

The System Name dialog box appears (see Figure 4.13), prompting you for the name of your GroupWise system.

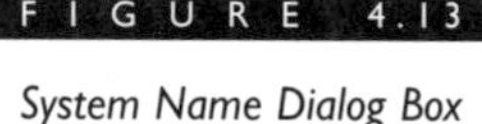
FIGURE 4.13

System Name Dialog Box

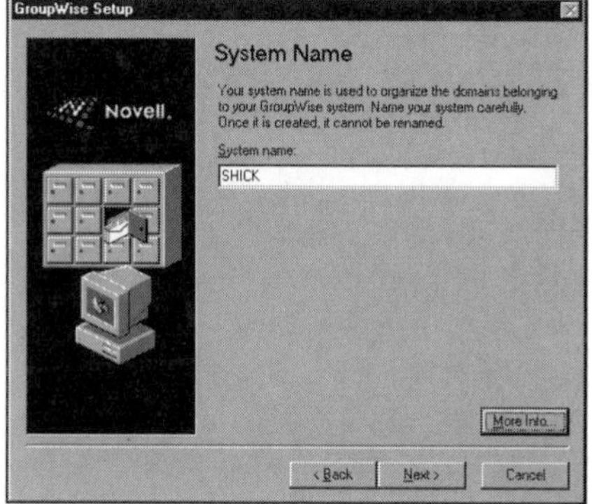

The name you give your system is used to synchronize GroupWise directory information between your GroupWise system and other GroupWise systems you connect to via an external domain link.

IMPORTANT

The system name cannot be changed. Make sure you have carefully selected the name for your system.

Enter the name of your GroupWise system and choose Enter. The Primary Domain dialog box, shown in Figure 4.14, will appear.

FIGURE 4.14

Primary Domain Dialog Box

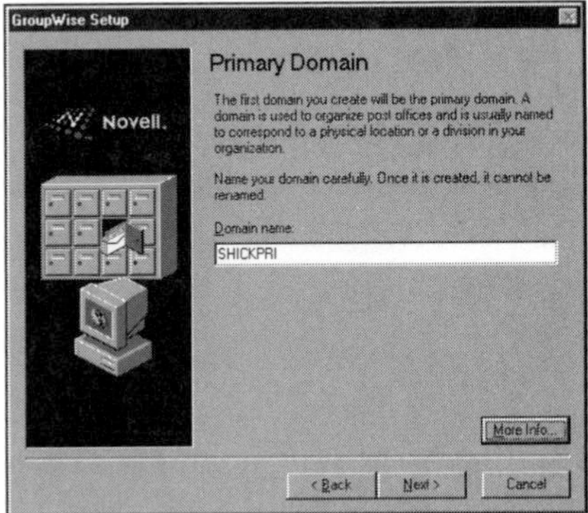

The domain name must be unique within your GroupWise system and the Domain object name must be unique in the NDS context in which the object will be created. The first domain you define becomes your primary domain.

IMPORTANT

The domain name cannot be changed. Be sure you've followed the domain naming guidelines provided in Chapter 3.

As discussed in Chapter 3, you should use a name that represents a physical location or division within the organization.

In the Primary Domain dialog box, enter the name and select Next. The Domain Directory dialog box appears (see Figure 4.15).

FIGURE 4.15

Domain Directory Dialog Box

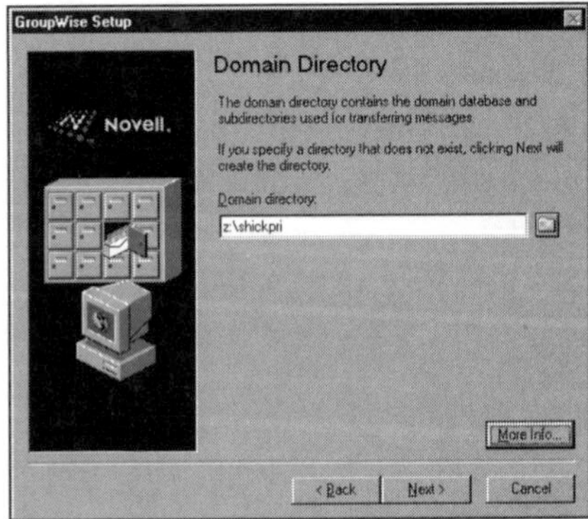

The domain directory contains the domain database and the domain message transfer subdirectories. The installation program will create the directory for you if it does not exist. You can specify a mapped drive or a UNC path for the domain directory.

Specify a domain directory and choose Next to continue. (If the domain directory doesn't exist, click on Yes when prompted to create the directory.)

You will next be prompted to enter the context in which the Domain object will be placed. (The Domain Context dialog box is shown in Figure 4.16.) Enter the context in which the Domain object should be placed. (You can browse to the domain's context by clicking on the Browse button).

NOTE

You'll recall from Chapter 3 that we recommend an NDS organizational unit called "GRPWISE" to contain all administrative-level GroupWise components.

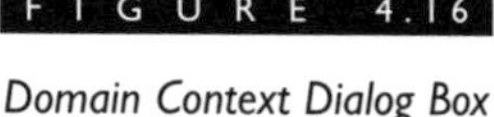
FIGURE 4.16

Domain Context Dialog Box

The Domain Language dialog box appears. Enter the language for the domain and click on Next. The Time Zone dialog box appears.

Select the Time Zone where the domain resides and click on Next.

Once you have entered the above information about the domain, you will be prompted for the same type of information for your first post office.

NOTE

Nothing has yet been created. You will have the opportunity to back up and make changes before the GroupWise components are "committed" to NDS and before the domain directory structure is created on a file server.

Creating Your First Post Office

The GroupWise Setup Advisor will next collect information about the first GroupWise post office in your system. Most of the information you entered for your domain will also be requested for your post office. Because the post office dialog boxes are so similar to those shown previously for the domain, they are not shown in this chapter.

IMPORTANT

You cannot change a post office name after it has been created.

The first dialog box prompts you for the name of the post office. Post office names must be unique within the domain and should be unique in your system to avoid confusion. The name of the post office object must also be unique within its NDS context.

1 • Enter the name of the post office and choose Next. You are prompted for the post office directory.

2 • Enter the post office directory and choose Next. Click on Yes if prompted to create the directory. You are prompted for the post office context.

3 • Enter the context in which the post office object should appear and click on Next. We recommend that you place the post office object in the same context as most of the users in the Post Office. You are prompted for the post office language.

4 • Select the language and choose Next. You are prompted for the time zone.

5 • Select the time zone for the post office and choose Next.

You will next be prompted to add existing NetWare users to the post office.

Adding Users to the Post Office

The Post Office Users dialog box, shown in Figure 4.17, lets you specify which existing NDS users should be given membership in the post office. This dialog box will not display any usernames until you specify the users' location in the NDS tree.

Typically, you will add users who belong to the organizational unit (OU) in which you created the post office. However, users can be added from different OUs.

FIGURE 4.17

Post Office Users Dialog Box

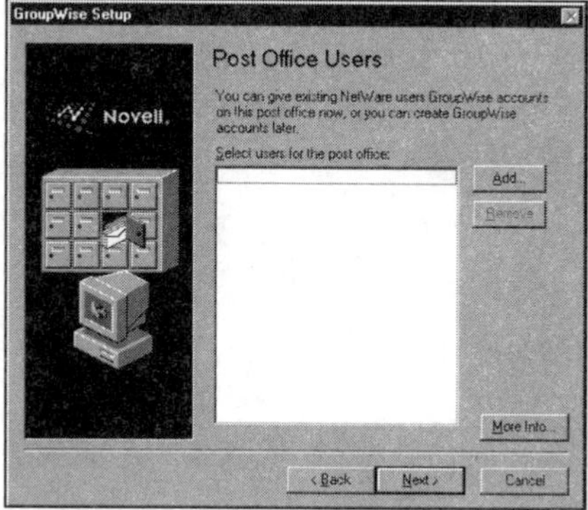

Click on the Add button to locate the users you want to add to this post office. The Select Object dialog box appears, as shown in Figure 4.18.

FIGURE 4.18

Select Object Dialog Box

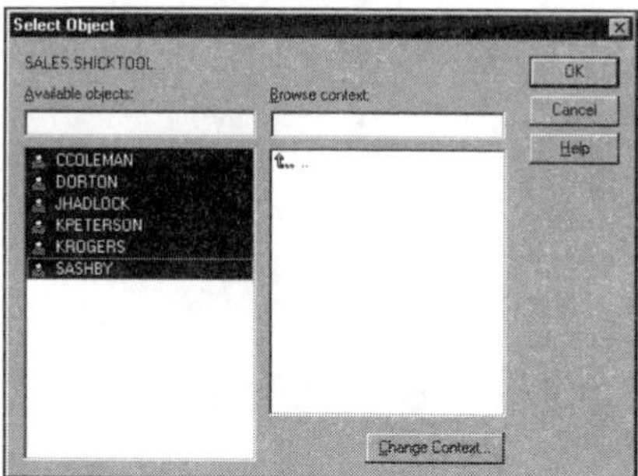

Browse to the container that holds the users, press the Ctrl key, and click to select multiple users. Then click on OK. The users will appear in the Post Office Users dialog box.

Repeat this step to add users from other contexts. When all of the users are listed in the Post Office Users dialog box, click on Next to continue.

The GroupWise Setup Progress dialog box again appears. Click on Next and the Summary dialog box appears.

The Summary dialog box (see Figure 4.19) shows you all of the information you have entered for the domain and post office. If any of the information is incorrect, click the Back button to correct it.

FIGURE 4.19

Summary Dialog Box

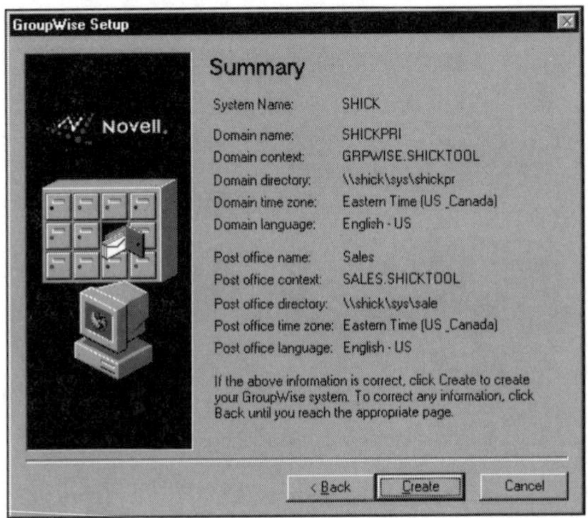

When the information is complete, click on Create to create the domain and post offices, and to add the user accounts. This is the point at which the actual GroupWise components are created. When you click Create, the following events occur in your system:

- The GroupWise Domain object is created in the context you specified.
- The GroupWise domain directories and domain database are created in the location you specified.
- The GroupWise MTA object is created as a subordinate object to the domain object.
- The GroupWise ADA object is created as a subordinate object to the domain object.

- The GroupWise Post Office object is created in the context you specified.
- The GroupWise post office directories and post office database are created in the location you specified.
- The Post Office Agent object is created as a subordinate object to the Post Office object.
- GroupWise user account properties are added for each user you added to the post office.

After you have created the GroupWise domain and post office objects, the GroupWise Setup Progress dialog box again appears. Click on Next and the Agent Information dialog box appears, as Figure 4.20 illustrates.

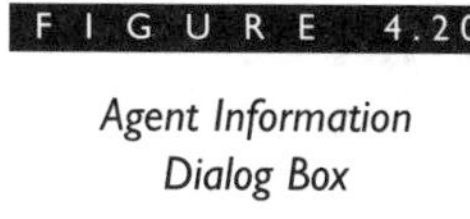

Agent Information Dialog Box

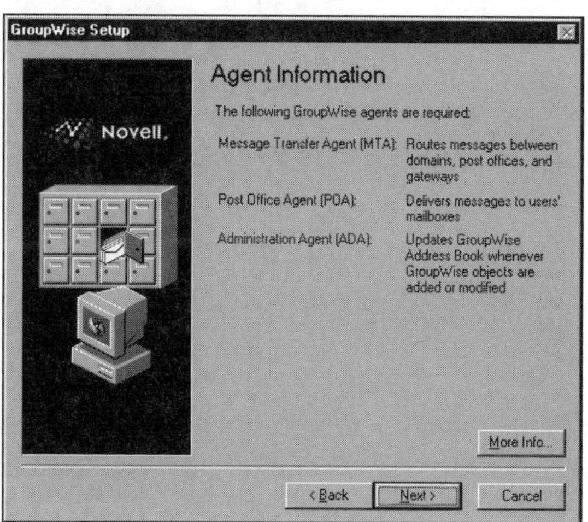

This dialog box gives you an overview of each agent.

Click on Next to proceed with the agent installation. The Agent Platform dialog box appears.

Installing the GroupWise Agents

You can choose to install the NLM or Windows NT versions of the GroupWise agents (ADA, MTA, and POA). Remember, the GroupWise agents are those "back-end" GroupWise programs that handle message delivery and administration-related tasks in the GroupWise system. They are discussed in greater detail in Chapter 12.

Installing the NLM Agents

To install the NLM agents:

1 • In the Agent Platform dialog box, select NetWare NLM and click on Next. The NetWare NLM Agent Setup dialog box appears.

2 • Click on the Install Agents button. The Agent Installation drive appears.

3 • Highlight the drive on which the agents will be installed and choose Next. The Language dialog box appears.

4 • Select the language and choose Next.

5 • Verify the information in the summary and choose Install to continue or Back to cycle back and make changes.

6 • When the installation process is finished, the Installation Complete dialog box appears. Click on Done to return to the NetWare NLM Agent Setup dialog box. (Notice that this is the same screen you saw before launching the Agent Installation routine. You can run the Agent Installation program again if you want to install the agents to another server.)

7 • Click on Next to continue.

The NLM agents are installed to the SYSTEM directory on the drive you specified.

At this point in the installation, you are prompted to run the agents. You can use the Remote Console program (RCONSOLE) to run the agents from the installation program as prompted by the dialog boxes. However, because we discuss how to load these agents in the next section, we recommend that you skip this step and complete it after the software installation and system configuration is complete. Trust us!

You have now installed the GroupWise software, defined your first GroupWise domain and post office, and installed the GroupWise agents. We'll now gracefully bow out of the GroupWise Setup Advisor:

1 • From the Load GroupWise Agents screen, click on Next. The GroupWise Setup Progress dialog box appears.

2 • From the GroupWise Setup progress screen, choose Next to continue. The Setup Client dialog box appears.

At this point you are given the opportunity to set up the client program on this computer. Remember, however, that this is the administration computer. While you *may* want the GroupWise client installed on this machine, in most cases you will run the client installation program from a user's workstation. We'll cover how to do that in the next chapter.

You can continue with the installation process by clicking on Install, or you can choose Next from the Setup Client screen. The System Creation Complete dialog box appears, as shown in Figure 4.21.

FIGURE 4.21

System Creation Complete Dialog Box

Running the GroupWise Agents

The NLM versions of the GroupWise agents are GWADA.NLM, GWMTA.NLM, and GWPOA.NLM.

Each of these agents has a startup file associated with it: STARTUP.ADA, STARTUP.MTA, and STARTUP.POA. These startup files are template startup files located in SYS:SYSTEM that are used to create custom startup files during the installation process. For example, if you name your domain "NEWYORK" and your post office "YANKEES," the ADA startup file will be named NEWYORK.ADA, the MTA startup file will be named NEWYORK.MTA, and the POA startup file will be named YANKEES.POA.

The startup files contain commands that are required to load the agents successfully. The startup files are ASCII format and can be edited by any text editor, including EDIT.NLM. Table 4.1 shows the commands required for each agent.

TABLE 4.1

Commands Required for Agents

AGENT	REQUIRED PARAMETERS
MTA	`/home-`*domain directory* `/password-`*password* `/userid-`*distinguished GWACCESS* *user ID*
ADA	`/home-`*domain directory* `/password-`*password* `/userid-`*distinguished GWACCESS* *user ID*
POA	`/home-`*post office directory*

Italicized text in Table 4.1 represents variables you will need to fill in according to your system's configuration.

The password and user ID information are for the GroupWise access user account (GWACCESS) you created prior to the installation. You need to use the fully distinguished name for GWACCESS. The format is as follows:

.GWACCESS.GRPWISE. *Organizational Unit.Organization*

Be sure to include the leading period when specifying the distinguished name for the GWACCESS user.

These switches are required when you have GroupWise domains and post offices on other file servers. If your domain and post office(s) are located on the same file server that will run the NLM agents, or if you are using TCP/IP links, these switches are not required.

Notice that the password appears in the startup file. To prevent a network security breach, you should make sure users do not have rights to read the contents of this file. The startup files are located in SYS:SYSTEM, which should already have minimum user rights.

To load an agent with the startup file, the syntax is as follows:

LOAD AGENT.NLM @*startup filename*

For example, to load the administration agent for the New York domain, you could type

```
LOAD GWADA @NEWYORK.ADA
```

The startup files are simply automation tools. You can enter the required parameters from the file server console prompt. For example, the following command would load the MTA:

```
LOAD GWMTA /home-SYS:\NEWYORK /user-.GWACESS.GRPWISE.SHICKDOM
           /password-grpwise
```

The GroupWise installation program takes one more step to automate the agent loading procedure. During the installation program, a GRPWISE.NCF file is created that contains the lines required to load all of the agents. Commands in the SYS:SYSTEM\GRPWISE.NCF are a simple ASCII text file that will load the agents with their startup files. A sample GRPWISE.NCF file would look like the following:

```
LOAD GWADA@NEWYORK.ADA
LOAD GWMTA@NEWYORK.MTA
LOAD GWPOA@YANKEES.POA
```

NOTE

If you placed the post office on a server other than the server containing the domain, the GRPWISE.NCF will only load the ADA and MTA.

If you want to take the automation one step further, you can add GRPWISE.NCF to the file server's AUTOEXEC.NCF. The agents will then load when the server is started. (Much like a DOS batch file, NetWare .NCF files are loaded by simply typing the filename at the console prompt. Don't use the LOAD command.)

Configuring Workstations for GroupWise Administration

The workstation you use to install GroupWise is automatically configured as a GroupWise administration workstation. In other words, it is configured with the NWADMN3X.INI file, any necessary .DLL files to run NetWare Administrator 4.11, and the GroupWise administration components.

You can configure other GroupWise administration machines with the SETUPGW.EXE file, located in the *software distribution directory* in the ADMIN directory.

To create another GroupWise administration machine, follow these steps from the machine you want to configure:

1. Click on Start.

2. Click on Run.

3 • Browse to the SOFTWARE\ADMIN directory or the ADMIN directory on the mounted GroupWise CD if you are using the CD software distribution option.

4 • Double-click on SETUPGW.EXE. The welcome screen appears.

5 • Click on Next.

6 • Specify the path to the domain.

7 • Modify the defaults for the program path and help file path if necessary, then choose Next.

8 • When the installation is complete, choose Done.

You should now be able to run NetWare Administrator 4.11 from this machine and administer the GroupWise system.

Installation Review

Whew! That was one whirlwind tour of the GroupWise installation process. Before we lead you into the next chapter and help you put the finishing touches on your GroupWise system, let's take a look at what happened during the installation and introduce you to the key NDS objects and physical directory structures that you just created. (We won't go into exhaustive detail about each of the objects, directories, and files. That's done throughout the rest of this book.)

Changes Made to NDS

Figure 4.22 shows the GroupWise objects in our ShickTools tree.

FIGURE 4.22

NDS Tree With Default GroupWise Objects

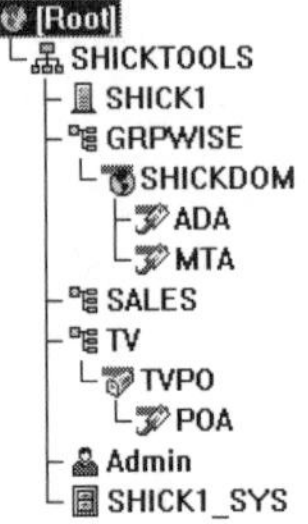

Notice that the Domain object has ADA and MTA objects as subordinate objects. Notice also that the Post Office object has the POA as a subordinate object. The ADA, MTA, and POA objects cannot be moved to other locations in the NDS tree.

Each of the GroupWise NDS objects has definable properties that are used to modify the object's default settings. When you run the GroupWise ADA, MTA, and POA during the installation, you run these agents with the default properties.

We'll teach you how to modify and fine-tune these objects throughout this book.

Next, find a User object you added to the post office. Right click on the User object and select details. A properties page like the one shown in Figure 4.23 appears.

FIGURE 4.23

NetWare User Properties

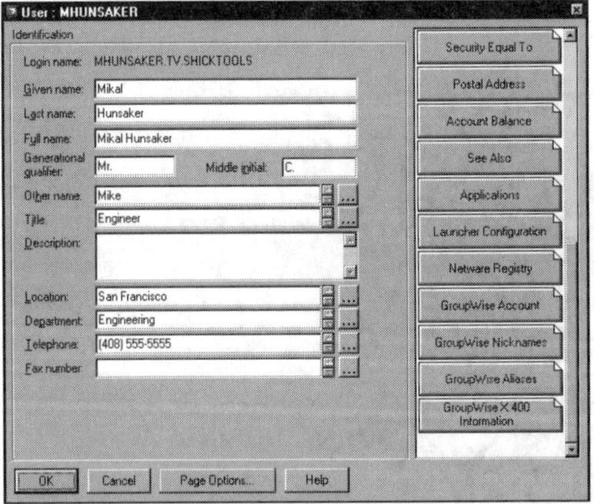

Notice the GroupWise pages that appear in the right column. The most important GroupWise properties for a User object are found in the GroupWise Account property page (see Figure 4.24).

FIGURE 4.24

GroupWise Account Properties

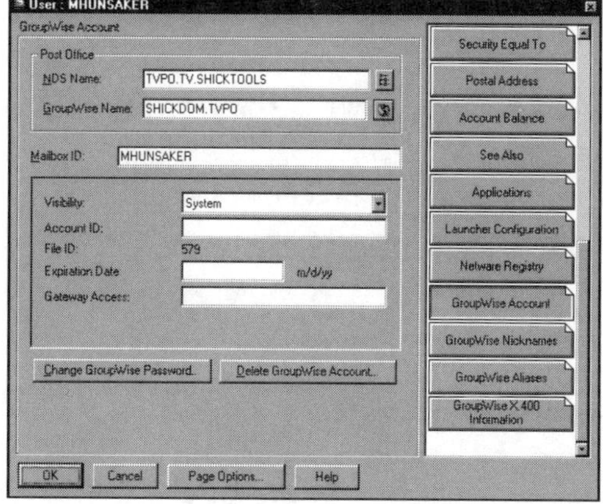

For now our purpose is to just familiarize you with these objects and properties. Each of the properties and how they work are discussed throughout the book.

GroupWise Files and Directories Created During Installation

During the GroupWise installation, three GroupWise-related directory structures are created and the physical GroupWise components are installed into these directory structures.

Domain Directory Structure

The domain directory is created in the location you specify during the installation. The domain directory for our SHICKDOM is shown in Figure 4.25.

FIGURE 4.25

Domain Directory Structure

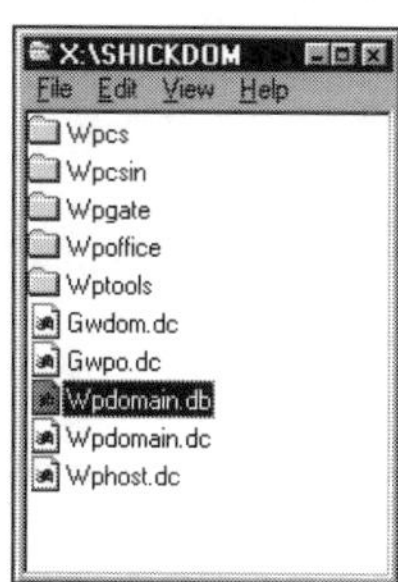

The most important file in the domain directory structure is the WPDOMAIN.DB file. This is known as the domain database, and it contains the directory information about all of the GroupWise components. This information is copied to each post office serviced by the domain and includes the information that displays in the GroupWise users' Address Books.

For now, don't worry about the function of each file and subdirectory under the domain. As we proceed through the book and provide you with diagrams showing how messages move through the system, we'll explain the directory structure in detail.

Post Office Directory Structure

The post office directory structure is installed in the location you specify during the installation. The post office directory structure for our TV post office is shown in Figure 4.26.

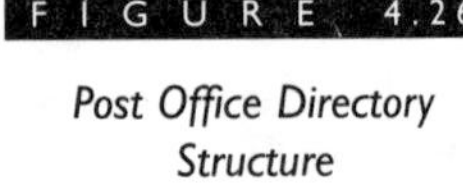

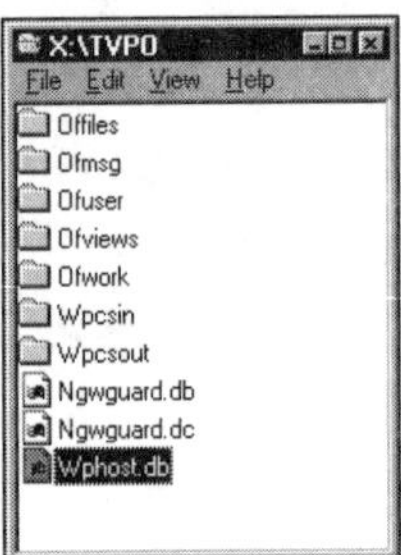

FIGURE 4.26

Post Office Directory Structure

The most important file in the post office directory structure is WPHOST.DB. This file contains the GroupWise directory information. The Address Book in the GroupWise client reads information contained in this file.

The OFUSERS, OFFILES, and OFMSG subdirectories contain the post office information store. This is where the messages for the users in the post office are stored. We'll explain how these directories work together to store messages in Chapter 7.

Software Directory Structure

The third major directory structure that is created during installation is the software directory. The software directory we installed for our ShickTools system is shown in Figure 4.27.

FIGURE 4.27

Software Directory

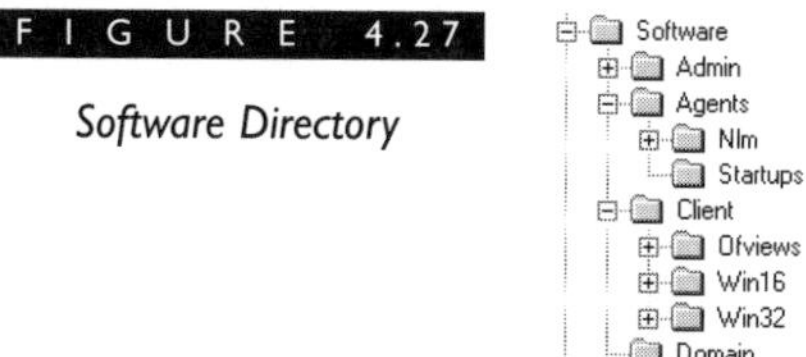

Users should have Read access to at least the client portion of the software directory structure so they can install the GroupWise client software from the network.

Summary

In this chapter you learned how to install GroupWise 5. In Chapter 5 you will learn how to install the GroupWise 5 client programs.

CHAPTER 5

Installing and Configuring the Client Software

In Chapter 4 we explained how to install the GroupWise system software, set up the GroupWise infrastructure, and run the GroupWise messaging agents. We basically gave you the keys to the car and let you start the ignition and rev the engine. We'll install the steering wheel (the GroupWise client) in this chapter.

The final component you need to set up in order to enable the messaging system is the GroupWise client program.

You have four choices for the client program:

- Windows 32-bit client for Windows 95 and Windows NT 4.0.
- Windows 16-bit client for Windows 3.1.
- Macintosh client.
- UNIX client.

We explain installation of the 32-bit client on a Windows 95 workstation in this chapter because it is by far the most widely used client in GroupWise 5. Refer to the WPSETUS.HLP file in the <software>\CLIENT\WIN16 directory for information on how to install the 16-bit Windows client.

For specific information on the installation of Macintosh and UNIX client software, refer to the documentation that comes with those client versions.

Installation of the Windows 95 Client Software

To install the client software on a Windows 95 workstation, you need to meet one of two requirements: you must either have the GroupWise CD in hand, or you must be able to access the GroupWise client software on the network.

In most cases, users need access to the SOFTWARE directory you set up during the initial installation of the GroupWise software.

In addition to having access to the GroupWise client software, you might need to have your Windows 95 setup disks handy. GroupWise requires the Windows messaging system files (MAPI32) to enable several messaging features, including the GroupWise Address Book.

If you see an In Box icon on your Windows desktop, you know that the Windows messaging system files have been installed, and you won't need the Windows setup disks. If you don't have an In Box icon on your Windows desktop, you will probably need to have the disks because GroupWise will prompt you for them during the installation. (Windows 95 looks for the Windows files in the directory from which they were originally installed. However, you can browse to a different directory to locate the Windows .CAB files.)

Beginning the Installation

Follow these steps to begin the installation routine for the GroupWise 32-bit client from within Windows 95 or Windows NT 4.0:

1. Click on Start.

2. Click on Run.

3. Browse to the GroupWise directory on either the network or CD-ROM. The SETUP.EXE file will be found in the CLIENT\WIN32 directory.

4. Double-click on SETUP.EXE. The Welcome dialog box appears.

5. Click on Next to continue.

The installation program first detects whether the Windows messaging system is installed. If it is not installed, the Windows Messaging System dialog box, shown in Figure 5.1, appears.

If the dialog box shown in Figure 5.1 does *not* appear, skip ahead to Step 8.

6. Choose Next to install the complete Windows messaging system. You will be prompted to insert the Windows 95 disk.

7. Insert the Windows disk and click on OK. You will see the message box shown in Figure 5.2.

FIGURE 5.1

Windows Messaging System Dialog Box

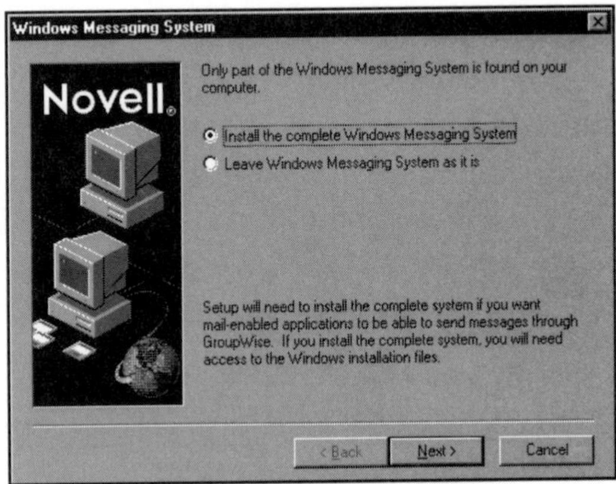

FIGURE 5.2

Restart Dialog Box

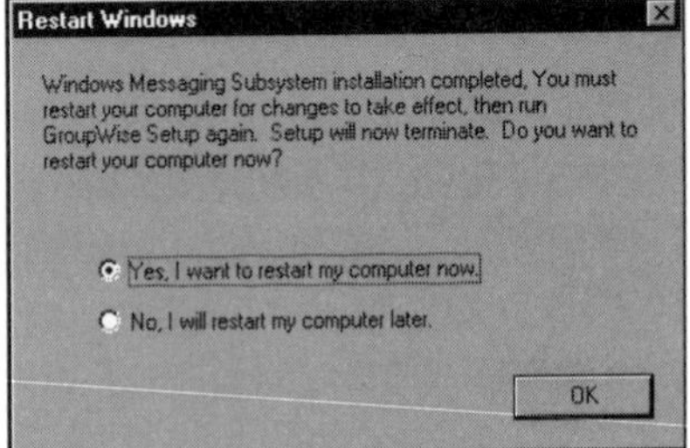

8 • Choose OK to restart your computer. The computer will restart and attempt to automatically restart the GroupWise setup program, picking up where you left off. If the attempt to resume the GroupWise setup routine fails, repeat Steps 1 through 5 above. The GroupWise Setup Options dialog box appears (see Figure 5.3).

You have two options for installing the 32-bit client: standard installation or workstation installation. Standard installation places all of the GroupWise program files on the local hard drive. Workstation installation leaves all of the GroupWise program files in a shared network directory that users access when launching the GroupWise client.

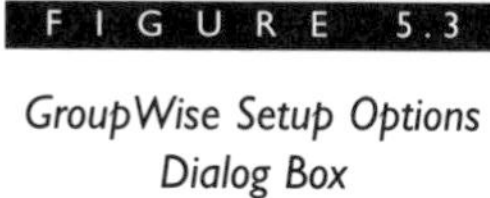

FIGURE 5.3

GroupWise Setup Options Dialog Box

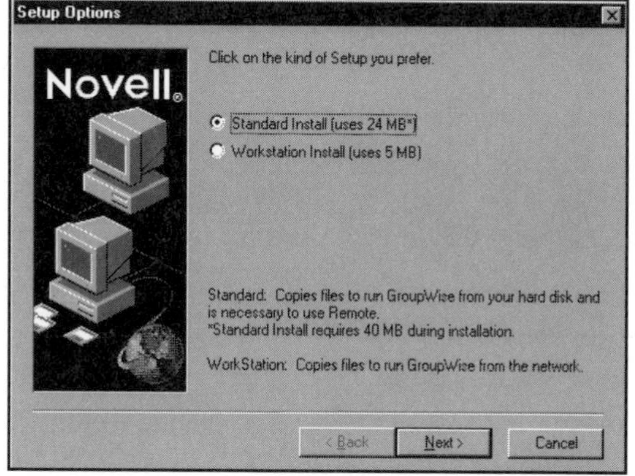

Standard Installation

When you choose *standard installation*, GroupWise copies the client software to the local hard drive. The advantages of standard installation include:

- Performance is enhanced because users do not load the program over the network.
- Network traffic is decreased because the client is accessed locally.
- Network is used more efficiently in a client/server environment.
- Users can run GroupWise in Remote mode on a mobile computer.

The main disadvantages of standard installation are:

- It takes about 24MB of hard disk space.
- You must run the installation program whenever new GroupWise code is installed on the network.

In most cases the advantages of standard installation outweigh the disadvantages.

Workstation Installation

The term *workstation installation* is a bit of a misnomer. When you perform a workstation installation, your computer is configured to run GroupWise from a network directory. The installation program registers the GroupWise components in the Windows Registry and adds GroupWise icons to your desktop. (The Windows Registry is discussed later in this chapter.) Workstation installation does not install the complete GroupWise client program to your hard drive. However, about 4MB of .DLL files are copied to the WINDOWS\SYSTEM directory.

The key advantage of the workstation installation is that users don't have to worry about reinstalling their GroupWise client whenever the GroupWise software is updated. You (as the administrator) update it on the network; users are therefore updated automatically. Another advantage is the local disk space savings, because the GroupWise client is accessed from the network and not from the local hard drive.

The disadvantages of the workstation installation are increased network traffic caused by users loading the GroupWise client across the network wire and the inability of users to run GroupWise in Remote mode. (It also takes slightly longer to load the client software when it is accessed from the network.)

You will likely use the workstation installation option when you don't want to bother your users with the task of updating their workstation when you upgrade the GroupWise client.

Completing the Installation

Picking up where we left off in the installation process (Step 8), we'll assume for the purposes of this illustration that you decide to perform a standard installation option.

9 • After you select either the Workstation Install or Standard Install option, click on Next. The Destination Directory dialog box appears.

10 • Select your desired destination directory for the GroupWise client files and click on Next. The Select Program Folder dialog box appears, as shown in Figure 5.4.

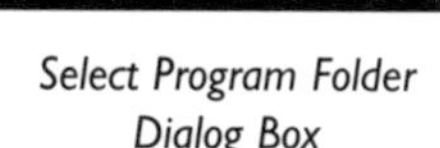

FIGURE 5.4

Select Program Folder Dialog Box

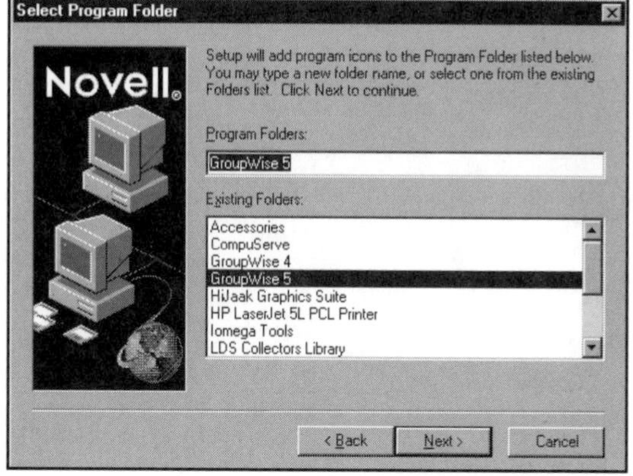

11 • Highlight the desired folder for the GroupWise program icons and click on Next. You'll see the Language Selection dialog box, shown in Figure 5.5.

12 • Highlight the desired language and click on Next. The Start Copying Files dialog box appears, as illustrated in Figure 5.6.

NOTE

The languages selected during the system installation appear in the Language Selection dialog box. If you only installed one language during system installation, only that language will appear in this dialog box.

FIGURE 5.5

Language Selection Dialog Box

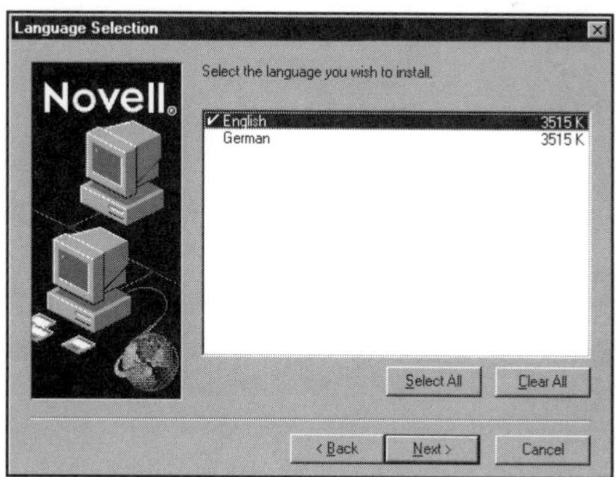

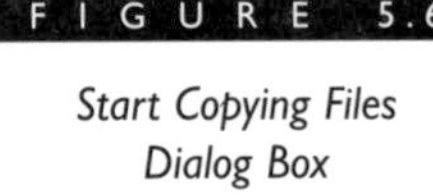

FIGURE 5.6

Start Copying Files Dialog Box

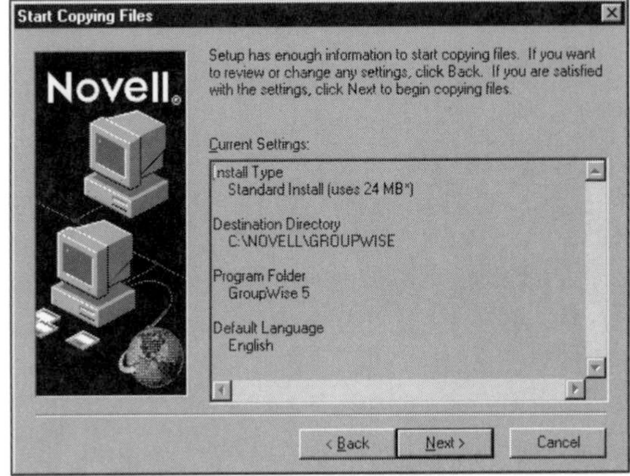

The Start Copying Files dialog box presents you with a summary of the options you have chosen up to this point in the client installation. If you want to alter any of the options displayed in this dialog box, click on the Back button to cycle back through the dialog boxes.

13 • Click on Next to begin the installation.

14 • You can view the progress of the installation in the Setup box, as shown in Figure 5.7.

FIGURE 5.7

Setup Box

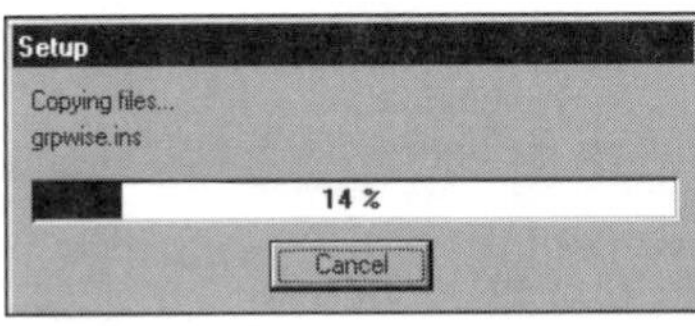

During installation, GroupWise checks your system for programs that can be integrated with GroupWise's document management programs. If it finds any, it presents you with the Software Integrations dialog box (see Figure 5.8) and enables you to select the applications for which you want the integration modules installed. (We explain much more about GroupWise document management in Chapter 17.)

FIGURE 5.8

Software Integrations Dialog Box

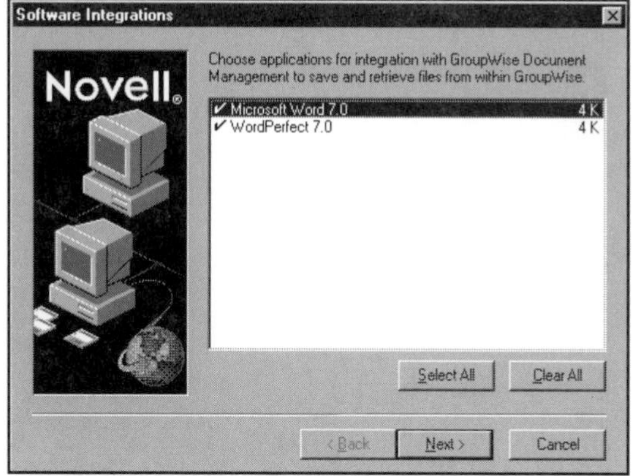

Select the applications you want integrated with GroupWise and choose Next. The file installation process resumes.

After the file installation is complete, the Installation program registers the necessary GroupWise components in your Windows Registry, explained later in this chapter. You can view the progress of the registration process, as shown in Figure 5.9.

FIGURE 5.9

Registration Progress

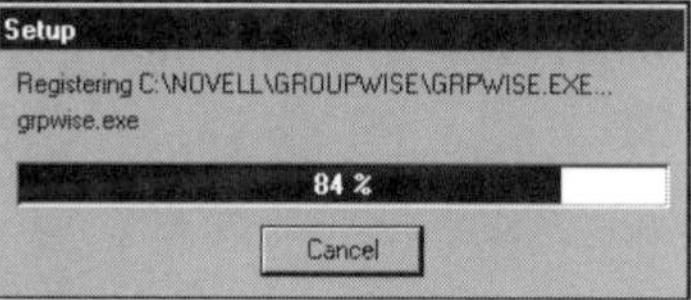

After the registration process is finished, the Setup Complete dialog box appears (see Figure 5.10). The Setup Complete dialog box lets you launch GroupWise and read the README file if desired. Click on Finish to exit the installation program.

FIGURE 5.10

Setup Complete Dialog Box

Behind the Scenes

For a system administrator, the GroupWise client installation process should be a "no-brainer." You see those percentage-complete bars in your sleep. But what happens behind the scenes?

When you launch the SETUP.EXE file from the network, the GroupWise installation program looks at the DATA.Z file. The DATA.Z file contains the GroupWise code accessed by the SETUP program.

Directories and Files

When you perform a standard installation, the GroupWise code is copied to the C:\NOVELL\GROUPWISE directory unless you specify otherwise.

The GroupWise executable files and directories that you should be familiar with are explained in Table 5.1.

TABLE 5.1

.EXE Files

FILES	EXPLANATION
ADDRBOOK.EXE	The GroupWise Address Book executable file (The Address Book can be launched outside of GroupWise as a stand-alone application or it can be called from the GroupWise screen.)
GRPWISE.EXE	The main GroupWise program executable file

TABLE 5.1
.EXE Files (continued)

FILES	EXPLANATION
OFVIEWS directory	The OFVIEWS directory contains the view files used for each GroupWise message type, such as the Appointment and Calendar views (Views are the graphical message display formats used when messages are created or viewed.)
PPFORMS directory	Calendar printing templates for day planner and other formats

You need to be familiar with these files and directories in order to troubleshoot problems with the GroupWise client.

The Windows Registry

The Windows 95 Registry is a database used by the Windows operating system to store the configuration information necessary to operate your computer and run the applications installed on it. In previous versions of GroupWise, the program preferences and settings were stored in a preferences file. (If you are familiar with earlier versions, you may recall the .BIF file.) In the GroupWise 32-bit client, all preferences and settings are now stored in the Windows Registry or in the user database.

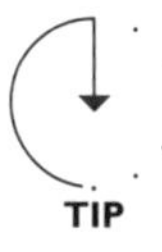

If you begin experiencing strange problems with the GroupWise 32-bit client, you may have a registry problem. The CD-ROM included with this book contains the Novell Registry Editor utility, SETUPNRE.EXE, which can be used to purge the Windows Registry of all GroupWise-related settings. After you run this utility, reinstall GroupWise to see if your problem has been fixed.

Running GroupWise

When you start GroupWise, it must first locate your post office. You will see this taking place when the GroupWise Startup dialog box appears (see Figure 5.11).

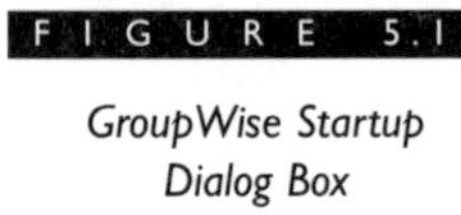

FIGURE 5.11

GroupWise Startup Dialog Box

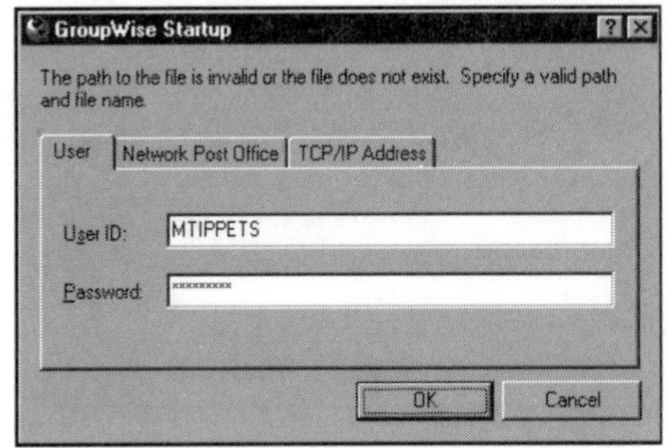

When you start the GroupWise client, it first tries to determine if a network is present by (1) looking for existing network drive mappings or post office agents running in client/server mode, (2) looking for any established dial-up network connections, and (3) checking for an auto-dial configuration for a dial-up network connection.

If GroupWise determines that a network is not present, it launches in Remote mode.

Automatic Search for a Network Post Office

If GroupWise determines that a network is present, it searches for a network post office. You need to know the search order when troubleshooting client-to-post office connection failures. GroupWise uses the following procedure to find your post office.

It checks the system memory to see if another GroupWise component, such as the Address Book or Notify, is loaded. If it finds another GroupWise component, the client will use the location of the post office that is already in memory.

The GroupWise client then checks the command-line parameters to see if a post office is specified. (The switches are explained in the next section.)

If NDS is present, the client reads the NDS information for the user object, the GroupWise Post Office object, and the GroupWise Post Office Agent (POA) object to determine which post office should be used and its location.

The NDS rights required of the logged-in user to perform a search of NDS are as follows:

- Browse Object right to the User object
  - Read and Compare to the NGW: Object ID property
  - Read to the NGW: Post Office property
- Browse Object right to the Post Office object
  - Read to the NGW: Access Mode property
  - Read to the NGW: Location property
- Browse Object right to the GroupWise Post Office Agent (POA) object
  - Read to the NGW: Type property
  - Read to the Network Address property

NOTE

The default NDS rights to objects in a user's container include Browse Object and Read rights to all properties. These rights must be granted to users of a post office when it is in a container other than the container in which the users are located.

The GroupWise client next searches the Windows Registry in the following key:

```
HKEY_CURRENT_USER\Software\Novell\GroupWise\Login
Parameters....
```

The client looks for the following values in that key:

- Account Name (user ID)
- PostOfficePath (path to post office)
- Path to Remote database
- TCP/IP Address (IP address where the POA is running)
- TCP/IP Port (IP port the POA is using for this post office)

The GroupWise client then looks for a post office agent running with the NDS host name of NGWNameServer. (Chapter 15 explains how the client/server GroupWise access mode is configured.)

The client will prompt the user to enter the information manually if it fails to find the post office automatically.

If the client does not find a valid post office after looking at these five sources three times in succession and if the user does not enter valid post office information, it will prompt the user to run in Remote mode. Remote mode is discussed in Chapter 19.

Client Startup Switches

You can force GroupWise to run in a specific way by manually adding switches to the command line, found under the GroupWise icon's properties. The GroupWise client switches shown in Table 5.2 are valid from the command line.

TABLE 5.2

Startup Switches

SWITCH	EXPLANATION
`/@u`-*userid*	Tells the GroupWise client the GroupWise user ID of the user launching the client (GroupWise will search the post office for a user with this ID.)
`/@la`-*login alias*	Tells the GroupWise client the network login name of the user launching GroupWise (GroupWise will look at the user properties to find a user whose network login ID matches the specified ID.)
`/ph`-*path to post office*	GroupWise will use this path to locate the desired GroupWise post office
`/ipa`-*IP address*	Tells GroupWise to look at the specified IP address to locate the correct POA
`/ipp`-*IP port*	Tells GroupWise to look to the specified IP port to find the desired POA
`/ps`-*path to remote post office*	Tells GroupWise to launch in Remote mode and look at the specified path to find the Remote database

Updating the Client Software

Before you receive an updated version of the GroupWise client software from Novell, you should have a strategy in mind for updating all of your GroupWise users' workstations.

When the GroupWise software is updated in the network SOFTWARE\CLIENT directory, the GroupWise Auto-Update feature will alert the client users that new software is available. Users can choose to update the software immediately or later.

The Auto-Update feature ensures that users who have installed the GroupWise client software to their hard drives will be alerted to newer code.

Summary

You now know what it takes to build a fully functional GroupWise system. At this point, your messaging system should be complete and operational. Go ahead — take a break for a while, come back, and send a few messages.

Chapter 6 will explain how you can customize your post office settings.

CHAPTER 6

Managing a GroupWise Post Office

It's time for a quick review of what you've already learned about GroupWise post offices:

- Post offices are used to group users together within geographical or organizational groups.
- User-level GroupWise objects—for example, User objects, Resource objects, and Distribution List objects—belong to Post Office objects.
- Each post office contains the information store (in other words, the mailboxes) for members of the post office.
- The post office agent (POA), which is the GroupWise workhorse, performs vital messaging and maintenance tasks for each post office.

In this chapter we will explain a variety of topics on the subject of post office administration.

As a GroupWise administrator, you need to understand the physical structure of a post office. The physical structure includes the post office databases and files and the information store for the users assigned to the post office. You also need to understand how the parts of a GroupWise message, such as the message header, the message body, and file attachments, are stored in the post office information store.

After we explain the physical structure of post offices, we'll show you how to customize some post office settings, including post office security settings and access modes. We'll explain how to optimize post office settings to best meet your message delivery and security needs.

Finally, we'll describe message flow within a post office. You'll see how post office access modes affect message delivery in a single post office system. As you examine the message flow diagrams at the end of this chapter, you'll learn to locate bottlenecks and troubleshoot problems in a single post office GroupWise system.

Physical Structure of a Post Office

In order to understand how messages are delivered and stored in a post office, you need to be familiar with the directories, databases, and files that make up a post office directory structure. In Chapter 2, we briefly explained the post office administrative directories and files and the information store. In this chapter, we'll show you the overall post office structure and explain in more detail how the various directories, subdirectories, and databases interact.

Two critical files are stored in the *<post office>* directory (in other words, the directory specified during post office installation; for example, Z:\SALESPO):

- **NGWGUARD.DC**. The template file for the Guardian database.
- **WPHOST.DB**. The post office database file. It contains the GroupWise system's directory (Address Book) information that is accessed by users within the post office.

A typical post office directory structure is shown in Figure 6.1. Note that the files are not shown in the diagram. A complete listing of the files and their functions is provided in Appendix E.

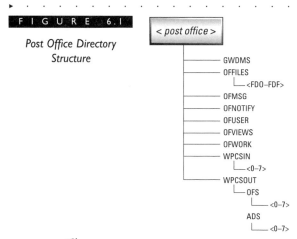

FIGURE 6.1

Post Office Directory Structure

```
< post office >
   |
   |-------- GWDMS
   |-------- OFFILES
   |           └── <FDO–FDF>
   |-------- OFMSG
   |-------- OFNOTIFY
   |-------- OFUSER
   |-------- OFVIEWS
   |-------- OFWORK
   |-------- WPCSIN
   |           └── <0–7>
   |-------- WPCSOUT
               └── OFS
                     └── <0–7>
                   ADS
                     └── <0–7>
```

NOTE

In all directory structure and message flow diagrams, pointed brackets (< and >) denote variables.

Table 6.1 describes the purposes of the different post office directories related to message storage and delivery. For detailed information on all of the directories in the post office directory structure, see Appendix E.

TABLE 6.1
Post Office Directories

DIRECTORY	PURPOSE
GWDMS	Contains information and databases that control GroupWise document management for the post office. This directory and its contents will be explained in Chapter 17.
OFFILES	Contains several subdirectories. These subdirectories are used to store file attachments that are sent along with GroupWise messages. The files are encrypted and cannot be viewed by standard viewing programs.
OFMSG	Contains the message databases that store GroupWise messages.
OFUSER	Contains the individual user database files (user mailboxes).
WPCSIN\<0–7>	Temporarily stores messages addressed to other post offices or domains. Messages stored here are received by the MTA and moved to other locations in the system. This is an MTA input queue. Think of this directory as the "EXIT" from your post office. The MTA constantly polls the WPCSIN\<0–7> directories for messages to move. Once a message is found, the Message Server places it in the appropriate Message Server Output Queue.

As indicated in Table 6.1, the WPCSIN\<0–7> directories are message queues used during the message delivery process.

Several of the directories listed in Table 6.1 contain directories numbered 0 through 7. These directories are known as *priority directories*. You will see this 0-7 pattern followed in various places within the GroupWise system; for example, in the WPSCSIN, WPCSOUT\OFS, and WPCSOUT\ADS directories. These numbered directories represent priority levels and are explained in Table 6.2.

You now have an overview of the post office directory structure. Now we'll explain in more detail those directories and databases that make up the post office information store.

TABLE 6.2 *Priority Directories*

PRIORITY DIRECTORY	PRIMARY USE
0	Busy Searches
1	Remote Requests
2	High Priority/Administrative Messages
3	High Priority Message Status
4	Normal Priority Messages
5	Normal Priority Status Messages
6	Low Priority Messages
7	Low Priority Status Messages

Post Office Information Store

As you saw in Chapter 2, the information store is where user messages and file attachments are stored. The information store is the heart of the GroupWise messaging system. A healthy information store will keep your users happy and productive.

To understand how the information store works, you need to understand the structure of GroupWise messages themselves. Messages can contain three parts: a message header, the message body, and attachments. The top part of Figure 6.2 shows a view of the GroupWise mailbox that displays a message reference. The message reference consists of the message header information (the mailbox can be customized to show other header fields not shown in the graphic). This header information is also displayed at the top of the mail message, shown in the bottom half of the graphic.

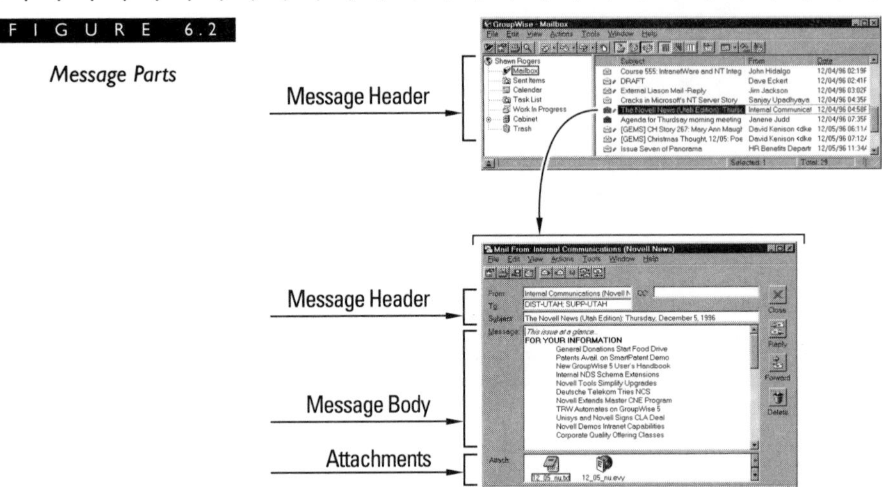

FIGURE 6.2

Message Parts

Notice the different parts of the message in Figure 6.2. These components of a message are stored in various locations within the information store and are linked together by *pointers*, which specify the exact location of the information in the information store. Pointers are references stored within the information store databases that link associated message components together. We'll explain more about pointers in a minute.

- *Message Header.* The sender, recipients, CC:, BC:, date, time, and subject make up the message header. The message header information appears in the items area of the GroupWise client when a folder is highlighted. The same information appears in the message itself when the message is opened.

- *Message Body.* The body, or text portion, of the message. The contents of the message, the details of the appointments request, task or note, as well as any embedded macros or RTF data that are part of the message. The message body is viewed when a particular message is opened with the client.

- *Attachment.* An attached file or object that is treated as an extension of the message. The attachment is transparently tied with a *pointer* to the message, and is accessed when the attachment is viewed in the client using the built-in file viewers, when it is saved, or when the associated application is launched.

Of the directories listed in Table 6.1, the OFUSER, OFMSG, and OFFILES directories are *information store directories*. These directories contain files and databases that store GroupWise message information. The other directories listed in Table 6.1 are explained later in this chapter and in Appendix E.

Figure 6.3 shows how the information store databases and OFFILES directory work together and how they relate to the information the user sees in the GroupWise client.

The arrows pointing from the user database to the message database and from the message database to the attachment directory represent pointers contained within the database that link the parts of the message together. These pointers are used when the message is opened and the various message parts are compiled into the message view seen by the user. The pointers point to the exact location in the message database and OFFILES directory where the message body and file attachments are stored.

FIGURE 6.3

GroupWise Information Store

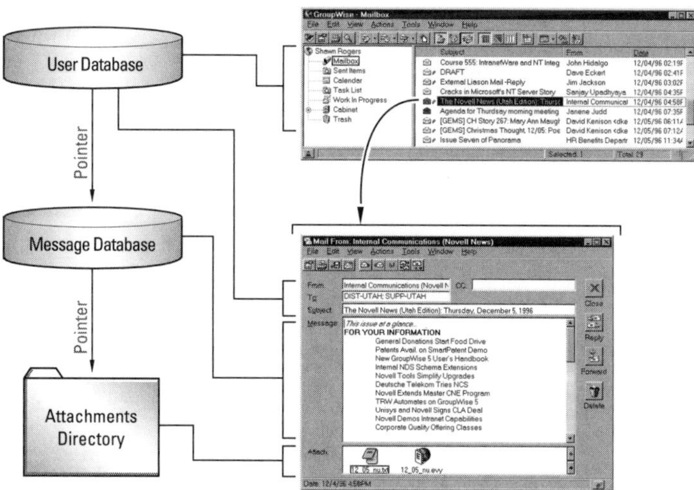

IMPORTANT

There are some exceptions to the message storage structure illustrated in Figure 6.3. For example, if file attachments do not exceed 2K, they are stored in the message database. Figure 6.3 provides a general overview of the relationship between the GroupWise client and the post office information store.

As illustrated in Figure 6.3, two different types of *information store databases* are stored in the information store directories: user databases and message databases.

User Databases

As you saw in Figure 6.1, the post office directory contains a subdirectory called OFUSER. This directory contains a database for every user and resource belonging to the post office. The term *user database* is used synonymously with the term *user mailbox*.

The naming convention for user databases is USER*xxx*.DB, where *xxx* is the user's GroupWise file ID. (You can find out a user's file ID in the Address Book or by checking the corresponding NDS User object's GroupWise Account properties page.)

User databases are not automatically created when you assign user accounts in NetWare Administrator. A user database is created when one of two events occurs: (1) the user runs the client for the first time, or (2) someone sends a message to that user account for the first time.

User databases contain the message header information. As you saw earlier in this chapter, header information includes the data in the To:, From:, CC:, BC:, and Subject: fields, as well as the date and time when the message was created.

User databases do not contain the messages themselves. However, they do store message header information, as well as pointers that indicate where the complete messages are stored in the message databases.

When a GroupWise user runs the client application, the user first sees the information stored in the user database. The mailbox displays the header information—that is, information in the message's To:, From:, CC:, BC:, Date:, Subject:, and Attach: fields.

The user accesses the message text (stored in the message database) by double-clicking on the message to open it.

IMPORTANT

Some configuration information is also stored in the user database. For example, if you lock a preference setting so that users cannot change it, this information is stored in the user database and recognized by the client upon startup.

Note that the OFMSG directory also contains databases named PU*xxxx*.DB. (The number of characters represented by *xxxx* may vary.) GroupWise uses these databases to track information stored in shared folders.

Message Databases

Another component of the post office structure is the OFMSG subdirectory (refer to Figure 6.1 at the beginning of the chapter). The OFMSG directory contains the *message database* files. The message databases in a post office are named MSG*xx*.DB, where *xx* represents a number from 0 to 24. There are usually 25 message databases in a post office. Each user in the post office is assigned to a message database containing messages the user sends. As new users are assigned to a post office, GroupWise assigns users to message databases in a way that keeps the size of the message databases roughly balanced.

All messages sent by an individual user go to the same message database. In other words, all messages stored in a user's Sent Items folder are stored in the same message database. Message recipients who reside in the same post office as the sender read the message from the sender's message database.

Messages coming into the post office from other locations in the GroupWise system are stored in these same message database files. While an incoming message may have several recipients in the post office, it will be added to only one message database—the one associated with the sender. Then pointers are added to each additional recipient's user database.

Note the efficiency of this message storage strategy. While a message may have several recipients within a post office, the message is only stored once. The same principle applies to the file attachments that accompany messages.

Understanding how message databases function can be invaluable to you as you attempt to troubleshoot users' problems. If some users in a post office can't access messages in their Sent Items folder while most of the other users in the post office aren't experiencing any difficulty, it's likely that the users experiencing problems have all been assigned to the same message database. Similarly, messages sent from a particular user that cannot be accessed by recipients could also indicate a problem with a specific message database. If so, that message database might need to be repaired (see Chapter 13).

Message Storage The following example may help you understand GroupWise message storage within a post office: Suppose you have a GroupWise account within a post office and you send a message to 20 recipients who also have GroupWise accounts within your post office. The message is placed into the message database that you are assigned to—say, for example, MSG2.DB. GroupWise places a pointer in each of the recipients' user databases pointing to the message stored in MSG2.DB. Likewise, GroupWise places a pointer to the message in your user database so you can access the message again, if necessary, through your Sent Items folder.

If the message contains file attachments that exceed 2K in size, GroupWise places those attachments in the OFFILES directory structure and places pointers to the attachment in the message database. (If the attachment is less than 2K, it is stored in the message database, with the message record.)

Note that in this scenario, the message and the file attachments are only stored once in the information store, even though 20 people received the message. If you had sent the message to users in other post offices, that message and its file attachments would only be stored once in each post office, even though multiple recipients may be located in that post office.

Message Deletion Now let's look at how a message is removed from the information store when it is no longer needed.

When a user deletes a message from his or her mailbox, the user is actually only deleting the pointer to the message from his or her user database (unless that user's pointer is the only one still pointing to the message, in which case the entire message is deleted). In the preceding example, the message you sent to 20 other users will not be deleted from the post office information store until all 20 of the recipients have archived or deleted the message from their mailbox and emptied it from their trash *and* you have deleted the message from your Sent Items folder and emptied it from the trash or archived it. You now should be able to see the importance of establishing information store cleanup policies and instructing your users to maintain their mailboxes. A single unmanaged user account can keep a message in the post office information store indefinitely.

File Attachments Directory

To prevent message databases from growing too large, messages, file attachments, and distribution lists that exceed 2K are stored in the post office's file attachments directory, OFFILES, as individual files. The files stored in this directory are encrypted with the GroupWise proprietary encryption technology and cannot be viewed or opened by standard document viewers or other programs. For added security, files in the attachments directory get renamed with a new date and time stamp, and in no way reflect the file's origins or contents.

When a message or file attachment is placed into the attachments directory, GroupWise places pointers in the message database pointing to that location. A single GroupWise message may contain up to 99 file attachments. The size of file attachments is limited only by available disk space.

Address Book Information

As mentioned earlier, the WPHOST.DB database stores the Address Book information accessed by users within the post office. When users run the client and access the Address Book, they read the information from this file.

The file is kept up-to-date by the administration agent (ADA). When changes are made in NetWare Administrator, the ADA updates domains and post offices throughout the GroupWise system.

Typically, the ADA runs at the domain level and has access rights to the WPHOST.DB file in each post office. However, it can also be run at the post office level. This is covered in Chapter 13, which explains how to optimize the GroupWise agents.

If you notice problems in the Address Book, such as user names that are missing or that appear multiple times, the problem is rooted in the WPHOST.DB file. Maintenance of the WPHOST.DB file is covered in Chapter 13.

Post Office Settings

Post office settings are used to customize the operation of your post office. They are found in the property pages of the Post Office object in the NDS tree.

You use the settings in the Post Office object properties page to control the post office security level, delivery mode, and access mode. You access a Post Office object's properties page in NetWare Administrator by right-clicking on the Post Office object and then choosing Details. Figure 6.4 shows a Post Office object properties page.

FIGURE 6.4

Post Office Object Properties

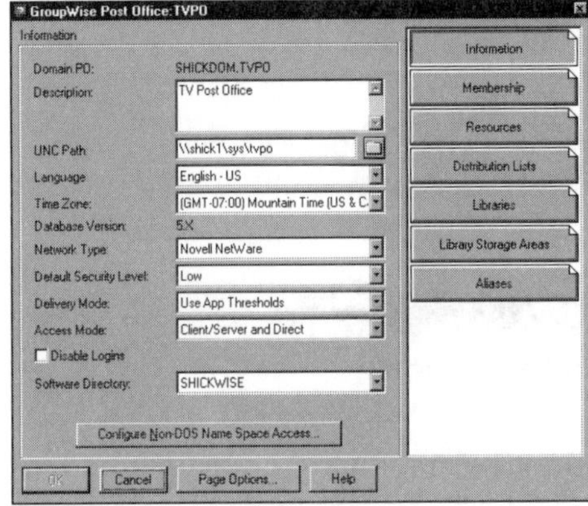

Setting the Security Level

As a GroupWise administrator, the security of users' GroupWise messages should be of the utmost importance to you. Security settings for the post office determine how and when users can access their messages and under what conditions users can access other users' messages.

In order to understand exactly how post office security works you first need to understand how the GroupWise system decides whether or not to allow the client program to access a particular user mailbox.

When GroupWise is launched (GRPWISE.EXE), GroupWise looks at the network login ID of the user currently logged in and tries to match the network ID with a GroupWise user account in the post office. (In most cases, the GroupWise account and the NDS user name should be identical.)

By adding *startup switches* to the GroupWise shortcut command line, you can change the default behavior of the client. For example, you can tell GroupWise to open a mailbox that doesn't match the login name of your current location. Two switches control which mailbox GroupWise will try to open:

- /@U-*user ID*
- /LA-*network login name*

The /@U-*user ID* switch tells GroupWise to ignore the network login information and open the mailbox for the GroupWise user ID specified on the command line. The most common use for the /@U-*user ID* switch is to gain access to a GroupWise mailbox from a workstation that is logged in under someone else's network login name.

For example, suppose that Jeff Ross, a GroupWise user with the user ID of JEFFR is temporarily working at Lisa's computer, which is logged in to the network with the login name LISAR. Jeff could modify the GroupWise command line property to have the switch /@U-JEFFR and then launch GroupWise to access his mailbox.

The /LA-*network login name* tells GroupWise to look for a mailbox that corresponds with a network login ID, rather than a GroupWise user ID. This switch is most commonly used when for some reason the GroupWise network login detection feature is not correctly locating a user's mailbox.

Another factor that affects how GroupWise accesses a user's mailbox is whether or not the user has set a password on the mailbox.

The post office security setting determines the conditions under which a user's mailbox can be accessed. As shown in figure 6.5, the post office has two security settings: low and high. To access the post office security setting, from NetWare Administrator right-click on the Post Office object and select Details.

FIGURE 6.5

Post Office Security Settings

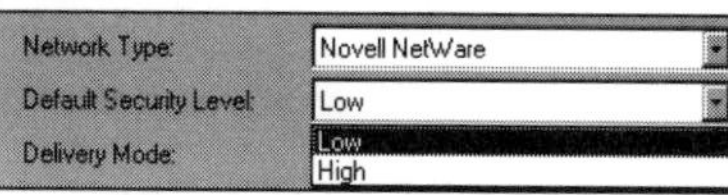

When GroupWise is set to low security, it is very trusting. When it encounters the /@U-*user ID* switch, it assumes that the person using the switch is really the user identified by the user ID. When GroupWise security is set to high, it becomes much more cautious. It requires the person using the switch to enter a password proving that access to the mailbox is warranted.

Setting Security to Low

When post office security is set to low, the /@U-*user ID* switch will let anyone access the mailbox, unless the mailbox's owner has set a mailbox password.

For example, suppose that Mark, a GroupWise user, logs in to NetWare with his network ID MSTEELE. If he launches GroupWise without the /@U-*user ID* switch, GroupWise checks the network login ID, matches his network ID (MSTEELE) with his mailbox, and opens that mailbox.

Suppose that Mark sits next to Brian and, for some reason, he would like to read some of Brian's mail messages. He knows that Brian's GroupWise ID is BJOHNSON, so he launches GroupWise with the /@U-BJOHNSON switch.

If the post office security is set to low, GroupWise will let Mark access Brian's mailbox. What can he do once he gets into Brian's mailbox? Everything! As far as GroupWise is concerned, he *is* Brian. He has complete access to Brian's mailbox and can do anything he wants as Brian. He can even send mail in Brian's name.

Now suppose that Brian is practicing safe messaging. He has set a password on his mailbox. Mark is now out of luck. When he tries to run GroupWise with the @U-BJOHNSON switch, GroupWise will require a password before entering. If he can't enter Brian's password, he can't get into Brian's mailbox.

In summary, if post office security is set to low, anybody can get into another user's mailbox with the /@U-*user ID* switch, unless passwords have been set on the mailboxes. A password on a mailbox effectively gives that mailbox high security.

Table 6.3 summaries how low security works in various circumstances.

TABLE 6.3

Low Security

POST OFFICE SECURITY	RESULT OF NETWORK LOGIN AUTO-DETECTION	PASSWORD SET	RESULT WHEN /@U-*USER ID* SWITCH IS USED
Low	Network login not validated	No	Access is granted to everybody
Low	Network login validated	No	Access is granted to everybody
Low	Network login not validated	Yes	Password must be entered before access is granted
Low	Network login validated	Yes	Access is granted to the logged-in network user without requiring a password

During GroupWise startup, the GroupWise client issues a query to the network operating system for the network ID of the user currently logged in. If this query returns a network ID that matches a GroupWise ID, the login is considered validated. In other words, GroupWise assumes that the GroupWise user has passed the security check when he or she logged in to the network, and that the user's mailbox can be opened without further security validation.

Most GroupWise installations do not use the low security setting because of the intrusion risks inherent with this setting.

Setting Security to High

If post office security is set to high and no password has been set on the mailbox, only the owner of the mailbox can gain access to that mailbox *and* only when the GroupWise client can successfully identify the network login ID. In this situation, GroupWise will grant access to a mailbox only when it can match the current network login ID with a mailbox in the post office.

If network detection fails, even the rightful owner of a mailbox will be denied access.

If post office security is set to high and no password has been set on a specific user's mailbox, GroupWise will return an Access Denied error when someone tries to gain access to a mailbox other than the one they are logged into the network as.

If post office security is set to high and a mailbox password has been set, GroupWise handles the `/@U-`*user ID* switch differently. In this situation, GroupWise will always prompt for the password, granting access if the person using the switch is able to enter the correct one.

GroupWise passwords are case-sensitive.

Let's go back to our friends Brian and Mark. Suppose that their post office security is set to high and Brian has not protected his mailbox with a password. Mark, who is as nosy as ever, wants to know what's in Brian's mailbox. He tries to run GroupWise with the `/@U-BJOHNSON` switch. In this situation, GroupWise will recognize that the request for access was not coming from a computer logged into the network as Brian, and will deny access.

If Brian had set a password and Mark was able to enter it, GroupWise would allow Mark to access Brian's mailbox.

There is one additional scenario that you need to be aware of. When users set a password in GroupWise, they have a checkbox option entitled "Remember My Password" that they can select in the password dialog. If the user selects this option, GroupWise will not prompt the user for a password if the network login detection validates the user's identity. If the user does not select this option, GroupWise will always prompt for the password. If the system's query for the login name does not confirm the user's identity, it will prompt for the password. In other words, this is a keystroke-saving feature that prevents the legitimate (logged in) user from having to enter the password every time he or she launches GroupWise.

Note that as an administrator, you have an option to restrict the *password caching* feature. The first time users access GroupWise, they have to enter the password. This feature, enabled by default, means that the user won't have to reenter the password if they close GroupWise and start it again in the same computer session (in other words, they have not shut down, restarted, or logged back in again). This could present a security breach if someone starts GroupWise, exits GroupWise, and walks away from their desk while still logged into the network.

To prohibit password caching:

1 • From NetWare Administrator, click on Tools.

2 • Click on Client Defaults.

3 • Click on Security.

4 • Clear the check box next to Allow Password Caching.

Table 6.4 summarizes how the high security setting works in various situations. (These settings assume that the Remember My Password option is selected.)

TABLE 6.4

High Security

POST OFFICE SECURITY	RESULT OF NETWORK LOGIN AUTO-DETECTION	PASSWORD SET	RESULT WHEN /@U-*USER ID* SWITCH IS USED
High	Network login not validated	No	Access is denied to everybody
High	Network login validated	No	Access is granted
High	Network login not validated	Yes	Password must be entered before access is granted
High	ID validated	Yes	Access is granted without prompting for password

Optimizing Post Office Security

In terms of message security, the most secure post office is accomplished when the following conditions are met:

- The post office security setting is high.
- Users set passwords on their mailboxes.
- Users do not select the "Remember My Password" option.
- The Allow Password Caching option is not selected.

With these settings in place, it is impossible to hack into another user's mailbox without knowing that user's password. Also, if a user walks away from an unattended, logged-in workstation, intruders would still need to know that user's GroupWise password to access the mailbox. Of course, if GroupWise is already running, there is no protection.

Optimizing Mailbox Security

The following checklist will help you and your users maintain secure GroupWise mailboxes:

- As an administrator, set post office security to high.

- Instruct users how to set passwords in the GroupWise client, and encourage this practice. The password dialog is accessed in the client by clicking on Tools, Options, and Security. (Instruct users that passwords are case-sensitive and to write them down in a secure place. If users select the Remember My Password option, they are likely to forget it.) Note that passwords are required if users will access GroupWise in Remote mode.

- Encourage users not to walk away from their computers while they are logged in to the network. Nothing can prevent someone from accessing an unattended computer.

- Encourage users to be selective when granting proxy rights to their mailboxes. When granting proxy rights, users should grant Write permissions *only* if they are absolutely sure they want that person to create messages in their name.

Setting the Delivery Mode

The security settings explained in the preceding section affect how users can access the information held in the information store. The *delivery mode settings* affect how the GroupWise client or the POA delivers messages within the information store.

NOTE

When we use the phrase "delivers messages" we are referring to (1) the process of updating the recipients' user database with pointers that link to the message in a message database, and (2) generation of status messages indicating delivery.

The delivery mode settings enable you to specify how the actual message delivery occurs within a post office. You use the delivery mode settings to specify if only the GroupWise client places the message in the information store, to specify if only the POA places the messages in the information store, or to establish settings that let these two components share message delivery duties.

Delivery mode settings affect the network rights that are required by the user to access the information store directories and files.

The post office information store is most secure if the POA handles message delivery, because users don't need rights to the post office directories and files.

The post office agent is perhaps the most critical component of your entire GroupWise system. When it runs efficiently, the system runs efficiently. The post office agent runs at the post office level and handles many messaging tasks, such as delivering messages, queuing messages to other locations in the system, generating status messages, maintaining the integrity of the post office databases, and overseeing the client/server connections.

Chapter 11, which covers optimization of the GroupWise agents, provides more detailed information on the operation of the post office agent.

You can take some of the burden off the POA and optimize the performance of your GroupWise system by adjusting the post office delivery mode. This setting enables you to balance some of the messaging tasks between the GroupWise client and the POA. The delivery mode settings are accessed by right-clicking on the Post Office object and selecting Details.

As shown in Figure 6.6, three message delivery modes are available: Use App Thresholds, Agent Always, and Client Delivers Locally. The default mode is Use App Thresholds. To understand the Use App Threshold setting, you first need to understand the other two settings.

FIGURE 6.6

Message Delivery Modes

Client Delivers Locally

In Client Delivers Locally mode, the GroupWise client performs all message delivery within the post office. This mode is practical only in very small GroupWise implementations. For example, if the delivery mode is set to Client Delivers Locally and a user sends a message to 100 recipients in the post office, that user would have to wait while the client at the workstation delivered all 100 messages.

After it delivers local messages, the client also creates status messages and delivers them to the sender.

Agent Always

In Agent Always mode, the POA handles all message delivery within the post office. When the post office operates in this mode, users do not need to have Write, Create, or Erase file system rights to the post office information store directories, because the client simply queues the message to a POA message queue and the POA assumes all delivery responsibilities. Therefore, users don't need rights to the OFUSER, OFMSG, and OFFILES directories. Consequently, this mode provides a high level of security for the post office. (In the other two modes, users need file system rights to the information store directories.)

However, this mode can have an adverse affect on system performance from an end user's perspective. In Agent Always mode, the POA performs all message delivery and creates all status updates, including updates to users' mailbox information (such as new passwords). Any action performed in the client that causes a change in an information store database generates a message to the POA to perform the change, and hence causes a delay in that change being reflected in the client. When Agent Always is selected, users must wait for all personal items to be processed. Nevertheless, if a user were to send a message to 100 users in the post office, the workstation would be freed up almost immediately.

NOTE

If you want the file system security provided by the Agent Always mode, you should consider using Client/Server access mode for the post office. Like Agent Always delivery mode, Client/Server access mode does not require that users have rights to the post office directories or files. Client/Server access mode is explained a little later in this chapter under the heading "Setting the Access Mode." Chapter 15 also gives detailed instructions for setting up a system to run in Client/Server mode.

Use App Thresholds

The Use App Thresholds setting enables you to determine how much work is handled by the client program and how much is handled by the POA. The *Application Threshold* is the number of "processes" involved in delivering a message to all of its recipients. The Use App Thresholds option is a setting that specifies how many processes will trigger message delivery by the POA. In this context, a *process* usually means message delivery to a single recipient. In other words, if a message is sent to ten recipients, at least ten processes are involved. However, depending upon other factors, such as Send options and the like, it may take more than one process to deliver a message to a single recipient.

Suppose the Application Threshold is set to 5. If a user runs the client and sends a message to four recipients within a post office, the user's client will deliver all of the messages. That is, the client will place the message in the information store and update all of the recipients' mailboxes.

NOTE

If a message is sent to recipients outside the post office, the client still delivers messages to the local users in the post office if the number of local users does not exceed the threshold. The client then puts the message in a queue so the MTA can deliver it to users outside the post office.

If the Application Threshold is set to 5 and a user sends a message to seven local recipients in the post office, the threshold is exceeded and the POA handles message delivery to *all* local recipients. The Application Threshold is an "all-or-nothing" setting. Either the client handles all local delivery of a message or the POA takes over and handles delivery of the message.

In order for the client to handle message delivery, users in the post office must be given certain file system rights to the post office. Special rights are needed because the client must write to several different post office files and databases.

IMPORTANT

The Use App Threshold setting is useless if the post office is operating in Client/Server access mode. In Client/Server access mode, the POA handles *all* message delivery.

Setting the Application Threshold Value Although you specify the delivery mode in the Post Office object's properties screen, the value of the application threshold cannot be set there. Instead, you set it on a per user, per post office, or per domain, basis. To set the Application Threshold for a domain, post office, or individual user:

1 • Highlight the Domain, Post Office, or User object in NetWare Administrator.

2 • Click on Tools.

3 • Click on GroupWise Utilities.

4 • Click on Client Options.

5 • Double-click on the Environment icon.

6 • Click on the Threshold Tab.

7 • Set the desired threshold value.

8 • Click on OK.

9 • Click on Close.

NOTE

An Application Threshold set for a specific user overrides settings for the user's post office or domain. Likewise, an Application Threshold set for a post office overrides the value set for the domain.

When you set Application Thresholds, consider both the message delivery load you're placing on the post office server and the level of performance users expect from the GroupWise client.

Novell recommends that you set the threshold to 3 or less. If the POA becomes bogged down with message delivery tasks at an Application Threshold of 3, increase it gradually until you find a good balance.

Setting the Application Threshold to 0 The default Application Threshold value is 0. Although at first you might think that an Application Threshold value of 0 is the equivalent of the Agent Always setting, in reality that is not the case. When the Application Threshold value is set to 0, the client program still handles certain message delivery tasks:

- Placing messages into message databases
- Placing file attachments into the OFFILES directory
- Adding pointers to senders' user databases

- Handling users' personal messages, such as Personal Appointments

With the setting at 0, the POA handles delivery to the recipients, but the client handles the creation of messages in the information store for the sender. When a user does something that only affects his or her own mailbox, the client handles the task and the results are immediate.

NOTE

When you use any Application Threshold value, users must have file system rights to some post office directories. Users need Read, Write, and Create (RWC) rights in the OFUSER and OFMSG directories, and Read, Write, Create, and Erase (RWCE) rights in the OFFILES directory.

Setting the Access Mode

The *access mode setting* controls how the GroupWise client program connects to the post office (see Figure 6.7). In other words, you use the access mode setting to specify whether the GroupWise client performs direct reads and writes to files and directories in the post office or whether the POA handles all reads and writes to the post office.

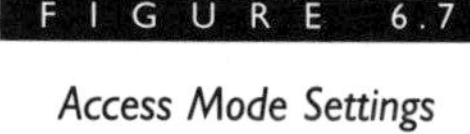
FIGURE 6.7

Access Mode Settings

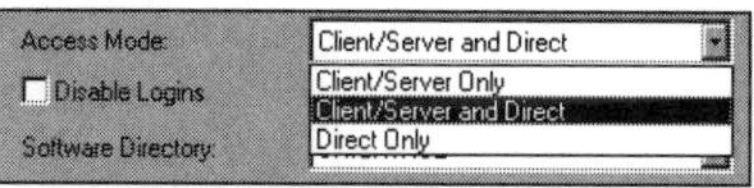

When deciding how users will access your post office, you have three choices:

- Client/Server Only
- Direct Only
- Client/Server and Direct

Client/Server Only

When a post office is set to Client/Server Only mode, the POA handles all interaction between the client and the post office directories and files. The client never directly reads or writes to the post office directories and files. The client program requests services from the POA via TCP/IP network transport protocol.

NOTE

When Client/Server Only mode is used, the delivery mode setting is irrelevant.

Client/Server Only mode has the following advantages:

- Because all read and write functions of the post office are handled by the POA, it is less likely that post office files will become corrupted. Most corruption of database files results from abnormal file writing and access.
- Problems caused by multiple workstations accessing information store databases and files concurrently are eliminated because all access is performed by the POA.
- Users do not need file system rights to post office files and directories.
- Fewer IntranetWare licenses are needed because you don't need a license for the client/server connection. Note, however, that if users must access the file server for file and print services, they will require a license.
- Because a drive mapping to the post office is not required, users can easily access their post office files from different post offices in the system.

The major disadvantage of Client/Server Only mode is the difficulty associated with configuring support for TCP/IP. TCP/IP must be configured at every workstation that will use client/server access.

Setting up a post office and POA for client/server access is discussed in Chapter 15.

Direct Only

Direct Only mode is the post office access mode used by previous versions of GroupWise. In Direct Only mode, users need file system rights and a drive mapping to the post office directory on the network. Consequently, users must have a file access connection to the file server on which the post office directory is located. Users also need network login IDs and passwords to access the post office directory.

The advantages of Direct Only mode are as follows:

- It's relatively easy to set up a post office in this mode.
- Within network segments, system performance is good.
- You do not need to configure TCP/IP support at the client workstations.

If you can't make up your mind which of the above access modes you want to use—or if you want some users to be able to use client/server access and some users to use direct access—the next option is the one for you.

Client/Server and Direct

When you choose the Client/Server and Direct mode, users can access the post office with either type of access.

Users can add two switches to the GroupWise shortcut command line to force the client to connect in Client/Server mode:

- `/ipa-`*IP address of POA*
- `/ipp-`*IP port of POA*

These switches can be used on the command line independently or together. (The command line is accessed by clicking the GroupWise icon, selecting Properties, and then choosing the Shortcut tab.)

For example, the shortcut command line for GroupWise to a post office using client/server connections might look something like the following:

```
C:\NOVELL\GROUPWISE\GRPWISE.EXE /ipa-155.151.233.2 /ipp-1677
```

If either (or both) of the switches appears on the command line, the client will attempt to connect in Client/Server mode. Otherwise, the client program will try to detect a drive mapping to the post office. If neither a switch nor a drive mapping is found, the client will prompt the user to enter the necessary information manually or else run GroupWise in Remote mode.

At startup, the GroupWise client looks at NDS to determine which access mode to use and which post office to access. This information is only available to the client if the user is logged in with an NDS connection. The user must also have object and property rights to certain NDS objects, as explained in the following lists.

The user needs the following NDS rights to his or her own User object:

- Browse Object rights to the User object itself
- Read rights to the NGW: Object ID property
- Read rights to the NGW: Post Office property
- Read rights to the Surname property

The user needs the following rights to the Post Office object:

- Browse Object rights for the Post Office object itself
- Read rights to the Network Address property
- Read rights to the NGW: Access Mode property
- Read rights to the NGW: Location property
- Read rights to the NGW: Type property

NOTE

In the above rights listings, *NGW* denotes a "Novell GroupWise" property. In other words, these are properties added by GroupWise when the NDS schema is extended.

Client/Server and Direct access mode provides the greatest flexibility because users can access their post offices according to their system capabilities, their network configurations, and their messaging needs.

Message Flow

Now that you understand the post office physical structure and you've seen how to adjust some of the post office settings, you're ready to start analyzing message flow.

If you understand how messages flow in a GroupWise system, you will be able to troubleshoot many problems by identifying the faulty process. Message flow in a single post office system is relatively simple. The processes are much more complicated in larger GroupWise systems with multiple post offices and domains. You'll see more complex message flow diagrams later in the book.

In this chapter, we explain three message flow scenarios for a single post office system. The scenarios correspond to the different settings you can choose for the message-delivery mode:

- Client Delivers Locally
- Agent Always
- Application Threshold = 0

These settings are explained earlier in this chapter in the section "Setting the Delivery Mode."

Client Delivers Locally

If the delivery mode is set to Client Delivers Locally, message delivery follows the path illustrated in Figure 6.8.

IMPORTANT

When the Application Threshold is not exceeded, message delivery is the same as in Client Delivers Locally mode.

FIGURE 6.8

Client Delivers Locally (or Threshold Not Exceeded)

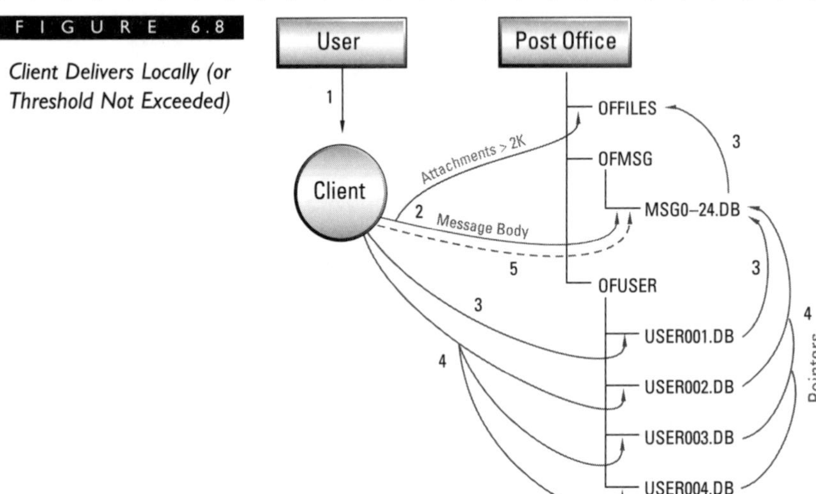

NOTE

For convenience, in Figure 6.8 the sender's user database is USER001.DB and the recipients' user databases are numbered 002, 003, and 004. In a real-world situation, these numbers would actually be the users' FIDs. As a general convention throughout this book, figures do not show all of the subdirectories and files in the post office.

Here are the steps shown in Figure 6.8:

1. The GroupWise user (001) runs the client and sends a message to three recipients whose user databases are numbered 002, 003, and 004 and who reside in the same post office. The message contains a file attachment that exceeds 2K in size.

2. The client places the message in the message database that has been assigned to the sender and places the attachment file in a subdirectory of the OFFILES directory. (If the message contains multiple file attachments, each attachment is stored as an individual file in the OFFILES subdirectories.)

3. The client places in the sender's user database (USER001.DB) the message header information and a pointer, which points to the

message stored in the message database. The client also places a pointer in the message database, which points to the attachment in the OFFILES directory. These pointers enable the sender to access the message through the client Sent Items folder.

4 • The client now assumes a message delivery role, placing message header information and a pointer in each of the recipients' user databases pointing to the message in the sender's message database. At this point, the message has been delivered and recipients can access the message with their client.

5 • The client updates the message database with a status message indicating that the message has been delivered. (Broken lines in the message flow diagrams represent status message updates.) If the sender checks the message status, the Delivered status will appear, along with the exact time the pointers were placed in the users' databases. When recipients open the message, their client will tag the status message to Opened by updating the status information in the message database.

NOTE

In Figure 6.8, the arrows on the right-hand side pointing to the message databases represent pointers in the user databases pointing to the message databases. For the sake of simplicity, these arrows will not be included in subsequent diagrams.

Notice that a client has a lot of work to do when it is responsible for message delivery. The user will notice this in the form of sluggish client performance. This is the biggest argument against using the Client Delivers Locally mode or setting the Application Threshold to a high value.

In short, when the client delivers locally, it handles message creation, message delivery, and status-message delivery.

Message Deletion

What happens when one of the recipients deletes the message? When a message is deleted in the client program, it moves to the Trash folder *in the user's database*. The Trash folder is similar to the Windows 95 Recycle Bin. When the user empties the Trash, that user's pointer to the message is deleted, but the message itself remains in the message database until two events occur: (1) all recipients delete the message and empty the message from their Trash; *and* (2) the sender deletes the message from the Sent Items folder and empties the Trash. When all pointers to the message have been deleted, the client removing the last pointer will perform the cleanup duties by deleting the message from the message database, along with any file attachments associated with that message.

Message Archival

GroupWise users also have an option to archive messages. When a user archives a message, the message and its file attachments are copied from the post office information store to a location on the user's hard drive or to a personal directory on the network. The location of the archive directory can be set in the GroupWise client preferences, or you can set it through NWAdmin (as you will see in Chapter 7). As far as the GroupWise master system is concerned, archival is the same as deletion.

The archive directory on a user's hard drive is very similar to the post office information store. The archive directory contains a user database (USER.DB) and a message database (MSG.DB). File attachments are stored in the same archive directory.

IMPORTANT

If a user "unarchives" a message, it is moved back to the post office information store. However, old pointers are *not* restored. The message and its attachments are placed back into the post office information store as a *new* message and new file attachments. Also, status information is no longer updated once a message has been archived.

Agent Always

Figure 6.9 shows the message delivery process when the delivery mode is set to Agent Always.

FIGURE 6.9

Agent Always

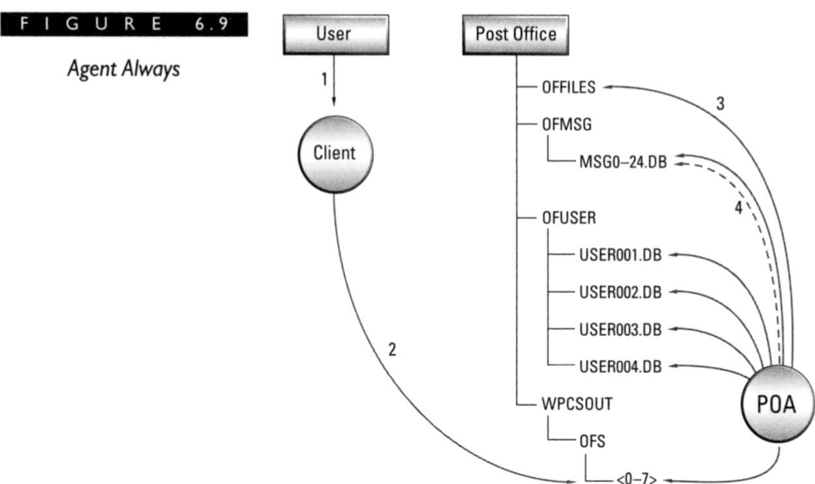

Here are the steps illustrated in Figure 6.9:

1 • The sender sends the message in the client application.

2 • The client writes the entire message and file attachments to a message file that is placed in the WPCSOUT\OFS\<0–7> subdirectory (the POA queue). This is the only directory to which users need Write, Create, or Erase file system rights if the message delivery mode is Agent Always.

3 • The POA reads the message file, placing the message in the message database and the file attachments in the OFFILES directory. It also updates the sender's user database with a pointer to the message, and it places pointers in all of the recipients' user databases.

4 • The POA then updates the message database marking the status of the "Delivered."

Notice that the client does not perform any message delivery tasks. Even if the sender is just placing a personal note in his or her personal calendar, the POA must handle delivery. This will be noticed by the user, because there will be a delay between the time the user presses Send and the time it appears in the user's calendar. This is the biggest disadvantage of the Agent Always setting. As mentioned earlier, if you want the file system security offered by this setting, you should consider using the Client/Server Only mode.

In summary, when the Agent Always setting is used, the client creates the message and passes the message to the POA, which handles all message delivery and status message delivery.

Application Threshold Value Exceeded or Set to 0

If the Application Threshold value is exceeded or set to 0, the message flow follows the path illustrated in Figure 6.10.

FIGURE 6.10

Application Threshold Exceeded

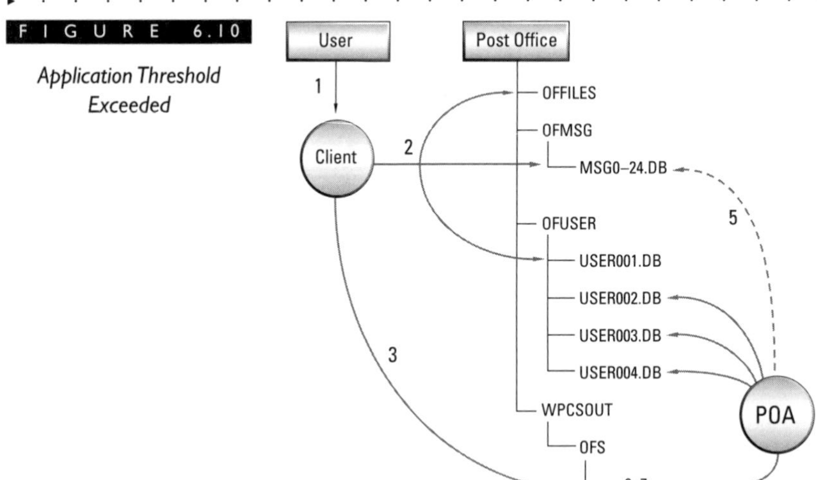

Figure 6.10 diagrams the following steps:

1 • The sender creates the message in the client.

2 • The client puts the message in the message database, places a pointer in the sender's user database to the message in the message database,

and places file attachments or messages over 2K in the attachments directory.

3 • The client places a file containing a list of the message recipients in the POA's queue.

4 • The POA reads the file from its queue and places pointers in the recipients' user databases.

5 • The POA updates the message database with "Delivered" status.

As indicated, when the Application Threshold is exceeded, the client creates the message and places the message in the sender's message database. The POA then handles message delivery to the recipients and also manages the status messages.

Summary

Now you have completed Post Office Management 101. Like a basic algebra class, this chapter has provided the groundwork for the concepts explained throughout the rest of this book.

You've now learned how post office security works. You should be aware of the ways users can attempt to hack into another user's mailbox, and how to prevent them from such nefarious activities by using the security settings.

You also learned how to configure inter-post-office messaging with delivery modes and access modes. These settings are used to control which GroupWise components can directly access the post office information store, and also allow you to optimize post office message management to meet your network configuration and messaging needs.

Finally, you saw how GroupWise messaging works behind the scenes within a post office. We sincerely hope that you like those nice message flow diagrams, because they get even better as your GroupWise system gets more complex.

CHAPTER 7

User-Level Administration

So far you have learned how to manage system-level objects—domains, post offices, gateways, and so forth. In this chapter you'll learn how to manage objects at the user level. As a GroupWise administrator, you need to decide which features you'll make available to the end users. The more features available, the more work you'll have to do to set up and manage the users in your system.

In this chapter, we show you how to make using GroupWise as easy as possible for your end users. As you read this chapter, keep in mind that you probably won't need to implement all of the features you'll learn about. For example, you'll learn how to create distribution lists so users can send messages to predefined groups of people. This is a nice feature for the end users, but it involves additional managerial tasks for the administrator. You'll need to decide which features are necessary for your end users and which features are not feasible from an administrative perspective.

We begin the chapter by showing you some tips for navigating through NDS using NetWare Administrator. Next, we'll look at the NDS properties relevant to GroupWise administration of User objects, showing you how to create, modify, and delete user accounts. Finally, you'll look at administration of Resource objects and Distribution List objects.

Using NetWare Administrator

In this section, you will learn how to get the most out of NetWare Administrator as you perform administrative tasks related to your GroupWise system. Although a complete discussion of IntranetWare, NetWare, and NetWare Administrator would be beyond the scope of this book, we want to give you a few tips to follow as you navigate through the NetWare Administrator interface. Remember, you use NetWare Administrator to modify the NDS tree containing the GroupWise objects in your system.

You can design (or update) your NDS tree to facilitate GroupWise administration. For example, you might decide to group users in a certain department in a single organizational unit (OU) to make the User objects easy to administer. Strategies for planning your implementation of GroupWise and NDS are explained in Chapter 3.

NetWare Administrator has a few handy features you should be familiar with as you modify and navigate through the NDS tree structure. Use the Sort and Include option under the View menu to choose specific types of NDS objects you want to view. For example, you can view only User objects and Distribution List objects. Also, you can right-click on an object to open its shortcut menu. Finally, the GroupWise View option in the Tools menu enables you to view only the GroupWise objects in the tree—such as domains, post offices, gateways, users, distribution lists, resources, libraries, and nicknames.

Using Sort and Include

You can use the Sort and Include option to display only certain objects in a container. For example, you might want to view only users, without having to scroll through all of the printers, volumes, and servers in the container.

To view only certain types of objects, follow these steps:

1. In the NetWare Administrator, select the appropriate container. Under the View menu, select Sort and Include. The default view shows you all objects in your system (see Figure 7.1).

2. Select the objects you *don't* want to appear in the "Included classes" column and click on the right-pointing arrow to move them to the "Available classes" column. You can press the Shift key as you click to select a range of objects. Press Ctrl and click to select nonadjacent objects.

3. Click on OK when your choice is complete. Double-click on the container object to close it, and then double-click again to open and refresh the list of objects under the container. NetWare Administrator now displays only the objects listed in the "Included classes" column of the Browser Sort and Include dialog box.

FIGURE 7.1

Browser Sort and Include Dialog Box

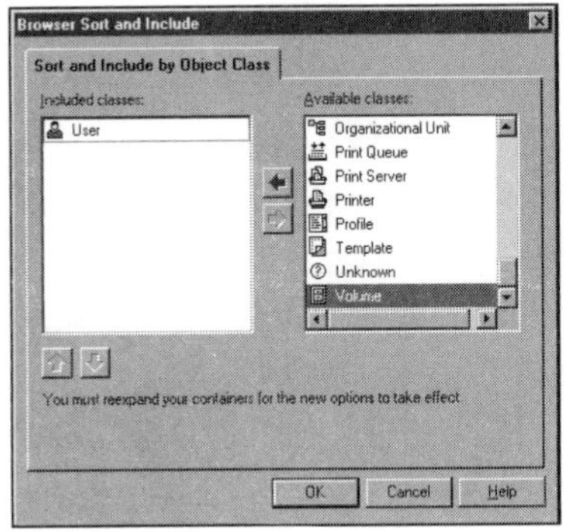

Right-Clicking

To access detailed information about an NDS object, right-click on the object and choose Details from the shortcut menu. You'll see a dialog box that shows general properties of the object. Additional properties are grouped together in property pages for the object, which appear as tabs along the right-hand side of the dialog box. Figure 7.2 shows a property page for a User object.

FIGURE 7.2

A User Object's Property Page

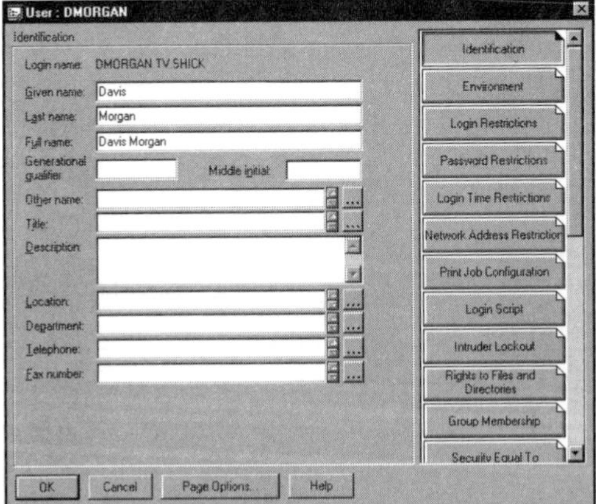

Avoid clicking and dragging in NetWare Administrator unless you are absolutely sure of what you're doing. Clicking on an object and dragging it to another object changes the first object into an NDS Trustee of the target object. This can have serious implications for NDS security.

Viewing Only GroupWise Objects

When you select *GroupWise View*, you can view only the GroupWise objects in your NDS tree. (In other words, no non-GroupWise NDS objects show up in this view.) Using GroupWise View can make GroupWise administration tasks much easier. To change NetWare Administrator to GroupWise View, choose GroupWise View from the Tools menu (see Figure 7.3).

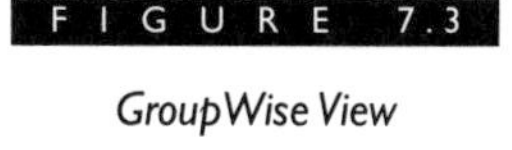

FIGURE 7.3

GroupWise View

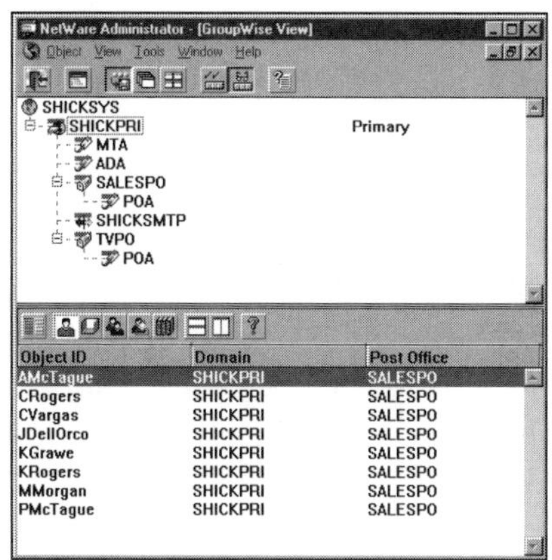

As you can see in Figure 7.3, GroupWise system-level components appear in the top portion of this window, and user-level objects are listed at the bottom.

You may see a plus sign (+) next to a domain or post office. This means that the display is collapsed; clicking on it will expand the view to show the objects underneath.

When you click on a post office or domain in the top portion of the window, objects belonging to that component are listed in the lower part of the window. For example, clicking on the SHICKPRI domain will list all of the users in the entire domain. Clicking on the SALESPO post office will display just the users in that post office.

The button bars of the lower window change which GroupWise objects (users, resources, distribution lists and nicknames) are listed. Leave your mouse pointer over a button for a few seconds to see a pop-up description of the button. Two buttons to the right of the Toolbar hide or modify the Toolbar. If you hide the Toolbar, you must close the GroupWise View window and choose View Toolbar from the View menu. Open the GroupWise View again to see the Toolbar.

As you will see in later chapters, some GroupWise features and settings are available only through the GroupWise View. For example, you can't create an external domain without opening GroupWise View.

Administering User Objects

Most user accounts listed in the GroupWise Address Book are actually NDS User objects that have been assigned GroupWise mailboxes. This assignment takes place when you manage the GroupWise properties of User objects. Remember, *properties* are categories of data that can be specified for an object in NDS, such as a phone number or the name of a GroupWise post office.

You can manage the GroupWise properties of objects at the same time you change their IntranetWare properties. This feature makes GroupWise administration exceptionally easy for network administrators. You can modify GroupWise properties when you create new User objects or when you modify existing NDS users' network information.

Creating New User Objects

Here are the steps for creating a new User object in an NDS tree:

1 • Right-click on the container in which you want to create the new User object and choose Create. You'll see a dialog box like the one shown in Figure 7.4.

2 • Enter information in the Login Name and Last Name fields. If you like, you can create a home directory for the new user at this time. You can also apply template properties if you choose.

3 • Click on OK.

FIGURE 7.4

Creating a New NDS User Object

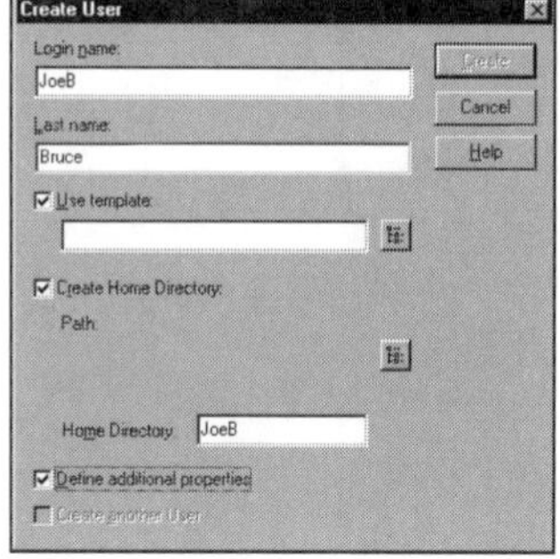

Changing an Existing User Object's Properties

To change the GroupWise properties of an existing User object, right-click on the User object in the NDS tree and choose Details from the shortcut menu. The Information property page appears.

NOTE

GroupWise properties are enabled for users when the NDS schema is extended, but actual properties are not assigned until users are added to a post office.

The properties window contains a separate property page for each of the four types of GroupWise properties: GroupWise Account, GroupWise Nicknames, Aliases, and GroupWise X.400 Information (see Figure 7.5).

FIGURE 7.5

GroupWise Property Pages

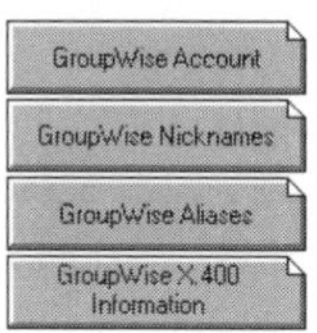

GroupWise Account

As Figure 7.6 shows, information on the GroupWise Account property page includes the name of the user's mailbox and the GroupWise domain name and post office name for the account.

FIGURE 7.6

GroupWise Account Information

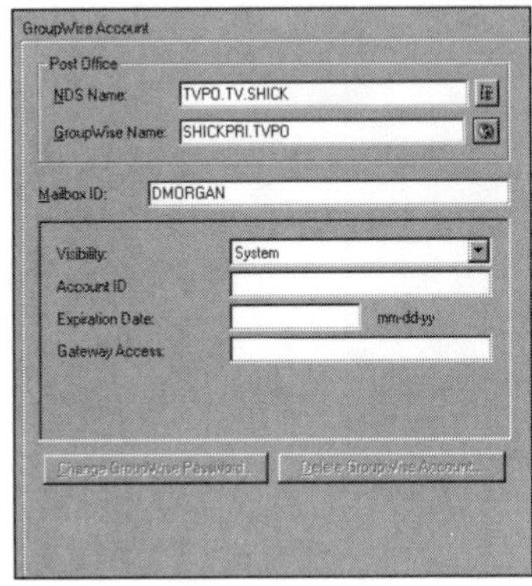

Follow these steps to add a user to a GroupWise post office:

1 • From the GroupWise Account property page, click on the browse button next to the GroupWise post office name.

2 • Select the user's post office from the list.

3 • Click on OK twice to complete the assignment.

Table 7.1 describes the various properties you can set on the GroupWise Account property page.

TABLE 7.1

GroupWise Account Properties

PROPERTY	DESCRIPTION
PO NDS Name	Distinguished NDS name of the post office
GroupWise Name	*domain.post office* for the post office
Mailbox ID	GroupWise mailbox account name
Visibility	System: Object will appear on all users' Address Books (Default) Domain: Object will appear in Address Book for the Domain only Post Office: Object will appear in Address Book for users in the same PO None: Object will not appear on any Address Book

TABLE 7.1

GroupWise Account Properties (continued)

PROPERTY	DESCRIPTION
Account ID	ID for gateway accounting (Optional)
File ID	Unique mailbox ID Note: the ID will appear only on mailboxes that have been created
Expiration Date	Date the mailbox will expire (Optional)
Gateway Access	Specify what gateways the user can access and how (Optional)

After you fill in the fields, choose OK to create the user's mailbox and update the GroupWise Address Books.

GroupWise Nicknames

The GroupWise Nicknames property page controls GroupWise nicknames. You can use the Create Nickname dialog box to specify an alternative name for a GroupWise object. Messages addressed using the nickname in the To: field are delivered to the mailbox associated with the nickname.

Follow these steps to create a nickname:

1 • From GroupWise View, highlight a GroupWise post office.

2 • Right-click and choose Add. The dialog box shown in Figure 7.7 appears.

3 • Choose the post office for the nickname. This will usually be the same post office where the nicknamed object is located.

4 • In the Object ID field, type the nickname. Choose the visibility level and click on OK.

FIGURE 7.7

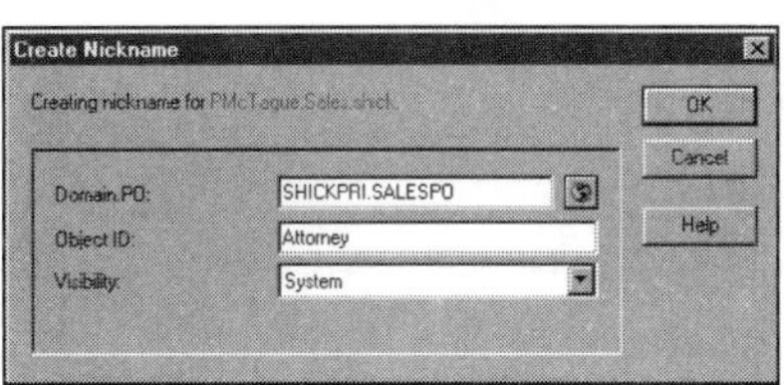

Create Nickname Dialog Box

Nicknames can be very useful when users need to direct mail to certain company positions or entities (such as "HELPDESK" or "SHIPPING"). Using a nickname you can route messages to a particular individual or distribution list.

GroupWise Aliases

Aliases can be used in conjunction with GroupWise gateways to simplify addressing when you don't want to use the GroupWise domain or post office name. For example, a GroupWise user with the GroupWise ID `crogers` could be given the alias `crogers@shick.com`. This enables outsiders to send messages to `crogers@shick.com` without having to include the post office and domain name in the address.

To create an alias for a user, you must first specify the *gateway alias type* for the gateway. Gateway alias types are covered in Chapter 19. Once you have a gateway alias type, follow these steps to create aliases for users:

1. From the GroupWise Aliases property page, click on the Add button. The dialog box shown in Figure 7.8 appears.
2. Click on the NDS symbol next to Gateway Alias Type and select the alias type from the list.
3. In Gateway Alias, enter the address to be used as an alias. Enter the address exactly as you want others outside the system to address messages to the user. In the example in Figure 7.8, an Internet address for Patty McTague (`pmctague@shick.com`) was added as an alias.
4. Click on OK to complete the alias assignment.

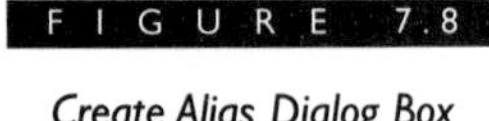
FIGURE 7.8

Create Alias Dialog Box

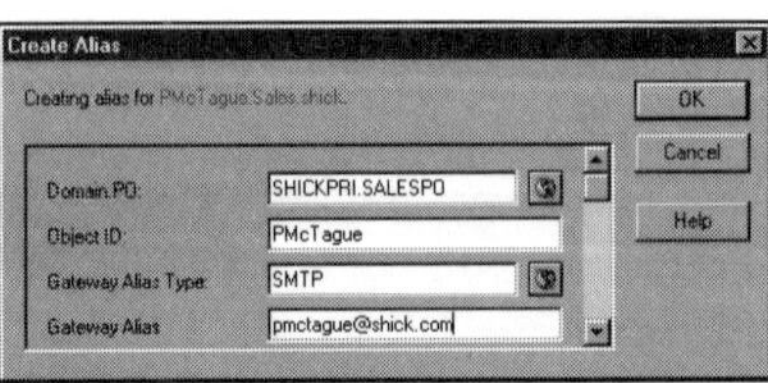

Aliases are primarily used for addressing messages from outside of GroupWise (for example, from the Internet). You'll learn more about aliases in Chapter 20, where we discuss Internet mail and GroupWise.

X.400 Information

X.400 is a messaging protocol that can be used to create, send, and route messages. It has very rigid addressing rules, which must be followed. These rules affect all three parts of a message—address, message body, and attachment. We'll say more about X.400 in Chapter 18, where we explain the X.400 gateway, which enables GroupWise to communicate with X.400 messaging networks.

The GroupWise X.400 Information property page enables you to create the address parts you need for using X.400 addresses.

More information on X.400 can be found in the X.400 white paper included on the companion CD-ROM that comes with this book.

Setting Defaults

Using NetWare Administrator, you can control several of the default preferences and options available to users in the GroupWise client. Most of these preferences are stored in the user database (USER*xxx*.DB) located in the post office. Users can access the preference settings with the client program.

Setting these options enables you to limit the size of mailboxes in your system. You can also use these settings to control network traffic. For example, you can adjust the maximum interval at which Notify scans mailboxes. If the interval is too short, your network may become bogged down with a lot of Notify traffic.

To set default preferences, select the appropriate domain, post office, user, or external entity in NetWare Administrator and then choose GroupWise Utilities from the Tools menu. Then select Client Options.

NOTE

The only way to change GroupWise client options for multiple users is to select the post office or domain to which those users belong.

Figure 7.9 shows the icons that correspond to the different categories of preferences (Environment, Send, Security, and Date & Time).

FIGURE 7.9

GroupWise Client Options

After you set preferences, you can lock the settings to prevent users from changing them. This prevents users at the corresponding level (domain, post office, user, or external entity) from changing the option setting within the GroupWise client program. The option is "grayed out" and cannot be changed.

Locking a preference only prevents users from changing the default setting within the client. A user can still change the setting for individual messages. For example, you can set the default message priority to normal and lock it so users can't change the default message priority setting within the client. However, users would still be able to set message priority to high for individual messages.

To lock a setting, click on the padlock button next to the option.

Depending on the level at which you make a setting—domain, post office, or user—you can lock settings for an entire group. When users try to access those settings from their client, the options will be grayed out and users won't be able to change them. Figure 7.10 shows the Mail and Phone Cleanup options (discussed later in this chapter) after they have been locked.

FIGURE 7.10

Locked Cleanup Settings

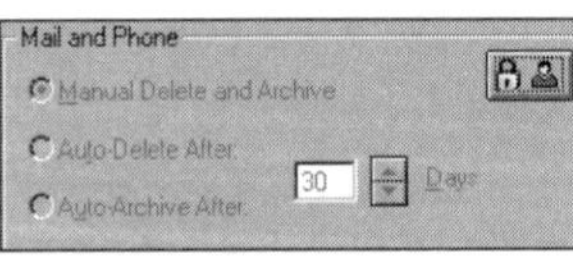

Let's take a closer look at each of the four categories of preferences.

Environment

Figure 7.11 shows the different kinds of options available when you double-click on the Environment icon.

FIGURE 7.11

Environment Options

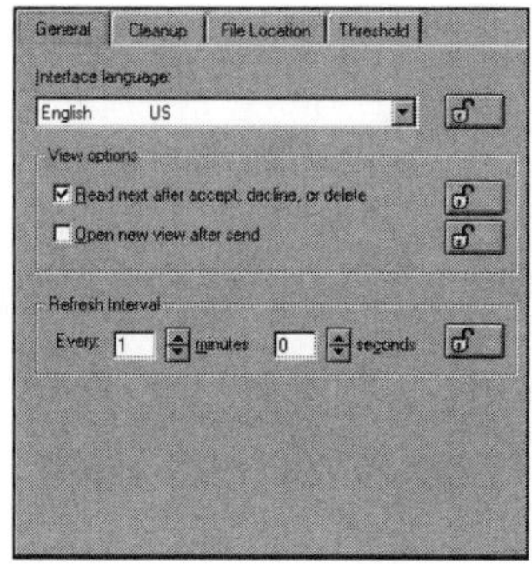

General Under the General tab, you can set the following preferences:

- *Interface Language*. This is the default language for the client interface (menus, views, and so forth). The languages available are those that were installed with GroupWise 5.
- *View Options*. Select "Read next after accept, decline or delete" to open the next message in the mailbox after accepting, declining, or deleting a message. Select "Open new view after send" to start up a new message of the same type immediately after sending a message.
- *Refresh Interval*. This setting determines how often the GroupWise client will check the user's mailbox for new messages. The default is once every minute. (The minimum setting is one minute; the maximum setting is 60 minutes and 59 seconds.)

Normally, you shouldn't need to change the default settings. However, in special cases, it may be beneficial to adjust the defaults. For example, in some cases, you may need to lower the Refresh Interval to reduce network traffic.

Cleanup The Cleanup options can be used to control the size of the information store and limit the number of Mail and Calendar items stored in user and message databases. If you use the default setting, Manual Delete and Archive, the post office information store can grow rapidly (and consume valuable disk space) because deletion and archival are left up to individual users.

We recommend that you establish message deletion and archival policies before you implement GroupWise so users are accustomed to limits from the outset. Typically, administrators settle on a 90-day deletion policy. This gives users ample time to process messages in their mailboxes. Users can then set their client software to automatically archive messages at any point before the 90-day period expires.

Figure 7.12 shows the preferences that can be set under the Cleanup tab.

FIGURE 7.12

Cleanup Options

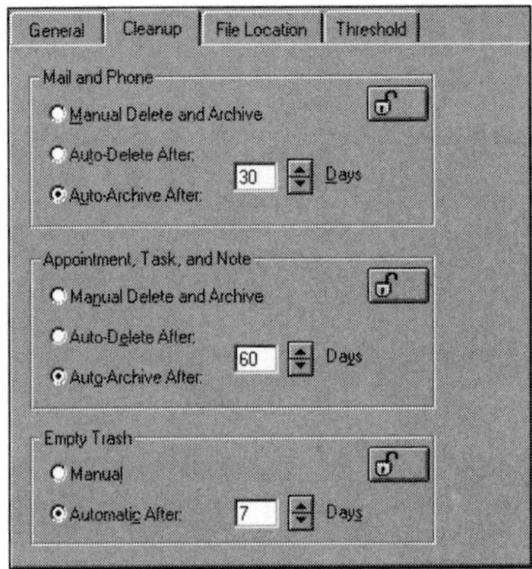

- *Mail and Phone.* This option specifies how long a Mail message or Phone message can remain in the information store before it is automatically archived or deleted by the client program. The period of time begins on the date of the message. The default is Manual Delete and Archive. (The minimum setting is one day; the maximum setting is 250 days.)

- *Appointment, Task, and Note.* This option specifies how long old Calendar information remains in the information store before it is automatically deleted or archived. The default is Manual Delete and Archive. (The minimum setting is one day; the maximum setting is 250 days.)

- *Empty Trash.* This option specifies how long deleted items can stay in the Trash folder before they are either permanently deleted or archived. The default is seven days. (The minimum is one day; the maximum is 250 days.)

IMPORTANT

Once messages have been emptied from the Trash folder, they are no longer retrievable.

Automatic deletion and archival occur when users exit GroupWise. For example, if you set Cleanup options so that messages are archived after ten days, the archiving occurs when users exit GroupWise on the tenth day after a message was received. The automatic Cleanup options may cause a slight delay when users exit GroupWise.

File Location Figure 7.13 shows the File Location options.

FIGURE 7.13

File Location Options

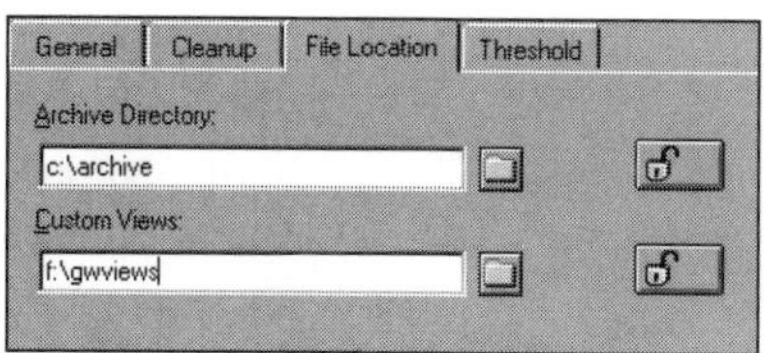

Use the *Archive Directory* setting to specify the location of the directory in which you want to archive messages. In this field you designate the directory under which the archive directory will be created. If you choose the local hard drive, you will save space on the file server, but will have no backup. If you choose a directory on the file server, the archive files will be backed up during your regular network backup process, but the archived messages will take up space on the server. We recommend placing these file on the network in the users' home directory, the directory to which users have extensive rights and where they store their own files, so the files are backed up.

Use the *Custom Views* setting to specify where custom view files are stored. (A *custom view* is a special GroupWise view you can create with a view-designer utility.) A good place to store custom view files is in the Software Management directory that was created when GroupWise was installed. (The default is SYS:SOFTWARE.)

Threshold Figure 7.14 shows the setting you can adjust under the Threshold tab. As you saw in Chapter 6, the Threshold setting determines the point at which the post office agent takes over local message delivery from the client when users send messages to other users in the same post office.

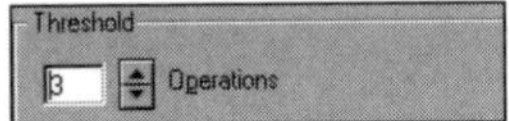

FIGURE 7.14 Threshold Setting

The default setting is 0. However, we recommend that the Threshold be set to 3 in most cases. You should increase the Threshold when you want the client to send more messages, and decrease it when you want the post office agent to send more messages.

NOTE

The Threshold setting only affects messages sent internally within a post office. Messages sent between post offices are *always* delivered by the receiving post office's POA.

By choosing the most appropriate default settings for the Environment options, you can greatly enhance the efficiency of the client program for your users.

Send

Click on the Send icon in the group of Client Options icons under Tools, GroupWise Utilities, Client Options. The Send options are used to configure the default settings that affect how messages are sent. For example, you can set preferences for message status and priority. You can also specify display options for different message types, such as Meeting Requests, Notes, and Tasks.

One reason you might want to change these defaults is to prevent users from sending every message as a high priority message.

The Mail/Phone, Appointment, Task, and Note tabs contain nearly identical options (see Figure 7.15). The Send options common to all four tabs are explained in Table 7.2.

Users can set message Send options on a message-by-message basis, but they cannot set these defaults if the administrator has locked them.

FIGURE 7.15

The Send Options Screen

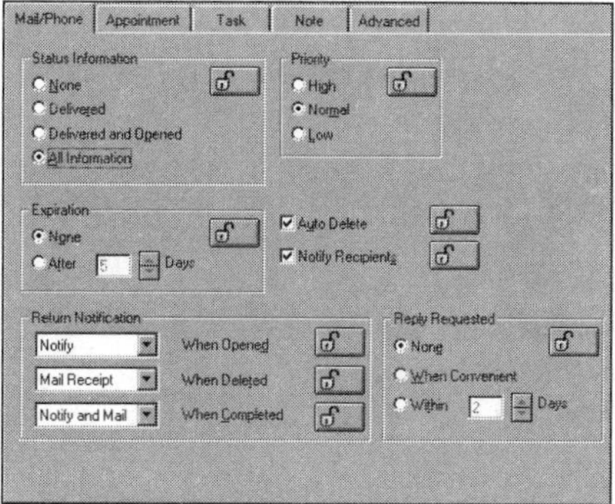

TABLE 7.2

Send Options for the Different Message Types

OPTION	FUNCTION	SETTINGS
Status Information	Determines how much information to track for each message type.	*None.* No status information will appear in the item properties. *Delivered.* Shows if and when the message was delivered to the recipient's mailbox. *Delivered and Opened.* Shows when the message was delivered and when the message was opened. *All Information.* Shows all of the above information, plus information about when the message was deleted, accepted, declined, etc.
Priority	Determines the default priority for each message type.	*High.* The message appears with a red icon in the recipient's mailbox, and may be delivered quicker by GroupWise. *Medium or Standard.* The message appears with a regular icon in the mailbox. *Low.* The message appears with a dimmed icon in the mailbox.

(continued)

TABLE 7.2

Send Options for the Different Message Types (continued)

OPTION	FUNCTION	SETTINGS
Return Notification	Specifies if and how the sender wants to be notified of events triggered by the recipient, such as when the recipient opened, deleted, accepted, declined, or completed, the message.	*Mail Receipt.* A mail message in your mailbox informs you of the event. *Notify.* An on-screen notification message informs you of the event. See Notify in the Appendix. *Notify and Mail.* You receive both of the above.
Notify Recipients	Specifies if the recipients receive a Notify message when the message arrives in their mailbox.	

Mail/Phone, Appointment, Task, and Note Options The Send options available under the Mail/Phone, Appointment, and Note tabs are explained in Table 7.3.

TABLE 7.3

Mail/Phone, Appointment, Task, and Note Options

OPTION	FUNCTION	SETTINGS
Reply Requested	Lets users inform message recipients that they would like replies to messages. When users set a Reply Requested option, GroupWise inserts text in the message body noting that a reply is requested and indicating when the reply is desired. The message icon shows two-way arrows, indicating that a reply is requested.	*When Convenient.* Inserts the following text in the message body: `Reply Requested: When Convenient` *Within X Days.* Inserts the following text in the message body: `Reply Requested: By` *`mm/dd/yy`*
Expiration	Lets users specify when a message will automatically be deleted from the recipient's mailbox if it is not opened.	
Auto-Delete	Automatically removes a message from the Sent Items folder after all recipients have deleted the item and emptied it from the Trash.	

Task The Task tab has one option not available under the other tabs: *Display due date length*. This option lets users specify whether they want the due date to appear as an ending date (for example, "Due on 10/15/1996") or as a length of time (for example, "Due in five days").

Advanced The options available under the Advanced tab are shown in Figure 7.16.

FIGURE 7.16

Advanced Send Options

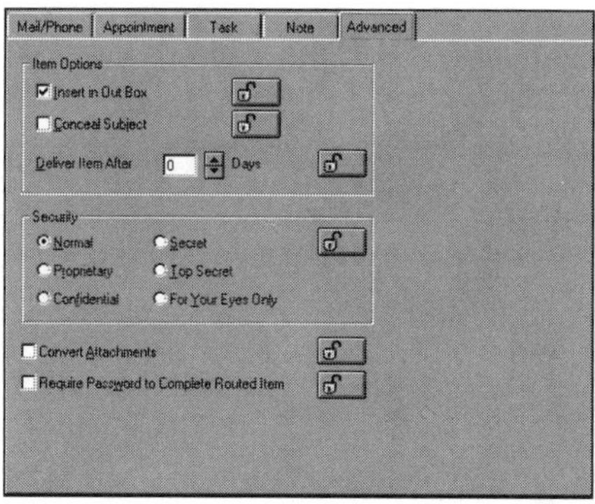

- *Insert in Out Box.* This option determines whether the message will be tracked in the Sent Items folder.

- *Conceal Subject.* This option prevents the message subject line from appearing in the recipient's mailbox. The subject line appears when the recipient opens the item. Use this feature as an additional security measure.

- *Deliver Item After.* This enables users to create a message now that will be automatically sent after a specified number of days.

- *Security.* This lets users tag messages with an introductory sentence indicating the messages security-level.

IMPORTANT

The Security option under the Advanced tab does *not* in any way place security restrictions on the message; it simply labels the message as having a particular security status.

- *Convert Attachments.* This option allows attachments to be converted when sent through a gateway.

- *Require Passwords to Complete Routed Item.* When someone sends a routed item, this setting requires each recipient to enter a password to mark the item "Completed." The item is then routed to the next recipient.

Security

Double-click on the Security icon under Client Options to manage users' mailbox passwords, macro playing, and message notification.

Password If a user forgets his or her password, or if you need to establish a new password, this is where you do it.

You can only change passwords for one user account at a time. Figure 7.17 shows the Password options.

FIGURE 7.17

Password Options

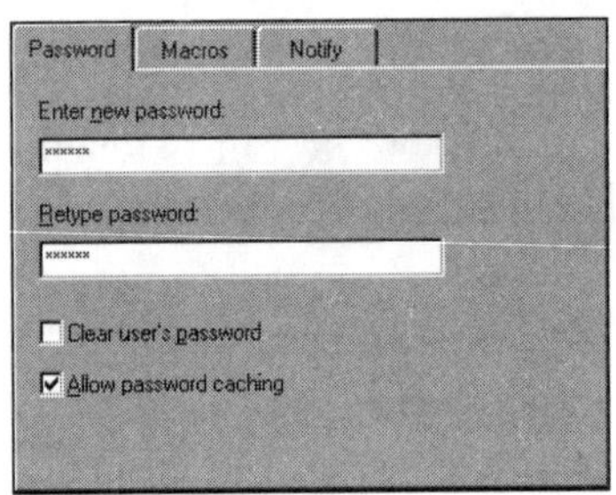

The options under the Password tab are as follows:

- *Enter new password.* Enter a case-sensitive password for the mailbox.

- *Retype password.* Verify the password by entering it again. If the password entered in this field doesn't exactly match the password entered above, you'll be prompted to enter the password again.

- *Clear user's password.* Remove the password for a mailbox without creating a new one.

- *Allow password caching.* When this checkbox is selected, users need not reenter passwords every time they start GroupWise during the same computer session. If users shut down their computers and restart (or log off the network and log in again), they'll still be required to enter a password. This checkbox is checked by default.

Macros Use the Macros setting to provide a higher level of security for users by selecting either "Never Play Received Macros" or "Always Prompt before Playing a Macro." It is possible for viruses to be embedded in message macros. If you are concerned about this threat, choose "Never Play Received Macros." The default is "Always Prompt before Playing a Macro," as shown in Figure 7.18.

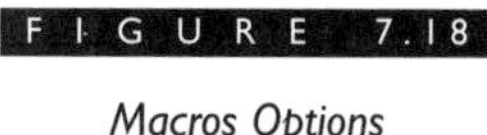

Macros Options

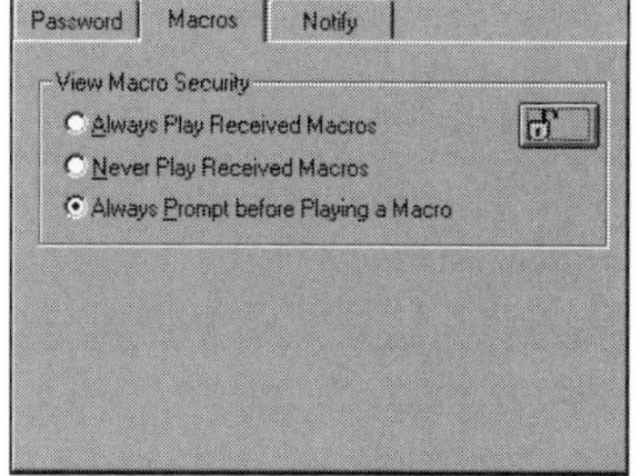

Notify Notify is a program that periodically scans the user's mailbox (USER*xxx*.DB) for new pointers that have been received. When a new message is received, either a dialog box appears on the user's screen or a sound can be played.

Notify adds some network traffic to accomplish this polling. Use the Notify setting to adjust the "polling interval" (see Figure 7.19). The *polling interval* is the period of time (in minutes and seconds) Notify waits before it regularly checks the user databases for new messages. If the polling interval is a larger number, Notify will check for new mail less often, and network traffic decreases. The lower the number, the greater the network traffic.

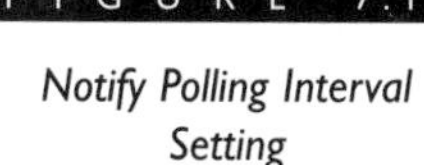

Notify Polling Interval Setting

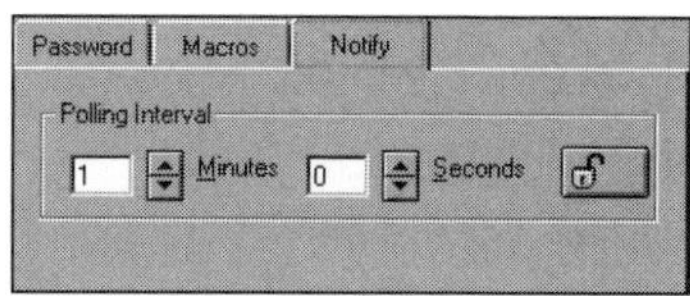

Date & Time

The Date & Time icon (one of the Client Options icons) opens the Date & Time dialog box, which contains two types of settings: Calendar options and Busy Search options. Even though most of these settings won't need to be set for most systems, you should understand them in case users have questions about how they function. Also, in some special cases, you may want to adjust or lock the default settings.

Calendar

The Calendar options are shown in Figure 7.20.

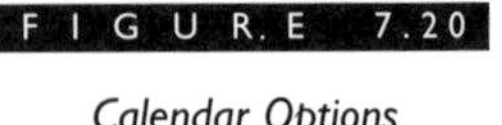

FIGURE 7.20

Calendar Options

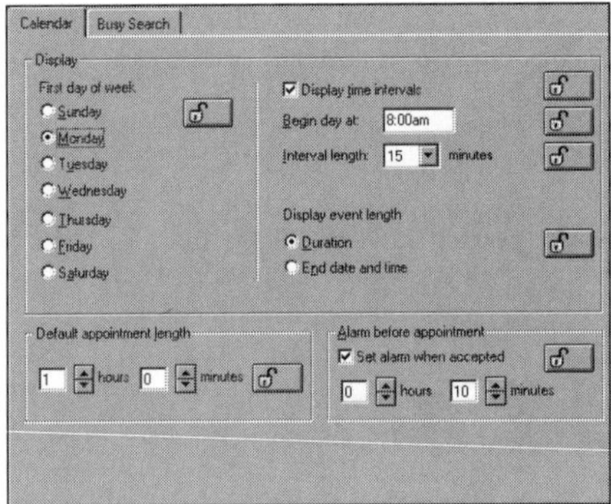

- *First day of week.* Lets users specify which day they want to display as the first day of the week in the Calendar.
- *Display time intervals.* Displays the time increments in the Calendar view. If this option is not selected, only the start and end times of appointments appear.
- *Begin day at.* Sets the starting time for the appointment list in the Calendar view.
- *Interval length.* Specifies the time intervals that appear in the Calendar view.
- *Display event length.* Specifies whether users want the event length to appear as a starting and ending time, or as a duration in the Calendar.

- *Default appointment length.* Specifies the default appointment length for the Appointment messages sent.

- *Alarm before appointment.* Specifies when the alarm should sound before appointments.

Busy Search

A *Busy Search* is a client process users can run to check the GroupWise calendars of meeting invitees. A Busy Search can tell you whether invitees are available for a meeting or not. The Busy Search options are shown in Figure 7.21.

FIGURE 7.21

Busy Search Options

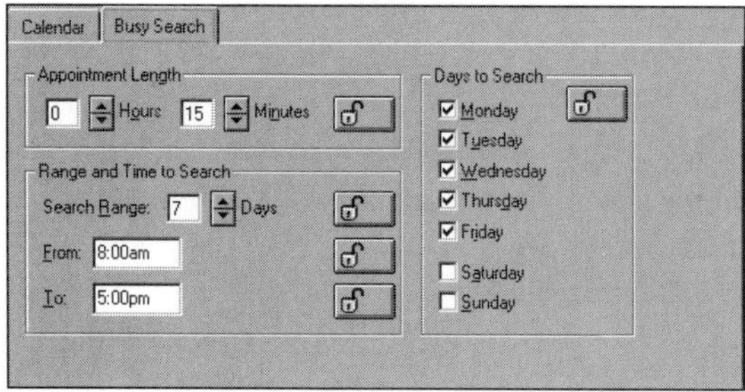

- *Appointment Length.* Specifies the default appointment length for Appointments created with the Busy Search feature.

- *Search Range.* Lets users specify the default number of days that should be searched.

- *From: and To: fields.* Lets users specify the default time ranges during each day that is searched.

- *Days to Search.* Lets users set the default days to be included in the Busy Search.

Modifying User Accounts

The relationship between NDS *objects* and GroupWise *mailboxes* is somewhat confusing. They appear as one in NetWare Administrator, but in reality they are two separate entities. NDS User objects show how users fit into the entire NDS structure.

The information associated with each User object is used to allow access to various resources available on the network. The GroupWise mailbox, on the other hand, is a database that contains GroupWise information for the associated user.

When you establish the GroupWise properties for an NDS User object, you create the relationship between the User object and a GroupWise mailbox. When users change positions in your organization, or if their personal information changes, you'll need to update this association. A change to the NDS tree does not automatically update the mailbox information.

When you move an NDS User object from one container to another, you need to update the GroupWise account information (domain, post office, FID, and so forth).

Renaming an Account

There are many reasons to rename a user account. For example, the user may have a new name, or your organization may have changed its naming conventions. Whatever the reason, you will need to modify both the NDS object and the GroupWise account.

The following steps should be taken in preparing to rename an account:

- Make sure the user has exited GroupWise and that Notify is turned off.
- Make sure the POA for the user's post office is up and running.
- If the user owns a resource, temporarily assign the resource to another owner.

Connecting to the Domain When renaming a GroupWise account, we recommend you first connect to the domain to which the user belongs. This helps to reduce synchronization traffic for the Address Books.

Follow these steps to connect to a specific domain:

1 • From the Tools menu, choose GroupWise System Operations.

2 • Double-click on the System Connection icon. You'll see the dialog box shown in Figure 7.22.

3 • Highlight the user's domain in the Current System window, and click on the Connect button. You will return to the GroupWise System Operations screen. Choose Close.

FIGURE 7.22

GroupWise System Connection

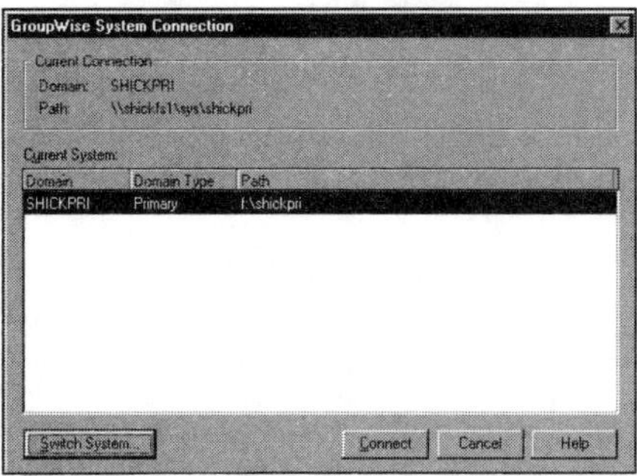

Changing the Account Properties To actually rename the GroupWise account, edit the properties of the NDS User object, changing the Mailbox ID property to reflect the new account name.

To rename a mailbox:

1 • Highlight the User or External Entity object.

2 • Right-click and choose Details.

3 • On the GroupWise Account property page, edit the Mailbox ID field and change the name.

4 • Click on OK to complete the change.

When you change the Mailbox ID property, the following events occur:

- The WPDOMAIN.DB of the domain you are currently connected to will be updated with the new mailbox name, and the distribution lists that contain the renamed user will be updated.
- The WPHOST.DB files in the current domain will be updated

- An update message will be sent to all of the other domains in the system, and their administrative databases will be updated with the renamed GroupWise account. The details of this activity are covered in Chapter 9, when we discuss multiple domains.

- An administrative message will be sent to the POA for the user's post office.

- The POA will rename the Mailbox ID record of the USER*xxx*.DB.

Once the account has been renamed, when the user starts the GroupWise client after you have renamed the domain, the GroupWise startup screen will appear and the user can enter the new user ID. This information will then be stored in the Windows Registry, and the user will not be prompted to enter the information again.

Other users' Personal Address Books are not updated when the change occurs, so you should tell the user to inform associates of the change.

Reply messages to the old address will not be delivered because the old account no longer exists. However, you can create a nickname using the old user ID so that reply messages are not lost.

Moving an Account

The steps for moving a user account are very similar to the steps for renaming an account. In fact, when you move an account, you simply modify the domain and/or post office portion of a GroupWise address. (Behind the scenes, the process is more complicated because the messages must be directed to the new post office. When you merely rename a user, the messages need not be directed to a different post office.)

There are two different scenarios for moving user accounts:

- Moving from one post office to another in the same domain.

- Moving from one post office to another in a different domain (in the same system).

In preparation for moving an account (in either scenario), you should take the following steps:

- Have the user delete any messages that are no longer necessary.

- Have the user archive all messages that will not be necessary immediately after the move takes place.
- Ask the user to save or print messages that are not necessary to move.
- Ask the user to save as many attachments as possible.
- Perform "mailbox maintenance" on the user's account. See Chapter 13 for details on mailbox maintenance.
- Make sure the user has exited GroupWise and that Notify is turned off.
- If the user owns a resource, permanently assign the resource to another owner.
- Make sure the administration agents (ADAs) and message transfer agents (MTAs) are up and running in all domains and post offices.
- Exit the POA for each post office involved in the move. This allows the synchronization of the administrative databases (WPDOMAIN.DB and WPHOST.DB) to take place before the user database and messages are moved. (Once the account change has been updated between all domains and post offices, reload the POAs for both post offices involved in the move.)

Connecting to a Relevant Domain When moving a GroupWise account, we recommend you first connect to one of the domains involved in the move. This allows you to access the domain database directly, making the move as simple as possible. The steps for connecting to a new domain are explained earlier in this chapter in the section called "Renaming an Account."

Moving the GroupWise Account

The steps for actually moving a GroupWise account from one post office to another are deceptively simple. After all of the prerequisite steps are completed, simply highlight the User object in the NetWare Administrator, right-click on the object, and choose Details from the shortcut menu. Then follow these steps:

1 • On the GroupWise Account page, click on the browse button to the right of the post office name.

2 • Browse the NDS tree until the target post office appears in the Available Objects portion of the window and choose OK.

3 • You will see the notification box shown in Figure 7.23.

4 • Choose Yes to move the user.

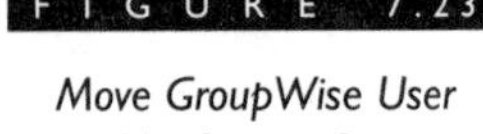

FIGURE 7.23

Move GroupWise User Notification Box

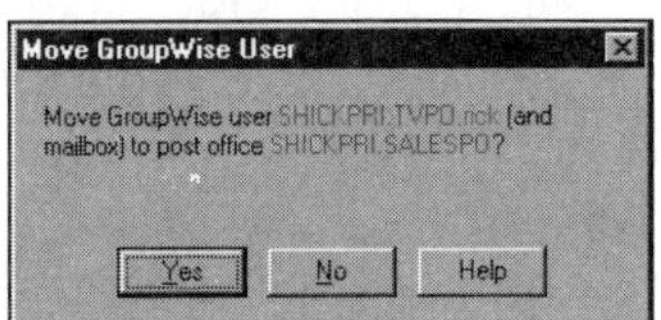

When you move a user from one post office to another, the following events take place:

- The WPDOMAIN.DB database of the domain you are currently connected to will be updated with the new mailbox name and distribution lists that the renamed user is a part of are updated.
- The WPHOST.DB database files are updated in the current domain.
- An update message is sent to all of the other domains in the system, and their administrative databases are updated with the renamed GroupWise account. The details of this activity are covered in Chapter 9, where we discuss multiple domain systems.
- An administrative message to move the user's database (USER*xxx*.DB) will be sent to the POA for the user's post office.
- The USER*xxx*.DB is sent to the target post office, where it is added to the OFUSER subdirectory.
- The target post office's POA sends a message back to the original post office to move the messages.

- The original post office's POA reads the message databases and creates a series of messages with attachments, which are sent to the target post office.
- The target post office's POA will add the messages to the MSG*xx*.DB files in its OFMSG directory.
- The original POA deletes the original USER*xxx*.DB.

After the account has been moved, the GroupWise startup screen appears the next time the user opens GroupWise. At that point, the path to the new post office can be entered. (If the user is to configure the client for accessing the new post office, this information must be given to the user.) This step is only required the first time the user starts GroupWise.

Personal Address Books are not updated by the change. You should tell the user to send a message to associates telling them to delete the old address and replace it with the new user ID.

Reply messages sent using the old post office name in the address will not be delivered because the old account no longer exists. However, you can create a nickname for the user so that reply messages are delivered.

Deleting User Accounts

To delete an NDS User object and the associated GroupWise account, highlight the User object in NetWare Administrator and press the delete key.

NOTE

If you want to keep the NDS User object but delete the GroupWise account, view the details of the User object and click on the Delete GroupWise Account button on the GroupWise Account property page.

When you delete the User object, you will see the dialog box shown in Figure 7.24.

FIGURE 7.24

Delete GroupWise Account Dialog Box

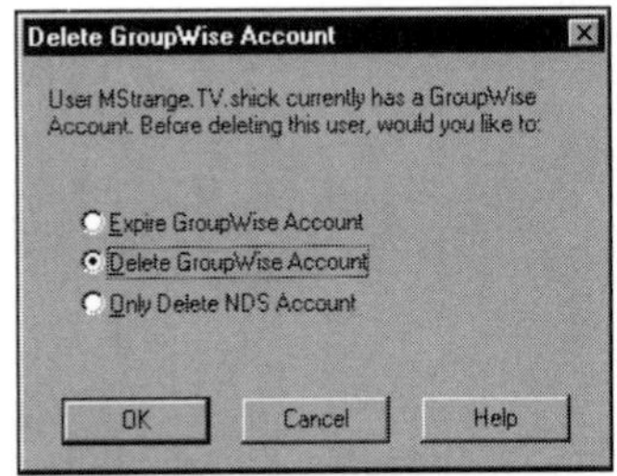

There are three options in the Delete GroupWise Account dialog box:

- *Expire GroupWise Account.* This option enables you to retain the GroupWise mailbox, but places an expired date on the mailbox. This is useful if you want to keep the messages in it and possibly associate it with another NDS user later. If anyone tries to use this account, they will be denied access. You can change this status by changing the expired date from the GroupWise View for the mailbox. You can then use the /@U-*user id* switch with the GroupWise client program to access the information contained in the GroupWise account.

- *Delete GroupWise Account.* This option permanently removes the GroupWise mailbox along with the NDS object. There is no way to recover from this, so before deleting make sure there are no messages in this account that might be needed later.

- *Only Delete NDS Account.* This option keeps the GroupWise account active, but deletes the NDS object. The user can still use the account through a client/server connection or through GroupWise running in Remote mode. This option will leave the GroupWise account in the GroupWise system. To again access this account, you will have to associate the account with an NDS user account by using the Graft GroupWise Objects feature. This is explained in Chapter 16.

Choosing "Expire GroupWise Account" or "Only Delete NDS Account" converts the mailbox to an external entity.

Creating Resource Objects

GroupWise Resource objects are very much like NDS User objects with associated GroupWise accounts. Each GroupWise Resource object has its own mailbox with Calendar information, preference settings, and messages.

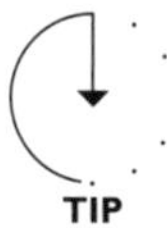

Using the GroupWise client, you can enter the name of a resource in the User ID field of the GroupWise Startup screen and go right into the mailbox for the Resource.

GroupWise Resource objects represent physical resources, such as conference rooms or equipment, that users can reserve. To reserve a resource, a user includes the resource as a recipient in a new meeting request. Figure 7.25 shows two resources for ShickTools, a conference room and the company Lear jet.

FIGURE 7.25

GroupWise Resources

Every GroupWise Resource object has an associated GroupWise user who manages the Calendar requests sent to the Resource object. This user, called the *resource owner*, has full access to the entire mailbox of the resource. The owner can then use the Proxy feature to view the Calendar of the resource. The owner can also be notified of messages that are sent to the resource, and accept or decline appointments for the resource. The resource and its owner must be in the same post office.

To create a GroupWise Resource object:

1 • Highlight the container that will hold the object, right-click on it, and choose Create from the shortcut menu. We recommend creating all Resource objects in the GRPWISE organizational unit. You might want to create a sub-OU called RESOURCE under GRPWISE. The resources will show up in the Address Book of the client, so users will never need to browse the NDS tree to find the resources. They will, however, need Browse Object and Read property rights to all properties of the Resource objects. You can grant these NDS rights at OU=RESOURCE and these rights will be inherited.

2 • Select GroupWise Resource from the list and click on OK. You will see the dialog box in Figure 7.26.

FIGURE 7.26

Create GroupWise Resource Dialog Box

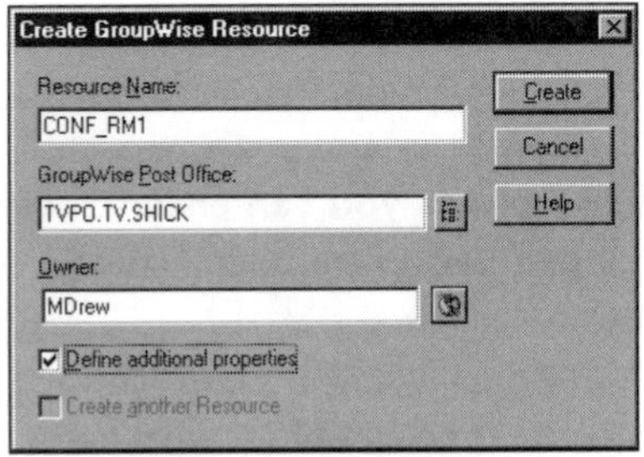

3 • Fill in the name of the resource and use the NDS browse button next to the Post Office field to select the post office the resource will belong to.

4 • Click on the GroupWise object browse button and select the resource's owner from the list of names. Notice that only names in the same post office as the resource are available.

5 • Select Define Additional Properties and click on OK to create the resource. You will see the resource property page shown in Figure 7.27.

6 • Specify a description, the visibility, and the resource type. If the resource is a place, select Place. This will cause the information in the Description field to be displayed in the Place field in an appointment request in the client program. Otherwise, choose Resource.

7 • You can choose to give the resource a nickname by clicking on the Nickname tab and adding a nickname. Messages sent to the nickname will go to the resource's mailbox.

8 • Once all information has been entered, choose OK.

FIGURE 7.27

Resource Details

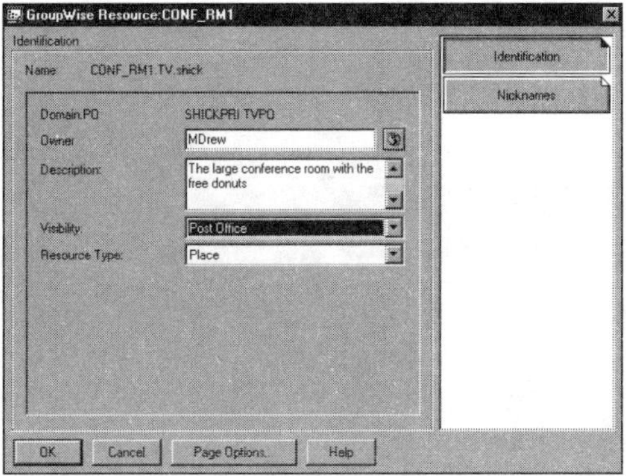

It is critical for you to manage the GroupWise resources so that your users can effectively use the powerful calendaring and scheduling features of GroupWise.

Creating Distribution List Objects

As system administrator, one of your duties is to maintain public distribution lists to facilitate sending messages to predefined groups of users. Developing a strategy of what distribution lists to make and who will maintain them is a wise topic to address in the planning stage, as covered in Chapter 3. We will look at the steps for creating and maintaining distribution lists in this section.

To create a distribution list:

1 • Highlight the container in which the Distribution List object will reside. Right-click and choose Create from the shortcut menu. We recommend creating all Distribution List objects in the GRPWISE organizational unit. You might want to create a sub-OU called DLIST under GRPWISE. The distribution lists will show up in the Address Book of the client, so users will never need to browse the NDS tree to find them. They will, however, need Browse Object and Read property rights to all properties of the Distribution List objects. You can grant these NDS rights at OU=DLIST and these rights will be inherited.

2 • Select GroupWise Distribution List from the list of object classes. You will see a dialog box for creating a distribution list, as shown in Figure 7.28.

FIGURE 7.28

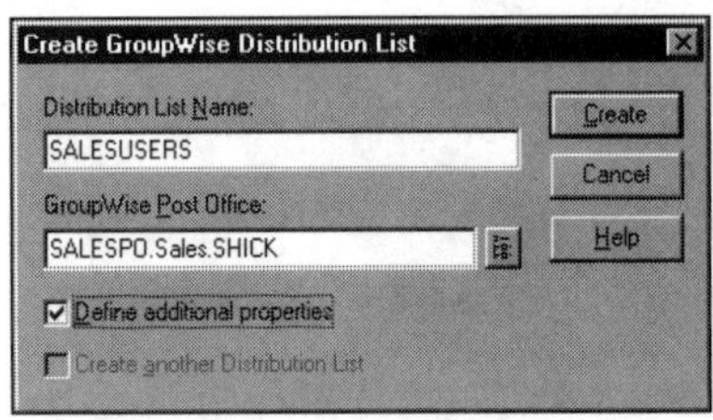

Create GroupWise Distribution List Dialog Box

3 • Enter a name for the distribution list and select the post office the distribution list will belong to by clicking on the NDS browse button next to the GroupWise Post Office field.

4 • Browse NDS until the post office appears in the Available Objects window and choose OK. Click on the box labeled Define Additional Properties and choose OK. The distribution list's property page will appear, as shown in Figure 7.29.

FIGURE 7.29

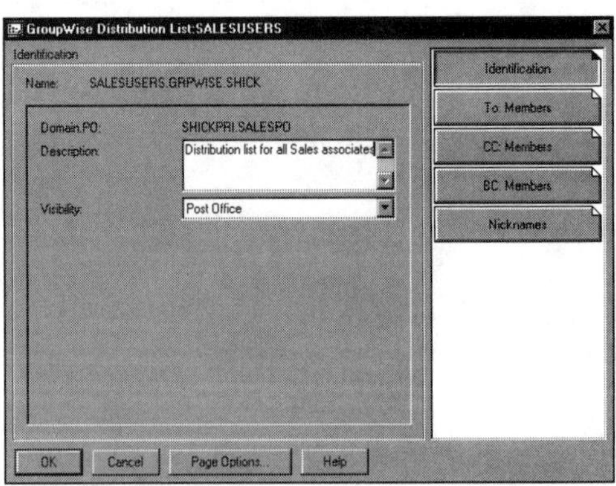

GroupWise Distribution List Details

5 • Type in a description if needed, and select the visibility. Click on the To: Member property page and choose Add. Browse NDS to select the members of the distribution list (see Figure 7.30). Note that the distribution list itself appears as a possible member. *Do not select the*

distribution list as a member. You'll get a cat-chasing-its-tail-as-the-mail-system-crashes effect.

6 • Press Shift and click to select a range of user names (or press Ctrl and click to select multiple nonadjacent user names) and choose OK to add them to the distribution list.

7 • Repeat Steps 5 and 6 for the CC: Members and BC: Members pages. The CC: members will be placed on the carbon copy line of messages and the BC: members will be placed on the blind copy line.

8 • Choose OK to create the Distribution List object.

Once users have been added to a distribution list, the Address Books will be updated. Messages sent to the distribution list will include the added users in the To:, CC:, or BC: field.

FIGURE 7.30

Adding Members to a Distribution List

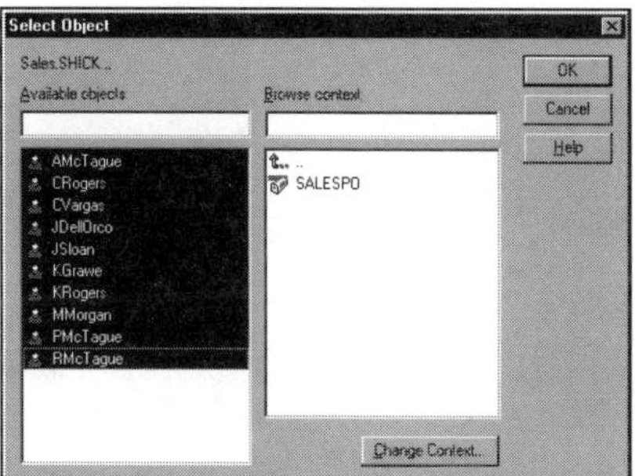

Summary

In this chapter, we explained how to create GroupWise accounts, Resource objects, and Distribution List objects. You learned how to rename and move user accounts and how to set and lock default settings for the GroupWise client program. In the next chapter, you'll learn how to add post offices to your system.

PART III

Complex GroupWise Systems

CHAPTER 8

Adding Post Offices

Up to this point we've explained GroupWise administration and implementation of small GroupWise systems consisting of a single domain with a single post office. We'll now look at more complex GroupWise systems. By "complex" we mean GroupWise systems that consist of multiple post offices within a domain, or multiple domains that each contain one or more post offices.

Usually, administrators don't base the decision to create multiple post offices solely on the number of users in the first post office. High-performance GroupWise servers can handle hundreds—even thousands—of users in a single post office. Instead, the decision to implement multiple post offices is typically based on administrative considerations.

NOTE

Earlier versions of GroupWise and WordPerfect Office generally recognized a practical limit of between 200 and 400 users in a post office. However, with the new multithreading capabilities of the MTA and POA, and with the ability to run multiple POA sessions for a single post office, these limits are no longer valid.

Here are some of the most common reasons for creating multiple post offices in a system:

- To organize post offices by departments or organizational units
- To group users by geographic location, thereby segmenting messaging traffic
- To conform the GroupWise system to the network configuration

We discuss post office planning issues at length in Chapter 3. If you are planning to create a multiple post office system, you should review the system planning information we present in that chapter.

This chapter explains messaging when multiple post offices have been implemented within a single domain. We show you how to define multiple post offices and install the required agents, wrapping up the chapter with an overview of message delivery among users who reside in the same domain but in different post offices.

Enabling Message Transfer

In Chapter 6 you saw how message delivery is handled within the post office. In a single post office system, message delivery is handled entirely by the client or by the POA, depending upon your message delivery mode setting.

When you add a second post office, message delivery becomes a bit more complex. When users send messages within one post office, message delivery is still handled by the client and the POA. But when users send messages between two post offices in the same domain, those messages are passed from one post office to the other by the message transfer agent (MTA).

NOTE

In GroupWise 5, the MTA is required in single post office systems to handle synchronization of messages received from the administration agent (ADA). However, in single post office systems, the MTA does not handle message delivery.

Using the Message Transfer Agent

The MTA works for the entire domain and its post offices and gateways. Besides delivering messages between post offices within its domain, the MTA also transfers messages to and from other domains in the GroupWise system. It also handles message transfer to and from gateways. We say more about the various MTA functions in Chapter 9, where we discuss multiple domain systems.

Figure 8.1 shows how the GroupWise agents process a message sent between two post offices.

As you saw in Chapter 2, when the MTA is running, it watches over the input queues. These queues are located in the post office directory structures. The input queues are named WPCSIN and the output queues are named WPCSOUT.

When the MTA finds a message in an input queue, it must deliver it to an output queue somewhere in the system. The input and output queues are located in the post office directory structures. The MTA constantly scans (or *polls*) its input queues for messages that need to be processed.

FIGURE 8.1

Message Delivery Between Post Offices

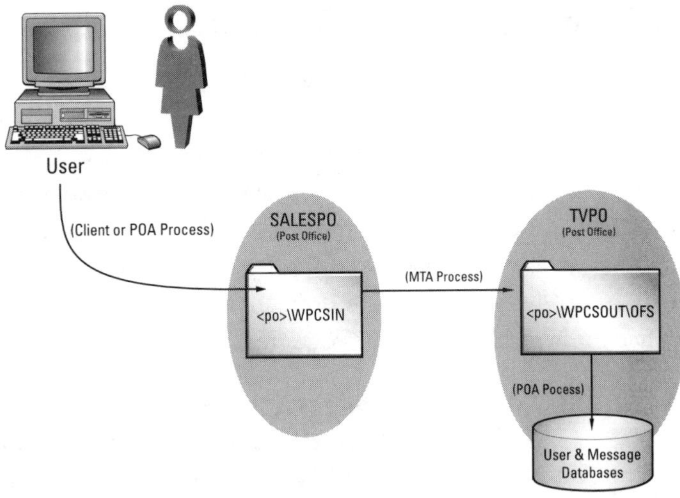

Notice that the POA always handles the last part of the message-delivery process. In other words, the MTA simply moves messages between input and output queues located in the post office directory structure, hence the term *transfer agent*. The MTA never touches the message store directories and databases. The POA always adds the message to the information store.

Later in this chapter, you'll see detailed message flow diagrams depicting message transfer between two post offices.

NOTE

In this section, we assume that traditional store-and-forward (file access) delivery mode is used; that is, the client and the POA are not operating in Client/Server mode, and the POA and MTA are not linked via TCP/IP connections. We explain how to configure TCP/IP connections in a GroupWise system in Chapter 10.

Configuring an Access Account

In Chapter 3, we recommend that you create an access account named GWACCESS in an organizational unit called GRPWISE. We also suggest that you grant the access account object and file system rights to enable message delivery between GroupWise components.

NOTE

If you have not yet created an access account, you may wish to review Chapter 3 before reading this section.

The access account is used by both the ADA and the MTA. (It is also used by the POA when the POA is running on a computer other than the server that houses the post office directory structure.)

You enable the access account by entering the GWACCESS user name and password in the POA startup file. The following example shows the proper syntax:

```
/user-GWACCESS
/password-ACCESS
```

As we explained, the access account is necessary in a single post office system so the ADA can gain access to NDS and perform NDS-to-GroupWise synchronization for user account properties. The GroupWise access account is also used by the MTA to retrieve files from the post office input queues and write files to the post office-level output queues.

Technically, you don't need to configure the access account in startup files for every agent if you have configured the agents to use TCP/IP. (Chapter 10 explains TCP/IP configuration in more detail.) However, the access account is necessary for the ADA, even if TCP/IP is configured for the agents, because the ADA needs access to NDS to handle user property synchronization with NDS.

When you add a new post office, you need to give the access account rights to the new post office directory. The access account needs the following file system rights to the MTA queues in the post office and the domain:

- Read
- Write
- Create
- Modify
- Erase

The access account also needs to support multiple concurrent logins, because several agents will log in to NDS at the same time using the same User object.

If you want to create a User object that is local to the context of the server on which the NLMs are loaded, you can create an NDS "alias object" in the server's container.

You can use an NDS *alias* if you want to have the User object on the same server on which the NLMs are loaded. To create an alias, follow these steps:

1 • Highlight the container in which you want to create the alias.

2 • Right-click on the container and choose Create from the Shortcut menu. You'll see a dialog box like the one shown in Figure 8.2.

Create Alias Dialog Box

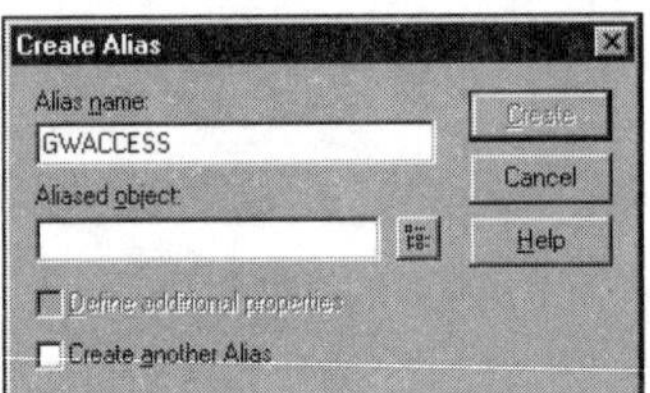

3 • Name the alias "GWACCESS."

4 • Click on the NDS browse button next to the Aliased Object field. Browse NDS until the original GWACCESS User object is listed in the list of available objects (see Figure 8.3).

5 • Click on OK to complete the creation of the alias.

To use the alias object in the startup file for the agents, add the distinguished name of the alias after the `/user` switch.

This ensures that a local object is used in the startup file (in the same container as the Server object), and any changes made to the original User object are automatically reflected in the alias.

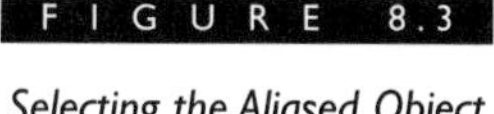
FIGURE 8.3

Selecting the Aliased Object

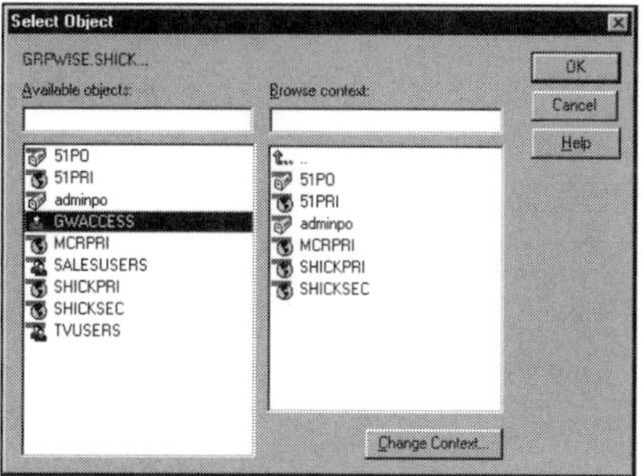

Adding a New Post Office

As discussed in Chapter 3, once you have decided that you want to add a new post office to your system, you need to decide which IntranetWare container (usually an organizational unit representing a division or department) will hold the Post Office object.

Usually the Post Office object resides in the same container as most of the members of the post office.

In our fictional company, ShickTools, the original post office was located in the TV organizational unit (see Chapter 4). Now we'll create a second post office in the Sales OU, called SALESPO.

To create a new post office, follow these steps:

NOTE

The ADA for the domain and first post office should be running during this entire process so that changes are replicated throughout the GroupWise system.

1 • Run NetWare Administrator and highlight the organizational unit that will contain the Post Office object.

2 • Right-click on the object and choose Create.

3 • Highlight GroupWise Post Office and click on OK. The Create GroupWise Post Office dialog box appears, as shown in Figure 8.4.

FIGURE 8.4

Create Post Office Dialog Box

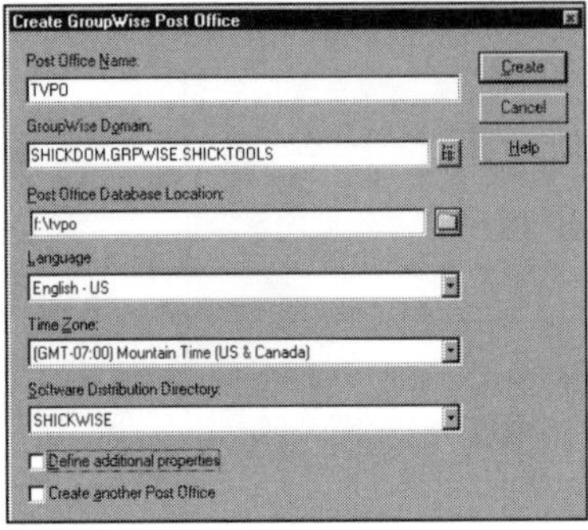

4 • Enter the name of the post office using the naming conventions you decided upon when you planned your GroupWise system (see Chapter 3). Remember, the name of the Post Office object cannot be the same as any other NDS object within the organizational unit.

5 • Select the domain that the post office will belong to by clicking on the NDS browse button to the right of the domain field. Browse the tree until the domain you want is displayed in the list of available objects and choose OK. Note that if you followed our recommendation, the domain will be in OU=GRPWISE.

6 • Enter the path of the post office directory. NetWare Administrator will create the path if it doesn't already exist.

7 • Select the language for the post office.

8 • Select the time zone where the post office resides.

9 • Specify the software distribution directory for the post office.

10 • Choose the Define Additional Properties option.

11 • Click on Create. The Post Office object is created and the post office page automatically appears, enabling you to continue configuring the post office.

12 • Change any of the post office defaults, such as Default Security Level, Delivery Mode, or Access Mode. These are discussed in more detail in Chapter 6.

13 • Click on the membership button. The Post Office Membership page appears, as shown in Figure 8.5.

14 • Click on Add. The Select Object dialog box appears (see Figure 8.6).

15 • Browse to the location of the users who will be added to this post office.

16 • Select users (remember, you can select multiple users by pressing the Shift or Ctrl key as you click), and then click on OK. The users are added to the post office membership page. To add members from different contexts, click on Add again and follow Steps 16 and 17.

17 • Click on OK. GroupWise properties are added for each user that you added to the post office.

FIGURE 8.5

Post Office Membership Page

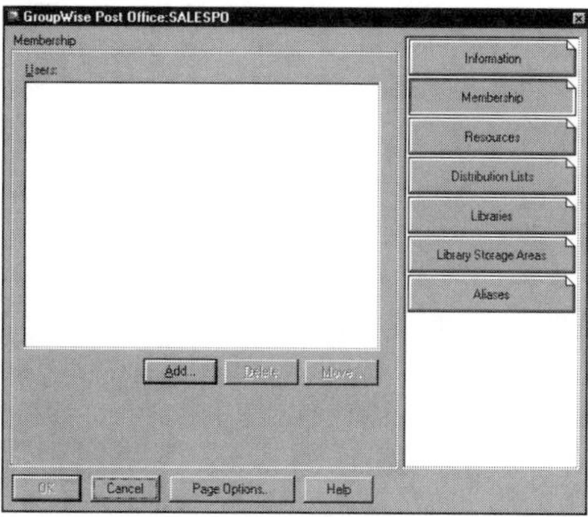

You have now created an additional post office and added members to it. You next need to install and run the POA for the new post office and enable the GroupWise client software for the users.

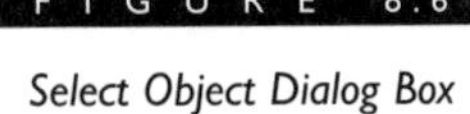

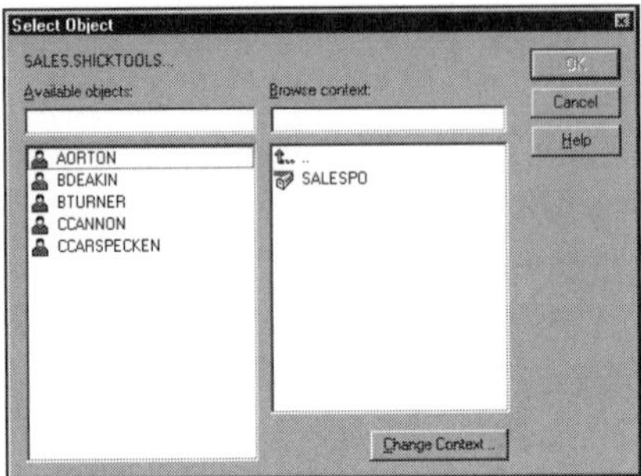

FIGURE 8.6

Select Object Dialog Box

Installing the Agents

After you have created a new post office and added members, you need to run the POA for the post office—and your users need access to the client software.

NOTE

Assume for the purposes of this discussion that the post office directory is located on a file server other than the one housing the domain directory and the directory for the first post office in the system.

When you initially install GroupWise, you create a directory containing the agent files and client files. You should use this software directory to install the agents. Users in the post office should be able to use the software directory to install the client files.

If users do not have access to the GroupWise software directory containing the client files, you can grant them the necessary rights to the software directory you established when you installed the first domain and post office, or you can create a new software directory on a server that the users can access.

Follow these steps to create a new software directory:

1. Map a drive to the new server and have a directory name in mind for the new software directory. A user logged in at the computer running NetWare Administrator must have Read and File Scan file system rights to the location of the software directory created during

installation and all rights except supervisory to the location of the new software directory.

2 • From NetWare Administrator, choose Tools and then GroupWise System Operations.

3 • Double-click on the Software Directory Management icon. A dialog box like the one shown in Figure 8.7 will appear.

4 • Choose Create and specify a name for the software directory. This name is not the name of the file system directory that will house the GroupWise files. Rather, it is the name of a GroupWise component, much like the domain and post office names you previously specified.

5 • Enter a description and the UNC path to the location where you want the directory to be created. If the target directory has not been created, you will be prompted to create the new directory.

6 • Select the "Copy software from" box that shows the name of your GroupWise system.

7 • Click on OK to copy the software—client, administration and agent software—from the original installation point to the new directory on the other file server.

FIGURE 8.7

Software Directory Management

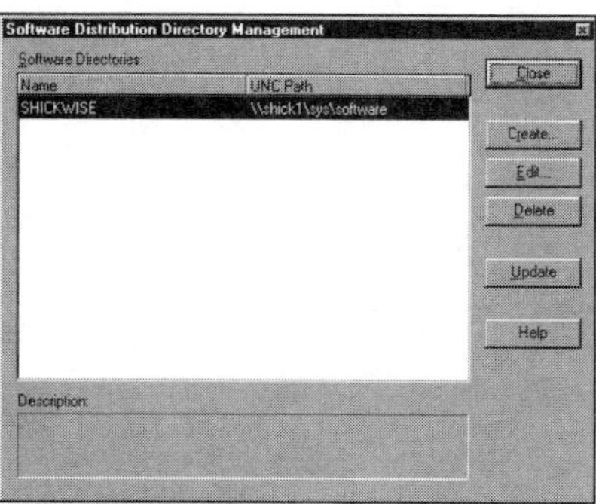

Now you can install the agents on the server that houses the new post office.

NOTE

The agent installation routine varies slightly from the installation routine you see when you initially install and configure software for the first domain and post office. The information you enter in Step 6 of the following steps updates the POA startup file and the GRPWISE.NCF file. If a file called GRPWISE.NCF already exists, this routine will replace it. Consequently, you may want to make a backup of the original GRPWISE.NCF file (or simply rename it) before you install the agents.

To install the agents, follow these steps:

1 • Click on Start from your Windows 95 Taskbar.

2 • Click on Run.

3 • Browse to the software directory.

4 • Navigate to the AGENTS directory.

5 • Double-click on the INSTALL.EXE file.

6 • Follow the prompts to install the agent software on the server's SYSTEM directory.

After the software is installed, you should check the POA's startup file and verify that the correct path to the post office directory is listed. After you launch the POA, the clients are ready to be installed and messages are ready to be sent. For instructions on installing the client files, see Chapter 5.

Installing Additional Post Offices

The installation procedures explained in this chapter can be followed to create a third, fourth, or even a hundredth post office in a single domain.

Although it is possible to create several post offices at once, we advise against it. In most cases, you should create a post office, establish membership, install the POA and client software, and test the messaging in the post office thoroughly.

Only after you have completed all these procedures should you consider adding the next post office.

Message Flow Between Two Post Offices

Figures 8.6 and 8.7 show how messages move from one GroupWise post office to another within the same domain and how the status message is processed.

NOTE

In Figures 8.8 and 8.9, and throughout the rest of this book, assume that the App Threshold delivery mode has been selected and that the threshold is not exceeded (unless otherwise indicated).

Figure 8.8 illustrates what happens when someone sends a message from TVPO to SALESPO.

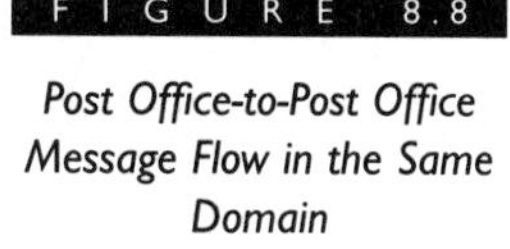

FIGURE 8.8

Post Office-to-Post Office Message Flow in the Same Domain

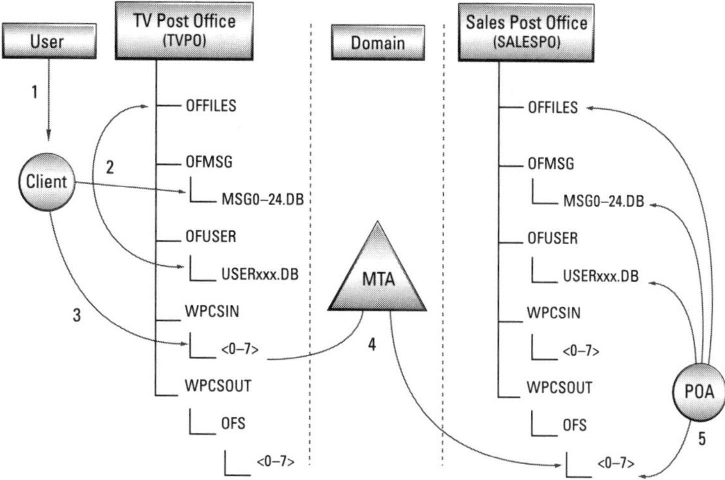

The following steps are shown in the diagram:

1 • The GroupWise user creates a message file addressed to a recipient who resides in another post office in the same domain.

2 • The client places the message in the sender's mailbox, inserts the message in the message database, adds pointers to the sender's user database, and places any message components that exceed 2K in the OFFILES directory.

3 • The client places a copy of the message file in the MTA input queue (TVPO\WPCSIN\<0–7).

4 • The MTA scans the input queue and detects the message file. It determines the message destination and places the message file in the SALESPO's POA input queue (SALESPO\WPSOUT\OFS\<0–7>).

5 • The POA in the recipient's post office detects the message file in the queue and completes the message delivery to the recipient's mailbox. The SALESPO's POA inserts the message in the message database, adds pointers to the recipient's user database, and places any file attachments over 2K in the OFFILES directory.

Figure 8.9 shows the path the status message takes back to the sender's mailbox.

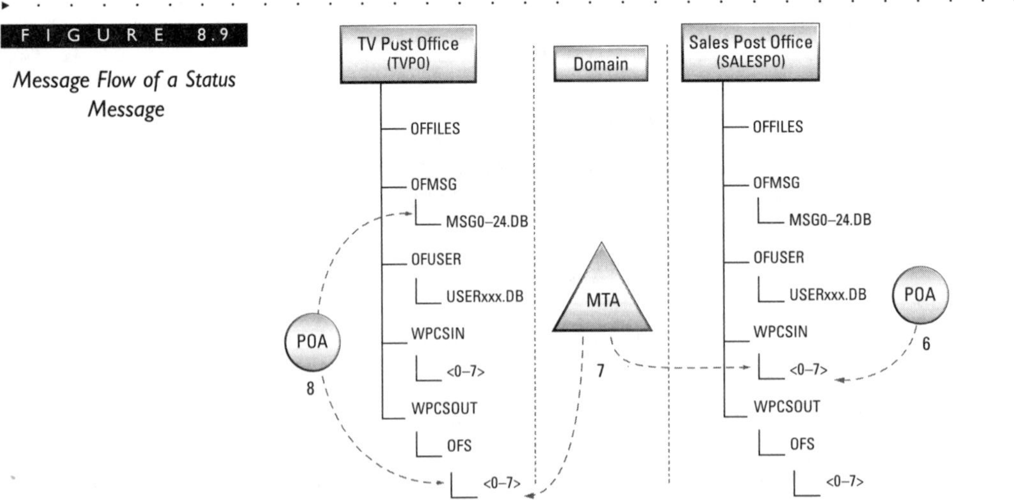

FIGURE 8.9

Message Flow of a Status Message

Following are the steps shown in Figure 8.9:

1 • The POA in the recipient's post office generates a "Delivered" status message addressed to the sender in the originating post office. It places the status message file in the MTA input queue, SALESPO\WPCSIN\<0–7>.

2 • The MTA picks up the message file and delivers it to the sender's post office MTA output queue, TVPO\WPCSOUT\OFS\<0–7>.

3 • The TVPO POA receives the status message and updates the sender's mailbox.

Notice that the POA for each post office deals only with its own message store. Also, the MTA simply moves message files from one post office to another via the WPCSIN and WPCSOUT directories. The MTA does *not* perform the final step in the message delivery process.

Summary

In Chapter 3 we explained how to plan GroupWise systems—from the most simple system to a complex system.

In this chapter, we explained how to increase the complexity of your GroupWise system by adding additional post offices within a domain. You learned how to create the Post Office object in NetWare Administrator, how to add members to the post office, and how to enable messaging by installing the required agents.

We then provided an overview of how messages are delivered from one post office to another within a single domain.

In the next chapter, we take GroupWise system complexity to the next level as we explain how to implement multiple domains.

CHAPTER 9

Creating Secondary Domains

You'll recall from Chapter 2 the main components of a domain:

- *Domain database.* Each domain has its own WPDOMAIN.DB that contains information about User objects and other objects in the system. The WPDOMAIN.DB is synchronized with NDS, as well as all other domain databases in the system and the post office databases within the domain.

- *Message transfer agent.* Every domain needs its own message transfer agent (MTA) to route messages to post offices and gateways within the domain and to transfer messages to and from other domains.

- *Administration agent.* The administration agent (ADA) for a domain is in charge of synchronization with NDS. The ADA also updates the WPDOMAIN.DB and WPHOST.DB files for the Address Book.

Now that you've had a mini refresher course in domains, you're ready to learn about multiple domain systems.

In this chapter, we show you the steps for creating additional domains. You'll also learn how to establish communication between two domains by running the MTA and ADA for the second domain. In addition, we discuss MTA configuration for multiple-domain systems, and examine the expanded role of the ADA. (Because multiple-domain systems have more than one domain database to be updated, the ADA has more to do than it does in a single-domain system.) Finally, at the end of the chapter, you'll find some useful message flow diagrams that show you how messages travel between two domains. Understanding these message flow diagrams is crucial for troubleshooting in multiple-domain systems.

Implementation of a Secondary Domain

In this section, we cover the steps for creating a secondary domain in an existing GroupWise system. We will use our fictional organization, ShickTools, as an example of a company that is ready to implement a multiple domain GroupWise system.

NOTE

You can follow the steps outlined in this chapter to add multiple domains to your system.

At ShickTools we have experienced phenomenal growth and have decided to open a research and development facility in another city. That office will have its own local area network, administrator, and about 200 users. We have decided (based on the criteria spelled out in Chapter 3) to create a secondary domain and a post office for the site.

The GroupWise components (and their fully distinguished names) are as follows:

- SHICKSEC.GRPWISE.SHICKTOOLS: Secondary Domain on file server SHICKFS2
- RDPO.R&D.SHICKTOOLS: Research and Development post office on file server SHICKFS2

The new site will be connected to the main office with a T1 link that will be used for both data and voice communications. We will have about 384K of available bandwidth for data.

Distinguishing Between Primary and Secondary Domains

The role of the first domain in a multiple-domain system is transparent from the user's perspective. In other words, it won't make much difference to a user whether he or she belongs to a primary or secondary domain. From the administrator's perspective, however, there is a significant difference, which lies in the answer to the following question: Which domain will contain the "master" domain database and, therefore, be responsible for synchronizing all of the other domains in the system?

Also, as the main GroupWise administrator, you should make sure that you have easy access to the primary domain's file server so you can perform system maintenance on it and access it directly.

As you will see, every time you start NetWare Administrator, you will be accessing a GroupWise domain database. It can be the primary or any secondary database. The domain's database you are accessing is known as the *connected domain*. You will see how to change this later in the chapter.

Changes you make to one domain database are replicated throughout the GroupWise system. This is known as "automatic directory synchronization," and is covered in the final portion of this chapter.

Preparing to Implement a New Domain

Before you create a secondary domain, be sure to:

- Determine which file server will hold the secondary domain
- Know what platform (NLM, NT, UNIX) the MTA and ADA for the new domain will run on
- Authenticate to the new server and map a drive to the volume that will hold the secondary domain
- Choose an administrator account (in other words, assign a GroupWise user) to receive error messages for the new domain
- Know which container will hold the new Domain object
- Have a plan for the post offices in the new domain
- Know which client platforms will be used in the new domain's post offices

Your first domain is created by the GroupWise installation program, as explained in Chapter 4. By default, this is the primary domain in your system. You can later change a secondary domain into a primary domain if you desire.

Adding a Domain Object in NDS

Follow these steps to create a secondary domain:

1. Authenticate and map a drive to the server that will hold the secondary domain directory.

2 • From NetWare Administrator, select the container that will hold the new Domain object. Since we recommended using one container for the Domain objects in Chapter 3 (because we have a centralized administration model), we will use OU=GRPWISE.

3 • Right-click and choose Create from the Shortcut menu. Select GroupWise Domain from the list of objects. You'll see the dialog box shown in Figure 9.1.

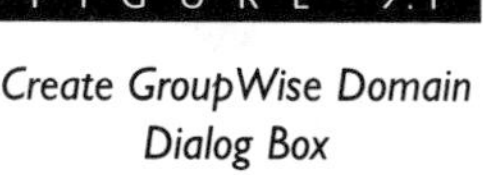

FIGURE 9.1

Create GroupWise Domain Dialog Box

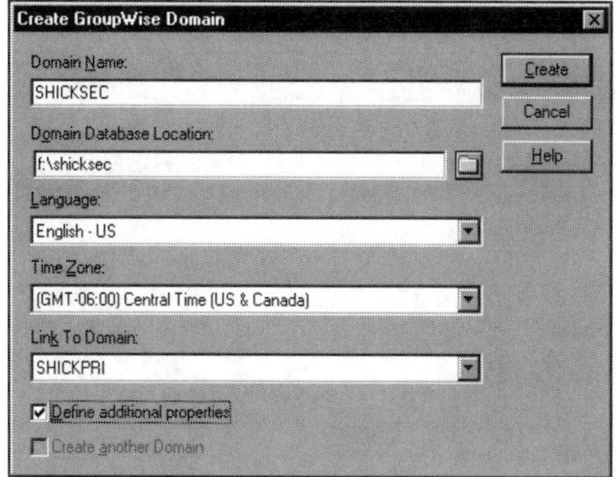

4 • Type in the domain name carefully because it *cannot* be renamed. Also pay attention to the case, because it will be displayed in NetWare Administrator exactly as you type it in here.

5 • In the Domain Database Location field, enter the DOS path to the secondary domain directory. If the directory doesn't exist, you will be prompted to create it. The name of the directory should match closely the name of the domain itself.

6 • Select the Language and Time Zone and verify that the primary domain is listed in the Link to Domain field. A direct link will automatically be established to this domain.

7 • Click on the Define Additional Properties box and choose OK to create the domain. Details for the domain appear, as shown in Figure 9.2.

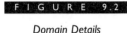

FIGURE 9.2

Domain Details

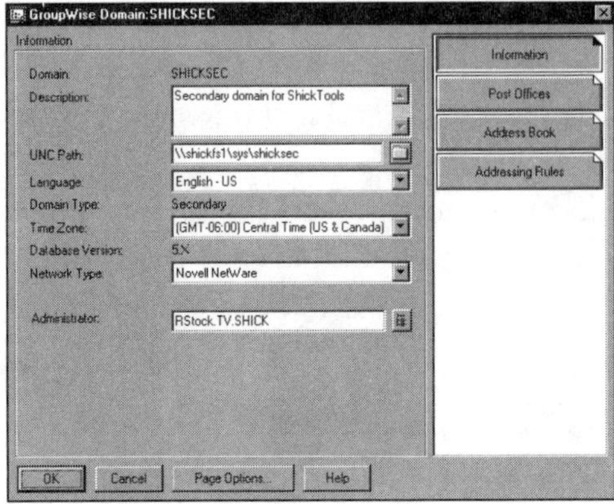

8 • Type in a description and verify the other entries on the Information page.

9 • To create an administrator account for receiving error messages for this domain, click on the NDS browse button to the right of the Administrator field and choose a user. You can change this assignment later if you need to.

10 • Once you create post offices for this domain, they will be added to the Post Offices property page. Chapters 4 and 8 cover how to create post offices, so we won't go into it here.

11 • The Address Book property page lets you configure the fields and sort order (Last Name, First Name or First Name, Last Name) for the Address Book. This is covered in more detail in Chapter 14.

12 • The Addressing Rules property page lets you associate an addressing rule with the domain. The rule can be either enabled or disabled for the entire domain, and you can choose the test button to see the effect of the rule. Creating addressing rules is covered in Chapter 14.

You have now created a brand-new domain. You will now need to create post offices in the new domain and add users and objects using the same techniques we outlined for the primary domain.

The new domain already knows how to talk to the primary domain. A direct link is automatically created between the two domains. The different link types and how you configure them is covered in Chapter 10.

Creating a Software Directory

If the new secondary domain is located across a wide area network router, or if you need to make another distribution point for the GroupWise software, the agent, administration, and client software need to be copied to the new domain's file server. This is best done by creating a new software directory. These steps are also explained in Chapter 8, but we'll repeat them here for your convenience. Of course, you don't have to perform them if you want users in the new domain accessing the client software from the original location.

Follow these steps to create a new software directory:

1. Map a drive to the new server and have a name in mind for the new software directory.

2. From NetWare Administrator, choose Tools and GroupWise System Operations.

3. Double-click on the Software Directory Management icon. The screen shown in Figure 9.3 will appear.

4. Choose Create and specify a name for the directory. This is not the file system directory name, but the name that it will be known by in GroupWise, much like a GroupWise Library Object.

5. Enter a description and the UNC path to the new server's location (where you want the directory created). If the target directory has not been created, you will be prompted to create the new directory.

6. Select the "Copy software from" box displaying the name of the original Software Distribution Directory. (The default is the name of your GroupWise system.)

7 • Click on OK to copy the software—client, administration, and agent software—from the original installation point to the new directory on the other file server.

NOTE

Only the software that was loaded to the original software distribution directory will be available to transfer to this new directory. For example, if you didn't load the NT agents (not knowing at the time that you would end up using them in the new domain), the NLM agents won't be available to copy into the new directory where they are needed. You'll need to run the INSTALL.EXE program from the GroupWise CD (in the AGENTS directory).

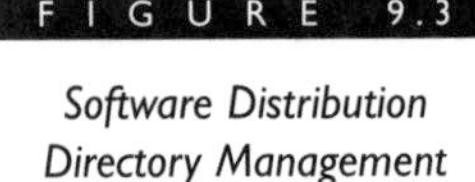

FIGURE 9.3

Software Distribution Directory Management

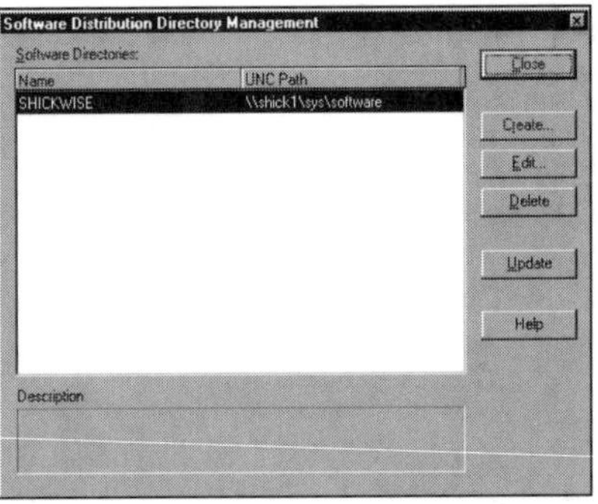

Installing the Agents

The process of installing the agent software must be performed on all servers on which agent software will run. For example, if a server will only house a post office, you must run INSTALL to install a copy of the agent software on it, even though you'll only be running the POA (and perhaps the ADA) on that server.

Follow these steps to install the agents on the new domain's server:

1 • Click on Start from your Windows 95 Taskbar (or choose Run from the File menu in the Windows 3.x Program Manager).

2 • Click on Run.

3 • Browse to the software directory.

4 • Navigate to the Agents directory.

5 • Double-click on the INSTALL.EXE file. Note: There are a few small differences in running the agent INSTALL program manually as compared to running it in the Setup Advisor.

6 • Once you read the Overview and License Agreement, select the platform (NT, NLM, or UNIX) of the agents you are installing, the path to the location of the agents, and the language.

7 • You will need to specify the domains and post offices that are part of this domain, and their path. Click on Add and you will see the dialog box shown in Figure 9.4.

8 • Click on Domain and fill in the Name field with the name of the domain.

9 • Enter the path to the domain database (or use the browse button) in the Path to Database field. Click on OK.

10 • Repeat Steps 7 through 9 for the post offices in the domain, selecting each post office appearing in the Post Office in the Facility Type field.

11 • Once the domains and post offices have been specified, click on Next.

12 • Verify the information on the Summary page and click on Install to install the agents on the server.

FIGURE 9.4

Domain / Post Office Information

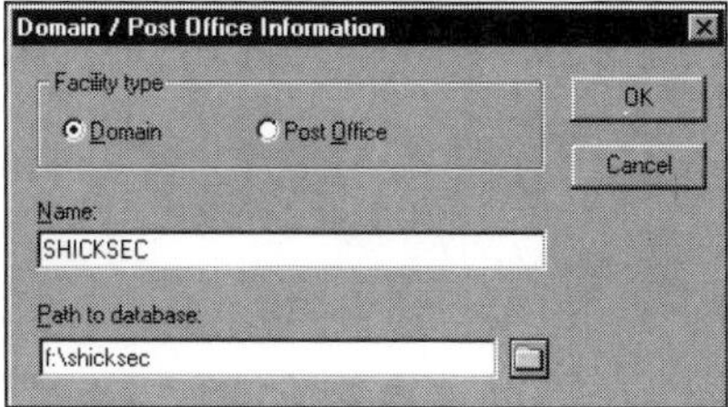

The installation program copies and creates the following files in the SYS:\SYSTEM directory:

- **STARTUP.MTA**. Blank startup file for the MTA
- ***<domain>*.MTA**. Configured MTA startup file for the domain specified in the installation program
- **STARTUP.ADA**. Blank startup file for the ADA
- ***<domain>*.ADA**. Configured ADA startup file for the domain specified in the installation program
- **STARTUP.POA**. Blank startup file for the POA
- ***<post office>*.POA**. Configured POA startup file for the post office(s) specified in the Installation program
- **GRPWISE.NCF**. Load script file for agents

Chapter 12 covers customizing the GroupWise agents, including the startup files.

Loading the Agents

Now that your new domain and its post offices have been created, you need to load the agents. Load the MTA and ADA for the domain, and the POA for the post office, by accessing the server prompt (at the server itself or by using Remote Console), entering

```
GRPWISE
```

and pressing the <Enter> key. The following commands were executed when we loaded the agents for our secondary domain SHICKSEC:

```
LOAD SYS:\SYSTEM\GWMTA @SHICKSEC.MTA

LOAD SYS:\SYSTEM\GWADA @SHICKSEC.ADA

LOAD SYS:\SYSTEM\GWPOA @RDPO.POA
```

The order in which you load the agents is not important.

Role of the Administration Agent

The administration agent (ADA) in GroupWise is the key to the integration of NDS and the GroupWise Address Book. The ADA has three jobs:

- Synchronizing NDS with the GroupWise domain databases. The ADA updates the domain database that you are connected to with information from NDS.
- Updating the GroupWise domain and post office databases. Once a domain database has been changed, the ADA confirms the change to the primary domain database and replicates the changes to secondary domains and post offices.
- Creating administrative and system error messages. The ADA creates synchronization, confirmation, and replication messages as well as error and diagnostic messages that are sent to the domain's administrator.

In a single-domain system, the ADA's role is more transparent because there is only one domain database and possibly a few post office databases to keep synchronized. When you add more domains to your system, the update functions of ADA become very crucial. If the ADA doesn't update the databases, the Address Books for that domain will not be up-to-date.

ADA Operation Modes

The ADA can be configured for either an entire domain or in dedicated Domain Only and Post Office Only modes. Table 9.1 shows the different modes for the ADA, the switches that enable the modes, the required path to the administrative database, and the minimum number of instances of ADA.

TABLE 9.1

ADA Modes

ADA MODE	SWITCH IN STARTUP FILE	/HOME SETTING	NUMBER OF INSTANCES OF ADA
Entire Domain	n/a	/home=<path to domain directory>	1
Domain Only	/domain	/home=<path to domain directory>	1 per domain
Post Office Only	/post	/home=<path to post office directory>	1 per post office

NOTE

To help keep track of the ADA's operating modes, you should choose either the Entire Domain mode or use both the other two modes. In other words, you should let one instance of ADA take care of all domain and post office databases in that domain, or configure and load a separate ADA for the domain, and for each post office in that domain. If necessary, you can create and load a Post Office Only mode ADA for just one post office in a domain, and let the domain's ADA handle the other post offices (and the domain itself). In this case, the post office for which the ADA was created and loaded will be designated as "Excluded" in the domain's ADA status screen on the server.

The default mode of operation for the ADA is for the entire domain. A single ADA object is configured in NetWare Administrator, and it is a subordinate object under the Domain object.

In some cases, you need to run a Post Office Only version of ADA. For example, if your domain is in one building and a post office is located on a server in another building, running a post office ADA will help the integrity of the post office database because it is updated by a local process. Otherwise, the ADA of the domain will update the post office database across the WAN, which is not as stable as a local update.

If you want to run in the Post Office Only mode, you must create a new ADA object under each post office:

1 • Highlight the Post Office object for which you are creating an ADA, right-click, and choose Create from the shortcut menu.

2 • Choose GroupWise Agent from the list of objects and click on OK. You will see the dialog box shown in Figure 9.5.

FIGURE 9.5

Create GroupWise Agent

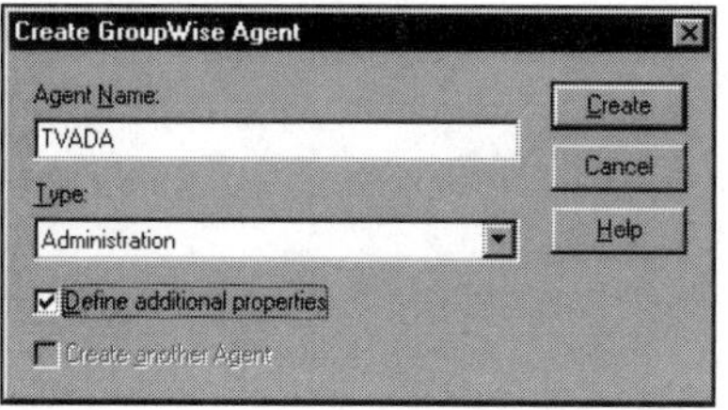

3 • Fill in a name for the agent (include the ADA in the name for clarity), specify Administration as the type of agent, click on Define Additional Properties, and choose OK. You will then see the ADA object detail screen shown in Figure 9.6.

The property pages for the ADA are as follows:

- *Information.* Platform (NLM, NT) for the agent, and a description
- *Agent Settings.* Scan cycles for the domain and post office WPCSOUT\ADS directories
- *Log Setting.* Log files path, age, maximum size, and logging level
- *Scheduled Events.* Events for notification based on preset thresholds. These are discussed in Chapter 14.

4 • Choose OK when you are finished to complete the creation of the new ADA object.

You are now ready to create a startup file for the post office's ADA called *<post office>*.ADA (using the switches mentioned earlier: `/home` and `/post`), and load the ADA. Remember to use the correct naming convention for the startup files, and place the `LOAD GWADA @<post office>.ADA` command in the GRPWISE.NCF file for automatic loading.

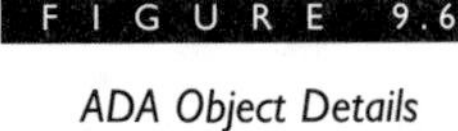

FIGURE 9.6

ADA Object Details

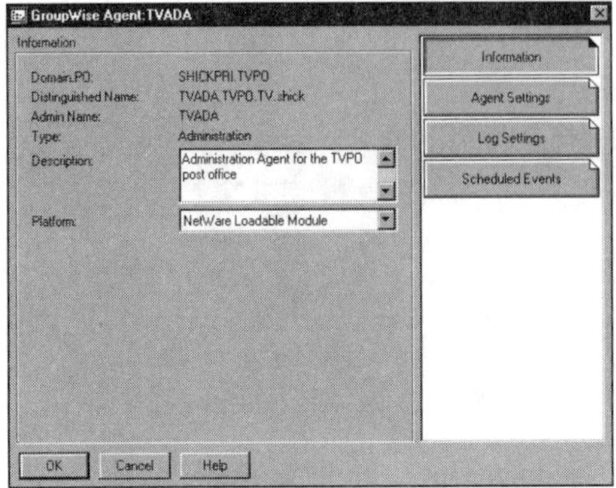

Directory Synchronization

Directory synchronization in a multiple-domain system has two facets: NDS synchronization and GroupWise synchronization. In order to understand synchronization between NDS and GroupWise, you need to keep in mind that when you have NetWare Administrator open, you are reading from and writing to both the NDS database and the GroupWise domain database of the system you are connected to at the time.

There are numerous reasons for this separation of NDS and GroupWise databases. One major reason is the speed of NDS synchronization. The Address Books would not be updated as quickly if they were drawn from NDS directly instead of coming from the GroupWise domain and post office databases. Another reason for separating NDS and the GroupWise administrative databases is because the Address Book, client program, and agents (except for the ADA) get information from the GroupWise domain and post office databases, not from NDS directly.

Another advantage of the separation is that it makes GroupWise more portable; GroupWise can run on many different platforms that may or may not support NDS. Since the domain and post office databases contain all pertinent GroupWise information, they are the only administrative databases needed to run GroupWise successfully on Windows NT, UNIX, NetWare 3.x, or even a NetWare 4.x server that doesn't have a local copy or replica of NDS.

NDS Synchronization

When you start NetWare Administrator, the program reads the GroupWise domain database to obtain some of the domain, post office, gateway, and linking information. This is shown in Figure 9.7.

FIGURE 9.7

NetWare Administrator, NDS, and GroupWise Databases

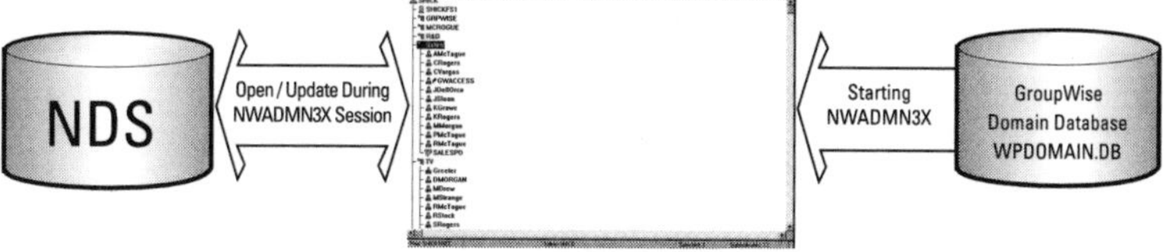

The domain database you will read on startup is specified in the C:\WINDOWS\NWADMN3X.INI file:

```
[GroupWise Snapin]

NetIDAsDn=TRUE

PathToDomain=\\SHICKFS1\SYS\shickpri
```

Once you have started NetWare Administrator, follow these steps to view the GroupWise domain you are connected to:

1 • Click on GroupWise System Operations from the Tools menu.

2 • Double-click on the System Connection icon. You'll see the dialog box shown in Figure 9.8.

3 • You can view and change the domain database you are connected to in this dialog box. The domains in your system will be listed; you can just highlight the other domain and click on Connect. Your session of NetWare Administrator will now be pointing to this domain database.

NOTE

The path-to-domain line in the NWADMN3X.INI file will be changed when you connect to another domain. If you exit NetWare Administrator and re-execute it, you will be connected to the domain you were connected to when you exited.

FIGURE 9.8

GroupWise System Connection

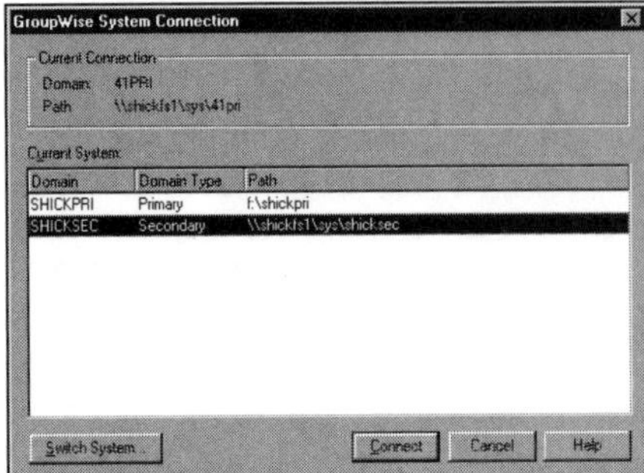

Some activities that you perform in NetWare Administrator, such as adding a new user, update the domain database directly (see Figure 9.9).

FIGURE 9.9

Databases Updated by NetWare Administrator

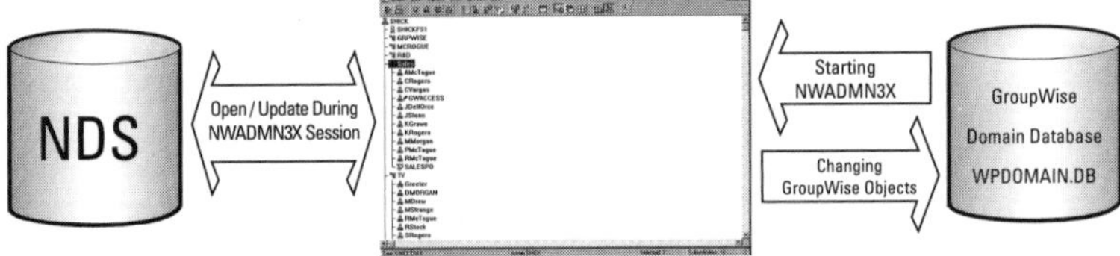

Other activities don't change the domain database directly, but rather NetWare Administrator creates a message for the ADA, which updates the domain database independently of NetWare Administrator. This is illustrated in Figure 9.10.

FIGURE 9.10

GroupWise Adminsitrative Databases Updated by the ADA

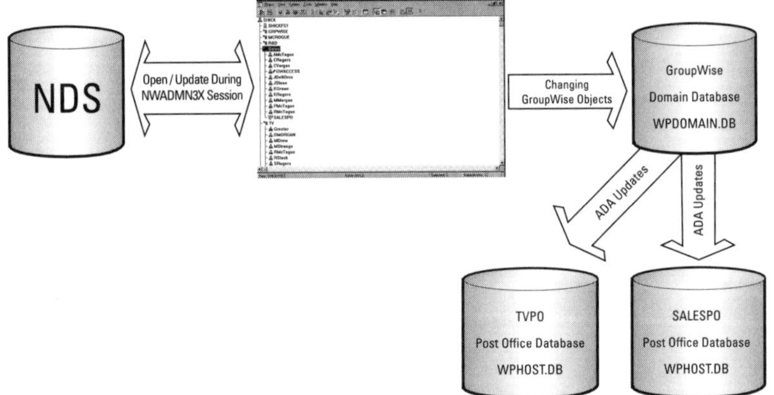

NOTE

When you see an "Adding User" or "Creating" message in NetWare Administrator, the domain database is being changed directly. The "Replicating to Local Post Offices" message creates the ADA message for updating the post office databases.

GroupWise Synchronization

Once the GroupWise domain database is changed, all of the other GroupWise administrative databases need to be updated as well. As you have seen before, there are two GroupWise administrative databases: domain (WPDOMAIN.DB) and post office (WPHOST.DB).

The domain database is primarily for administration through NetWare Administrator, while the post office database is used by the GroupWise client as the system Address Book. When a change is made to a domain database, that change needs to be replicated, or copied, to that domain's post office databases. This is shown in Figure 9.11.

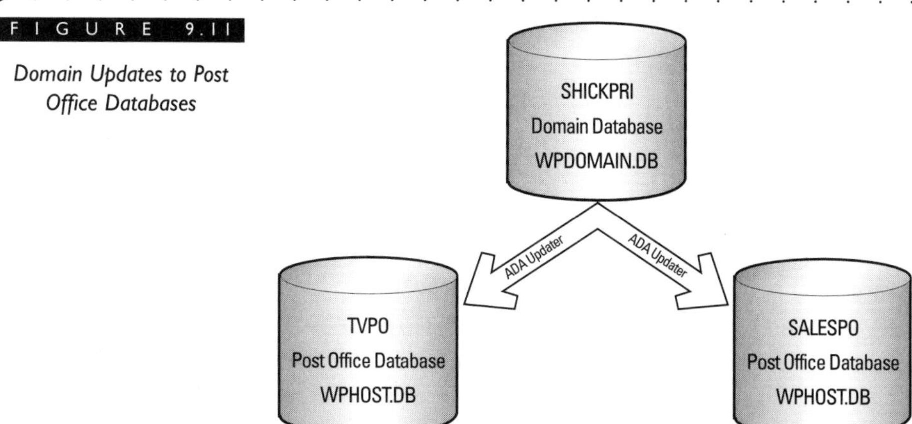

FIGURE 9.11

Domain Updates to Post Office Databases

As explained in Chapter 8, the ADA is responsible for updating the post office databases with a domain.

When you have a multiple-domain system, the domain databases need to be synchronized, which is also handled by the ADA for each domain. Of course, the MTA sends the replication messages to the domains, as shown in Figure 9.12.

FIGURE 9.12

Multiple Domain Replication

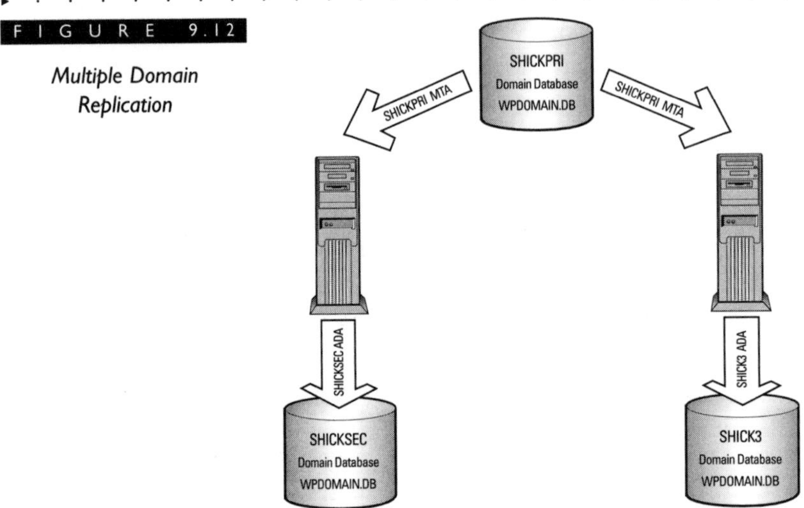

In Figure 9.12, we show the primary domain receiving an update from NetWare Administrator, and the change being sent to the other secondary domains in the system, SHICKSEC and SHICK3. Once those domains are updated, their post office databases are updated also.

If NetWare Administrator is connected to a secondary domain, the change is sent immediately to the primary domain, which then replicates to the other secondary domains. It is important to note that the secondary domain receiving the change from NetWare Administrator is *not* responsible for telling all of the other domains in the system about it! All it has to do is to send the update to the primary domain (whose domain database is updated), and then the primary domain has to replicate to all of the other secondary domains (see Figure 9.13).

An easy way to remember this is to keep the following rule in mind: The primary domain database is the master GroupWise database and has to be kept up-to-date by confirmation messages sent from the secondary domain that was changed. When the primary domain database is changed, all of the other secondary domains will be updated with replication messages.

FIGURE 9.13

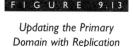

Updating the Primary Domain with Replication

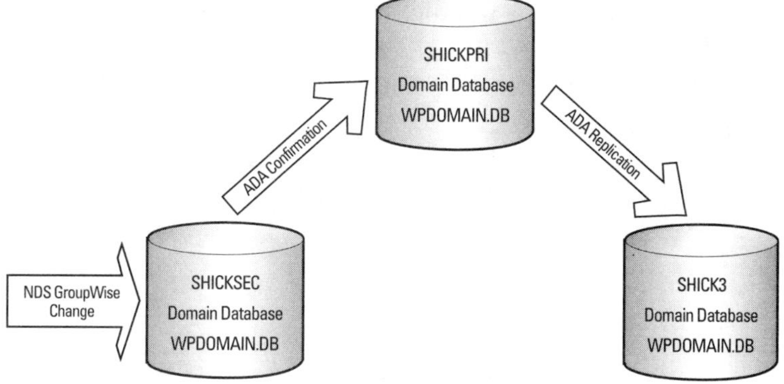

You should note the following points with regard to domain synchronization:

- The MTA from one domain always picks up messages from its own WPCSIN directory and places messages in the target domain's WPCSIN directory.
- The MTA for a domain is the only process that can hand messages off to that domain's processes via the WPCSOUT\ADS directories in the domain and post office.
- The ADA for the domain is the only agent that will ever change the domain (WPDOMAIN.DB) and post office (WPHOST.DB) databases.
- All confirmation and replication messages are created by the ADA in the WPCSIN directory.

Message Flow Between Two Domains

Understanding message flow between domains can be extremely useful when you're troubleshooting problems with your system. If messages are not being transferred, you can look in the actual directories and discover which process is malfunctioning.

The MTA of one domain in a two-domain system moves message files from its own input queues to other input queues of the other domain's MTA. Figure 9.14 show this process.

FIGURE 9.14

MTA in a Two-Domain System

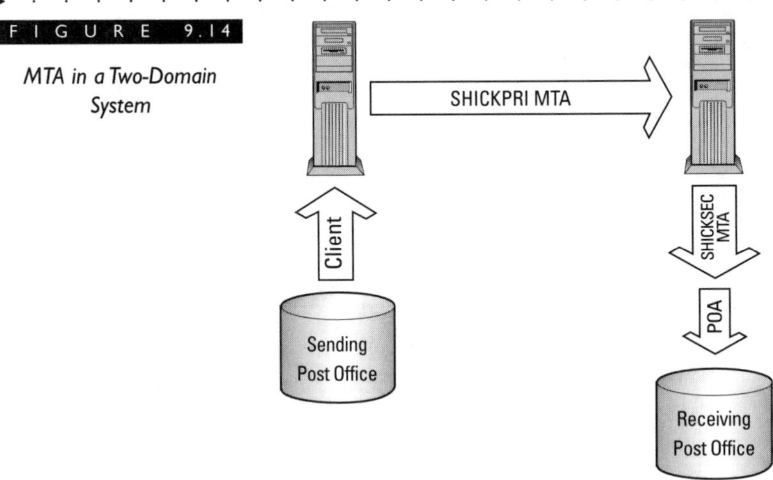

The ultimate goal is to get the message to the recipient's post office. Consequently, the MTA wants to always "push" messages to the recipient's domain. But the MTA can only get messages to the post offices in its own domain, so it needs to hand off the message to the recipient domain's MTA.

Figure 9.15 illustrates the flow of a message sent from a user on the TVPO post office in the SHICKPRI domain to a user on the RDPO post office in the SHICKSEC domain.

FIGURE 9.15

Detailed Message Flow

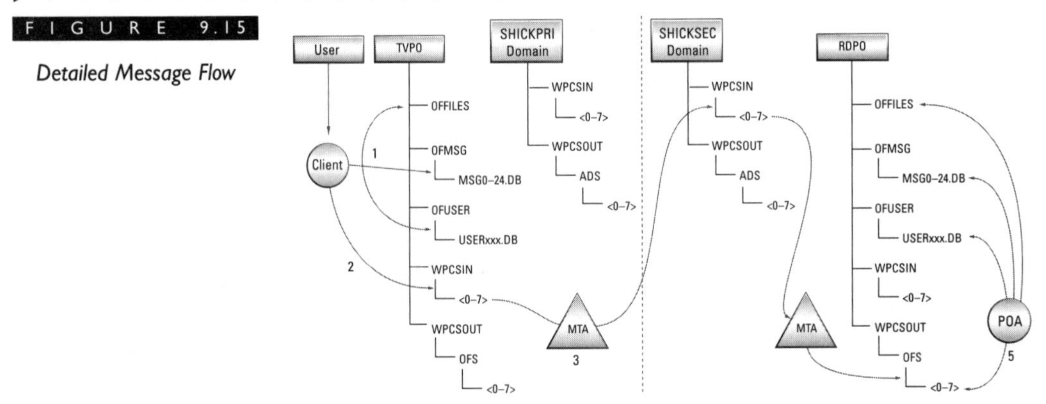

The following steps are shown in Figure 9.15:

1 • The sender's client program creates the message as a record in a message database (TVPO\OFMSG\MSG*xx*.DB); a pointer is created in the sender's user database (TVPO\OFUSER\USER*xxx*.DB); and any part of the message that is less than 2K in size is created as a file in a subdirectory under TVPO\OFFILES.

2 • A message file is created in the MTA input queue on the TVPO post office in TVPO\WPCSIN\0–7.

3 • The SHICKPRI MTA picks up the message file on one of its scans and reads the address portion of the message. The MTA reads its link records to determine how it can find the target domain (SHICKSEC). Since a direct link was automatically created, the UNC path to SHICKSEC is used by the MTA to forward the message file to the SHICKSEC domain directory, in SHICKSEC\WPCSIN\0–7.

NOTE

The GroupWise Access User (GWACCESS) that was specified in the startup files with the `/user` and `/password` switches allows the authentication to this other server.

4 • The SHICKSEC MTA sees a new message in its domain directory input queue and reads the address portion of the message. The SHICKSEC MTA uses the UNC path to the RDPO post office to forward the message to RDPO\WPCSOUT\OFS\0–7.

5 • The RDPO POA reads the message file from its input queue and creates the message in the RDPO information store. The message is created as a record in a message database (MSG*xx*.DB) in RDPO\OFMSG; the recipient's user database (RDPO\OFUSER\USER*xxx*.DB) is updated with a pointer to the new message record; and any portion of the message less than 2K is created as a file in a subdirectory under RDPO\OFFILES.

Figure 9.16 shows the message flow for the return status message.

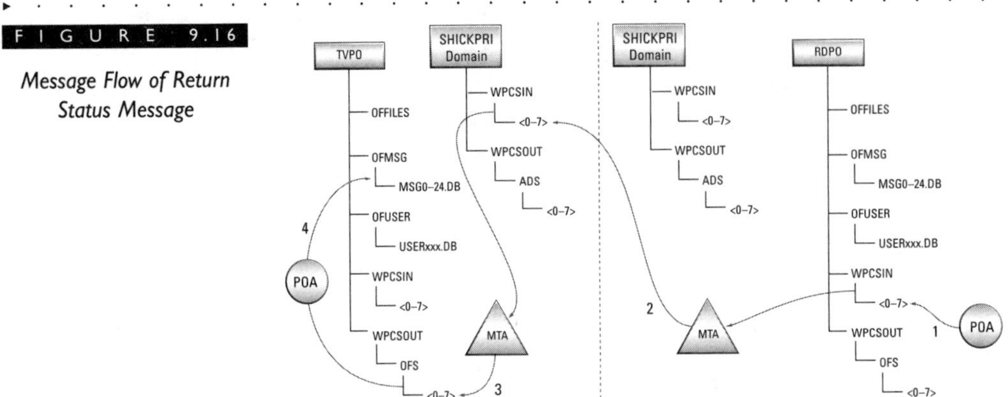

FIGURE 9.16

Message Flow of Return Status Message

Following are the steps depicted in Figure 9.16:

1. The RDPO POA creates a Delivered status message file addressed to TVPO in RDPO\WPCSIN\0–7.

2. The SHICKSEC MTA picks up the message file and, by reading the address and using the direct link path, places it into the SHICKPRI\WPCSIN\0–7.

3. The SHICKPRI MTA forwards the message file to TVPO\WPCSOUT\OFS\0–7.

4. The TVPO POA updates the original message record in the MSG*xx*.DB file with the Delivered status.

This message flow chart can be very helpful for troubleshooting. For example, if you send a message and the recipient gets it but you get no Delivered status, you can use this chart to backtrack and find out that either 1) the sender's POA didn't update the message database with the status, 2) the recipient's POA didn't create the status message, or 3) one of the MTAs didn't move the message. Of course, the answer could be that the sender specified No Status when he or she sent the message to begin with.

Summary

This chapter covered the steps for creating a secondary domain and establishing communication and synchronization between them. In addition, you should have a better understanding of the role of the ADA in a multiple-domain system. You also learned how GroupWise gets Address Book information from NDS. Chapter 10 will cover how to change and define different types of links for the MTA to pass messages between post offices and domains.

CHAPTER 10

Linking System Components

In this chapter, you'll learn about the different ways to link system-level GroupWise components such as post offices, domains, and gateways.

A *link* enables a domain's MTA to find the input queue of other domains so the target domain's MTA can transfer the message to the recipient's post office. Links provide the means by which MTAs can direct messages to other MTAs. For example, a direct link from one domain to another creates a path to the target domain's directory, so the sending domain's MTA can direct messages to the receiving domain.

As you learned in Chapter 8, a domain's MTA moves messages among post offices within the domain by passing the messages to the POA (see Figure 10.1).

FIGURE 10.1

Message Transfer Within a Domain

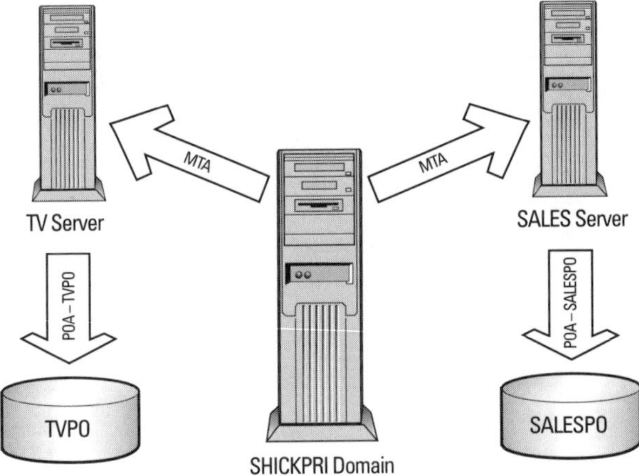

In Chapter 9 you learned that the MTA process also moves messages among domains. Typically, it pushes messages from the domain's input queues to other domains. The MTA also moves messages to gateways. (We discuss that process in more detail later in the book.)

When a message is sent from one domain to another, the MTA of the sender's domain pushes the message to the target domain. Once the message arrives at the target domain, that domain's MTA forwards it to the appropriate output queue for message delivery (see Figure 10.2).

FIGURE 10.2

Message Transfer Between Domains

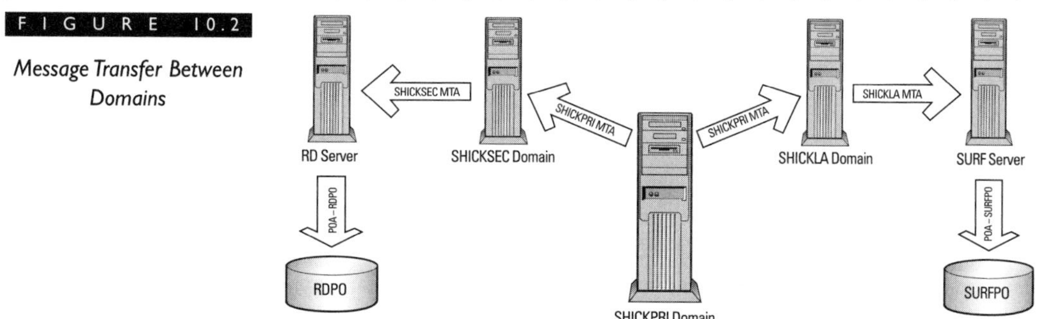

In this chapter, you'll learn exactly how to set up your system-level components so that the MTAs can efficiently route messages to the proper locations. We introduce you to the different types of links available for connecting post offices and domains. You'll also learn how to use the Link Configuration Utility. We provide message flow diagrams throughout the chapter, which can help you better understand the linking process at the file and directory level.

Link Types

As we've explained, links are used to connect GroupWise components together. In this chapter, we'll discuss several types of links, which can be grouped into two categories:

- Post office-to-post office links
- Domain-to-domain links

Post Office-to-Post Office Links

Within a domain, the MTA only moves messages between post offices and gateways. A domain's MTA uses the post office links to transfer messages to post offices within the domain.

At the network level, the MTA moves message files by sending packets on the wire (just like any other network signal). GroupWise can be run on many different types of networks using many different packet styles, or protocols. A *protocol* is a combination of an addressing scheme and a packet format.

Three protocols are available for post office links:

- **Mapped.** This is the DOS path to the post office, used by the Windows NT agents.
- **UNC.** This is the Universal Naming Convention (UNC) path to the post office, automatically defined when you create the post office. It is used by the NLM and Windows NT versions of the agents.
- **TCP/IP.** This is the TCP/IP address and port number of the MTA for the post office. We'll say more about TCP/IP later in this chapter in the section named "Link Configuration Tool."

When you create a post office, a direct link is automatically set up for the MTA to find the post office directory. You can change this link using the Link Configuration Tool, a special utility we explain later in this chapter.

Domain-to-Domain Links

The link between two domains defines the path messages take from one domain to the other. The link you define is used by the sending domain's MTA to find the target domain's directory. The link configuration should match your physical network layer. For example, if you have domains set up in multiple buildings, the links between them should closely match the network connections between the buildings.

If you are routing TCP/IP traffic through relatively slow WAN routers such as 56K or Frame Relay, you should use TCP/IP links to the domains at the respective sites. If the WAN lines run from many "remote" sites to a central building, then you should set up indirect links through that main building, letting that domain act as a message routing hub.

If you have a relatively fast network—100M Ethernet, T1, or Fiber—you should use UNC paths between the domains.

If a physical connection is too costly or not possible, you will need to set up a gateway link between the domains.

NOTE

The second domain you create in a system automatically has a direct link to and from the primary domain. If the agent platform is NLM or Windows NT, this direct link will use UNC paths by default.

You can define three types of links between domains:

- Direct
- Indirect
- Gateway

Direct Links

A *direct link* is a physical network connection from one MTA to another domain's directory, as shown in Figure 10.3.

FIGURE 10.3

Direct Link

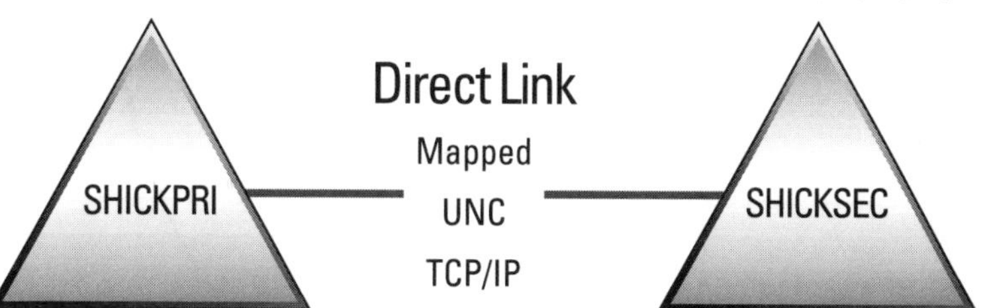

There are three connection protocols you can use for a direct link. They are the same protocols used for post office links:

- **Mapped.** This uses a DOS path to the target domain's directory for the Windows NT version of the agent software. A licensed authenticated connection will be used between the servers and will be kept open all of the time.

  Example: `H:\SHICKSEC` (This is a drive map that is accurate and consistent on the administration workstation.)

- **UNC.** Used by the NLM and Windows NT versions of the MTA, the UNC path is a different, more universal, style for defining the target domain's directory. A licensed authenticated connection will be used between the servers, and it will be kept open all of the time. UNC paths use the following syntax:

```
\\server\volume\domain directory
```

Example: `\\SHICKFS1\SYS\SHICKSEC` (This would be the UNC path for the secondary domain named SHICKSEC.)

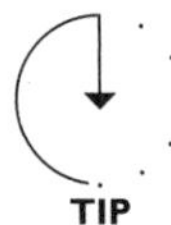

TIP

You can quickly display the UNC path of any directory by opening a DOS prompt, changing to the directory you want to get the UNC path for, and entering the command `TRUENAME`.

- **TCP/IP.** This is the IP address of the server on which the MTA is running for the other domain. The TCP/IP link between domains is best on a Wide Area Network (WAN) or when the GroupWise domains are on different operating system platforms, such as NetWare, Windows NT, and UNIX. The TCP/IP link opens a TCP/IP socket session only when messages need to be transferred; and a licensed, authenticated connection is *not* required. GroupWise moves message files by sending IP packets on the wire with this protocol.

  Example: 202.133.122.5

Indirect Links

An *indirect link* enables one domain to act as a "hub" or routing domain for passing messages on to other domains. The sender's domain transfers the message to the indirect link domain, which then transfers the message to the recipient's domain or to other domains indirectly (see Figure 10.4).

The advantage of indirect links over direct links is that they greatly decrease network traffic. The routing domain is like a telephone call center. Rather than setting up direct telephone lines to everyone you communicate with, it is more efficient to route your calls through a hub. Similarly, indirect links can be more efficient than direct links between each and every domain.

In a real-world scenario, you should match your domain links to the connections between your locations that house domains. For example, if all of the WAN connections are routed through a home office, then messages from remote sites should be routed indirectly to one another through a "hub" domain located in the home office.

FIGURE 10.4

Indirect Link

If there are more than three domains in your system, and you are setting up indirect links, you only have to specify which domain is next in the path that the message will take; you need not define all of the domains the message will pass through on its way to the recipient's domain.

NOTE

The third domain you create automatically has an indirect link to the second domain in the system via the primary domain.

Care must be taken when setting up indirect links. You should avoid redundant links that can result in circular message routes (the GroupWise equivalent of Abbott and Costello's "Who's on First?" routine). To guard against this, GroupWise has a built-in *hop count* of ten. In other words, if the same message hits the same MTA ten times, the message is returned to the sender.

To avoid redundant links, make a simple drawing of the domains in your system and how they are linked together (such as Figure 10.4 above) to help illustrate the message paths.

Gateway Links

Gateway links can be used to connect multiple GroupWise domains where direct links are very expensive or not feasible. International companies often use gateway links between domains. As shown in Figure 10.5, both domains must use the same gateway in order for messages to be transferred. You'll learn more about gateway links in Chapter 17.

FIGURE 10.5

Gateway Link

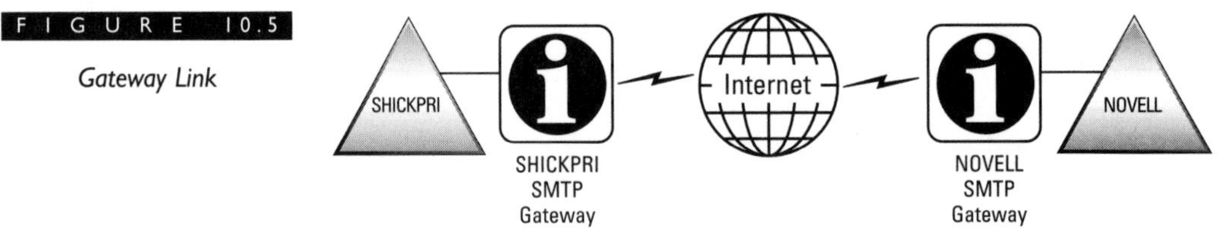

Link Configuration Tool

You can use the Link Configuration Tool, or LCT, to set up and manage links between system-level components. The LCT is a utility within NetWare Administrator. With the LCT you can set up all links from one screen without changing to another program.

To start the Link Configuration Tool, follow these steps:

1 • Choose GroupWise Utilities from the Tools menu in NetWare Administrator.

2 • Select Link Configuration from the menu.

Figure 10.6 show the main screen of the Link Configuration Tool.

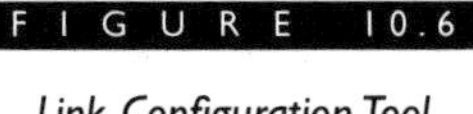

Link Configuration Tool

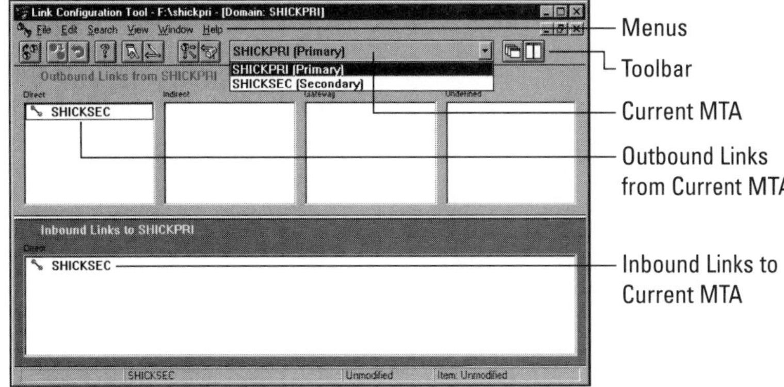

The main parts of the LCT interface are as follows:

- *Menus.* The drop-down menus you use to perform LCT actions.
- *Toolbar.* Shortcuts to frequently used menu choices. The toolbar cannot be customized.
- *Current MTA.* The domain that houses the MTA whose links you wish to view or change. To change the MTA, select the domain name from the list.

The Current MTA field *does not* show the name of the domain database to which you are connected. You should always verify which domain database you are changing with The LCT. The Current MTA field indicates the links for a particular domain's MTA as it is recorded in the WPDOMAIN.DB in the domain to which you are connected. In other words, the Current MTA field is simply your "point of view" for configuring links. The next section explains how to change the current domain.

- *Outbound Links.* Domains and post offices to which the Current MTA can send messages.
- *Inbound Links.* Known links from other domains to the Current MTA as recorded in the domain database to which the LCT is connected.

Connecting to a Domain

When using the LCT, you should always be conscious of the GroupWise domain you are connected to because that is the domain database you will be changing.

Here is an example of why you need to be careful: Suppose you are connected to the New York domain database and start the Link Configuration Tool. The outbound links for the New York MTA appear. Using the LCT, you can also configure the inbound link from the Miami domain. If you change the outbound link from New York to Miami to TCP/IP, the New York MTA will restart immediately and try to establish a TCP/IP connection with Miami's MTA. However, the Miami MTA doesn't know that it's supposed to use TCP/IP also because the update never made it there! Its domain database wasn't updated because of the new link. The MTAs can't connect because the New York MTA is trying to use TCP/IP, and Miami's MTA is still using UNC.

This whole problem can be avoided if NetWare Administrator is pointing to each domain database when the domain's MTA is changed. *Make sure you always connect to the domain that houses the MTA whose link you want to change* (so that MTA is the current MTA).

To connect to a specific domain database from the Link Configuration Tool, map a drive to the domain's server and volume and follow these steps:

1 • Choose Open from the File menu, or click on the icon on the Toolbar.

2 • Browse to the other domain database to which you want to connect and choose OK.

IMPORTANT

Connecting to a new domain in the LCT only changes the connection for the LCT; you are not changing the domain for NetWare Administrator.

As you saw in Chapter 9, a direct link is automatically configured from the primary domain to secondary domains; however, you can change those links using the Link Configuration Tool if you'd like.

Configuring Domain Links

When you start the LCT, you view the domain links for the MTA. The links are listed in four separate boxes, one for each type of link, as shown Figure 10.7.

FIGURE 10.7

Link Types

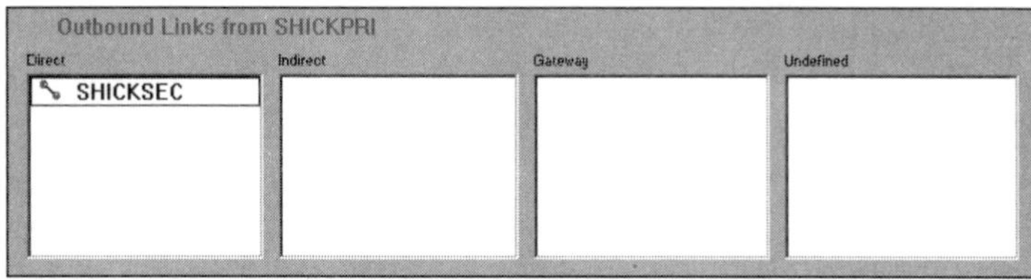

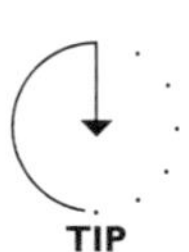

TIP

To view the different link types, select them from the View menu.

Follow these steps to edit the characteristics of the link for the current MTA to another domain:

1. In the LCT, double-click on the domain name listed that you want to change the link to. You will see the dialog box shown in Figure 10.8.

2. Click on the Link Type drop-down list to view the four types of links and select the desired link type.

3. Based on the type of link you chose, you will see one of the following settings boxes. Complete the settings and choose OK to create or change the link.

FIGURE 10.8

Edit Domain Link Dialog Box

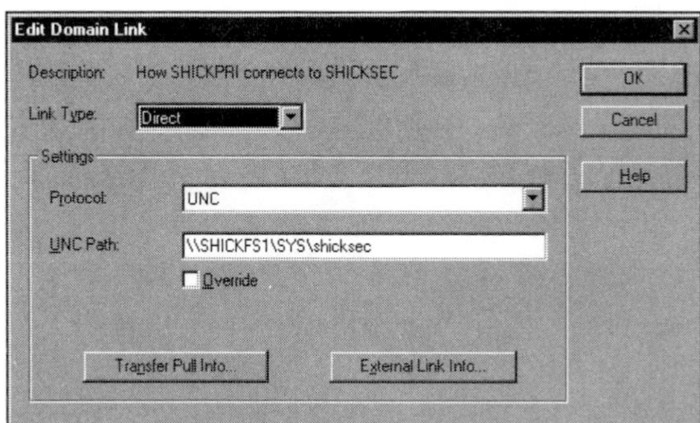

Direct Link Settings

The direct link settings screen (see Figure 10.9) enables you to specify the connection protocol used by the direct link—mapped, UNC, or TCP/IP. You can also set up *transfer pull directories* in this dialog box. Transfer pull directories are described later in this chapter.

FIGURE 10.9

Direct Link Settings

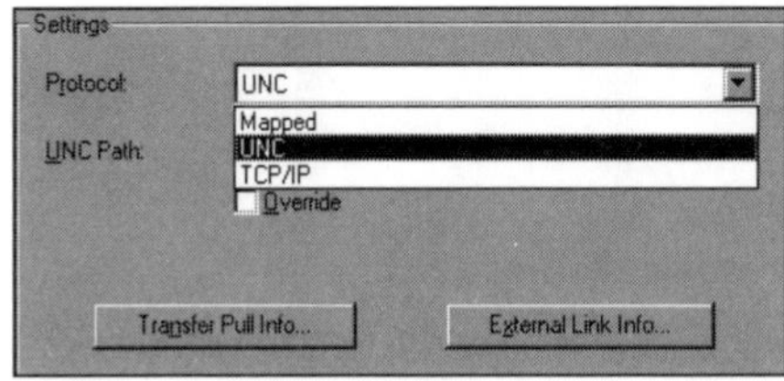

Table 10.1 shows the three different protocols for direct links, with definitions and examples of each.

TABLE 10.1

Direct Link Settings

PROTOCOL	PATH OR ADDRESS	EXAMPLE
Mapped	DOS path to domain directory	h:\SHICKSEC
UNC	UNC path to domain directory	\\SHICKFS2\SYS\SHICKSEC
TCP/IP	IP address and port # of target domain	203.120.134.6:7100

In the Settings dialog box, select the protocol and enter the required path information. Click on OK to complete the link assignment.

Indirect Link Setting

To specify an indirect link from one domain to another, follow these steps:

1 • Double-click on the target domain to which you are linking (as listed in the main screen of the Link Configuration Tool).

2 • In the Edit Domain Link dialog box, select Indirect from the Link Type drop-down list. You'll see the Settings dialog box shown in Figure 10.10.

FIGURE 10.10

Indirect Settings

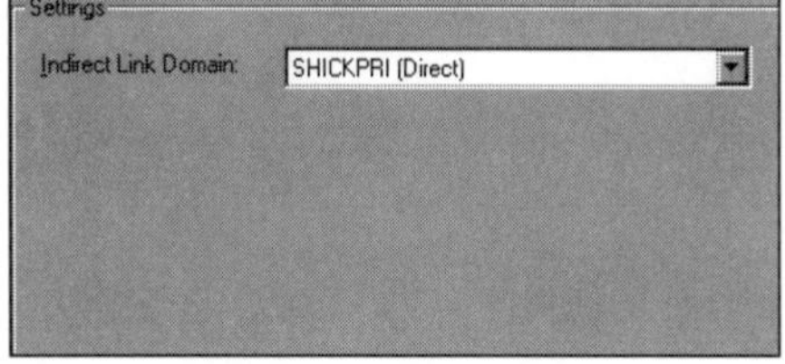

3 • In the Indirect Link Domain field, select the domain to which you want to forward messages and click on OK.

Gateway Link Settings

Gateways are used to connect together domains using different messaging protocols, such as SMTP (for messaging over the Internet), or X.400. To get messages routed through a gateway, you identify a gateway link to the target domain. To do so, follow these steps:

1 • In the main screen of the LCT, double-click on the domain you want to create a gateway link to.

2 • In the Edit Domain Link dialog box, click on the Link Type drop-down list, and select Gateway from the list. You will see the Settings dialog box shown in Figure 10.11.

3 • Enter the appropriate information in the fields and click on OK to continue.

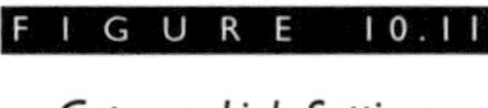

FIGURE 10.11

Gateway Link Settings

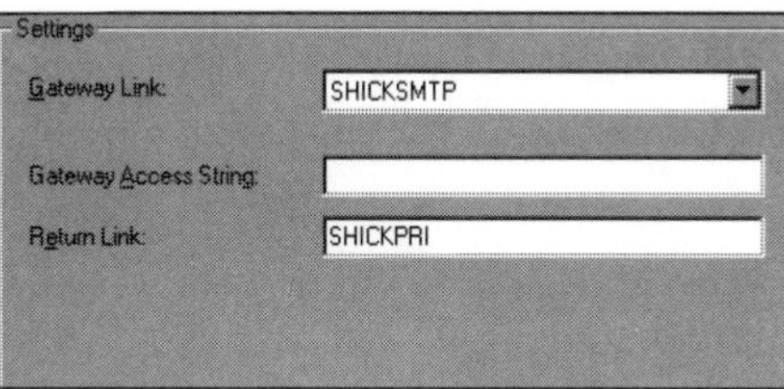

The Settings dialog box contains the following fields:

- *Gateway Link.* The gateway to use as the linking method to the target domain.

- *Gateway Access String.* An optional data string to pass to the gateway to find and connect with the matching gateway at the domain the link is for.
- *Return Link Domain.* The name of the domain that foreign mail systems should use for routing.

Chapters 19 and 20 cover connecting domains using the Async and SMTP gateways in more detail.

As a shortcut for selecting domain links, follow these steps.

1 • From the View menu in the LCT, make sure Direct, Indirect, and Gateway are selected. You should be able to see all three link boxes, as shown in Figure 10.7.

2 • Move your mouse pointer to a domain listed in one of the link boxes. Notice that as you do this, the pointer changes to a hand.

3 • When the pointer changes to a hand, you can pick up this domain and move it to another link type by clicking on the domain in the list and dragging it to another link type box.

For example, to change a link to a domain from gateway to indirect, simply click on the domain in the gateway link box and drag it to the indirect box. You will then be able to specify the indirect link domain as normal.

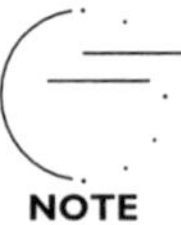
NOTE

Be sure to choose the Save option from the Edit menu when you change links so the MTA can restart and use the new link information.

Configuring Post Office Links

To view the post office links within a domain, choose Post Office Links from the View menu. You will see only the post offices belonging to the domain in the Current MTA box. Notice that we have SHICKPRI as the Current MTA, so the two post offices that belong to the SHICKPRI domain—TVPO and SALESPO—appear (see Figure 10.12).

Post Office Links

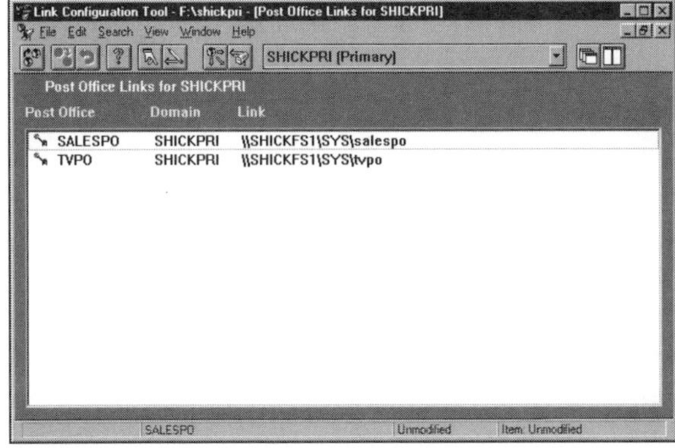

To view the details of the post office link, or to change the configuration of the link, double-click on the post office (see Figure 10.13).

FIGURE 10.13

Post Office Link Details

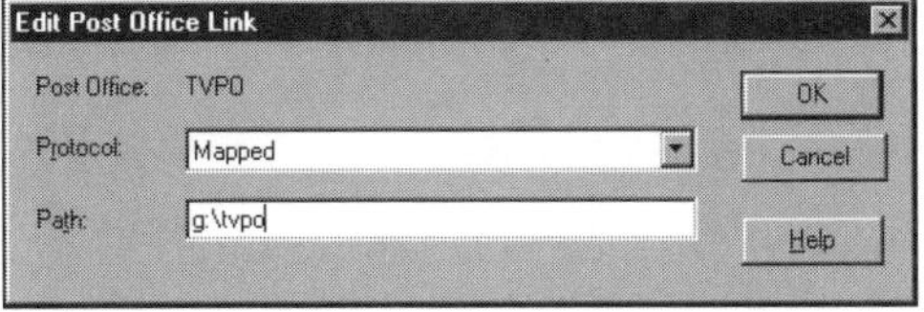

The protocol choices enable you to select the method by which the MTA to the post office will send messages. The choices are listed in Table 10.2.

TABLE 10.2

Post Office Link Settings

PROTOCOL	PATH OR ADDRESS	USAGE	EXAMPLE
Mapped	DOS path to the post office	Local area network	G:\TVPO
UNC	UNC path to the post office	Local area network (This is the default.)	\\SHICKFS1\SYS\TVPO
TCP/IP	TCP/IP address and port of the server on which the POA is loaded	Wide area network/ IP network	203.145.201.6:6700

Once you have changed the link information for the post office, the MTA will automatically restart and begin using the link you defined.

To use a mapped or UNC path as the link to a post office, verify that the path listed accurately reflects the path to the post office directory. As noted in Table 10.2, this is the default path type for a direct link.

The mapped option is rarely used, if at all. If you are using a mapped connection, be sure the driver letter is accurately pointing to the post office directory.

To view the UNC path, open a DOS prompt, change to the post office directory, and execute the TRUENAME command. The UNC path will be displayed on the screen. TRUENAME is an undocumented DOS command, which we provide to you free of charge.

There are three steps for using TCP/IP as the protocol for a post office:

- First configure the TCP/IP protocol and make sure DNS is set up properly. (Use the Ping or Telnet utility to verify the TCP/IP connection.)
- Next, create an MTA for the post office, edit its startup file, and load the MTA for the post office.
- Finally, configure the domain's MTA to use TCP/IP.

Configuring the TCP/IP Protocol on an IntranetWare, NetWare, or Windows NT Server

At the file server prompt, enter the `CONFIG` command to display the network configuration. If you see TCP/IP and an address for the file server, things are looking good! If not, you need to enable your server to talk TCP/IP.

When you configure TCP/IP on IntranetWare or NetWare servers, NetWare IP is not required—just the TCP/IP protocol.

Follow these steps to configure basic TCP/IP on an IntranetWare or NetWare file server:

1 • Edit the SYS:ETC\RESOLV.CFG file to include the domain name and TCP/IP address of your DNS server, as shown below:

Domain: shicktools.com

Nameserver: 203.145.201.20

Note: DNS doesn't have to be configured if you use IP addresses to define all links.

2 • At the NetWare server prompt, type the following commands:

```
LOAD TCPIP
```

(This command loads the TCPIP.NLM)

```
LOAD NE2000 INT=5 PORT=320 FRAME=ETHERNET_II NAME=EII
```

(This command loads the ETHERNET_II frame for TCP/IP. Replace NE2000 and the values for INT= and PORT= with the settings for the network card in your server.)

```
BIND IP TO EII ADDR=203.145.201.21 FORWARD=YES
GATEWAY=203.145.201.22 MASK=255.255.255.0
```

(This command binds the TCP/IP protocol to the network card and assigns it the IP address. The gateway parameter is the IP address of the router on this network segment.)

```
CONFIG
```

(This command displays the network configuration.)

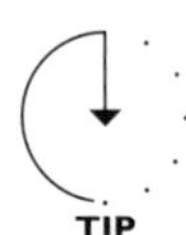

TIP

An alternative way to configure TCP/IP is by using INETCFG.NLM.

To configure TCP/IP on a Windows NT server, follow these steps:

1. From the Control Panel, double-click on the Network icon.
2. Scroll through the configured services and if you see TCP/IP, you can highlight it and click on the Properties button to see the address.
3. If TCP/IP has not been loaded, click on the Add Software button and select TCP/IP from the list. You will need the Windows NT server CD for this step.
4. Enter the TCP/IP address, gateway address, subnet mask, and DNS information in the appropriate fields. If this server obtains its IP address from a DHCP server, make sure you configure DHCP to always assign the same IP address to this server.
5. Click on OK twice to complete the addition. You'll be prompted to restart your machine, and after you do, TCP/IP will be loaded. Refer to Windows NT documentation for further details.

We won't get much deeper into TCP/IP because it can get complicated rather quickly. For more information about TCP/IP configuration, see Drew Heywood's *Novell's Guide to TCP/IP and IntranetWare*, published by Novell Press and IDG Books Worldwide.

Creating an MTA for the Post Office

To create a TCP/IP post office link, you need to create an MTA just for that post office. Use the following steps:

1. Right-click on the Post Office object and choose GroupWise Agent from the short menu. You will see the dialog box shown in Figure 10.14.

2 • Complete the name of the Agent object. It is a good idea to be descriptive when choosing a name, something reflecting the function of the MTA, as you can see from our example.

FIGURE 10.14

Create GroupWise Agent Dialog Box

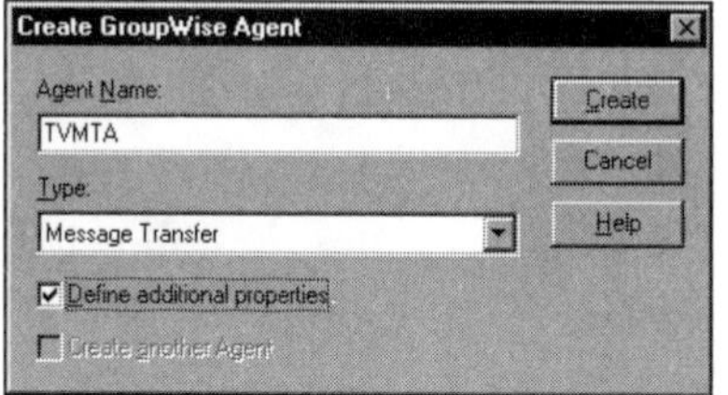

3 • Click on the drop-down list for Type and choose Message Transfer. Select Define additional properties and choose OK. You will see the property pages for the MTA. The fields are as follows:

- *Information.* Enter a description and change the platform if necessary.
- *Network Address.* Click on Add to define the TCP/IP address of the server on which the MTA will be running. If DNS is configured to associate a host name (such as TVPO. SHICKTOOLS.COM) with an IP address, you can enter it as an alternative.
- *Agent Settings.* Define Scan Cycles and additional message handlers for this process. Unless you have a large number of users in the post office, you probably won't need to change the defaults.
- *Log Settings.* Define the log path, age, maximum size, and logging level.
- *Message Log Settings.* This advanced data collection option creates databases for reporting programs that can be written. See Chapter 14 for more information.

4 • Once you have defined all settings, click on OK to complete the creation of the post office MTA.

5 • You now need to create a startup file for the post office MTA and load the agent. The startup file, called *<post office>*.MTA (for example, TVPO.MTA) needs the following definitions:

```
/home=<file server>\<volume>:<post office directory>

/postoffice
```

6 • To load the post office MTA, enter the following command at the server prompt:

```
LOAD GWMTA @<post office>.MTA
```

For example,

```
LOAD GWMTA @TVPO.MTA
```

(You can also add this command to the GRPWISE.NCF file on the file server.)

Once the post office's MTA has been created and configured, you can set up TCP/IP links to the post office as described earlier in this chapter. When the links have been saved, each MTA will restart and begin to communicate using TCP/IP.

Configuring the Domain's MTA to use TCP/IP

The last step in successfully setting up a TCP/IP link is verifying that the domain's MTA is configured to use TCP/IP. The following steps explain how to configure each domain's MTA to use TCP/IP links in order to connect to one another.

1 • Right-click on the MTA object and choose Details from the shortcut menu.

2 • From the Network Address property page, add a TCP/IP address and port number for the server on which the MTA is loaded.

3 • Click on OK to complete the change.

4 • Edit the domain's links using the Link Configuration Tool as described earlier in this chapter.

Once the link information has been saved, the MTA will restart using the TCP/IP links you have set up.

Other LCT Tasks

Now that you understand how to configure links for the domains and post office, we'll take a look at some of the other link-related tasks you can perform with the LCT.

Copying Links

You can use the Copy Links feature to quickly apply one MTA's link configuration to another domain's MTA. The MTA you are copying from is known as the *default MTA*.

This is useful, of course, when you have a lot of domains to manage. With just two or three domains, copying the links really isn't necessary. But with 12 or 14 domains, copying links can be very handy.

The steps for copying one domain's links to another are as follows:

1 • Select the domain you want to copy the link *to* in the Current MTA window.

2 • Choose the Default option from the Edit menu. The dialog box shown in Figure 10.15 appears.

3 • Highlight the domain in the list that you want to copy the link configuration *from*, choose to copy Inbound links and/or Outbound links, and click on OK.

4 • The links from the domain you selected in the preceding step will be copied to the domain listed in the Current MTA box.

FIGURE 10.15

Copying Default Links

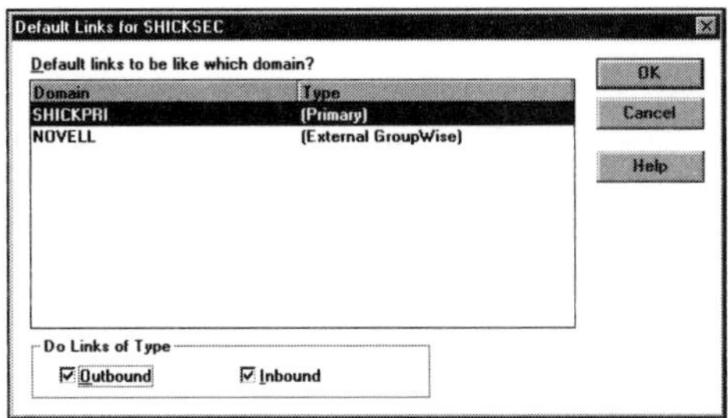

Creating a Transfer Pull Directory

The normal flow of messages between domains is a movement by the MTA of a message from one domain to another domain's directory. Sometimes, however, you may decide not to create connections (or you may be unable to create them) to a particular server on which a GroupWise domain is located. Following are some cases in which a connection may not be possible:

- Licensed connections are not available
- You want to specify the period during which messages flow across a WAN link
- Security issues prevent authentication to a server
- File Access/Transfer is not supported from a domain's particular platform

In all of these cases, you can use a *transfer pull directory* to work around the problem. A transfer pull directory works much like the milkman who, in the good old days, used to come around and pick up empty milk bottles left out on the porch. In GroupWise, instead of empty milk bottles, a domain's MTA sets out messages for pickup. Another domain's MTA grabs those messages and also delivers fresh messages to the domain. The transfer pull directory creates a local site where a sending domain's MTA can place messages destined for another domain. The receiving domain's MTA will scan that local queue and "pull" messages into its own queues for delivery to the post office.

Since two MTAs are involved in the transfer, you will need to edit link information for both domains.

As an example, we'll use our fictional company, ShickTools, to demonstrate how this works. Imagine that the SHICKPRI domain has run out of license connections and can't enable SHICKSEC's MTA to transfer messages to its domain directory. Consequently, SHICKSEC will drop the messages off in a directory on its own server, and SHICKPRI's MTA will retrieve them (see Figure 10.16).

FIGURE 10.16

Transfer Pull Directory

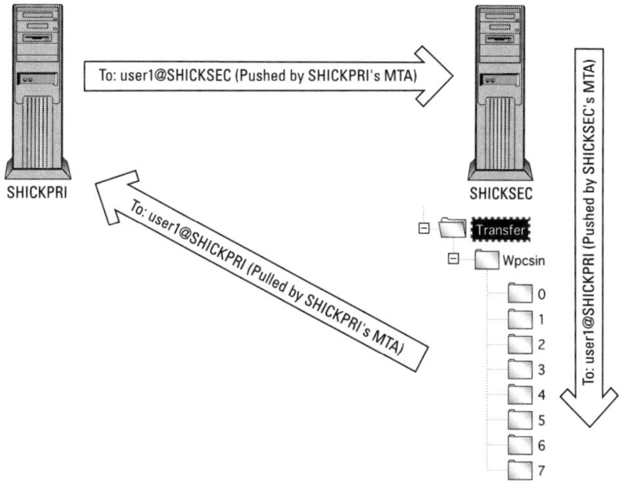

To configure a transfer pull directory for ShickTools, you would follow these steps:

1. On the SHICKSEC file server, create a directory to be used for transfer. Using a de facto standard, make a directory called TRANSFER under the SHICKSEC domain.

2. Under the TRANSFER directory, create a directory structure like the one shown in Figure 10.17. The SHICKPRI will use this structure as one of its input queues.

3. In the Link Configuration Tool, set the current domain database to SHICKSEC by selecting File, Open, and then browsing to the SHICKSEC domain directory.

FIGURE 10.17

Transfer Pull Directory Structure

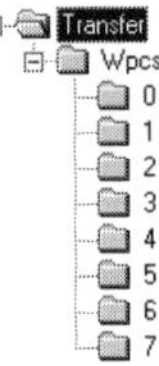

4 • Verify that the SHICKSEC domain is displayed in the Current MTA box.

5 • Double-click on the direct link to SHICKPRI.

6 • Click on the Override check box and you will see an extra field called UNC Override, as shown in Figure 10.18.

FIGURE 10.18

UNC Override

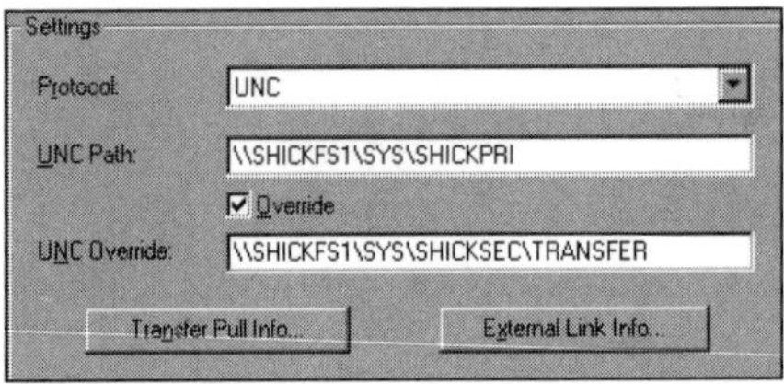

7 • Enter the UNC path to the directory you made in Step 1 and click on OK. The MTA for SHICKSEC will now move messages addressed to SHICKPRI to the TRANSFER directory.

8 • Set the current domain database to SHICKPRI by selecting File, Open, and then browsing to the SHICKPRI domain directory. Verify that the SHICKPRI domain is displayed in the Current MTA box.

9 • Double-click on the SHICKSEC domain to edit the link. Click on the Transfer Pull Information button to open a dialog box like the one shown in Figure 10.19.

Transfer Pull Information

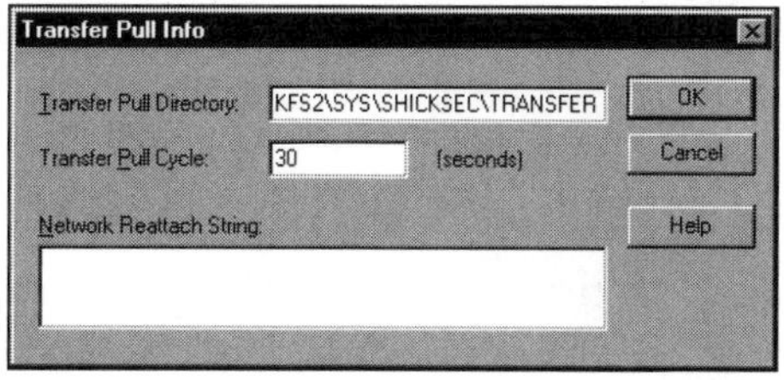

10 • In the Transfer Pull Directory field, enter the UNC path to the directory you made in Step 1. In the Transfer Pull Cycle field, enter the time interval in seconds that you want the SHICKPRI MTA to poll the TRANSFER directory for messages addressed to SHICKPRI from SHICKSEC.

11 • Click on OK.

Remember that messages going to SHICKSEC from SHICKPRI will still go directly to the domain. The messages going to SHICKPRI from SHICKSEC, however, will be placed in the TRANSFER directory, waiting for the SHICKPRI MTA to come and get them.

You can verify the configuration by examining both MTA screens and making sure that domains are open, and by viewing the details under Status Configuration.

Saving and Undoing Changes

The Save option under the Edit menu is used to update the current MTA's domain database with changes that have been made. The MTA (if it is loaded) will restart and use the new link information.

The Undo option lets you cancel any changes you have made, as long as they have not been saved.

Updating Other Domains

Select Synchronize under the Edit menu to update the link configuration for the current MTA in all of the other domains in the system. This happens automatically via the ADA process, but if an immediate update is necessary—in other words, you need the other domain databases to know about it immediately—you should use the Synchronize option.

Viewing Link Hops

To help you see the path that a message will take to a particular domain, you can use the Link Hop option under the View menu. Select a domain from the list and a quick calculation will be done by the LCT to determine which domains use the selected domain as a hop. Figure 10.20 shows the type of information you get when you use the Link Hop option. You can see that the SHICKSEC uses an indirect link through SHICKPRI to send messages to the NOVELL domain.

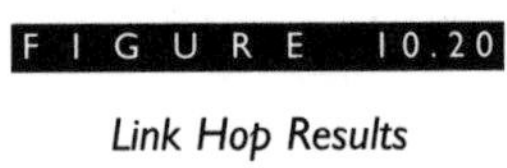

FIGURE 10.20

Link Hop Results

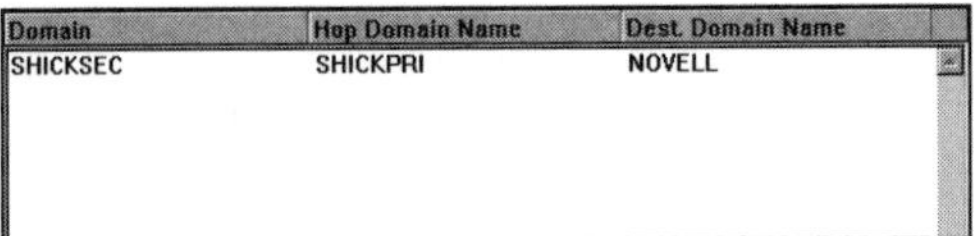

Domain	Hop Domain Name	Dest. Domain Name
SHICKSEC	SHICKPRI	NOVELL

Viewing Gateway Hops

The Gateway Hop option under the View menu brings up a list of the gateways in your system. After you select a gateway and click on OK, you will see a screen that lists the domains accessed through the chosen gateway (see Figure 10.21).

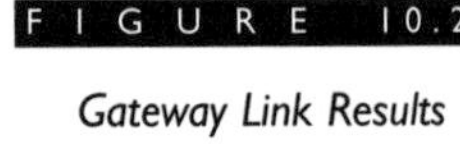

FIGURE 10.21

Gateway Link Results

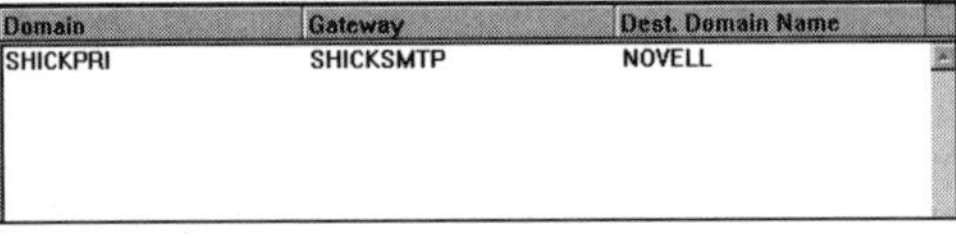

Domain	Gateway	Dest. Domain Name
SHICKPRI	SHICKSMTP	NOVELL

Figure 10.21 shows that the SHICKPRI domain uses the SHICKSMTP gateway to send messages to the NOVELL domain.

Quickly Changing the Current MTA

To quickly change the current MTA, go to the View menu and choose Selected. You will have a choice of either domain or post office links.

If you choose Domain under this option, whatever domain you have highlighted at the moment will become your current MTA, and its domain links appear.

If you choose Post Office, the current MTA will change to the highlighted domain and its post office links will appear.

WARNING

This procedure does *not* change the current domain database.

Use the Selected option as a shortcut to changing the current MTA.

Viewing Multiple Domain Links

All of the normal window options are available in the LCT: Cascade, Tile, Arrange Icons, and Close All. In addition, you have a list of all open link windows you can readily switch to. Use the Cascade and Tile options to display multiple domain links simultaneously.

Using the Toolbar

The symbols on the Toolbar of the LCT have two different kinds of tool tips: The title bar of the LCT has a longer explanation of the buttons function, and if you leave the mouse pointer on a button for a short period of time, a label with a short description of the button's function pops up.

The two most handy buttons are to the left of the Current MTA box. They quickly switch between domain and post office links.

Advanced Message Flow Diagrams

In this section we'll review the steps you need to take in order to enable the MTA to use the TCP/IP protocol for sending messages between post offices within a domain. We'll explain how messages are transferred, and we'll examine message flow between two domains.

TCP/IP Link to the Post Office

When you set up a TCP/IP link to a post office, you must load an MTA for the post office. This MTA actually behaves like a separate post office, with its own directory input queues that the TCP/IP transfer can take place in. This directory is created under the domain's working directory as specified by the `/WORK` switch in the domain's MTA startup file.

Using our Primary domain SHICKPRI as an example, the Inbound TCP/IP queue is as follows:

```
shickfs1/sys:shickpri/mslocal/msibound
```

This incoming TCP/IP path to the SHICKPRI domain is viewed from the main screen of the MTA by pressing the F10 key and highlighting Configuration Status. Highlight the entry `*Inbound Queue` and press Enter (see Figure 10.22).

FIGURE 10.22

MSINBOUND TCP/IP Transfer Module Queue

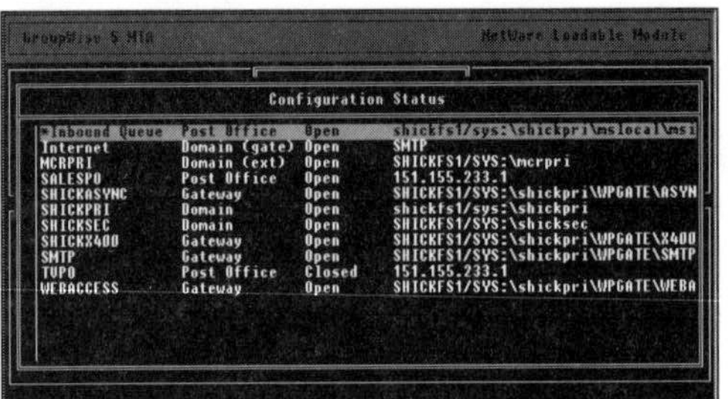

Notice that the post office to which the MTA is connected using TCP/IP is designated by the TCP/IP address.

In order to obtain more specific information regarding the actual TCP/IP transfer, a TCP process screen is automatically loaded when the TCP/IP-enabled MTA is loaded. This screen appears as a separate screen you can view from the file server console. If you don't want this screen loaded, remove the comment symbol (;) from the `/notcpscreen` switch in the domain's MTA startup file.

Figure 10.23 shows how messages flow to a post office using TCP/IP links.

FIGURE 10.23

TCP/IP Message Flow from TVPO to SALESPO

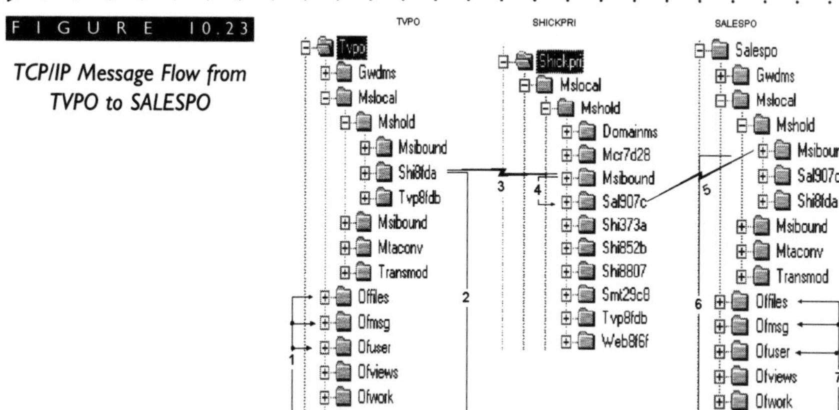

This figure shows the following processes:

1 • A user in the TVPO post office creates and sends a message to a user in the SALESPO post office in the SHICKPRI domain, placing it in the Information Store in TVPO and in the TVPO\WPCSIN\0–7 directory.

2 • The TVPO MTA picks up the message file in the TVPO\WPCSIN\0–7 directory and places it in the MTA Transport Module Input queue for the SHICKPRI domain (TVPO\<mslocal>MSHOLD\SHI8FDA).

3 • The TVPO MTA Transport Module establishes a TCP/IP connection with the SHICKPRI MTA Transport Module and transfers the message file to the SHICKPRI MTA Transport Module, which places the message file in the MSIBOUND Input queue for the SHICKPRI MTA..

4 • The SHICKPRI MTA routes the message file to the holding queue for the SALESPO post office (SHICKPRI\<mslocal>\MSHOLD\SAL907C).

5 • The SHICKPRI MTA Transport Module establishes a TCP/IP connection with the SALESPO MTA Transport Module and transfers the message file in TCP/IP packets to the SALESPO MTA Transport Module, which places the message file in the MSIBOUND Input queue for the SALESPO MTA.

6 • The SALESPO MTA transfers the message file to the SALESPO POA input queue, SALESPO\WPCSOUT\OFS\0–7.

7 • The SALESPO POA delivers the message to the SALESPO information Store.

Figure 10.24 shows how status messages flow return to the sender's post office using TCP/IP links.

FIGURE 10.24

TCP/IP Status Message Flow from SALESPO to TVPO

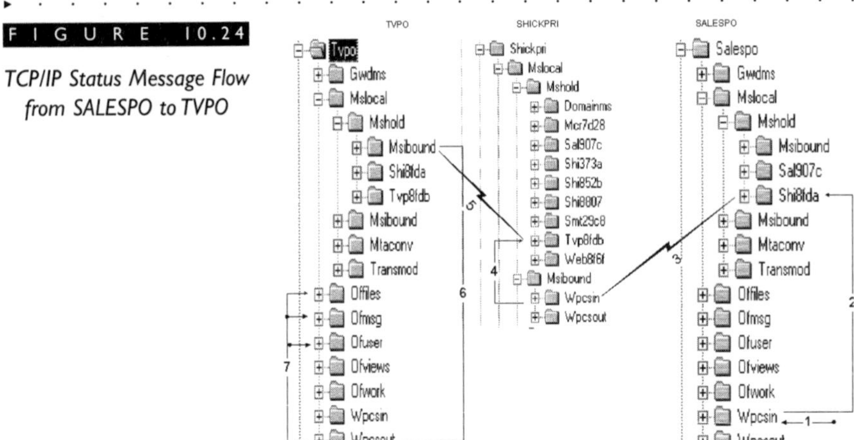

This figure shows the following processes:

1 • The SALESPO POA creates a delivered status message file and places it in the SALESPO\WPCSIN\0–7 directory.

2 • The SALESPO MTA picks up the status message file in the SALESPO\WPCSIN\0–7 directory and places it in the MTA Transport Module Input queue for the SHICKPRI domain (SALESPO\<mslocal> MSHOLD\SHI8FDA).

3 • The SALESPO MTA Transport Module establishes a TCP/IP connection with the SHICKPRI MTA Transport Module and transfers the status message file in TCP/IP packets to the SHICKPRI MTA Transport Module, which places the status message file in the MSIBOUND Input queue for the SHICKPRI MTA.

4 • The SHICKPRI MTA routes the status message file to the holding queue for the TVPO post office (SHICKPRI\<mslocal>\MSHOLD\TVP8FDB).

5 • The SHICKPRI MTA Transport Module establishes a TCP/IP connection with the TVPO MTA Transport Module and transfers the status message file to the TVPO MTA Transport Module, which places the status message file in the MSIBOUND Input queue for the TVPO MTA.

6 • The TVPO MTA transfers the status message file to the TVPO POA Input queue, TVPO\WPCSOUT\OFS\0–7.

7 • The TVPO POA delivers the status message to the TVPO information Store.

TCP/IP Between Domains

The message flow diagram in Figure 10.25 shows the movement of a message sent from the TVPO post office in the SHICKPRI domain to the RDPO post office in the SHICKSEC domain. These two domains are connected using TCP/IP links.

FIGURE 10.25

TCP/IP Message Flow

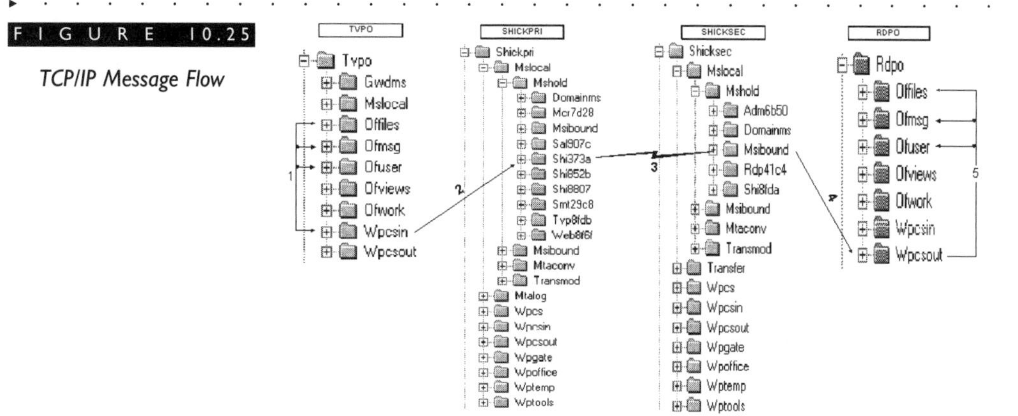

The steps shown in Figure 10.25 are as follows:

1 • The user in the TVPO post office creates and sends a message to a user in the RDPO post office in the SHICKSEC domain. The

GroupWise client adds the message to the message database, the user database, and the OFFILES directory (if necessary). The client places the outbound message file in the TVPO\WPCSIN\<0–7> directory.

2 • The MTA for the SHICKPRI domain detects the message file in the input queue and places the message file in the SHICKPRI\MSLOCAL\MSHOLD\SHI373a\<0–7> directory.

3 • The TCP/IP symbiont running for SHICKPRI's MTA sends the file in TCP/IP packets to the TCP/IP symbiont running for the SHICKSEC MTA, which assembles the packets into a file in the MSIBOUND input queue for the SHICKSEC MTA in the SHICKSEC domain.

4 • SHICKSEC's MTA moves the message file to the MTA output queue in the RDPO post office.

5 • RDPO's POA finishes the message file delivery to the RDPO information store.

Figure 10.26 shows the message flow for the status message. (Note: The steps in Figure 10.26 pick up where Figure 10.25 leaves off.)

FIGURE 10.26

TCP/IP Status Back

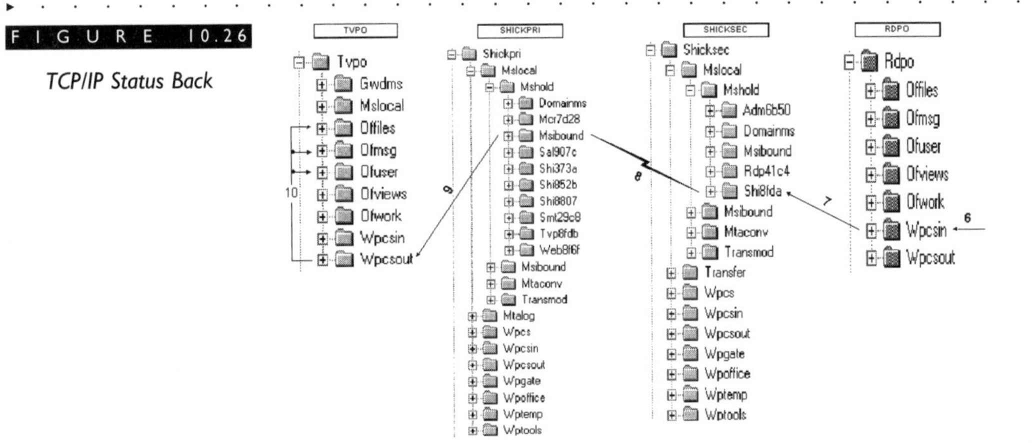

6 • RDPO's POA generates a Delivered status message file and places it in the RDPO\WPCSIN\<0–7> directory.

7 • SHICKSEC's MTA detects the message file and places it in the SHICKSEC\MSLOCAL\MSHOLD\SHICKPRI\<0–7> directory.

8 • The TCP/IP symbiont running for SHICKSEC's MTA sends the file in TCP/IP packets to the TCP/IP symbiont running for SHICKPRI's MTA, which assembles the packets into a file in the MSIBOUND input queue for the SHICKPRI MTA in the SHICKPRI domain.

9 • SHICKPRI's MTA places the status message file in the post office output queue.

10 • The POA updates the message database with the Delivered status.

Transfer Pull

The message flow diagram in Figure 10.27 illustrates the path of a message from RDPO on the SHICKSEC domain to a user in the TVPO post office under the SHICKPRI domain. The administrator has configured the transfer pull directory in the SHICKSEC domain and pointed SHICKSEC's link for SHICKPRI to that transfer pull directory. The SHICKPRI MTA will "go get them" because SHICKPRI's link for SHICKSEC has been configured to get the transfer pull directory in SHICKSEC's domain directory.

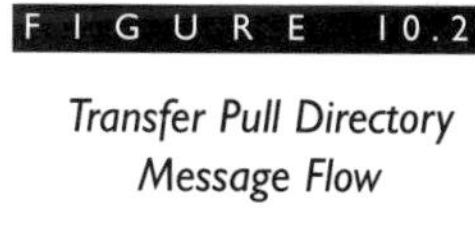

FIGURE 10.27

Transfer Pull Directory Message Flow

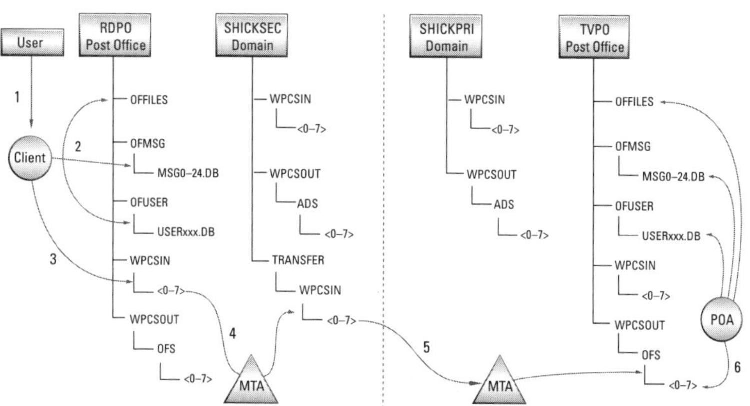

The steps shown in Figure 10.27 are as follows:

1 • A user in the RDPO post office in the SHICKSEC domain creates and sends a message to a user in the TVPO post office in the SHICKPRI domain.

2 • The GroupWise client adds the message to the message database, the user database, and the OFFILES directory (if necessary).

3 • The GroupWise client places the outbound message in the RDPO\WPCSIN\<0–7> directory.

4 • The MTA for SHICKSEC detects the message in the post office MTA input queue and places the message in the SHICKSEC\TRANSFER\WPCSIN\<0–7> directory created for the SHICKSEC domain.

5 • The MTA for SHICKPRI scans the SHICKSEC\TRANSFER\WPCSIN\<0–7> directory at the intervals specified in the transfer poll cycle and detects the message. It places the message in the TVPO\WPCSOUT\\OFS\<0–7> directory.

6 • TVPO's POA finishes the message delivery.

Figure 10.28 shows the message flow of the status message. (Note: The steps in Figure 10.28 pick up where Figure 10.27 leaves off.)

7 • The POA for the TVPO post office generates a Delivered status message and places it in the TVPO\WPCSIN\<0–7> directory.

8 • The MTA for SHICKPRI detects the message and places it directly in the SHICKSEC\WPCSIN\<0–7> directory.

9 • SHICKSEC's MTA places the status message in the MTA output queue of the post office.

10 • The POA for RDPO updates the message database with the Delivered status.

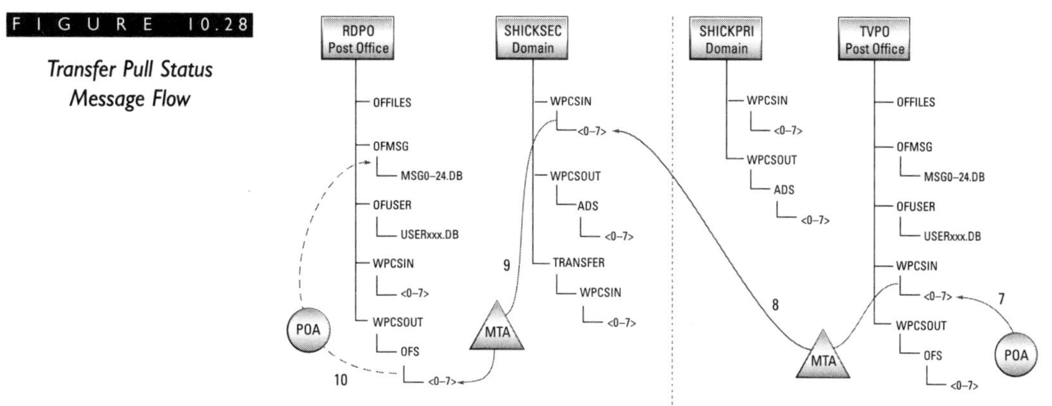

FIGURE 10.28

Transfer Pull Status Message Flow

Notice in Figure 10.28 that messages traveling from SHICKPRI to SHICKSEC do *not* go through the transfer pull directory structure. Only messages going from SHICKSEC to SHICKPRI pass through the transfer pull directories.

Summary

In this chapter we explained your options for linking your domains and post offices together, and how to create and manage links with the Link Configuration Tool. You learned how to create and manage different types of links, and how messages move between domains and post offices with both UNC and TCP/IP linking methods.

In the next chapter you will learn how to expand a closed GroupWise system to allow communication with domains, post offices, and users in other GroupWise systems. You will use the links that you learned about in this chapter to establish connections between the different GroupWise systems.

CHAPTER 11

Connecting to an External System

You have already learned how to create a multiple-domain GroupWise system and how to link the domains together. Now we'll explain how to open up your messaging system to communicate with the outside world. In this chapter, we show you how to connect your system with external GroupWise systems. Later in the book (in Chapters 18 through 20), we'll show you how to connect your system to non-GroupWise systems and the Internet.

External domains are used to connect separate GroupWise systems. Companies often decide they want to connect their GroupWise systems to other companies' GroupWise systems. Also, sometimes a single enterprise has separate GroupWise systems (for security or administrative reasons) that it wants to connect. In either case, the solution is to set up an external domain.

You can use *external GroupWise objects* to set up a communication link between two independent GroupWise systems. There are three kinds of external GroupWise objects: external Domain objects, external Post Office objects, and external User objects. All three types are used to connect independent GroupWise systems. Once you have connected your system with an external system, users in your system can see the names of the external users in the Address Book and send them messages to them as if they were part of your system.

When you set up external objects in your system, you are only entering information about existing objects in the other system. You are not actually creating mailboxes for the other system, and you have no administrative control over the domains, post offices, or users in the external system.

Some of the major benefits provided by the ability to define external GroupWise systems include the following:

- Users in another GroupWise system appear in your system's Address Book to facilitate messaging.
- Messages transferred between the GroupWise systems are maintained in the GroupWise message format, even when transferred through a gateway. This preserves security because messages are never translated to a less-secure messaging format.
- Users in the separate system can share custom GroupWise message types and custom GroupWise views.

- The separate systems remain autonomous because they are maintained and administered separately.

However, there are also a few drawbacks:

- If you want the other system's users to appear in your Address Book, you must recreate the external system's domain and post office structure in your system.

- Because the systems are administered separately, you have to continually verify that the other system's information is correctly maintained in your system.

NOTE

In previous versions of GroupWise, you had to manually synchronize the user information between separate GroupWise systems. However, GroupWise 5 has added automatic synchronization of user information between external systems, thereby reducing the administrative work involved in maintaining external connections.

This chapter explains how to create external domains and post offices and how to add external users to your system. It also covers synchronization of directory information between external systems.

We assume that you will include all of the users in the external system in your system's Address Book. You could, however, selectively define only those external domains and post offices that contain users you want in your Address Book.

There are four main tasks involved in establishing communication with an external GroupWise system:

- Planning your connection strategy

- Creating the external domains

- Creating the external post offices

- Enabling synchronization

Planning Your Connection Strategy

When connecting with an external system, you must define every domain in the external system containing external users whom you want your users to see in their Address Books.

At least one domain in your system and one domain in the external system must serve as connecting points between the two systems, with either a direct network link or a gateway link.

In theory, you could create just one external domain representing one domain in the other system and then set up a link to it, and messaging would be enabled. However, in order to send messages to a user in the other system, you would have to use the exact e-mail address, which includes the user's domain, post office, and user ID. In some cases, you'll want to create multiple external domains and post offices to represent multiple domains and post offices in the other system. That way, your system's Address Book can display the other system's users.

Usually, you will establish a single domain in each system as the connecting point between the two systems. All domains in your system (other than the domain that serves as the connecting point) can then connect via indirect links through the two connected domains. The same is true of the external system also. Each one of their domains will be indirectly linked to all of your domains through the domain of theirs that serves as the connecting point.

Figure 11.1 shows an example of two GroupWise systems linked together by a direct connection between their primary domains. Notice that each system has the other system's domains defined in the GroupWise directory store.

External GroupWise objects *do not* have corresponding NDS objects in your NDS tree. External objects are defined and administered through the GroupWise view of NetWare Administrator. They exist only in the GroupWise directory databases, not in the NDS database.

FIGURE 11.1

Connected GroupWise Systems

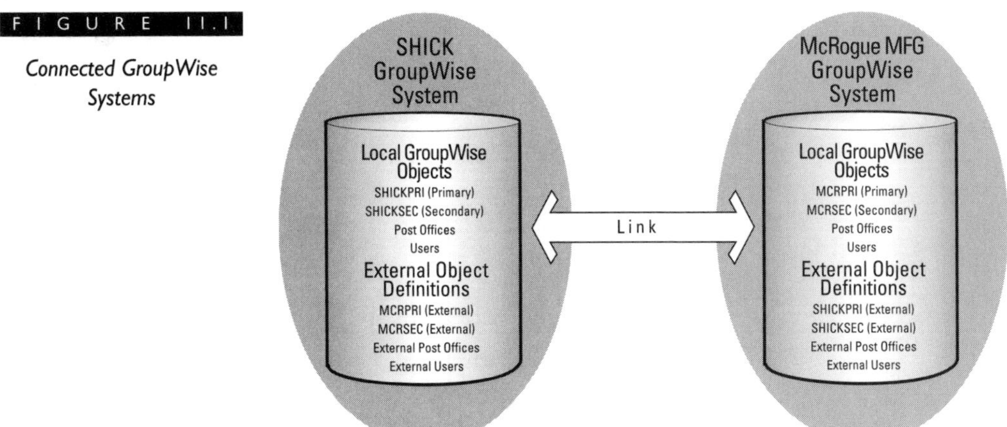

As you learned in Chapter 3, the most important step you need to take when implementing system-level changes is spending sufficient time planning. When you're planning to connect your system to an external GroupWise system, you need to first answer the following questions:

- Which domains will serve as connecting domains?
- Will you have a direct network link (i.e., can you set a UNC path between the domains) or will you have to create a gateway link?
- What information do you want to automatically synchronize between the systems?
- Who is the administrator for the external GroupWise system, and how will you coordinate the connection with that person?

Determining Which Domains to Connect

Usually, it is fairly obvious which domains should serve as connecting points between the two systems. In most cases, the connecting domains should be the primary domains. By connecting primary domains, you minimize the synchronization traffic that will occur throughout both GroupWise systems.

The only exception to this general rule is when you want to isolate traffic. If you have users in a secondary domain who will cause most of the messaging traffic between the systems, you might decide to use that secondary domain as the connecting domain. This would be the case if you have a secondary domain that only contains gateways, if a gateway will be used to connect to the other system.

Choosing a Link Type

The link type between your systems will be determined by the physical connections between your networks. For example, if you have a 56K Frame Relay wide area connection between your company and the network on which the other system is located, you will want a direct network link between the two connecting systems. A direct link between the two systems is best if possible, especially if you want to take advantage of the external synchronization features of GroupWise 5.

You only need a direct link between one domain in each system, not a direct link from every domain in your system to every domain in the other system.

Other than a direct link using a physical WAN connection, a GroupWise gateway would provide another viable connection option. You could use the SMTP, Async, or X.400 gateway to accomplish this. Of course, the gateway needs to be installed at both domains. We will cover gateways more fully in Chapter 19.

If you will be using an Async gateway, you will want to set your connection options so that the systems connect fairly frequently. This ensures that GroupWise messages and synchronization traffic will occur regularly.

Deciding How to Set Up Synchronization

When you establish automatic synchronization between the systems, you have the option to synchronize users, groups, and resources.

In most cases, users in your system will not need to see the external system's groups and resources. Therefore, synchronizing these objects will only clutter your Address Books and cause unnecessary administration traffic. Decide in advance which objects you want synchronized between the systems.

If you are connecting to an external GroupWise 4 system, you will have to perform all synchronization manually, unless you can persuade the other system's movers and shakers to upgrade to the most powerful messaging system available.

For detailed information about manually synchronizing with a GroupWise 4 system, see *Novell's GroupWise 4 Administrator's Guide*, published by Novell Press and IDG Books Worldwide.

Contacting the External System

Because you have no administrative control over the external GroupWise system, the success or failure of your communication with the other system hinges upon your ability to work effectively with the external system's administrator.

The external system's administrator will have to mirror the steps you perform on your system in his or her system. You will need to share information about your systems, such as domain and post office names. You will also need to be able to work together to make the connection function smoothly.

It is a good idea to stay in close contact with the external system's administrator.

Defining an External Domain

After you have established a clear-cut strategy for connecting the two GroupWise systems, you are ready to begin defining the external objects in your GroupWise system.

Notice that we did not use the word *create*. Information for the external system is defined using NetWare Administrator and entered into your GroupWise databases for the purpose of connecting to the system and addressing messages to the system. No directories or databases are created on your system's file servers; the information is simply entered into your databases.

In Figure 11.2, ShickTool's primary domain, SHICKPRI, will serve as the connecting point to McRogue Manufacturing's primary domain, MCRPRI. All messages sent from any domain in the ShickTools system will be routed through the SHICKPRI domain, and all messages sent from McRogue Manufacturing's system will be routed through the MCRPRI domain.

FIGURE 11.2

Connecting Points

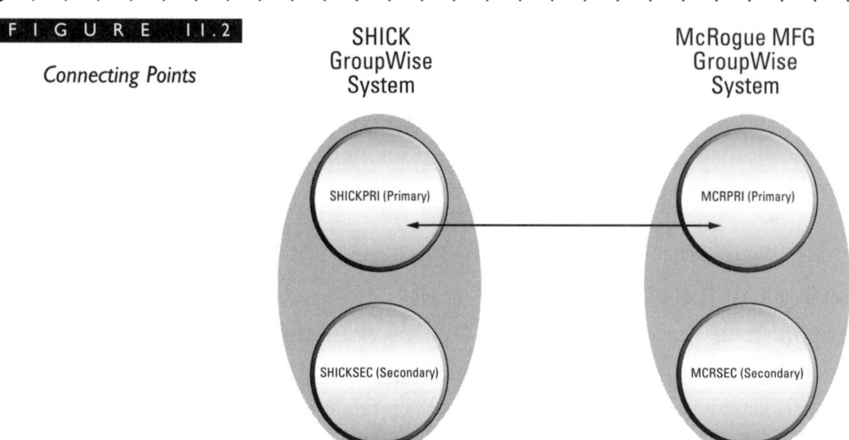

Figure 11.2 illustrates just one possible configuration. There is no reason why a secondary domain in the McRogue Manufacturing system could not link directly to a domain in the ShickTools system. Any number of domains in your system can connect to any number of domains in the external system, as long as the amount of message traffic justifies the additional use of network bandwidth.

To create an external domain, follow these steps:

1 • In NetWare Administrator, click on the Tools menu.

2 • Click on GroupWise View. The GroupWise view appears.

3 • Right-click on the object that represents your system and click on Create. You'll see the Create External Object dialog box, as shown in Figure 11.3

FIGURE 11.3

Create External Object Options

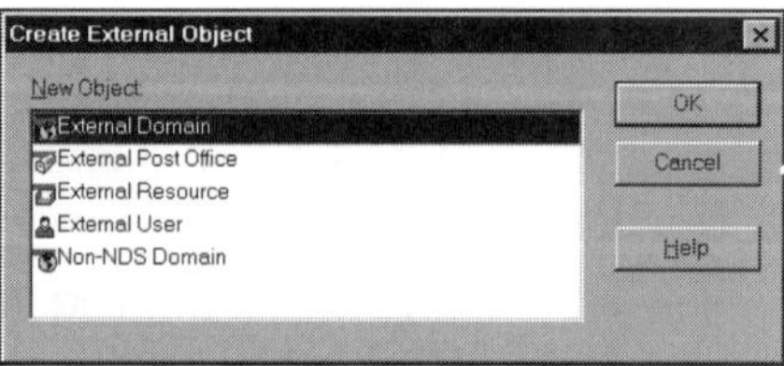

4 • Highlight External Domain, and click on OK. The Create External Domain dialog box appears, as shown in Figure 11.4.

FIGURE 11.4

Create External Domain

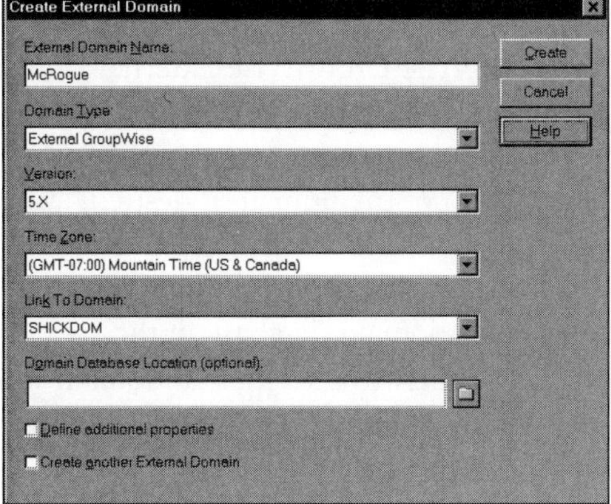

5 • Enter the name of the external domain in the External Domain Name field.

6 • Set Domain Type to External GroupWise

7 • Set the database type to version 5.x if the external domain is using any version of GroupWise 5 (e.g., 5.01, 5.1, etc.). Select 4.x if the other system is using GroupWise 4.1 or WordPerfect Office 4.0a. Note: You can set up external domains with GroupWise 4, but external domain directory synchronization is not supported.

8 • Set the Time Zone field to the time zone that corresponds to the location of the external domain.

9 • Make sure that the domain in your system that will connect to this external domain is listed in the Link To Domain field.

10 • (Optional) Enter the path to the domain database in the Domain Database Location field. If you will use a direct link to the other domain, you must use a UNC path here. This field is where the MTA

finds the other domain directory. Of course, you can override it in the Link Configuration Utility if you'd like.

11 • Click on the Define Additional Properties check box.

12 • Click on Create. The GroupWise External Domain properties dialog box appears (see Figure 11.5).

13 • Add a description of the domain if desired.

14 • If you have a direct network link to the external domain, enter the UNC path to the domain database in the UNC Path field. This will establish a direct link to the external domain when you close the dialog box. If you entered this information in the Create dialog box, it will appear here. If you leave this field blank, you will need to create a gateway link using the Link Configuration Tool. The LCT was covered extensively in Chapter 10, and creating gateway links will be covered in Chapter 19.

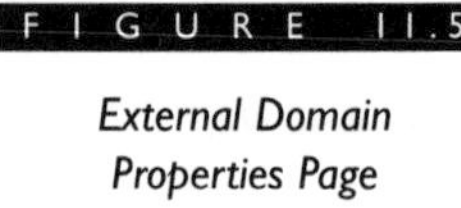
FIGURE 11.5

External Domain Properties Page

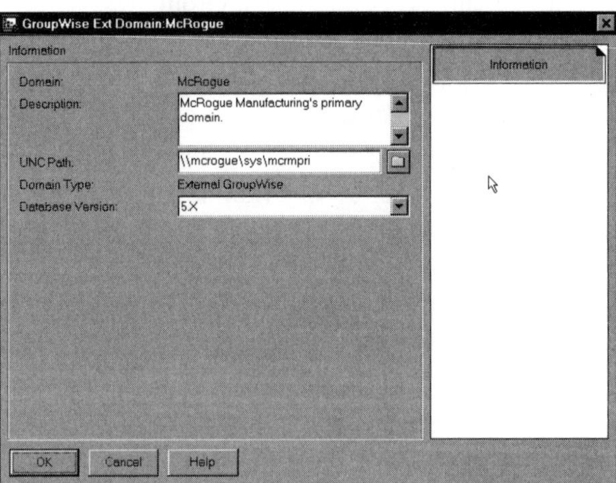

Repeat the preceding steps to define the other domains in the external system. If the other domains will link via indirect links through the connecting domain, leave the UNC Path field blank (Step 14) and create the indirect links in the Link Configuration Tool.

If you are using a direct link to the other system and its server is located in your NDS tree, grant file system rights to the other system's domain directory to the GWACCESS user. This will allow your MTA to authenticate to the other domain directory. You will likely need to work with the other system's administrator to have these rights granted to your GWACCESS user.

If the other system's domains are in a separate tree (which will be the majority of cases), the other system administrator must create a user in their domain server's bindery context with the exact same name (GWACCESS) and password.

TIP

The best and easiest method of linking domains in separate NDS trees is to use TCP/IP.

Creating an External Post Office

The next step in setting up messaging to an external GroupWise system is defining the external system's post offices. Again, this is done from the GroupWise view using NetWare Administrator.

The steps for creating external post offices are as follows:

1. From the GroupWise view, right-click on the external domain that will contain the post office you are defining and select Create.
2. Highlight External Post Office and click on OK. The Create External GroupWise Post Office dialog box appears (see Figure 11.6).
3. Enter the name of the external post office. Note: This name must match *exactly* the name of the post office in the external system.
4. Verify that the correct external domain name appears in the External Domain field.
5. Select the time zone of the post office.
6. (Optional) If you want to enter a description of the external post office, choose the Define Additional Properties check box.

7 • Click on Create. If you selected the Define Additional Properties option, you will be prompted to enter the description. After you enter this information click on OK.

FIGURE 11.6

Create External Post Office

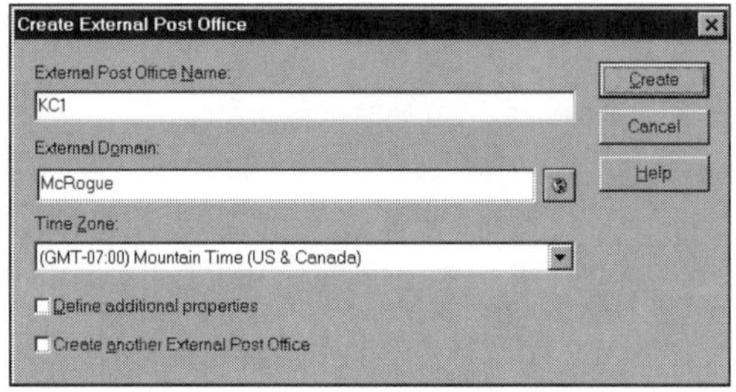

The post office will appear subordinate to the external domain in the GroupWise view.

Adding External Users

Before you set up automatic synchronization to occur between the two systems, or if you want to manually administer the user information from the external system, you can create users in the external post offices with the GroupWise view. This information is added only to the GroupWise databases in your system, not NDS.

NOTE

If you are going to set up automatic synchronization with the external system, you do not need to follow the steps explained in this section. You can skip ahead to the "Synchronizing the Systems" section later in this chapter.

This approach is useful if only some of the external system's users need to appear in your system's Address Book; otherwise, skip to the next section to find out how to set up automatic synchronization with the external system.

1 • From the GroupWise view, right-click on the external post office.

2 • Click on Create.

3 • Highlight External User and click on OK. The Create External User dialog box appears (see Figure 11.7).

4 • Enter the GroupWise user name. This must match the GroupWise mailbox ID in the external system.

5 • Verify that the correct post office is listed.

6 • (Optional) If you want to define additional information about the user, such as the user's telephone number or network address, click on the Define Additional Properties option. The additional properties are for informational purposes only. The information will appear in the Address Book in your system.

7 • (Optional) If you want to enter specific GroupWise account information, click on the GroupWise Account button and change the information. This should be unnecessary in most cases.

8 • Click on OK. The external GroupWise user will appear in the external post office and be added to the Address Books throughout your system.

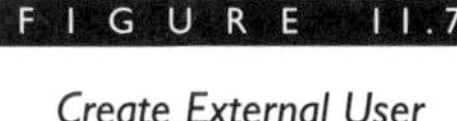

FIGURE 11.7

Create External User

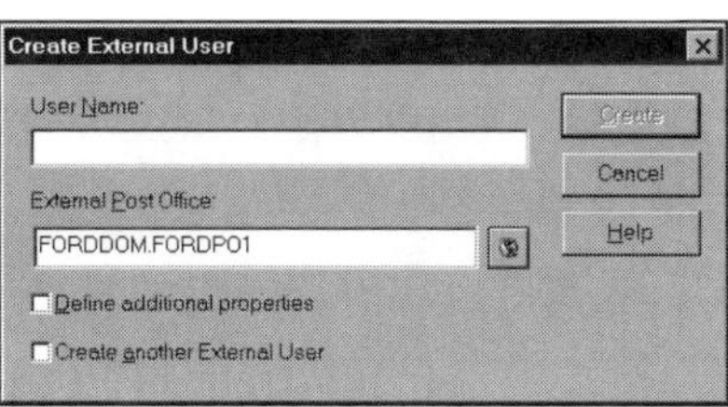

If the other administrator sends you an exported file of the other system's users for updating into your Address Book, don't be afraid to delete the external users and then import them. Remember, you are not deleting any mailboxes or actual users, just your *representation* of them.

Exporting Users

If you are setting up a connection to an external GroupWise 4.x system, or if you will not be using the user synchronization options in GroupWise 5, you can use the manual export and import features to keep user information in sync. If you choose to use this method, you will have to exchange export files with the external system's administrator on a regular basis. For information on exporting and importing user information in GroupWise 4, see *Novell's GroupWise 4 Administrator's Guide*, published by Novell Press and IDG Books Worldwide.

Follow these steps to export GroupWise information to an export file:

1 • From the NetWare Administrator view, use Ctrl-click or Shift-click to select the users you want to export. (Don't use the GroupWise view, because you can't select more than one user.)

2 • Click on Tools, GroupWise Utilities, and Export. The GroupWise Export dialog box appears (see Figure 11.8).

3 • Make the following selections:

- For the NDS/GroupWise class, select Users from the drop-down list.
- Select the post office that the users belong to.
- Enter the name of the Export file in the Export File field. (Suggestion: name the export file after the name of the post office, e.g., SALESPO.TXT.)
- In the Class Attributes field, use Ctrl-click to select all items that have an exclamation point. These are the required fields. Select any other fields that should display in the receiving system's Address Book.
- In the Starting Context field, click on the browse button to go to the context containing the objects you selected above.

4 • Now that you have specified the export parameters, save these parameters in a configuration file by using these steps:

a. Click on the Save button under the Configuration field.

b. Enter the path and name for the configuration file. (Suggestion: Use the name of the post office with the .CFG extension, e.g., SALESPO.CFG.)

c. Click on OK to save the configuration file.

5 • Begin exporting by clicking on the Run button. The information you specified will be added to the export file.

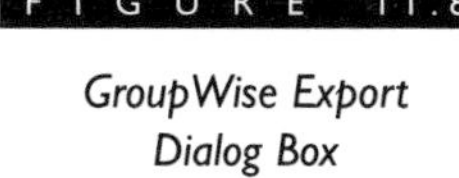
FIGURE 11.8

GroupWise Export Dialog Box

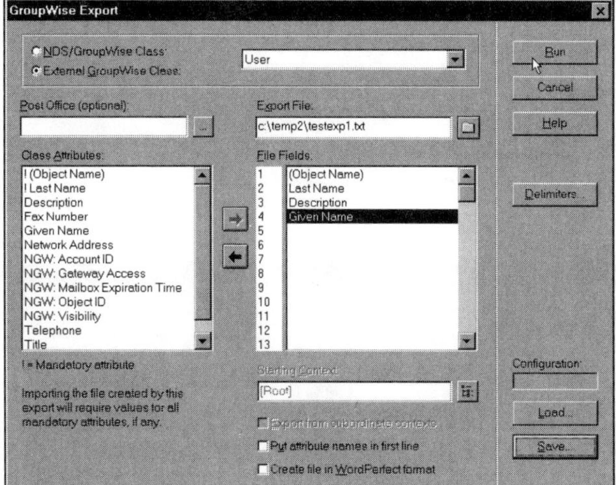

Importing Users

When you need to import Address Book information from the other system, you will need both the .TXT export file and the .CFG import file.

To import a file that you have received from the other system, follow these steps:

1 • Click on Tools, GroupWise Utilities, and Import. The GroupWise Import dialog box appears (see Figure 11.9).

2 • Click on the Load button, browse to the location of the configuration file, highlight it, and select OK.

3 • Click on the browse button next to the Import File field, locate the import file, and choose OK.

4 • Click on External GroupWise Class and choose Yes when prompted to keep the field assignments the same.

5 • Click on Post Office and highlight the name of the external post office to which the users will be added.

6 • Specify the post office that will receive the information.

7 • Click on Run to import the information.

8 • Open the GroupWise view and click on the external post office. The users should show in the bottom windows.

9 • Double-click on any of the imported users to see the imported information.

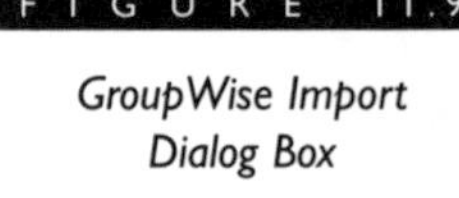

FIGURE 11.9

GroupWise Import Dialog Box

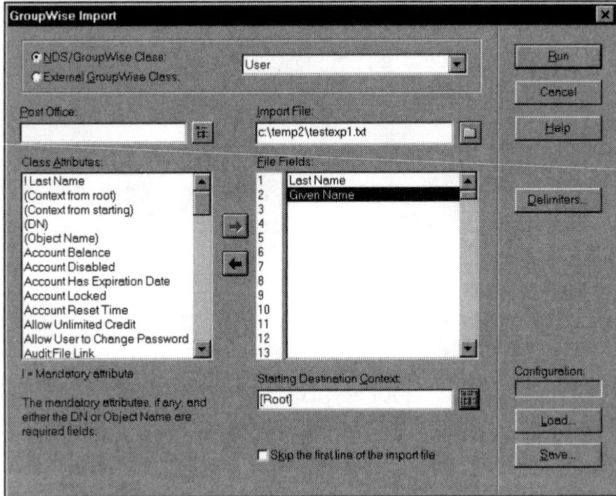

Synchronizing the Systems

The ability to synchronize information with an external GroupWise system is new to GroupWise 5. Both systems must be using GroupWise 5.

As the system administrator for your domains, you define what information you want to send from your system to the external system and what information you want to receive from the external system (users, resources and/or distribution lists).

IMPORTANT

Synchronization information is defined at the system level, not the domain level.

To define synchronization, follow these steps:

1 • From the main NDS window (not the GroupWise view screen), click on Tools.

2 • Click on GroupWise System Operations.

3 • Double-click on the External System Synchronization icon. The External System Synchronization dialog box appears (see Figure 11.10).

FIGURE 11.10

External System Synchronization

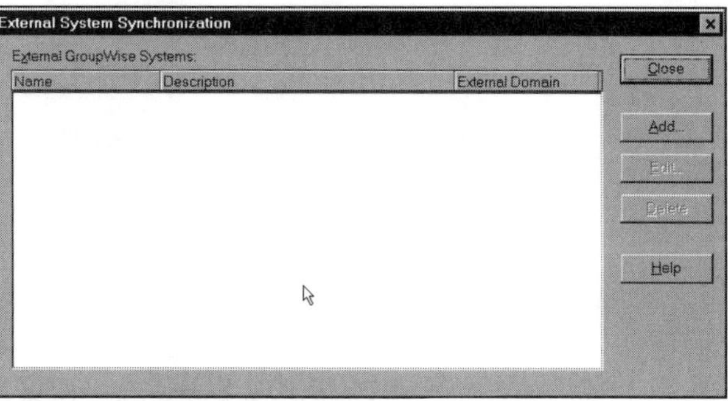

4 • Click on Add. The Add External GroupWise System dialog box appears (see Figure 11.11).

5 • Enter the name of the external system. You will need to obtain this information from the external system's administrator.

6 • Enter a description of the external system.

FIGURE 11.11

Add External GroupWise System

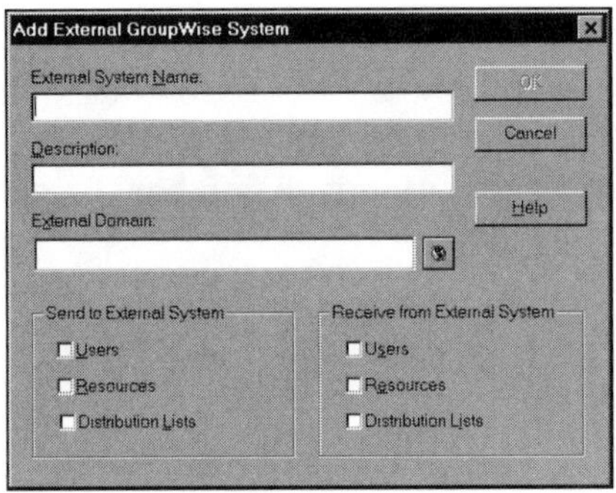

7 • Click on the icon next to the External Domain field. A list of external domains that you have defined appears in the Select GroupWise Object dialog box (see Figure 11.12).

FIGURE 11.12

Select GroupWise Object

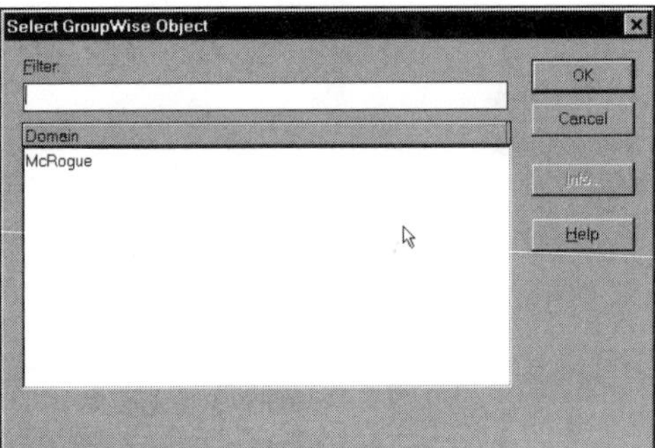

If you highlight a domain in this dialog box and click on Info, a dialog box listing extensive information about this domain appears (see Figure 11.11).

8 • Double-click on the external domain that is serving as the connecting domain in the external system.

9 • In the Send to External System area of the Add External GroupWise System dialog box, click on the boxes next to the information you want to send to the external domain.

10 • In the Receive from External System area of the dialog box, select the information you want to receive from the external system.

11 • Click on OK.

12 • Click on Close to exit from the External System Synchronization dialog box.

13 • Click Close to exit from the GroupWise System Operations dialog box.

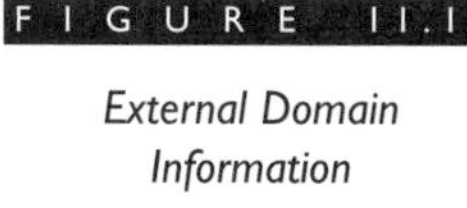
FIGURE 11.13

External Domain Information

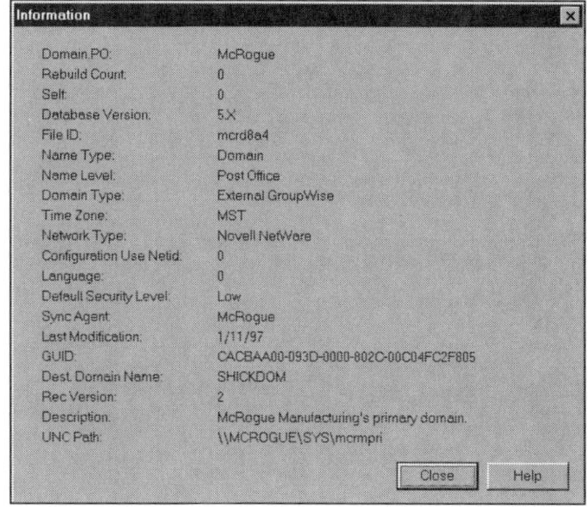

IMPORTANT

Both system administrators must have completed all synchronization options before they both complete the next steps.

After you have set synchronization options, you have to manually initiate synchronization the first time. To manually initiate a synchronization, follow these steps:

1 • Go to the main NetWare Administrator view (i.e., not the GroupWise view).

2 • Use Ctrl-click to select the users that need to be synchronized.

3 • Click on Tools.

4 • Click on GroupWise Utilities.

5 • Click on Synchronization and choose Yes to synchronize the information.

When you click on Yes, NWAdmin generates an administration message to the external GroupWise system that begins the synchronization process. The ADAs for the connecting domains exchange synchronization information, and the information is replicated to other domains and post offices in both systems. Of course, this information is passed through the link that you set up earlier.

When synchronization is established, user information from the external system (and any other information you requested) will be added to the GroupWise databases in your system. If you go into the GroupWise view, you will see the external users in the external post office you created previously. (But be patient, it will take a little while for this to occur after the systems begin the synchronization process.)

Message Flow Between Domains

Message flow between external domains is identical to the message flow between domains in the same GroupWise system.

See Chapter 9 for diagrams explaining the message flow between domains linked by direct network links. See Chapter 20 for diagrams explaining the message flow between domains linked by gateway links.

Summary

In this chapter you learned how to enable communication with an external GroupWise system by configuring external GroupWise domains. You also learned how to establish automatic synchronization between two systems that are both using GroupWise 5.

In the next chapter, we'll explain how to customize and optimize the GroupWise agents.

PART IV

Advanced Administration

CHAPTER 12

Customizing the GroupWise Agents

In this chapter we'll look at all three GroupWise agents—POA, MTA and ADA—together in one place. We have discussed the agents in several different contexts so far, but we have yet to explore each of the agents in depth.

We'll begin with a refresher course on each of the agents and then proceed to discuss each individual agent in detail. We will explain how to load the agents and discuss each agent's NDS properties and startup options. We'll also explain methods for optimizing the performance of the agents.

Review of the GroupWise Agents

When you first start working as a GroupWise system administrator, you may wonder why the system has separate agents. Some novice administrators even conclude that the sole purpose of the various agents must be to make their lives more complicated.

That conclusion couldn't be farther from the truth. In fact, having separate agents is beneficial for a number of reasons:

- *Fault Tolerance.* If one agent stops working the others continue to process messages.
- *Efficiency.* Since the GroupWise agents are multitasking, as the POA is delivering messages, the MTA can be transferring message files.
- *Optimization.* There are many different thread, scan rate, and timeout switches unique to each agent.
- *Load Balancing.* You can load multiple agents on behalf of the same GroupWise component and dedicate them to a specific task. For example, you can create and load a POA that does nothing but client/server connections.

Before discussing the agents in detail, let's review the primary functions of each.

The *post office agent* (POA) is responsible for delivering messages into the information store databases and directories, and other ancillary tasks, such as Quick Finder indexing for GroupWise Document Management. The POA (the workhorse of the GroupWise system) interacts directly with the information store. It handles a wider variety of tasks than any other GroupWise agent. A sound understanding of how the POA works is critical to successfully administering a GroupWise system.

The *message transfer agent* (MTA) has the least demanding role of the three GroupWise agents. It just moves message files from one directory (input queue) to another (output queue). Messages that move between post offices, domains, and gateways are moved by the MTA, as are any administrative confirmation, replication, or error messages.

The *administration agent* (ADA) is responsible for synchronizing NDS with the GroupWise domain databases, and for synchronizing the GroupWise domain and post office databases. It also creates all administration, replication, confirmation, and error messages. The ADA keeps the GroupWise directory store databases (user Address Books) synchronized and current.

In addition to the agents themselves, you should be familiar with a set of library routines shared by all three agents. These routines are known as the *GWENN1 Module*. The first agent loads GWENN1; subsequent agents use GWENN1, which is stored in memory. GWENN1 has the following responsibilities:

- Database management
- Message handling
- Thread management
- Semaphores (file and record locking)
- Date and time services

You'll see the GWENN1.NLM loaded one time on every server running a GroupWise agent (or gateway). The GWENN1.NLM is the "glue" that holds the GroupWise NLMs together on a particular server.

Post Office Agent

The POA is responsible for the following actions:

- *Local message delivery.* The POA places the messages into the information store databases and directories.
- *Creating status messages.* As it delivers messages, the POA creates a "Delivered" status message in the WPCSIN directory so the MTA can transfer it to the originating post office.
- *Information store maintenance.* The POA performs user and message database maintenance, checking the integrity and structure of the databases each time it delivers a message. When the administrator chooses the Information Store Maintenance option from the Tools menu in NetWare Administrator, task messages are sent to the POA to perform the actual maintenance. Database maintenance is covered in Chapter 13.
- *Client/server requests.* Workstations running the GroupWise client in Client/Server mode connect to the POA using TCP/IP. The POA handles all client/server requests and delivers the messages using the TCP/IP connection to the workstation. Client/Server mode is discussed more fully in Chapter 15.
- *Miscellaneous activities.* The POA runs the Quick Finder indexing for GroupWise Document Management (Chapter 17), executes rules set up by the end users, and creates a number of log files to catalog the activities of the POA.

Viewing a POA Object's Properties

By default, one POA is created for each post office. To *view* the POA object properties for a post office, double-click on the Post Office object in NetWare Administrator. The POA for the post office will appear as a subordinate object.

There are four property pages for a Post Office Agent (POA) object in addition to the main Information page:

- Agent Settings
- Log Settings
- Scheduled Events
- Network Address

The POA object's Information page contains a description of the POA and identifies its platform (see Figure 12.1).

FIGURE 12.1

POA Information Page

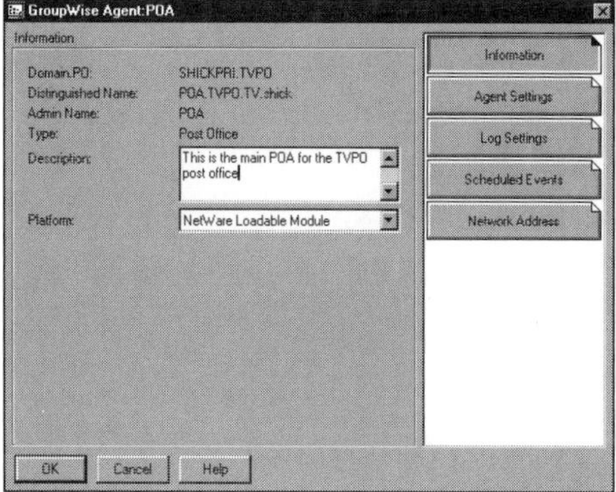

The Agent Settings page, shown in Figure 12.2, contains numerous settings for the POA.

Table 12.1 describes each of the settings you can adjust on the Agent Settings page.

FIGURE 12.2

Agent Settings Page

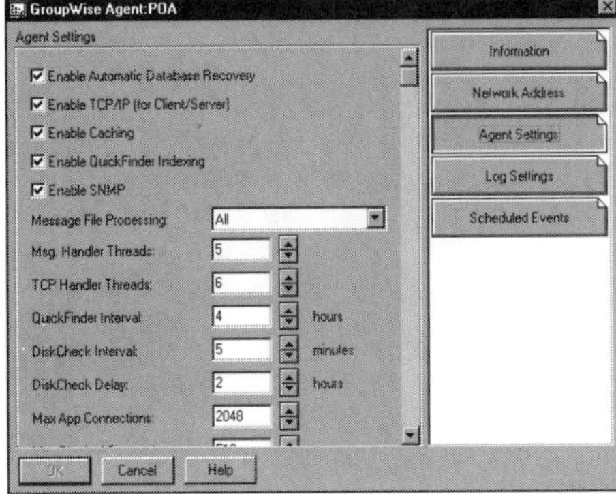

TABLE 12.1

POA Settings

SETTING	DESCRIPTION	DEFAULT VALUE
Automatic DB Recovery	Automatically rebuild and recover damaged user and message databases	Enabled
Enable TCP/IP	Client/server connections	Enabled
Enable Caching	Cache data to be written to the information store	Enabled
Message File Processing	Use this POA to deliver messages to the information store	Enabled
Total Threads	Message handlers used to scan queues and update message and user databases	5
Quick Finder Interval	Period to update Quick Finder Index	4 Hours
Disk Check Interval	Period to check for available disk space	5 Minutes
Disk Check Delay	After the first notification, wait this period of time before notifying the administrator of the disk alert	2 Hours
Max Physical Connections	Maximum number of TCP/IP connections for client/server	512
Max App Connections	Maximum number of application connections (virtual connections) for client/server	2048
CPU Utilization (NLM)	Threshold percent for utilization on the NetWare server. The POA will not cause the server to go above this utilization percentage	65

TABLE 12.1

POA Settings (continued)

SETTING	DESCRIPTION	DEFAULT VALUE
Delay Time	Period of time the POA will "sleep," waiting for the utilization to decrease	400 ms
Enable SMP (NLM)	For Symmetric Multi-Processing NetWare servers	Enabled
Enable SNMP	Register this POA NLM with applications that use the Simple Network Management Protocol (such as ManageWise)	Enabled

On the Log Settings page, you can modify the log path, age (that is, the number of days old log files are kept; the default is seven); size (the amount of disk space to be used by all POA log files; the default is 1024K); and level of logging (the amount of information logged) for the POA log files. These are stored in the path specified in the Log Path property, or in <*postoffice*>\WPCSOUT\OFS by default (see Figure 12.3).

FIGURE 12.3

Log Settings Page

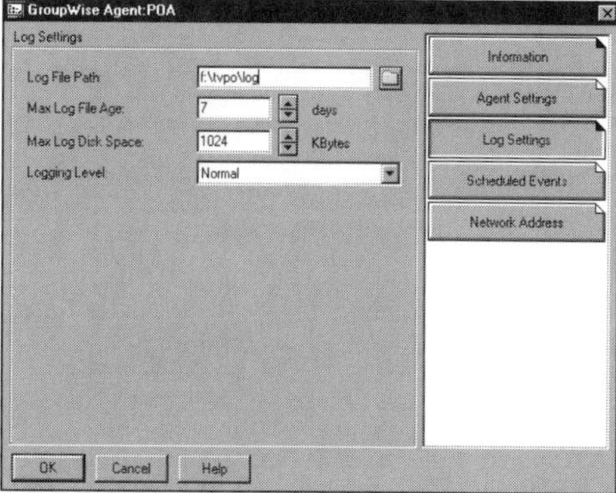

The Network Address page contains a definition of the TCP/IP address associated with the POA. This is the address used in client/server connections, discussed in Chapter 15. To add the TCP/IP address, click on the Add button and enter the TCP/IP address and port number (1677 by default), or enter the name of the server as it is known in Domain Name Services (the Internet process that resolves an Internet domain name, such as shickfs1.shicktools.com, with an IP address). Figure 12.4 shows an example of the Network Address page.

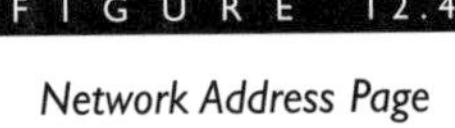

FIGURE 12.4

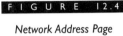

Network Address Page

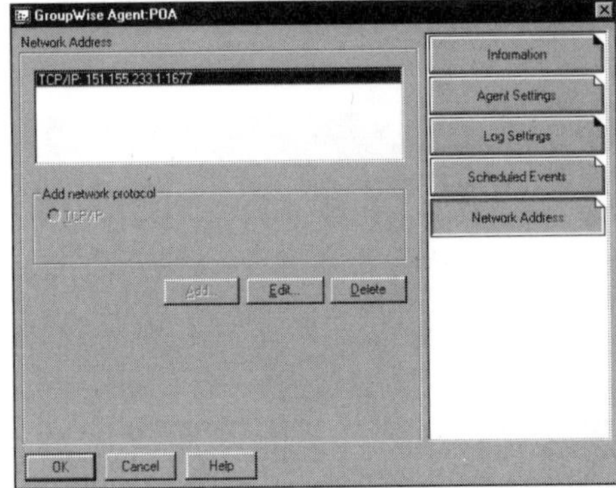

With the Scheduled Events page you can view, modify, create, and enable or disable Scheduled Events for the POA (see Figure 12.5). See Chapter 14 for more information about Scheduled Events for the POA and other agents.

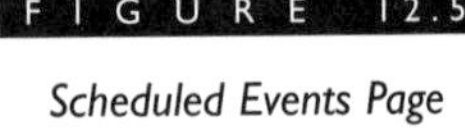

FIGURE 12.5

Scheduled Events Page

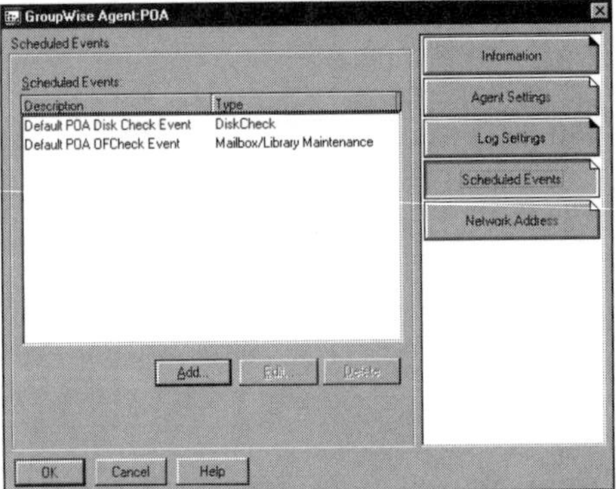

Editing Startup Files

Startup files are created during the installation of the GroupWise agents. Each agent has a template startup file that contains all of the options available for that agent. The template startup file for the POA is STARTUP.POA.

When you install the agents, the template startup file is used to automatically create a startup file for the post office you specify during installation. For example, suppose you were to install the agents for your sales department's post office (named SALESPO). The startup file would be named SALESPO.POA. This file contains the default options required in order to load the POA for the SALESPO post office.

You should not use the original STARTUP.POA file to load your POA. This is the template startup file. Instead, use the startup file that is automatically created, or make a working copy with a meaningful name (for example, SALESPO.POA).

The startup file is an ASCII file that can be edited with any text editor. Using a switch in the startup file is the same as entering the startup switches on the command line. An advantage to using the startup files is that you can use comments to explain what a particular switch does. The semicolon (;) is a comment character. To enable a switch, remove the semicolon and fill in any required information, such as a directory path. When you fill in information and remove the semicolon, be sure to remove the brackets from the comment line as well.

Settings in NetWare Administrator and the startup file may conflict with each other. The startup file switches take precedence over the settings you choose in NetWare Administrator. For example, if you set the logging level to normal on the Log Settings property page in NetWare Administrator but then added the `/loglevel-verbose` switch to the startup file, the POA would use verbose logging. You can change a number of these settings right from the POA screen on the server console, but they are not saved unless they are added to the startup file.

Most settings can also be adjusted in NetWare Administrator. If a setting is changed in NetWare Administrator while the agent is running, a restart message will be sent to the agent. It will then restart making the new setting take effect without reading the startup file. When the agent is reloaded, the new setting is overridden with the startup file switch.

The startup file is only read when you *load* the agent at the server prompt. The startup file is not read again each time you *restart* the agent (with the Restart option). Consequently, in order to initiate changes to the startup file, you must completely exit and reload the agent.

You can edit the startup file directly from the POA screen on the server console by pressing F10 and selecting Edit Startup File. Remember, though, that you will have to exit and restart the agent for the changes to take effect.

Optimizing the POA

This section examines in detail the STARTUP.POA file created when the agents are installed. The file includes all of the startup switches for the POA.

The STARTUP.POA file is divided into two sections:

- Settings you can only modify using startup switches
- Settings that you should adjust with NetWare Administrator (but that can also be determined with startup switches)

The first part of the startup file contains the startup-file-only switches; the second part contains the settings that should be modified in NetWare Administrator.

TIP

As a general rule, we recommend you make most changes to the agents using NetWare Administrator, instead of editing the startup files. This allows other administrators centralized access to the options for the agents, and it is a much easier method of customizing the agents when compared to editing many different startup files. However, some switches can only be modified in the startup file, such as `/user` and `/password`.

Startup-File-Only POA Switches

The startup-file-only switches can only be set by editing the POA's startup file. Other settings are configured using NetWare Administrator. (The other settings are discussed in the following section.) Switches unique to the startup file for the POA are explained in Table 12.2.

TABLE 12.2

Startup-File-Only POA Switches

SWITCH	DESCRIPTION
`/home-\\[server]\[volume]\[directory]`	Required NetWare path to the post office directory
`/name-[string]`	Name of POA object to read configuration information from. If the post office has been set up with different configurations through NetWare Administrator, the `/name` switch *must be used* to specify which configuration this instance the POA should use.
`/convert`	Converts GroupWise 4.x databases to GroupWise 5.x format
`/noconfig`	Do not read any configuration information from the database; use only the settings in the startup file.
`/language-[ US | DE | JP ]`	Two-letter language code
`/noerrormail`	Do not send error messages to the defined administrator
`/user-[user ID]`	Distinguished name of the GroupWise access account
`/password-[password]`	Case-sensitive password of the GroupWise access account

NetWare Administrator Settings

Switches in the second part of the startup file affect the following features of the POA:

- Performance
- Event logging
- Client/server
- Message file processing

These switches are for settings that should be modified using NetWare Administrator, but they can also be adjusted in the startup file. Table 12.3 describes each of these switches.

TABLE 12.3

Switches Corresponding to NetWare Administrator Settings

SWITCH	DESCRIPTION
/cpu-[percentage]	CPU utilization threshold level
/sleep-[milli-seconds]	Time interval the POA sleeps when CPU threshold is reached
/nosmp	Disable Symmetric Multi-Processing (SMP) (Enabled by default)
/nosnmp	Disable Simple Network Management Protocol (SNMP) (Enabled by default)
/loglevel-[Normal | Verbose]	Selects error logging only (Normal) or more details (Verbose)
/logdiskoff	Disables writing log file to disk
/log-\\[server]\ [volume]\[directory]	Path for log files
/logdays-[days]	How long (number of days) a log file resides on the disk before being automatically deleted
/logmax-[K]	Determines the maximum disk space (kilobytes) used for all log files
/threads-[number]	Sets how many threads the POA spawns. The default is 5.
/nocache	Disables database caching feature. Use this option if you are running NFS, if your backup system cannot back up open files, or if your LAN file server is not stable.
/norecover	Disables automatic online database repairs
/qfinterval-[hours]	Time interval (in hours) for updating the Quick Finder indexes. The default is 4 hours and the minimum is 1 hour.
/notcpip	Disables processing of client/server requests from users in the post office
/port-[number]	Specifies the port number that the POA will check for client/server requests. The default port is 1677.
/iploglevel-[Normal, Verbose]	Amount of information logged for a TCP/IP link to the post office. The default is Normal. Short syntax: /ipll
/maxappconns-[number]	Number of client/server application connections the server will allow. The default is 2048.

TABLE 12.3

Switches Corresponding to NetWare Administrator Settings (continued)

SWITCH	DESCRIPTION
`/maxphysconns-[number]`	Number of physical client/server connections the server will allow. The default is 512.
`/nomf`	Disables directory scanning for all incoming message files
`/nomflow`	Disables directory scanning for low-priority message files
`/nomfhigh`	Disables directory scanning for high-priority message files

Loading the POA

Loading the POA is accomplished by entering the following command at the server prompt:

```
LOAD GWPOA @<postoffice>.POA
```

Loading the POA can be done from either the server's console or by loading the Remote Console (RCONSOLE) utility of NetWare.

To use RCONSOLE, follow these steps:

1. At the server prompt, type the following two commands to enable RCONSOLE:

   ```
   LOAD REMOTE <password>
   ```

   ```
   LOAD RSPX
   ```

2. Type `RCONSOLE` at a DOS command prompt. You may get a warning about RCONSOLE causing Windows to behave erratically.

3. Select the desired file server from the list and press Enter. You will be prompted for your RCONSOLE password.

4 • After entering the password, you'll see the file server console. You can then use the keyboard commands listed in Table 12.4 to navigate through RCONSOLE.

TABLE 12.4

RCONSOLE Navigation Keys

FUNCTION KEY	PURPOSE
Alt-F1	RCONSOLE menu
Alt-F2	Exit RCONSOLE
Alt-F3	Toggle forward through NLM screens
Alt-F4	Toggle backward through NLM screens

Viewing the POA Screen

When you view the POA screen (after toggling through the other screens or selecting it from the list of screens to view from the RCONSOLE menu), you can tell a lot about what the POA is actually doing after the agent has been loaded.

The POA screen, shown in Figure 12.6, is divided into three main sections:

- Status
- Statistics
- Log display

FIGURE 12.6

POA Screen

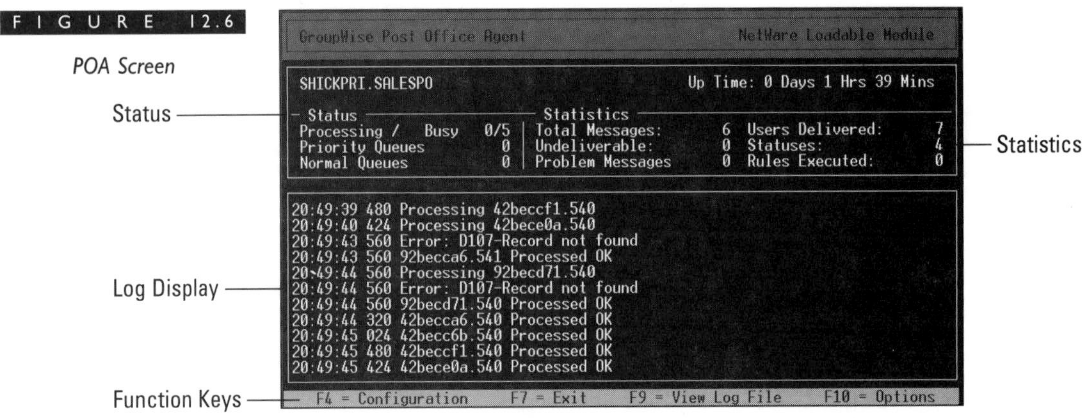

Status

The status portion of the POA screen displays a summary of the activity that the POA is performing during the current session.

- *Processing.* This indicator tells you whether the process is still active.
- *Busy.* This is a ratio of busy message-handlers to available message-handlers. Message-handlers are subprocesses that scan the input queues for the POA.
- *Normal Queues.* This is the number of messages waiting in <PO>\WPCSOUT\OFS\2–7 directories.
- *Priority Queues.* This is the number of messages waiting in the <PO>\WPCSOUT\OFS\0–1 directories.

By viewing the status area of the POA you can tell at a glance whether the POA is active and how many messages are waiting to be processed. If there is a problem, the Busy indicator will be very slow or even stopped, and the number of messages in the queues will either decrease slowly, stay the same, or increase.

Statistics

The statistics area of the POA screen displays a summary of the messaging activity the POA has performed throughout a session. It contains the following information:

- *Total Messages.* The total number of message files processed by the POA since the POA was loaded.
- *Undeliverable.* The number of messages that couldn't be delivered because a database was closed, the index was incorrect, or some other structural reason. The problem was probably fixed by the POA, using its ability to rebuild and repair databases.
- *Problem Messages.* These are message with a corruption in the message file itself. They are kept in the <PO>\WPCSOUT\PROBLEM directory. Normally, these messages are sent to the administrator for the domain as attachments.

- *Users Delivered.* The number of user databases that were updated with pointers to messages in the message databases. This is helpful, because it is a truer indication of the traffic on the post office, as the messages exist only once per post office.
- *Statuses.* When the POA delivers a message, it also creates a status message. This is the tally of status messages created by the POA.
- *Rules Executed.* GroupWise rules are server-based, and the POA is the server process that executes the rules.

The statistics area is very useful for the administrator because it shows how busy the POA is performing different tasks (such as message processing, status delivery, and rules processing), and you can then determine whether you need to possibly load additional instances of the POA to distribute this task load across multiple POAs. Creating and loading multiple POAs is discussed in Chapter 15.

Log Display

This is an active display of what the POA is doing at the moment. The amount of information in this portion of the POA varies, depending on the logging level you have chosen: Normal, Verbose, or Off.

If you have set the logging level to *Normal*, the screen displays the configuration information on startup and when a message is processed. It gives the message file number, but not the name of the recipient. This is a good setting for a typical POA that functions properly.

When you set the logging level to *Verbose*, the screen displays user information as the databases are updated, and it includes the most complete logging information available for the POA. This setting is useful when you are first bringing up the POA. It provides as much troubleshooting information as possible.

You can also turn off logging completely in NetWare Administrator. However, we recommended that you do not turn off logging.

Additional logging options for client/server activity are covered in Chapter 15.

Using the POA Screen

A description of the function keys appears at the bottom of the POA screen. The function keys can be used to perform the following tasks:

- **F4.** Displays the current configuration being used, in a nice summary format.
- **F7 or Esc.** Exits and unloads the POA from memory.
- **F9.** Views the active log file. When Verbose logging is being used, you can see the POA scan the input queues.
- **F10.** Accesses the menu options in Table 12.5.

TABLE 12.5

POA Screen Menu Options

MENU OPTION	DESCRIPTION
View Log Files	View past log files stored on disk
Logging	Change the name of the log file, level, enabled or not, age, and disk space
Configuration	Display current configuration (Same as pressing F4)
Cycle Log	Close the current log file and open a new one
Actions	View the message file queues, enable or disable auto-rebuild of databases and Quick Finder options
Edit Startup File	Open an editor to change the current startup file

There are many more configuration options for client/server operation. Those options are discussed in Chapter 15. Options related to GroupWise Document Management are discussed in Chapter 17.

Message Transfer Agent

The GroupWise Message Transfer Agent (MTA) is the process that transports the messages to and from the following GroupWise components:

- Two post offices in the same domain

- Two domains
- A post office and a gateway in the same domain

The MTA can also move corrupt messages to a directory designated for problem messages. In addition, a special MTA can be set up for a *post office* to enable TCP/IP transfers to the post office. It handles the TCP/IP connection from the domain's MTA.

Viewing an MTA Object's Properties

By default, an MTA is created whenever a domain is created. The MTA object is a subordinate under the Domain object and can be accessed by double-clicking on the Domain object.

In addition to the Information page, an MTA object has the following property pages:

- Network Address
- Agent Settings
- Log Settings
- Message Logging

The MTA object's Information page contains a description of the MTA and identifies its platform.

The Network Address property page contains a definition of the TCP/IP address associated with the MTA. This address is used to connect two domains together using TCP/IP, or to use TCP/IP connections between post offices. To add the TCP/IP address, click on the Add button and enter the TCP/IP address and port number (7100 by default), or enter the name of the server as it is known in Domain Name Services.

The Agent Settings page, shown in Figure 12.7 contains numerous settings for the MTA.

FIGURE 12.7

Agent Settings Page

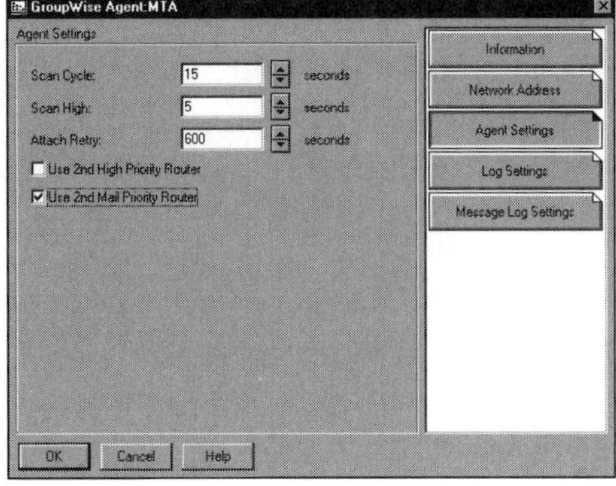

Table 12.6 describes each of the settings you can adjust on an MTA object's Agent Settings page.

TABLE 12.6

MTA Agent Settings the NetWare Administrator

SETTING	DESCRIPTION	DEFAULT VALUE
Scan Cycle	Interval that the MTA waits to check all WPCSIN\2–7 directories for messages	15 Seconds
Scan High	Interval that the MTA waits to check all WPCSIN\0–1 directories for messages	5 Seconds
Attach Retry	Interval that the MTA waits to open a connection to a closed component	600 Seconds
Use 2nd High Priority Mail Router	Adds a thread to handle high levels of Remote access or Busy Search activity	Disabled
Use 2nd Mail Priority Router	Adds a thread to handle higher levels of normal or administrative messages	Disabled

On the Log Settings page, you can modify settings for the MTA log files: the log path (location for the log files; <domain>\ MSLOCAL is the default); age (number of days old log files are kept); size of all MTA log files on the disk (1024 is the default); and level of logging (the amount of information stored in the log files).

The Message Logging page controls application programming hooks into GroupWise activity. These settings are discussed in Chapter 22.

Optimizing the MTA

This section examines in detail the STARTUP.MTA file created when the agents are installed. This file includes all of the startup switches for the MTA.

The STARTUP.MTA file is divided into two sections:

- Settings you can only modify using switches in the startup file
- Settings that you should adjust with NetWare Administrator (but that can also be determined with startup switches)

The first part of the MTA startup file contains the MTA startup-file-only switches; the second part contains the switches for settings that should be modified in NetWare Administrator.

MTA Startup-File-Only Switches

The settings available only as startup switches control the following kinds of functions handled by the MTA:

- General
- NLM-specific
- NT-specific
- Running mode (address lookup, post office, backup)
- TCP/IP Transport Module

Table 12.7 explains the switches in the first part of the MTA startup file.

TABLE 12.7

MTA's Startup-File-Only Switches

SWITCH	DESCRIPTION
/home-\\[server]\[volume]\[directory]	Required NetWare path to the domain directory
/work-\\[server]\[volume]\[directory]	MTA work directory (If not specified the MTA will create the MSLOCAL directory under the domain directory.)
/language-[US | DE | JP]	Two-letter language code
/noerrormail	Do not send error messages to the defined administrator
/user-[user ID]	Distinguished name of the GroupWise access account
/password-[password]	Case-sensitive password of the GroupWise access account
/nosmp	Disable Symmetric Multi-Processing (SMP) (The MTA is SMP-enabled by default.)
/nosnmp	Disable Simple Network Management Protocol (SNMP) (The MTA is SNMP-enabled by default.)
/activelog	Display the active log window initially (For Windows NT agent only)
/postoffice	Run on behalf of a post office so that TCP/IP communication can be used between domain and post office (The /home switch needs to point to the post office directory if this switch is used.) Short syntax: /post
/addresslookup	The MTA looks up users from the domain database if no domain.po is specified in the address.
/hubgate	Designates this MTA as a hub gate
/backup	Designates this MTA as the backup MTA
/primary	Designates this MTA as the primary MTA
/heartbeat-[minutes]	Sets the time (in minutes) after which the backup MTA becomes active if the primary MTA stops responding. The default is 5 minutes.
/tcpboot	Allows the TCP/IP Transport Module to be loaded even if there are no outgoing links configured. Short syntax: /tcpb

(continued)

TABLE 12.7

MTA's Startup-File-Only Switches (continued)

SWITCH	DESCRIPTION
/tcptransport-[path]	Path to the GroupWise TCP/IP transport module (symbiont) Short syntax: /tcptm Alternate syntax: /tcpsymbiont
/tcpinbound-[connections]	Maximum inbound TCP/IP connections
/tcpport-[portnumber]	TCP Port for incoming connections (The default is 7100)
/notcpscreen	Do not provide a separate screen for the TCP/IP Transport Module
/tcptrunkwidth-[number]	Number of sending threads dedicated for each TCP/IP link, from 1 to 4. (The default is 1.) Short syntax: /tcpt or /tcptrunk
/tcpwaitconnect-[seconds]	The maximum time MTA waits for a TPC/IP connection to another MTA
/tcpwaitdata-[seconds]	The maximum time MTA attempts to send data
/tracelogin-[1] [2]	Displays MTA login messages on the console to help determine problems the MTA is having when logging into a remote server. [1] displays login problems; [2] displays all login messages Short syntax: /tl

NetWare Administrator Settings

Switches in the second part of the MTA startup file affect the following features of the MTA:

- Event logging
- Performance
- Message logging

These switches are for settings that should be modified using NetWare Administrator, but they can also be adjusted in the startup file. Table 12.8 describes each of these switches.

TABLE 12.8

Switches Corresponding to NetWare Administrator Settings

SWITCH	DESCRIPTION
/loglevel-[Normal | Verbose]	Selects error logging only (Normal) or more details (Verbose)
/logdiskoff	Disables writing log file to disk
/log-\\[server]\[volume]\[directory]	Path for log files
/logdays-[days]	How long (number of days) a log file resides on the disk before being automatically deleted
/logmax-[kb]	Determines the maximum disk space (kilobytes) used for all log files
/fast0	Routes priority 0 & 1 messages separately (Use if you have frequent remote access or Busy Search requests.)
/fast4	Routes priority 2–3 and 4–7 messages separately (Use if there are large numbers of high-priority messages.)
/cylo-[seconds]	Time in seconds to scan priority queues 2–7. The default is 15 seconds.
/cyhi-[seconds]	Time in seconds to scan priority queues 0–1. The default is 5 seconds.
/messagelogpath-\\[server]\[volume]\[directory]	Path for message log databases (See Chapter 14) Short syntax: /mlp-<path>
/messagelogsettings-[evrsoc]	Message logging settings. Include any combination of the following: e Enabled. This option has to be specified in order for message logging to be active. All mail messages are logged. v Verbose (Includes all information for the logged messages.) r Log delivery/nondelivery reports. s Log GroupWise statuses. o Log all other message types (e.g., administrative messages). c Correlate reports with messages. Short syntax: /mls-<settings>

We recommend using NetWare Administrator wherever possible to change these settings. You should only edit the startup file to change settings that aren't available in NetWare Administrator. This way, you can keep the majority of the settings under control by using one program (NetWare Administrator) instead of having to edit many different files.

Loading the MTA

To load the MTA, enter the following command at the server's console:

```
LOAD GWMTA @<domain>.MTA
```

Alternatively, you can run RCONSOLE, as described earlier in this chapter.

Viewing the MTA Screen

Once the MTA is loaded, you can get a lot of useful information about the MTA's performance from the MTA screen. (You view this screen on the server console.) The three main parts of the MTA screen, shown in Figure 12.8, are as follows:

- Status
- Statistics
- Log display

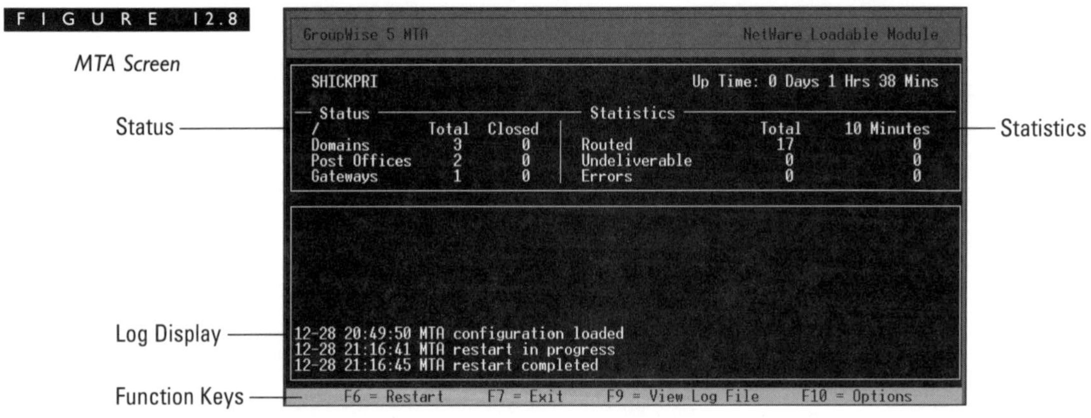

FIGURE 12.8

MTA Screen

Status

The status portion of the MTA screen displays the number of GroupWise facilities (domains, post offices, or gateways) the MTA is communicating (or not communicating) with.

- *Domains Total / Closed.* This is the total number of domains that have been defined. Closed domains cannot be reached by the MTA for some reason. Select Configuration Status under the Options menu for the closed domain to see the reason for the closure. Note: A transfer pull configuration will increment the domain count for the MTA.
- *Post Offices Total / Closed.* This is the number of post offices in this domain that this MTA has to pass messages between. Note: An additional post office will be counted if TCP/IP links are used as the protocol for the MTA to reach a post office. Refer to Chapter 10 for more information.
- *Gateways Total / Closed.* This is the number of gateways in this domain.

Statistics

The statistics portion of the screen displays numeric summaries of the messaging activity that has been performed by the MTA for the current session.

- *Routed.* This is the total number of messages processed by this MTA. The screen displays a total (since the MTA was first loaded), and the number of messages within the last ten minutes.
- *Undeliverable.* The number of undeliverable messages as a total and within the last ten minutes. When this happens, a message file is created and queued back to the sender as an undeliverable message. The sender can try again to send the message. Undeliverable messages are often the result of faulty addressing information. For example, perhaps the user addressed the message using an address stored in his or her personal Address Book, but the recipient's account information has changed since the address was initially stored.

- *Errors.* The number of messages (as a total and in the last ten minutes) that are corrupted in their format and sent to the domain's administrator as attachments with instructions on what to do with them. Usually, they can be placed back into a WPCSIN directory to give the MTA another shot at delivering the messages.

Information in the statistics area of the MTA screen is useful for monitoring the MTA's message load and for troubleshooting.

Log Display

Even if you change the logging level, the amount of information in the live log window of the MTA screen does not vary.

The log display provides important information about facilities (domains, post offices, and gateways) that have been closed for some reason. In addition, the log display gives the status of TCP/IP links (if applicable).

Using the MTA Screen

A description of the function keys appears at the bottom of the MTA screen. The function keys can be used to perform the following tasks:

- **F6.** Restarts the MTA, re-reading its configuration information from the domain database in the `/home` switch in the startup file. (Note: Restarting the MTA does not cause the startup file to be read again. To reload the startup, you must exit and reload the MTA.)

- **F7.** Exits and unloads the MTA from memory.

- **F9.** Switches to a static view of the current log file.

- **F10.** Accesses the menus for the MTA. The menu options are explained in Table 12.9.

TABLE 12.9
MTA Menu Options

MENU OPTION	DESCRIPTION
Configuration Status	Displays details; suspends or resumes any facility this MTA is communicating with
Active Log	Dynamic view of the current log file
View Log Files	Opens old MTA and TCP/IP log files
Log Settings	Changes Log Name, Level, Write to Disk, Age, and Space
Cycle Log	Opens a new log file
Edit Startup File	Opens the current startup file for the MTA

Administration Agent

The administration agent (ADA) performs the following tasks:

- Reads NDS for changes pertaining to GroupWise
- Synchronizes all GroupWise domain and post office databases
- Creates administrative messages (confirmation, replication, and error messages)
- Automatically repairs domain and post office databases

Viewing an ADA Object's Properties

By default, there is one ADA object created for every domain, and it has to update the domain and post office databases for the entire domain. (Creating additional ADA objects is explained in Chapter 9.) You will find the ADA object under the domain by double-clicking on the Domain object in NetWare Administrator. Double-click on the ADA object to access its property pages. In addition to the Information property page, an ADA object has the following three property pages:

- Agent Settings

- Log Settings
- Scheduled Events

The Information property page contains a description of the ADA object and identifies its platform.

The Agent Settings page, shown in Figure 12.9, has several settings.

FIGURE 12.9

ADA's Agent Settings Page

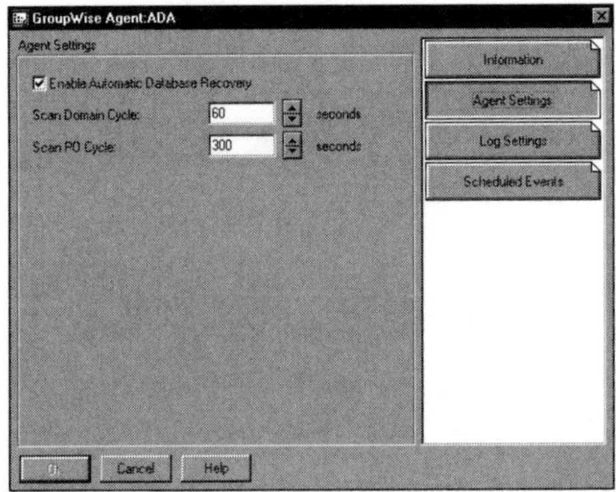

The Agent Settings for an ADA are explained in Table 12.10.

TABLE 12.10

ADA Settings

SETTING	DESCRIPTION	DEFAULT VALUE
`Enable Automatic Database Recovery`	Automatically recovers or rebuilds databases that have structural problems. (See Chapter 13)	Enabled
`Scan Domain Cycle`	Interval after which the <*domain*>WPCSOUT\ADS directories are scanned for messages.	60 Seconds
`Scan PO Cycle`	Interval after which the <*postoffice*>WPCSOUT\ADS directories are scanned for messages.	300 Seconds

On the Log Settings page, you can modify the log path (location), age (days to keep log files before automatically deleting them), size (total size in kilobytes for all ADA log files), and level of logging (amount of information).

On the ADA Scheduled Events page, you can view, modify, and create Scheduled Events for the ADA to automatically perform. The settings on the Scheduled Events page are discussed in more detail in Chapter 14.

Optimizing the ADA

This section examines in detail the STARTUP.ADA file created when the agents are installed. The file includes all of the startup switches for the ADA.

The STARTUP.ADA file, like the STARTUP.POA file and the STARTUP.MTA file, is divided into two sections:

- Settings you can only modify using startup switches
- Settings that you should adjust with NetWare Administrator (but that can also be determined with startup switches)

The first part of the startup file contains the ADA startup-file-only switches; the second part contains the switches for settings that should be modified in NetWare Administrator.

ADA Startup-File-Only Switches

Switches in the first part of the startup file control the following aspects of the ADA's performance:

- General
- NLM-specific

These switches are explained in Table 12.11.

TABLE 12.11

ADA's Startup-File-Only Switches

SWITCH	DESCRIPTION
/home-\\[server]\[volume]\[directory]	Required NetWare path to the domain (or post office) directory
/domain	Puts the ADA into Domain-Only mode. The /home switch must point to the domain directory with this switch.
/post	Puts the ADA into Post office–Only mode. The /home switch must point to the post office directory with this switch.
/language-[US | DE | JP]	Two-letter language code
/noerrormail	Do not send error messages to the defined administrator
/nondssync	Disable NDS User Synchronization
/user-[user ID]	Distinguished name of the GroupWise access account
/password-[password]	The case-sensitive password for the GroupWise access account
/nosmp	Disable Symmetric Multi-Processing (SMP) (SMP-enabled by default)
/nosnmp	Disable Simple Network Management Protocol (SNMP) (SNMP-enabled by default)

NetWare Administrator Settings

The second part of the startup file contains switches for settings that we recommend you modify from NetWare Administrator, but they are also available as startup switches. These switches affect the following aspects of the ADA:

- Event Logging
- Performance
- Operation Mode

Table 12.12 describes each of these switches.

TABLE 12.12

ADA Startup Switches Corresponding to NetWare Administrator Settings

SWITCH	DESCRIPTION
/loglevel-[Normal | Verbose]	Selects error logging only (Normal) or more details (Verbose)
/logdiskoff	Disables writing log file to disk
/log-\\[server]\[volume]\[directory]	Path for log files
/logdays-[days]	How long (number of days) a log file resides on the disk before being automatically deleted
/logmax-[kb]	Determines the maximum disk space (kilobytes) used for all log files
/dscan-[seconds]	Domain directory scanning interval
/pscan-[seconds]	Post office directory scanning interval
/norecover	Disables automatic online database repairs
/start1-[hh]:[mm] /end1-[hh]:[mm]	Idle times are entered using 24-hour time syntax. For example, to put the ADA into an idle state between 11:30 p.m. and 1:00 a.m., the following switches would be set: /start1-23:30 /end1-1:00 Using idle periods is necessary if your backup software cannot back up open files, for database maintenance, or administrative traffic control.
/start2-[hh]:[mm] /end2-[hh]:[mm]	Performs the same function as /start1 and /end1, but allows a second idle state time setting.

Loading the ADA

To load the ADA, enter the following command at the server prompt:

```
LOAD GWADA /@<domain>.ADA
```

Alternatively, you can use RCONSOLE to access the server.

Viewing the ADA Screen

To view the ADA screen, access the server console (by using RCONSOLE or physically going to the file server) and toggle through the NLM screens until the ADA screen is displayed.

The ADA screen, shown in Figure 12.10, is divided into three main parts:

- Status
- Statistics
- Log display

FIGURE 12.10

ADA Screen

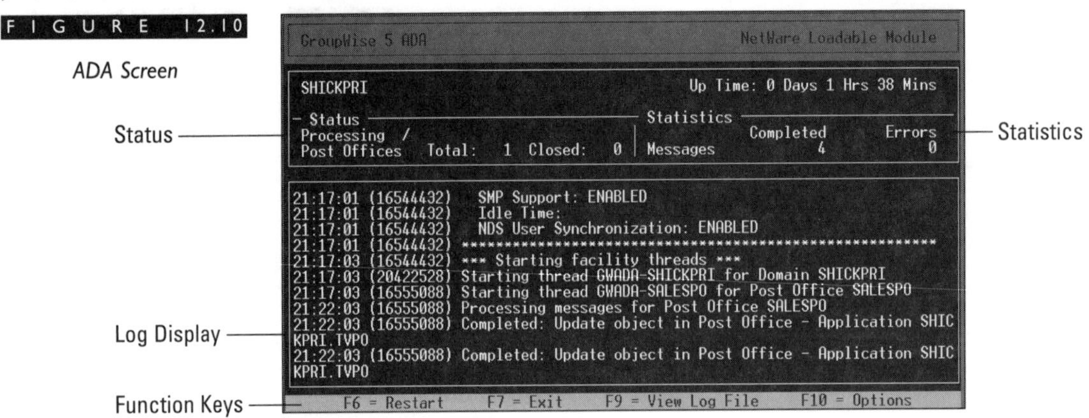

Status

The status area displays the total number of post offices that the ADA is responsible for in the domain. This number will not reflect the number of post offices in the domain if you create and enable an ADA for a post office. For example, if you have three post offices, and one of them has its own ADA, the domain's ADA screen will reflect that it is updating two post offices. If any post offices cannot be accessed, a number will appear in the Closed column.

If any post offices are closed, the ADA is unable update the post office database, and the Address Book is not updated. The closed state needs to be resolved before the ADA can perform the update.

To determine the reason for the closure, you can use the Configuration Status information for the closed post office. This is done by pressing F10 and choosing Configuration Status and viewing the details of the post office. Usually, the path to the post office is not available because of a network problem or an incorrect UNC path or TCP/IP address.

NOTE

If a post office appears as Excluded, an ADA has been created and loaded for that post office, and the domain's ADA is not responsible for updating that post office's database. See Chapter 9 for more information.

Statistics

The statistics area of the ADA screen displays the total number of completed messages and error messages processed by the ADA. This is important because it shows how busy the ADA is and how many Address Book update messages it has handled.

If the ADA is swamped or you're having difficulties with the post office databases, you can consider creating, configuring, and loading multiple ADAs, possibly placing them in Post Office–Only mode. (This is discussed in Chapter 9.) In most situations, however, a single ADA running at the domain is sufficient for day-to-day GroupWise operations. Creating an ADA at the post office is most useful when the post office is located in a remote location across a WAN link.

Log Display

The configuration of the ADA appears here, along with any actions taken by the ADA, such as updating specific objects or rebuilding certain databases. You can see the most information if the logging level is set to Verbose.

Using the ADA Screen

A description of the function keys appears at the bottom of the ADA screen. The function keys can be used to perform the following tasks:

- **F6.** Restarts the ADA, re-rereading its configuration information from the domain or post office database in the `/home` switch in the startup file.

- **F7.** Exits and unloads the ADA from memory.
- **F9.** Statically views the current log file.
- **F10.** Accesses the ADA menu options shown in Table 12.13.

TABLE 12.13

ADA Menu Options

MENU OPTION	DESCRIPTION
Configuration Status	Displays Details; suspends or resumes any facility the ADA is updating
View Log Files	Views old log files
Log Settings	Changes Log Name, Level, Write to Disk, Age, and Space
Cycle Log	Opens a new log file
Edit Startup file	Opens the current startup file for editing

Updating the Agents

It is extremely important to contact Novell regularly for version updates and patches for the agent software (As well as the client software). The best way to do this is to access the Internet and point your Web browser to the following URL:

```
http://support.novell.com/search/patlst.htm
```

There you'll find a list of the most current and necessary patches for all Novell products.

For GroupWise 5 product information, use the following URL:

```
http://support.novell.com/home/groupwar/gw5/
```

The latest GroupWise files can be found here, with links to patch files. Once you download update files for an agent, copy them to a working directory on your hard drive or on the network. The patch files are self-extracting, so you need to type the name of the patch file in at a command prompt and press Enter, which will create a series of files.

The expanded patch files include a text file with instructions on how to apply the patch. As of this writing, no patch files for GroupWise 5 are available. Nevertheless, here are some tips for installing the new patches:

- Exit or unload every GroupWise NLM on the server you are updating. Messages sent by users during this "down" time will be kept in the queue directories.
- Manually unload GWENN1.NLM; it does not always unload automatically.
- Read the README.TXT files that come with the patches to see what problems it fixes and what enhancements there are.
- The Startup files will not change from the update.

It is a good idea to load each agent with the `/help` switch to see the new options for the agent. For example, :LOAD GWMTA /help will display a list of all available startup switches for the MTA, which you can add to the startup file.

Summary

In this chapter, you learned about every aspect of day-to-day life with the GroupWise agents. We discussed the properties, startup files, loading procedures, and screens of the post office agent, message transfer agent, and administration agent. In the next chapter, you'll learn about a most intriguing topic, GroupWise database maintenance.

CHAPTER 13

Maintaining GroupWise Databases

The GroupWise databases are the heart of your GroupWise system. When the GroupWise databases are in good shape, you have a healthy messaging system. One of your major responsibilities as a GroupWise administrator is to maintain the GroupWise databases.

In Chapter 2 you learned that there are two basic types of GroupWise databases: directory store databases and information store databases (which include document storage databases for GroupWise Document Management Services). The *directory store databases* contain information found in the Address Book, such as user IDs, telephone numbers, departments, and so forth. The *information store databases* contain all messages and associated file attachments.

NOTE

There is a third type of GroupWise database that hasn't been mentioned yet, the *document store database*. These databases contain the documents stored in GroupWise libraries. Document store databases are discussed in Chapter 17.

GroupWise databases have the following characteristics:

- *Proprietary*. These databases are encrypted in Novell's proprietary format for the GroupWise system. They cannot be viewed, changed, or "hacked" with any software outside of the utilities and programs that are part of the GroupWise system.

- *Fault-tolerant*. The databases in GroupWise are analyzed each time an agent (ADA or POA) accesses them for structural problems, and are automatically repaired. They also support full transaction tracking and rollback, which means all writes to database files are monitored until they are complete. In the event of a server failure, any writes to the database that were not completed before the failure will not be committed to disk.

- *Sharable*. Each database can be opened by many users at the same time, while maintaining the privacy of the information.

- *Portable*. The databases are not tied to any particular operating or file system, so they can be placed on a wide variety of network operating systems.

Before we explain how to maintain your GroupWise databases, you need to understand the two basic types of problems that can occur with the databases: physical problems and content problems. *Physical problems* (sometimes called "structural" problems) relate to the database structure itself and occur if the database is saved to the disk in an abnormal way. Physical problems prohibit GroupWise components from successfully reading from or writing to the database. *Content problems* are problems with the information stored in the database, not problems relating to the database structure itself. A content problem occurs when data held in the database is modified or corrupted in such a way as to make it unreadable by GroupWise.

Some of the most common symptoms of directory store database errors include the following:

- Users not appearing in all Address Books throughout the system
- Users appearing multiple times in an Address Book
- Undeliverable messages to certain users, even when the users appear in the Address Books
- Synchronization errors, such as distribution list membership that is not consistent from one database to the next

Some of the most common symptoms of information store database problems include the following:

- `Record not found` errors in the GroupWise client
- Users are unable to open or delete certain messages
- The GroupWise client is denied access to the mailbox
- Strange errors appear when running the GroupWise client program

A complete listing of the GroupWise error messages is located in the troubleshooting section of online help.

Synchronization of GroupWise and NDS

Before we explain how to maintain GroupWise directory databases, we'll briefly review how directory synchronization works between NDS and GroupWise 5.

GroupWise is administered through NetWare Administrator, the front-end browser and administration program for NDS. The GroupWise directory and NDS are two separate and distinct entities, but they have a very close relationship.

Take, for example, the process of adding a network user. You run NetWare Administrator and complete the user creation process. A record is created for the User object, and the properties associated with that user—for example, the user's name, telephone number, department, and password—are stored in NDS (see Figure 13.1).

FIGURE 13.1

Creating a User Account in NetWare Administrator

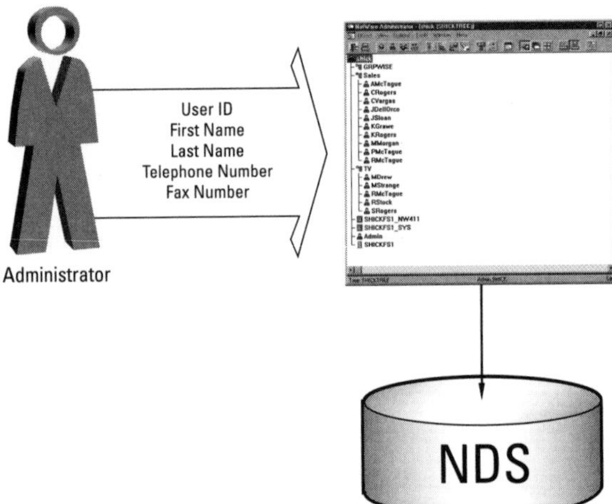

When you create a network user account and give the User object GroupWise properties, the user's regular NDS properties *and* the GroupWise properties (such as mailbox ID, post office name, and domain name) are added to the GroupWise directory store, the domain database. That information is then replicated by the GroupWise administration agent and message transfer agent to the rest of the domains and post offices in the GroupWise system.

When you assign GroupWise properties to a User object, the GroupWise properties are stored in NDS for that user, along with the user's default NDS properties. The User properties needed by the GroupWise system are sent to the GroupWise directory databases. Not all of the User object's NDS properties are sent to the GroupWise directory, only those properties needed by the GroupWise system and the GroupWise Address Book. In other words, all NDS User objects' GroupWise-related properties are *stored* in NDS, but not all of the objects' properties are *sent* to the GroupWise directory.

Note that the information stored in the GroupWise directory is a combination of the User object's default NDS properties and its GroupWise properties.

When you initially create a user and assign that user a GroupWise account, or when you manually edit a User object's GroupWise properties, those changes are passed from NetWare Administrator to the GroupWise ADA. The ADA, using the MTA for transportation, then replicates those changes to the rest of the GroupWise system.

Updating GroupWise Databases

In certain situations, modifications to user accounts are not automatically queued to the GroupWise ADA. This might occur if changes are made to a user account by an administrator running a version of NetWare Administrator that does not have the GroupWise administration components installed. How, then, are these changes made in the GroupWise directory?

Using an NDS-Enabled ADA

In this situation, the GroupWise ADA must be set up to run in *NDS Synchronization mode*. As shown in Figure 13.2, when the ADA is running in NDS Synchronization mode, it monitors changes to NDS and replicates to the appropriate GroupWise databases any changes affecting the GroupWise directory.

At press time, only the NLM version of the ADA is NDS-synchronization-enabled. If you are running a GroupWise ADA on the NT or Unix platforms, you must assign another domain's GWADA.NLM process to update the domain running the non-NDS-enabled ADA.

FIGURE 13.2

NDS Synchronization with GroupWise ADA

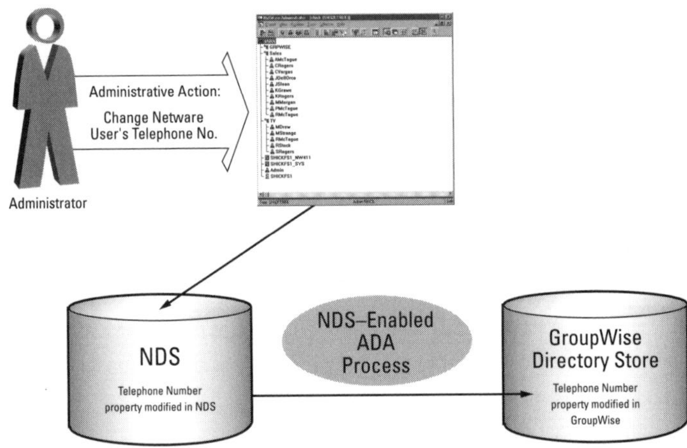

NOTE

At least one but not all ADAs in your system must be NDS-synchronization-enabled. The changes in NDS that are read are replicated throughout the GroupWise system. If you have a wide area network, for example, you can set up multiple NDS-synchronization-enabled ADAs to help balance the load.

In order to enable synchronization for the NLM version of the ADA, you need to provide a user name and password for the GroupWise Access account in the ADA startup file. When the ADA loads, you should see the message *NDS User Synchronization Enabled* in the logging screen.

In addition, you need to create a "scheduled event" in order for the ADA to perform the synchronization from NDS to the GroupWise directory store. (A *scheduled event* is a set of preconfigured instructions for the ADA to perform at intervals you manually specify.) If you don't create the scheduled event for the ADA, it will not be an NDS-enabled agent. This type of scheduled event is explained further in Chapter 14.

Using a Non-NDS-Enabled ADA

For a domain running a non-NDS-enabled ADA (for example, a domain using the NT platform of the ADA), you must use the ADA Synchronization Configuration dialog box to associate another domain's ADA with the domain requiring NDS synchronization. The server running the ADA must be in the same

NDS tree as the GroupWise system. If it is not, the agent cannot authenticate to Directory Services and cannot perform the synchronization.

To enable synchronization for a domain with a non-NDS-synchronization-enabled ADA, follow these steps:

1 • Click on Tools.

2 • Click on GroupWise System Operations.

3 • Double-click on the ADA Synchronization icon. All domains in the system are listed on the left side of the dialog box, and domains with synchronization-enabled ADA processes appear on the right (see Figure 13.3).

4 • Click on the domain on the left for which NDS synchronization needs to be enabled.

5 • Highlight the agent that needs to be assigned to handle synchronization for that domain.

6 • Click on the Arrow button to assign synchronization to the NDS-enabled agent you selected in Step 5.

7 • Click on OK.

FIGURE 13.3

ADA Synchronization Configuration

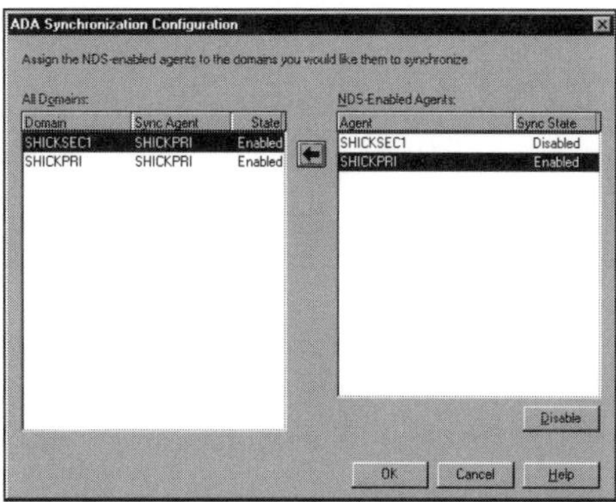

Notice in Figure 13.3 that the SHICKSEC1 domain appears to be disabled. Consequently, the ADA for SHICKPRI has been assigned to handle NDS synchronization for SHICKSEC1.

IMPORTANT

Even though the NT version of the ADA cannot perform NDS user synchronization, it receives messages from NetWare Administrator to perform all other ADA activities, such as directory database updates, synchronization between domains, and automatic database recovery.

Manually Synchronizing the Directory Store with NDS

If you add (or modify) GroupWise properties of a User object but the changes aren't reflected in the GroupWise system, a failure may have occurred in the synchronization process between NDS and the GroupWise ADA process.

In order to manually synchronize GroupWise databases and NDS, follow these steps:

1 • Verify that the administration agent for the connected domain is running and that NDS synchronization is enabled. Also verify that all ADAs and MTAs in the system are running, so synchronization will be completed properly.

2 • From the NetWare Administrator screen, highlight the object you want to synchronize. You can use Ctrl-click or Shift-click to select multiple objects.

3 • Click on Tools and on GroupWise Utilities. A message appears indicating that the selected objects will be synchronized.

4 • Click on Yes.

This procedure reads the information about the selected object(s) and sends an update message via the ADA to the GroupWise directory store. The information is replicated to the domain and post office databases, which are updated to reflect the correct information.

Keep in mind that the information you see about an object in NetWare Administrator is stored in the domain you are connected to at the moment. When you manually synchronize databases, your goal is to "push" this information to the other domain databases.

NOTE

In order to tell which domain you are connected to, under the Tools menu select the GroupWise System Operations option, and then double-click on System Connection.

Directory Store Database Maintenance

The preceding section explained how synchronization occurs between the network directory (NDS) and the GroupWise directory. Now we'll look at how you keep all of the GroupWise directory databases (as opposed to individual objects) intact and synchronized with one another.

As you know, the directory store databases are the domain and post office databases, WPDOMAIN.DB and WPHOST.DB.

As a general rule, these databases do not need much maintenance. This is because the ADA is able to fix most problems automatically before you need to get involved. However, two common situations do require some administrative intervention:

- When the databases become damaged due to internal system errors, network failures, or file corruption
- When the databases become "out-of-sync" with databases in other domains. In other words, when some databases hold information that does not exactly match all other databases in the system, you will need to take action to get them back in sync. This problem occurs most often in a GroupWise system that is administered from multiple locations in the system (i.e., a distributed administration model).

When you perform operations on a GroupWise directory database, the tasks are performed by the GroupWise administration tools found in NetWare Administrator. Therefore, when you run NetWare Administrator, you must have direct network access to these databases (see Figure 13.4). The GroupWise maintenance options in NetWare Administrator operate directly on these databases.

FIGURE 13.4

Directory Store Maintenance

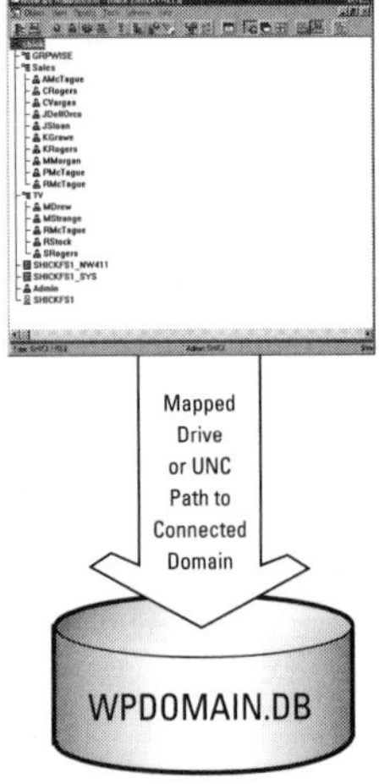

Notice that all of the options relating to maintaining the GroupWise directory databases require direct access from NetWare Administrator to the databases being affected. In other words, the administrator must be able to specify a path (either in the form of a UNC path or mapped drive) to the location of the databases. The administrator must have the following rights to the files: Read, Write, Create, Modify, and File Scan.

Do all users need to log off of GroupWise before you can perform directory store maintenance? That depends on which database(s) you are working on and which procedure you are performing. Different maintenance procedures are explained in this chapter. For each procedure, we'll advise you on whether users can be logged in to the system or whether they need to exit GroupWise.

Two different kinds of problems require administrative intervention: database corruption and synchronization difficulties. Although they involve separate administrative tasks, you use the same dialog box, the GroupWise System Maintenance dialog box, to correct both (see Figure 13.5).

Before you use the System Maintenance dialog box, make sure you are connected to the right domain. To work on post office databases, the current domain you are connected to should be the domain in which those post offices are located. To fix a secondary domain database, you need to be connected to the primary domain.

FIGURE 13.5

GroupWise System Maintenance Dialog Box

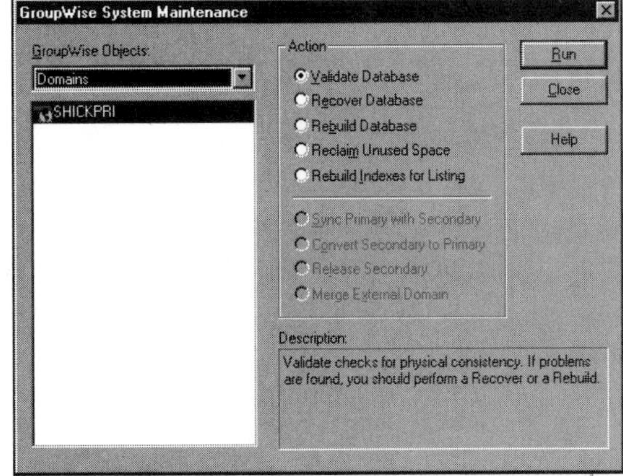

To connect to the right domain, follow these steps:

1 • In NetWare Administrator, click on the Tools menu.

2 • Select GroupWise System Operations.

3 • Double-click on the System Connection icon.

4 • Select the correct domain and click on Connect.

When you want to perform maintenance on any GroupWise domain or post office database, access the GroupWise System Maintenance dialog box by following these steps:

1 • In NetWare Administrator, highlight the problematic domain or post office object in the NDS tree.

2 • Click on the Tools menu and select GroupWise Utilities.

3 • Click on System Maintenance. The GroupWise System Maintenance dialog box will appear.

The Action portion of the System Maintenance dialog box contains nine options. The first five options can be used to fix problems with the domain or post office databases, WPDOMAIN.DB and WPHOST.DB. The last four options are used to perform database synchronization and domain operations in multiple-domain systems. If there is only one domain in the system, the last four options are not available.

Fixing Corrupt Directory Store Databases

Sometimes you will encounter problems with the physical structure of a database, the information contained within the database, or both. The first five options in the GroupWise System Maintenance dialog box can be used to fix such problems.

NOTE

The information in this section pertains only to domain and post office databases (WPDOMAIN.DB and WPHOST.DB). Changes you make to these databases do not affect the information store or document store in any way.

We address the five options in the order of least to greatest impact on the databases. This is the same order in which the options appear in the dialog box (refer to Figure 13.5). As you move down the list, from the Validate Database option to the Rebuild Indexes for Listing option, each option you select replaces more data. Also as you move down the list, the options are more likely to require downtime for the end users. When you attempt to fix directory store problems, you should select these options in the order in which they appear in the System Maintenance dialog box. If one options fails to correct the problem, then you should try the next.

Validate Database

When you select the Validate Database option, the System Maintenance utility checks for physical problems with the domain or post office databases. In other words, the utility checks and verifies the structural integrity of the databases.

IMPORTANT

The utility does not actually fix database problems when you select the Validate Database option. This option is similar to the CHKDSK utility for DOS in that it only detects and reports problems. It doesn't correct them unless you select additional options.

The Validate Database option is a quick way to determine whether a database is structurally sound. You can run this option at any time, and you don't have to shut down the GroupWise agents or disable client connections to the post office. You should validate the databases regularly to detect structural problems.

The steps for validating a domain or post office database are as follows:

1. In NetWare Administrator or in the GroupWise view, highlight the domain or post office object that you want to validate. You can highlight multiple objects by pressing the Ctrl key when you click. Then you can select each object individually once you open the GroupWise System Maintenance dialog box.
2. Click on Tools.
3. Click on GroupWise Utilities.
4. Click on System Maintenance.
5. Select the Validate Database option.
6. Click on Run.
7. Specify the path (a UNC path or mapped drive) to the database and click on OK.

If the validation finds no errors, the message *Database passed validation check* will appear. A successful validation means that no structural problems were discovered. If problems are encountered during validation, you should use the Recover Database or Rebuild Database option.

Recover Database

If an error is discovered during validation, your next option is Recover Database. You should also select this option if you receive an administration message informing you of internal database errors or if you receive other error messages regarding the domain or post office databases.

When you select Recover Database, the System Maintenance utility will correct physical problems with the structure of the domain or post office database.

However, it does not correct content problems. Basically, you use the Recover Database option to create a new structure for the database while maintaining the content of the original database.

The major advantage of the Recover Database option is that it can be used when the domain or post office database is in use by other GroupWise processes, such as the ADA, MTA, POA, or the GroupWise client software. Therefore, you don't have to take the GroupWise system offline to run the Recover Database option.

Follow these steps to recover a database:

1. In NetWare Administrator, highlight the domain or post office object you need to recover.
2. Click on Tools.
3. Click on GroupWise Utilities.
4. Click on System Maintenance.
5. Select the Recover Database option.
6. Click on Run.
7. Specify the path to the database and click on OK.

When you select the Recover Database option, the System Maintenance utility creates a new database structure. When the process is finished, you'll see the message *Database recovery completed.* If information is lost during the process, the person designated as the administrator for the domain should receive an e-mail message to that effect.

The following events occur behind the scenes when you select the Recover Database option:

- The existing domain or post office database is queried to determine the number of records it contains.
- A backup file of the domain or post office database is created to ensure recovery if the operation fails. (If you are running Recover

Database on a domain database, the backup file is named RECOVER.DDB. If you are recovering a post office database, the backup file is named RECOVER.HDB.) The original domain or post office database is left intact so that it can be accessed by other GroupWise processes while you run the Recover Database option.

If the process hangs or fails, you should rename the RECOVER file with the original name of the database file and retry the operation.

- The GroupWise System Maintenance utility next creates a new database structure based on the domain or post office database template file (GWDOM.DC or GWPO.DC). This file is temporarily named CREATING.DDB if you are recovering a domain database, or CREATING.HDB if you are recovering a post office database.
- The System Maintenance utility populates the CREATING.*x*DB file (where *x* stands for either *D* or *H*) with the information from the existing domain or post office database. If invalid records are discovered in the original, they are skipped and therefore not added to the CREATING.*x*DB file.
- The CREATING.*x*DB database is then renamed to WPDOMAIN.DB or WPHOST.DB, replacing the original file.
- The System Maintenance utility then queries the new database to determine how many records it contains. If the number of records in the new database does not equal the number of records in the original database, an administration message is generated indicating that data has been lost. The message is sent to the person or distribution list designated as the administrator on the Domain object's property page.
- The backup file (RECOVER.HDB or RECOVER.DDB) is then deleted.

If you receive an administration message indicating that data was lost, you should then select the Rebuild Database option, or else you can synchronize the database with an undamaged database. (See the following sections "Rebuild Database" and "Correcting Database Synchronization Problems.")

The important point to remember about the Recover Database option is that the System Maintenance utility recreates the database structure and populates it with information in the existing WPDOMAIN.DB or WPHOST.DB file. Corrupted records from the original database are not included in the new database.

Rebuild Database

Use the Rebuild Database option to fix physical *and* content problems with the database. The major prerequisite to running the Rebuild Database option is that you must have exclusive access to the database before you can rebuild it.

Unlike the Recover Database option, when you select the Rebuild Database option, the System Maintenance utility creates a new database structure and then populates it based on information from a "parent source," rather than from the existing database.

If you are rebuilding a secondary domain database, a new database is created and the information is extracted from the primary domain database (the parent source in this case) and added to the new database.

If you are rebuilding a primary domain database, the database rebuilds itself based upon information contained in the existing primary domain database. In other words, a new database is created, but information might be lost if the original domain database had corrupt records. If you suspect that the primary WPDOMAIN.DB file is corrupted, you should use the most recent uncorrupted backup file. (This underscores the importance of maintaining regular backups of the primary domain WPDOMAIN.DB file.)

If you are rebuilding a post office database, the database is rebuilt and populated with information from the domain's database, which is the parent source in this case.

You should rebuild a database if it appears that User objects (or other GroupWise objects) are not being replicated to other domains in the GroupWise system. You should also select the Rebuild Database option if you suspect database corruption has caused data to be lost, or if the Recover Database option did not recover all records in the original domain or post office database file. The Rebuild Database option can also be used to force directory synchronization or to fix a database index. Therefore, this option can correct synchronization problems as well as database problems.

Before rebuilding a domain or post office database, disable all processes that are accessing the domain or post office database. If you are rebuilding a domain database, you must shut down the ADA and MTA and any gateways that are running. If you are rebuilding a post office database, you must shut down the POA and make sure no users are running the GroupWise client.

You can prevent users from logging in to the post office by following these steps:

1. Right-click on the Post Office object and select Details.
2. Click on the Disable Logins option.
3. Click on OK.
4. Repeat these steps to again enable logins to the post office.

The steps for rebuilding a database are as follows:

1. In NetWare Administrator, locate the Domain object or Post Office object and highlight it.
2. Click on Tools.
3. Click on GroupWise Utilities.
4. Click on System Maintenance.
5. Select the Rebuild Database option.
6. Click on Run.
7. Specify the path to the database and click on OK. The rebuild process runs. When the process is over, the message *Database rebuild complete* should appear.

TIP

If it is not possible to take a domain or post office offline to rebuild a database, you can change the *Path to Domain* or *Path to Post Office* setting while rebuilding to a temporary directory on your hard drive. A brand-new database will be created in that directory. You can then replace the existing database file with the rebuilt file at your convenience. Make sure that no ADA replication traffic occurs before you have a chance to replace the file, as that would result in an unsynchronized condition.

If you rebuild a copy of the database in a temporary directory, copy it over the existing database in the domain or post office directory.

When you rebuild a database, the following events occur:

- A backup copy of the original database is created and named RECOVER.DDB (domain database) or RECOVER.HDB (post office database.)
- An empty domain or post office database is created based on the database template file and named CREATING.DDB or CREATING.HDB.
- The new database is populated with the contents of its parent database. If you are rebuilding a secondary domain database, the contents are extracted from the primary domain database. If you are rebuilding a primary domain database, the contents are extracted from the RECOVER.DDB file. If it is a post office database, the contents are extracted from its parent domain database.
- The CREATING.*x*DB file is renamed (to WPDOMAIN.DB or WPHOST.DB).
- The backup file, RECOVER.*x*DB is deleted.

Reclaim Unused Space

As records are added, modified, and deleted, pockets of wasted space can be left in the domain and post office database. You can eliminate the extra space by using the Reclaim Unused Space option.

GroupWise will use free space in the database before it requires more disk space. Reclaim Unused Space is most useful immediately after you have deleted several objects from your GroupWise system.

The benefit of this option is the disk space savings that results. It will not necessarily improve message delivery performance. When the free space is removed from the databases, the GroupWise agents will actually have to expand the database to add more messages, and this can result in a performance decrease in some situations.

Rebuild Indexes for Listing

In the domain database, indexes are used to display how GroupWise object information displays in the GroupWise view. In the post office databases, indexes are used to define how directory information can be displayed in the client Address Book.

The Rebuild Indexes for Listing option is used to correct problems with object lists.

The clearest indicator that there is a problem with a database index is the Address Book. A user who is added to a database may not appear in the Address Book, or a user's name may appear two or more times.

When users report problems with information contained in the Address Book, or if you notice that there are problems with the user display in the GroupWise view in NetWare Administrator, the Rebuild Indexes for Listing option can be used to rebuild the indexes.

When you run this option, NetWare Administrator goes through each record in the domain or post office database and makes sure each record has a corresponding listing in the indexes within the database.

Sometimes users will not appear in the Address Book because of visibility settings. The visibility setting is the first thing you should check when users do not appear in the Address Book.

Synchronizing GroupWise Databases

In large, multiple-domain systems, you occasionally need to use the GroupWise System Maintenance options to synchronize all directory store databases throughout the system with identical information.

Because a GroupWise system can be administered from different points in the system, and because an administrator can connect to either a primary or secondary domain when making changes to the GroupWise system, databases may get out of sync. In other words, all databases in the system might not contain identical user addressing information.

Synchronization problems between domains usually occur when you are using a distributed GroupWise administration model. If GroupWise administration is performed by several administrators who are responsible for their own GroupWise domains, it is possible for secondary domains to contain user information that has not been replicated to the primary domain.

The Sync Primary with Secondary option looks at records in the secondary domain database and verifies that corresponding records are found in the primary domain database. Remember that the primary domain database is responsible for updating all domains in the system. If records are found in the secondary domain that do not exist in the primary domain, those records are added to the primary domain database and then replicated to other domains in the system.

If you think a secondary domain's database has bad information, use the Rebuild Database option. If you think a secondary domain's database is correct and the primary domain's database is inaccurate or incomplete, use the synchronization option.

Follow these steps to synchronize a primary domain with a secondary domain:

1 • Highlight the secondary domain in NetWare Administrator.

2 • Click on Tools and on GroupWise Maintenance.

3 • Click on Sync Primary with Secondary.

4 • Click on Run.

Records in the secondary domain will be compared with records in the primary domain. Any records found in the secondary domain for objects owned by that secondary that are not found in the primary domain will be added to the primary domain. The ADA running for the primary domain will then replicate these records to all other secondary domains in the system.

IMPORTANT

Synchronization problems can also be corrected by running the Rebuild Database option on secondary domains. This ensures that the secondary domains contain all of the records found in the primary domain. This is the exact opposite of the Sync Primary with Secondary option. Because of a risk of losing information in a secondary domain by doing a rebuild, we recommend that you use the Sync Primary to Secondary option before rebuilding.

Note: The Convert Secondary to Primary, Release Secondary, and Merge External Domain options are used for administrative tasks unrelated to regular database maintenance. These options are discussed in Chapter 14.

Information Store Database Maintenance

Now we turn our attention to maintenance of the information store databases. The information store databases are where users' messages are stored. The information store consists of the user databases, the message databases, the file attachments directory, and the document management databases.

The operations on the directory store databases explained earlier in this chapter are performed by NetWare Administrator directly accessing the databases (refer to Figure 13.4). Maintenance you perform on the information store databases is not performed directly by NetWare Administrator, but by the post office agent (see Figure 13.6).

However, you initiate these actions from within NetWare Administrator using the Mailbox/Library Maintenance option, which is located under GroupWise Utilities in the Tools menu (see Figure 13.7). NetWare Administrator then sends task messages to the POA.

FIGURE 13.6

Information Store Maintenance

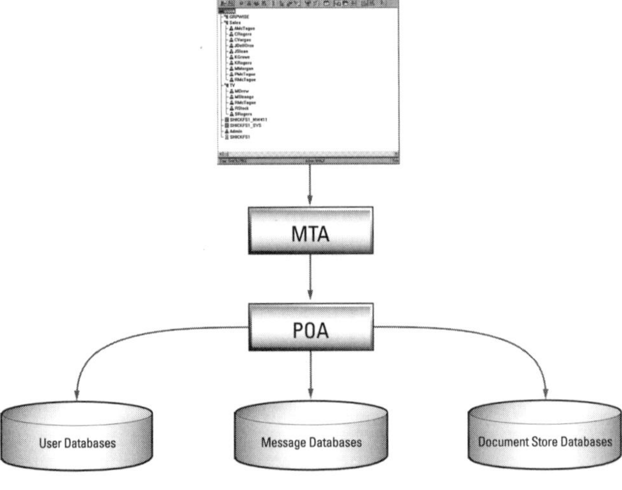

FIGURE 13.7

Mailbox/Library Maintenance Dialog Box

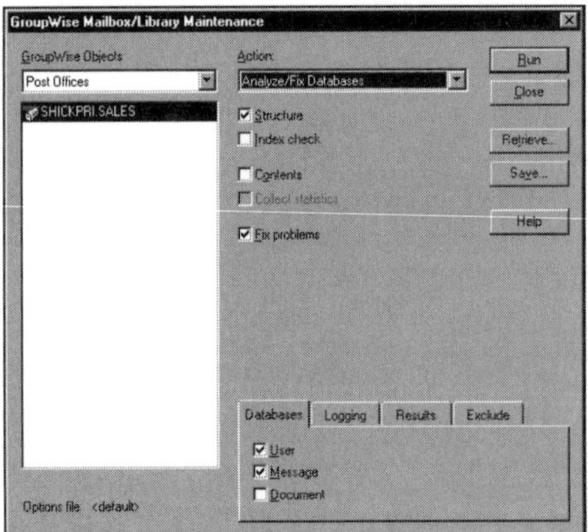

There are several different situations for which the Mailbox/Library Maintenance options can be useful. They include the following:

- *Problems with the client program*. Users are unable to access or open messages or documents, or are receiving error messages in GroupWise.
- *Regulating disk space*. You will need to remove old message records and attachments from the information store, therefore saving disk space.

- *A User forgets his or her password.* The new password for the mailbox will need to be written into the user's database.
- *Periodic Maintenance.* Detect problems or errors before they become severe enough to affect the performance of the client program.

NOTE

In earlier versions of GroupWise, the information store database maintenance utility was called OFCHECK.EXE, which could be run from the command prompt or from the DOS-based GroupWise Administrator program. All database maintenance is now done from within NetWare Administrator. There are no stand-alone or command-line utilities to administer databases.

Information store maintenance options can be run for a post office or for individual users. (These options are not available for domains because domains do not store users' messages.)

When you run maintenance options on post offices, the maintenance options affect all the users within that post office. (You can exclude specific users with the Exclude option, explained in Table 13.1.) When you run maintenance options on individual users, only those users' databases are affected. Some of the options that are available for individual users are not available for the entire post office. We'll point out instances for which the options are not available for entire post offices.

To run the information store maintenance options for a post office or for individual users, follow these steps:

1. Highlight one or more Post Office objects or User objects in the NetWare Administrator main browser screen. Note: You can highlight multiple Post Office objects or multiple User objects before going to the maintenance screen. This enables you to administer objects without having to continually exit the dialog box and select objects. You cannot select multiple objects in the GroupWise View, so use the main screen of NetWare Administrator.
2. Click on Tools and on GroupWise Utilities
3. Click on Mailbox/Library Maintenance. The GroupWise Mailbox/ Library Maintenance dialog box appears, as shown in Figure 13.7.

4 • Select the post office or users from the GroupWise Objects drop-down list.

5 • Select the maintenance action from the drop-down list. For each action you select, a list of available settings will appear below the drop-down list.

6 • Select the specific settings you want applied to the action. These settings vary depending upon the action you select.

7 • In the bottom right-hand corner of the dialog box, select the databases for which the option should be run. If you are running the maintenance option for a post office, your choices are User databases, Message databases, or Document databases.

8 • Click on Run.

A message appears stating that the maintenance task instruction has been sent.

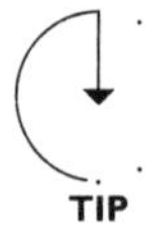

TIP

You should check the Novell's Web site at `www.support.novell.com` for updates to the post office agent. Always use the newest versions of the agents (after testing them on your system) so you have the latest enhancements, including mailbox maintenance routines.

Mailbox/Library Maintenance Dialog Box Settings

Table 13.1 explains the settings, tabs, and buttons in the Mailbox/Library Maintenance dialog box. The specific options are explained a little later in the chapter.

TABLE 13.1

Mailbox/Library Maintenance Settings

SETTING	EXPLANATION
GroupWise Objects	Allows you to select the users/resources, post office, or library(s) on which you want to perform maintenance
Action	What the POA will do to the selected objects' user and message databases (explained below)
Databases	Allows you to select what databases are manipulated

TABLE 13.1
Mailbox/Library Maintenance Settings (continued)

SETTING	EXPLANATION
Logging	Allows you to specify the resulting log file name, and to enable verbose (maximum) logging to this file
Results	Selects administrator or users who should receive the results of the maintenance action
Exclude	Adds users for whom the maintenance options should not be run (Available only when a post office has been highlighted.)
Run	Sends task message to POA to run maintenance routine
Close	Finishes the Mailbox/Library Maintenance session
Retrieve	Reads a saved settings file. (Displays in lower left-hand corner of dialog box.)
Save	Saves the current settings in a file

After you click on Run, a *Maintenance task has been sent* message tells you that a request for the POA to perform the task has been sent to the POA for processing (refer to Figure 13.6). NetWare Administrator queues this request to the domain's MTA, and the MTA forwards the message to the POA for processing.

Mailbox/Library Maintenance Options

This section outlines the options that can be used for maintaining GroupWise information store databases.

NOTE

Maintenance of the document management databases is covered in Chapter 17.

Analyze/Fix Databases

The Analyze/Fix Databases option is available for both post offices and users. When run against a post office, this options looks for errors in all the user, message, and document databases in the post office. When run against individual users, only those users' databases are analyzed. Detected errors are then fixed. This should be the first option you run if there are problems with users being able to send or receive messages, or users are getting errors when starting the GroupWise client program. Refer to Figure 13.7 in the preceding section to see an example of the Mailbox/Library Maintenance dialog box with the Analyze/Fix Databases option selected.

Settings for the Analyze/Fix Databases option let you explicitly specify what should be checked and fixed during the operation. For example, you could check only the structure or the index, but not the database contents. Options under Analyze/Fix Databases are as follows:

- *Structure.* The integrity of the selected databases is checked, assuming the data is correct. Use this option first when you are having problems. The majority of database problems are fixed with this option.
- *Index check.* If a user opens a message and gets a read error, or if delivered messages do not appear in the recipient's mailbox, use this option. This option will often solve problems with users' folder structures. Because this option requires the POA to do a lot of work, it should be run during off-peak hours.
- *Contents.* In the user database, pointers to message records are checked. In the message databases, pointers to attachments are checked. Rules, personal groups, and distribution list membership are also checked. This option is time-consuming.
- *Fix problems.* This tells the POA to fix any problems that are found. If this option is not checked, they are only reported in the log file.

It is wise to run these options individually, rather than in combination. This allows the results to be more easily analyzed and interpreted, and to justify further action if necessary.

Expire/Reduce Messages

The Expire/Reduce Messages option (see Figure 13.8) is available for both post offices and users. When run against a post office, this option deletes expired messages and documents in the information store database, and then reduces the databases to reclaim the disk space freed by the deleted messages and documents. This option should be part of your regular maintenance routine.

FIGURE 13.8

Expire/Reduce Messages Option

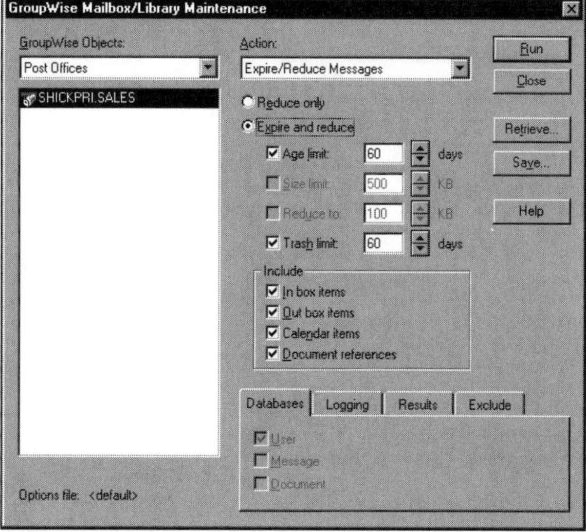

Notice that you can further customize the actions performed by the Expire/Reduce Messages option. For example, you could select `Reduce only` and thereby only reclaim the free disk space that is already available in the databases. Or, you can choose the Expire and Reduce option and explicitly state the age of the items to expire, and which parts of the user databases to analyze, such as In Box, Out Box, and Document References. The Expire/Reduce Messages option gives you control over the size of your information store. A policy for using this option should be established, and users should be clearly informed that they will lose messages that are older than a specific number of days unless they save or archive them.

Mailbox Statistics

The Mailbox Statistics option (see Figure 13.9) is available for both post offices and individual users. This option is a useful tool for helping you analyze how disk space is being used by users in the post office. This option generates statistics about the number of messages and appointments in the post office, and the average number per user.

From these statistics you can determine your policy for deleting information from the post office.

FIGURE 13.9

Mailbox Statistics

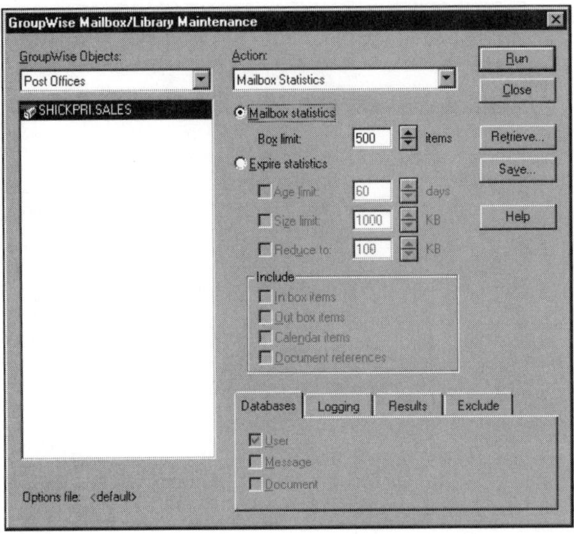

When you run this option, a report is generated and sent to the person designated as the administrator. (This option is defined in the Domain object details screen.) You specify the name of the log file under the Logging tab at the bottom of the Maintenance dialog box. If you want to send the results to an individual user, you can use the Results tab.

A sample of the report that can be generated is shown in Figure 13.10. This report was generated using Verbose logging. Notice the useful information presented in this report, such as number of messages in each user's In Box, Out Box, and Trash, the name of the user's database, and the user's File ID (FID).

If you choose the Verbose logging setting with this option, be prepared to get a fairly large log file.

The three options that follow, Reset Client Options, Recreate User Database, and Structural Rebuild, are only available on a per-user basis. They cannot be performed on an entire post office.

Statistical Report

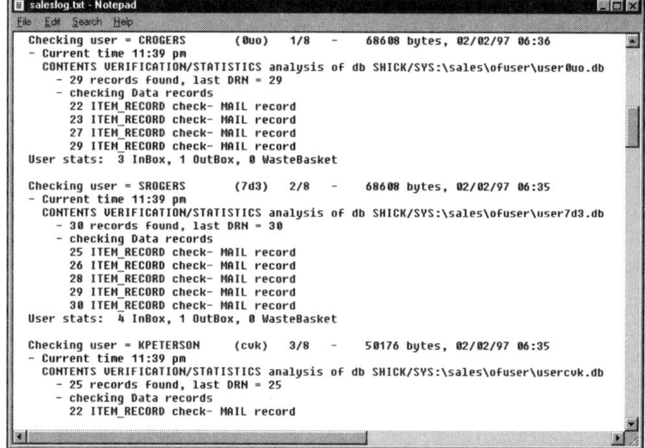

saleslog.txt - Notepad

File Edit Search Help

```
Checking user = CROGERS       (0uo)   1/8   -    68608 bytes, 02/02/97 06:36
- Current time 11:39 pm
  CONTENTS VERIFICATION/STATISTICS analysis of db SHICK/SYS:\sales\ofuser\user0uo.db
    - 29 records found, last DRN = 29
    - checking Data records
      22 ITEM_RECORD check- MAIL record
      23 ITEM_RECORD check- MAIL record
      27 ITEM_RECORD check- MAIL record
      29 ITEM_RECORD check- MAIL record
User stats:  3 InBox, 1 OutBox, 0 WasteBasket

Checking user = SROGERS       (7d3)   2/8   -    68608 bytes, 02/02/97 06:35
- Current time 11:39 pm
  CONTENTS VERIFICATION/STATISTICS analysis of db SHICK/SYS:\sales\ofuser\user7d3.db
    - 30 records found, last DRN = 30
    - checking Data records
      25 ITEM_RECORD check- MAIL record
      26 ITEM_RECORD check- MAIL record
      28 ITEM_RECORD check- MAIL record
      29 ITEM_RECORD check- MAIL record
      30 ITEM_RECORD check- MAIL record
User stats:  4 InBox, 1 OutBox, 0 WasteBasket

Checking user = KPETERSON     (cvk)   3/8   -    50176 bytes, 02/02/97 06:35
- Current time 11:39 pm
  CONTENTS VERIFICATION/STATISTICS analysis of db SHICK/SYS:\sales\ofuser\usercvk.db
    - 25 records found, last DRN = 25
    - checking Data records
      22 ITEM_RECORD check- MAIL record
```

Reset Client Options

You have the ability as the administrator to establish default or mandatory options for the users' client. (Refer to Chapter 7 for more information about setting defaults.) For example, you can set the archive option to archive users' messages to their local hard drives instead of the network.

Reset Client Options is used to update user databases if you alter the client options available under Tools, GroupWise Utilities, Client Options. This is because NetWare Administrator *never* touches the user databases directly! It only changes the directory store (the domain and post office databases), and the information needs to get into the user database, where the changes are seen with the GroupWise client program.

If a user forgets his or her password and you reset that password through NetWare Administrator, you should run this option for that user so the new password takes effect. Be advised that this option resets all of the client options, not just the ones you change. It resets them to the defaults specified in NetWare Administrator, possibly overwriting a user's customization of the GroupWise client.

Recreate User Database

The Recreate User Database option will build a new user database based upon the information contained in the message databases. This option is rarely necessary because most problems are fixed with the Analyze/Fix option.

This option should only be used when a user's database has been deleted or completely destroyed. Rebuilding a user's database may result in the loss of folders and personal messages. This process deletes the existing user database file and then reads each message database, creating pointers to every message the affected user has ever touched—as a recipient or sender. This means that old messages deleted by the user months ago may show up again in the user's mailbox.

Structural Rebuild

This option performs a complete structural reconstruction of the database. Like the Recreate User Database option, this action is usually unnecessary because the problems it can fix are usually fixed by the Analyze/Fix option. The data is not recreated, but the database itself is.

NOTE

When a structural problem is fixed by the GroupWise maintenance options, the damaged database is saved for future reference and as a backup. The old database is saved with the same filename, with a third letter added to the file extension. For example, a rebuilt user database might be given the filename USERSBR.DBA. If the database has been fixed, you can safely delete these backup files if you are certain they won't be needed for recovery purposes.

You can have the POA automatically perform database maintenance options by creating a scheduled event, a set of manually created instructions that the agent performs at intervals you specify. POA scheduled events are covered in detail in Chapter 14.

Summary

In this chapter you learned how to keep your GroupWise directory store and information store databases ship-shape. You should incorporate the database maintenance techniques discussed in this chapter into your GroupWise administration strategy. In the next chapter, you will learn some important advanced administration tasks.

CHAPTER 14

Special Administrative Tasks

In this chapter, we tie up a few loose ends. We'll explain several tasks that you won't do on a daily basis but will likely need to perform at some point as a GroupWise administrator:

- **Combining GroupWise systems.** In this section we explain how to combine domains and post offices from several systems into one.
- **Changing a secondary domain to a primary domain.** We'll discuss the situations that might require you to promote a secondary domain to a primary domain for synchronization reasons.
- **Using GroupWise 5's software directory management features.** This subsection explains how to create additional software directories so you have installation points for GroupWise software.
- **Using advanced addressing.** We'll explain how to use GroupWise advanced addressing techniques, which are useful when troubleshooting and sending messages through gateways.
- **Adding fields to the GroupWise Address Book.** You can add additional fields to the GroupWise Address Book for informational purposes.
- **Defining scheduled events.** Scheduled events are POA and ADA agent actions that occur automatically or when triggered by certain system events.
- **Configuring MTA message logging.** We'll explain how to configure the MTA to establish log files for other applications.

Once you master these topics, you will have plunged to the depths of GroupWise administration. So hold your breath and dive in.

Combining GroupWise Systems

In Chapter 2, you saw that a GroupWise system consists of one or more GroupWise domains. The first domain created is the *primary domain*; subsequent domains are called *secondary domains*.

In Chapter 11, you learned how to define external domains and establish communication with outside systems. External domains are domains in other GroupWise systems. Usually, a company or enterprise will have only one GroupWise system.

What if you want to merge one system with another (for example, when one company merges with another)? The next section deals specifically with that circumstance.

Preparing to Merge

This section covers the steps that need to be taken before you combine two GroupWise systems into one. We will use our fictional company, ShickTools, Inc., and another company as an example.

Imagine that ShickTools, Inc., has just had a banner year and has a lot of extra cash sitting around. So the board of directors decides to expand into hardware by buying the Nuts 'n Bolts company.

Nuts 'n Bolts has two locations in Detroit, Michigan, and has been using GroupWise 5 (on NetWare 4.1) for quite some time. As a matter of fact, ShickTools and Nuts 'n Bolts have been communicating using GroupWise, as depicted in Figure 14.1.

Each system has the other's domains defined as external GroupWise domains, and they have been using the GroupWise SMTP gateway to send messages back and forth. In addition, each system has a capable administrator (who, being capable, must have read this book).

Prior to merging two GroupWise systems some external domain definitions must be made. In the system being merged, you must define an external domain for the new system's primary domain, and set up a link to it. In the system performing the merge, you must define all domains you want to merge as external domains with links set up and open. The process of creating external domains is explained in detail in Chapter 11.

FIGURE 14.1

The ShickTools and Nuts 'n Bolts Systems

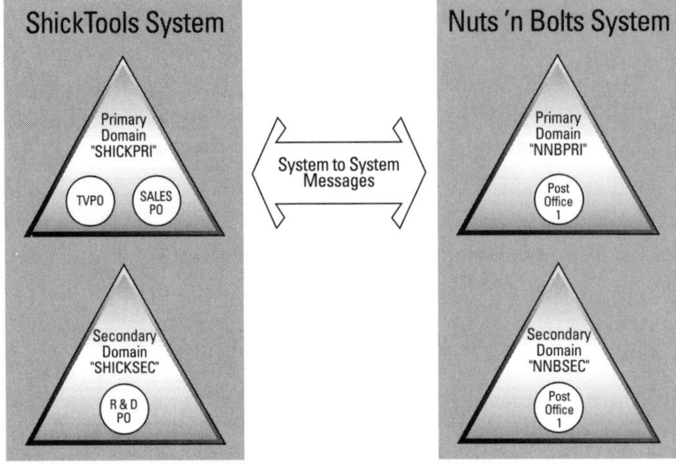

Once the external domains have been defined, the two GroupWise systems can become one. The goal is to have all employees from both companies use the same Address Book, and administrators from both systems will have the power to perform GroupWise administration.

To accomplish these goals, the following tasks need to be performed:

- To enable centralized administration of all domains, the NDS trees need to be combined.
- Determine which domain will be the primary domain in the new system.
- Make complete backups of all domain and post office databases in the system to be acquired.
- Release all secondary domains. For example, before the Nuts 'n Bolts domains can be merged into the ShickTools system, the secondary domain in the Nuts 'n Bolts system must be released, thereby becoming a separate GroupWise system.

- Merge external domains. For example, in this step the external domains from the Nuts 'n Bolts system would be added to the ShickTools system.

- Rebuild databases. Once the merging process is complete, the accurate view of the newly enlarged system must be applied to all other domains and post offices. This will create one system-wide Address Book.

Merging NDS Trees

Since NDS is designed to be an enterprise database, there are many good reasons to combine the NDS trees of ShickTools and Nuts 'n Bolts. The administrative staffs of both companies will need to agree on one strategy for naming, groups, resources, and licensing.

Since the GroupWise domains are currently linked together with the SMTP gateway, combining the NDS trees is not a requirement for message exchanged. Making one NDS tree will give the administrators an advantage (because you are administering one NDS database), but will be mostly transparent to the end user.

Follow these steps to switch NDS trees that you are administering with NetWare Administrator:

1. From the View menu, choose Set Context.

2. Click on the Tree symbol next to the Tree field, select the tree from the list, and click on OK.

3. Enter your user name and password for the new tree and click on OK.

4. Change your context in the new tree by selecting the NDS browse button next to the Context field and click on OK.

NetWare Administrator will now be pointing to the new NDS tree where the GroupWise components it contains can be administered.

NOTE

We will assume for the purpose of this example that the NDS trees for both companies will merge into one tree. For more detailed information on the considerations and procedures involved in combining NDS trees, we recommend Jeffrey F. Hughes and Blair W. Thomas's *Novell's Guide to IntranetWare Networks*, published by Novell Press and IDG Books Worldwide.

As long as the domains and post offices contained in the different NDS trees are connected with TCP/IP links (see Chapter 10), you can avoid a lot of headaches. If you need to use UNC paths to connect GroupWise components between two NDS trees, you need to use the same GroupWise access account and password in both trees.

The GroupWise access account User object (GWACCESS, for example) must be located in the bindery context in both trees so a connection can be made. That way, you can use the common name (GWACCESS) instead of the distinguished name in the startup files for the components that span the two trees.

Choosing the Primary Domain

Before you actually get started, you need to determine which domain will be the primary domain for the combined system. In Chapter 9, you learned that the primary domain is responsible for all replication and synchronization of changes between the GroupWise domains in a system.

You should also keep the physical location of the primary domain in mind. Make sure it is located on a file server the main administrator can access. We will cover how to make a secondary domain into a primary domain later in this chapter.

In our example, the ShickTools primary domain, SHICKPRI, will be the primary domain for the combined system because ShickTools is buying Nuts 'n Bolts.

Backing Up the Domain and Post Office Databases

As you are well aware, e-mail administrators worth their pay will always provide a safety net for themselves, ere something fails and they need to get back to the system's initial state.

The next step in the process is to release all secondary domains from an existing GroupWise system, thereby breaking each domain into individual GroupWise systems. If we were doctors, we'd consider this to be radical surgery, sort of like taking a big toe and sewing it on for a missing thumb. Before you dissect an existing GroupWise system into several individual systems, make complete backups of at least all of the domain databases. It wouldn't hurt to run complete system backups if you have the time and the necessary bandwidth.

At a minimum, you should back up the primary domain databases before you begin the release process. You can reconstruct secondary domains from the primary domain database if necessary.

If you choose not to back up your systems . . . well, let's just say we warned you.

Releasing a Domain

Before a domain can be merged into another system, it needs to be a single, stand-alone domain. In other words, if there are two domains (one primary and one secondary) in the Nuts 'n Bolts GroupWise system, the primary has to "divorce" from the secondary, since both of them are betrothed to the SHICKPRI domain.

Before the release, make sure that the MTA and ADA for all domains in the Nuts 'n Bolts system are operating, and that all facilities are open.

To release a domain from another domain, follow these steps:

1. From the NetWare Administrator screen for the NDS tree, click on the domain to be released.
2. From the Tools menu, choose GroupWise Utilities and then System Maintenance. You'll see the dialog box shown in Figure 14.2.
3. Select Release Secondary and click on Run.
4. The Release Domain wizard starts. Click on Next.
5. Read the Pending operations warning and click on Next.
6. Enter the path to the domain directory you are releasing (NNBSEC, in our example) and click on Next.

FIGURE 14.2

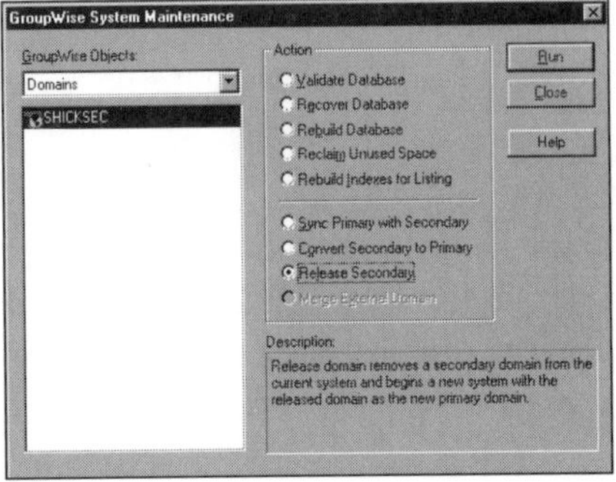

GroupWise System Maintenance Dialog Box

7 • Since this new domain will temporarily become a primary domain, you need to specify a new GroupWise system name. Enter a new system name (using a temporary system name such as TEMPSYS), and click on Next.

8 • You now have the option to transfer objects to another location in the same tree or to a different tree (see Figure 14.3). Choose the appropriate context for the newly released domain and click on Next. We recommend a container called GRPWISE to hold all of the Domain objects (see Chapter 3).

FIGURE 14.3

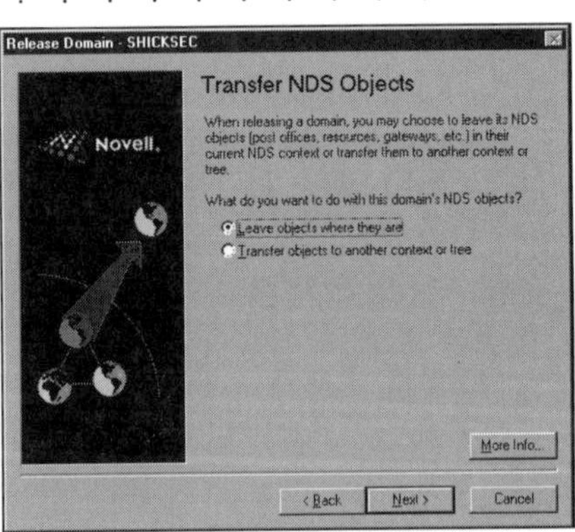

Transferring NDS Objects During Release

9 • You are now prompted to shut down the agents for the domain you are about to release. You can either use RCONSOLE or go to the

server itself to exit out of the MTA and ADA for the domain you are releasing. Once you have shut the agents down, click on Next.

10 • Click on Release to release the domain from your system.

11 • The release process will take a few moments (see Figure 14.4), depending on how large the database is and the speed of the network connection to the domain directory.

12 • You will see a notification once the domain release is complete. Restart the MTA and ADA agents for the domain and click on Done to continue.

FIGURE 14.4

Release Domain Notification

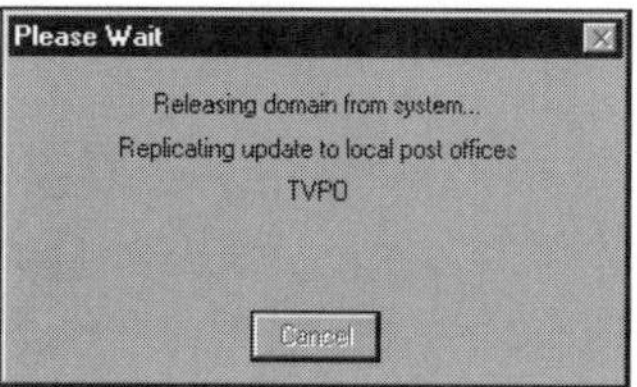

Applying the preceding steps to our ShickTools example, the NNBSEC domain would now be separated from the NNBPRI domain. If we connected to the NNBSEC domain database, the NNBSEC domain would now be a primary domain.

NOTE

If your company decided to sell off a business entity, you could use Release to allow their secondary domain to become a primary domain (and therefore its own GroupWise system). This newly released domain becomes an external domain, and external directory synchronization is automatically set up.

Merging a Domain into a System

The next step in actually combining the GroupWise systems into one is a process called "merging a domain." In our example, the SHICKPRI domain will "gobble up" the NNBPRI and NNBSEC domains, thus merging them into one system.

Before you merge a domain into your system, you need access to its domain database. The easiest way to do this (unless you have a WAN connection and can map a drive to the other domain directory) is to obtain a local copy of the domain database:

1 • Make two folders on your local hard drive named after the names of the domains you are merging. In our example, the folders are named NNBPRI and NNBSEC, after the names of Nuts 'n Bolts' primary and secondary domains.

2 • Have the other administrator (for example, the NNBPRI administrator) send a message to you with each file as an attachment. It is a good idea to send two separate messages so the databases don't get mixed up, which could happen because both domain databases are called WPDOMAIN.DB. It's a good idea to place them in separate directories. Note: Any changes that the Nuts 'n Bolts administrator makes to the "live" domain databases will be lost, because they will be replaced with the modified WPDOMAIN.DB files that you will send back to the administrator after the merge is complete. We suggest that the ADA for the domain being merged be unloaded during the merge and not loaded again until the merged copy of the domain database is returned to the domain directory.

3 • Once you have received the messages, save the attached WPDOMAIN.DB files in their respective folders.

You need to know the location of the domain database you want to merge. Because external GroupWise domains are not available in the regular NetWare Administrator screens, the only way to accomplish this is by following these steps:

1 • In NetWare Administrator, choose GroupWise View from the Tools menu.

2 • Highlight the domain to be merged, and choose GroupWise Utilities from the Tools menu. Click on System Maintenance. You'll see the dialog box shown in Figure 14.5.

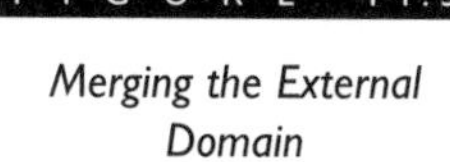

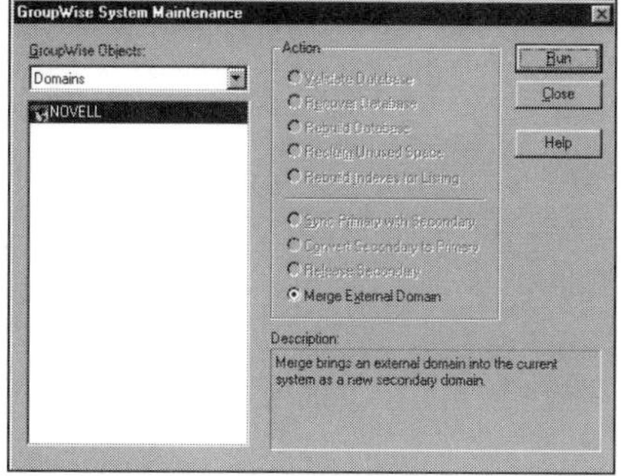

FIGURE 14.5

Merging the External Domain

3 • The only selection available is Merge External Domain. Verify that this is selected and click on Run.

4 • The Merge Domain Into System wizard will start. Click on Next.

5 • Enter the path to the domain database for the domain being merged (for example, C:\NNBPRI).

6 • You are now prompted to bring information about other external domains that the domain you are merging knows about into your system. Normally, you would answer no to this screen because all of the domain databases will get rebuilt later.

7 • You are prompted to shut down the agents for the domain you are merging. From the server console, or by using RCONSOLE, exit the ADA and MTA for the domain you are merging (NNBPRI, in our example). Once the agents are unloaded, click on Next to continue. Note: If you are working with a copy of the domain database on your local drive, you don't need to shut down the agents. Just click on Next to continue.

8 • Click on Merge to perform the merge process, which will take a few minutes, depending on the size of it. During the process, you'll see the box shown in Figure 14.6. You will be notified when it is complete. Click on Done and restart the ADA and MTA for the NNBPRI domain.

Repeat these steps for all other domains you wish to merge into the GroupWise system (for example, the NNBSEC domain).

FIGURE 14.6

Merge Process Notification

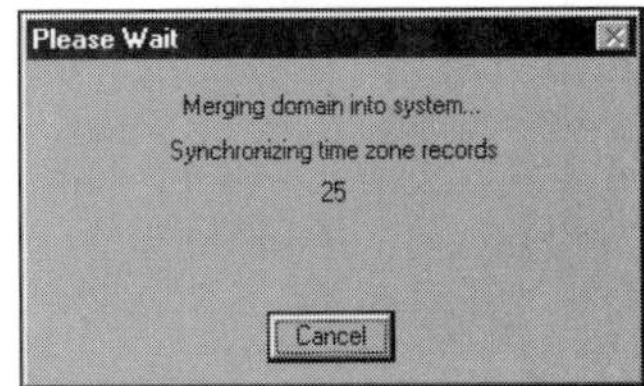

At this point, you have changed only copies of the actual domain databases. The databases now need to be rebuilt so they contain accurate information about the domain definitions.

In our example, the ShickTools GroupWise system is now set up as illustrated in Figure 14.7.

FIGURE 14.7

ShickTools' System after Merge

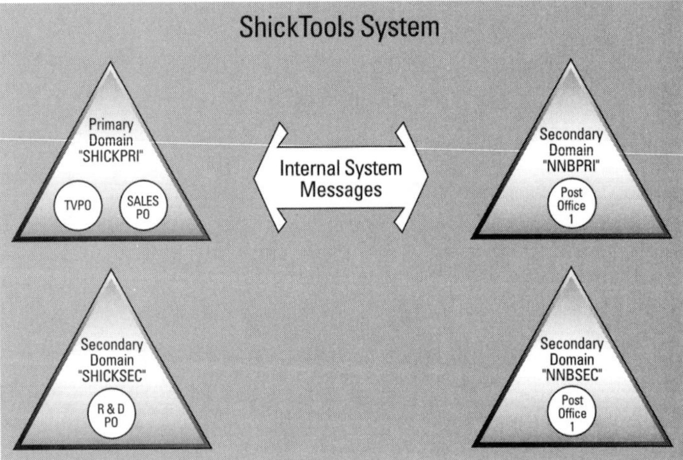

Note that the NNBPRI and NNBSEC domains are now secondary domains to the SHICKPRI primary domain.

Rebuilding the Databases

Once the merge has been completed, it is critical that you rebuild all of the domain and post office databases. You could let the ADA for each domain perform the synchronization, but such a fundamental change in the GroupWise system structure demands immediate update of the administrative databases.

During a release or merge operation, only the domain databases immediately affected are updated about the operation. Consequently, other domain databases not directly involved, and all post office databases, are all in need of updated information before the release or merge operation takes place. To correct this situation, the administrative databases need to be rebuilt.

Domain Databases

In Chapter 13, you learned about the process for rebuilding domain databases. When you rebuild a domain database, you replace the existing database with a new one, which is built from the primary domain database.

In our ShickTools example, we would rebuild three domain databases, one for each of the secondary domains (SHICKSEC, NNBPRI, and NNBSEC).

To rebuild a domain database, follow these steps:

1. Prevent other processes from accessing the database by unloading the ADA agents for the domain database you are rebuilding. Rebuilding requires exclusive access to the database. No other process (for example, the ADA or NetWare Administrator) should have access to it at the time.

2. In NetWare, make sure you have access to the path for the domain database you are rebuilding (the SHICKSEC domain, in our example).

3. Highlight the Domain object representing the domain database you are rebuilding (the SHICKSEC domain, in our example), and choose GroupWise Utilities from the Tools menu.

4. Select System Maintenance and then Rebuild Domain Database from the Actions box, as shown in Figure 14.8. Click on Run.

5. In the Rebuild Destination Path dialog box, enter the path to the secondary domain database (either the actual domain directory or the local directory where the copy of the WPDOMAIN.DB is).

6 • Click on OK to rebuild the domain database, and click on OK and Close when it is finished. It might take some time, depending on the size of the database and network traffic.

7 • If domain databases were rebuilt in the domain directory, reload the MTA and ADA agents for the rebuilt domain.

Repeat these steps for each of the secondary domains in your system.

Domain Database Copies

Once you have finished rebuilding the administrative databases, you need to send the rebuilt copies of the domain databases to the administrator of the domains that were merged into your system. If the domain administrator has local post offices, he or she will need to rebuild the post office databases in their domain, which is explained below.

In our example, we would send the WPDOMAIN.DB files for the NNBPRI and NNBSEC domains back to the Nuts 'n Bolts administrator. Remember, these were kept temporarily in C:\NNBPRI and C:\NNBSEC. We can simply send two mail messages with the corresponding WPDOMAIN.DB files attached. The receiving administrator would save these files in the actual NNBPRI and NNBSEC domain directories and reload the MTA and ADA for the domains.

FIGURE 14.8

Rebuilding the Secondary Domain

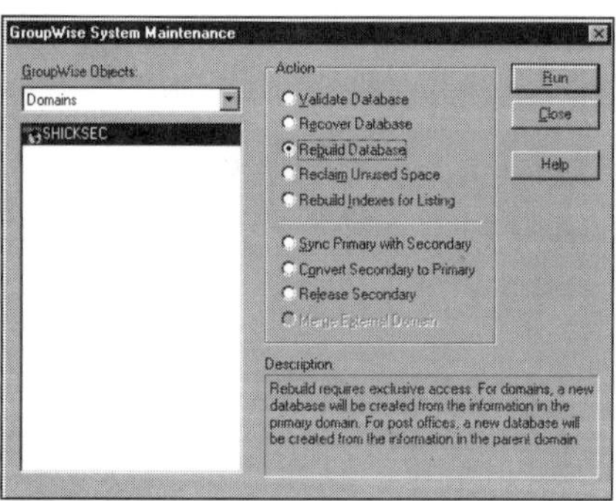

Post Office Databases

The post office databases need to be rebuilt to make sure the domain relationships are accurately in the Address Books. You can only rebuild the *current* domain's post office databases. In other words, if we were connected to the SHICKPRI domain, we would only be able to rebuild the TVPO and SALESPO post office databases.

Follow these steps to rebuild post office databases:

1. Rebuilding a post office database requires exclusive access, so make sure nothing is holding it open. The only two processes that use the post office database are the POA and the client program. Therefore, you need to unload the POA and make sure everyone who is accessing this post office gets out of GroupWise. Obviously, rebuilding databases is a good operation to perform during off hours.

2. In NetWare Administrator, verify which domain you are connected to by choosing GroupWise System Operations from the Tools menu. Double-click on the System Connection. Click on OK when you have selected the right domain.

3. From the main screen of NetWare Administrator, single-click the first post office in the current domain.

4. Choose GroupWise Utilities from the Tools menu. Click on System Maintenance.

5. Select Rebuild Database, as shown in Figure 14.9. Choose Run.

6. Enter the path to the post office directory and click on OK to rebuild the post office database. Click on OK when it is finished and choose Close to go back to the main NetWare Administrator screen.

7. Reload the POA for the post office you rebuilt.

Repeat these steps for each post office in the current domain. To rebuild the post office databases for post offices in another domain, you need to make that domain the current domain (see Step 2).

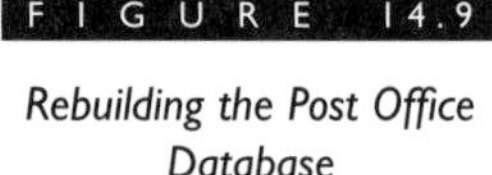

FIGURE 14.9

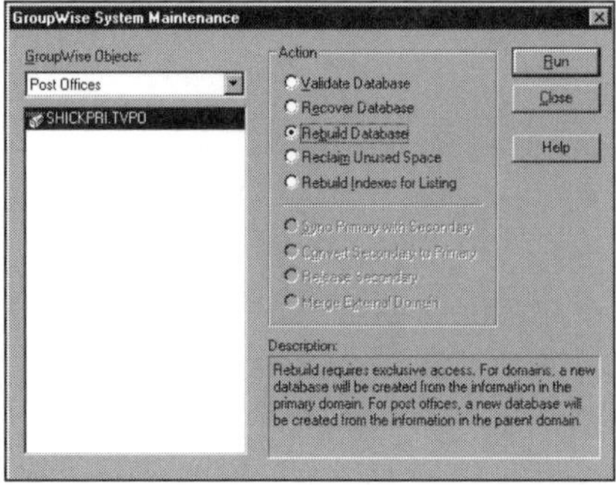

Rebuilding the Post Office Database

Managing the New System

After you combine two systems into one, you'll undoubtedly notice that system administration is easier for one large system than it was for a smaller system with an external domain.

For one thing, it is now easier to move users from one domain to another. You can only move users within the same system. You cannot move users from an external domain to a secondary domain in your system. So, now that the Nuts 'n Bolts users belong to the ShickTools system, they can be moved wherever they are needed within the system.

Also, you'll discover that links work the same way they did before. When you combine GroupWise systems, you change only the domain type (from external to secondary). You do not have to change the links at all. Changes to domain types have no effect on links.

Finally, you don't need to worry about coming up with new post office and domain names. In our example, the names of the Nuts 'n Bolts domains and post offices could remain unchanged to reduce the disruption to end users.

Changing a Secondary Domain to a Primary

After your system has been up and running for a while, you may decide you want to change a secondary domain into a primary domain. For example, you may notice that one of your secondary domains has relatively light message traffic. Or the primary domain's server may need to move to a location that is less convenient for you to access. Or you may want to promote a secondary domain to a primary domain if you have lost confidence in the structure or content of the primary domain database but are reasonably sure that the secondary domain is reliable. You could promote the secondary domain to primary, and then rebuild all other domains based on the new primary domain.

Whatever the reason, the promotion of a secondary domain to primary—while easy to perform—is a fundamental change in the structure for synchronization. Make sure you have good backups of the domain databases involved before you make the change.

Also, make sure automatic directory synchronization has finished its activities before attempting this procedure. A quick way to do this is to use the F6 key to restart the ADA from the screen of the ADA on the server console for both domains involved in this procedure. After the restart, if there is no update activity on the main part of screen, the ADA has settled down.

This is important because the primary domain is in charge of replication; changing the primary domain will pull the rug out from under the feet of the ADA.

To convert a secondary domain into the primary domain, follow these steps:

1. In NetWare Administrator, verify which domain you are connected to by choosing GroupWise System Operations from the Tools menu. Double-click on the System Connection. Click on OK when you have selected the primary domain.

2. From the NetWare Administrator main screen highlight the secondary domain you want to become primary.

3. Choose GroupWise Utilities from the Tools menu and then select System Maintenance from the menu.

4. Choose Convert Secondary to Primary from the Action box and click on Run to continue (see Figure 14.10).

5. Enter the path to the secondary domain database, and click OK. Click OK when the domain has been successfully converted and choose Close to return to the main NetWare Administrator screen.

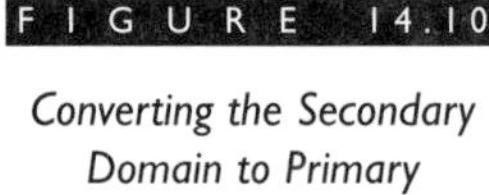

FIGURE 14.10

Converting the Secondary Domain to Primary

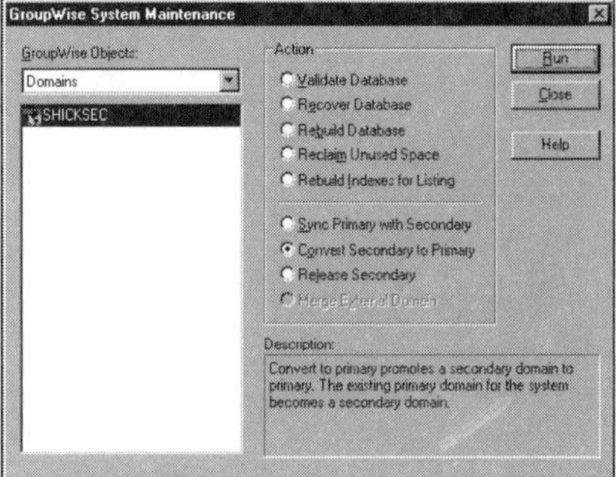

The implications of this change are not felt at the user level. Rather, the load on the new primary domain's MTA is now increased, as it is in charge of replicating all administrative changes to the other secondary domains.

Using Software Directory Management

The agent, administration, and client software can easily be copied to a new file server by creating a new software directory. When you create additional software directories on file servers throughout your system, you make it easier for users to access the most recent versions of GroupWise software.

Follow these steps to create a new software directory:

1 • Map a drive to the new server and have a directory name in mind for the new software directory.

2 • From the NetWare Administrator, choose Tools and GroupWise System Operations.

3 • Double-click on the Software Directory Management icon. The dialog box in Figure 14.11 will appear.

4 • Choose Create and specify a name for the directory. This is not the file system directory name, but the name that it will be known by in GroupWise (much like the name of a GroupWise Library object). The

default name is the name of the GroupWise system created during the initial installation.

5 • Complete a description and the UNC path to the new server's location where you want the directory to hold the GroupWise client, agent, and other software created. If the target directory has not been created, you will be prompted to create the new directory.

6 • Select the `Copy software from` box, which displays the name of your GroupWise system or other software distribution directories that have been created. Click on the name of the source software directory from the drop-down list.

7 • Click OK to copy the software—client, administration and agent software—from the original installation point to the new directory on the other file server.

FIGURE 14.11

Software Directory Management

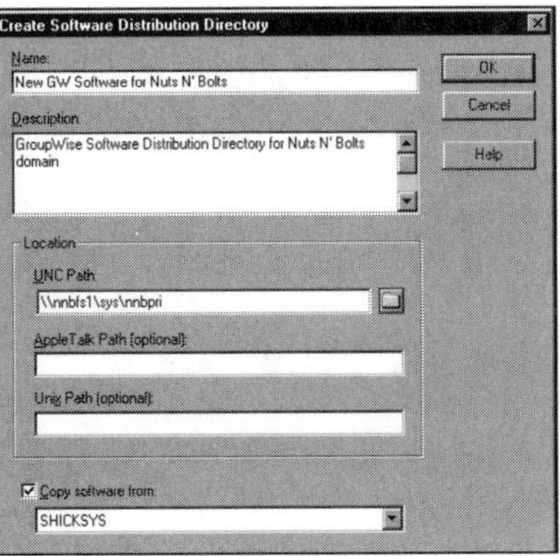

Using Addressing Rules

The GroupWise system uses an Internet-style address for each mailbox. This is mostly transparent to end users because they normally use the Address Book to address messages.

The default format of an address in GroupWise 5 is:

user@domain.post office

where *user* is the user's GroupWise name, *domain* is the name of the domain, and *post office* is the name of the GroupWise post office suffix. For example, if a GroupWise user with the user name MSTRANGE belongs to the TVPO post office in the SHICKPRI domain, the GroupWise address would be

mstrange@shickpri.tvpo

Users don't have to use this default Internet address. You can customize each user's Internet address. This procedure is explained in Chapter 20.

GroupWise has a handy feature called *addressing rules*. You can use a series of wildcard characters (? represents a single character and * represents multiple characters) and variables to convert short addresses entered by end users into longer, more complex addresses.

If a large number of users need to send mail to an Internet address with a long and unwieldy address, you can create a rule to help them. This enables users to enter a short and simple address, and GroupWise replaces the short format with its long counterpart.

For example, suppose users need to send e-mail to users at a government agency with the following address:

user@gw5.highway.kdot.ks.state.us.gov

You can create an addressing rule that would let users enter "*user*@kdot.gov" instead of the complete Internet address.

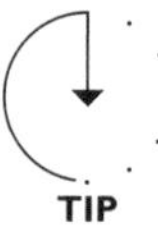

Don't confuse addressing rules with *explicit addressing*. Explicit addressing adds routing information in front of a recipient's regular GroupWise Address. An example of an explicit address is: INET:jdellorco@usckc.com. In this example INET is a foreign domain that represents the Internet to which the domain has an SMTP gateway link. Explicit addressing is typically used along with gateways, and is discussed more fully in Chapters 19 and 20.

Creating an Addressing Rule

To create an addressing rule, follow these steps:

1. From the Tools menu, choose GroupWise System Operations and double-click on the Addressing Rules icon.
2. A list of available addressing rules appears. (There are no addressing rules by default.) Click on the New button to create a new rule. You'll see the dialog box shown in Figure 14.12.
3. Enter a descriptive name in the Name field, and a short description in the Description field.
4. Type in a string for the rule to look for in the Search String field (for example, *@kdot.gov). In this field, you enter the characters you want users to type. The field can include wildcard characters (* or ?).
5. In the Replace With field, type in a string for the address that the rule should convert the search string into (for example, %1@gw5.highway.kdot.ks.state.us.gov). This is what you want the address to be converted to. This field can include variables that represent input (%1, %2, and so on).
6. Enter a sample address in the Test Rule field and click on the Test button.
7. The result of the rule appears under the sample address. If this is the result you want, click on OK to save the rule and add it to the list.

FIGURE 14.12

Creating an Addressing Rule

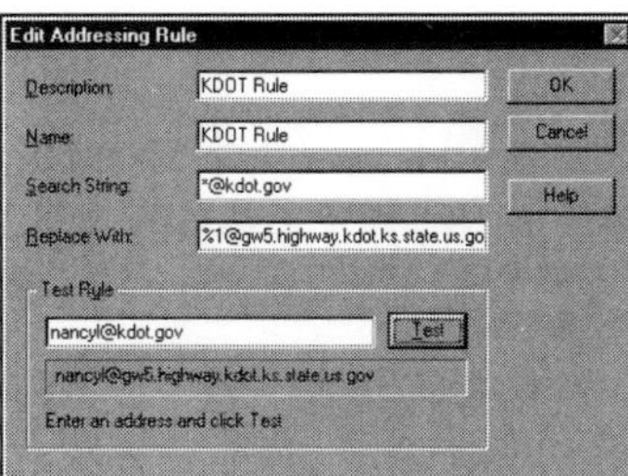

Be very careful when creating a rule that adds anything to the left of the user name (for explicit addressing purposes) in a standard Internet-style address (for instance, user@whatever.com). For example, if you make a rule to add the foreign domain INTERNET to all Internet-style addresses, GroupWise will try to send all mail to the Internet, even internal mail. This is because GroupWise uses Internet-style addressing natively—with the mailbox, domain, and post office names forming the address (*mailbox@domain.postoffice*).

Suppose the mailbox for a user named Maggie in the TVPO post office of the domain SHICKPRI has the default address maggie@shickpri.tvpo. If you create an addressing rule adding "INTERNET:" at the beginning of all Internet-style addresses, the internal GroupWise address of maggie@shickpri.tvpo would be resolved to INTERNET:maggie@shickpri.tvpo, and therefore would be routed through the SMTP gateway (instead of going to Maggie's mailbox in GroupWise).

Adding an Addressing Rule to a Domain

Simply creating an addressing rule doesn't automatically enable end users to start using the shorter address format. Before they can do that, you need to add the rule to the specific domain's properties.

To enable an addressing rule for a domain, follow these steps:

1 • Right-click on the Domain object and choose Details from the shortcut menu.

2 • Click on the Addressing Rules property page, as shown in Figure 14.13.

3 • The available Addressing Rules are listed. Click on the check box next to the rule (s) that you want to enable.

4 • To test the Rule, click on the Test button.

5 • Enter a sample address in the Enter a test address field, and click on the Test button. You will see the resulting address in the Results field (see Figure 14.14). Click on Close.

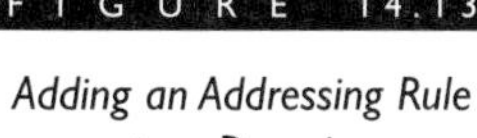

Adding an Addressing Rule to a Domain

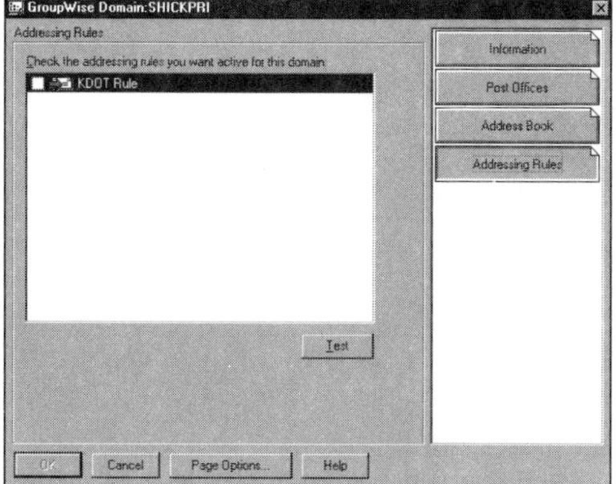

FIGURE 14.14

Testing an Addressing Rule

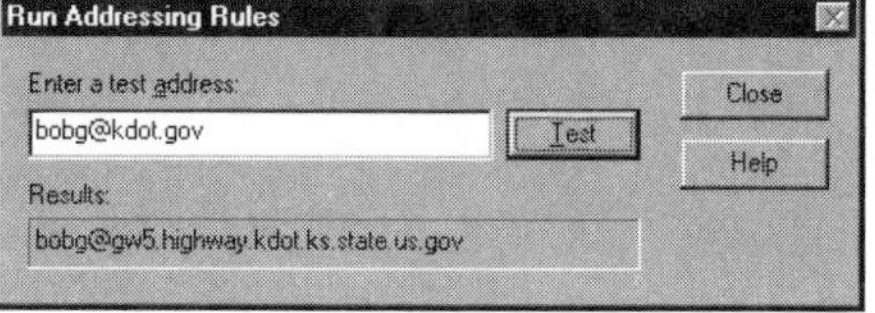

When you assign an addressing rule to a domain, a series of administrative messages are created, and the current domain's domain and post office databases are updated by its ADA. Users in the current domain will see the immediate effects of it. We highly recommend that you send out a message to everyone in the domain informing them about the rule, what its purpose is, and how to use it.

Normal replication then takes place via the MTA and ADA, and all other domain and post office databases are updated with the information that the original domain can use the addressing rule.

When a user addresses a message using the proper syntax, the address will be resolved to the result of the rule, and the message will be sent.

Adding Fields to the Address Book

As the administrator, you might need to define additional information about users and want that information viewable in the Address Book. You can accomplish this by defining additional properties for NDS User objects with GroupWise properties.

There are two types of additional fields: NDS fields and administrator-defined fields.

With NDS fields, you specify new NDS properties to appear in the Address Book (such as the Postal Zip Code property, which would not normally appear). Existing NDS information will be read and added to the Address Book, or you can enter new information after the fields have been added.

With administrator-defined fields, the administrator can create unique properties in NDS and then define them in NetWare Administrator so they appear in the GroupWise Address Book.

Adding new fields to the Address Book is domain-specific; in other words, the new fields are used only in the domain whose details you are editing. The additional fields themselves can be added to the Address Book for any domain in your system.

To specify additional NDS fields or to create new administrator-defined fields, follow these steps:

1 • In the Tools menu of NetWare Administrator, click on GroupWise System Operations and double-click on the Admin-Defined Fields icon.

2 • Double-click on a property currently defined as unused.

3 • Click on the NDS User properties you want to appear in the Address Book, and click Select (see Figure 14.15). Repeat this step until all desired NDS properties have been selected. If you do not want to create new NDS properties, skip to Step 10.

4 • To create new administrator-defined fields, click on Create from this screen. The Extend NDS Schema dialog box appears (see Figure 14.16).

5 • In the `Properties will be created in` *`tree name`*`:` field, enter the name of the new property and click on Add.

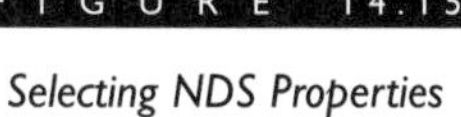

FIGURE 14.15

Selecting NDS Properties

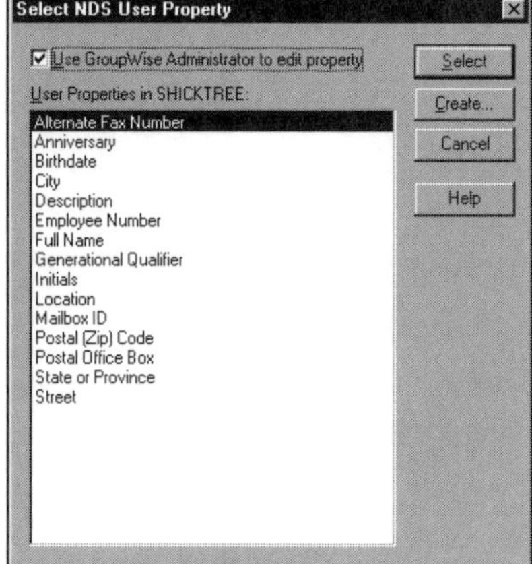

FIGURE 14.16

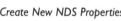

Create New NDS Properties

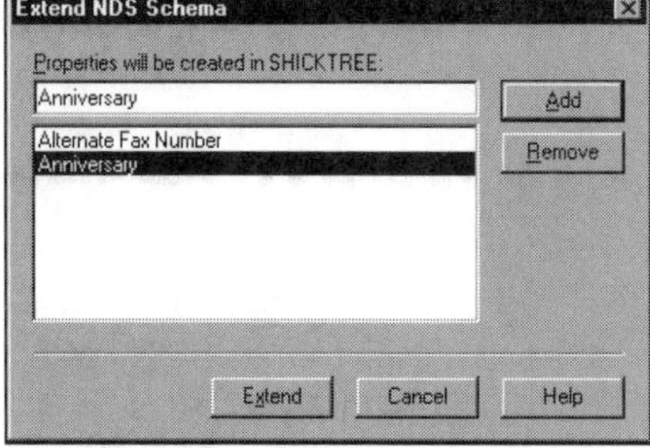

6 • Repeat Step 5, defining additional new properties. Click on Extend when finished. Note: This step will extend the schema of the specified NDS tree permanently. Be sure you have an adequate backup before performing this step.

7 • Read the warning on the screen about extending the schema and click on Yes when you are ready.

8 • Once the schema has been extended, you'll see the message shown in Figure 14.17. Click on OK to continue.

9 • Click on the name of the new field to appear in the Address Book, choose the Use GroupWise Administrator to Edit property, and then click on Select (see Figure 14.18).

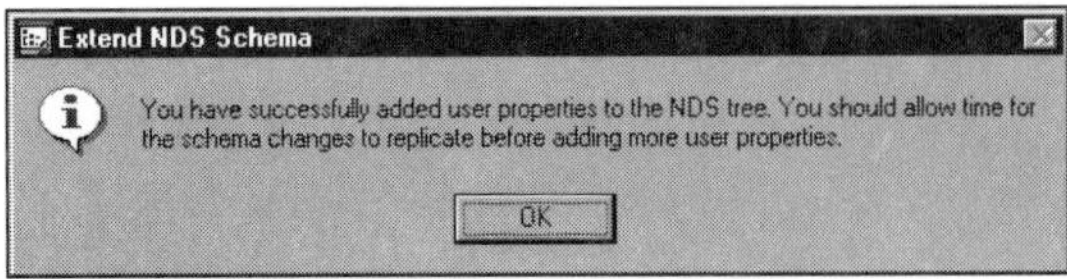

FIGURE 14.17

Schema Extension Alert

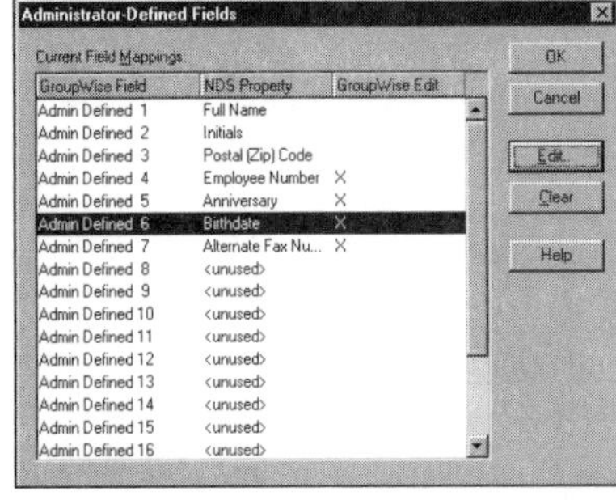

FIGURE 14.18

Administrator-Defined Fields

10 • Repeat Step 9 until all new fields have been added. Click on OK when you have added all of the desired fields.

11 • Choose Close to return to the main screen of NetWare Administrator.

Editing New NDS Properties

To change a new property for an NDS User object, follow these steps:

1 • From the main screen of NetWare Administrator, right-click on a User object and choose Details from the shortcut menu.

2 • Click on the GroupWise Account property page and scroll through the account fields until the new properties appear (see Figure 14.19).

3 • Click on OK to complete the change.

Once the fields have been made available to the domain, you need to enable the domain's Address Book to display them.

FIGURE 14.19

Editing New NDS Properties

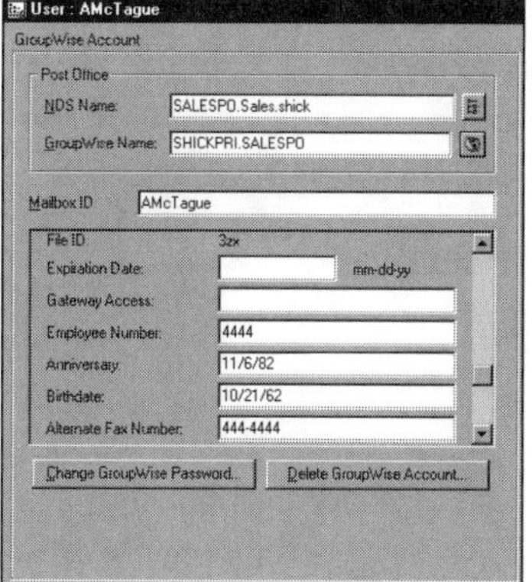

Enabling the Address Book to Display New Properties

To enable a domain's Address Book to display new properties, follow these steps:

1. Right-click on the Domain object and choose Details from the shortcut menu.
2. Click on the Address Book property page (see Figure 14.20).
3. In the Available Fields column, select (by clicking or pressing Shift-click or Ctrl-click) the properties you wish to be added to the Address Book.
4. Click on the left arrow to add them to the list of Address Book Fields.
5. To remove any fields from the Address Book, select them from the Address Book Fields list and click on the right-pointing arrow to move them to the Available Fields list.
6. Click on OK to complete the change.

NOTE

To see the new properties in the Address Book of the GroupWise client, right-click on the column headings to see the new fields; select the fields, and the properties will be displayed.

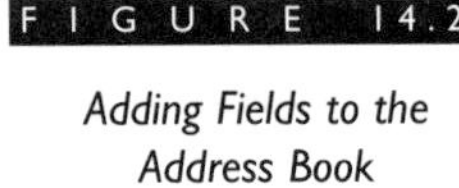

FIGURE 14.20

Adding Fields to the Address Book

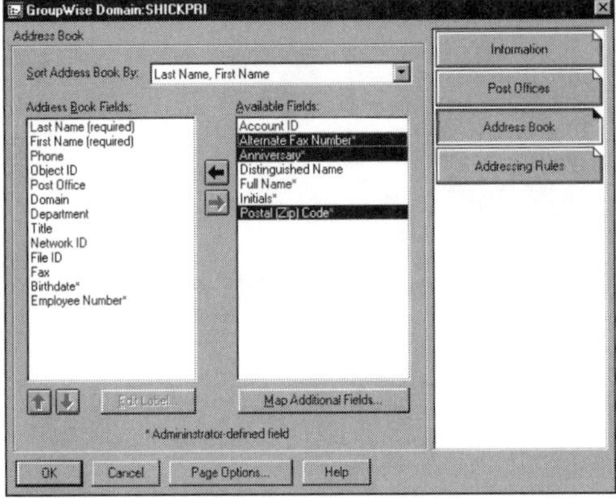

You can use additional fields to add administrator-defined properties in the GroupWise Address Book for users, such as a birthday or employee number. You can also use this information in other NDS-aware programs, since the information is entered into NDS.

Defining Scheduled Events

The GroupWise POA and ADA can be enhanced to perform many different types of activities, from warning you about low disk space to performing maintenance on the information store.

Each event has three components: event type, event trigger, and action to perform. The *event type* is a pre-defined category of the available Scheduled Events, and are different for the POA and ADA. The *event trigger* is a measured quantity (for example, disk space or a time interval) that initiates the action that the agent is configured to perform. The *action(s) to perform* defines procedures for the agent to perform when activated by the trigger (for example, "perform a statistical check every Friday at 3:00 p.m. of the post office information store and send the log file to the administrator").

Once the event has been defined in NetWare Administrator, you need to restart the agent to enable the event. The agent will then check the trigger and perform the action that was defined.

POA Scheduled Events

POA Scheduled Events can be viewed in NetWare Administrator on the Scheduled Events property page for the POA object. Two POA events are created by default:

- Disk check event
- OFCheck event

These default Scheduled Events can be modified, added to, or deleted. You can add other actions to these events. Once you know how to create them, you'll probably want to create custom Scheduled Events to meet your own needs.

Disk Check Event

The *Disk Check event* for the POA will periodically check the amount of drive space available to the information store for which the POA is running. This is displayed in Figure 14.21.

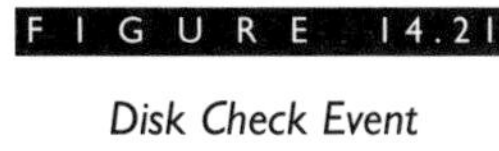

FIGURE 14.21

Disk Check Event

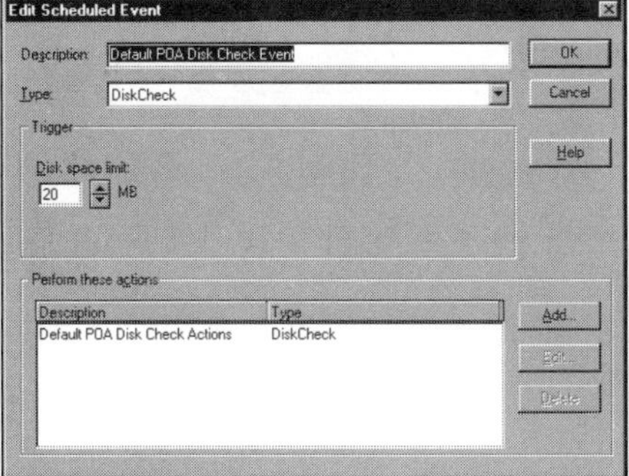

Based on a specified amount of disk space, the POA Disk Check event runs Mailbox/Library Maintenance and performs one of the following actions:

- *Send Begin.* Sends a message to the domain administrator when the disk limit has been reached.
- *Send Failed.* Sends a message to the domain's administrator if Mailbox/Library Maintenance doesn't free up enough disk space.

- *Send End.* Sends a message to the administrator with the amount of disk space that was recovered with Mailbox/Library Maintenance.

To add an action to the Disk Check event, click on the Add button and select an appropriate action, as shown in Figure 14.22.

FIGURE 14.22

Disk Check Actions

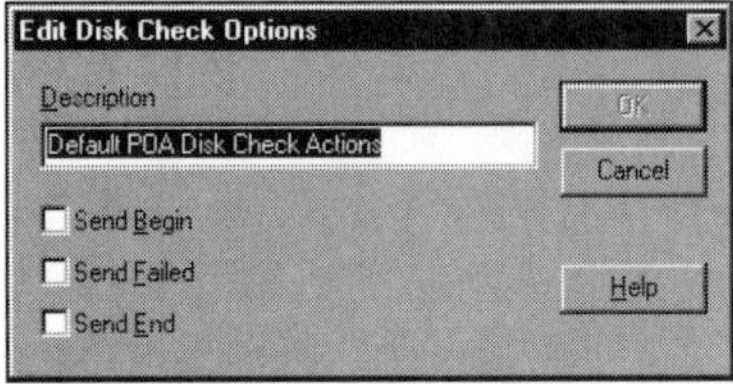

OFCheck Event

The second POA default Scheduled Event, the *OFCheck event*, performs a regular check of the information store and sends the resulting log file to the configured administrator's mailbox. Details of the OFCheck event can be seen in Figure 14.23.

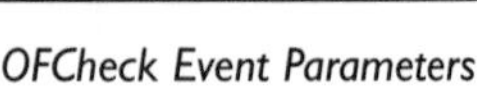
FIGURE 14.23

OFCheck Event Parameters

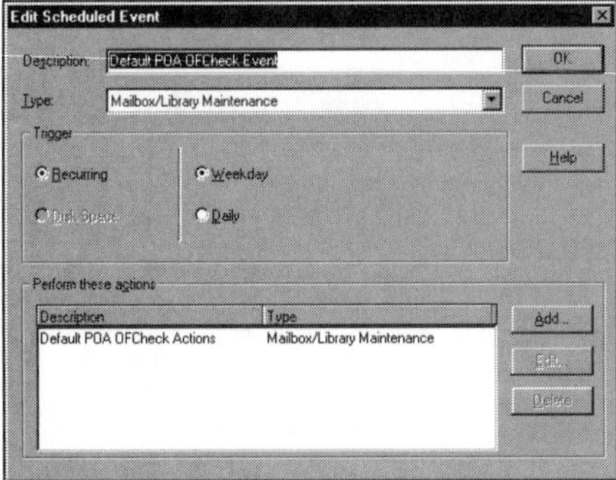

Based on either a weekly or daily schedule, or based on available disk space, the Scheduled Event runs OFCheck with the specified parameters.

By highlighting the OFCheck action, you can click on the Edit button to change the options (see Figure 14.24). These options are discussed in more detail in Chapter 13.

FIGURE 14.24
OFCheck Options

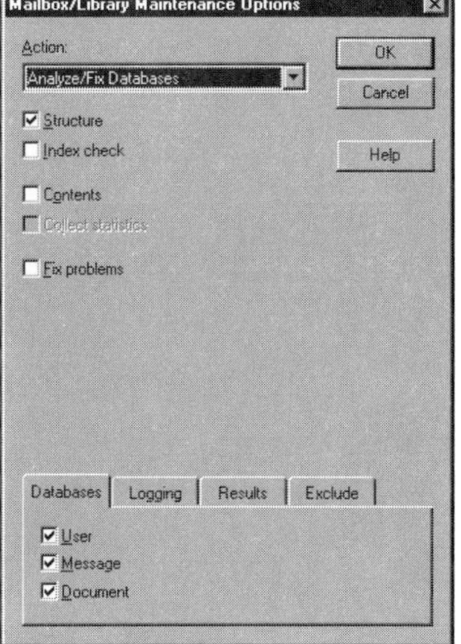

ADA Scheduled Events

There two ADA Scheduled Event types: NDS User Synchronization and ADA Idle events. Unlike the POA, there are no default ADA Scheduled Events. At the least, we recommend that you create an NDS User Synchronization Scheduled Event to update the Address Book with information about changes that occur in NDS. To allow administration database backup and maintenance on a regular basis, the ADA Idle Time event can be created.

NDS User Synchronization

The GroupWise administration portion of NetWare Administrator (GWADA) has to be told when and how to synchronize with NDS. This event isn't scheduled by default; it needs to be created with NetWare Administrator. If NDS User Synchronization is not performed by this Scheduled Event, changes in NDS that do not create a replication message (such as a change made by a non-GroupWise-enabled version of NetWare Administrator) will not be reflected in the GroupWise Address Book.

1. Right-click on the ADA object for the domain. Choose Details from the shortcut menu.

2 • Select the Scheduled Events property page.

3 • Choose Add and then Create. You'll see the dialog box shown in Figure 14.25.

4 • Fill in the name, select type as NDS User synchronization, select the interval (Daily or Weekday) and choose OK to save.

5 • To enable the ADA for NDS synchronization, you must use the GWACCESS account. The following must be placed in the startup file for the ADA:

```
/user-.GWACCESS.GRPWISE.SHICKTOOLS
/password-chiefs
```

FIGURE 14.25

Creating an NDS Scheduled Event

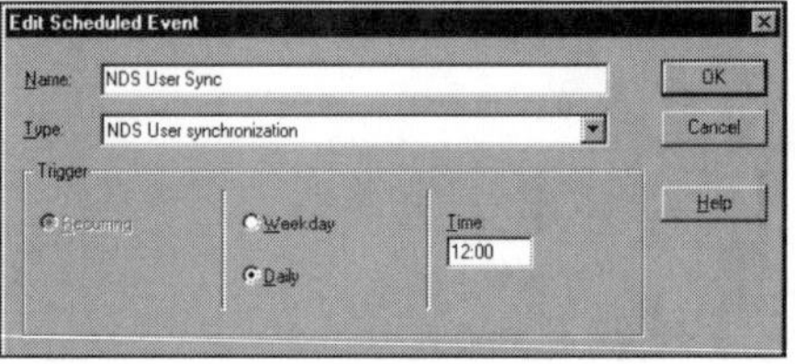

The ADA will now look at NDS at the specified interval (see Step 4) for changes, and update the GroupWise administrative databases.

ADA Idle

The other type of Scheduled Event that can be created for the ADA is the ADA Idle event. This event suspends the ADA process from updating the GroupWise databases. This is very good for backups, troubleshooting, and maintenance of the databases. With an ADA Idle event, you can specify the time (weekly or daily) and duration (the default is 1 minute) after which you want the ADA to not process updates (and therefore access the domain and/or post office databases).

Once the Scheduled Events are created, they will be listed in the Scheduled Events property page of the ADA object in NetWare Administrator. To enable (or disable) a particular event, check (or uncheck) the check box next to the event. The ADA agent will restart, and the Scheduled Event will be performed at the time interval specified.

Configuring MTA Message Logging

The MTA can provide very in-depth message log reports of message activity. These reports are in the form of GroupWise databases, which can only be read with the Message Logging API in the GroupWise Software Developer's Kit (SDK). The GroupWise SDK is found on the CD included with this book.

It is beyond the scope of this discussion to go into how to use these reports; you have to use the aforementioned API to access the databases with value-added programs. Instead, we will tell you how to start the logging process, furnishing a brief description of the different amounts and types of information you can obtain.

To enable MTA message logging, follow these steps:

1 • In NetWare Administrator, right-click on the MTA object and choose Details from the short menu.

2 • Click on the Message Logging property page. You'll see the property page shown in Figure 14.26.

3 • Make your selections and click on OK, and restart the MTA to enable message logging.

FIGURE 14.26

MTA Message Logging Property Page

Table 14.1 describes the fields on the Message Logging property page.

TABLE 14.1

Message Logging Options

FIELD	DESCRIPTION
`Logging Level`	`Brief`. Message data for billing and tracking (message identifier, type, sender, priority, next hop, final destination, and customizable flags) `Full`. In addition to the Brief information, Full includes arrival time, queued time, send time at each hop, completed time, connection count, and transport information
`Log File Path`	The directory that will hold the databases (The GWACCESS user needs full rights to this directory.)
`Message Correlation`	Keeps a live connection between the delivery report and the delivered status for the original message record
`Include Reports`	Include delivery reports from messages that are delivered
`Include User Statistics`	Additional status information from user-prompted actions, such as when the message was opened or deleted
Include Other Messages	Log administrative messages in addition to user messages

Instead of specifying these options in NetWare Administrator, you can edit the following switches in the MTA startup file:

```
/messagelogpath-\\[server]\[volume]\[directory] - Message
Logging Directory

/messagelogsettings-[ evrsoc ]
```

e Enabled. This option has to be specified for the message logging to be active.
v Verbose. Includes all information for the logged messages.
r Log delivery/nondelivery reports.
s Log GroupWise statuses.
o Log all other message types (e.g., administrative messages).
c Correlate reports with messages.

Once you have made the changes to the MTA startup file, you must exit and reload the MTA in order for the new switches to be read.

Summary

This chapter covered the special topics that administrators typically don't have to deal with every day, such as combining GroupWise systems, changing a secondary domain to a primary domain, software directory management, advanced addressing, additional fields, Scheduled Events, and MTA message logging. Chapter 15 covers Client/Server access mode in GroupWise 5.

CHAPTER 15

Client/Server Access Mode

In this chapter, we focus on enabling GroupWise 5's Client/Server access mode. With GroupWise 5 you have a choice between classic file-sharing messaging (called *Direct Only access mode*) and more state-of-the-art client/server messaging (*Client/Server Only access mode* and *Client/Server and Direct access mode*).

When you use GroupWise 5's Direct Only access mode, your system relies on an access method called *file sharing*. This type of access has the following characteristics:

- *Restrictive network protocols*. Each client must use the same network protocol as the server on which the messages are stored in order to access them.
- *Licensed connections*. Each client uses a licensed connection to the file server on which messages are stored, and each license costs money.
- *File system rights*. The user must be granted file system Read rights to the databases and files, and Write and Create rights to send messages and change databases.
- *Open files*. When a client has the messaging program open on a computer, it holds files open on the server. Therefore, it is very difficult to perform maintenance or backup the message store during normal operating hours.

When you use client/server messaging, on the other hand, you can take advantage of the client/server architecture's many strengths. The main benefit of using the Client/Server access mode is that the processing load is split between the client computer and the server computer. The client program runs on a user's computer, and the server program (POA) runs on the network server. In terms of GroupWise components specifically, the GroupWise client runs in the client mode on the user's workstation, and the POA runs in server mode on the file server. These two programs use a TCP/IP network connection to exchange information.

Other benefits of client/server messaging are as follows:

- *Flexible network protocol*. Using TCP/IP provides today's users with access to most information they need to do their jobs: the messaging system, the Internet, and corporate intranets as well. In addition,

GroupWise 5 supports other Internet/intranet-related capabilities, such as HTML data types and URL references in messages and folders. TCP/IP also offers a more open platform for development, and is a very open standard.

- *No licenses needed.* Client/server connections do not take any licensed connections on a server, since one application (the client program) is communicating with another application (the POA). This saves money! As a matter of fact, you can use a two-user version of NetWare 4.x or 3.x on one server to support many users without the requirement of a NetWare license for each (the caveat is that the NetWare server can't be used for anything else besides GroupWise via Client/Server access, such as file or print services).
- *No file system rights needed.* GroupWise users who access their post office with a client/server connection do not need any file system rights; since they are not opening files, they don't need to be authenticated to any files on the server. The POA will access the files on their behalf. Of course, network security is the big winner here.
- *No open files.* If everyone in a given post office has access using client/server connections, the POA is the only process that opens files. Users do not open files on the server with client/server connections. This gives you greater flexibility in performing backups and maintenance, and also reduces the likelihood of file and database corruption caused by irregular access by the client application.
- *More reliability.* Compared to Direct Only access, Client/Server access mode boasts greater functionality and maintains better integrity of the information store, which results in reduced downtime for end users.
- *Easier link management.* When you use client/server messaging, you'll find it's much easier to deploy and track links that are normally defined with UNC or DOS paths in file-sharing messaging.
- *Less chance of database corruption.* Because only the POA directly accesses the information store and directory store databases,

corruption caused by concurrent client access is completely eliminated.

To enjoy the benefits of Client/Server access mode, several preparatory steps must be taken. These steps are covered in the next section.

Network Requirements

The network requirements for Client/Server access mode are straightforward: You need a TCP/IP network. All servers running the GroupWise post office agent need to be able to send out and receive TCP/IP network packets. Workstations must be configured to receive these TCP/IP packets and send out their own. Figure 15.1 illustrates a GroupWise system using Client/Server access mode.

FIGURE 15.1

Client/Server Access Mode

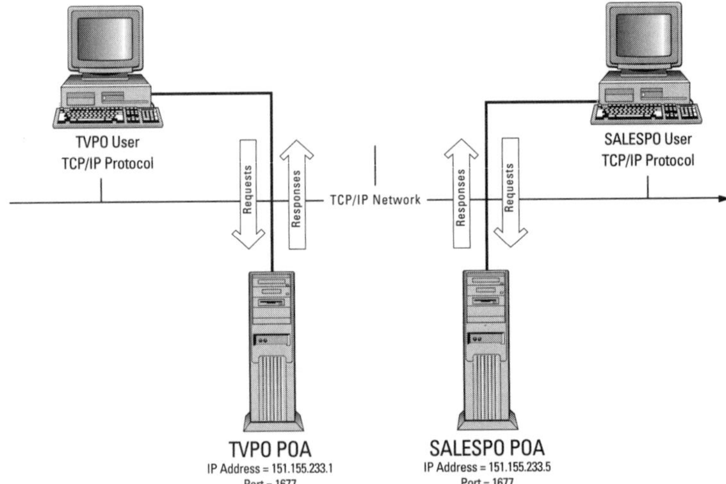

As mentioned previously, with the advent of the Internet and intranets (closed, customized versions of the Internet for private organizations), there is a good chance that you already have TCP/IP running on your network.

If not, there are many things to consider if you are thinking about setting up your system for client/server messaging. Let's briefly look at those considerations next.

TCP/IP Addressing

The TCP/IP address uniquely identifies each computer on your network. An example of a TCP/IP address is: 151.155.233.7. The range of valid IP addresses is provided to you by InterNic when you obtain your connection to the Internet.

Each workstation needs a unique IP address. In addition, each server running a POA in Client/Server access mode needs a unique IP address.

If you are not planning to connect to the Internet, you can use any series of addresses you like, but be forewarned: There are serious implications if you connect a nonregistered set of IP-addressed computers to the Internet (due to the risk of duplicated IP addresses).

One solution to this problem is to use an IP proxy server, which holds a pool of IP addresses and passes them out as workstations request them. IntraNetWare has an IP/IPX gateway that allows you to use a nonregistered IP address scheme using as many nodes as you want, connected through the gateway to the Internet with one registered IP address. The NetWare DHCP portion of IntraNetWare allocates IP addresses with or without any of these other components. You specify a range of IP addresses for the DHCP server to "hand out" and when the workstations attach to the network, they are provided an IP address.

Domain Names

If your company plans to send and receive e-mail on the Internet using an address that reflects the company name, you need to register for an Internet domain name with InterNic. For example, our fictitious company, ShickTools, Inc., might register for the domain name "shicktools.com." The e-mail address for ShickTools employees would then have the following format: *user*@shicktools.com. There is a fee associated with the process of obtaining a registered domain name. Also, the domain name must be unique throughout the Internet.

DNS Configuration

The Domain Name System, or *DNS*, is a series of distributed databases that resolve an Internet domain name to a TCP/IP address. Each DNS database entry for e-mail routing purposes has the format of the following example:

```
shicktools.com    MX    10    151.155.233.87
```

DNS also includes routing information that helps requests find the computer with the associated IP address. "MX" stands for Mail Exchange and is used to route Internet mail, and the 10 is a preference number (the lower the number, the more preferable the record to use). We discuss this more fully in Chapter 20.

When you obtain your IP addresses and domain name, this information is entered into DNS so the entire Internet will know that any mail sent to "kgrawe@ shicktools.com" will go to 151.155.233.87, which is a specific computer connected to the Internet.

Each workstation needs to know how to find one (and possibly two) DNS servers. This is specified in the setup for the TCP/IP on the workstation.

Firewalls

An effective firewall protects your internal network from the outside world. The firewall will block certain kinds of traffic and allow other types of traffic to pass through. Many types of firewalls are available, from both a hardware and software perspective. A complete discussion of firewalls is outside the scope of this book. You may want to contact your Internet Service Provider or a TCP/IP networking consultant for more information.

TCP/IP Stacks

The servers and workstations need to load and bind to their network interface cards the TCP/IP protocol stack. When you bind the TCP/IP protocol, you are telling the network card to start speaking the language of TCP/IP, and assigning an address to the card.

The client/server configuration needs to be implemented between all of your post offices in order to fully maximize the benefits. A few utilities, programs, and files are needed to implement the TCP/IP protocol on your network, which are included with IntraNetWare and NetWare 4.x.

INETCFG.NLM

On NetWare servers, you can use this NLM at the file server to enter all of the pertinent TCP/IP information.

At the server console, or by using RCONSOLE, enter the following command and press Enter:

```
load inetcfg
```

You will see the menu shown in Figure 15.2, which you can use to configure the server for TCP/IP.

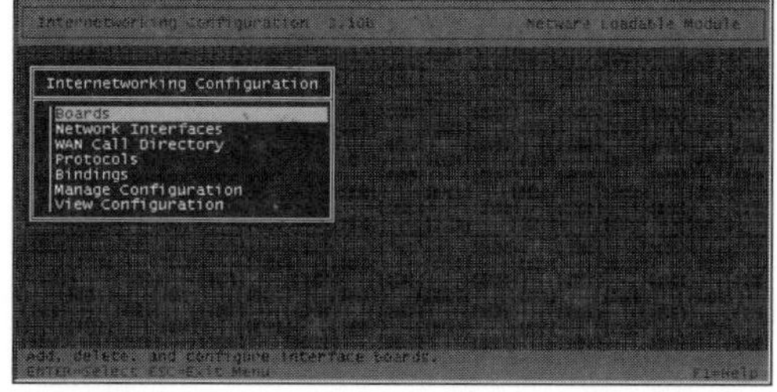

FIGURE 15.2

The INETCFG Screen

RESOLV.CFG

This file is created to tell the TCP/IP NLM what the host name of the computer is and where to find DNS. The file is located in the SYS:ETC directory on NetWare 3.x and 4.x servers.

Following is a sample RESOLV.CFG file:

```
domain        shicktools.com
nameserver    155.151.233.67
```

`domain shicktools.com` (This is the registered domain name.)

`nameserver 155.151.233.67` (This is the IP address of the DNS server.)

TCP/IP Console for NetWare

The TCP/IP Console for NetWare (TCPCON) is an excellent method of tracking TCP/IP traffic. To load the TCP/IP Console, enter the following command at the server console and press Enter:

```
load tcpcon
```

Figure 15.3 shows the TCP/IP Console.

You can use the menus and options in this utility to view TCP/IP traffic on this server. This would be an excellent addition to the AUTOEXEC.NCF file, which would then load the TCP/IP Console program automatically when the server is started.

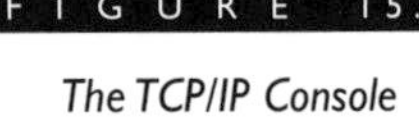

FIGURE 15.3

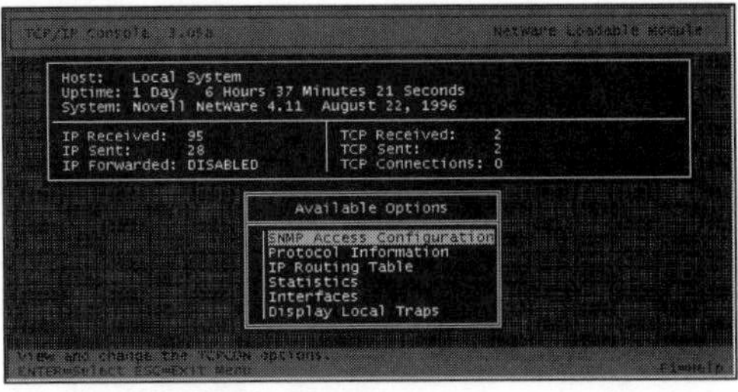

The TCP/IP Console

This is merely an overview of the things you need to accomplish. A detailed explanation of these tasks is beyond the scope of this book. However, you should check out an excellent resource on the subject: *Novell's Guide to TCP/IP and IntranetWare* by Drew Heywood (published by Novell Press and IDG Books Worldwide).

Server Configuration

This section covers the server-level setup to enable Client/Server access mode for GroupWise. Here we explain the necessary post office settings, designation of a post office agent (POA) as the NGWNameServer, POA settings, and use of multiple POAs for load-balancing.

Post Office Settings

In NetWare Administrator, you need to configure the Post Office object to use Client/Server access mode for its users. This is done by editing the properties of the Post Office object:

1. Right-click on the Post Office object and choose Details from the shortcut menu (see Figure 15.4). There are three possible settings for the access mode:
    - *Direct Only*. All users access this post office using file-sharing messaging.

- *Client/Server Only*. All users access the post office using TCP/IP.
- *Client/Server and Direct*. Both types of access mode are used in the post office.

2 • Choose either *Client/Server Only* or *Client/Server and Direct* and then click on OK.

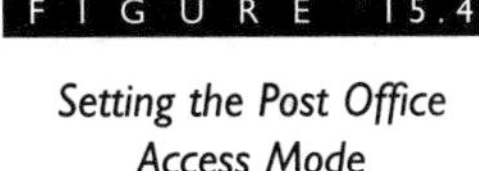
FIGURE 15.4

Setting the Post Office Access Mode

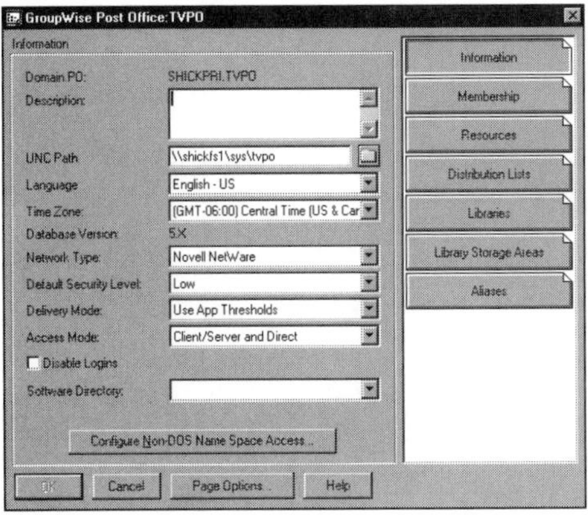

The ADA will update the domain and post office databases with the change, and clients will need to be configured to use the access mode you specified.

NGWNameServer

NGWNameServer is a special entry in DNS for the post office agents. It points the client to the POA's IP address. The format of the DNS entry is as follows:

```
Ngwnameserver <post office agent IP address>
```

When you set up Client/Server access mode, you need to select one low-traffic POA to be the NGWNameServer POA. Once you have chosen a POA, you need to add the POA's IP address into DNS.

To add the NGWNameServer entry to DNS, you need to edit the DNS databases on the DNS server for your company. The database may be on a local server or at an Internet Service Provider. Because the procedures for editing the DNS database vary widely from company to company, the specific steps are not covered here. As a system administrator, you should have access to the procedures to edit the DNS database used by your organization. You can check with your Internet Service Provider or the documentation that was included with your DNS software, if you have an internal DNS server.

We recommend that you specify a second POA to serve as a backup NGWNAMESERVER. To specify a second POA as a backup NGWNameServer, add the following entry to DNS:

```
ngwnameserver2 <post office agent IP address>
```

When a client starts GroupWise in Client/Server Access mode, the client program determines the POA's IP address through the following process:

- The client first reads any startup switches for the shortcut that designates the IP address.
- The client reads the Windows registry for a TCP/IP address for the POA.
- The client looks at Novell Directory Services (NDS) to determine the IP address of the POA object.
- The client reads the DNS entry for NGWNameServer to get an IP address for a POA.

Once the client can find a POA running TCP/IP, GroupWise is then connected to the user's home POA with TCP/IP. This happens because the post office database (of the POA that the client found) has all of the address information about each POA.

POA Settings and Startup Files

Once you have configured the Post Office object for Client/Server access mode, you need to change the properties of the POA object. You may need to make changes in two different places: in NetWare Administrator and in the POA startup file. For most environments, it is usually only necessary to make all changes to the POA using only NetWare Administrator. (In fact, that is the recommended way to make changes.)

NetWare Administrator Settings

To modify the Client/Server Access mode setting for a POA in NetWare Administrator, follow these steps:

1 • Right-click on the POA object and choose Details.

2 • Click on the Agent Settings. You will see a property page like the one shown in Figure 15.5.

FIGURE 15.5

POA Client/Server Settings

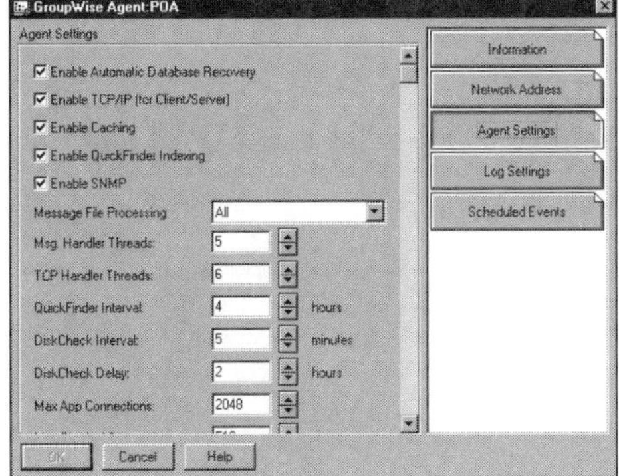

The following settings affect client/server configuration:

- *Enable TCP/IP (for Client/Server)*. Loads the GroupWise TCP/IP support NLM when the POA is loaded.
- *Max Physical Connections*. Specifies the maximum number of physical connections from workstations to the POA. Physical connections are established IP connections between the client and the server. The default is 512.
- *Max App Connections*. Specifies the maximum number of "virtual applications" that can connect to this POA. *Virtual applications* include custom applications, the Address Book, the proxy feature, shared folders, and the Personal Address Book. These virtual connections can share one physical connection. The default is 2048 connections. Note: Each virtual connection takes up 2 to 3K of server memory. It is

estimated that each user will have an average of three to four virtual connections sharing the same physical connection at one time. Virtual connections exist as long as the client software is loaded. Physical connections take up very little memory on the server and are terminated by the client software after they are inactive for ten seconds. The server will terminate physical and virtual connections if they are inactive for 15 minutes.

3 • Once the settings have been selected, click on the Network Address property page.

4 • To assign an IP address to the POA, click on Add. You'll see the dialog box shown in Figure 15.6.

FIGURE 15.6

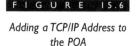

Adding a TCP/IP Address to the POA

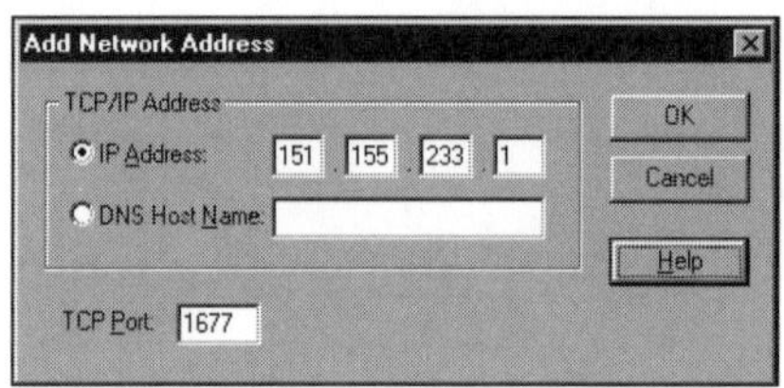

5 • Enter either the TCP/IP address of the server on which the POA will be loaded, or enter the DNS host name of the computer on which the POA is loaded.

6 • Notice that the port number defaults to 1677. If multiple POAs will be loaded on the same server, you will need to specify other port numbers here and in the startup files.

7 • Click on OK to assign the IP address to the POA, and click on OK to return to the main screen of NetWare Administrator. If the POA is already loaded, you will need to unload it and reload it to read the new configuration information.

Now that the POA object has been configured, you need to make sure that the POA's startup file is configured properly for Client/Server access mode.

Startup File Switches

The POA startup file has several switches that can be used to configure client/server messaging. All of these switches are also available as settings in NetWare Administrator. Therefore, you do not need to use these switches in the startup file unless you want to override the values in NetWare Administrator on a temporary basis, or to tune a particular server.

NOTE

The POA startup file can be edited by pressing the F10 key and choosing Edit Startup File from the POA screen on the server console. Any changes made to the startup file will not go into effect until the POA is unloaded and then reloaded.

Table 15.1 lists and describes the various client/server configuration switches.

TABLE 15.1

Client/Server Configuration Switches

SWITCH	DESCRIPTION
/notcpip	Disables processing of client/server requests from users on the post office
/port-[number]	Specifies the port number that the POA will poll for client/server requests (The default port is 1677.)
/maxappconns-[number]	Number of client/server application connections the server will allow (The default is 2048. Note: The number of applications that will use the POA could be greater than the number of users because each GroupWise session opens more than one application connection)
/maxphysconns-[number]	Number of physical client/server connections the server will allow (The default is 512. This number could be greater than the number of users on the post office because of passthrough client/server requests to other POAs.)

Once you have edited and saved the file, you need to unload and reload the POA to re-read the startup file.

Multiple POAs

To help with load-balancing in a large environment, you can create and load multiple POAs for a given post office.

You can create, configure, and load a separate POA to perform any of the following dedicated tasks:

- Provide Client/Server access to the post office
- Provide Direct Only access to the post office
- Perform QuickFinder Indexing
- Perform normal-priority message delivery
- Perform high-priority message delivery

Creating multiple POAs for a single post office is a four-step procedure:

- Creating and configuring the POA object
- Specifying the POA settings
- Creating and editing the POA's startup file
- Loading the POA

Creating a New POA Object

To create a new POA for a post office, follow these steps:

1. In NetWare Administrator, right-click on the Post Office object and choose Create from the shortcut menu. Note: You can only perform this step in the main NetWare Administrator screen, not in GroupWise View.

2. Select GroupWise Agent from the list of available objects and click on OK.

3. Enter a name for the new POA that relates to its function. In our example in Figure 15.7, we are creating a TVCSPOA for the TVPO post office that will handle all of its client/server functions.

4 • Select Post Office type, click on Additional Properties, and choose OK.

5 • Fill in the appropriate property pages, based on the role for the new POA. (See Table 15.2 for a description of these settings.)

FIGURE 15.7

Creating a New POA Object

Creating the POA's Startup File

Each of the POAs in a post office uses a separate startup file. After you create the new POA object, you need to create a new startup file for the POA. You should copy an existing POA startup file and rename it to reflect the POA's function. For example, you could use a dedicated POA for providing client/server access, using "CS" in the file name and "POA" as the extension (for example, TVCS.POA for the TVPO post office's dedicated client/server POA).

Specifying POA Settings

You can (and should) specify the agent settings in NetWare Administrator. Optionally, you can use the startup file switches described in Table 15.2 to make the POA run in a particular mode.

TABLE 15.2

POA Mode Switches

POA MODE	STARTUP FILE SWITCHES AND DESCRIPTIONS	
Dedicated Client/Server	`/nomf`	Disables directory scanning for all incoming (directories 0–7) message files
	`/nomflow`	Disables directory scanning for low-priority (directories 2–7) message files
	`/nomfhigh`	Disables directory scanning for high-priority (directories 0 and 1) message files
	`/noqf`	Disables QuickFinder indexing

(continued)

TABLE 15.2

POA Mode Switches (continued)

POA MODE	STARTUP FILE SWITCHES AND DESCRIPTIONS	
Dedicated Direct Access	/notcp	Disables processing of client/server requests from users
	/noqf	Disables QuickFinder indexing
Dedicated QuickFinder Index	/qfinterval-[hours]	Time interval (in hours) for updating the Quick Finder indexes (The default is 4 hours and the minimum is 1 hour.)
	/notcp	Disables processing of client/server requests from users
	/nomf	Disables directory scanning for all incoming message files
	/nomflow	Disables directory scanning for low-priority message files
	/nomfhigh	Disables directory scanning for high-priority message files
Dedicated Normal Priority Message Delivery	/nomflow	Disables directory scanning for low priority message files
	/nomfhigh	Disables directory scanning for high-priority message files
	/notcp	Disables processing of client/server requests from users
	/noqf	Disables QuickFinder indexing
Dedicated High Priority Message Delivery	/nomflow	Disables directory scanning for low-priority Message Files
	/notcp	Disables processing of client/server requests from users
	/noqf	Disables QuickFinder indexing

In addition to the switches listed in Table 15.2, the startup file must include the standard POA switches (for example, `/home-`*<path to post office>*) in order to make the POA run correctly.

IMPORTANT

If you use multiple POAs, you must use the `/name` switch to specify the POA's common name in NDS. This is required when you have created multiple POAs for a given post office. For example, `/name-TVCS` would use the properties of the POA object called TVPOCS.

Loading the POA

Once you have created the POA objects and specified the settings for each, you need to load the GWPOA.NLM by entering the following command at the file server console and pressing Enter:

```
load gwpoa @TVCS.POA
```

Be sure to use the correct startup file. We suggest naming the POA startup file using a reference to the function it serves; for example, "TVCS.POA" for a client/server POA to be used by the TVPO post office.

Client Configuration

After you have set up the server for Client/Server access mode, you need to focus on the client. This usually means visiting each workstation, so you might want to combine the client setup with other workstation activities, such as upgrading the operating system or drivers.

Before we get into the details of client configuration, it is important that you understand the process the client goes through during the startup sequence. You need to understand where the client looks for settings—the IP address of the POA, the user ID, the path to the post office, and so forth—to know how to properly configure the client software for your network.

The client startup sequence is as follows:

- The client first looks for a GroupWise component loaded in memory (Address Book or Notify).
- Next, GroupWise looks at the command line for switches.
- GroupWise then looks to NDS (if present) and reads the NDS properties that would specify a connection method.

- Then, if you're running the client on Windows 95 or Windows NT, the client checks the Windows Registry in the following key for configuration data:

  ```
  HKEY_CURRENT_USER\Software\Novell\GroupWise\Login
  Parameters
  ```

- GroupWise then looks for NGWNameServer in DNS.
- The GroupWise startup screen appears, prompting the user for connection information such as the IP address and port number of the POA.
- If a network connection is not available, GroupWise starts in Remote mode.

In order to enable users to connect to the POA in Client/Server access mode, you must tell the GroupWise client the IP address of the POA that it should connect to. Once you have specified the address, GroupWise will remember the IP address and store it in the Registry. Thereafter, when you double-click on the GroupWise client, it will by default connect to the POA via a client/server connection.

As mentioned before, it doesn't really matter which POA you connect to. The POA will send the client the IP address and port of the user's home POA, where it is stored in the Registry. This is very handy if you have users who travel between offices connected by TCP/IP over a WAN.

You need to perform three main steps at each workstation that will use client/server messaging:

- Setting up TCP/IP on the workstation
- Specifying the IP address of the POA
- Tracking the client/server activity of the POA

NOTE

A major benefit of Client/Server access mode is that it supports proxying among all users in your system. In previous versions of GroupWise (and in GroupWise 5 in Direct Only access mode) users can serve as proxies only for other users in the same post office.

Setting up TCP/IP

Many different options are available for enabling TCP/IP at workstations. We cover only the TCP/IP configuration options recommended by Novell for use with GroupWise in Client/Server access mode:

- Windows 95: Microsoft TCP/IP IP stack
- Windows 3.1: LAN WorkPlace 5 for MS Windows and DOS

Before you set up TCP/IP on a workstation, you need to obtain the following background information for the workstation:

- *TCP/IP address*. Each workstation needs a full-time permanent IP address assigned to it, or it must obtain one each time it logs into the network.
- *DNS Address*. The IP address of the DNS server that will translate Internet host names to IP addresses must be specified on each workstation. Usually one or two DNS servers are used by each workstation. Note: The DNS server will be used by the GroupWise client only if it needs to find the default POA using the NGWNameServer entry in DNS.
- *Gateway Address*. The address of the gateway machine (usually a router) to allow access beyond the local network segment.

Windows 95: Microsoft TCP/IP IP Stack

To set up TCP/IP on a Windows 95 workstation, follow these steps:

1. From the Start menu, choose Settings and then Control Panel.

2 • Double-click on the Network icon. You should see the Configuration sheet shown in Figure 15.8.

3 • Click on the Add button, select Protocol from the Select Network Component Type dialog box, and then click on Add.

4 • From the Select Network Protocol screen, click on Microsoft in the Manufacturers box, and click on TCP/IP in the Network Protocol dialog box (see Figure 15.9). Click on OK.

FIGURE 15.8

NetWork Dialog Box

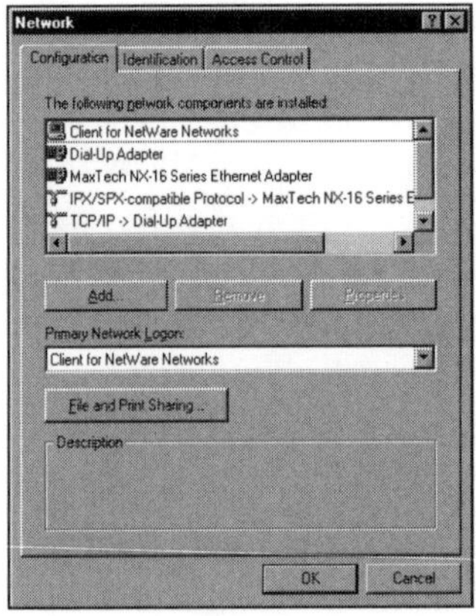

FIGURE 15.9

Adding the TCP/IP Protocol

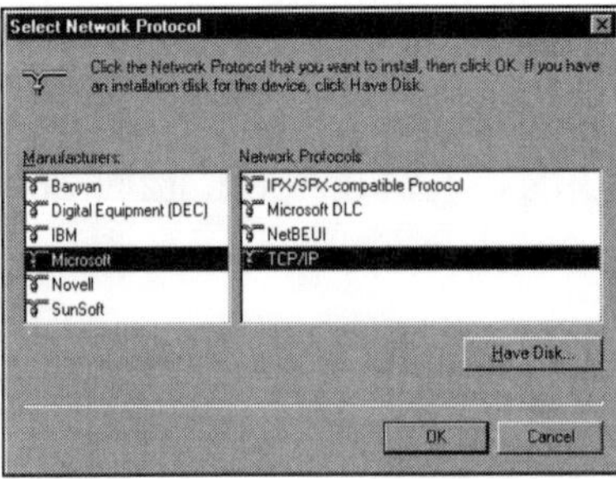

5 • The TCP/IP protocol will now be listed in the network components list. Highlight the entry for TCP/IP for the network card and click on Properties. (Refer to Figure 15.8 for an example of the network component list.)

6 • Enter the TCP/IP address for the workstation, as shown in Figure 15.10. If IP addresses are being allocated dynamically through a service such as DHCP, you can skip to Step 9.

7 • Enter the gateway address, as shown in Figure 15.11, and click on Add to add it to the list of IP gateway addresses.

FIGURE 15.10

IP Address Sheet

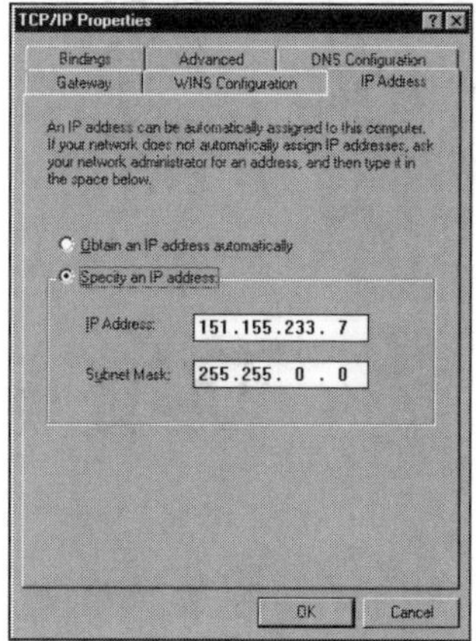

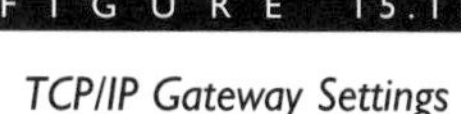
FIGURE 15.11

TCP/IP Gateway Settings

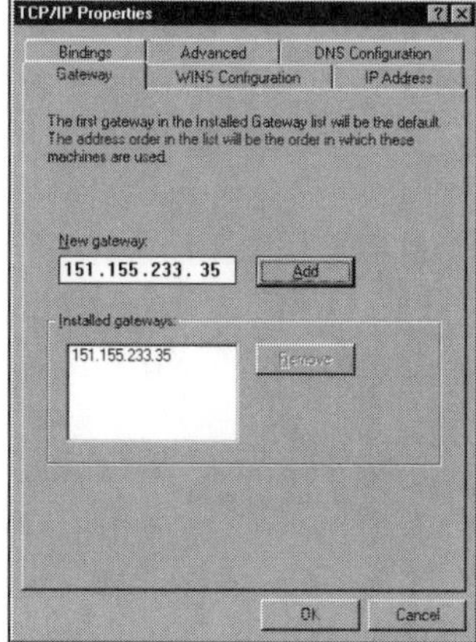

8 • Click on the DNS Configuration tab, click on Enable DNS, and enter the IP addresses of the DNS servers for your network (see Figure 15.12). Click on Add after each entry to add the address to the list.

9 • Click on OK twice. You might be prompted to insert the Windows 95 CD, after which you will need to restart your PC in order for the changes to take affect.

FIGURE 15.12

DNS Configuration Sheet

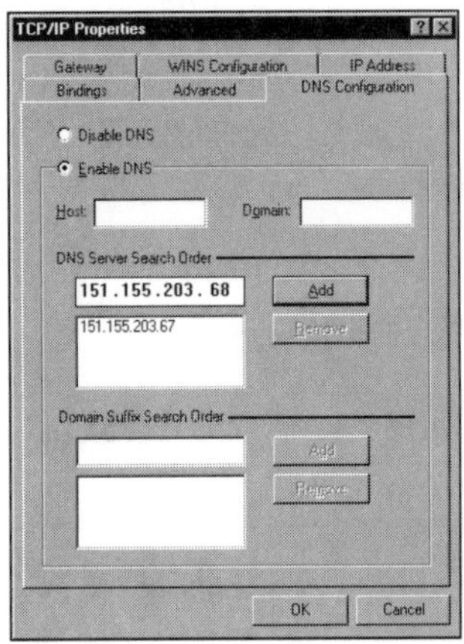

To verify that you have successfully loaded TCP/IP on the workstation, open a command prompt window, change to the C:\WINDOWS directory, type the following command, and then press Enter:

```
PING dnsservername
```

For example, to ping Novell, you would enter the following:

```
PING NOVELL.COM
```

You should see a series of replies. This confirms that the TCP/IP protocol is working, that the DNS server was found to resolve "novell.com" to an IP address, and that the IP address was found on the Internet through the gateway.

Windows 3.1: LAN WorkPlace 5 for MS Windows and DOS

Refer to the documentation included with Novell's LAN WorkPlace 5 for MS Windows and DOS to install the TCP/IP protocol on Windows 3.x workstations.

Optionally, you can use a third party TCP/IP stack, such as Trumpet WinSock or NetManage's Chameleon Suite.

Specifying the IP Address of the POA

Each workstation needs to know the IP address of the POA it should connect to. You can furnish this information to GroupWise in a number of ways. Regardless of how it finds the IP address of the POA, GroupWise will read the Access Mode property of the Post Office NDS object to find out whether the access mode has been set up as Client/Server Only, Direct Only, or Client/Server and Direct. Once it is read, GroupWise will try to access that post office using that mode. If it is set to either Client/Server Only or Client/Server and Direct, GroupWise will try to establish a client/server connection.

The different methods for indicating the IP address of the POA for clients include the following:

- Specifying the address in the GroupWise startup screen
- Adding startup switches to the GroupWise shortcut in Windows 95
- Modifying the Windows 95 Registry
- Specifying the IP address of the POA in NDS
- Using the default address NGWNameServer

GroupWise Startup Screen

As Figure 15.13 shows, you can enter the IP address and port number of the POA under the TCP/IP Address tab of GroupWise 5's Startup screen, which is displayed when you start GroupWise the first time (and if you have added startup switches to the shortcut).

FIGURE 15.13

Client Startup Screen

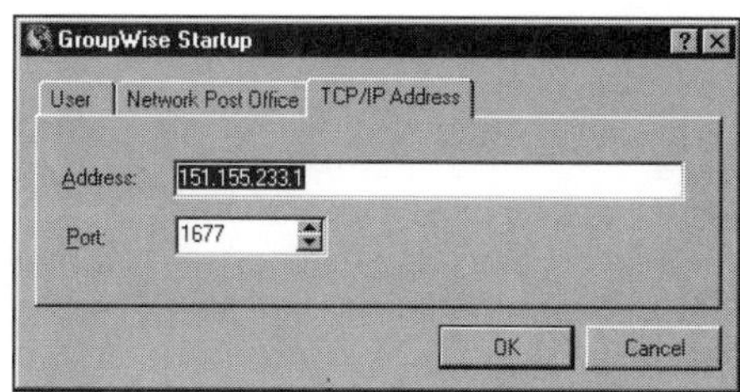

Shortcut Startup Switches

You can add two startup switches to the GroupWise shortcut. Be sure to separate these with a space. Both switches (IP address and port number) are required if you use this method.

```
/ipa-<IP address of POA>

/ipp-<port number of POA>
```

To add the startup switches to the shortcut, follow these steps:

1 • Right-click on the GroupWise shortcut and choose Properties from the shortcut menu.

2 • Click on the Shortcut tab (see Figure 15.14) and add the switches to the end of the Target entry of the path to the executable file. Remember to insert a space between each one.

3 • Click on OK.

FIGURE 15.14

Shortcut Startup Switches

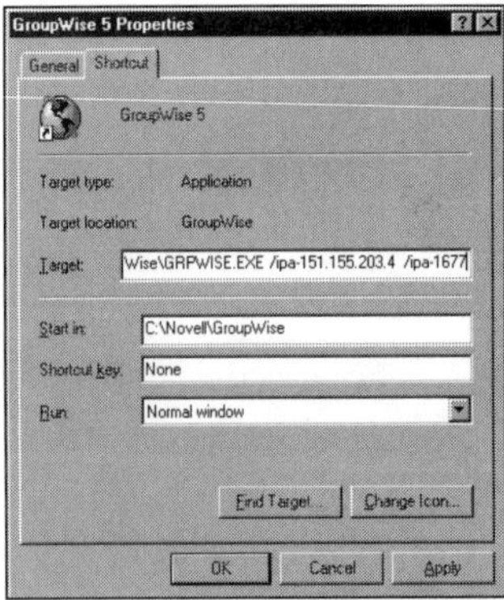

When you double-click on the shortcut, it will run using the switches you added.

Windows 95 Registry

The Windows 95 Registry contains TCP/IP information in the HKEY_CURRENT_USER\Software\Novell\GroupWise\Login Parameters key. The values in this key are as follows:

- Account Name = user ID
- PostOfficePath = path to post office
- Path to Remote Database = path to remote database
- TCP/IP Address = IP address of the POA
- TCP/IP Port = IP port used by the POA

This is given for informational purposes only. As a last resort, you can enter this information into the Registry using the REGEDIT program that is furnished with Windows 95.

WARNING

Be extremely careful when using the REGEDIT program, and make sure you have a good backup before saving any changes you make.

POA IP Address Property

The GroupWise client will read the NDS database to determine the IP address and port number of the POA for the post office to which the NDS-authenticated user belongs. This takes place automatically, and no client-side configuration is needed to make it happen

Default Setting

As mentioned earlier in the chapter, if the client does not find all the information it needs in one of the previous steps, then it will look for the NGWNameServer entry in DNS, which will point GroupWise to the default POA to which it should connect. Once this connection is made, the client will be connected to the home post office's POA.

The benefit of this feature is that it should connect all GroupWise clients who have not yet established a client/server connection to their POA. Every TCP/IP protocol-enabled computer will be configured to find the DNS server, where the

NGWNameServer setting is placed. To use this method, users simply double-click on the GroupWise shortcut and the client program will use NGWNameServer if none of the methods mentioned above have been configured.

Client/Server Tracking

For troubleshooting and administrative purposes, it is important to know what client/server activity is taking place. This section explains the information available with regard to client/server messaging and how much IP traffic it generates.

The main place to track client/server activity is at the POA screen in NetWare Administrator. This screen includes all available information about current client/server activity. The different categories of logging information are placed into the log files for the POA. If you don't change the Log Path property of the POA in NetWare Administrator (or use the `/logpath` switch in the startup file), the log files are placed in the <*post office*>\WPCSOUT\OFS directory.

Basic Information

As shown in Figure 15.15, you can use the POA screen to track the total number of "C/S Requests" (client/server requests). This tells you how many TCP/IP requests have been generated and serviced by both the GroupWise clients and the POA. If you know users have been set up to run GroupWise in Client/Server access mode and the total number of C/S Requests is not increasing, you can expect to hear your help desk phone ring at any moment.

Client/Server Requests

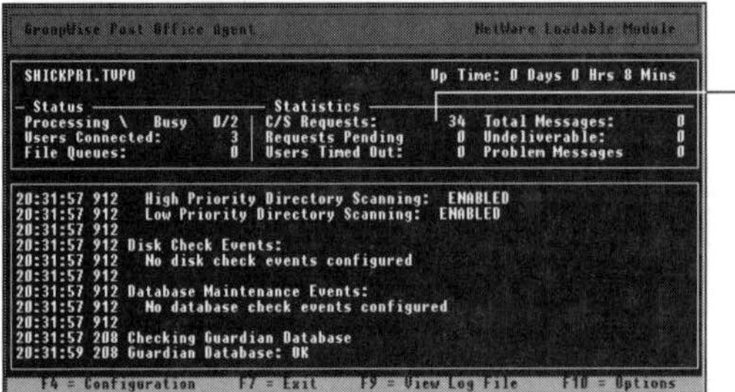

Every four minutes, the GroupWise client sends out an "I'm Alive" message to the POA. If there is no interaction between client and POA for 28 minutes, the POA will disconnect the client.

Detailed Information

To view more detailed client/server information, press the F10 key, highlight Configuration Options, and then press Enter. You will be presented with the options shown in Figure 15.16.

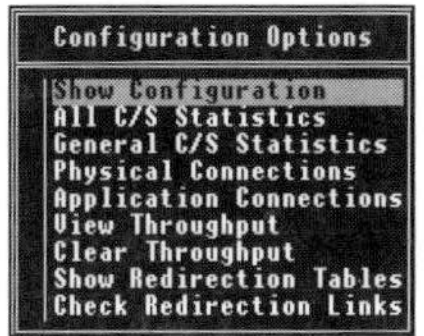

FIGURE 15.16

Client/Server Activity Options

Show Configuration Displays and enters into the log file all of the following settings: General, Log, Performance, Client/Server, Message File Processing, Disk Check Events, Database Maintenance Events.

All C/S Statistics A combination of all available classes of client/server categories. These are available individually, as shown in Figure 15-16, above.

General C/S Statistics Displays and adds physical and application connection information to the log file.

Physical Connections Displays the numbers of active physical connections.

Application Connections Displays information about user connections, such as the user login name, IP address, and connection time.

View Throughput Displays TCP/IP packet information from a performance perspective.

Clear Throughput Resets all throughput statistics.

Show Redirection Tables Displays a table of all other post offices in the system and the current status of how client/server requests are passed to them. The following is an example of a redirection table:

```
SHICKPRI.SALESPO POA—TCP/IP disabled

SHICKPRI.TVPO POA—151.155.233.1:1677

SHICKSEC.RDPO POA—Agent with no TCP/IP address configured
```

Information in the redirection table is taken from the WPHOST.DB file. When you check the redirection table, the POA pretends to be a client and attempts to open a physical connection with each of the POAs it is aware of. If it can establish a physical connection, it assumes the POA is functioning.

Check Redirection Links Performs a check on the current status of the connection to the other post offices' POAs within the system. The resulting redirection table is displayed on the screen, as shown in the following example:

```
SHICKPRI.SALESPO
    POA—TCP/IP disabled
SHICKPRI.TVPO
    POA—151.155.233.1:1677     Connectable
SHICKSEC.RDPO
    POA—Agent with no TCP/IP address configured
```

The order in which the POAs are listed in the redirection table (alphabetical by domain; and alphabetical by post office within the domain) of the NGWNameServer POA can affect the speed at which clients can access their messages if they are being passed through to their home Post Office Agent instead of accessing it directly.

Message Flow

This section will help you understand the path of messages through a GroupWise system when Client/Server access mode has been enabled. Figure 15.17 illustrates the path a message takes from a user in the same post office as the recipient, with both users accessing the post office with client/server connections.

Following are the steps shown in Figure 15.17:

1. The user creates and sends a message to users in the same post office, which has been configured to use Client/Server access via TCP/IP.

2. The GroupWise client transmits the message to the POA using TCP/IP.

FIGURE 15.17

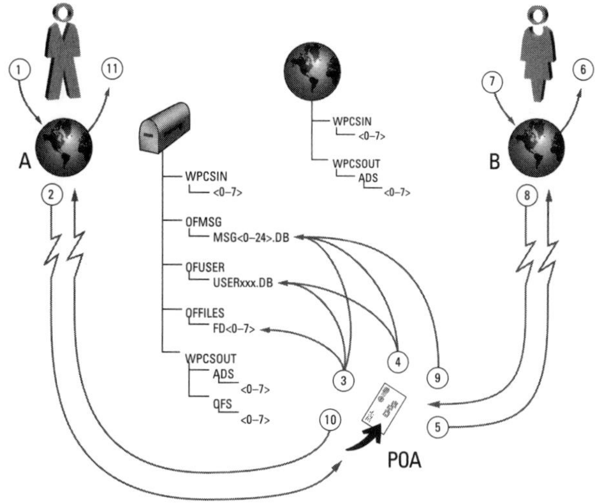

Message Flow in Client/Server Access Mode

3 • The POA adds the message to the message store with the following actions:

a. It places the message in a <PO>\OFMSG\MSG<0–24>.DB message database

b. It adds a pointer to the message record in the sender's <PO>\OFUSER\USER*xxx*.DB user database

c. It places any portion of the message (attachment, message text, or recipient list) greater than or equal to 2K in <PO>\OFFILES\FD<0–7F>. The message record has a pointer to this file.

4 • The POA also delivers the message:

a. It adds pointers to each of the recipient's <PO>\OFUSER\ USER*xxx*.DB files

b. It updates the message record with a Delivered status

5 • The POA uses TCP/IP to communicate with the GroupWise client for each recipient.

6 • (*Optional*) Each recipient's Notify program tells them that a new message has arrived.

7 • The recipient opens and reads the message using the GroupWise client. The message is still stored in the message store, and its contents are transmitted in the form of TCP/IP packets to the GroupWise client for reading.

8 • The GroupWise client sends a TCP/IP message to the POA with an Opened status. The client also transmits the appropriate status information when the action is taken: deleted, completed, accepted, or declined.

9 • The POA updates the message record with the Opened status. Each time a different recipient opens the message, it is updated.

10 • The POA sends an Opened status TCP/IP communication to the sender's GroupWise client.

11 • The sender, when viewing the message information in his or her Sent Items folder, will see the status information displayed.

Understanding the flow of messages with client/server connections is very useful when troubleshooting, as you can check the directories to which messages were transferred if there is a problem. Other troubleshooting tips are described in the next section.

Client/Server Troubleshooting

Following are some suggestions for troubleshooting client/server messaging problems:

- **Check the access mode.** In NetWare Administrator, check the Post Office object for access mode. It needs to be set to either Client/Server Only or Client/Server and Direct. Check the POA object's Network

Address setting in NetWare Administrator, and verify the proper TCP/IP address and port number.

- **Check the POA's IP address and port number.** Check the IP address and port number of the POA on the server and in the startup files.
- **Use Telnet.** Use the Windows Telnet utility to check between client and server. To use the utility, follow these steps:
    1. Click on Start and Run. Enter `telnet` in the open field and click on OK.
    2. Choose Remote System from the Connect menu.
    3. Enter the host name of the computer on which the POA is running in the Host Name field (see Figure 15.18), and click on OK.
    4. If you get connected to the other computer, you have verified that the TCP/IP connection can be made from the workstation to the server.

FIGURE 15.18

Host Name Entry in Telnet

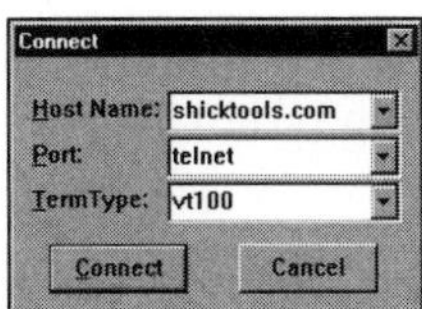

- **Try Ping.** At the workstation, you can use Ping to check the TCP/IP path between client and server. At a command prompt, enter the following command:

```
ping <ip address or hostname>
```

You should be rewarded with a series of replies from the target computer. If you get no reply, you may have a problem with the gateway address specified in the workstation's TCP/IP configuration.

- **Use the Config utility to check TCP/IP addressing.** To display the NetWare server's TCP/IP address, you can enter the following command at the server prompt:

  ```
  config
  ```

- **Check location of DNS server.** The text file in the path SYS:ETC\RESOLV.CFG can be viewed to determine the location of the DNS server. It will be under the heading "nameserver" in this file.

- **Verify IP address in DNS.** Verify that an accurate IP address is entered into DNS for the NGWNameServer entry.

- **Check TEMP variable.** GroupWise places temporary files in the directory specified by the TEMP variable for each workstation. These temporary files are always changing, and new ones are being added with every action that is taken while using Client/Server access in GroupWise. You must make sure that the TEMP variable points to a directory on the local hard drive and that the drive has plenty of available space. To view the directory setup for the TEMP variable, type `SET` at the command prompt.

For more information on troubleshooting, you can refer to online help. Most problems with client/server messaging can be solved by examining configuration details.

Summary

You have now examined every little nook and cranny of client/server access with GroupWise. You learned how to set up the server for TCP/IP and client/server connections and how the workstation needs to be configured. You have also seen how understanding the detailed client/server message flow will help you troubleshoot problems.

In the next chapter, you will learn how to migrate from a GroupWise 4.x system to GroupWise 5.

CHAPTER 16

Migrating to GroupWise 5

Migration means upgrading your messaging system from one version to another (or completely changing from one messaging system to another) and bringing stored messages from the old system into the new one. In this chapter we explain the steps for migrating from earlier versions of GroupWise to GroupWise 5.

When a company or organization decides to upgrade its messaging system, it must determine the best way to handle the conversion. At a large organization with many users, it may not be feasible to convert all of the existing messages in the old system to make them compatible with the new system. There are basically three different approaches to dealing with this problem:

- You can have users print out messages they want to save from the old system. This approach to message conversion is the easiest from the administrator's perspective, but it is the least convenient for users.
- You can migrate only certain people (you can probably figure out which ones we're talking about) and have everyone else print out the messages they want to keep.
- You can migrate the entire system. This approach is the most convenient from the user's perspective, but it requires more work for system administrators.

You will need to decide what level of migration to undertake before you upgrade from one version of GroupWise to another.

We wrote this chapter with two goals in mind: (1) to help you migrate your system as fast as possible, and (2) to help you prevent data loss during migration. We have focused extensively on the preparatory steps you should take to make the migration go smoothly.

Deciding to Migrate

Before you decide to migrate, you need to determine what your options are and whether it even makes sense for you to migrate.

The migration process we explain in this chapter only works for an upgrade from GroupWise 4.1 to GroupWise 5 (or later). Before you can migrate to GroupWise 5 from WordPerfect Office, you must first upgrade to GroupWise 4.1 (see Figure 16.1).

FIGURE 16.1

Upgrading to GroupWise 5

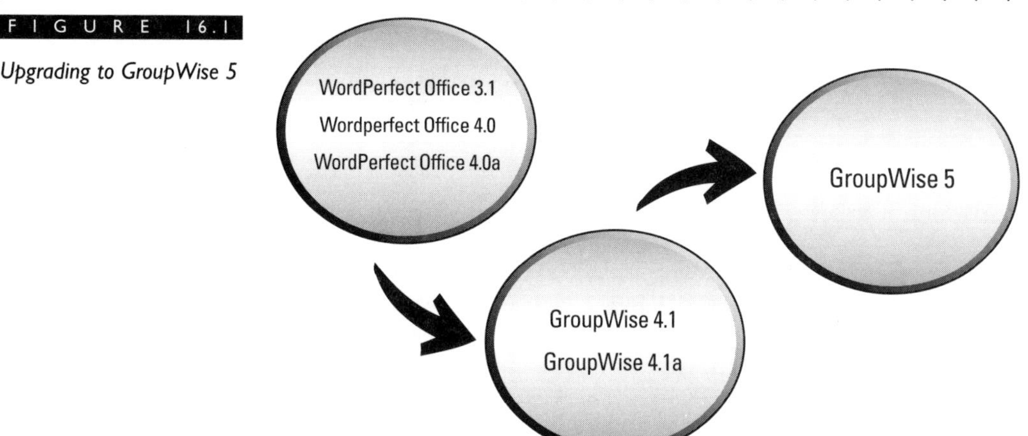

Before you start the migration, make sure you are using GroupWise 5.1 (or a later release). If you are using a GroupWise 5 release dated before February 1997, you should contact Novell to obtain the GroupWise 5.1 release, which is free to anyone who purchased the initial release of GroupWise 5. Make sure you also check Novell's Support Web site for any additional patches or updates: `http://support.novell.com`.

Another consideration is that old versions of GroupWise may support client platforms that are not supported in the newer version. If that is the case, you must keep the old system around. For example, GroupWise 4 shipped with a DOS client, but GroupWise 5 does not. Therefore, if you have DOS users (and you don't plan to upgrade their operating system to Windows), then you *must* maintain at least one GroupWise 4.1 post office.

Following are some other factors to think about as you consider migrating from GroupWise 4.1 to GroupWise 5:

- Once a domain is migrated to GroupWise 5 it can no longer be administered with the GroupWise 4.1 AD.EXE program. It must be administered with the GroupWise administration tools in NetWare

Administrator. Note: You should never run AD.EXE on a domain that has been converted to GroupWise 5.

- Once you have migrated the primary domain to GroupWise 5, you can no longer use the Rebuild option on the secondary domain databases. The Rebuild option uses the primary domain to populate the rebuilt database; once the primary domain database has been converted to the GroupWise 5 format, you cannot use it to rebuild secondary domain databases.

- GroupWise 4.1 post offices can reside within a domain that has been converted to GroupWise 5. Note: It's a good idea to maintain a GroupWise 4.1 post office if you need to support GroupWise 4.1 client programs. You may want to consider creating a single domain with GroupWise 4.1 post offices somewhere in your system until the need to support the GroupWise 4.1 client no longer exists.

- Post office and client software versions must match. Once a post office has been migrated to GroupWise 5, only the GroupWise 5 client software can be used. Conversely, the GroupWise 5 client software cannot be used on a GroupWise 4 post office.

- Personal groups will be converted, but the CC: and BC: information in those groups will not be retained.

- Users' rules will be converted to the GroupWise 5 rule language and should work correctly after the migration.

- Remote users can continue to use the GroupWise 4.1 Remote client even after their post offices are upgraded to GroupWise 5. However, they should install the GroupWise 5 client software as soon as possible to take advantage of the new features.

- Any macros that users have created will only be available in the 16-bit version of the GroupWise 5 client.

- Links will still be maintained between GroupWise 4 and GroupWise 5 after the conversion of the primary domain. Directory synchronization will still occur even after the primary domain is converted to GroupWise 5.
- GroupWise 4.1 gateways are completely compatible with GroupWise 5. After you migrate a domain that contains gateways, you administer the gateways through the NDS Gateway objects in NetWare Administrator.

As you decide whether to migrate your system (or how much of your system to migrate), you should take each of these considerations into account.

Getting the Big Picture

Before you actually get started with migration, it is critical that you understand how the migration process works. Following are the main steps in the migration process:

1. The GroupWise 4.1 primary domain database is converted to GroupWise 5.
2. The GroupWise 4.1 message transfer components (MS, ADS, and OFS) are updated to the GroupWise 5 agents (MTA, ADA, and POA) and the new MTA and ADA are run for the new GroupWise 5 domain.
3. GroupWise 4.1 post offices, gateways, users, resources, and groups (distribution lists) are "grafted" onto NDS. In other words, for each object in the existing GroupWise 4.1 system, new NDS objects are created so you can administer the objects from NetWare Administrator.
4. The GroupWise 4.1 post office database (WPHOST.DB) is converted to GroupWise 5.

5. The GroupWise 4.1 post office message store is converted to GroupWise 5 format.

6. The GroupWise 5 client software is installed.

7. The migration process for other post offices within the primary domain is continued by repeating Steps 3–6.

8. Secondary domains and their post offices are migrated to GroupWise 5 by repeating Steps 1–8.

The rest of this chapter explains these steps in more detail and leads you through all of the procedures necessary for a successful migration.

Planning Your Migration Strategy

Now that you know what happens when you perform a migration, you can successfully plan your migration strategy. Planning a migration is very similar to planning a new GroupWise 5 system implementation (see Chapter 3).

In our discussion of migration planning, we assume your system meets the following criteria:

- The GroupWise 4.1 system is operational and adequately patched.
- You have an existing NetWare 4.1 (or later) or IntranetWare system with a fully implemented NDS tree.
- Your server hardware meets the requirements for GroupWise 5. GroupWise system components are covered in Chapter 3.
- Your users' hardware meets the requirements for a GroupWise 5 client (either the 16-bit or 32-bit version). These requirements are discussed in Chapter 3.

The key to a successful migration is good planning. Migration planning involves seven main tasks:

- Collecting information
- Deciding on a primary domain
- Determining a schedule
- Mapping the existing system to NDS
- Administering the system during migration
- Informing users about the migration
- Training users and administrators

The following sections advise you about each of these important steps to planning a successful migration.

Collecting Information

You probably know your GroupWise 4.1 system inside and out, but you should thoroughly document it before you start.

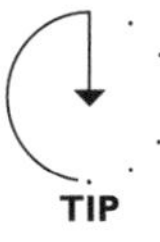
TIP

Now is the time to change the names of your GroupWise domains, post offices, and gateway because you will *not* have a chance to change them later. It is also important to make sure that the 4.1 objects (users, resources, groups, and nicknames) are in the post offices that you want them in after the migration is complete. In other words, make any system changes (i.e., moving or renaming users) to GroupWise 4.1 *before* the migration and verify those changes before you start the migration.

You need to plan for the proper platform of the GroupWise 5 agents. The GroupWise agents are available in NetWare Loadable Modules (NLMs), Windows NT, or UNIX platforms. If you were using the DOS or OS/2 version of the GroupWise 4.1 servers, you need to select one of these new platforms for the GroupWise 5 agents.

A migration worksheet containing all of the information that you will be asked for during the migration process can be found in the GroupWise 5 online help system under "How Do I Migrate to GroupWise 5?"

Print out a copy of this worksheet and carefully fill in each field before you begin your migration to GroupWise 5.

Deciding on a Primary Domain

The GroupWise 5 migration procedures require that you start with the GroupWise 4.1 primary domain. The GroupWise primary domain is the master domain in the entire GroupWise system because it contains the most accurate and complete information about the entire system.

As you now know, the primary domain is the most critical domain in your GroupWise system. Not only is it responsible for the replication of directory information to other domains in the system, it is also the domain from which all secondary domains receive their information during rebuilds of the domain database.

The GroupWise 5 migration process needs the information in the primary domain database so that it can properly insert objects for the rest of the system's domains, post offices, and users into NDS.

In most cases, beginning with the existing primary domain is a very safe and reliable approach, even if it does seem risky. However, you have some options if you don't want to start with the current GroupWise 4.1 primary domain.

Releasing a Domain for Migration

As you learned in Chapter 14, when you release a domain from your GroupWise system, it becomes a primary domain in its own GroupWise system.

If you have a domain in your system that you would like to use as a test domain for the migration, you can release that domain and migrate it to GroupWise 5. It will continue to communicate with the rest of the GroupWise system normally as an external GroupWise domain. The drawback to this strategy is that it will not take advantage of automatic directory synchronization.

You could approach the entire migration in this manner if you desire. The process would be as follows:

1. Release a domain from the GroupWise 4.1 system.

2 • Migrate it to GroupWise 5. It then becomes a GroupWise 5 primary domain in a new GroupWise 5 system.

3 • Release another domain from the GroupWise 4.1 system.

4 • Migrate it to GroupWise 5.

5 • Merge it with the domain you upgraded to GroupWise 5 in Step 2.

6 • Continue with the release, upgrade, and merge cycle until all GroupWise 4.1 domains are upgraded and merged into the GroupWise 5 system.

This manner of migrating should not be necessary in most situations. Personally, we don't recommend it. But it is a good option if you feel the need to take a very cautious approach to your migration.

Promoting an Existing Secondary Domain to Primary

If you have a domain that you would prefer to use as the first domain migrated to GroupWise 5, you can promote it to primary domain and then run migration on that domain.

While there is no inherent administrative benefit to this approach, it gives you the flexibility to start the migration process on a domain other than your current primary domain.

Determining a Schedule

As you learned in the preceding section, when you migrate from GroupWise 4 to GroupWise 5, you must begin with your primary domain. After the primary domain, you need to establish a schedule for migrating the other domains and post offices in your system.

Remember that this process cannot be done overnight, or even in a week. You should plan to migrate your system gradually. Depending upon its size and complexity, you should be prepared for this process to take several weeks.

In reality, you will need to balance several priorities during this process:

- You need to be concerned with the ongoing migration of the domains and post offices.
- You need to be concerned about maintaining connectivity to the parts of the system that have not been migrated.
- You need to manage the day-to-day administration of the *entire* system, regardless of the version of the components.
- You need to be prepared to troubleshoot problems reported by individual users as they are migrated to GroupWise 5.

A deliberate and organized approach, especially with large GroupWise systems, will be the least stressful and most successful.

We recommend that after you migrate the primary domain and its post offices, you then move to secondary domains that are geographically close to the primary domain. In other words, start with the primary domain, move to secondary domains directly linked to the primary or in close proximity to it, and then move to domains and post offices located in other offices or connected through gateways.

Mapping the Existing System to NDS

Because the NDS schema did not include definitions for GroupWise 4.1 components, it was administered entirely from the DOS AD.EXE program. The most dramatic change made in GroupWise 5 is the integration of its components—domains, post offices, and gateways—with NDS and the procedures by which administration is done in NetWare Administrator.

During the migration process, you will be prompted to "graft" the GroupWise objects that exist in the GroupWise 4.1 system onto NDS. This process will create an object for each GroupWise component in the NDS tree containers you specify.

Before you begin the migration, you should know exactly where each domain and post office will reside. You might even need to modify your NDS structure to accommodate the new GroupWise 5 system.

We highly recommend creating all GroupWise 4.1 users as NDS users before you begin the migration. This will simplify the association of GroupWise 4.1 users with NDS User objects. Of course, this might also entail upgrading the network client software to allow NDS login and authentication.

You should create new container objects to hold GroupWise components before you start the GroupWise 5 Migration utility.

For more information about mapping your GroupWise system to NDS, refer to Chapter 3.

Administering the System During Migration

When migrating from GroupWise 4.1 to GroupWise 5, you will essentially be maintaining two messaging systems.

While it is true that both systems are GroupWise and function in a similar manner, they are administered separately.

After you migrate the GroupWise 4.1 primary domain to GroupWise 5, you must administer it with the GroupWise tools in NetWare Administrator. You must administer the GroupWise 4.1 secondary domains with AD.EXE.

If you administer your GroupWise 4.1 system centrally by making all changes to the primary domain, you will have to temporarily change your administration model. You will have to run the AD.EXE program for each secondary domain if you need to make changes to the domain or post offices within the domain.

NOTE

Automatic directory synchronization will still occur between GroupWise 4.1 and GroupWise 5 domains, but changes to information in secondary domains will need to be made directly to the secondary domain databases with AD.EXE. You can use the `/ph-path to secondary domain` **switch with the AD.EXE program to accomplish this, or run AD.EXE from the secondary domain directory.**

Based on this information, you should devise a plan for administering the migrated GroupWise 5 domains and the rest of the GroupWise 4 domains during the migration.

Informing Users About the Migration

It is absolutely vital that you keep your GroupWise users informed about the migration plan and its progress.

Having the cooperation of your GroupWise users is a key to your success. You will need to ask them to help with the migration process by cleaning out their mailboxes prior to the conversion of the message store. While the migration is in process, there will be times when users will not have access to their mailboxes. They will need to know about the GroupWise "outage" before it occurs.

Once the post office is upgraded to GroupWise 5, users will see a notice about new GroupWise software being available on the post office (see Figure 16.2).

FIGURE 16.2

Auto-Update Notice

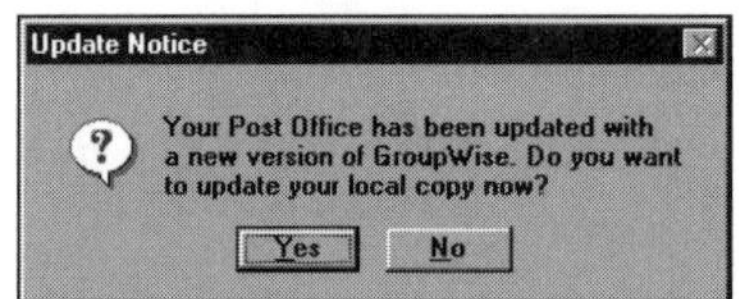

Depending upon your level of confidence in your users, you may be comfortable instructing them how to install the GroupWise 5 client program on their computers. Once the post office is upgraded, the GroupWise 4 client will not read the contents of their mailboxes.

NOTE

A migrated post office will affect *all* users in the post office, requiring them to use the GroupWise 5 client software.

When Novell migrated its internal system to GroupWise 5 (over a period of several months), the IS staff was careful to keep users updated on when their post offices would be migrated to GroupWise 5.

Novell kept employees informed in the following ways:

- It posted a migration schedule on the corporate intranet.
- It sent regular messages about the progress of the migration.
- It continually placed update articles in the company newsletter.
- It set up an internal GroupWise hotline to answer users' questions about the upgrade.

- It set up a GroupWise account where users could send messages asking questions or reporting problems. (Of course, this did not help if users had problems with e-mail.)
- Instructions were sent to each user immediately before his or her post office was upgraded. These instructions contained instructions about how to install the GroupWise client, appropriate cautions, and estimates of projected downtime.

You might decide to use a combination of the above approaches to keep your users informed and content during the upgrade to GroupWise 5.

Training Users and Administrators

Novell has provided extensive resources for training users and administrators on GroupWise 5. The following resources are available from Novell and from Novell Authorized Education Centers:

- *Novell's GroupWise 5 User's Handbook*, by your humble authors (published by Novell Press and IDG Books Worldwide).
- Novell education courses on using the GroupWise 5 client, and also several courses on administering GroupWise 5. Contact your local Novell Authorized Education Center for information on these courses.
- Novell technical support information in Novell's GroupWise support forum. See `http://support.novell.com/home/groupwar/gw5`.

Preparing Your System for Migration

Now that you're familiar with migration issues and have developed a strategy for the migration, you should be ready to start the migration process.

You will make your migration to GroupWise 5 much easier if you spend time prepping your GroupWise 4.1 system before the migration. This section explains several tasks that should be completed on the 4.1 system to save time (and prevent headaches) during the migration.

These tasks fall into three categories:

- Optimization and cleanup
- NDS tree development
- Final preparations

Optimization and Cleanup

If you are running a lean, mean, and clean GroupWise 4.1 system, the migration to GroupWise 5 will go smoothly. During the migration process, the Migration Utility must do the following:

- Create NDS objects for all of your GroupWise 4.1 domains, post offices, gateways, resources, and distribution lists
- Match up the GroupWise 4.1 user objects with existing NDS users
- Convert all of the users' messages into GroupWise 5 format

Obviously, the fewer the objects and messages in the GroupWise 4.1 system, the faster and more efficient the migration will be.

You can perform the following checklist of tasks to streamline your GroupWise 4.1 system:

√ Delete all users, resources, and distributions lists that are not being used.

√ Ask users to clean out their mailboxes. Have them delete all messages they don't need, empty their Trash, and archive as many of the remaining messages as possible. (Users will have the option to convert their archived messages to GroupWise 5 when they run the GroupWise 5 client.) You might also want to inform users that messages older than a certain number of days will be deleted. You can then use OFCHECK.EXE to delete these messages from the system.

- √ Run Check GroupWise (OFCHECK.EXE) on the GroupWise 4.1 message stores. Use the most recent version of OFCHECK.EXE (available from Novell's Web site, `http://support.novell.com/home/groupwar/grpwise`). Run OFCHECK with the Check/Fix option, the Index Check option, the Check Contents option, and the Orphan Files Cleanup option. These options will fix problems with the GroupWise 4.1 databases, delete orphaned file attachments, and delete expired messages from the message store. Note: The safest method for performing these options is to perform them individually instead of together in the same operation. This is explained in Chapter 13.

- √ Run AD.EXE for each domain that will be converted and place UNC paths in the domain and post office path fields. (Note: Mapped drives will work if the drive mappings are valid from the computer that runs the Migration utility. However, UNC paths are preferred.)

- √ In AD.EXE, verify that each user has his or her full NDS context entered in the Network ID field. This will expedite the grafting process.

- √ If you want to take the most cautious approach, you can use the Rebuild option on all secondary domains and post offices to ensure that all information is completely synchronized throughout the entire system. This is time-consuming and requires some post office downtime.

NDS Tree Development

Next, you need to take a close look at your NDS tree and determine if you need to make any additions to accommodate the GroupWise 5 system. Chapter 3 provides a methodology for locating GroupWise 5 components in the NDS tree.

Make sure you know into which containers you will place the Domain objects and Post Office objects.

You will not have the option of creating new User objects or container objects in NDS once you begin the migration process. You should make sure NDS user objects already exist for each of the users in the GroupWise 4.1 system. If you have users on non-NetWare networks that will eventually have NDS user accounts, you should consider creating NetWare accounts for them so their mailboxes can be matched to NDS user accounts during the migration.

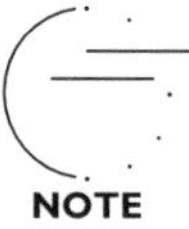
NOTE

If you have GroupWise 4.1 users who will not have NDS accounts, you can convert their messages and associate them with an external entity object. We'll explain how this works later in this chapter.

Final Preparations

Complete the following checklist of tasks just before you begin the migration. Note: These tasks relate mainly to converting post office message stores. If you have completed the preparations above, you are basically ready to convert the domain to GroupWise 5. The steps discussed so far require very little, if any, disruption to GroupWise users. Until you actually prepare the information store for the migration, the preparation process is transparent to users.

√ The POA will handle the conversion of all messages in a given post office within a domain. Verify that the server running the POA that will convert the messages is loaded on the same server that the post office is located on and that the server has enough memory. If you've worked with NetWare much, you've probably heard the old saying "You can never have too much memory." The best place to check this is with the Monitor utility, on the Resource Utilization menu. The Percent of Cache Buffers should be above 70, preferably in the 80–90 range. If this percentage is below 50, you *must* add memory to keep the server in good health. (This is a NetWare warning, not necessarily a GroupWise warning.)

√ Run one final OFCHECK on the post office to be converted using only the Check/Fix, Index Check, and Structure Check options.

√ Verify that the post office to be migrated has a complete backup.

- √ Verify that all users in the post office to be migrated have exited from the GroupWise 4.1 system. You can use the File Open/Lock Activity in the Monitor utility running on the NetWare server and view the WPHOST.DB file in the post office directory. If no one has it open, no one is in GroupWise.
- √ Terminate the OFS agent running for the post office to be migrated.
- √ If you have a backup server available, copy the WPHOST.DB file, the contents of the OFUSER directory, the contents of the OFMSG directory, and the .DC files to a backup server. (You do not need to copy the OFFILES directories.) This allows you to quickly recover from any conversion problems that might occur during the message conversion portion of the migration.

Performing the Migration

Once the preparations have been made, it's time to get the process underway. The migration process consists of four phases:

- Starting the Migration utility
- Converting the GroupWise 4.1 primary domain to GroupWise 5
- Grafting GroupWise 4.1 objects into NDS
- Migrating a post office to GroupWise 5 and enabling the GroupWise 5 client

Beginning the Migration

The Migration utility can be accessed in two different ways, depending upon the state of your network and your NDS tree.

If you haven't installed GroupWise 5 in the existing tree, you can access the Migration utility when you begin the GroupWise 5 installation.

If you have previously installed the GroupWise 5 software and extended the NDS schema, you can access the Migration utility from the Tools menu.

As you begin this process, you should have your completed migration worksheet available.

NOTE

The Migration utility will present many different GroupWise dialog boxes as you migrate your system. We don't show every migration screen in this chapter, but we will describe the steps in enough detail that you will be able to complete each screen.

Using the Installation Program

You will use this method to begin the migration process if you've never installed GroupWise 5 into the NDS tree. Complete the following steps to begin the migration process at the same time you install the GroupWise software:

1. Run Install.
2. Choose the *Migrate an existing GroupWise 4.1 system* option in the Welcome to GroupWise Setup dialog box.
3. Click on Next.
4. Follow the prompts for extending the schema and installing the GroupWise software, as previously explained. After you have completed these steps, the GroupWise Migration dialog box will appear, as shown in Figure 16.3.

FIGURE 16.3

GroupWise Migration Dialog Box

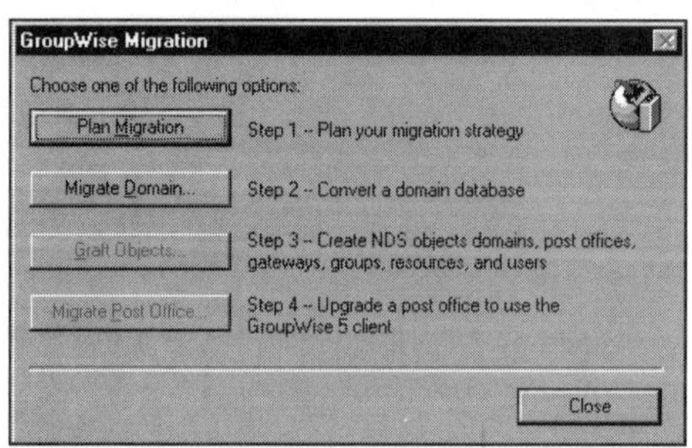

You are now ready to continue with the migration, as described in the section named "Converting a Domain Database" later in this chapter.

Using NetWare Administrator

If you have previously installed GroupWise 5 in your NDS tree, the schema has been extended and the GroupWise tools have been added to the NetWare Administrator menu. (This is often the case because most system administrators have set up a test GroupWise domain and post office as part of a pilot test of GroupWise.)

To start the migration from NetWare Administrator, follow these steps:

1 • Click on Tools.

2 • Click on GroupWise System Operations.

3 • Double-click on the System Connection icon.

4 • Click on the Switch System button.

5 • Browse to the GroupWise 4.1 primary domain and choose Connect. This will make the GroupWise primary domain your connected domain.

6 • Click on Close. You are now connected to the GroupWise 4.1 primary domain.

7 • Click on Tools and then on GroupWise Utilities.

8 • Click on GroupWise 4.1 Migration. The GroupWise Migration dialog box shown in Figure 16.3 appears.

The GroupWise Migration dialog will appear at four different points throughout the migration process. Each represents a logical division of the migration tasks.

Notice that Step 1 is "Plan your migration strategy." If you click on the Plan Migration button, online help launches and takes you through an overview of the migration process. If you have carefully read the information presented thus far in this chapter, you can skip this step and move to Step 2: "Convert a domain database."

Converting a Domain Database

The Migrate Domain phase of the migration process converts the GroupWise 4.1 domain database, WPDOMAIN.DB, to the GroupWise 5 domain database format. Once you have converted this database, it should not be accessed by the GroupWise 4.1 AD.EXE program, and cannot be used by the GroupWise 4.1 agents. It cannot be converted back to GroupWise 4.1 format, so make sure you have backed up this database before you begin.

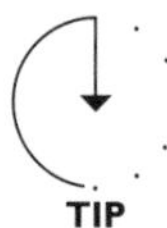

Make a backup of the .DC files, which are the GroupWise 4.1 database template files. These files are replaced by the migration process.

1 • Click on the Migrate Domain button to begin the process of converting the domain database. The GroupWise Migration Overview dialog box appears, as shown in Figure 16.4.

2 • Click on Next. The Software distribution dialog box appears.

3 • Specify the directory that stores the GroupWise software files. (You created this directory during the initial installation of the GroupWise software, prior to the beginning of the migration.)

4 • Click on Next. The Migrate Primary Domain dialog box appears. The name of your GroupWise 4.1 primary domain should be listed.

5 • Click on Next. The System Name dialog box appears. Guidelines for choosing the system name are covered in Chapter 3. You must enter a unique name for your GroupWise 5 system.

6 • Enter the system name and click on Next. The Shut Down Agents dialog box appears. You must shut down any agent that accesses the WPDOMAIN.DB file, namely the MTA and ADA processes.

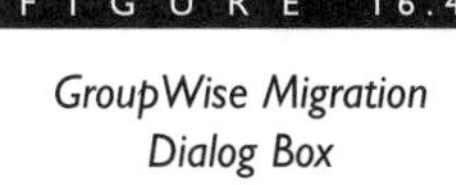

FIGURE 16.4

GroupWise Migration Dialog Box

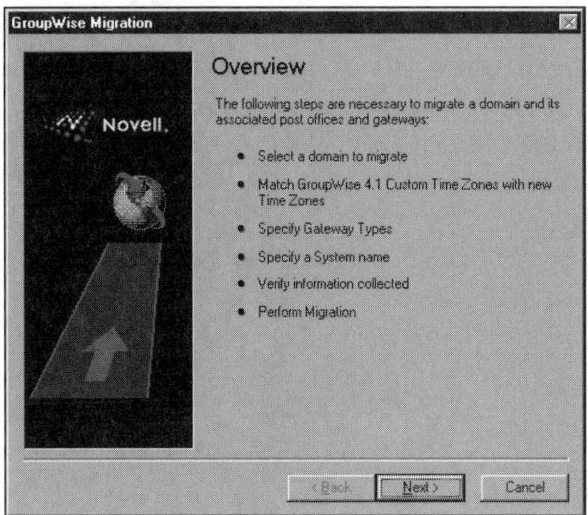
GroupWise Migration
Novell.
Overview
The following steps are necessary to migrate a domain and its associated post offices and gateways:
Select a domain to migrate
Match GroupWise 4.1 Custom Time Zones with new Time Zones
Specify Gateway Types
Specify a System name
Verify information collected
Perform Migration
< Back
Next >
Cancel

7 • Shut down any ADS, OFS, ADA, or MTA processes that might be accessing the domain. If there are no other GroupWise NLMs loaded, you need to manually unload NGWLIB.NLM at this point. You will need to either run an RCONSOLE session to the server or go to the server console to terminate the agents. If you are using DOS or OS/2 GroupWise 4.1 servers, unload them from the workstation they are running on.

8 • Click on Next in the Shut Down Agents dialog box. The Domain Directory dialog box appears.

9 • Enter the UNC or DOS path to the domain directory for the domain you are migrating and click on Next. The Post Office Directories dialog box appears. All of the post offices within the domain database are listed.

10 • Verify that the directories to the post offices are correct and click on Next. The Temporary Directory dialog box appears.

11 • Specify a temporary directory and click on Next. The Summary dialog box appears.

TIP

To speed up the process of converting the database, the Migration utility can use a directory to store temporary files during the conversion of the WPDOMAIN.DB file. If the domain database is large, you can speed up the conversion if you specify a directory on the local hard drive. Make sure you have free disk space at least two-and-a-half times the size of the WPDOMAIN.DB file.

12 • Summary dialog boxes appear at various points during the migration. These dialog boxes represent your "last chance" to make changes before the options you have specified are implemented. If you need to change any of the information displayed in the Summary dialog boxes, click Back to cycle back through the previous dialog boxes and change the information.

13 • When the information is correct, click on Finish to convert the WPDOMAIN.DB file. A "Please Wait" message appears while the domain database is converted. The Agent Information dialog box then appears. Click on Next. The Software Distribution dialog box appears.

14 • The Migration utility needs to know where the agent software is located so the GroupWise 5 agents can be installed. Highlight the software distribution directory and click on Next. The Agent Platform dialog box appears.

15 • Select the version of the GroupWise agents you will use and click on Next. Install Agents dialog box appears.

16 • Click on Install Agents and follow the prompts presented by the installation program to install the agents to your desired location. (Installing the agents is covered in Chapter 4.) When the installation is finished, the Install Agents dialog box will again appear, indicating that the agent installation program is finished and you can proceed.

17 • Click on Next in the Agent Installation dialog box. The Load GroupWise Agents dialog box appears.

18 • You now need to load the ADA and the MTA for the domain that you just converted. You can do this through RCONSOLE or from the server console on which the agents were installed. Once the ADA and MTA have been successfully loaded, click on Next. The GroupWise Migration dialog box appears again.

NOTE

You will need to customize these agents once the migration is complete. See Chapter 12 for more information about customizing the agents.

When the domain is migrated, many (often hundreds) of administrative messages are generated and passed to the ADA. These messages are generated because of the implementation of the *guardian databases* in GroupWise 5. Guardian databases track each GroupWise object by its *Global Unique Identifier*, or *GUID* (pronounced "GWID"). The administrative messages you see at this stage are caused by the system assigning a GUID to each GroupWise object.

The domain database has now been converted to the GroupWise 5 format. This means that all of the information about the other domains, post offices, gateways, users, resources, and groups is now stored in the GroupWise 5 primary domain database.

However, there is only one program that can administer a GroupWise 5 system: NetWare Administrator. NetWare Administrator only operates on objects in the NDS tree, and at this point no GroupWise objects are found in your NDS tree. The NDS schema has been extended, but the NDS database is not yet populated with any GroupWise information. This process occurs in the next phase of the migration when GroupWise objects, such as Domain objects, Post Office objects, and Gateway objects, are "grafted" onto the NDS tree.

Grafting GroupWise Objects onto NDS

This phase of the migration adds GroupWise objects to containers in your NDS tree. When this phase is complete, you will be able to administer your GroupWise system from NetWare Administrator.

There are two phases to grafting GroupWise objects:

- Grafting the GroupWise system components (domains, post offices, and gateways)
- Grafting the GroupWise objects (users, resources, and distribution lists)

To begin grafting GroupWise objects onto NDS, click on the Graft Objects button in the GroupWise Migration dialog box. The Welcome dialog box appears, as shown in Figure 16.5.

NOTE

This is the same dialog box that appears if you select Graft GroupWise Objects from the GroupWise Utilities option under Tools in NetWare Administrator.

FIGURE 16.5

Welcome Dialog Box

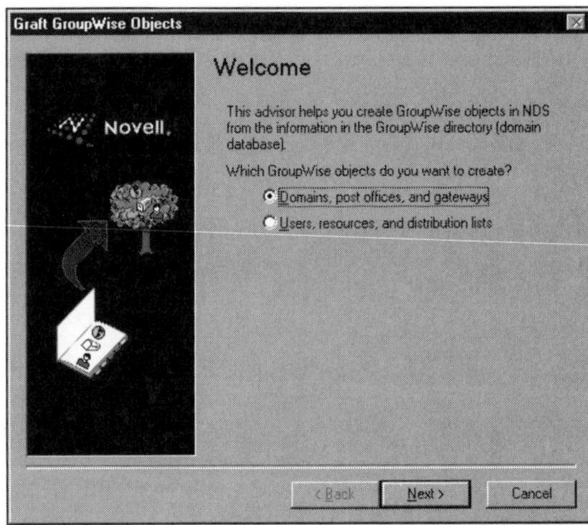

Notice that the dialog box presents the two options mentioned above. You must add Domain, Post Office, and Gateway objects to your NDS tree before you can add Resource objects, Distribution List objects, and GroupWise properties to existing NDS user accounts.

Domains, Post Offices, and Gateways

This next step grafts the GroupWise objects in a domain onto the NDS tree structure. Be sure to have the location planned out and the containers created before proceeding.

1 • Select the "Domains, post offices, and gateways" option, and click on Next. The Overview dialog box appears (see Figure 16.6).

2 • Click on Next in the Overview dialog box. The Select Domain dialog box appears. This dialog box lists only the GroupWise 5 domains found in the system.

3 • Highlight the name of the primary domain and click on Next. The Domain Context dialog box appears.

4 • Enter the NDS context in which the Domain object should be created and click on Next. The Post Office Context dialog box appears. Each post office within the domain is listed in this dialog box.

5 • If the context listed in the dialog box is not the context in which the Post Office object should be created, click on the Edit Context button and specify the correct context for each Post Office object. When the context is listed correctly, click on Next. The Summary dialog box appears.

6 • Verify that the information in the Summary dialog box is correct. If necessary, click on Back to change any incorrect information. When the summary information is correct, click Finish. A Please Wait dialog box appears while the Domain and Post Office objects are added to the NDS tree. When the process is complete, the Graft More Objects dialog box appears.

7 • Choose Yes in the Graft More Objects dialog box and click on Next. The Welcome dialog box again appears.

Graft Objects Overview

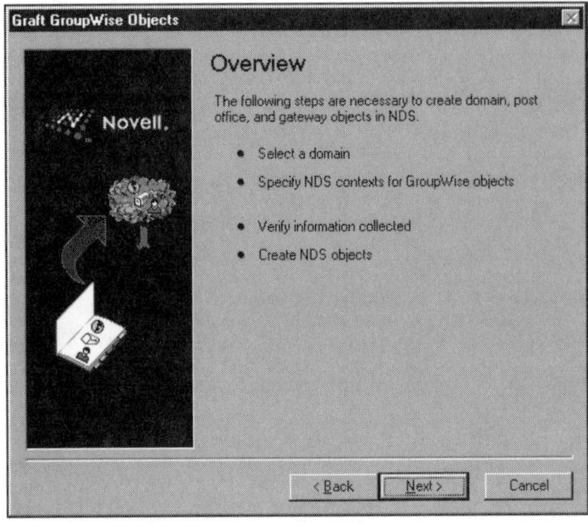

Users, Resources, and Distribution Lists

This step grafts Resource objects and Distribution List objects for a particular post office onto the NDS locations for each. GroupWise users for the newly migrated post office will be associated with existing NDS users.

1. Select the "Users, resources, and distribution lists" option, then click on Next. The Overview dialog box appears, listing the steps for grafting these objects onto NDS (see Figure 16.7).

Graft GroupWise Objects

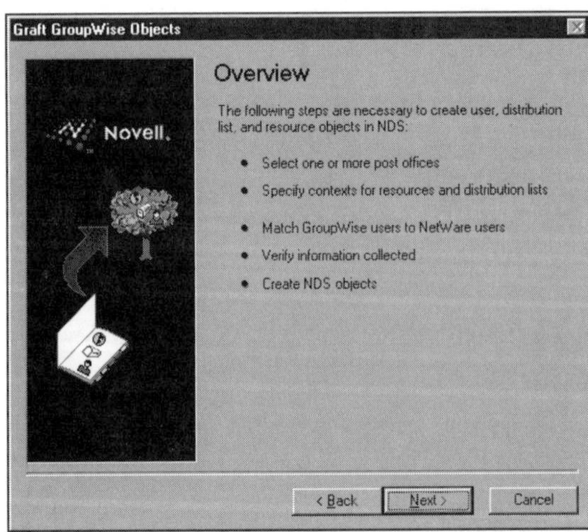

2 • Click on Next. The Select Post Offices dialog box appears.

3 • Highlight the post office that contains the users, resources, or distribution lists you are grafting and click on Next. (You can use Ctrl+click to select multiple post offices. If you select multiple post offices, objects from each post office will be grafted in this phase of the migration.) The Additional User Fields dialog box appears.

4 • The Additional User Fields dialog box lets you match custom additional address fields you might have assigned in your GroupWise 4.1 system with existing NDS fields. Make your desired selection and click on Next. The Resources Context dialog box appears.

5 • Enter the context in which the Resource objects should exist and click on Next. The Distribution List Context dialog box appears.

6 • Enter the context in which the Distribution List objects should be created and click on Next. The Match Users dialog box appears, as shown in Figure 16.8. This dialog box lets you select contexts (NDS containers) in which the Migration utility should look to find existing NDS User objects that match the User objects you are grafting from the GroupWise domain database. This step requires that you know where your User objects exist in your NDS tree. The user accounts in the post office might exist in several different contexts in the NDS tree. Because it is inefficient for the Migration utility to search your entire NDS tree in its attempt to match GroupWise User objects to NDS users, you must specify which contexts contain the NDS users.

7 • To add contexts, click on the Add button.

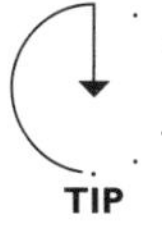
TIP

Notice that you can specify several contexts in this dialog box. You should specify contexts containing the users in descending order in this dialog box, with the contexts containing the most matching User objects first. The search for NDS objects will cascade down the tree from the contexts you specify. You should minimize the number of WAN links traversed by the search for objects.

FIGURE 16.8

Match GroupWise Users

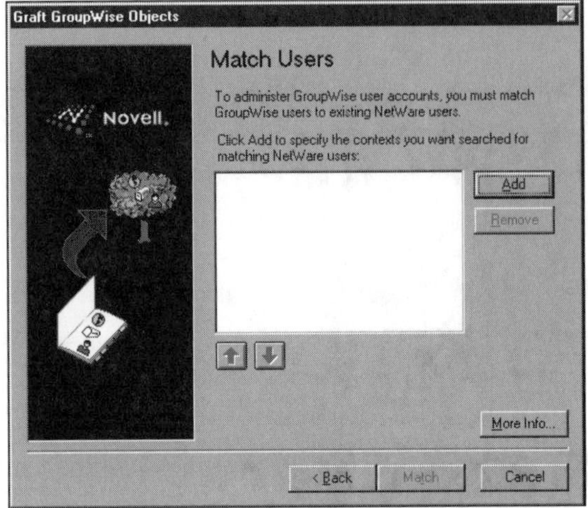

8 • Highlight a context that you want to search and click on OK.

9 • Repeat Steps 7 and 8 to add all contexts that should be searched.

10 • Use the up and down arrow keys to adjust the order in which the contexts should be searched.

11 • When all of the contexts are listed, click on the Match button. The Migration utility looks at the users in the GroupWise database and attempts to match these users with existing NDS user accounts. When the process is finished, a dialog box appears showing the users who were not matched (see Figure 16.9).

Time for a brief intermission. The Unmatched Users dialog box gives you four options for dealing with unmatched users:

- Specify more search contexts and try again
- Create these users as GroupWise external entities
- Save to a text file and go on
- Ignore

FIGURE 16.9

Results of Matching Process

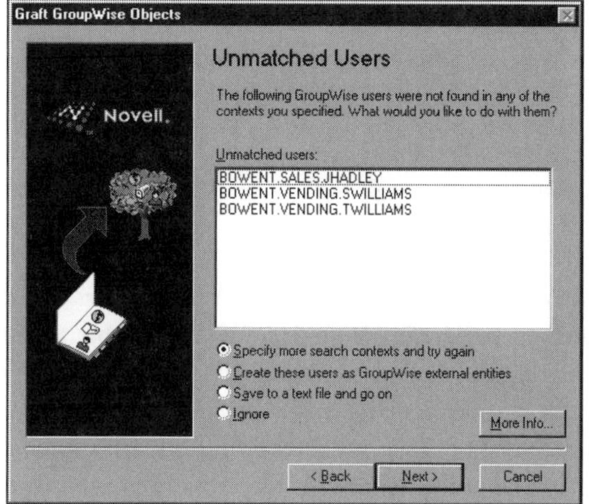

If you choose the *Specify more search contexts and try again* option, you can enter the contexts for other container objects that contain users. Use this option if you did not specify all of the search contexts in the Match Users dialog box.

The second option is to create the users as external entities. A GroupWise external entity is an NDS object for a GroupWise user who does not have an NDS user account; for example, users on non-NetWare networks. An external entity has a mailbox in the GroupWise system and is displayed in the Address Book. As system administrator, you can manage that user's GroupWise account by using the external entity object.

If the unmatched users will eventually have NDS user accounts, you should consider creating these user accounts prior to your migration, as we explained previously.

External entities cannot be automatically converted to NetWare users. If you create external entity objects and later want the external entity's mailbox associated with an NDS user account, you must delete the external entity object and then graft the user onto NDS.

However, you must be careful that you do not delete the mailbox associated with the external entity when you delete the external entity object. Use the "Delete Object (NDS Only)" option from the GroupWise diagnostics menu to delete the external entity object and leave the mailbox intact.

The *Save to a text file and go on* option allows you to proceed with the migration and preserve a record of the users that were not matched to NDS User objects.

If you select this option, you can later use the text file as a reference and create NDS objects for these users. You can then use the Graft option to associate the mailboxes with NDS user accounts.

If you choose the `Ignore` option, you can proceed without acting on the unmatched users.

IMPORTANT

Mailboxes associated with unmatched users are preserved and converted to GroupWise 5, no matter which option you select. The mailboxes and their associated messages will be converted and placed into the post office message store awaiting further action. However, if you choose the Save to a Text File option or the Ignore option, you will have no administrative abilities for these mailboxes or the users that own the mailboxes. You will have to use the Graft option to gain administrative control over these users and mailboxes.

Now, back to our feature presentation . . .

12 • Select an option for the unmatched users and click on Next. The Graft GroupWise Objects Summary dialog box appears, as shown in Figure 16.10. The Summary dialog box presents you with one last chance to change your mind about the graft process. If necessary, you can use the Back button to make changes.

13 • Click on the Finish button to associate the GroupWise users, resources, and distribution lists with NDS objects. The associations are created, and the Graft More Objects? dialog box appears. If you want to graft more objects, choose Yes. Otherwise, choose No and then click on Done to return to the GroupWise Migration dialog box.

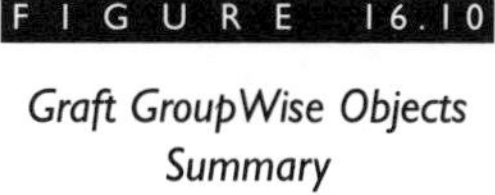

FIGURE 16.10

Graft GroupWise Objects Summary

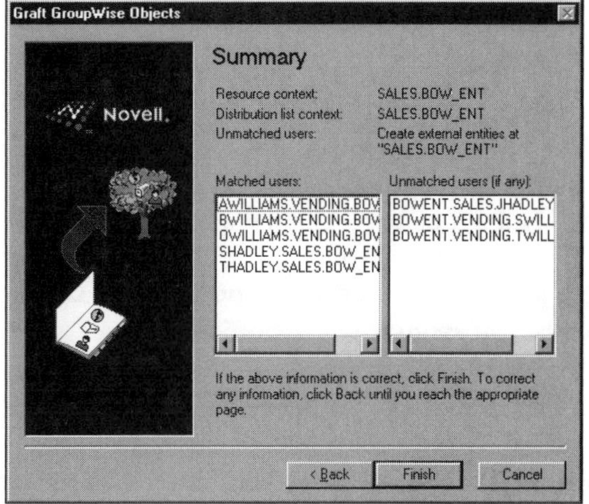

Let's take a breather for a moment and review what has happened thus far in the migration.

At this point, the following tasks have been completed:

- The GroupWise 4.1 domain was converted to the GroupWise 5 format.
- The GroupWise 5 agents have been installed.
- NDS objects have been created for the GroupWise domain and at least one post office.
- NDS objects have been created for distribution lists and resources that were found in the post office or post offices that you are migrating.
- Users in the GroupWise post office have been matched with NDS user accounts, and GroupWise properties have been added to those NDS user accounts.

The next phase is the most critical and probably the most time-consuming—converting the users' messages into GroupWise 5 format.

Migrating a Post Office to GroupWise 5

The next phase of the migration converts the post office database (WPHOST.DB) to GroupWise 5 and then converts the post office message store (user and message databases) to GroupWise 5 format.

When this phase is complete, the post office and its messages will no longer be accessible to users running either the GroupWise 4.1 or GroupWise 5 client program. Access will not be restored until all remaining steps have been completed.

WARNING

At this point in the migration, no users or GroupWise processes should be accessing the post office.

To proceed with the post office conversion, follow these steps:

1. Click on the Migrate Post Office button in the GroupWise Migration dialog box. The Overview dialog box appears, as shown in Figure 16.11.

2. Click on Next on the Overview screen. The Close Post Office dialog box appears. You might need to force users out of the post office by terminating logins to the server that holds the post office files.

3. Select the post office that is being migrated and click on Next. The Shut Down Agents dialog box appears.

FIGURE 16.11

Post Office Overview

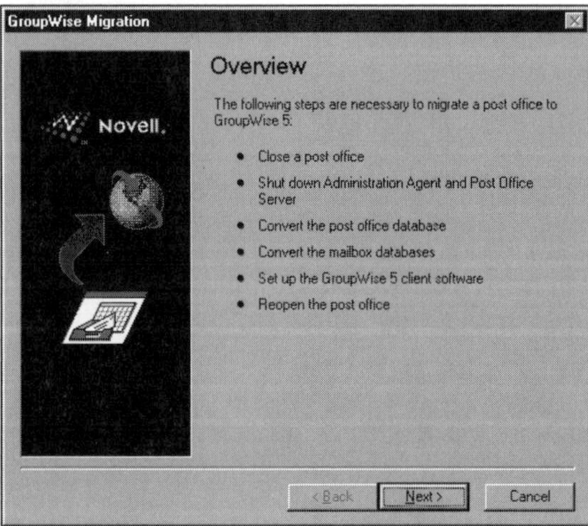

4 • You need to shut down the ADA you loaded after you converted the domain database earlier in the migration. Depending upon the platform you are using for the GroupWise OFS agent, take the steps necessary to terminate it. If you are using the NLM version, use RCONSOLE or go to the server console and manually exit the OFS process.

5 • After you have shut down the agents, click on Next. The Software Distribution directory appears.

6 • Highlight the software distribution directory that will provide users in this post office with access to the GroupWise software and then click on Next. The Convert Post Office Database dialog box appears.

7 • Specify a temporary directory (if desired) and click on Convert to convert the WPHOST.DB file to GroupWise 5. When you click on Convert, the NetWare Administrator copies GroupWise 5 dictionary files to the post office directory and then rebuilds the existing WPHOST.DB file based upon these dictionary files. This process converts the database to GroupWise 5 format. When this process is finished, the Convert Mailbox Overview dialog box appears.

8 • After you review the steps involved in converting the mailboxes, click on Next. The Agent Platform dialog box appears. This dialog box is used to initiate the agent installation program for installing the GroupWise 5 POA that will service the post office.

9 • Earlier in the migration, you installed the ADA and MTA for the domain you migrated. In this phase, you install the POA. Follow the prompts for installing the POA. When the Agent Installation Complete dialog box appears, Click on Done to return to the NLM Agent Installation dialog box. Click on Next to continue. The Convert Mailboxes dialog box appears, as shown in Figure 16.12.

The Convert Mailboxes dialog box explains how to convert the post office information store to the GroupWise 5 format.

FIGURE 16.12

Convert Mailboxes Dialog Box

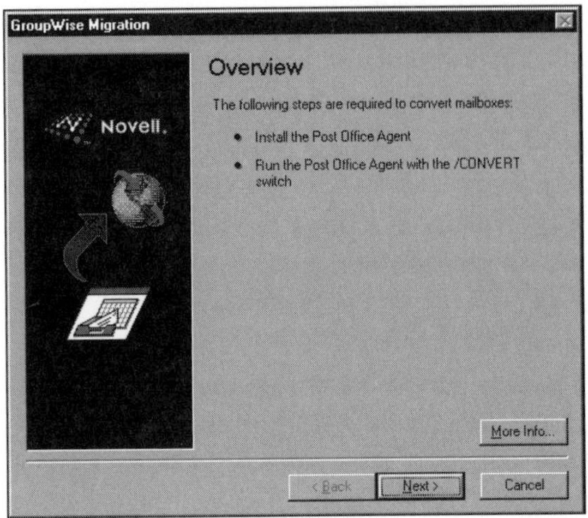

The conversion is performed by the GroupWise 5 POA running in a special conversion mode. To launch the POA in the conversion mode, you run the POA with the `/convert` parameter. You can use the following syntax to load the POA in the conversion mode:

```
LOAD GWPOA /home-<path to post office> /convert
```

For example,

```
LOAD GWPOA /home-shickfs1\sys:tvpo /convert
```

10 • Load the POA in the convert mode as instructed in the Convert Mailboxes dialog box. If you are converting a post office that holds a lot of messages, it's time for a coffee break. A log file is created for the post office conversion. You can use the log file to identify and troubleshoot problems that might have occurred during the message conversion. To view the log file, press F9 from the POA monitor screen. The top of the screen will show you the log filename and the directory where it is stored. You can retrieve the log file into an editor program if you need to print it.

WARNING

Do not re-open the post office until this process has completely finished.

11 • When the POA has finished converting the information store, the message "Conversion Complete!" appears on the POA monitor screen. Exit the POA and reload it without the `/convert` switch.

12 • Reload the GroupWise agents for the domain you converted.

Congratulations! You now have a functional GroupWise 5 domain and post office.

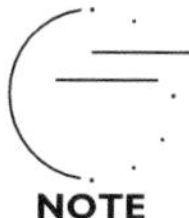
NOTE

Now that you have completely upgraded the domain and post office to GroupWise 5, it's time to run another backup, because all backups of the 4.1-level system are now useless for this domain and post office.

The rest of the dialog boxes presented by the Migration utility will assist you in installing the GroupWise 5 client on the computer that is running NetWare Administrator.

If you want to install the client software on this computer, you can continue through the Migration utility screens.

Before you completely exit out of the migration process, you will be prompted to open the post offices. Make sure that you open the post offices and that you then launch the ADA, MTA, and POA before testing the results of the migration.

You can run the setup program at your convenience from the software distribution directory. You need to test the migration by loading the GroupWise 5 client software on a few workstations and accessing the mailboxes. After testing the first migration, you can return to the main NetWare Administrator screen. If users attempt to access the post office with the GroupWise 4.1 client, they will get a message prompting them to update their client to GroupWise 5.

Migrating More Domains, Post Offices, and Objects

You have now completed the process of migrating the GroupWise 4.1 primary domain to GroupWise 5. You've also migrated a GroupWise post office and its objects to NDS, and converted a post office message store to GroupWise 5.

To finish your migration, you will need to migrate the rest of the post offices in the primary domain, and then migrate your secondary domains and their post offices and users.

Because the process is very similar to the process previously explained in this chapter, we'll simply give you the steps to get each task going, and let you take it from there.

Additional Domains

To migrate additional domains, follow these steps:

1. In NetWare Administrator, click on Tools.
2. Click on GroupWise System Operations.
3. Double-click on the System Connection icon.
4. Connect to the GroupWise 4.1 domain that you want to migrate.
5. Click on Close to exit from the GroupWise System Operations dialog box.
6. Click on Tools.
7. Click on GroupWise Utilities.
8. Click on GroupWise 4.1 Migration. The GroupWise Migration dialog box appears.
9. Click on Migrate Domain and follow the prompts you have seen previously in this chapter to migrate the secondary domain.

Additional Post Offices

To migrate additional post offices in the primary domain, or to migrate post offices in a secondary domain after you have converted the domain database to GroupWise 5, use the following steps:

1. Verify that you are connected to the domain containing the post office.

2 • Click on Tools.

3 • Click on GroupWise Utilities.

4 • Click on GroupWise 4.1 Migration.

5 • Choose the Migrate Post Office button.

6 • Follow the Migration utility's prompts as previously explained.

Previously Unmatched Users

If you had unmatched users that you either ignored or saved to a log file when you initially migrated users into GroupWise 5, use the following steps to migrate those users to GroupWise 5:

1 • Verify that an NDS User object exists for each user previously unmatched. Create any User objects that are needed.

2 • Connect to the domain containing the unmatched users' post office.

3 • Click on Tools.

4 • Click on GroupWise Utilities.

5 • Select Graft GroupWise Objects.

6 • Choose the "Users, resources, and distribution lists" option from the Graft GroupWise Objects Welcome screen.

7 • Use the steps presented previously in this chapter for matching GroupWise users with NDS users.

Converting External Entities to NDS User Objects

There is no automatic upgrade path for converting an external entity into an NDS User object with GroupWise properties. If a GroupWise user is initially represented in NDS as an external entity and you later need to associate the external entity's GroupWise mailbox with an NDS User object, follow the steps outlined in this section:

Do not delete the external entity object before completing these steps. If you delete the external entity object with the GroupWise administration features enabled in NetWare Administrator, the GroupWise mailbox that corresponds to the object will also be deleted.

1 • On the computer that you use to administer GroupWise, exit NetWare Administrator.

2 • Using Windows Explorer, browse to the WINDOWS directory and locate the NWADMN3X.INI file.

3 • Rename NWADMN3X.INI to NWADMN3X.OLD.

4 • Run NetWare Administrator. Because you renamed the INI file, all GroupWise objects will be represented with question marks instead of the regular icons.

5 • Locate the external entity object that currently represents the GroupWise user account.

6 • Delete the external entity object.

7 • Exit from NetWare Administrator.

8 • Using Explorer, go to the WINDOWS directory and delete the NWADMN3X.INI file that was created automatically.

9 • Rename NWADMN3X.OLD to NWADMN3X.INI.

10 • Run NetWare Administrator.

11 • Create the NDS User object that needs to be associated with the GroupWise mailbox.

12 • Go to the User object's GroupWise property page.

13 • Fill in the GroupWise Mailbox ID field so that it corresponds with the mailbox that formerly belonged to the external entity.

14 • When you exit that field, you will be asked if that NDS object corresponds with the GroupWise object. Select Yes. The NDS user account is now associated with the mailbox that formerly belonged to the external entity object.

Summary

This chapter showed you how to plan a migration, what you need to do to prepare your GroupWise 4.1 system for the migration, and the procedures for migrating a GroupWise 4.1 system to GroupWise 5.

Remember: The key to a successful migration is the planning and preparatory steps that you take before you actually migrate the GroupWise 4.1 system to GroupWise 5.

In the next chapter, you'll learn how to implement GroupWise 5 document management.

PART V

Connectivity and Mobile Computing

CHAPTER 17

Document Management

A major set of new features was added to GroupWise with the release of GroupWise 5: GroupWise Document Management Services (GWDMS). GroupWise Document Management Services lets GroupWise users store and manage their documents in the GroupWise system. With the addition of GWDMS, GroupWise 5 combines electronic messaging with document management technology.

NOTE

Some publications refer to Document Management Services as DMS. Because the acronym "DMS" has another, totally different, meaning in the electronic messaging industry (it stands for "Defense Messaging System"), we use the acronym GWDMS in this chapter to refer to GroupWise Document Management Services.

GWDMS is not automatically implemented when you install GroupWise 5. There are special steps for setting it up and enabling users to access it. Implementing document management services in a GroupWise system is a big step with wide-sweeping implications. A successful implementation involves planning, testing, and some extra work on the part of the GroupWise administrator. Consequently, you should consider carefully whether or not it make sense to implement document management services in your system.

Following are a few general guidelines for deciding whether or not to implement GWDMS in your system:

- If you are already using a full-featured document management program, it's possible you won't need to utilize GroupWise 5's document management features. If that's the case, you can save yourself the time and effort it takes to install GWDMS and convert your existing documents.

- If you have been using SoftSolutions as your document management system, you should evaluate the capabilities of GWDMS to see if it will provide adequate document management features for your organization's needs.

- If you don't currently have a document management system but feel that you could benefit from one, you should try out the GroupWise document management capabilities to see if they meet your needs.

If you think your organization might benefit from GroupWise 5's document management capabilities, you should read this chapter. We explain GroupWise 5 Document Management Services and tell you how to plan and carry out its implementation. We also give some basic maintenance and troubleshooting pointers.

A thorough explanation of GroupWise 5 document management could fill an entire book. Although we can't cover everything in one chapter, we'll give you the basic information you need to get started with GWDMS, and we'll point you to additional references for more detailed information.

In this chapter, we will not explain how to use the document management features available in the GroupWise 5 client program. This chapter focuses exclusively on how to set up and administer GroupWise document management. For an in-depth explanation of how end users can use GroupWise document management features, refer to *Novell's GroupWise 5 User's Handbook*, published by Novell Press and IDG Books Worldwide.

What Is Document Management?

Although document management programs have been around for years, many computer users are not familiar with their capabilities. Most people are, however, very familiar with file management techniques. Therefore, we'll begin our discussion of document management by comparing it to more traditional file management concepts.

In a traditional *file management* system, files are saved in directories or folders. Users organize their files with intuitively named directories and subdirectories. For example, uses might save spreadsheet files in C:\QUATTRO\FILES, or word processing documents in U:\USERS\BOYD\WPDOCS.

You are undoubtedly already familiar with the drawbacks of standard file management systems (but you've probably learned to live with them). In standard file management, you need to remember directory names, filenames, where files are located, and so on. To compensate for these limitations, file management utilities have been developed to ease the burden of organizing and searching for files. However, those utilities still fall short of the power and flexibility of document management systems.

Although recent advances in computer operating systems have largely overcome limitations on the length of filenames, many users still use the traditional "eight-dot-three" convention (an eight-character filename followed by a three-character extension). That convention is still necessary for compatibility with programs that do not support newer naming conventions of operating systems like Windows 95.

In contrast to traditional file management techniques, document management programs typically offer the following features:

- Multiple versions of documents (for tracking revisions). With a document management program, it is easy to find the original draft, a recent draft, or the final draft, of a specific document.
- Shared documents with large groups of individuals
- Security protection for personal and business documents
- Document-access auditing capabilities
- Document searches based on a wide variety of criteria, such as the content of the document, version number, name, creation date, and so forth
- Reliable backup of documents
- Document archiving (to conserve disk space)
- Extended file naming capabilities, such as long filenames and support of spaces, symbols, and punctuation in filenames
- Extensive administrative control over documents

Document management programs, such as SoftSolutions and PC-DOCS, have traditionally met the needs of several niche markets (for example, the legal or insurance industries) that have to manage extremely large quantities of documents.

GroupWise is the first messaging system to integrate document management and electronic messaging.

Components of GWDMS

In this section, you'll learn about the main components of GWDMS:

- Documents
- Libraries
- The document store
- The GroupWise client
- Integrated applications
- The post office agent (POA)

After we describe each of these components, we'll explain how they all work together.

Documents

First we need to explain exactly what we mean by *document*. A document is any file that can be stored in the GroupWise document management system. Documents are not only word-processing files. They can be spreadsheets, presentation files, and basically any other type of file you can create with an application.

All documents in GWDMS are categorized by *document type*. Each document type (for instance, Contract or Memo) has a specific set of *default document properties* (for example, a property indicating when documents should be archived or deleted). Several standard document types are available in GWDMS. Popular document types include Contract, Form, Memo, Minutes, and Proposal. As a

GroupWise administrator, you can create custom document types if the default standard types do not meet your needs.

Each individual document stored in GroupWise has its own set of "document properties." *Document properties* are fields that describe a document's attributes. Some common document properties include the Subject, Document Type, Author, Creation Date, and Version. Document properties provide a way to organize documents and enable users to quickly find documents stored in the document management system.

Figure 17.1 shows NetWare Administrator's Document Properties Maintenance screen. Notice the default document types listed and the various properties assigned to each.

FIGURE 17.1

Document Properties Maintenance in NetWare Administrator

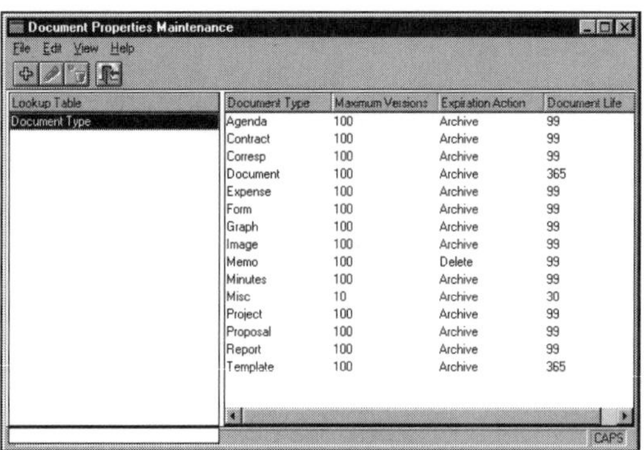

Each document type has three critical document properties:

- Maximum Versions
- Expiration Action
- Document Life

The *Maximum Versions property* determines how many versions of a document can be maintained in the library. The *Expiration Action property* determines whether a document will be deleted or archived when the retention period expires. The *Document Life property* specifies how long a document can remain in the library before it is either automatically archived or deleted according to the options specified in the Expiration Action field.

Libraries

In GWDMS, all documents are stored in *libraries*. A library is a set of directories and databases in a GroupWise system. These directories and databases store and maintain both documents and document properties. Each library in your system is an NDS object that can be configured, customized, and optimized to best suit your document management needs. Figure 17.2 shows a Library object in an NDS tree. Before users can use GroupWise Document Management Services, you must create at least one library to hold the GWDMS documents.

FIGURE 17.2

A Library Object in NDS

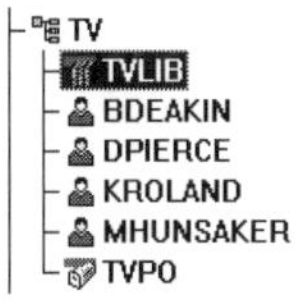

TV
TVLIB
BDEAKIN
DPIERCE
KROLAND
MHUNSAKER
TVPO

When libraries are added to a GroupWise system, a GWDMS directory structure is created in each post office directory. Just as messages are stored as records in message databases, documents are located in a series of databases. The GWDMS directory contains the master GroupWise library database, DMSH.DB, and subdirectories for each library associated with the post office. The individual library directories are named LIB*xxxx*, where *xxxx* represents a library number.

The DMSH.DB database holds lookup tables for all libraries in the GroupWise system. When a user runs the GroupWise client and views the list of available libraries, it reads the contents of the DMSH.DB file.

Each LIB*xxxx* directory also contains a collection of library databases used to store document properties, document logging information, and so forth.

The Document Store

Documents reside in the individual library storage areas, which are collectively known as the *document store*. The document store contains the databases that store the documents. These databases are called *Binary Large Objects*, or *BLOBs*. The databases in the LIB*xxxx* directory use pointers to reference the individual documents stored in the BLOBs. (This is similar to how GroupWise stores mail messages insofar as the message databases contain pointers to file attachments stored in the OFFILES directories.)

One of the main benefits of storing documents in BLOBs is that the document files are compressed and take up only about one-half the disk space consumed by documents stored as individual files. Documents stored in BLOBs are encrypted in the GroupWise 5 database encryption format for security.

NOTE

The document store can be located within a post office directory structure or in other document storage locations elsewhere in the network.

The GroupWise Client

End users access GroupWise Document Management Services using the GroupWise client interface. Using the GroupWise client, end users can manage their documents with the same program they use for electronic messaging.

In the GroupWise client, documents stored in a GroupWise library are listed as *document references*. As shown in Figure 17.3, document references are listed along with other messages. Users can also create folders within the GroupWise Cabinet to store document references.

FIGURE 17.3

Document References

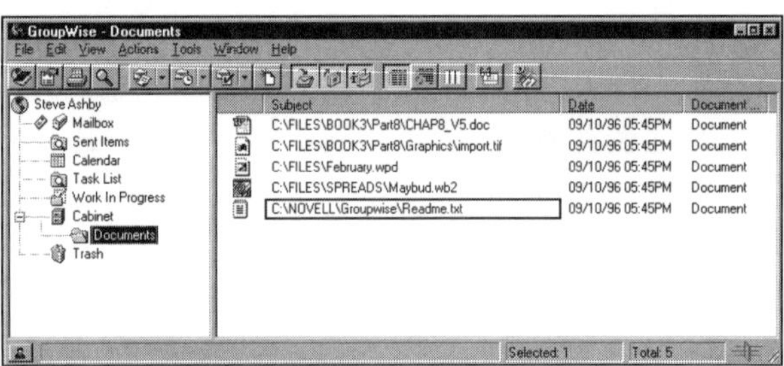

With the GroupWise client, users can perform the following document management tasks:

- Import documents into a library
- Create new documents
- Manage their personal documents

- Access public documents
- Check documents out of the library for use outside of the GroupWise system
- Check documents back into the library after working on them outside of the GroupWise system
- Send document references to other users

IMPORTANT

You need the 32-bit GroupWise 5 client, such as the Windows 95/NT client or the Macintosh client in order to use GWDMS. The 16-bit version of the GroupWise client does not support GWDMS.

Integrated Applications

You can access documents stored in libraries not only through the GroupWise client program but also when you use *integrated applications*, applications that can be integrated with GroupWise 5.

When an application is integrated with GWDMS, users can use the GWDMS interface *within that application* to save and retrieve documents stored in the GroupWise system. When you choose standard file management menu commands in an integrated office productivity application such as WordPerfect (for example, File → Open), you can automatically access the GWDMS interface. You also access the GWDMS interface whenever you need to access files (for example, when attaching a file to an e-mail message with the GroupWise client). Figure 17.4 shows the GWDMS interface within a common integrated application, Microsoft Word. The figure shows the GWDMS dialog box that appears for saving a document in a library.

GroupWise 5 supports document integration with the following applications: Corel WordPerfect, Corel Quattro Pro, Lotus WordPro, Microsoft Word, and Microsoft Excel. Also, any applications that are compliant with the 32-bit Open Document Management API (ODMA) are supported by GWDMS. (We explain more about integration with other applications later in this chapter.)

FIGURE 17.4

GWDMS Integrated with Word

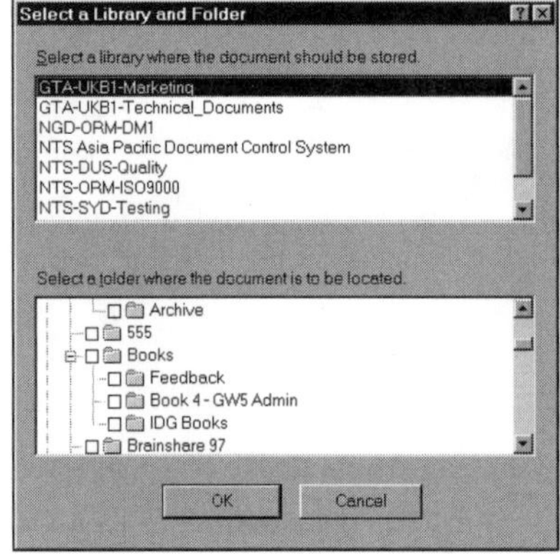

The Post Office Agent

Along with its message delivery duties and its mailbox maintenance duties, the post office agent also manages the GroupWise document store.

The POA's biggest document management responsibility is to generate indexes of the GroupWise document store. Indexing provides quick access to documents by expediting the search for and retrieval of documents. The POA also maintains and compresses the document store databases each night to ensure that disk space is used efficiently by the databases. If the POA is running in Client/Server mode, it also responds to all user requests to retrieve and save documents.

If you have a large document store (or if the POA already handles a large messaging load), you should consider setting up a dedicated POA for indexing. We explain this procedure later in the chapter.

How the Components Work Together

Figure 17.5 is a simplified diagram that shows how the GWDMS components work together.

FIGURE 17.5

GWDMS Components

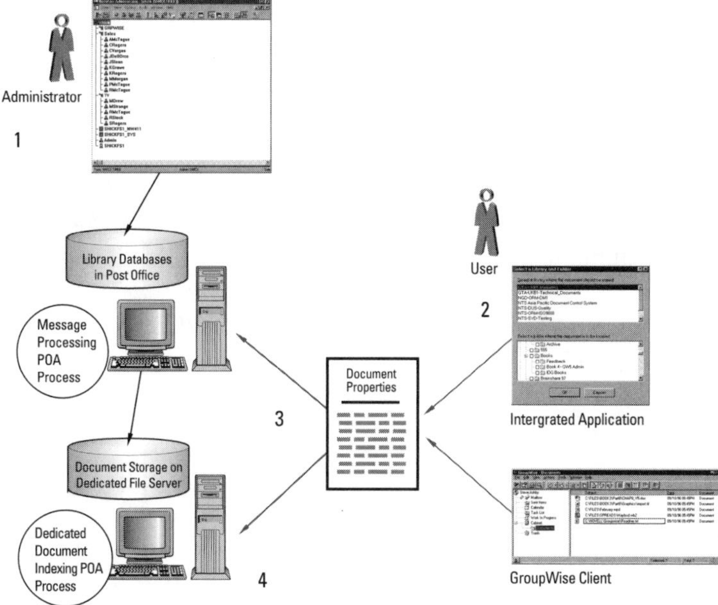

The events illustrated in the graphic are as follows:

1 • The system administrator uses NetWare Administrator to create and configure the library. This process creates a Library object in NDS, the library directories, databases, and (if desired) the document storage locations.

2 • Users run the GroupWise client and import documents into the library or create new documents with integrated applications.

3 • These documents are stored in the library. The document properties and logging information are stored in the library databases and the document is stored in the document store. (Note: This process could be handled by either the client or the POA, depending upon the post office configuration.)

4 • The POA manages the documents stored in the document store and performs document indexing on a regular basis.

Now that you're familiar with the basic components of GWDMS, you're ready to begin planning your GWDMS implementation.

Planning an Implementation of GWDMS

In this section we discuss some of the planning issues you should consider if you are thinking about implementing GroupWise document management services:

- Centralized and distributed GWDMS strategies
- Library functions
- Document storage
- Disk space requirements
- User access
- Indexing strategies
- Other planning considerations

For more information about planning a GroupWise 5 document management implementation, see Novell Technical Document ID # 2915907, "Plan a GW5 System with GW5 Document Management," included as file PLANDMS.DOC on the CD-ROM that comes with this book.

Centralized and Distributed GWDMS Strategies

As you design your document management strategy, you should consider whether you will use a *centralized strategy* or a *distributed strategy*.

In a *centralized document management strategy*, all libraries are located within one dedicated post office in the GroupWise 5 system, and document stores are located on dedicated servers or storage devices.

The benefits of a centralized document strategy include the following:

- You can use dedicated hardware, such as servers, optical drives, RAID, backup devices, etc.
- You centralize your library maintenance and administration.
- Backups of library data are greatly simplified.

In order to use a centralized configuration, users must be using the TCP/IP-based Client/Server access mode so they can access the TCP/IP-enabled POA of the post office that houses the libraries (just as TCP/IP enables users to serve as proxies in other post offices).

In a *distributed document management strategy*, libraries are spread throughout the entire GroupWise system in multiple post offices.

The advantages of a distributed strategy include the following:

- *Performance.* Users can access documents stored locally faster than documents stored in post offices that must be accessed via WAN links.
- *Specialization.* Libraries can be customized to meet the needs of the workgroups within a post office.
- *Flexibility.* Users can access the libraries using Direct Only access mode instead of having to use client/server messaging.
- *Fault-tolerance.* If one server goes down, it only affects libraries housed on that server, while other libraries continue to function.

You are not required to choose between the two strategies. You could implement a combination of centralized and decentralized document management. For example, some central libraries might house general documents that can be used by all employees, and specialized libraries might be created in individual post offices.

Library Functions

Each library's intended purpose determines where you should place that library in the GroupWise system and which library rights you should assign to users of the library.

If a library will serve as a repository for official corporate documents, you should place that library in the post office that hosts the users responsible for official documents. You should be very conservative in assigning user access rights to the library.

If a library is to serve as a storage location for users' personal documents, you should place that library in the post office that contains the user accounts. In this situation, you must be very liberal in the assignment of access rights. In order to manage their personal documents, users will need most (if not all) of the available library rights.

Document Storage

Planning your document storage strategy involves determining the location of the document databases themselves. As mentioned previously, you have two options for storing documents: in the post office or in dedicated document storage locations outside of the post office.

If you anticipate low message storage requirements and low levels of library usage, you can store documents under the post office without much difficulty. The possible disadvantages of storing documents in the post office include the following:

- Limitations on disk capacity.
- Immobility of document storage location. (In other words, you can't easily move your document storage to another location once you've established the post office as the storage location.)

If you expect heavy usage of the GroupWise document management features and large storage requirements, we recommend that you create a storage location outside of the post office directory, such as on a dedicated disk, server, or volume.

The advantages of storing documents in separate storage locations are as follows:

- Document storage locations can be moved if necessary.
- You can assign multiple storage locations to a post office.
- The disk space on the drive that stores the GroupWise message store is not used up by documents.

Whichever option you choose, you should put the POA that performs indexing for a library on the same computer that houses the document storage location. This prevents the POA from generating across-the-wire network traffic during indexing.

Disk Space Requirements

Estimating disk space for a document management system is difficult. When you add GroupWise Document Management Services to your existing GroupWise messaging system, you substantially increase the amount of disk space required by GroupWise, because documents are usually much larger than GroupWise messages.

A good place to start is by determining how much disk space is currently being allocated to documents. Your best estimates for disk space required by GroupWise libraries will probably be obtained through in-house experimentation. You also need to determine what percentage of documents will be handled by GWDMS. For example, are you going to have users store their personal documents in the GWDMS document store, or as individual files? Will 100 percent of the spreadsheets created by your company be managed by GWDMS?

Keep in mind that you can set up libraries with multiple document storage areas to spread the demand for disk space across multiple servers or multiple volumes.

Also keep in mind that because GroupWise stores documents in BLOB databases, the documents will be compressed by as much as 50 percent.

User Access

When a library is created in the GroupWise system, it becomes visible to all users in the GroupWise system. However, whether or not a GroupWise user can access the library depends upon the type of access available to the user: Client/Server or Direct.

If your post offices are configured with the Direct-Only access mode, only the libraries associated with a user's post office are available to users within the post office. If your post offices are configured with client/server messaging, users can access libraries located in other post offices. There are two requirements for this: (1) the POAs must communicate using client/server messaging, and (2) the users accessing the library in a different post office must access the local post office in Client/Server access mode.

Indexing Strategies

When you implement GroupWise document management services, you need to consider how indexing will be handled.

The GroupWise POA automatically indexes the document property information, the complete text of documents, and GroupWise messages.

If the library usage will be light, a single POA within a post office can handle both the messaging demands and the library indexing demands. However, if you anticipate that the libraries will be used heavily and if users expect changes made to documents to be indexed quickly, you should dedicate one or more POA processes to library indexing.

For a detailed description of the GWDMS indexing process, see Technical Document ID # 2921069, "The GroupWise 5 Library Indexing Process." This document is available as DMSINDEX.DOC on the companion CD-ROM for this book.

Other Planning Considerations

Other factors may influence your document management implementation:

- The number of users in a post office who will access a local library

- The number of users who will access a library from other post offices in the system
- The number of existing documents that will be stored in the library

We've now explained the planning issues involved in implementing GWDMS. Make sure you have adequately addressed these issues before you begin creating and configuring GroupWise document libraries.

Creating Libraries in GroupWise 5

After you have planned your document management strategy and determined where documents will be stored, you are ready to create the GWDMS system. The creation of a library within a post office involves three main tasks:

- Defining library storage areas
- Creating the Library object
- Assigning library rights

Defining Library Storage Areas

If you determine that you will use a storage area outside of the post office directory structure, you must define a library storage area.

NOTE

This step is not necessary if you will store documents within the post office's directory structure.

To define a document storage area:

1. In NetWare Administrator, right-click on the Post Office object and choose Details.
2. Click on the Library Storage Areas page.

3 • Click on Add. The Create Document Storage Area dialog box appears, as shown in Figure 17.6.

4 • Enter a description that identifies the storage area.

5 • Enter a UNC path to the document storage area.

6 • Click on OK to close the dialog box, and then click OK to close the Post Office property page.

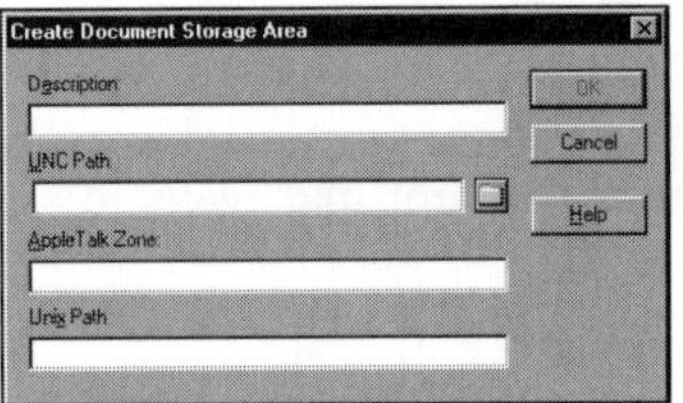

FIGURE 17.6

Creating a Document Storage Area

Creating the Library Object

The Library object can be created in any NDS container; however, we recommend that you store it either in the same organizational unit (OU) as the Post Office object with which the library is associated or store it in an OU dedicated to GroupWise objects or libraries.

Follow these steps to create the Library object:

1 • In NetWare Administrator, highlight the container object in which the Library object will reside.

2 • Right-click on the container object and click on Create.

3 • Double-click on GroupWise Library. The Create GroupWise Library dialog box appears (see Figure 17.7).

4 • Enter a name for the library. This name must be unique within the post office and within the container.

FIGURE 17.7

Create GroupWise Library

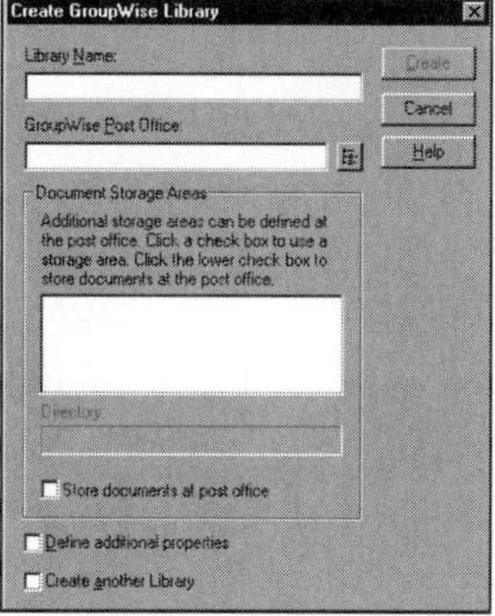

5 • Select the post office with which this library will be associated.

6 • Choose one of these options:

- Choose the Store Documents at Post Office option if the document storage location for the library will be the post office directory.
- Click in the box next to a document storage area that you created previously.

7 • Select the Define Additional Properties option and click on Create. The Library object will be created and the library properties screen will appear (see Figure 17.8).

8 • Enter a description for the library. We suggest that you include the name of the post office that the library is associated with and the types of documents that will be stored in the library.

9 • Specify any other parameters that you desire for the library. The available parameters are listed and described in Table 17.1.

10 • Click on OK when finished.

FIGURE 17.8

Library Properties

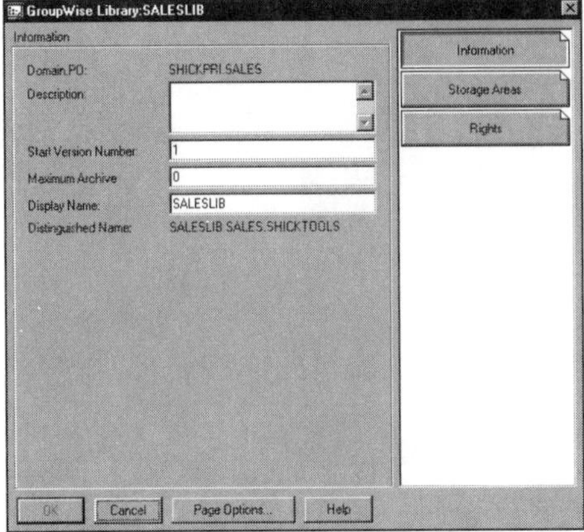

Table 17.1 explains the various options that are available in the GroupWise Library properties page.

TABLE 17.1

Library Parameters

OPTION	EXPLANATION
Start Version Number	The number assigned to the first version of a document stored in the library. Typically, you should start with 0 or 1. The default is 1.
Maximum Archive Size	When GroupWise archives a document, it moves the document's BLOB to a subdirectory under the ARCHIVE directory. The maximum archive size is the maximum size for the ARCHIVE subdirectory containing the archive files. When the maximum archive size is reached, GroupWise creates another archive subdirectory. You should consider the capacity of your backup medium and match the maximum archive size to the backup medium's capacity.
Display Name	This is the name of the library that will appear in the GroupWise client. By default, the distinguished name of the GroupWise Library object will appear.

Assigning Library Rights

Library rights control who has access to the library and what individual library members can do in the library.

For example, some users may only need to read documents in the library, while others may need rights to import, create, edit, and delete documents.

Follow these steps to assign rights to a library:

1 • Right-click on the Library object and select Details.

2 • Choose the Rights page. The Rights options are shown in Figure 17.9.

FIGURE 17.9

Library Rights

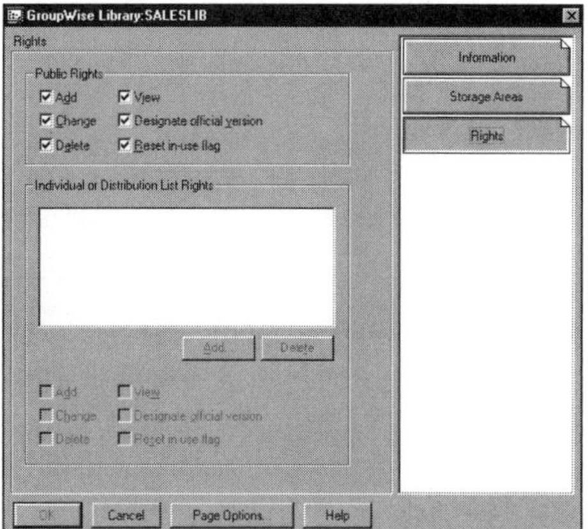

Public rights are rights that are given to everyone in the GroupWise system with access to the library. By default, all rights are granted, as shown in Figure 17.9.

If you leave the settings at the default, there is no need to grant individual rights because everyone will have complete access privileges to the library, including users in other post offices who have a TCP/IP connection to the POA running for the library.

The rights are described in Table 17.2.

TABLE 17.2

Description of Library Rights

RIGHT	DESCRIPTION
Add	Allows users to add new documents to the library.
Change	Allows users to make changes to documents in the library.
Delete	Allows users to delete documents, regardless of who created or has rights to the documents.
View	Allows users to view or copy documents, but not change them. This right is required in order for users to be able to find documents using the GroupWise client Find feature.
Designate Official Version	Allows users to designate which version of a specific document is the official version. The official version of a document is the one that library users will find when they perform a search. For example, a document may have seven versions stored in the library, but version 6 might be the official version, because version 7 is being updated but is not finalized.
Reset In-Use Flag	Allows users to reset the In-Use flag. The In-Use flag protects against data loss by preventing users from opening and editing the same document concurrently.
	When a document is opened by a user, the In-Use flag is set to On to prevent modifications by another user. The flag is reset to Off when the document is closed. If a system failure occurs when the document is open, the flag may remain in the On state, even if no users have the document open. This situation requires the In-Use flag to be reset before the document can again be accessed.

If you restrict public rights, you will need to grant some users additional rights for administrative purposes. For example, if you have a library that contains official corporate documents and most GroupWise users should only be able to view these documents, you should grant the public only the View right, and then grant other users the rights to add, change, and delete documents so they could administer the library's contents.

The rights referred to in this section apply only to documents accessed through the GWDMS system, not the file system. Users need no additional file system rights to use documents in GWDMS. Access to documents in the GWDMS system is controlled by the following steps.

Follow these steps to assign rights to individual users:

1 • From NetWare Administrator, double-click on the Library object.

2 • Click on the Rights page.

3 • Clear the boxes in the Public Rights area of the dialog box to remove rights that should not be assigned to all users.

4 • Click on Add.

5 • Browse to the context that contains the User or Group objects that need additional rights.

6 • Highlight the users or groups and choose OK. The users will be added to the rights list box.

7 • Highlight one or more users in the rights list.

8 • With the users highlighted, click on the rights you want them to have. Notice that rights already granted to the public are not available to be assigned to individual users.

9 • Click on OK when finished.

Users who places their personal documents into a library own those documents. Unless the document owner grants public access or grants access to other users, those documents are completely private and cannot be accessed by anyone else in the GroupWise system, regardless of the rights assigned to the library.

Not even you, as system administrator, can take ownership of those documents or access them in any way. You cannot even generate activity reports on those documents unless the owner gives you the rights necessary to do so.

The public rights you assign for the library determine the actions that individual users can perform in the library. If you are restrictive in your rights assignments, users will not be able to store and manage their personal documents in the library.

For this reason, it is important that you determine the library's purpose in advance of creating it, as discussed in the planning section earlier in this chapter. If the library is to be used by users to store their own documents, they will need all of the library rights in order to effectively manage their documents.

Understanding How Libraries Work

In this section, we'll explain the physical structure of the library directories and files, how indexing works, and how documents are stored in BLOBs.

In a GroupWise post office, document management information is stored in PO\GWDMS\ directory structure. A typical library directory structure is shown in Figure 17.10:

FIGURE 17.10

Library Directory Structure

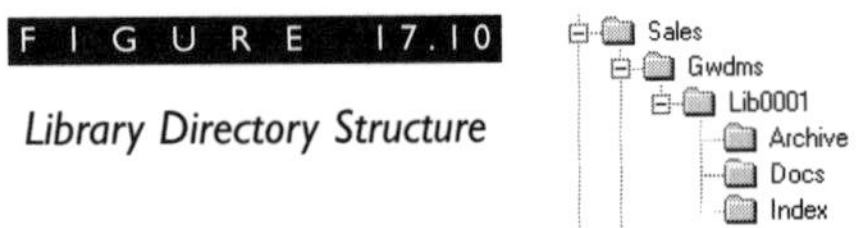

There are two important document management directories in the post office directory:

- The *post office*\GWDMS directory
- The *post office*\GWDMS\LIB*xxxx* directory (or directories)

The GWDMS Directory

The GWDMS directory is located under the post office directory, as shown in Figure 17.10, regardless of the document storage location. The GWDMS directory contains the main GroupWise document management database, DMSH.DB. This database is shared by all of the libraries associated with a post office.

The DMSH.DB database file stores information about every library in the GroupWise system. When users view a list of libraries in the GroupWise client, they are reading the contents of DMSH.DB.

Library Directories

The GWDMS\LIB*xxxx* directory, where *xxxx* represents a library number, contains the database files for a specific library. Every library associated with a specific post office will have a LIB*xxxx* directory under the GWDMS directory. Therefore, if multiple libraries are associated with a post office, each will have a LIB*xxxx* directory under the GWDMS directory.

Three types of database files are stored within a library: DMDL*xxxx*.DB, DMSD*xxxx*.DB, and DMDD*xxxx*.DB. Table 17.3 explains the functions of these database files.

TABLE 17.3

Library Database Types

DATABASE	FUNCTION
DMDL*xxxx*.DB	The DMDL*xxxx*.DB files contain the activity logs for documents stored within the library. Library users can access document activity logs with the GroupWise client. The document activity logs track all transactions associated with a document, such as when the document was opened, edited, checked out or checked in, and by whom the activities were performed.
DMSD*xxxx*.DB	Each library will have one DMSD*xxxx*.DB file. This database file contains library configuration information.
DMDD*xxxx*.DB	The DMDD*xxxx*.DB database files contain the profile information for each document stored in the library. Small documents might also be stored in the DMDD*xxxx*.DB files for efficiency.

The GWDMS\LIB*xxxx* directory contains three important subdirectories: ARCHIVE, DOCS, and INDEX.

The ARCHIVE Directory

The ARCHIVE directory contains subdirectories that hold documents that have been moved from the main GroupWise document storage areas. The subdirectories are numbered sequentially.

When a document is archived from the document store, it is saved to the ARCHIVE directory under the PO\GWDMS\LIB*xxxx*\ARCHIVE directory, even if the document storage location is not in the post office. This can have serious implications for the amount of disk space available in your post office. Consider migrating these archived documents to tape or some other storage medium.

The DOCS Directory

The DOCS directory, its subdirectories, and the BLOB files stored in the subdirectories constitute the GroupWise document storage location, or document store, if the documents are stored in the post office. If you specify a separate document storage location, the DOCS directory will be empty.

The INDEX Directory

GWDMS uses QuickFinder technology to enable rapid searching of documents in a library. The INDEX directory contains the QuickFinder indexes for the library. The POA indexes the documents stored in the document store and creates IDX files in the INDEX directory.

BLOB Storage

Storing documents inside of databases provides two distinct advantages: security and file compression.

By storing documents in databases, the files are encrypted with GroupWise's proprietary database encryption. This allows increased security of the documents because they can only be accessed through the GroupWise Document Management Services interfaces (the GroupWise client or a supported integrated application).

Also, the storage of documents within a database provides up to 50 percent compression on the files.

A BLOB is actually a database file stored in the document storage location you specify. Figure 17.11 shows the directory structure of a document storage location, with individual BLOB files.

FIGURE 17.11

BLOB Files

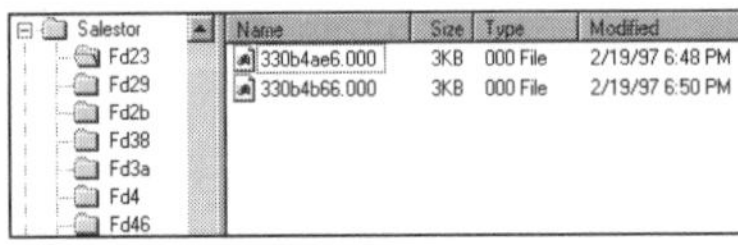

To find out which BLOB a specific document is stored in, run the GroupWise client and view the document properties under the Activity Log tab (see Figure 17.12).

FIGURE 17.12

Document Properties

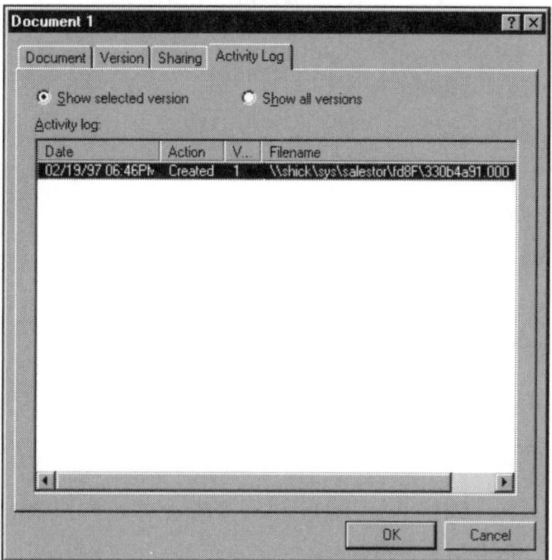

Integrating GWDMS with Other Applications

Before you can use GWDMS in conjunction with certain integrated applications, you need to enable integration. But first you need to understand the different types of integration that are possible.

GWDMS can be integrated with other applications in three ways:

- ODMA integration
- Point-to-point integration
- Loose integration

ODMA Integration

GroupWise supports integration with applications that meet the Open Document Management API (ODMA) specification. Integration with ODMA-compliant applications is sometimes known as *tight integration*.

When you integrate the GroupWise client with an ODMA-complaint application, the GroupWise document management dialog boxes appear when you use the application to open or save files.

When the client is installed, the GroupWise installation procedure will detect any ODMA-compliant applications that are installed, presenting the user with the option of integrating at that time.

The most common ODMA-compliant applications include Corel WordPerfect, Corel Quattro Pro, Lotus WordPro, Microsoft Word (version 8 or later), and Microsoft Excel (version 8 or later).

Enabling ODMA Integration

When users install the GroupWise client, the installation program will detect the installed ODMA-compliant applications and present a dialog box that gives the user the opportunity to install the integration files for the application.

To enable integration after GroupWise has been installed, the user must use GroupWise to open a document into an integrated application. When GroupWise opens a document into an integrated application, the GroupWise library keys are written to the Windows Registry; from that time on, the application is integrated.

After the first document is opened, users can open documents from GroupWise or from within the application.

Once integration has been enabled, users should be prepared to see the GWDMS interface whenever they perform file access tasks in integrated applications. If GroupWise is not running, users will get a dialog box warning them that GroupWise is not running.

Disabling ODMA Integration

The easiest way to disable integration is to run the GroupWise client and complete these steps:

1. Click on Tools and then Options.

2. Double-click on the Document icon.

3 • Clear the check mark next to the "Enable integration with other applications" check box.

This procedure will disable integrations with all ODMA-compliant applications on the system.

If you want to disable integrations for a specific application, you can manually edit the GWAPPINT.INF file, which is located in the WINDOWS\SYSTEM directory. This file can be edited with any text editing program, such as NotePad.

Follow these steps to disable an application through the GWAPPINT.INF file:

1 • Open the GWAPPINT.INF file in a text editor.

2 • Search the file for the name of the application for which you want to disable integrations; for example, Excel.

3 • Locate the line labeled Integrations=*value*.

4 • Set the value to 0.

5 • Save and close the file.

For additional information on GroupWise integrated applications, see Novell Technical Document ID # 2917418, "Applications Integrations," available as file APP_INT.DOC on the CD-ROM that comes with this book.

Point-to-Point Integration

Point-to-point integration is very similar to ODMA integration, except that the applications themselves are not ODMA-compliant. To achieve point-to-point integration with non-ODMA-compliant applications, Novell has created custom macros to allow these applications to integrate with GWDMS. These macros are installed automatically when the GroupWise client is installed.

The custom macros allow for tight integrations with these non-ODMA-compliant applications. As of this writing, only two applications are integrated through macros: Microsoft Word 7 and Microsoft Excel 7.

Loose Integration

If an application is not ODMA-compliant and cannot be integrated with point-to-point integration, a limited measure of integration can be achieved by using the application's default file extensions, which are registered with the Windows operating system.

When an application is integrated based only on file extensions, it is said to have a "loose integration" with GWDMS.

When an application is loosely integrated, the application must be launched from within GroupWise, and the file must not be given a filename other than that assigned by GroupWise.

Maintaining GWDMS Databases

Maintaining GWDMS databases is very similar to maintaining message store databases (see Chapter 13).

To access the document management database maintenance options, follow these steps:

1. In NetWare Administrator, highlight the library that you want to administer.
2. Click on Tools.
3. Click on GroupWise Utilities.
4. Click on Mailbox/Library Maintenance. You'll see the dialog box shown in Figure 17.13.
5. In the GroupWise Objects field, verify that Libraries is selected.
6. Select the maintenance options you want to perform on the Library.
7. Click on Run.

The available library maintenance options are explained thoroughly in online help. The options are very similar to the database maintenance options explained in Chapter 13.

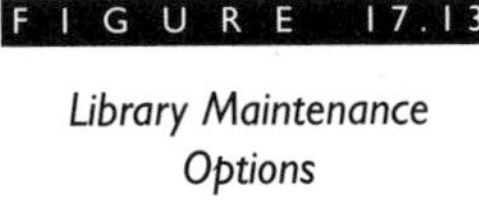

Library Maintenance Options

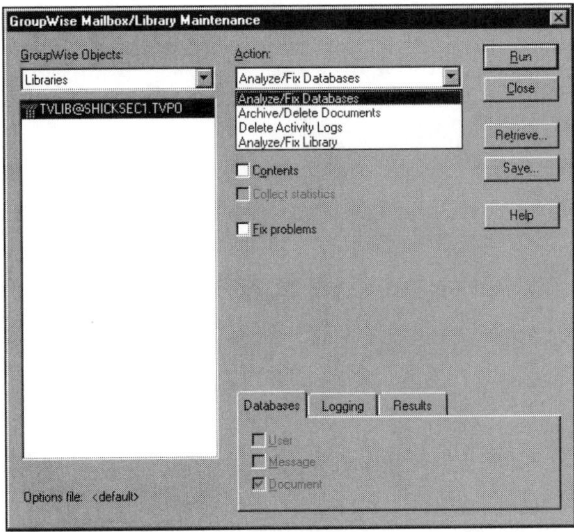

Setting Up a Dedicated POA for Indexing

One of the POA's biggest responsibilities in managing a library is indexing. Indexes allow users to rapidly search for and retrieve documents contained within the library.

Because libraries change rapidly as users add, delete, and modify documents, it is important that the library's documents be reindexed often to keep the library functional and efficient.

When the POA indexes a library, it generates word lists and associates words in the word lists with documents that contain the words. By default, a POA running for a post office will perform library indexing every four hours.

You must have a regular POA to handle message flow traffic and client/server requests. The dedicated POA in this subsection performs one function, updating the QuickFinder Index.

You should consider setting up a dedicated POA process to handle document indexing in the following situations:

- You are importing a large number of documents into the library at one time.
- The default POA in a post office is working at or near capacity, and adding indexing responsibilities will hinder message delivery performance.
- You have large libraries or several libraries within the post office.
- You have a need for continual indexing to ensure that changes made to documents are reflected very quickly in the indexes.

The only overhead associated with adding a dedicated POA is processing power and memory.

Follow these steps to set up a dedicated indexing POA:

1. In NetWare Administrator, right-click on the Post Office object and choose Create.
2. Double-click on GroupWise Agent.
3. Name the agent and specify Post Office Agent as the agent type.
4. Click on the Define Additional Properties check box and then click on Create.
5. Click on the Agent Settings page. The dialog box shown in Figure 17.14 will appear.
6. Click on the drop-down list next to Message File Processing and select Off. This disables message processing for this POA.
7. Change the QuickFinder Interval to a low value or to 0. A setting of 0 causes the POA to index continuously.

FIGURE 17.4

GroupWise POA Settings

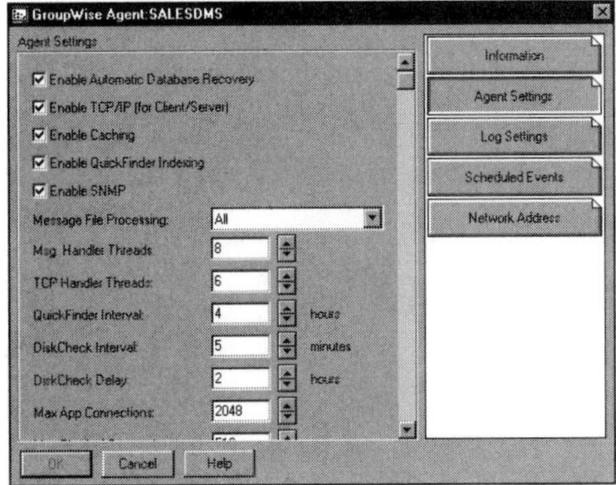

8 • Click on the Network Address page.

9 • Clear the Enable TCP/IP for Client/Server setting.

10 • Click on OK.

11 • Make a copy of the existing POA startup file and name it INDEX.POA.

12 • Edit the INDEX.POA file, making sure to use the switches listed in Table 17.4.

13 • At the server prompt, enter the following command:

```
:LOAD GWPOA @INDEX.POA
```

Table 17.4 lists the switches that should appear in the INDEX.POA file.

TABLE 17.4

INDEX.POA Switches

SWITCH	DESCRIPTION
`/home-\\[server]\[volume]\[directory]`	Required NetWare path to the post office directory
`/qfinterval-[hours]`	Time interval (in hours) for updating the Quick Finder indexes. The default is four hours and the minimum is one hour.

(continued)

TABLE 17.4 *INDEX.POA Switches (continued)*

SWITCH	DESCRIPTION
/notcpip	Disables processing of client/server requests from users in the post office
/nomf	Disables directory scanning for all incoming message files
/name-	Indicates the POA's NDS name to allow the settings made in NetWare Administrator to be read

You can make a POA create an index immediately by using the following steps at the POA screen in NetWare Administrator:

1 • Press F10.

2 • Select Actions.

3 • Select QuickFinder.

4 • Select Update QuickFinder References.

A dedicated indexing POA will offload the GWDMS indexing burden and prevent the indexing processes from interfering with GroupWise message delivery. If you decide not to use a dedicated indexing POA, you should carefully monitor your regular messaging POA to ensure that it isn't overloading with indexing tasks.

Summary

This chapter provided you with an overview of the document management features available in GroupWise 5. You learned the basics of how to plan, implement, and maintain GWDMS.

We recommend that you look at the documents referenced in this section for more details on specific GWDMS topics. For a detailed description of document management from an end user's perspective, we recommend our last book, *Novell's GroupWise 5 User's Handbook*, published by Novell Press and IDG Books Worldwide.

CHAPTER 18

Gateway Overview

The basic purpose of all GroupWise gateways is to convert messages from one format to another. Gateways serve as message translators. You can use gateways to provide your users with many different communication options. You can also use gateways to open up your GroupWise system to the entire world.

In Part V of this book, we describe the different types of gateways and explain how to install and use them in your GroupWise system. In this chapter we cover gateways in general, explaining some things that all gateways have in common, and covering basic concepts that aren't tied to any particular gateway. We also give you an overview of some of the most useful gateways. In Chapter 19, we offer a more detailed explanation of the *Asynchronous gateway*, or *Async gateway*, which can be used both to connect domains and to configure GroupWise for remote access. In Chapter 20, you'll learn about the SMTP/MIME gateway, which connects GroupWise systems to other mail systems over the Internet.

This chapter covers the following topics:

- Gateway functions
- Types of gateways
- Gateway installation
- Gateway administration
- Gateway troubleshooting

Gateway Functions

Gateways serve two basic purposes. One, you can use gateways to add functionality to your own GroupWise system. For example, you can enable users to retrieve voice mail and faxes in GroupWise by adding certain gateways to your system. Two, you can use gateways to communicate with other messaging systems, including non-GroupWise systems, and to send and receive Internet e-mail.

Adding Functionality

Although GroupWise is extremely powerful right out of the box, you can enhance your system by adding one or more gateways. It's like buying a new car. Even though the car may be well-equipped to begin with (perhaps even more so than other cars), you can always add features that provide greater functionality and make the car even more valuable. So too with GroupWise.

Of course, not every gateway is necessary for every system. When deciding whether to add gateways to your system, you should consider whom your users need to communicate with outside the system (for example, vendors, specific customers, the general public, and so on) and what forms of communication will best meet their needs (such as e-mail, faxing, voice mail, and paging).

Each GroupWise gateway has a specific set of hardware, software, and network requirements. We'll refer you to a number of Novell technical documents (included on the CD-ROM that comes with this book) for detailed information about the requirements of each gateway discussed in this chapter.

Connecting GroupWise Domains

An important use of gateways is connecting two GroupWise domains. These domains may be in the same system or in different systems. The most common implementation for gateway as the connection between domains is when a physical network (i.e., WAN) connection is impossible or not feasible.

Usually, this limitation occurs between domains that are located in different systems (which most often reside at different companies).

As shown in Figure 18.1, both domains must have the same type of gateway installed in order to communicate with each other.

FIGURE 18.1

A Gateway Connection Between Domains

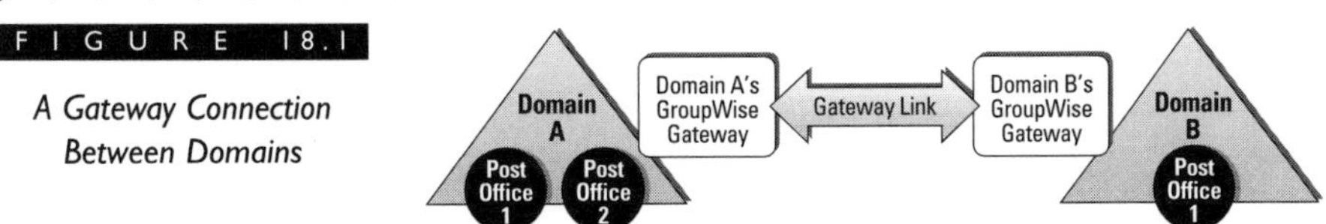

Benefits of Using Gateways Between Domains

Using gateways to connect domains can provide a number of benefits. For one thing, you have fewer network security issues to resolve. Because a network connection is not required between the two domains, you need not worry about the networking concerns typically associated with domain connections—for example, authentication, licenses, and file rights.

Also, using gateways between domains gives you greater flexibility in the types of connections you choose. For example, you could link the domains using modems and analog telephone lines, or you might decide to use the MHS services of an online provider such as CompuServe. Your company can choose the method of communication that makes most sense for it. An efficient use of gateways can actually save money for your company by maximizing services.

Using gateways between domains also provides standards-based messaging in your system. Certain gateways (for example, the SMTP and X.400 gateways) adhere to messaging standards that are internationally recognized.

Finally, with a gateway link between domains, you can achieve *passthrough messaging*. When you use the same type of gateway between two domains, no message conversion takes place, so original messages are left intact. This benefit is discussed in more detail in the following section.

Passthrough Messaging

When you use the same type of gateway to connect two GroupWise domains, messages are transmitted in a manner known as *passthrough messaging*. Passthrough messaging essentially means that messages are received in exactly the same form as they are sent because certain parts need not be converted (see Figure 18.2). Most GroupWise gateways can provide passthrough services.

Normally, a gateway converts each part of a message—address, body, and attachments—to a different format. Just as some words in French do not have exact counterparts in English, not all message systems have the same features. The potential for mistranslation exists whenever you use gateways to connect mail systems. The problem of mistranslation can be avoided, however, by using passthrough messaging.

FIGURE 18.2

Passthrough Messaging

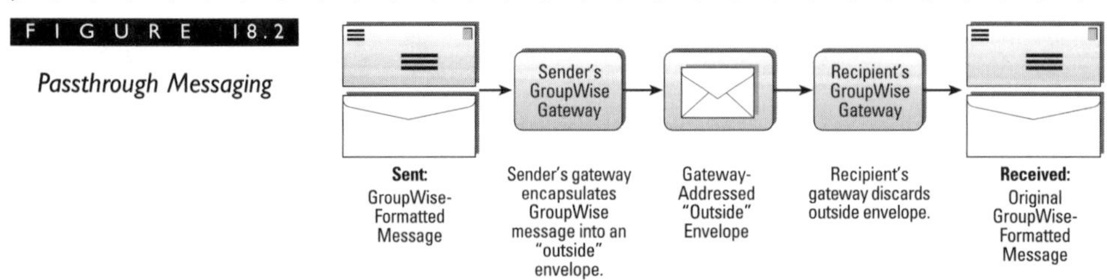

When you use the same gateway to communicate between GroupWise domains, conversion doesn't take place. The sending gateway leaves the original message intact and sends it through the gateway (provided by the gateway link to the other domain) with a routing address added. The receiving gateway receives the message, removes the extra routing information, and transfers the message to the recipient. The gateway link is defined when you use the Link Configuration Tool to connect two GroupWise domains.

Communicating with Other Mail Systems

The most common use of gateways is as translators of message formats. GroupWise speaks its own proprietary language that only GroupWise systems can understand. This is true of all messaging systems today that are not based on messaging standards such as POP3 or SMTP.

Because today's enterprises are open, multiplatform environments with many different systems trying to get along, many gateways are available from Novell to connect GroupWise to other mail systems, such as Lotus Notes, Microsoft Mail, and many others.

These gateways all perform the same two basic tasks: message conversion and message transfer. Of course, each specific gateway has its own set of features, requirements, and limitations, which is covered later in this chapter. Additionally, some gateways provide services such as synchronization and migration of users from another system to GroupWise.

Message Conversion

When an outgoing message hits the gateway, each of the three message parts are converted from their original GroupWise format into the target format of the gateway, i.e., Lotus Notes, MSMail, or X.400.

As shown in Figure 18.3, the address, message body, and attachment are all converted according to the formatting rules of the gateway.

FIGURE 18.3

Message Translation

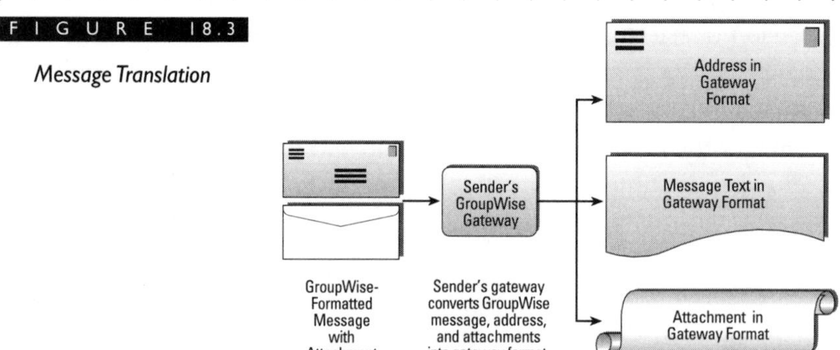

Conversion presents certain difficulties that gateways must contend with, including the following:

- *Long Reply Addresses Format*. Because other mail systems have their own address formats, the "Reply To:" address format can be rather lengthy, potentially resulting in the unsuccessful routing of the message.

- *Incompatible Message Types*. Not all GroupWise message types (e.g., Appointment messages and Task messages) are supported by other mail systems, so the gateway will convert it to the nearest message type it can, which is usually just a regular mail message.

- *Attachment Encoding*. Each mail system has its own set of rules regarding attachments, and the resulting encoding of attachments can result in the loss of printing and other formatting codes in the attached file.

- *Reduced Security*. Any time you establish communications with an outside mail system, you open your company up to possible security breaches, such as reduced or nonexistent message encryption in the other system.

These and other gateway issues are discussed at the end of this chapter, in the section titled "Gateway Troubleshooting."

Message Transfer

The message-transfer component of a gateway moves newly converted messages to their destination, whether it is the Internet, an X.25 network, cc:Mail, or some other mail system.

Each gateway has its own set of requirements for physically connecting to other systems, and each has its own set of challenges. You need to be aware of the communication requirements for each gateway you will use. We'll have more to say about physically connecting to other systems in the "Common Problems" section of this chapter.

Types of Gateways

This section summarizes the gateways offered by Novell for GroupWise, along with a description of the platforms they are available on, the purpose of each gateway, and a *brief* requirements list.

NOTE

The requirements listed for each gateway are intended only as a basic starting point. Please refer to the documentation on the companion CD for complete technical descriptions of the hardware and software requirements for each gateway.

The various GroupWise gateways sold by Novell can be grouped into three categories:

- System enhancement gateways
- Messaging standard gateways
- Messaging-system-specific gateways

Table 18.1 lists many of the most popular gateways in each of these categories.

TABLE 18.1

Types of Gateways

SYSTEM ENHANCEMENT GATEWAYS	MESSAGING STANDARD GATEWAYS	MESSAGING-SYSTEM-SPECIFIC GATEWAYS
WebAccess	MHS	cc:Mail
PhoneAccess	X.400	Lotus Notes Mail
Pager	SMTP/MIME	Microsoft Mail
Fax/Print	SNADS	PROFS/OfficeVision—VM
API		Banyan Vines—IM
X.25		VMS Mail
Asynchronous Gateway		DEC Message Router

System Enhancement Gateways

System enhancement gateways add functionality to GroupWise and make your users more productive by expanding the ways they share information. For each gateway we describe, we'll indicate the platforms for which the gateway is available, the basic installation requirements, and the relevant documents on the CD-ROM that comes with this book.

WebAccess

The WebAccess gateway works together with NetWare 4.11's Web Server to allow users complete, secure, and encrypted access to their GroupWise mailbox by using an HTML browser, such as NetScape Navigator. Chapter 21 explains the WebAccess Server.

Platforms: NetWare Loadable Module, Windows NT Server, UNIX

Basic Requirements: On the server side, the server on which the WebAccess NLM is loaded must be running a suitable HTTP server, such as NetWare Web Server. On the client side, you will need a Web browser, connection to the Internet, and a GroupWise mailbox.

CD Documents: WEBACCES.DOC, WEBPAPER.DOC

Figure 18.4 shows the main menu of WebAccess.

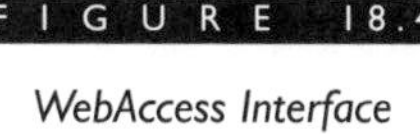

FIGURE 18.4

WebAccess Interface

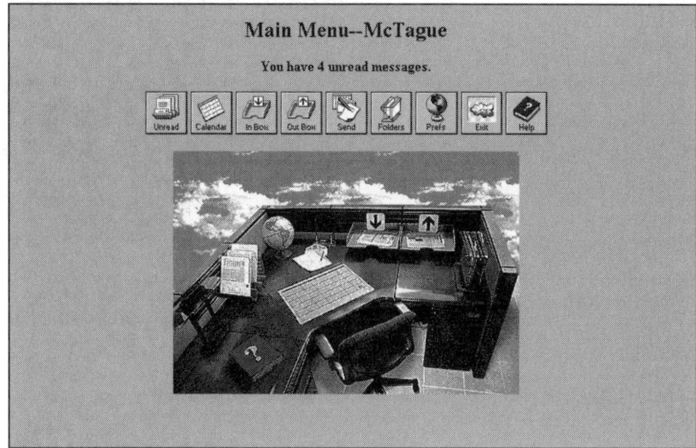

PhoneAccess

The PhoneAccess gateway adds two levels of additional functionality: access to your entire mailbox via a touchtone phone, and voice mail messages in your mailbox. The gateway works with a digital-to-analog converter, converting digital messages (e-mails, meeting requests, tasks, notes, or phone messages) typed in from any user, or any other information in your mailbox (calendar items, etc.) into a computer-generated audio signal. Conversely, any voice-generated messages that you create and send using the PhoneAccess gateway are attached as a .WAV file to a mail message.

Platforms: OS/2

Basic Requirements: The PhoneAccess gateway requires a dedicated OS/2 workstation with a digital-to-analog board made by Dialogic. The components you need to set up PhoneAccess depend on the PBX integration method you will use—Telephony Services API (TSAPI) or Simplified Message Desk Interface (SMDI). See the PhoneAccess Configuration guide on the CD for more information.

CD Documents: TAS.DOC, PACONFIG.DOC

Pager

The Pager gateway allows users to be able to forward the date, time, sender, and subject line of a message to alphanumeric pagers and PCMCIA paging receivers.

The Pager gateway works with the Site Connect Server from Motorola and the Vendor Independent Paging API to translate the message to provide this integrated paging service. The Site Connect Server then sends the message to a pager via private transmitter or a public paging service.

On the client side, you can send a page directly to someone else by creating a specially addressed mail message that includes the pager's phone number, or use Rules in your mailbox to have high-priority messages forwarded to your pager using this gateway, or to page you so many minutes before an appointment.

Platforms: OS/2, NLM

Basic Requirements: OS/2 workstation with a modem for dialing the pager numbers.

CD Document: PAGER.DOC

Fax/Print

The Fax/Print gateway was originally created to allow calendar printing from the GroupWise DOS client (which didn't ship with printer driver software). The current use of the Fax/Print gateway is to allow outbound and inbound faxes using the GroupWise client software.

Outbound faxes are sent using properly formatted addresses (including the fax number), and are routed via the GroupWise message flow processes to a fax server running the gateway software.

Inbound faxes are received by the gateway computer, converted by the gateway to GroupWise messages, and routed to recipients' mailboxes. Identification and resolution to the correct mailboxes are dependent upon the telephone system's use of direct inward dial (DID) identification of extensions. These extensions are then associated with GroupWise mailboxes.

Platforms: OS/2, NLM

Basic Requirements: A single OS/2 computer with an internal fax/modem can run the gateway software.

CD Document: FAXPRINT.DOC

API

The Application Programming Interface (API) gateway is the programmer's entrance into the information store and directory store of GroupWise. By using a series of programming function calls in their applications, information can be placed into the GroupWise message store and treated as a message. The API gateway can also place entries into the Address Book by adding information into the WPDOMAIN.DB files, where it is replicated throughout the GroupWise system.

In addition to adding information into the system, the API gateway can also be used to extract information from GroupWise. For example, if your GroupWise system is connected to many different e-mail systems, you can use the API gateway to achieve directory synchronization between them.

NOTE

The directory synchronization function is version-specific. In other words, only an API gateway for GroupWise 5 can synchronize the GroupWise 5 directory, while the API for GroupWise 4 should only be used to synchronize GroupWise 4 directories. See `http://support.novell.com` **for more information.**

The API gateway can be used to extract the GroupWise Address Book. This message is then sent to a central location where all of the other e-mail systems have extracted their changes. A compilation of changes is done, a new change message is sent back to all of the systems (including GroupWise), and the new updates are imported into the system through the API gateway.

Platforms: DOS, OS/2, NLM

Basic Requirements: No additional hardware or software is needed.

CD Document: API.DOC

GroupWise Asynchronous Gateway

The Asynchronous gateway (also known as the Async gateway) serves two main purposes: to connect two GroupWise domains by using modems and to provide connections for remote users. The Async gateway includes its own database with modem definitions because the gateway initializes and controls the modems. These modems must be physically attached to the same computer running the gateway software.

You can attach up to four modems directly to serial ports COM1–COM4, or you can attach up to 32 modems per gateway using multiport boards, such as DigiBoards.

Chapter 19 explains the Async gateway in more detail.

Platforms: OS/2, NLM

Basic Requirements: The Asynchronous gateway requires at least one modem physically attached to the computer running the gateway software, along with a phone line for dialing out and dialing in.

CD Document: DIGIBD.DOC

X.25

The X.25 gateway allows your system to connect domains together using a packet-switched X.25 (or synchronous) network. Each domain's network would connect to the X.25 network via X.25 modems, and the gateway is used to send messages between the domains using this link. The X.25 gateway provides functionality identical to the Async gateway, except it substitutes an X.25 PAD (packet assembler deassembler) for the modem in Async.

Remote users can configure GroupWise to use an X.25 connection to connect to their mailboxes through the X.25 gateway.

Platforms: OS/2

Basic Requirements: The GroupWise X.25 gateway requires that an EiconCard (various models are available) be installed in a network workstation, along with the Eicon OSI LAN gateway for OS/2.

CD Document: X25GATE.DOC

Messaging Standard Gateways

These gateways are written to conform to a specific messaging standard recognized by standards bodies and used by many other e-mail systems. Therefore, these gateways are used to provide connectivity to the specific messaging standard with which you need to communicate.

MHS

The MHS (Message Handling Service) gateway provides message translation to and from Novell's Global MHS (GMHS) messaging backbone. GMHS runs as a NetWare Loadable Module and provides many connectivity options to a wide variety of e-mail programs, mail services, and bulletin board systems.

The GroupWise MHS gateway runs as an NLM on the same NetWare server and converts GroupWise messages to either SMF (Standard Message Format) version 70 or 71.

Platforms: DOS, NLM

Basic Requirements: The MHS gateway requires Novell's Global MHS Version 2.0d, with appropriate patches applied, and a dedicated DOS workstation to run the message daemon, which scans the MHS input queues and moves the messages to and from the GMHS NLM and the other mail system you are communicating with.

CD Documents: MHS.DOC

Also included on the CD is a migration utility (MHSMCU.EXE) that will migrate an MHS-based mailbox to a GroupWise mailbox. The GroupWise Mailbox Conversion Utility for MHS (MHS MCU) is a user migration tool that converts MHS user mailboxes to GroupWise via the GroupWise API gateway. Conversions from Da Vinci, BeyondMail, and FirstMail systems are supported. The MHS MCU can also convert e-mail from other SMF mail clients that store messages as individual SMFv70 and SMFv71 format files.

X.400

The GroupWise X.400 gateway converts GroupWise messages to and from X.400 format and provides communication with an X.400 MTA. Once the X.400 message reaches the X.400 MTA, it is transferred to the target e-mail system that uses X.400 as a message format. Optionally, X.400 can be used as the message backbone between two dissimilar e-mail systems, such as GroupWise and Microsoft Exchange.

Each user has an X.400 Address property that you can configure to provide an X.400 address in the Address Book. Figure 18.5 shows an example of an X.400 Address property page.

Platforms: OS/2, NLM

Basic Requirements: A suitable X.400 MTA is required, and is not part of the GroupWise X.400 gateway. The GroupWise X.400 gateway only provides conversion of the message to and from GroupWise and X.400 format, but does *not* provide the transfer of the converted message. The gateway supports any XAPIA-based MTA, including Retrix's OpenServer, ISOCOR X.400 Lite, ISOCOR/ISOPLEX 400, and ISOCOR/ISOPLEX 800.

FIGURE 18.5

X.400 Address Property Page

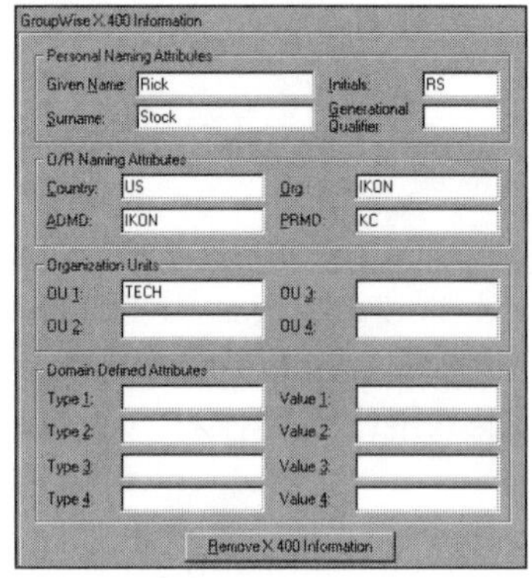

CD Document: X400GATE.DOC

SMTP/MIME

The SMTP/MIME gateway converts GroupWise messages to and from the Internet messaging standard of SMTP (Simple Mail Transfer Protocol). It also supports multimedia attachments in MIME format or UUENCODE format. These formats are important to know about because the receiving mail system must be able to understand them in order to have attachments received accurately. The UUENCODE format is the oldest and most widely used format, but MIME is much more flexible and efficient.

You can use this gateway to connect two GroupWise domains over the Internet, or to communicate with anyone on the Internet using e-mail. The many strategies for connecting GroupWise to the Internet are discussed in Chapter 21.

Platforms: NLM, UNIX

Basic Requirements: The computer running the gateway software needs either a physical connection to the Internet, or to be able to access an Internet Service Provider (ISP) using PPP (Point-to-Point Protocol) via a dial -p connection.

The domain portion of your company's desired Internet mail address (the information to the right of the "@" sign, such as "shicktools.com" or "novell.com") must be registered with InterNIC. In addition, the IP address of the computer running the gateway must be associated with this domain in the Mail Exchange (MX) record in Domain Name Systems (DNS) so incoming mail will find the gateway.

CD Document: SMTPGATE.DOC

SNADS

The Systems Network Architecture Distribution Services (SNADS) gateway enables GroupWise to communicate with five mainframe-based e-mail packages: MEMO/VM, OfficeVision on MVS Systems, MEMO/MVS, OfficeVision for the AS/400, and IBM's Message Exchange.

This gateway supports directory exchange between the two mail systems and is very dependent on the communication between the OS/2 workstation and the mainframe session. The gateway operates as a single Distribution Service Unit (DSU) and SNADS host. The GroupWise SNADS gateway also converts GroupWise message text from Novell format to an FFT, RFT, or EBCDIC Document. This allows users on the host system to read the document. Messages sent from hosts to GroupWise are automatically translated to the GroupWise message format.

Platforms: OS/2, NLM

Basic Requirements: The OS/2 workstation requires IBM's Communication Manager/2 to be loaded and configured correctly. This requires extensive cooperation and information from the mainframe system's administrators and operators. A Token Ring Adapter or SDLC connection to the mainframe is also required.

CD Document: SNADS.DOC

VMS

The purpose of the VMS gateway is to communicate with mail systems that exist on VAX VMS systems, such as Leverage or Pathworks. Leverage and Pathworks are not mail systems; they are file system connectivity packages. The VMS gateway works with generic VMS mail that comes free with VMS.

Platforms: DOS

Basic Requirements: This gateway requires that the API gateway be installed specifically for use with the VMS gateway. Because a drive must be mapped to a VAX disk on which the VAX software will be installed, the DOS workstation must have connectivity to the VAX system. This drive letter and/or path will be used in the API gateway-specific setup.

Messaging-System-Specific Gateways

These gateways are very specific in their purpose: they all attach GroupWise to a different e-mail product. The most common application is for migration or connectivity to a legacy system inside of your company, or for communicating with an outside company on a large enough scale that it justifies the configuration of a specific gateway.

cc:Mail

The cc:Mail gateway provides messaging, directory synchronization and exchange, administration, and migration between GroupWise and Lotus' cc:Mail. The installation of the cc:Mail gateway creates one foreign domain and additional post offices for each of the cc:Mail post offices. On the cc:Mail side, each GroupWise post office is represented by a cc:Mail external post office.

The gateway uses the cc:Mail Import and Export programs to transfer messages between the systems, and it strictly provides for conversion of GroupWise messages to and from cc:Mail format.

Platforms: DOS, OS/2

Basic Requirements: For directory synchronization and/or exchange, the cc:Mail Automatic Directory Exchange (ADE) program is required. The cc:Mail Migrate utility is required to move a user's messages from cc:Mail to a GroupWise mailbox.

CD Document: CCMAIL.DOC

Lotus Notes

The GroupWise Lotus Notes gateway enables users of both systems to exchange mail messages. The gateway creates a mailbox in the Lotus Notes system, which represents the GroupWise gateway. All mail between the systems passes through this mailbox.

Notes documents, which form the basic building blocks of each Notes database, are not transferable in their original, proprietary state. In other words, you can't open a Notes document from GroupWise. You are limited to exchanging mail messages.

The Notes gateway supports Address Book exchange and synchronization, and migration of a converted user's mail from Notes to GroupWise.

Platforms: OS/2

Basic Requirements: The only requirement on the OS/2 workstation is connectivity between the two mail systems' platforms. For directory synchronization, the GroupWise Notes gateway must be running on the same computer that functions as the Notes Server version 3.0 or later.

CD Document: NOTES.DOC

Microsoft Mail

The GroupWise Microsoft Mail gateway allows the exchange of messages between these two mail systems. It also provides directory synchronization through MAPI and provides for migration from MSMail to GroupWise.

NOTE

There is also an MSMail Conversion utility that works with the GroupWise API gateway to convert MSMail messages to GroupWise format, storing them in the GroupWise information store. This utility is included on the CD in the UTILITY directory; the filename is MSMCU.EXE.

Platforms: OS/2

Basic Requirements: On the MSMail side, this gateway works with Microsoft Mail for PC Networks, version 3.2 and 3.5. The OS/2 workstation has to be able to connect to the two mail systems over the network.

OfficeVision/VM

The OfficeVision gateway provides communication between users on GroupWise and OfficeVision on VM systems (OfficeVision on MVS or AS/400 systems are supported by the SNADS gateway). This communication can be either e-mail messages or calendar requests—GroupWise mail messages, phone messages, and notes are converted to an OVVM or PROFS note. You can also view users on the other system for available times for scheduling appointments. ASCII text file attachments sent through the gateway are converted to EBCDIC files. All other file types are left in their original format.

Directory synchronization and migration are supported through this gateway.

Platforms: OS/2, NLM

Basic Requirements: The OVVM Gateway is an OS/2-based gateway requiring OS/2 2.0 or higher and OS/2 Communications Manager/2 version 1, which establishes the logical link to the mainframe. The gateway station is attached to the mainframe by an IBM Token Ring Adapter or SDLC.

CD Document: OVVMGATE.DOC

DEC Message Router for VMS

This gateway provides message communication between the DEC Message Router mail system for VMS (VAX) systems.

Platforms: DOS

Basic Requirements: This gateway requires that the API gateway be installed specifically for use with the Message Router gateway. Because a drive must be mapped to a VAX disk on which the VAX software will be installed, the DOS workstation must have connectivity to the VAX system. This drive letter and/or path will be used in the API gateway-specific setup.

Banyan IM

This gateway allows communication to take place between the GroupWise system and Banyan's IM (Intelligent Messaging) III mail package. This gateway also provides directory synchronization with Banyan's STDA.

Platforms: DOS

Basic Requirements: This gateway requires Banyan 5.5x on the Banyan server, including STDA Services and Intelligent Messaging III. The DOS workstation running the gateway must connect to both the Novell server (if the domain is on a Novell server) on which the gateway is installed and the VINES server. The VINES Proxy Service must also be installed.

Gateway Installation

In this section, we explain how to install and run the gateway software. We also explain how to add gateways after your GroupWise installation is complete.

Installing and Creating Gateways

In a GroupWise system, each gateway belongs to a GroupWise domain and can be viewed in the same way you view a post office. Figure 18.6 shows a gateway within the structure of a GroupWise domain.

FIGURE 18.6

Gateway in a Domain

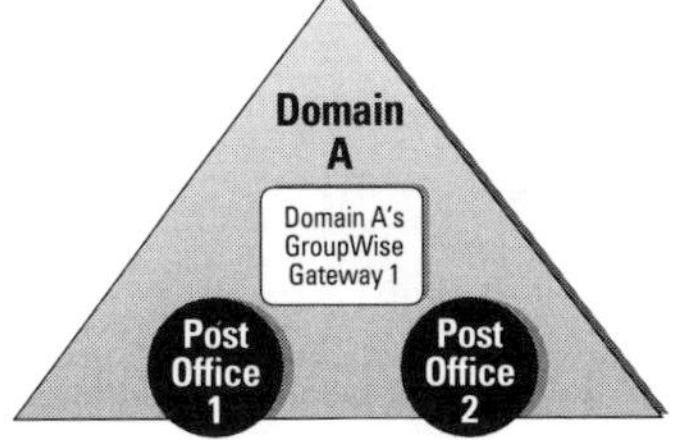

Structurally speaking, gateways are similar to GroupWise post offices. All gateways have a directory, database, and input and output queues for the message transfer agent. And like a post office, the MTA for the domain to which the gateway belongs is responsible for moving messages into and out of the gateway.

The main steps to using a gateway are the same no matter which type of gateway you are installing:

1 • Decide which domain will hold the gateway.

2 • Decide what platform the gateway software will run on.

3 • Install the gateway software. (You usually install the gateway in the <*domain*>\WPGATE\<*gateway*> directory.)

4 • Create the gateway object in NetWare Administrator under the Domain object, selecting the appropriate gateway type (see Figure 18.7).

5 • Configure the gateway properties (Times, Administrator, Access, etc.) and configuration files.

WARNING

Make sure you choose the correct version, 4.X or 5.X. If you're configuring a GroupWise 4 gateway, it will not work if you do not change the default version, which is 5.X.

6 • Set up the network connection to the other system.

7 • Run the gateway software.

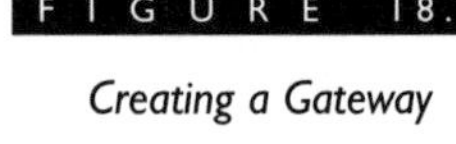

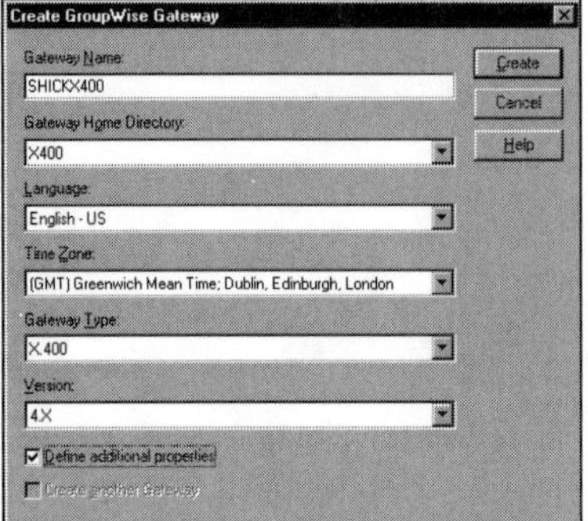

Creating a Gateway

Adding Gateways After GroupWise Installation

NetWare Administrator is used to administer a GroupWise gateway, and the gateway will be represented in NDS as a subordinate object under the Domain object. Since each gateway has a gateway-specific set of properties, GroupWise needs to run different DLLs to access and configure these properties.

In Chapter 4, we explained that you can choose which gateway DLLs are copied during the installation program. At that time, we recommended that you select all gateways so the DLLs would be ready. Use the following steps to install the DLL if you are in doubt or if you need to add a gateway DLL after GroupWise was initially installed:

1 • Insert the GroupWise CD into a local CD-ROM drive.

2 • On your Windows 95 Taskbar, click on the Start button and choose Run from the list.

4 • In the command line field, type D:\SETUP.EXE, where D is your CD-ROM drive letter.

5 • Go through the setup program until you see Figure 18.8.

6 • Check all appropriate gateways and click on Next.

7 • You don't have to select any client or agent platforms, so you can click on Next until the Summary page appears. Click on Finish to complete the installation of the new gateway's DLL files.

Gateway Administration

All GroupWise gateways share a common set of administrative features. In addition, all gateways can be administered using a common interface: NetWare Administrator.

FIGURE 18.8

GroupWise Gateway Setup

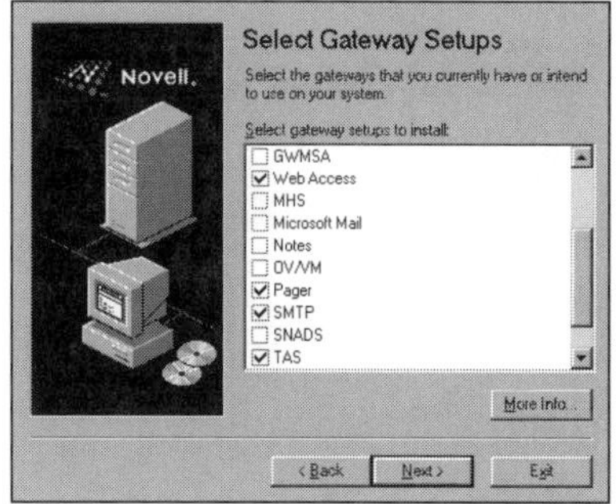

Gateway Property Pages

Gateway objects in NDS are created as subordinates of Domain objects. Figure 18.9 shows that the SHICKPRI domain has three objects beneath it, the MTA, ADA, and SHICKSMTP, which is the SMTP gateway for the SHICKPRI domain.

FIGURE 18.9

Gateway Objects in a Domain

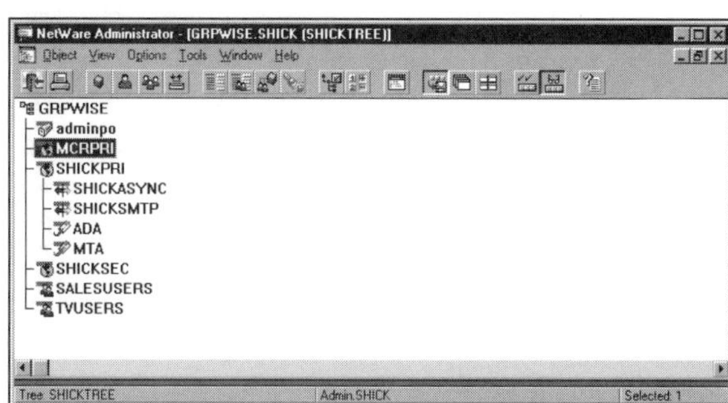

The property pages and settings for gateway objects are described in the following sections.

Information

The Information property page is the main page that is displayed when you access the details of a gateway object, and it contains general information about the gateway (see Figure 18.10).

FIGURE 18.10

Gateway Information Page

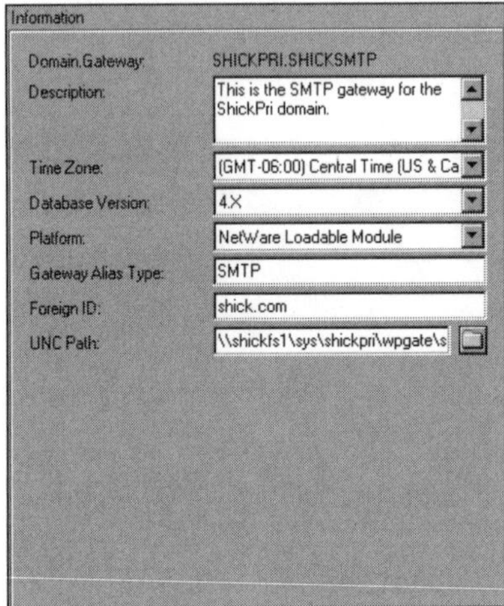

The various settings on the Information property page are described in Table 18.2

TABLE 18.2

Information Page Settings

PROPERTY	DESCRIPTION	EXAMPLE
Domain.Gateway	The GroupWise name of the gateway, showing which domain the gateway belongs to	SHICKPRI.SHICKSMTP
Description	A description of the gateway	SMTP gateway for SHICKPRI users
Time Zone	The time zone this gateway will operate in—message times will be adjusted accordingly	Central Time (US & Canada)
Database Version	The version of the gateway's database	4.X

TABLE 18.2

Information Page Settings (continued)

PROPERTY	DESCRIPTION	EXAMPLE
Platform	The operating system the gateway will run on	NetWare Loadable Module
Gateway Alias Type	A label for creating alias addresses for users, using the target system's address format	SMTP
Foreign ID	The name that the gateway will be known as to the other mail system	shick.com
UNC Path	The UNC path on which the gateway database is located	\\SHICKFS1\SYS\SHICKPRI\WPGATE\SMTP

Gateway Time Settings

The Gateway Time Settings page lets the administrator configure how often the conversion process takes place. In other words, these time intervals affect how often the gateway software checks its queues for messages to be converted and eventually transferred. (see Figure 18.11).

FIGURE 18.11

Gateway Time Settings

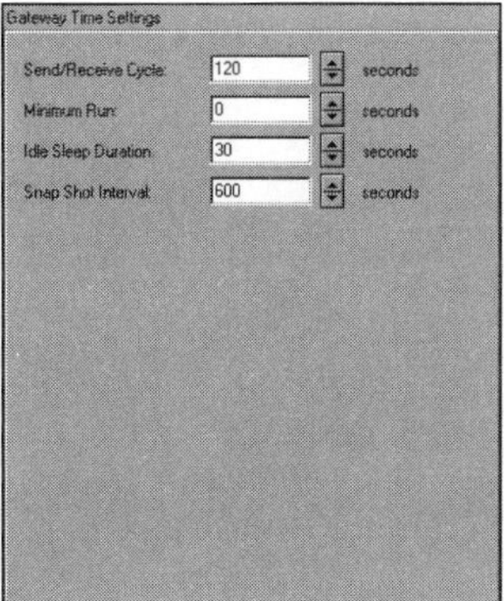

The time settings are described in Table 18.3.

TABLE 18.3

Gateway Time Settings

PROPERTY	DESCRIPTION	EXAMPLE
Send/Receive Cycle	The period of time, in seconds, that the gateway polls its input queue for messages	1–9999 Seconds (120 is default)
Minimum Run	The period of time, in seconds, that the gateway will stay connected to the other mail system (regardless of other settings). Should be 0 unless you are charged for opening the connection by a provider	0–9999 (0 is default)
Idle Sleep Duration	The period of time you want the gateway to not use any processing cycles to check for new messages.	0–999 (30 is default)
Snap Shot Interval	How often you want statistics on the gateway's screen to be updated with new information from the gateway's operations	0–9999 (600 is default)

Log Settings

The Gateway Log Settings page configures the gateway's logging level, as shown in Figure 18.12.

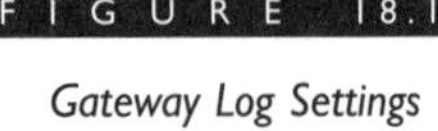

FIGURE 18.12

Gateway Log Settings

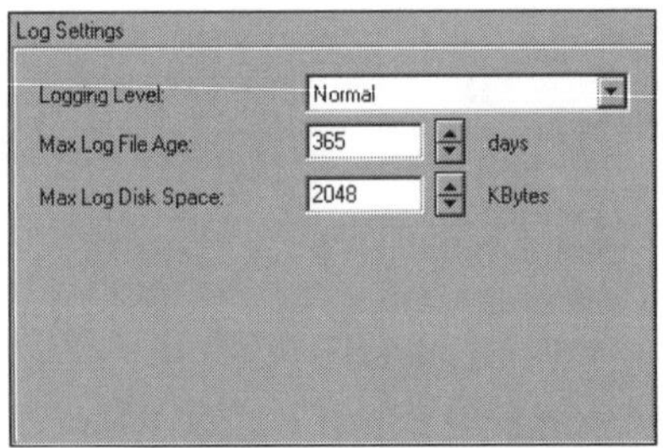

Settings that can be adjusted on this property page are as follows:

- *Logging Level*. The amount of information placed into the log files (Normal, Verbose, Diagnostic, or None)
- *Max Log File Age*. The maximum time you want to keep old log files on disk before they are deleted.
- *Max Log Disk Space*. The maximum amount of disk space to hold log files. When this limit is reached, old log files are deleted. (Maximum

is 32, 767K). If you set this to 0, the log disk space is limited only by the physical space available on the disk.

Optional Gateway Settings

The Optional Gateway Settings page (see Figure 18.13) controls different conversion, synchronization, and recovery settings for the gateway. Each gateway is very specific as to the supported settings on this page, so you *must* refer to the instructions for the specific gateway you are setting up.

Optional Gateway Settings

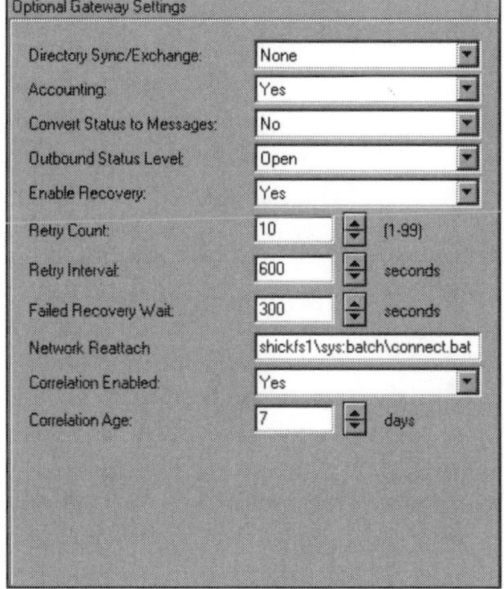

The optional gateway settings are described in Table 18.4.

TABLE 18.4

Optional Gateway Settings

PROPERTY	DESCRIPTION
Directory Sync/ Exchange	Tells the gateway how you will be communicating with users of the other system: synchronizing (sending each change) or exchanging (sending the entire directory). Both can be enabled.
Accounting	Enables or disables the gathering of accounting information reports for the administrator
Convert Status to Messages	Enables or disables creating a mail message of status information (delivered and opened)

(continued)

TABLE 18.4

Optional Gateway Settings (continued)

PROPERTY	DESCRIPTION
Outbound Status Level	Level of message activity of status information (Open, Full, Undelivered, Delivered, or None)
Enable Recovery	Enables or disables the gateway's automated recovery of lost connections to the other mail system
Retry Count	The number of times (from 10–99) that the gateway will attempt the recovery of a lost connection
Retry Interval	The period of time (0–999 seconds) the gateway will wait before attempting to recover a lost connection
Failed Recovery Wait	The period of time (0–999 seconds) the gateway will wait between retries on recovering a lost connection
Network Reattach	The path to a command (or batch file) to reattach the gateway computer to the network
Correlation Enabled	Enables or disables inbound status messages from the other mail system to be converted to a GroupWise status message
Correlation Age	The number of days (0–999) the correlation message will remain in the gateway's correlation database (*gatewaydirectory*\GWCORR.DB)

Gateway Administrators

The Gateway Administrators page, shown in Figure 18.14, lets you configure administrators to receive reports and error messages from the gateway. These administrators could be individual mailboxes or distribution lists for people who are responsible for the gateway's operation and who need to be notified if there is a problem.

NOTE

The different administrator types are explained in the following section.

FIGURE 18.14

Gateway Administrator Property Page

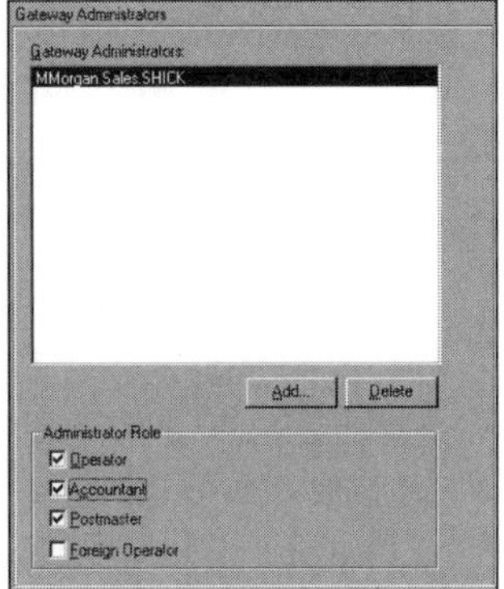

To add an administrator for a gateway, follow these steps:

1 • Right-click on the gateway object under the domain and choose Details from the short menu.

2 • Click on the Gateway Administrators tab.

3 • Click on Add and browse NDS until the desired user or Distribution List is displayed in the Available Objects window. Click on OK.

4 • With the user or distribution list highlighted, select the appropriate administrator type.

5 • Click on OK to complete the assignment.

Additional Administrative Features

Each gateway is different in the additional specific and administrator settings that need to be specified. For example, if you are using the Async gateway, you need to configure the modem and times it dials to the other system (covered in Chapter 20). These settings do not apply to the SMTP gateway, which are covered in Chapter 21. Therefore, for these specific and administrative gateway settings we must refer you to the Instant Expert Guide on the companion CD.

Gateway-Specific Settings

Gateway-specific settings are accessed in NetWare Administrator as additional property pages. These are enabled during the installation of GroupWise by specifying the gateways you will use. Dynamic Link Library (DLL) files are copied to the SYS:PUBLIC directory to let you perform the specific setup in NetWare Administrator for each gateway.

Administrator Types

You can create administrators to fulfill different functions for each gateway. For example, you can set up the "Admin" distribution list to be the Operator for the SMTP gateway, and a manager to be the Accountant who receives a list of who uses the gateway every day.

You can create four types of administrators:

- *Operator*. Receives error messages from the gateway.
- *Accountant.* The Accountant receives a daily text-based report as an attachment to a message from the gateway; it describes the numbers of messages sent and received on that day; who the recipients are; and other message header information, such as the date, time, and subject of the message.
- *Postmaster*. Some gateways require the configuration of a "postmaster general." For mail systems that require a Postmaster (such as MHS), you can specify this administrator account to receive from the other system messages intended for this postmaster.
- *Foreign Operator*. This administrator account lets the administrator of the foreign mail system "query" your gateway for status information.

Not every gateway supports all four types. Refer to the *Instant Expert Guide* to find out what administrator types are available for the gateway you are configuring.

Gateway Access Control

You can control the access users have to specific gateways by configuring an NDS User's Gateway Access property on the GroupWise Account property page in NetWare Administrator (see Figure 18.15). Refer to a specific gateway's documentation to see if it supports access control. If you don't enter a value in this field, access to all gateways is unrestricted. These values are useful for establishing access controls to gateways, which have usage limitations based on the number of licenses purchased.

Gateway Troubleshooting

Keep in mind two important goals when troubleshooting gateways: understand how messages are supposed to flow from one system to another and don't overlook common problems.

Message Flow

The important thing to remember about message flow through a gateway is that there are always two processes to control:

- *Gateway Polling Interval*. The period of time after which gateway software polls its input queue for messages from the MTA.
- *Gateway Connection Interval*. The basis for the period of time that an actual connection is established. This can be based on the number of messages or a period of elapsed time.

Knowing this fact will help you troubleshoot the gateway.

The exact path that messages take through a gateway are specific to the gateway you are using. Refer to online help in NetWare Administrator (press F1) for details.

Common Problems

Check the following list if you're experiencing difficulties with a gateway:

√ *Network Connection*. This could be on the GroupWise side or in the system you are trying to communicate with. Most protocols can be tested with utilities, such as testing TCP/IP connections using the PING or TELNET utilities. These connections can also be tested with a workstation acting as an end user. See if the network connection can be made generically, eliminating the complexity of the gateway software itself.

- *System Requirements.* For some gateways, the system-level requirements can be pretty straightforward, such as using a TCP/IP protocol stack to connect the SMTP gateway to the Internet. On the other hand, a Master's degree in Computer Systems Design and Technology plus 5–10 years working with IBM mainframes would help in setting up the SNADS gateway. Other gateways fall somewhere in the middle of these two in terms of the technical knowledge required to successfully set up, run and maintain them. Novell provides a lot of good technical information to help you set up any GroupWise gateway. We have included the *Instant Expert Guide* on the CD that comes with this book. This guide includes detailed system requirements and instructions for setting up every GroupWise gateway. The technical support teams at Novell update this information regularly, so be sure to check out the latest version of the Instant Expert Guide on Novell's Web site at `http://support.novell.com`. You should verify with Novell or an authorized dealer that you have the most current gateway solution for your system.

- *Network Requestor Configuration.* Special versions of the network drivers needed to make the connection between the two systems must be installed.

- *Required Patch Files. Novell* places patch files for gateways that are "stability challenged" on two FTP sites:

  `ftp.novell.com/updates/gateways`

  and

  `http://support.novell.com/Ftp/Updates/gateways/Date0.html`

  Also make sure that appropriate or required patches from companies other than Novell are installed.

- √ *File SystemRights*. Make sure the file system rights of the user you are attaching to the other system with are adequate.

- √ *Gateway-Specific Information*. For most gateways, the properties of the gateway object in NetWare Administrator need to match *exactly* the information defined in the other mail system. Be sure to match uppercase and lowercase in addition to spelling.

- √ *Software Versions*. Most gateways are very particular about which versions of the other system's software they will work with. Be sure to research this during the gateway planning phase.

- √ *Addressing*. Each gateway has its own format for addressing, but you can usually "force" a message to be routed directly through the gateway with an explicit address (instead of relying on potentially incorrect link information). The format for an explicit address is as follows:

  ```
  <domain>.<gateway name>:"<native mail system address>"
  ```

  For example,

  ```
  SHICKPRI.SMTP:"cvargas@usckc.com"
  ```

- √ *User Permissions*. The user trying desperately to send a message might not have been given the proper access, based on message priority to the gateway. See "Gateway Access Control" earlier in this chapter for more information. You need to be aware of the other system's addressing limitations. For example, the Microsoft Mail address of a recipient's mailbox can be 10 characters or less, and older versions of MHS support addresses of 8 characters or less.

- √ *Conversion Problems*. The mail system you are communicating with won't support all of the message types that GroupWise does, so the gateway will change special message types in GroupWise to their regular message equivalents in the other mail system.

- √ *Attachment Problems*. Each mail system has its own rules about the number, format, and character set of file attachments. Be sure to consult the *Instant Expert Guide* about how to handle attachments for the specific gateway.

Summary

In this chapter, we introduced GroupWise gateways: their purpose, installation, administration, and troubleshooting. The next two chapters deal specifically with a couple of very important gateways: the GroupWise Asynchronous gateway and the GroupWise SMTP/MIME gateway.

PART VI

Additional GroupWise Technologies

CHAPTER 19

The Async Gateway

In this chapter, you will learn how to do the following:

- Plan for an Async gateway implementation
- Plan for remote access
- Install the NLM Async gateway software
- Create and configure an Async gateway in NetWare Administrator
- Configure an Async gateway to connect with another GroupWise domain
- Configure an Async gateway to support GroupWise Remote users
- Load and run an Async gateway

In Chapter 18, we introduced you to GroupWise gateways, how they generally work, and the roles they perform in a GroupWise system. In this chapter, we explain the GroupWise Async gateway in much greater detail, describing the two main functions it serves in GroupWise systems.

One primary function of Async gateways is to connect domains together. Often a network connection between domains is too expensive or simply not available. When that is the case, an Async gateway can be very useful. An Async gateway can connect domains together within the same GroupWise system or it can connect domains located in other (external) GroupWise systems.

Another important function of Async gateways is to enable remote access for users who need to access their mailboxes through a modem connection. (In this chapter, we use the term *remote user* to describe a user who accesses a GroupWise mailbox using the Remote mode of the GroupWise client.)

Preparing to Implement Async Gateways

Before you implement an Async gateway, you should devote some time to planning the installation. This is especially true if you have never implemented an Async gateway before. If the purpose of the Async gateway is to provide your users with remote access to GroupWise, then there are some additional considerations you need to take into account. This section covers both general planning issues and considerations that are specific to setting up an Async gateway for remote access.

General Async Gateway Planning

Planning the installation of Async gateways involves making decisions about several key questions:

- How many Async gateways are needed in the GroupWise system, and how many modems should be installed at each gateway?
- In which domains should the Async gateways be located?
- Which Async gateway platform should be used?

Number of Gateways

The number of Async gateways needed in a GroupWise system depends on the following factors:

- The configuration of the GroupWise system
- The volume of gateway traffic that will be generated
- How quickly messages need to be delivered through the gateway

If you plan to use an Async gateway to connect a remote domain to a local domain within your GroupWise system, you need a minimum of two Async gateways—one in the remote domain and one in a local domain. As shown in Figure 19.1, other domains can then be linked indirectly to the remote domain through the local domain that houses the Async gateway.

FIGURE 19.1

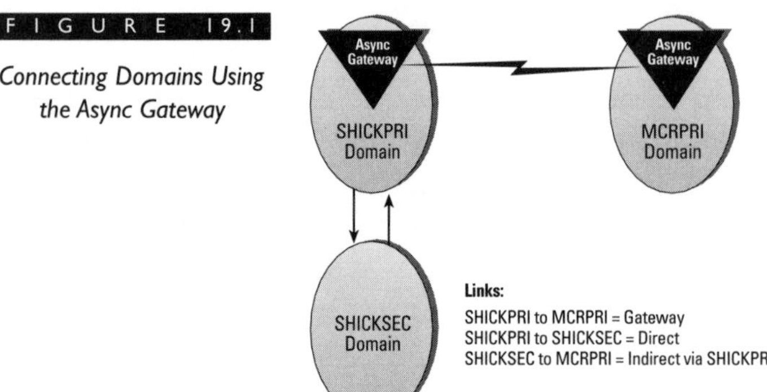

Connecting Domains Using the Async Gateway

NOTE

When used in this context, the term *remote* refers to a domain that is not connected to the other domains in a GroupWise system through a network link. The term *local* is used to describe a domain or gateway located on the same network as most of the other domains in a GroupWise system.

In a large GroupWise system, a dedicated gateway domain can be established. This type of configuration is shown in Figure 19.2.

FIGURE 19.2

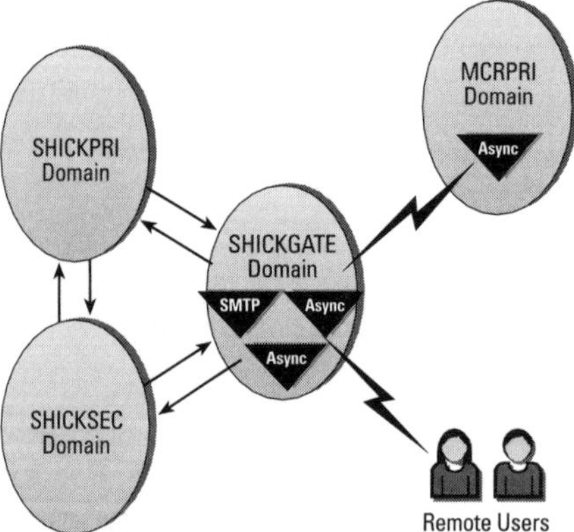

Dedicated Gateway Domain

When you have a dedicated gateway domain, at least two domain transfers occur for every message sent between the remote location and the main GroupWise system. This configuration is best if the anticipated Async traffic is scattered throughout the system. Notice in Figure 19.2 that the SHICKGATE domain is a dedicated gateway domain. It houses an Async gateway that connects to the MCRPRI domain, another Async gateway that supports remote users, and an SMTP gateway.

If one domain has a larger number of remote GroupWise users, or if the Async traffic is more concentrated to a particular domain, you should create an Async gateway for that domain.

A single domain can have multiple Async gateways. Likewise, each Async gateway can have multiple modems. Therefore, you have some flexibility as you decide how many Async gateways you need and where you should locate them.

Placement

You should have two goals in mind as you determine which domains will house your Async gateways:

- Gateways should be located where they will provide the most efficient message delivery between domains and for remote GroupWise users.
- Gateways should be located where they can be easily administered and maintained.

As a general rule, try to place a gateway close to the users who will generate the most traffic through the gateway. If you can identify a specific domain that will generate a lot of traffic to a remote site—or if you can identify a domain that services a large number of remote GroupWise users—it makes sense to place an Async gateway in that domain.

Your goal should be to place gateways so that message delivery will be the fastest possible. Remember: An Async gateway in one domain can also service users who belong to other domains in the system. It simply adds extra MTA transfers between the domains to their final destination.

Ease of maintenance is another important consideration. In a large GroupWise system, maintenance considerations often make a dedicated "gateway domain" a good idea because all gateways are centrally located.

Also, if all domains generate about the same amount of gateway traffic, or if remote users are scattered throughout the domains in the system, a centrally located gateway domain usually provides the best overall message delivery speed because all recipients have the same number of domain transfers between their domain and the gateway.

Platforms

The GroupWise Async gateway is available in two versions: NLM and OS/2. While this chapter focuses primarily on the NLM version, an overview of the advantages and disadvantages of both versions is provided.

NLM Async Gateway For NetWare networks, the NLM Async gateway is undoubtedly the best version of the gateway. It provides the following advantages:

- The NLM Async gateway can be run on the same file server that holds the domain directory structure. This eliminates the across-the-wire network traffic you encounter with other versions of the Async gateway, because the gateway is located on the same machine as the domain MTA queues and the gateway's queues.
- There is no need for a dedicated Async gateway workstation because the NLM Async gateway runs on the file server.
- It supports up to 32 modems on a single machine.

One possible disadvantage of the NLM Async gateway is that modems must be installed directly on a file server machine. In some organizations, this setup may violate network security policies. However, even with modems installed on file servers, potential intruders cannot use the Async gateway as an entry point into the network file system because they are controlled by the Async gateway exclusively. Only a valid GroupWise client in Remote mode or another GroupWise Async gateway can "talk" to it.

Following are the hardware requirements for running an GroupWise 4.1-level NLM Async gateway:

- 80486 PC or above
- Novell NetWare 3.x or above
- 3MB free disk space for installation files
- GroupWise MTA
- Novell NetWare CLIB.NLM version 3.12g or later

- 14.4K or faster AT command-set-compatible modem
- 590K memory for a single port (one modem) installation and 57K for each additional port that is configured
- NGWLIB.NLM and AIO.NLM modules

NOTE

The NGWLIB.NLM will not interfere with the GroupWise 5 agents' library NLM, called GWENN1.NLM. But if other GroupWise 4 gateways are being loaded on the same server, be sure to use the latest version of NGWLIB.NLM, which can be found on Novell's support site at `http://support.novell.com`**.**

Depending upon the configuration, one or more of the following NLMs may also be necessary: AIOCOMX.NLM (when modems are attached to a file server's ports), AIODGMEM.NLM, AIODGXI.NLM, AIODGXEM.NLM (when DigiBoards are connected to a file server), or other NLMs specific to the type of multiport board being used.

Specific instructions for installing, configuring, and running NLM Async gateways are given later in this chapter.

OS/2 Async Gateway The OS/2 Async gateway ranks second in performance, behind the NLM Async gateway. The OS/2 Async gateway is recommended by Novell for non-NetWare networks. It is a high performance gateway offering the following advantages:

- Its multithreading capabilities provide a solid, high-performance operating system for handling Async gateway processes.
- All gateway processes are handled by a single executable. Therefore, you only need one dedicated machine for the gateway.
- The OS/2 Async gateway supports up to 32 modems on a single gateway machine.
- It can be configured to access different network file systems at the same time. For example, it could run for domains located on UNIX NFS, Banyan Vines, or NT server file systems.

There are two disadvantages to using the OS/2 gateway: (1) it requires a dedicated workstation; and (2) across-the-wire network traffic is generated because the gateway runs on a computer other than the file server housing the domain.

The requirements for the OS/2 Async gateway are as follows:

- OS/2 2.1 or later workstation with proper network requestors
- Minimum of 16MB RAM
- 120MB hard drive space
- 14.4K AT command-set-compatible modem

Once you have chosen the platform for the Async gateway, you can plan for supporting remote GroupWise users.

Remote Access Planning

Most organizations that implement a GroupWise system eventually decide to enable support for the Remote mode of the GroupWise client. By supporting GroupWise in Remote mode, users can access their GroupWise master mailboxes without requiring a network connection to a post office.

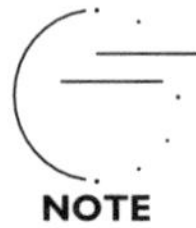

Remote GroupWise users can also connect to their mailboxes via a network connection. This could be an actual network connection or a dial-in "remote mode" solution, such as NetWare Connect.

This section covers the following tasks related to planning the implementation of GroupWise Remote mode at an organization:

- Deciding on the number of Async gateways
- Placement of the gateways
- Identifying the types of remote users
- Safeguarding system security

Deciding on the Number of Gateways

The first step in implementing GroupWise Remote involves deciding how many Async gateways you need.

A system that supports remote GroupWise connections must have at least one Async gateway. If you already have an Async gateway in your system, you will need to decide if that single Async gateway can handle remote GroupWise access or if you should install more Async gateways.

Remote users of GroupWise will call intermittently to upload and download new messages and then disconnect. The client program works offline, and messages are sent and calendar appointments are made, along with other changes, to the remote mailbox.

Once those changes are complete, remote users will dial into the Async gateway to synchronize their remote mailbox with the "master" mailbox on the server. The connection is terminated after the file transfer is complete.

If an existing Async gateway connects two GroupWise domains, you do not want GroupWise remote traffic to bog down the gateway and interfere with domain-to-domain message traffic. Before you allow that gateway to handle remote GroupWise connections, you need to determine if the gateway has the capacity to handle the extra work created by remote requests. You may also need to add modems to the existing gateway.

Often, dedicated Async gateways should be installed to support remote users. If you do not already have an Async gateway—or if you need additional gateways—you must first determine the best locations for the Async gateways to be used for remote access.

Placement of the Gateways

Ask yourself three questions as you decide where to locate the gateways that will support remote GroupWise access:

- Where are the remote users located in the system?
- What will remote access patterns be like?
- Will there be users who always use GroupWise in remote mode, users who only occasionally use GroupWise in remote mode, or both?

As a general rule, you should locate the Async gateway as close as possible to remote users' post offices. This strategy has two advantages: (1) it avoids causing a lot of extra domain-to-domain message traffic and therefore does not put a strain on domain MTAs; and (2) it provides the fastest performance for remote users.

If you can predict which domains will service a large number of remote users, you should consider placing an Async gateway in those domains. For example, if your system supports a large number of sales reps located throughout the country, it makes sense to place an Async gateway in a domain used by the sales department. This would isolate a good portion of the remote access traffic to a single domain. No additional burden would be placed on MTAs in other domains.

If the group of remote users is relatively large, consider making a post office for that group of users. Then create and install an Async gateway in their domain.

You should also try to predict the usage patterns of the GroupWise remote users. This will help you determine where to locate Async gateways and how to configure them. A pilot test of GroupWise Remote can be used to help you answer the following questions:

- When will the majority of remote users call in for their messages?
- Will users be uploading and downloading large messages and file attachments? How large will the file attachments be?
- Will users expect their requests to be received immediately? Are they willing to upload their requests, disconnect, and then reconnect later to receive the information requested?
- How fast are the users' modems?

Call-In Times If you know that many remote users will call in for their messages at certain times (for example, around 5:00 p.m.), you can adjust your Async gateways to accommodate the increased traffic generated at that time.

File Attachments The size of users' messages and file attachments can affect connection time and thereby reduce the amount of traffic an Async gateway can handle. Large file attachments significantly increase connection time. You can mitigate this problem by instructing remote users on how to use the remote download options in the GroupWise client.

Performance Goals Remote users' needs and expectations with regard to remote access performance should influence your decision about where to locate Async gateways and how to configure them.

If users expect messages to be immediately downloaded from their mailboxes when they connect to the gateway, you should place the Async gateways close to the users' mailboxes. Also, to meet the users' expectations, you should use high-performance gateways, MTAs, and POAs.

NOTE

If a post office houses a large number of remote users, consider setting up a POA dedicated to servicing the high-priority message queues. This strategy provides remote users with the fastest response time.

On the other hand, if users are willing to call in and upload message requests and then disconnect and wait for some time before reconnecting, you will have more flexibility as you plan your gateways.

Modem Speed If both the users and the Async gateway have high-speed modems, download time can be reduced significantly.

TIP

If possible, use the same type (manufacture and model) of modem in the Async gateway and in the remote users' machines—or at least test different modems to make sure they work well together. Modem incompatibilities can cause connections to fail or to be unreliable. Also, you should disable any compression that may be performed by the modems. GroupWise takes care of all necessary file compression and decompression.

Identifying the Types of Remote Users

The different types of remote users in your system are another important factor to consider as you plan the implementation of remote access. Determining the usage patterns of different types of users will help you decide where to place the Async gateways and which hardware resources to devote to them. There are two distinct types of remote users:

- Users who use the Remote mode only when traveling (and occasionally from home). We refer to these users as *occasional* remote users.

- Users who work away from the main offices and who can only contact the GroupWise system using the GroupWise Remote access mode. We refer to these users as *routine* remote users.

Occasional Remote Users Occasional remote users typically access their master mailboxes during business trips (often from hotels or trade shows). Sometimes these users work at home in the evening and want to connect to the main GroupWise system. When they're not traveling or at home, these remote users almost always access their mailboxes using the regular network connection for the GroupWise client.

In most systems, you will not be able to group all of the occasional remote users into a single domain. Therefore, you probably won't be able to place an Async gateway in every domain that has occasional remote users. When you are faced with this situation, the best solution is to place an Async gateway in a centrally located domain that can be easily accessed by all domains.

Routine Remote Users Routine remote users never (or very seldom) use the network GroupWise client to access their mailboxes. Instead, they routinely use the GroupWise Remote access mode to communicate with other employees.

If your organization has a substantial number of routine remote users, you should strongly consider grouping them into a domain that can contain one or more dedicated Async gateways.

There are two advantages to this strategy. First, the remote users get a better response time. Because they rely so heavily on remote access, they are bound to be concerned about message delivery speed. Second, grouping these users into one domain reduces the impact that processing their messages will have on the rest of the system.

Offsite employees often work in the same department. For example, a sales department may have a large number of offsite sales reps. These employees often send a lot of messages among themselves. By placing them in their own domain, a large percentage of their messages are isolated within that domain.

The demands that routine remote users place on a GroupWise system are very different from the demands of occasional remote users. You need to consider the needs of each type of remote user as you plan your Remote access support.

Safeguarding System Security

One of the most common concerns administrators have about implementing remote GroupWise support is the potential for security breaches. You can rest assured that GroupWise in Remote mode does not pose a security risk.

GroupWise in Remote mode operates on a request-and-response basis. Remote GroupWise users who use modem connections to an Async gateway never log in to the network and never have live access to network file servers, volumes, or directories. Therefore, providing GroupWise users with remote access does not pose a security risk to your network.

After you have planned your Async gateway strategy—for both connecting to other domains and for enabling remote access for GroupWise users—you are ready to install and run the Async gateway.

Setting Up an Async Gateway

This section explains how to set up an Async gateway in your system. The steps are the same regardless of how the gateway will be used. After you learn how to set up the gateway, you'll learn how to use it to connect domains together and how to set it up to support GroupWise Remote access.

Setting up an Async gateway involves the following:

- Installing the Async gateway software
- Creating the gateway in NetWare Administrator
- Configuring the gateway

Installing the Software

Each Async gateway platform has its own installation routine. The OS/2 Async gateway is installed from a workstation running OS/2; the NLM Async gateway is installed on a NetWare file server.

Refer to the OS/2 Async gateway manual for instructions on how to install gateways for OS/2. The steps for installing the NLM Async gateway are as follows:

1 • Place the gateway installation disk in drive A: on the NetWare file server.

2 • From the system console, type

```
LOAD A:\PINSTALL.NLM.
```

NOTE

The NLM Async gateway installation program is an NLM. It must be run from the file server console. You could copy the gateway software to an installation directory—for example, SYS:SOFTWARE\ASYNC—and use that path in the LOAD command.

Figure 19.3 shows the installation screen for the NLM version of the Async gateway.

FIGURE 19.3

Async Gateway Installation

```
                    Async Gateway Installation
Install From              A:\
Install NLM To            SYS:\SYSTEM
Install Shared NLM's To   SYS:\SYSTEM
Domain Path               SYS:\DOMAIN
Gateway Directory (under <domain>\wpgate\): ASYNC

          Install...      Press ESC to exit.
```

3 • In the Install NLM To: field, enter the directory where the NLM Async gateway (NGWASYNC.NLM) will be installed. You should install this file in the SYS:\SYSTEM directory because that directory is the default location for NLMs.

4 • In the Install Shared NLMs To: field, enter the directory where the shared NLMs will be installed. Again, the SYS:\SYSTEM directory is the recommended location for shared NLMs. Note: The primary shared NLM file to manage is NGWLIB.NLM. (Be sure not to overwrite a new version of this file with an older version of the Async gateway software.)

5 • In the Domain Path: field, enter the path to the GroupWise domain that will contain the Async gateway. Use the NetWare path syntax. For example, you would type SYS:HEADQRTS if you were installing

to the SYS volume on the file server and HEADQRTS were the name of the domain directory.

6 • In the Gateway Directory: field, enter the name of the subdirectory that will hold the Async gateway files. This should be the *domain*\WPGATE*async* directory, where *domain* is the name of the domain and *async* is the name of the subdirectory. The default name for the gateway subdirectory is ASYNC, but you can change that name if you wish.

7 • Select Install.

8 • After the installation process is complete, load AIO.NLM by typing

```
LOAD AIO.NLM
```

9 • Next, load AIOCOMX.NLM for each port/modem you intend to use by typing

```
LOAD AIOCOMX.NLM
```

Make a note of the board number (the number that identifies the modem that is installed) as you load AIOCOMX.NLM. This information will be needed later, and is only displayed when AIOCOMX.NLM is loaded.

NOTE

There are no required parameters to load these NLMs, but you need to use startup options if you want to override any of the default settings (such as the IRQ or port settings). Refer to the NLM Async gateway documentation or NetWare documentation for a list of possible startup options for AIO or AIOCOMX.

Creating the Gateway Object

At this point, you have installed the files for the NLM Async gateway. Now you need to run NetWare Administrator to create the Gateway object.

In Chapter 18, you saw that all gateways are administered from NetWare Administrator. During the GroupWise installation process, you had an option to install supporting administration files for each gateway type you use in your system. At that time, you should have installed the Async gateway administration DLL files. If you did not install the Async gateway administration DLL files during your GroupWise installation, refer to Chapter 18 for installation instructions. You should make sure these DLLs have been installed before proceeding.

To create the Async Gateway object in NetWare Administrator, follow these steps:

1 • Right-click the Domain object containing the Async Gateway object and choose Create. This must be the same domain as the domain directory you installed the gateway under in the steps on the previous pages.

2 • Highlight GroupWise Gateway and click on OK. The Create GroupWise Gateway dialog box appears (see Figure 19.4).

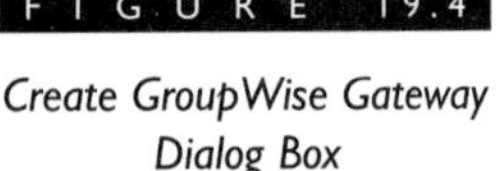

Create GroupWise Gateway Dialog Box

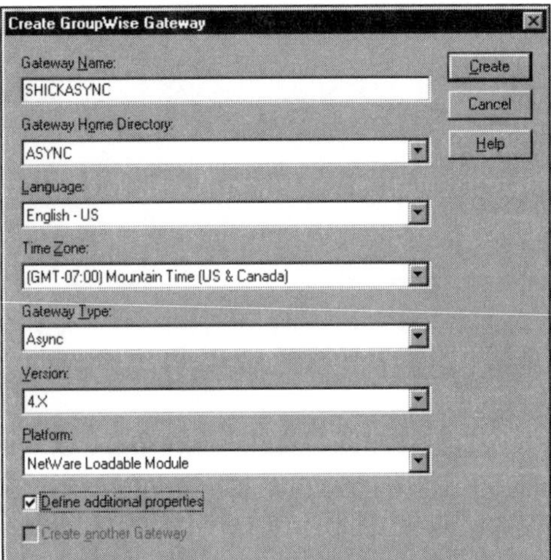

3 • Enter the name of the gateway in the Gateway Name field. Keep this name short but descriptive. Naming gateways is similar to naming post offices and domains. The name you choose will be the name that is used when addressing this gateway.

4 • Enter the gateway directory in the Gateway Home Directory field by clicking on the drop-down list and choosing ASYNC. (Note: If you do not see a choice for the Async gateway, you have chosen the wrong

domain to install the gateway in or you named the gateway directory something besides ASYNC during the installation process.)

5 • Verify the language and the time zone. Change these options if necessary.

6 • Select Async in the Gateway Type field.

7 • Select 4.x in the version field. (Note: As of this writing, the 4.x gateways are the most current versions. If you have a later version, select it.)

8 • Select NetWare Loadable Module in the Platform field.

9 • Click on Create.

The gateway object is created under the Domain object, and the information you entered is added to the WPDOMAIN.DB file. To confirm the creation of the gateway object, look at the MTA screen: you should see the number of gateways in the domain increase by one.

Next you must configure the Async gateway.

Configuring the Gateway

In order to configure the gateway properly, you must complete the following tasks:

- Define port settings
- Establish other elective gateway options. These options are found in the Gateway Time Settings, Log Settings, Optional Gateway Settings, Network Address, and Gateway Administrators pages in the Gateway Properties dialog box.

Defining Port Settings

You need to establish port settings for your Async gateway. To set the port, click on the Ports page and then click on Create. (Note: You can create multiple ports if you have multiple modems installed in the server running the Async gateway NLM.) The Port Information dialog box appears, as shown in Figure 19.5.

FIGURE 19.5

Port Information Dialog Box

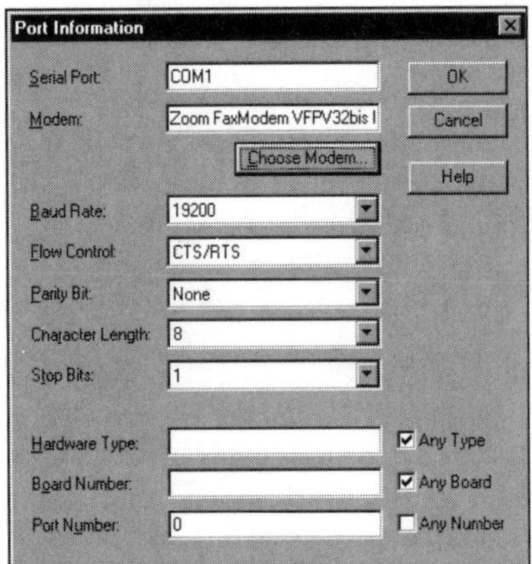

Once you have accessed the Port Information dialog box, follow these steps to establish the port settings for the Async gateway:

1 • Enter a name for the port in the Serial Port: field. This is the descriptive name for the first modem you are defining. "COM1" is fine.

2 • Click on the Choose Modem button and select the type of modem you are using.

3 • Verify that the information in the Baud Rate, Flow Control, Parity Bit, Character Length, and Stop Bits fields is correct for your modem.

4 • If you have only one modem installed, you can leave the Any Type and Any Board options defined. If you have multiple modems or a multiport device, such as a DigiBoard, you must specify the hardware type, the port number, and the board numbers in the corresponding fields. These values are reported when you load the device drivers.

5 • Click on OK when you finish setting the port values.

NOTE

The preceding steps only apply when modems are connected to a standard serial port on a file server. If you are using a multiport DigiBoard, refer to the NLM Async gateway documentation and the DigiBoard documentation for instructions on how to configure those ports. In addition, see the white paper called DIGIBD.DOC on the CD.

Defining Other Gateway Settings

Several optional settings that can be used to customize and optimize the gateway appear on the GroupWise properties pages:

- **Gateway Time Settings.** The properties in the Time Settings page let you control how often the gateway performs routing message processing tasks.
- **Log Settings.** All GroupWise gateways can create log files that register information about the gateway's activities. Click on the Log Settings page to access the log file options.
- **Optional Gateway Settings.** This option lets you customize and optimize your Async gateway.
- **Queue Maintenance.** The Queue Maintenance option is used to synchronize the Async gateway queue directory structure with the Async database. When you run the Queue Maintenance option, the gateway deletes directories for any connections no longer listed in the database, and creates directories for any connections that have entries in the database but don't have associated queue directories.

These settings are covered more fully in Chapter 18.

You have now established all of the settings required in order for the Async gateway to operate. Depending upon how the gateway is to be used, you now need to define connections to other domains or establish settings for supporting GroupWise remote users.

Defining Domain Connections

Let's now look at the main use of Async gateways: linking domains together. The domains may be primary, secondary, or external domains. The steps for defining connections between two domains are the same in all three cases:

- Create Domain Connection definitions for the Async gateways your Async gateway will connect to.
- Establish Calling Schedules and Intervals
- Set the Master Schedule

Creating Domain Connections

Domain connections contain the information that your local gateway needs in order to connect with the remote gateways. To create a domain connection, click on the Domain Connections page from the Async Gateway properties screen, then click on Create.

FIGURE 19.6

Domain Connections Page

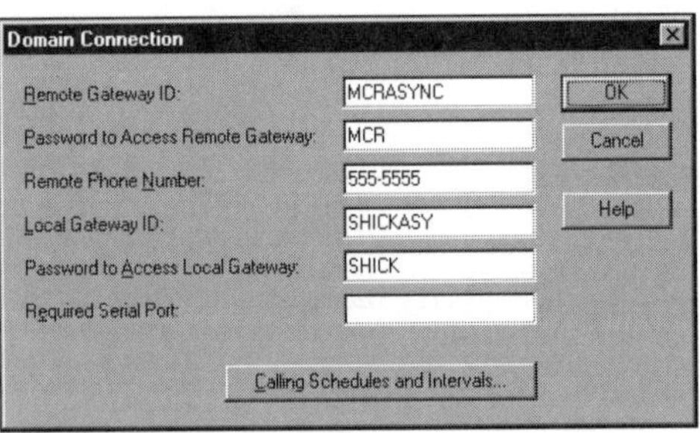

Figure 19.6 shows the fields you must complete when you create a domain connection.

To define a domain connection, follow these steps:

1. Enter the gateway ID for the remote Async gateway. You will need to obtain this information from the remote gateway's administrator.

2 • Enter the password for the remote Async gateway. You will need to obtain this information from the remote gateway's administrator. Remember: the password is case-sensitive.

3 • Enter the phone number of the remote gateway.

4 • Enter a local gateway ID that the remote gateway should use when calling your gateway. You will need to tell this to the other domain's administrator. This gateway ID can be unique—with a unique password for connections to multiple domains—or you can use a common ID and password for all domain connections.

6 • Enter a local gateway password that the remote gateway must use when connecting to your Async gateway.

7 • (*Optional*) Enter the name of a required serial port.

The optional step (Step 7) makes all outgoing messages travel through one port (in other words, through a specific modem). Leave this field blank if you do not want to designate a required port. This option can be very useful if you want to designate a high-speed modem for connection to a certain remote gateway. Along the same lines, if a remote gateway has a low-speed modem installed, you may wish to designate a low-speed modem on the local gateway so that high-speed modems are reserved for connections to other domains with high-speed modems (or for GroupWise remote users who have fast modems).

The next step is to configure Calling Schedules and Intervals.

Configuring Calling Schedules and Intervals

Configuring Calling Schedules and Intervals is a vital part of Async gateway setup. These settings enable you to establish the parameters a local gateway will follow when initiating a connection to a specific remote gateway.

Before you complete the Calling Schedules and Intervals portion of the domain connection, you need to answer the following questions:

- On which days should the Async gateway call the other gateway?

- At what time of day should calls be made?
- Should the local gateway or the other gateway initiate all calls, or should both gateways be allowed to initiate calls?
- Should calls be initiated whenever a certain period of time has elapsed? Should calls be initiated only when a certain number of messages are waiting? Should all message priorities be treated the same? Should all three factors be considered when determining when to initiate calls?
- If the other gateway cannot receive a call (e.g., the line is busy), how many times should the Async gateway attempt to establish a connection?

Calling Schedules and Intervals are used to optimize message delivery between domains. You can also use these options to take advantage of discount telephone rates.

The settings for Calling Schedules and Intervals are discussed in the following section.

Settings

After you have entered the domain connection information, you need to configure the calling options for your gateway. To access these options, click on the Calling Schedules and Intervals button in the Domain Connection dialog box. The Calling Schedules and Intervals dialog box will appear (see Figure 19.7).

FIGURE 19.7

Calling Schedules and Intervals Dialog Box

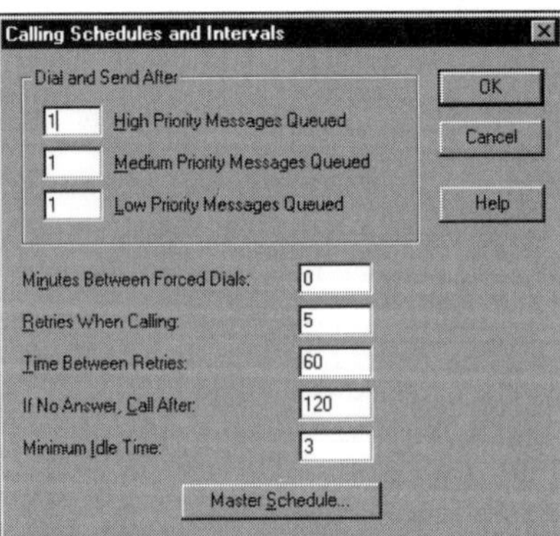

The options in the Dial and Send After area of the dialog box let you set different parameters for the number of high-, medium-, and low -priority messages that must be queued before a call will be initiated. These parameters, in conjunction with the settings you configure in the Master Schedule, determine when calls will be made.

Specific definitions for each option in this dialog box can be found in online help.

NOTE

The Time Between Retries option is counted in *seconds.* The If No Answer Call After option and Minimum Idle Time option are counted in *minutes.*

It is important for you to understand how these options work in relation to the Master Schedule options. We'll explain the Master Schedule and then provide an example that explains how these options work together.

The Master Schedule

The Master Schedule lets you adjust an Async gateway's sending schedule to optimize message delivery and take advantage of discount calling periods. A sample Master Schedule screen is shown in Figure 19.8.

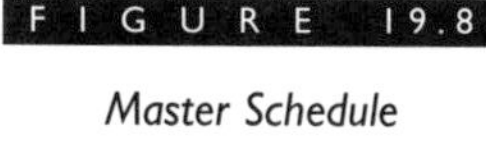

FIGURE 19.8

Master Schedule

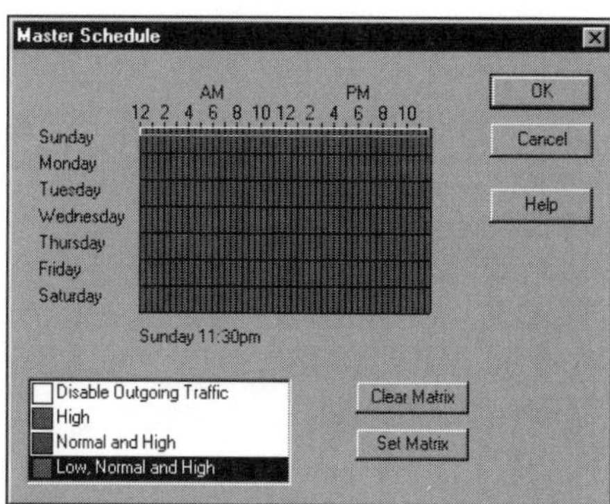

On the Master Schedule, you can specify the time of day and the days of the week during which calls can be made. Notice that you can set specific times when only high-priority messages will trigger calls, when both normal and high-priority messages trigger calls, or when all messages trigger calls. You can also specify periods when the gateway can never initiate a call.

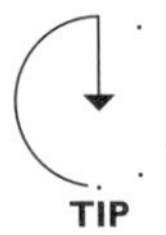
TIP

Completely clearing the matrix prevents the gateway from initiating calls to the remote gateway. If you want the remote gateway to initiate all calls, you can clear the entire matrix.

Figures 19.9 and 19.10 show examples of how one might configure the options in the Calling Schedules and Intervals dialog box and configure a Master Schedule.

Suppose that an administrator at ShickTools configures the Calling Schedules and Intervals options as shown in Figure 19.9.

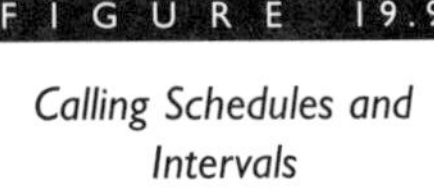
FIGURE 19.9

Calling Schedules and Intervals

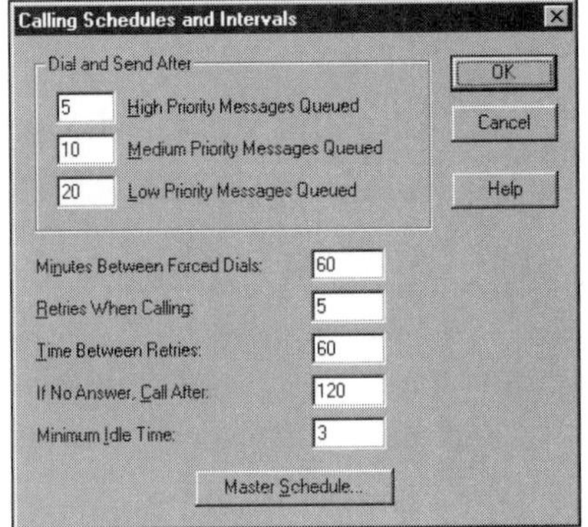

In this example, the ShickTools Async gateway SHICKASYNC may initiate a call to the remote Async gateway (let's call it the MCRASYNC for the McRogue Manufacturing Company's Async gateway) if 60 minutes have passed since the last call and *any one* of the following conditions has been met:

- Five high-priority messages are queued
- Ten normal priority messages are queued
- Twenty low-priority messages are queued

However, a call will be initiated only if the Master Schedule for SHICKASYNC permits the gateway to call MCRASYNC at that time.

Now suppose the ShickTools administrator has configured the Master Schedule for SHICKASYNC as shown in Figure 19.10.

IMPORTANT

The Master Schedule always has the last word. No calls can be initiated if the Master Schedule does not permit calls at a given time. The Master Schedule also overrides the Minutes Between Forced Dials setting.

FIGURE 19.10

Sample Master Calling Schedule

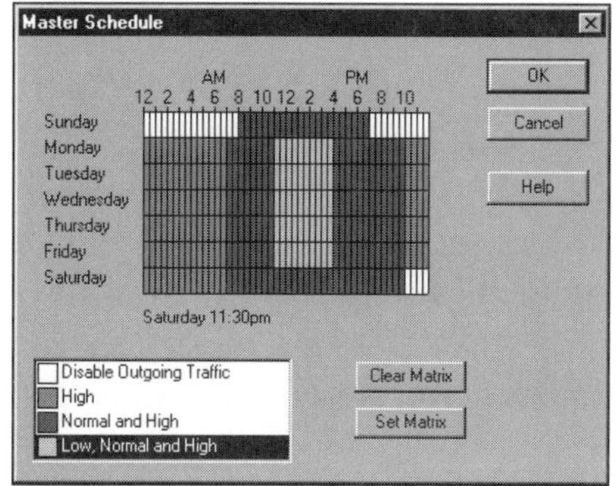

At certain times, the ShickTools Async gateway cannot call McRogue's gateway at all. For example, from 10:00 p.m. on Saturday until 8:00 a.m. on Sunday, SHICKASYNC cannot make any calls to MCRASYNC. During this period, it does not matter how many high-, normal-, or low-priority messages are in the queue.

At other times, the ShickTools Async gateway can only call when the high-priority message count is met (i.e., when there are five or more high-priority messages queued). For example, on weekdays between 12:00 a.m. and 7:00 a.m., only high-priority messages can trigger a call. However, because the Minutes Between Forced Dial options is set to 60, SHICKASYNC will call MCRASYNC gateway every 60 minutes during this time—regardless of how many messages are queued.

IMPORTANT

All queued messages are sent when a connection is established, not just messages with the priority level that triggered the call.

When a call is initiated and received, all messages are sent. For example, suppose that on Monday morning at 4:00 a.m., 30 normal priority messages are in the queue waiting to be sent from SHICKASYNC. Even though the message count for normal priority messages has been exceeded, the Master Schedule is set so that only high-priority messages can trigger a call at that time (refer to Figure 19.8). Now suppose that at 4:15 a.m., five high-priority messages arrive in the queue @ enough to trigger a call. When the connection is established, all messages will be sent to MCRASYNC, including the 30 normal-priority messages that were waiting in the queue. Furthermore, when the connection is established, all messages in the queues of both domains are sent.

Refer to Figures 19.9 and 19.10 again. Between the hours of 7:00 a.m. and 11:00 a.m. on weekdays, both normal and high priority message counts can trigger calls. Weekdays between 11:00 a.m. and 4:00 p.m., the message counts for all three priority levels can trigger calls.

When you establish a Master Schedule, you should keep in mind that the default priority level for messages is normal. However, users can specify different priority levels by using the Send Options feature in the client. Administrative messages (e.g., directory synchronization messages), GroupWise Remote user requests, and busy searches are all high-priority messages (i.e., they are sent through the <0–3> message queue directories). Status messages have the same priority level as the messages that initiate them. In other words, a status message for a high-priority message comes back as a high-priority status message. Normal priority messages use the number 4 or 5 queue directories, and low-priority messages use the number 6 and 7 queue directories.

The Minimum Idle Time option in the Calling Schedules and Intervals dialog box determines how long a connection remains open when there is no activity through the connection. If this setting is set to a high value, Delivered status messages can make it back to the gateway before the connection is broken. However, setting this too high causes wasted connection time, which is often expensive. The timer that keeps track of idle time is reset every time a message reaches either gateway through the connection.

Linking Domains

After you have created an Async gateway, established the local domain profile, configured the ports, completed a remote domain profile, and configured calling schedules and intervals, you still need to create gateway links between the domains. As explained in Chapter 10, there are three different kinds of domain links: direct, indirect, and gateway. When you use Async gateways to connect domains, you must configure a *gateway link* between the domains.

In NetWare Administrator, follow these steps to create a gateway link between domains:

1 • Click on Tools, GroupWise Utilities, Link Configuration.

2 • Double-click the outbound link to the domain that contains the remote gateway.

3 • Click the Link Type drop-down list box and select Gateway.

4 • Click the Gateway Link drop-down list and select the name of the Async gateway in your domain.

5 • In the Gateway Access String: field, type the name of the Remote domain connection you created to connect to the other domain. (Note: This field must specify the Remote Gateway Login ID in order to enable your gateway to connect to the remote gateway.)

6 • Click on OK.

The administrator for the domain that contains the remote Async gateway must also perform these steps.

NOTE

The Return Link option is not required for the Async gateway.

The following section explains how to configure the gateway to support remote access. If your Async gateway will not support remote GroupWise access, you can skip ahead to the section entitled "Running the Async Gateway NLM."

Configuring Remote Access

To support remote GroupWise access, you must configure an Async gateway as instructed in the "Setting Up an Async Gateway" section earlier in this chapter, and then complete the following two tasks:

- Create one or more GroupWise remote profiles
- Ensure that remote users have passwords on their mailboxes

GroupWise Remote Profiles

A *GroupWise remote profile* establishes the parameters that GroupWise remote users must use when they define the connection to the Async gateway in the GroupWise client options screens.

In order to enable your Async gateway to support GroupWise remote users, you must configure a GroupWise remote profile:

1. In NetWare Administrator, double-click the Async gateway object.
2. Click the GroupWise Remote properties page.
3. Click on Create. The Remote Profile dialog box appears (see Figure 19.11).

FIGURE 19.11

Remote Profile Dialog Box

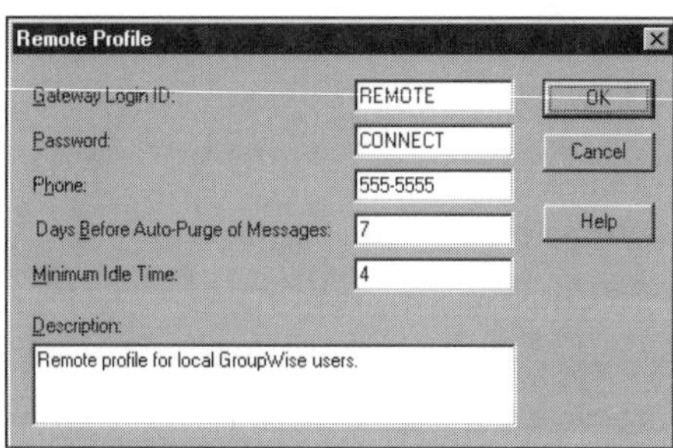

4. Enter a Gateway Login ID. Remote users will have to place this ID in their GroupWise remote access options.
5. Enter a password. This password is case-sensitive. Remote users will have to enter this password in their GroupWise options in order to connect to your gateway.
6. Enter the gateway telephone number. Users will use this number to connect to the gateway.

7 • *(Optional)* Change the default settings for Days Before Auto-Purge of Messages and Minimum Idle Time. These options are explained in Table 19.1.

8 • *(Optional)* Enter a description for the GroupWise remote profile.

9 • Click on OK.

TABLE 19.1

Remote Profile Options

OPTION	DESCRIPTION
Days Before Auto-Purge of Messages	The first time a remote user connects to the system, an account is created for that user. This account is a subdirectory under the Async gateway directory structure, and it is used to store responses that arrive at the gateway after the user has disconnected. This option lets you specify the number of days before the responses are deleted if the user does not reconnect.
Minimum Idle Time	Minimum Idle Time is the amount of time in minutes that the Async gateway will remain connected while waiting for responses to be received from the GroupWise system.

NOTE

If a remote user's account in the Async gateway directory structure is deleted, the user does not lose messages. The messages are still available in the user's master mailbox. Only the responses that were not downloaded during the previous connection are deleted. The remote user would need to request that information again.

As you create GroupWise remote profiles, you can employ a couple of different strategies. One strategy is to create a single profile that all GroupWise remote users share when accessing the main GroupWise system. Another strategy is to create remote user profiles for individual users or for groups of users. The second strategy is particularly useful when you have certain users who need unique remote profile settings (for example, if they need longer Minimum Idle Time settings because they prefer not to connect more than once to receive responses.)

WARNING

If you set Minimum Idle time to 0, the Async gateway will disconnect immediately after a user uploads requests. Users will have to initiate another connection to receive responses to requests. If you want to keep the connection open for a while to give users an opportunity to receive responses, you can specify a period of time (in minutes).

Master Mailbox Passwords

There is one last matter to take care of before GroupWise remote users can establish a connection to their mailboxes. All GroupWise remote users must set passwords for their master mailboxes (assuming post office security has been set to high). Setting a password is easy for occasional remote users because they can set the password from within the regular network GroupWise client.

However, for routine remote users, you usually need to set a password on their master mailboxes using NetWare Administrator. You cannot set a global password for multiple users. Passwords must be set individually.

Following are the steps for setting a master mailbox password:

1. Right-click a User object and click on Details.
2. Click the GroupWise Account page.
3. Click the Change GroupWise Password option.
4. Enter and confirm the password.
5. Click on OK to close the Security Options dialog box.
6. Click on OK to close the User property page.
7. Repeat Steps 1–6 for each GroupWise user needing a password.

IMPORTANT

The password is case-sensitive. You will need to provide the routine remote user with the password that you set in GroupWise Admin.

8. Highlight the user or users in NetWare Administrator.
9. Click on Tools, GroupWise Utilities, Mailbox/Library Maintenance.

10 • Click the Action drop-down list and choose Reset Client Options.

11 • Click on Run.

NOTE

Steps 8 through 11 cause the user's preferences to be reset and add the password information to the user's USERxxx.DB file.

In the above steps, we are assuming that the user has an existing master mailbox in the post office message store. If this is a new network user or if the user has never had a GroupWise account, there is a preliminary step you must take before you can set the password for the user—you must cause the user's USER*xxx*.DB file to be created in the post office message store.

The easiest way to force the creation of a USER*xxx*.DB file is to send a message to that user from a GroupWise client. You may want to send users a message welcoming them to GroupWise. This has two benefits: (1) it creates users' USER*xxx*.DB files, and (2) it provides users with something to download, for testing purposes, the first time they connect to the GroupWise system.

Running the Async Gateway NLM

Once you have completed the steps for either connecting domains or supporting remote GroupWise access, you are ready to run the Async gateway NLM.

IMPORTANT

Before you launch the Async gateway, you must run the domain's MTA (if it is not already running). The MTA will create the required input and output queues in the gateway subdirectory.

Loading the Async gateway NLM is very similar to loading other GroupWise NLMs. The default name of the Async gateway NLM startup file is STARTUP.ASY. You need to modify the /HOME switch in the startup file to point to the gateway directory. For example, if the name of the local domain's directory is SHICKPRI and it is located in the file server's SYS volume, the switch should look as follows:

```
/HOME-SYS:SHICKPRI\WPGATE\ASYNC
```

Table 19.2 lists optional gateway switches, with a brief description of each. (Italics indicate variable information.)

NOTE

As a general rule, you should use the options available in NetWare Administrator to configure the gateway, rather than overriding the NetWare Administrator settings with startup file switches.

TABLE 19.2

Optional Gateway Switches

SWITCH	DESCRIPTION
`/user`-*user ID*	Provides the NLM with the remote file server's NetWare user ID. Include this switch only if the Async gateway NLM is running on a file server other than the domain's file server. Use the GWACCESS account discussed earlier in this book.
`/password`-*NetWare password*	Provides the NLM with the remote file server's NetWare password. Include this switch only if the Async gateway NLM is running on a file server other than the domain's file server.
`/help`	Displays the startup switch help screen.
`/loglevel`-*log level*	Overrides the logging level for the log files. The logging levels—from the most detailed to the least—are diagnostic, verbose, and normal. The default value is set in NetWare Administrator.
`/log`-*pathname*	Points the NLM to the path on which the log files are written. This path must point to a directory on the local server or to the server on which the GroupWise domain directory resides.
`/logdays`-*number of days*	Sets the number of days that a log file resides on the disk before it is automatically deleted. The default is set in NetWare Administrator.
`/logmax`-*kilobytes*	Determines the maximum disk space used for all log files. The default is set in NetWare Administrator.

IMPORTANT

The `/user` and `/password` switches are used only if the Async gateway NLM is running on a file server other than the file server that holds the domain subdirectory. In most cases, these switches should not be used because the Async gateway is running on the same file server that houses the domain.

Follow these steps to start an Async gateway from the file server's console prompt or from a workstation running RCONSOLE:

1 • Load AIO.NLM.

2 • Load AIOCOMX.NLM for each port that has a modem connected to it.

3 • Load NGWASYNC.NLM with the @startup filename option. For example, type LOAD NGWASYNC.NLM @STARTUP.ASY. The Async gateway NLM screen will appear.

You can automate the loading of these NLMs by adding the load commands to the file server's AUTOEXEC.NCF file or the GRPWISE.NCF file.

Once you have completed these procedures, your Async gateway is ready to accept dial-in phone calls from remote GroupWise users.

Remote GroupWise users must configure the GroupWise client program to dial and log in to the gateway. For information on configuring the client for remote access, we refer you to our last book, *Novell's GroupWise 5 User's Handbook* published by Novell Press and IDG Books Worldwide, in which the GroupWise Remote mode is discussed thoroughly.

Understanding Message Flow

In this section we explain some message flow diagrams for Async gateways. These diagrams show how messages flow in three different scenarios: a domain-to-domain connection, a GroupWise remote connection, and a remote network connection. (In a *remote network connection* a GroupWise user runs GroupWise in Remote mode but connects to the GroupWise system through a network connection, rather than a modem connection. This special remote configuration of the client program is also explained in *Novell's GroupWise 5 User's Handbook.*)

Domain-to-Domain Traffic

Figure 19.12 shows how a message travels between a sender and a recipient when their domains are connected by an Async gateway.

FIGURE 19.12

Message Flow Through an Async Gateway

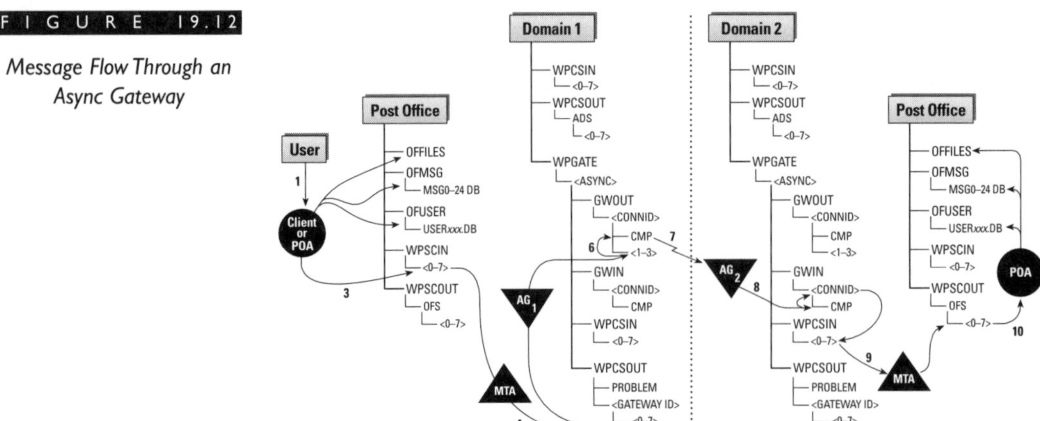

The following steps are depicted in Figure 19.12:

1 • Using the GroupWise client, a user in Domain 1 creates and sends a message to a user in Domain 2.

2 • The GroupWise client or the POA adds the message to the sender's message database, user database, and OFFILES directory (if necessary).

3 • The GroupWise client or the POA places the outbound message in Domain 1's message server input queue directory (<post office>\WPCSIN\<0–7>).

4 • The MTA for Domain 1 detects the message in its input queue (<po>\WPCSIN\<0–7>) and places the message in Domain 1's Async gateway's input queue subdirectory (<domain>\WPGATE\<async>\WPCSOUT\<gateway ID>\<0–7>). (Note: A gateway ID subdirectory is created under the WPCSOUT subdirectory for every gateway that has a remote domain profile defined. This is the MTA output queue for that specific gateway.)

5 • NGWASYNC.NLM reads the message to determine which connection directory to place the message in. Then it places the message in the <domain>\WPGATE\<async>\GWOUT\<connection ID>\<1–3>

directory. The connection ID directory corresponds to the port through which the connection is to be established. The message is placed in the 1, 2, or 3 directory depending upon its priority. The Master Schedule and calling intervals will use the different priority-level message counts in these directories to determine when the gateway initiates a call.

6 • When a connection is triggered, NGWASYNC.NLM reads the messages in the <connection ID>\<1–3> directory, compresses it, and moves it to the <domain>\WPGATE\<async>\GWOUT\<connection ID>\CMP directory. This is the directory where compression (hence, CMP) is performed prior to the message being transmitted to the other Async gateway.

7 • NGWASYNC.NLM transmits the message through the modem to the receiving Async gateway in Domain 2.

8 • Domain 2's NGWASYNC.NLM receives the message in the <domain>\WPGATE\<async>\GWIN\<connection ID>\CMP directory. Domain 2's Async gateway then decompresses the file and places it in the <domain>\WPGATE\<async>\GWIN\<connection ID> directory and moves it to the Async gateway's MTA input queue directory (<domain>\WPGATE\<async>\WPCSIN\<0–7>).

9 • Domain 2's MTA transfers the message from the domain>\WPGATE\<async>\WPCSIN\<0–7> directory to the receiving post office's MTA output queue (<po>\WPCSOUT\OFS\<0–7>).

10 • The POA delivers the message to the recipient by placing the message in the message database, adding file attachments to the OFFILES directory, and placing a pointer in the user database.

GroupWise Remote

Because each GroupWise remote user works offline, when a user creates a message and chooses the Send option, the message is not sent at that time. It goes to the pending requests queue until the user connects. The following steps detail what happens when a user sends a message from GroupWise running in remote mode to the main system via a modem connection to an Async gateway (see Figure 19.13).

FIGURE 19.13

Message Flow Through a Modem Connection

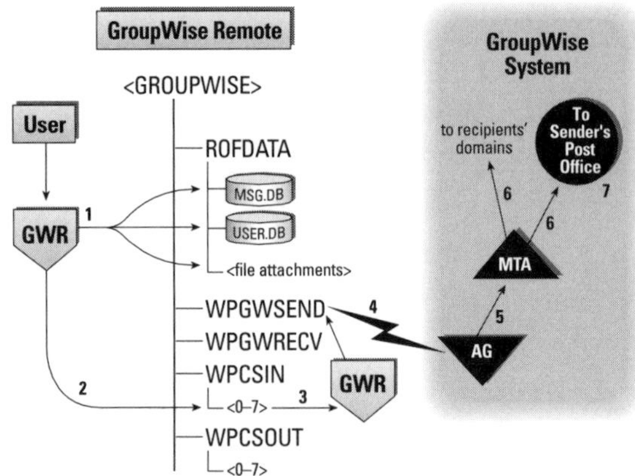

1 • A GroupWise remote user creates a message and chooses Send. GroupWise Remote updates the message database and the user database and adds any file attachments to the ROFDATA directory in the GroupWise Remote message store. This is usually located under the directory where GroupWise is installed; for example, C:\NOVELL\GROUPWISE\ROFDATA.

2 • GroupWise Remote places the message in the WPCSIN\<1–7> directory in the GroupWise Remote subdirectory structure. All remote requests are priority 0 or 1, where 0 is the highest priority.

3 • When the user initiates a connection, GroupWise Remote checks the WPCSIN directory for messages that are waiting to be uploaded to the main GroupWise system. GroupWise Remote reads the information in the WPCSIN directory, compresses the information into one or more files (to reduce connection time), and then moves the file to the WPGWSEND directory. (Note: File compression takes place before GroupWise Remote calls the gateway.)

4 • GroupWise Remote then dials the Async gateway, establishes a connection, and sends the file to the Async gateway.

5 • The Async gateway passes the message to the MTA.

6 • The MTA delivers the message to the recipients' domains and to the sender's POA (assuming the gateway is located in the sender's domain).

7 • The sender's POA updates the sender's user database, the message database, and the file attachments directory.

When information is downloaded from the main GroupWise system, the following events occur (see Figure 19.14).

FIGURE 19.14

Message Flow of Information Downloaded from Main System

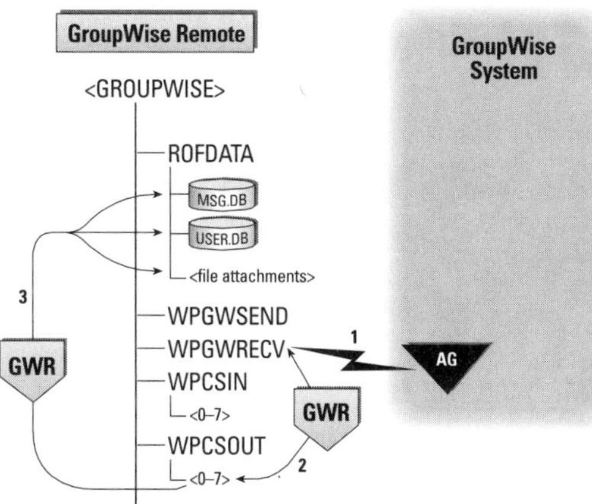

1 • When a message is received from the Async gateway, GroupWise receives the information and builds a response file in the WPGWRECV directory.

2 • When the download is complete, GroupWise disconnects and decompresses the downloaded response file. The response file may contain more than one message. As the information is decompressed, the individual messages are moved to the WPCSOUT directory.

3 • GroupWise then reads the information in the WPCSOUT directory and updates the information in the USER.DB, MSG.DB, and ROFDATA directories.

Remote Network Connection

If a user needs remote access to the network (to transfer files or to run applications), a "remote node" access program such as NetWare Connect can be used. This type of access to the network can be used by GroupWise to synchronize the remote mailbox with the master mailbox, using the Network Connection option.

When a user uses the GroupWise client in Remote mode configured with a network connection instead of a modem connection, the Async gateway is not used, and the message follows the path illustrated in Figure 19.15. (Note the file system rights that the user needs to the <post office>\OFWORK\OFDIRECT\ <CONN ID> directory.)

FIGURE 19.15

Message Flow Through a Network Connection

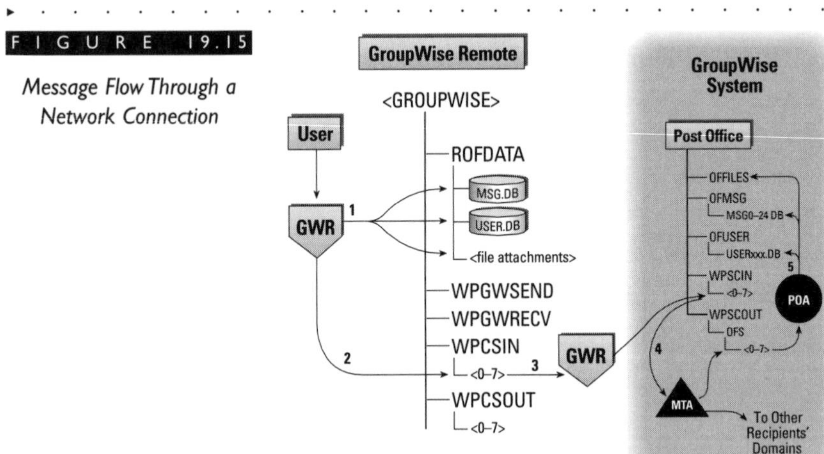

The steps are as follows:

1 • A remote user creates a request. GroupWise Remote places a copy of the message in the MSG.DB, updates the USER.DB, and places any file attachments in the ROFDATA directory.

2 • The GroupWise client running in Remote mode then inserts the request in the local post office's WPCSIN\1 directory.

3 • When a connection is initiated by the user, GroupWise Remote places the message or the request in the post office WPCSIN\1 directory. (Note: GroupWise users will need Write, Create, Modify, and File Scan rights to this directory if using a network connection in Remote mode.)

4 • The MTA delivers the request to the WPCSOUT\OFS\1 directory. (In the diagram, we assume that the user connects to the home post office. If the user accesses a post office other than the home post office, the MTA will route the request to the appropriate MTA for processing.)

5 • The POA processes the request by updating the message store databases or retrieving the requested information.

Figure 19.16 shows the *status back*—the response being delivered back to the GroupWise Remote user through the network connection.

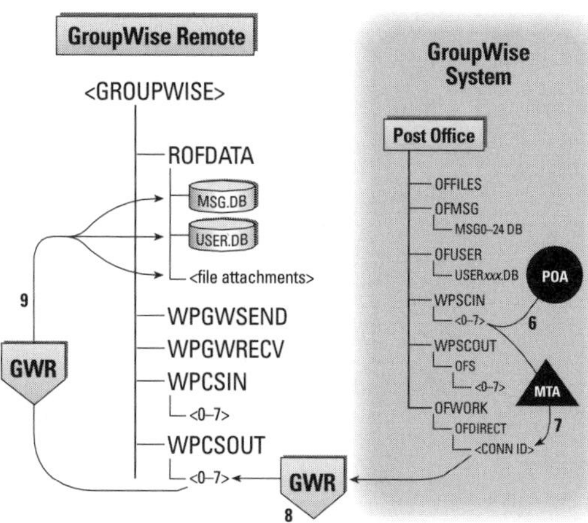

FIGURE 19.16

Response Delivered to the GroupWise Remote Client

The next steps are as follows:

6 • The POA places the status message or the response in the post office WPCSIN\1 directory.

7 • The MTA picks up the message and places it in the OFWORK\DIRECT\<*connection ID*> directory specific to the remote user.

8 • If the remote connection is still valid—in other words, if the GroupWise client is still polling the post office for the response—GroupWise picks up the message from the <*connection ID*> directory and inserts the message into the local WPCSOUT\OFS\1 directory.

GroupWise then updates the remote databases.

Summary

In this chapter, you learned how to plan an Async gateway implementation and how to install, set up, and configure an Async gateway to connect domains and support GroupWise remote users. You also learned how messages flow through an Async configuration.

CHAPTER 20

The SMTP/MIME Gateway and Internet Mail

This chapter explains the steps necessary to connect your GroupWise system to the Internet.

We focus on the GroupWise SMTP/MIME gateway installation and configuration. We also explain how to create a foreign domain to simplify addressing, and we give you some tips on gateway maintenance and troubleshooting.

The chapter covers TCP/IP and Internet connectivity basics. As with earlier chapters dealing with TCP/IP (for example, Chapter 12 and Chapter 15), we won't go into much detail about DNS server configuration, router technology, or firewalls. For more information about these topics, refer to *Novell's Guide to TCP/IP and IntranetWare* by Drew Heywood (published by Novell Press and IDG Books Worldwide), or take one of Novell Education's TCP/IP courses.

SMTP/MIME Gateway Overview

The SMTP/MIME gateway for GroupWise provides message translation and transfer to and from the Internet. This translation is necessary because GroupWise's message format is very proprietary, and it is not compatible (natively) with Internet mail.

The Internet's standard for e-mail is Simple Mail Transfer Protocol (SMTP). This standard was developed by RFC 821 in 1982 and has certain rules. In June of 1992, a new Internet mail standard was approved (RFC 1341). This new standard is known as MIME, which stands for Multipurpose Internet Mail Extensions. MIME builds upon the SMTP standard by adding new fields for mail message headers that describe new types of message content.

Novell created the latest version of the SMTP gateway in 1996 to allow MIME support, and they continue to update the gateway's process and capabilities.

As of this writing, the most current version is v. 4.11. The 4.1 SMTP gateway works fine with GroupWise 5 as long as you apply the patch. We have included the patch for the SMTP/MIME gateway on the CD, in a file called SMTP1.EXE. You can obtain the latest file updates for GroupWise gateways on the Internet at

```
http://support.novell.com/Ftp/Updates/gateways/Date0.html
```

(Note: This URL is case-sensitive.)

This self-extracting file will create a SMTP1.TXT file that leads you through installation of the patch.

The gateway is available in three platforms: NetWare Loadable Module (NLM), Windows NT, and UNIX. We will focus on the NLM version of the gateway, to stay consistent with the rest of the book.

As we stated before, the main purpose of the SMTP/MIME gateway is to communicate with anyone over the Internet. You could also use this gateway to communicate with other GroupWise domains over the Internet. To do this, install and configure the SMTP/MIME gateway for both domains, follow the procedures in Chapter 11 for setting up external domains, and configure a gateway link between them as detailed in Chapter 10.

This chapter focuses on using the gateway to communicate with e-mail users on the Internet.

Planning

Planning the SMTP gateway involves four areas:

- TCP/IP
- Mail Routing
- Internet Addressing
- GroupWise Requirements

TCP/IP

The SMTP/MIME gateway uses a TCP/IP connection to send messages to another SMTP mail host.

FIGURE 20.1

Sending SMTP Mail

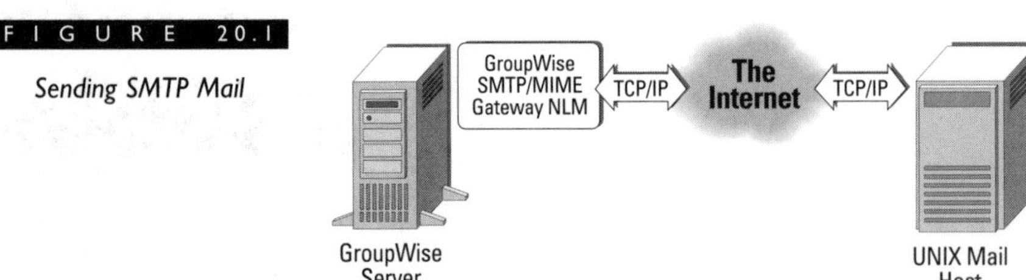

As you can see in Figure 20.1, the main requirement for your system is loading TCP/IP.NLM on the server (NetWare in this case), and specifying all of the accompanying settings:

- *IP Address.* The server must have its own unique IP address, such as the following example:

  `151.155.233.1`

- *DNS.* The server must be able to find the Domain Name System (DNS) to resolve the host name in the mail address (to the right of the "@" sign) to an IP address. This is accomplished in the SYS:ETC\RESOLV.CFG file:

  `domain       shicktools.com` (The host name of this server)

  `nameserver  151.155.233.6` (The IP address of the DNS server)

  In addition to finding the DNS server, the DNS database itself must be changed to allow mail addressed to users at the host name for your company to be routed to the server running the gateway software.

  This is done by adding or changing the Mail Exchange (MX) record in the DNS database. (Note: The exact steps for editing the DNS database depend on which version of DNS software you or your ISP are running.)

  The record that needs to be added will look like the following:

  ```
  shicktools.com    MX    151.155.233.1
  ```

When anyone sends mail to users at "shicktools.com," the mail will be routed to the server at 151.155.233.1, and the sending mail host will make a connection to the GroupWise SMTP/MIME gateway on that server.

- *Gateway.* The gateway setting is specified when the IP protocol is bound to the network interface card. It identifies the IP address of the server acting as a portal to the Internet. This could be a firewall server or physical router to the Internet.

To verify that TCP/IP has been loaded on the NetWare server, follow these steps:

1 • At the server console, type LOAD PING.

2 • Enter the IP address of the DNS server in the IP address field, press Enter, and Escape.

3 • If you have a valid IP data packet transmit and receive rate, the server can route TCP/IP packets.

To verify DNS and Internet connectivity, follow these steps:

1 • From a workstation with TCP/IP loaded on it, log into the network.

2 • From a DOS prompt, enter the following command:
C:\WINDOWS>ping novell.com

3 • If you get a response from an IP address, you have TCP/IP packets routing to Novell's server, and DNS successfully translated the "novell.com" host name to an IP address.

If you don't get a response, you still may have set things up right. It might be that your router doesn't allow "ping traffic" through to the Internet, but SMTP traffic will go just fine.

Mail Routing

The SMTP gateway has two options for sending mail to the Internet. The gateway can either send mail to any host on the Internet, or it can forward all outgoing mail to another mail host, possibly the mail host of your ISP. From there, the ISP's mail host would forward the mail to its destination.

The Direct to Recipient option assumes that the server on which the gateway is running can make an SMTP connection to another host anywhere on the Internet. Furthermore, it also assumes that any mail host on the Internet can connect to TCP/IP port 25 (the port that is dedicated for SMTP mail) on your server.

Certain firewalls and routers disallow this open connectivity, and your physical connection—for example, through an Internet service provider (ISP)—might also limit your connectivity. In this case, you would use the Forward to Mail Host option.

TABLE 20.1

Mail Send Options Advantages and Disadvantages

MAIL SEND OPTION	ADVANTAGES	DISADVANTAGES
Direct to Recipient	Faster throughput	Open ports to the Internet
	End-to-End messaging	
Forward to Mail Host	One connection open to known quantity	Slower throughput
		ISP can intercept messages

Internet Addressing

We will examine later how to set up Internet addresses for the GroupWise system and its users. In the planning phase, your company has to register a host name with InterNIC. (See Chapter 15 for more information about IP addresses.) Most Internet service providers offer domain name registration as a service, and for a reasonable price they will manage the process of obtaining a unique host name for your company on the Internet. In an Internet mail address, this is the information to the right of the @ symbol, such as "shicktools.com."

GroupWise Requirements

In order to install the SMTP/MIME gateway, the MTA, ADA, and POA processes must be up and running with no closed facilities because the SMTP/MIME gateway acts very much like a post office. This means the MTA will move messages from the sender's post office to the gateway. Message flow is covered later in the chapter.

As we explain in Chapter 3, you need to know in which domain the gateway will be located, who is going to have access to it, and on which server the gateway software will run.

Installation and Configuration

Once you have formulated a plan for connecting your GroupWise system to the Internet, you are ready to begin the process of installing and configuring the SMTP/MIME gateway.

Installing the Software

The SMTP/MIME gateway software needs to be installed on the server from which it is going to be executed. This server needs physical connectivity to the server on which the domain is located, because some files will be installed in the domain directory.

Before you install the gateway, the gateway software needs to be accessible from the server. If the SMTP/MIME gateway software is on a CD, you need to mount the CD on the server as a volume. If it is on a diskette, insert it in the floppy drive of the server. You do not need to unload any of the GroupWise agents to install or run the SMTP / MIME gateway.

Follow these steps to install the SMTP/MIME gateway:

1. At the server prompt, type LOAD INSTALL.
2. Choose Product Options and then Install a Product not Listed.
3. If the software is in the floppy drive, press Enter. If it is on a CD-ROM mounted as a volume, press the F3 key and enter the path to the

SMTP/MIME gateway software; for example, GW5CD:SMTP\NLM. You'll see the SMTP Gateway Installation screen shown in Figure 20.2.

FIGURE 20.2

SMTP/MIME Gateway Installation

4 • Fill in the fields of the Installation screen (table 20.2 explains them) then use the arrow keys to highlight Install. Press Enter.

5 • The files will be installed to the location you specified and you will return to the Install/Product Options screen. Press Esc to exit Install.

TABLE 20.2

Install Field Description

INSTALL FIELD	DESCRIPTION
Install From	Location of source files
Domain path	NetWare path to the domain the gateway will belong to
Gateway Directory	Directory name under *domain*\WPGATE where the gateway's database will be located
Gateway NLMs	NetWare path of the location of the gateway NLMs
Convert drivers	NetWare path of the files used to convert messages between GroupWise and the Internet
Load Script	NetWare path to where the SMTP.NCF load file is stored

Creating the Gateway Object

Once the software has been installed, the next step is creating the gateway object in NDS.

NOTE

This step assumes that the SMTP gateway DLL was copied to the SYS:PUBLIC directory during the original software installation. If it was not, refer to Chapter 18 for instructions on installing the gateway administration DLL files to NetWare Administrator.

To create the SMTP/MIME gateway object, follow these steps:

1 • From NetWare Administrator, choose GroupWise System Operations from the Tools menu.

2 • Double-click the System Connection icon and select the domain to which the gateway will belong. Click on Connect to continue.

3 • From the main screen of NetWare Administrator, highlight the domain to which the gateway will belong. Right-click and select Create from the shortcut menu.

4 • Select GroupWise Gateway from the list and click OK. You'll see the dialog box shown in Figure 20.3.

FIGURE 20.3

Creating the SMTP/MIME Gateway

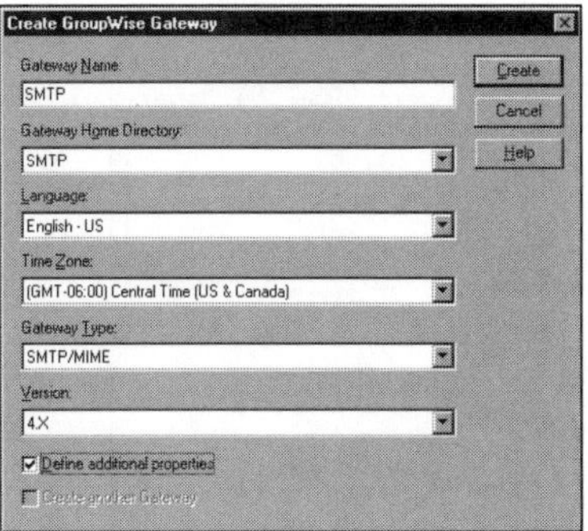

5 • Fill in the following fields (see Figure 20.3).

- *Gateway Name.* A name for the gateway, such as "SMTP."
- *Gateway Home Directory.* Select the SMTP directory (the location of the gateway database).
- *Language.* English-US

- *Time Zone.* Time zone of the computer running the gateway software.
- *Gateway Type.* SMTP/MIME
- Version. 4.x

6 • Select Define Additional Properties and click on OK to continue (see Figure 20.4).

7 • Define the additional properties as specified in the following list and click OK (see Figure 20.4).

- *Description.* A description of the gateway.
- *Platform.* Select NetWare Loadable Module.
- *Gateway Alias Type.* Used to customize addresses for users, usually the same name as the gateway.
- *Foreign ID.* The Internet host name for use in Internet messages and addresses, e.g., shicktools.com.

FIGURE 20.4

SMTP/MIME Information Page

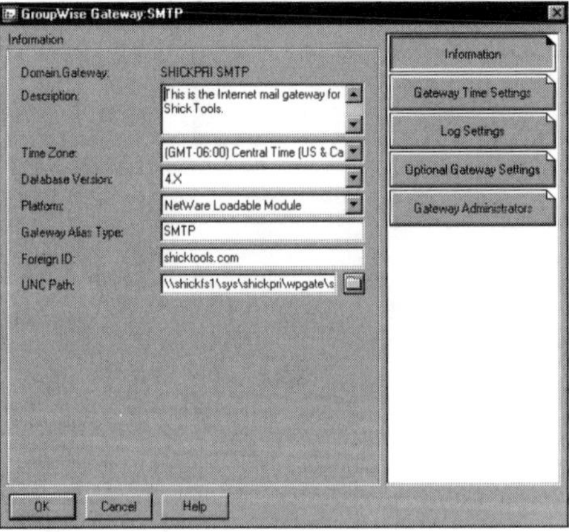

After the Gateway object has been created, you will still need to configure the gateway before it can be loaded.

Configuring the Gateway

You can configure the SMTP/MIME gateway in three places:

- The gateway property pages in NetWare Administrator
- The gateway configuration file
- The gateway screen

Property Pages

By editing the Gateway object in NetWare Administrator and accessing the property pages, you can change the standard information about the gateway. The standard gateway information includes time settings, log settings, optional settings, and gateway administrator.

Gateway Time Settings The gateway time settings, shown in Figure 20.5, tell the SMTP/MIME gateway how often to poll its message queues for messages to and from the Internet.

FIGURE 20.5

Gateway Time Settings

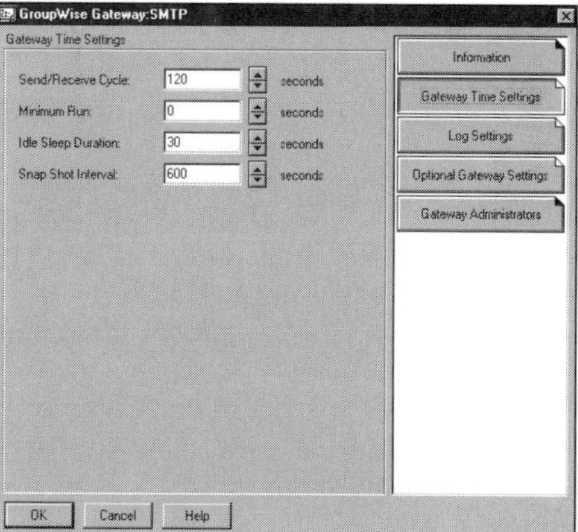

- *Send/Receive Cycle.* Total amount of time the gateway spends sending and receiving messages. The time is split in half for sending and receiving. For example, the default of 120 seconds means that 60 seconds will be used to send messages and 60 seconds will be used to receive messages.

- *Minimum Run.* Amount of time to stay connected to the other system; should be zero in most cases.
- *Idle Sleep Duration.* Time between scans of the input queues in and out of the gateway.
- *Snap Shot Interval.* Time interval between gateway screen updates.

Log Settings The log settings control the following logging features:

- *Logging Level.* Sets the amount of log information (Off, Normal, Verbose, or Diagnostic) to be displayed on the gateway screen and added to the log file on the disk.
- *Max Log File Age.* Age at which old log files are removed from the server.
- *Max Log File Disk Space.* Maximum size for log files (0 is unlimited).

Optional Gateway Settings The optional settings are as follows:

- *Directory/Sync.* Not applicable to the SMTP/MIME gateway.
- *Accounting.* Change to "Yes" if you configure an accountant administrator (see below).
- *Convert Status to Messages.* Select "No" for the SMTP/MIME gateway.
- *Outbound Status Level.* GroupWise action to trigger a message returned to the sender. "Undeliverable" is a good choice.
- *Enable Recovery.* Select "Yes" so the gateway will try to reestablish the connection to the Internet.
- *Retry Count.* Number of times the gateway tries to reconnect.
- *Retry Interval.* Interval between reconnect tries.

- *Failed Recovery Wait.* Interval to wait between a failed recovery and a retry.
- *Network Reattach.* Commands for reattaching to the foreign system.
- *Correlation Enabled.* Enable or disable correlation of foreign status messages to known GroupWise messages. Not used with the SMTP/MIME gateway.
- *Correlation Age.* Number of days the correlation record will be kept in the correlation database, GWCORR.DB.

Gateway Administrator You can also designate gateway administrators on the Gateway Administrators property page. The *gateway administrator* is the person who receives error messages and other reports related to the operation of the SMTP/MIME gateway.

Follow these steps to designate a gateway administrator:

1 • From the Gateway Administrator page, click on Add, select a user or distribution list as an administrator, and select the administrator type applicable to the SMTP/MIME gateway:
   - *Operator.* Receives error messages
   - *Accountant.* Receives a daily message with an attachment of all gateway activity—incoming and outgoing messages, with user information.

2 • Click OK to return to the main NetWare Administrator screen.

Gateway Configuration File (GWSMTP.CFG)

In addition to configuring the gateway using NetWare Administrator, you need to correctly specify some additional settings in the gateway configuration file (GWSMTP.CFG). You can use this file (for purposes ranging from customization to troubleshooting) to override the settings made in NetWare Administrator.

The GWSMTP.CFG file contains the most comprehensive collection of settings for the SMTP/MIME gateway. An ASCII text file located in the directory *domain*\WPGATE\SMTP, it tells the SMTP NLMs how to behave.

NOTE

There are two other configuration files: ACCESS.CFG (for restricting access to the gateway based on the Internet domain name), and MIMETYPE.CFG (for configuring file attachment associations for MIME attachments). Refer to the GroupWise SMTP/MIME gateway documentation and the files themselves for more information.

The GWSMTP.CFG file is divided into the following sections:

- **Required Switches.** Switches required for the SMTP/MIME gateway.
- **Outbound Encoding Switches.** Switches that specify the default outbound gateway encoding. The gateway will automatically process any type of inbound message received according to the message's format type.
- **Optional Gateway Switches.** Optional switches for customizing the behavior of the gateway for your environment.
- **Log File Switches.** Settings for the logging of the gateway.
- **Daemon Switches.** Switches that apply to the daemon portion of the gateway only. A *daemon* is a secondary portion of the gateway—GWSMTPD.NLM—that connects with other SMTP mail hosts and actually transfers the messages.
- **Daemon Timeouts.** Daemon timeout parameters are provided if you have a slow network connection. They specify how long (in minutes) the daemon will wait before giving up on necessary data. Do not change these settings unless you are experiencing communication problems.

Table 20.3 describes the most critical switches. For more information, see the actual GWSMTP.CFG file.

TABLE 20.3

Gateway Configuration Switches

SWITCH	DESCRIPTION
`/home`-*path to gateway*	This switch sets the full path to the location of the gateway under the domain directory.
`/dhome`-*path to daemon's send/receive queues*	This switch sets the path to the daemon's send and receive queues.
`/ARI=never`	This switch turns off additional routing information for return mail.
`/user`-*GroupWise access account*	This switch sets the login ID used to log into a remote file server to access the domain database and gateway directories.
`/password`-*access account password*	This switch sets the password used to log into a remote file server to access the domain database and gateway directories.
`/hn`-*registered domain name*	This switch sets the registered Internet domain host name to be used in the SMTP connection dialog. It should be set to your Internet domain name, including the suffix (for example, .com).

In addition to using NetWare Administrator and the GWSMTP.CFG file, you can configure some of these settings directly from the SMTP/MIME gateway monitor screen (see the section "Using the Gateway Monitor"). This is discussed in the next section. Once the SMTP/MIME gateway has been configured, you are ready to run the gateway software.

Loading the SMTP/MIME Gateway

The SMTP.NCF file is created when you install the SMTP/MIME gateway. It is used to load the two SMTP NLMs: GWSMTP.NLM and SMTPD.NLM. The GWSMTP.NLM is the main SMTP gateway program and the SMTPD.NLM is the SMTP daemon.

We recommend that you call the SMTP.NCF file from the AUTOEXEC.NCF file for the file server running the gateway. You can do this by adding the `smtp` command after the GroupWise NLMs are loaded (by invoking the GRPWISE command):

```
search add sys:gwroute\wpgate\smtp

search add sys:gwroute\wpgate\smtp\gwcnvrt

load sys:gwroute\wpgate\smtp\gwsmtpd @gwsmtp.cfg

load sys:gwroute\wpgate\smtp\gwsmtp @gwsmtp.cfg
```

When you need to unload the gateway, be sure to unload the two NLMs in reverse order. When you exit the gateway, only the GWSMTP.NLM file is removed from memory. You must manually unload the daemon program, SMTPD.NLM, by using the UNLOAD command at the server prompt:

```
UNLOAD GWSMTPD
```

Using the Gateway Monitor

The *gateway monitor* is used to view all gateway activity as well as to change a few settings for the current session. Changes that you make in the gateway monitor are not saved; the next time that the gateway loads, it will use the settings specified in NDS and the GWSMTP.CFG file. Figure 20.6 shows a sample gateway monitor screen.

FIGURE 20.6

SMTP/MIME Gateway Monitor

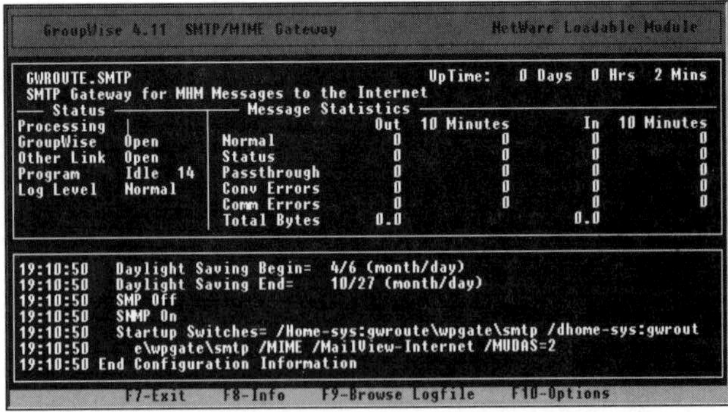

The following areas of the gateway monitor are important for gateway administration:

- *Gateway Operations.* Displays the processing status and the idle time between scans for messages to send or translate.
- *Message Statistics.* Displays the number of incoming and outgoing messages of different types (messages, status, etc.) as a total and within the last 10 minutes. This information is updated by the "Snap Shot Interval" setting in NetWare Administrator.
- *Log Window.* The information that scrolls through this portion of the screen is being written to the log file. If the log level is set to diagnostic, detailed information about gateway commands will appear in this screen.
- *Hotkey Operations.* The following hotkey operations are enabled for the SMTP/MIME gateway:
  - **F7** Exits and unloads the GWSMTP.NLM.
  - **F8** Displays settings for the gateway in the Log Window.
  - **F9** Opens the current log file for browsing, (Arrow keys and PgUp and PgDn are used for navigating the log files; F1 returns to the main screen.)
  - **F10** Displays options for the gateway.
  - **F2** Toggles the log level, which is displayed in the Gateway Operations portion of the gateway monitor.
  - **F6** Allows you to change the colors of the gateway monitor.
  - **F8** Used to "zero out" the message statistics.
  - **F9** Replaces the message statistics with daemon statistics (see Figure 20.7).

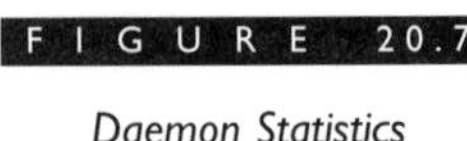

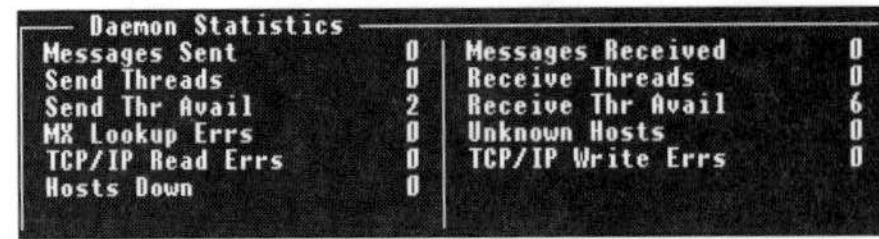

FIGURE 20.7

Daemon Statistics

Addressing

In the past, when you wanted to contact someone, you would ask for a phone number. Today it's becoming more common to ask for an e-mail address. If you had to give your full GroupWise address (domain, post office, and user ID) to everyone who asked for your e-mail address, people would probably stop asking you for it before too long. That's why most users prefer to give out Internet-style addresses.

The purpose of this subsection is to explain how common Internet mail addresses can be defined and managed in GroupWise.

Unless you've been on Mars for the last five years, you probably already know that an Internet mail address looks something like the following:

```
user@domain.suffix
```

For example,

```
carlys@acme.com
```

The rest of this section talks about how to set up Internet addressing for easy management and use.

Foreign ID of the SMTP/MIME Gateway

The first task in building an Internet address is defining the information about your company (for example, ShickTools). This is done in the "Foreign ID" field of the SMTP/MIME gateway in NetWare Administrator.

You should place in this field the Internet domain name and suffix that was assigned to your company. Your entry in this field will be placed to the right of the @ symbol in the From: field of every piece of Internet mail that your users send out.

By specifying an Internet domain name for the gateway, it is assumed that DNS has been changed to route Internet mail for that domain to the server running the GroupWise SMTP/MIME gateway. For information about configuring DNS, see the TCP/IP section earlier in this chapter.

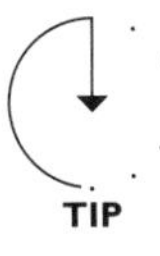
TIP

It is possible to specify more than one Internet domain name in the Foreign ID field of the gateway. Simply separate them with a space. This is useful if you want the same gateway to route messages for more than one Internet domain name. For more information, see the technical document called NGOUSSMT.EXE about the SMTP/MIME gateway on this book's companion CD.

Gateway Alias Type

The next piece of information you need to specify is the Gateway Alias Type (see Figure 20.8). This is an identifier of the custom address type you can define for each user. It is used together with the user's properties to allow messages to be sent to an Internet address with one user ID and to be delivered into another GroupWise mailbox with a different user ID.

The Gateway Alias Type is a property of the gateway object, and it is specified with NetWare Administrator.

Gateway Alias User Property

If you want a user's GroupWise ID to be different from his or her Internet e-mail address user ID, you can define it with the Gateway Alias User Property. All of the user aliases are built into an alias table, to be used by the gateway for routing the mail.

FIGURE 20.8

Gateway Alias User Property

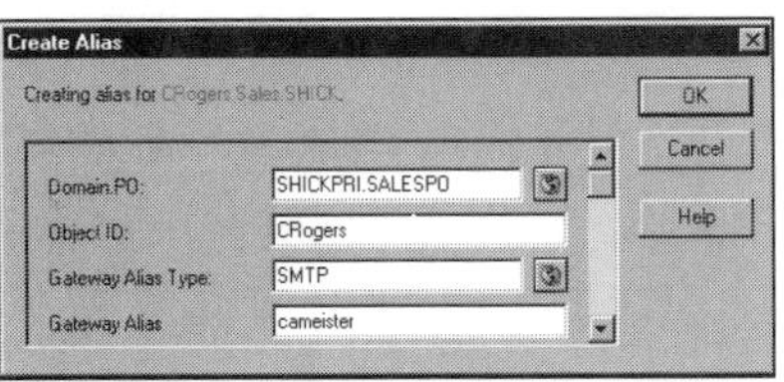

For outgoing Internet mail, the information specified here will be placed to the left of the @ symbol in the From: field of the message.

For incoming Internet mail, the address in the To: field of the message will be compared with the alias table. If a match is found, the gateway cross-references the alias with the GroupWise User ID and sends the message on its way.

Foreign Domains

Using foreign domains is the most straightforward way you can enable Internet mail addressing for your users. The foreign domain is used to represent any non-GroupWise mail system, and the link from GroupWise to the foreign domain is always a gateway link.

We recommend creating a foreign domain called INTERNET, and using it for addressing messages to the Internet. The SMTP/MIME gateway will be the link to the Internet foreign domain.

The addressing form for sending Internet mail will look like the following:

Internet:user@whatever.com

Follow these steps to create a foreign domain and set up a gateway link to it:

1 • From NetWare Administrator, choose the GroupWise View option under the Tools menu.

2 • Right-click the GroupWise system and choose Create from the short menu.

3 • Select External Domain from the list of new objects (see Figure 20.9).

4 • Fill in the External Domain name as Internet, change the Domain Type Field to External Foreign and click on Create. (Note: Details about external domains are covered in Chapter 11.)

5 • To set up the link from the GroupWise domain to the foreign domain, click on GroupWise Utilities from the Tools menu and select Link Configuration Tool (see Figure 20.10).

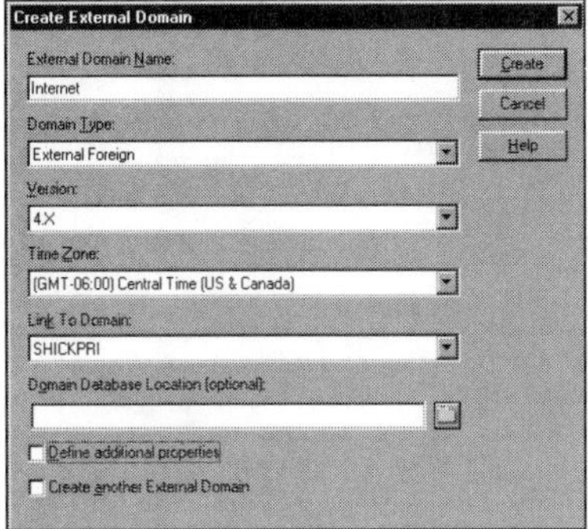

FIGURE 20.9

Foreign Domain Detail

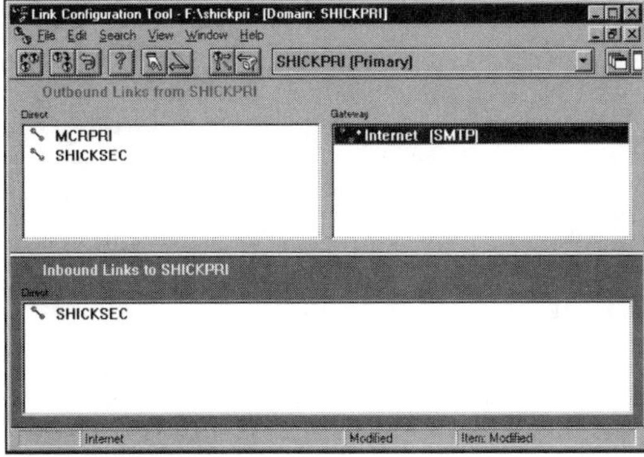

FIGURE 20.10

Gateway Link to the Internet Foreign Domain

6 • In the Current Domain drop-down list box, select the Primary domain of your system.

7 • From the View menu, select Gateway to view the gateway link box.

8 • Click the Internet domain in the Direct Link box, and drag it to the Gateway link box. You'll see the dialog box in Figure 20.11.

9 • In the Edit Link dialog box, select the SMTP/MIME gateway (by name) from the Gateway Link drop-down list. Click OK.

10 • Click the Save option from the Edit menu to save the link to the current domain database.

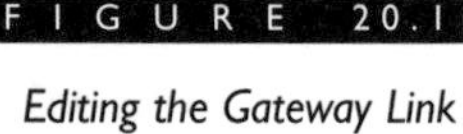
FIGURE 20.11

Editing the Gateway Link

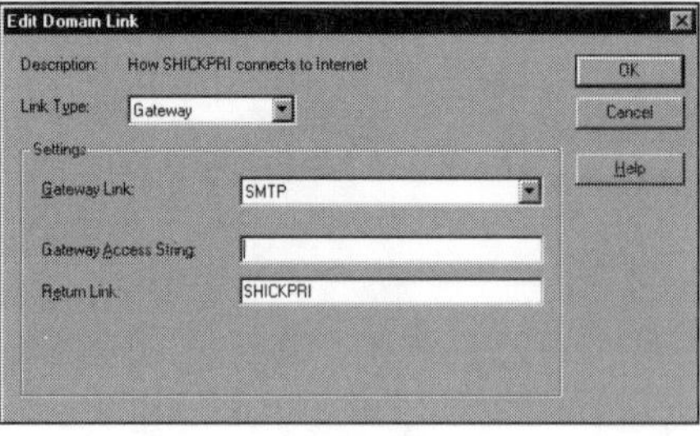

From the MTA screen, verify that the MTA restarts and that the link to the Internet foreign domain is defined as a gateway link. Also verify that the gateway is listed in the Status area and that it is in an open state. Use the F10 key to see details about the link to the foreign domain.

See Chapter 12 for information about setting up the agents.

You are now ready to send messages between GroupWise and the Internet.

Operation of the Gateway

As discussed in the previous section, you can use explicit addressing to send a message to the Internet from the GroupWise client. A GroupWise foreign domain with an SMTP/MIME gateway link is used to route Internet mail. As we explained in Chapter 3, when you plan your GroupWise system, you will specify which domain the gateways will belong to. As long as the sender's domain has a link to the gateway's domain, explicit addressing can be used. The message will hop from one domain to another until it reaches the gateway's domain.

Once the message has reached the gateway's domain, the MTA will route any messages to the Internet foreign domain to the SMTP/MIME gateway, where the Internet address, message body, and attachments will be converted, and the SMTP-formatted message will be sent on its way. The details of this message flow are discussed later in this chapter.

As an administrator, you should tell your users about the following potential limitations of sending mail over the Internet:

- **Security.** SMTP-formatted messages are not encrypted with the same encryption that GroupWise uses internally. Messages sent over the

Internet can be read by any number of Internet mail client programs. GroupWise-specific message types (such as a phone message, for example) will be converted to a regular text message, and any special formatting will be lost (such as colors, fonts, and other rich text). As a general rule, sensitive material should not be sent over the Internet. (Note: Any recipients placed in the blind copy (BC:) field in a GroupWise message addressed to someone over the Internet will be displayed as recipients of the message, thereby defeating the purpose of blind copy.)

- **Throughput.** Once the message leaves your SMTP/MIME gateway, there is a potential for delays as the message makes its way over the Internet to the recipient's mail host.
- **Attachment Conversions.** Because attachments to Internet messages are encoded for transfer over the Internet, they stand a chance of losing some formatting or other important characters during the conversion process.

Maintenance

The SMTP/MIME gateway is pretty much maintenance-free once it is set up and working correctly. The only ongoing maintenance is running "PURGE/ALL" from the volume on which the gateway is installed, to purge the queue directories of sent and received messages that have been deleted by the gateway.

Log Files

The log files, created in the <domain>\WPGATE\SMTP\000.PRC directory, are standard ASCII text files. The information contained in them will help you troubleshoot problems and give you an idea of the current settings that are being used by the gateway.

The log level, specified in NetWare Administrator, GWSMTP.CFG, and on the gateway monitor screen itself, will determine how much information is contained in the log files. We recommend using "Verbose" when you are installing the gateway, and "Normal" after it is stable.

The SMTP/MIME Gateway Directory Structure

Table 20.1 gives you an idea of the more important files and directories used by the SMTP/MIME gateway. All of these files and directories are located under the SYS:<*domain*>\WPGATE\SMTP directory, with the exception of the SMTP.NCF file, which is located in the SYS:SYSTEM directory.

TABLE 20.4

Gateway Files and Directories

FILES AND DIRECTORIES	EXPLANATION
SMTP.NCF	Load script for the gateway
README.TXT	Informational file about the gateway
GWSMTP.NLM	Main SMTP/MIME gateway NLM file
GWSMTPD.NLM	SMTP/MIME daemon NLM file
GWSMTP.MIB	SNMP MIB file for the gateway
ACCESS.CFG	Text configuration file for controlling access to the gateway
MIMETYPE.CFG	Configuration file for MIME encoding
GWCORR.DC	Correlation database template
GWSMTP.CFG	Main SMTP/MIME configuration file
GWCNVRT directory	Working directory for conversion of messages and attachments
WPCSIN directory	MTA input queue for messages from the Internet
WPCSOUT directory	MTA output queue for messages going out to the Internet

Message Flow

Understanding the flow of messages between the SMTP/MIME gateway and the GroupWise system is extremely useful for troubleshooting. This subsection discusses the flow of messages in both directions: from GroupWise to the Internet and from the Internet into the GroupWise system.

GroupWise to the Internet

Figure 20.12 shows the flow of a message sent from GroupWise to an Internet user through the SMTP/MIME gateway.

FIGURE 20.12

GroupWise to Internet Message Flow

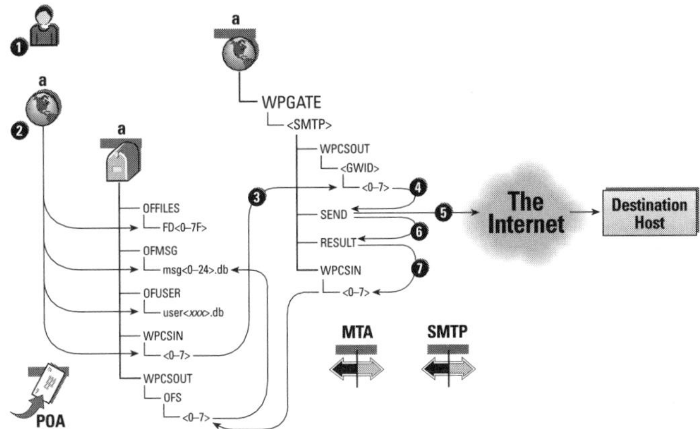

The following steps describe what happens when a message is sent from GroupWise to an Internet user:

1. The GroupWise client addresses an Internet mail message and chooses "Send."

2. The message is stored in the information store of the sender, and is copied to the <post office>\WPCSIN\0–7 directory for transfer out of the post office.

3. The MTA picks up the message, determines from the address format and link information that it needs to be passed to the SMTP/MIME gateway, and moves it to the <domain>\WPGATE\SMTP\WPCSOUT\<gateway ID>\0–7 directory.

4. The SMTP/MIME gateway, on one of its scan cycles, picks up the message file, converts the address, message body, and attachment(s) to SMTP format, and places the message file into the <domain>\WPGATE\SMTP\SEND directory. (Note: The message file name has the letter "S" as the first character at this point.)

5 • The SMTP/MIME gateway daemon scans the SEND directory, establishes a connection with the destination SMTP mail host (which is found by looking up the IP address using DNS), and transfers the SMTP message to the recipient's SMTP mail host.

6 • The SMTP/MIME gateway daemon creates a results file (named with the same filename as above, but with an "R" as the first character) in the <domain>\WPGATE\SMTP\RESULT directory. The "S" file is also moved to the RESULT directory.

7 • The SMTP/MIME gateway analyzes the "R" and "S" files, comparing the result codes. If there is a code of 250 in the "R" file, a "Transferred" status message is created in the <domain>\WPGATE\SMTP\WPCSIN\0–7 directory, after which the MTA moves it to the sender's post office. The POA then updates the message record with the Transferred status.

For more information on other result codes, see the online help file called GWGSS.HLP in the SYS:PUBLIC\NLS\ENGLISH directory.

Internet to the GroupWise System

Figure 20.13 shows the flow of an Internet message through the SMTP/MIME gateway into a GroupWise system.

FIGURE 20.13

Internet Mail Message Flow Into the GroupWise System

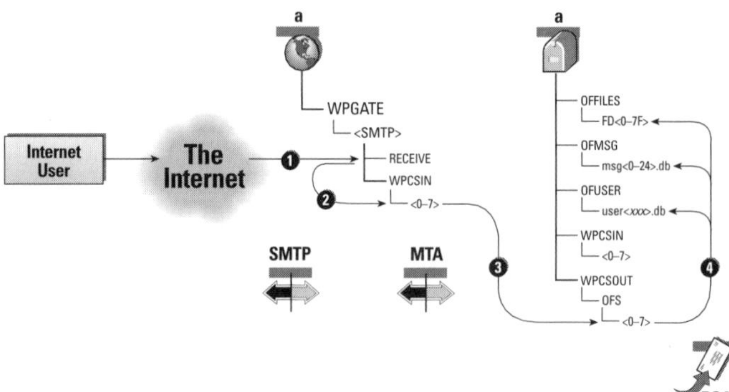

The following steps describe the flow of an Internet message into the GroupWise system.

1 • An Internet mail user addresses a message to a GroupWise user, and the sender's SMTP mail host establishes a connection (found by the MX record in DNS for the GroupWise system) to the SMTP/MIME gateway daemon, which creates a message file in the <domain>\WPGATE\SMTP\RECEIVE directory.

2 • The SMTP/MIME gateway scans the RECEIVE directory, converts the SMTP address, message body, and attachment(s) to GroupWise format, and places the GroupWise message file in the <domain>\WPGATE\SMTP\WPCSIN\4 directory.

3 • The MTA picks up the message file on one of its scan cycles, and transfers the message file to the recipient's <post office>\WPCSOUT\OFS\0–7 directory.

4 • The POA then delivers the message into the recipient's information store.

SMTP/MIME Gateway Troubleshooting

Most of the troubleshooting tasks involve Ping and Telnet. PING.NLM is available on the file server, but is limited to using the SYS:\ETC\HOSTS file. It does not use DNS. In order to overcome these limitations, we recommend that you try PING.NLM with host entries, or use a separate workstation if you are using DNS. If you need to use a separate workstation, try to make sure it is on the same LAN segment as the file server with the SMTP NLM gateway. It should have a TCP/IP stack loaded on it and *must* be using the same DNS server. (When a troubleshooting procedure requires using Ping or Telnet, you should use a TCP/IP-enabled workstation due to these limitations.)

The remainder of this section explains some of the most common error messages encountered by GroupWise administrators. Most of the solutions presented are configuration changes, by editing either NetWare Administrator or the GWSMTP.CFG or other configuration files.

`NGWSMTP: NGWLIB version sync error - load library 101`

This error indicates you are using the incorrect version of NGWLIB. Remove all copies of NGWLIB.NLM and only use the NGWLIB.NLM in the *domain*\WPGATE\SMTP directory.

NOTE

This is only an issue if you are using GroupWise 4 message servers. If you are using GroupWise 5 agents on the server, the GroupWise 4 gateways will be the only processes using the NGWLIB.NLM file.

The GroupWise 4.1 Message Server NLM pack copies its NGWLIB.NLM into the SYSTEM directory, but the SMTP NLM gateway installation copies its upgraded version of NGWLIB.NLM into the *domain*\WPGATE\SMTP directory. It is usually sufficient to copy the WPGATE\SMTP\NGWLIB.NLM into the system directory and restart the gateway.

`SMTP Daemon-Error: /HN-host name must be specified`

All mail in and out of the gateway has stopped. This error indicates that the gateway cannot identify its host name.

Define the `/hn-`*host* startup option in the GWSMTP.CFG file. See "Gateway Configuration Files" earlier in this chapter.

Alternately, you could add the server's host name and IP address to the SYS:\ETC\HOSTS file.

`Error 550 host unknown`

This error message indicates that the gateway daemon is unable to resolve an alphanumeric address (Internet domain name) to an IP address (numeric).

Make sure the address is correct. Try to ping the alphanumeric address from a workstation. If you can ping the alphanumeric address, the gateway should not get a 550 host unknown error.

Next, configure the TCP/IP kernel on the server to use a Domain Name System (DNS) server.

`Error 450 MX Record Lookup Failure`

This error message indicates that the gateway daemon's attempt to query a Domain Name System server to resolve an alphanumeric address to an IP address has failed. The Gateway will attempt to deliver the message again later.

The TCP/IP kernel may not be configured properly to query DNS. See "TCP/IP" earlier in this chapter for information on configuring a RESOLV.CFG for DNS.

GWSMTPD may have been executed with an incorrect address format following the `/mh` switch. When using the `/mh` switch, you *must* use the numeric IP address.

Correct format: `gwsmtpd /hn-orem.novell.com /mh-151.155.225.124`

Incorrect format: `gwsmtpd /hn-orem.novell.com /mh-bolo.orem.novell.com`

If you can ping the desired address, log in to the DNS machine and type `nslookup` *`alphanumeric address`*. If the nslookup command can resolve the address, the SMTP gateway will be able to resolve it (as long as the IN A record or IN MX record is correct).

Example: `nslookup honey.utah.orem.com`

Error 450 host down

This error message indicates that the sending portion of the SMTP gateway has successfully resolved the alphanumeric address to an IP address, but the attempt to connect to port 25 of that IP address has failed. The SMTP gateway will attempt to send the message again later.

From the troubleshooting workstation suggested in the introduction above, telnet to port 25 of the intended machine (for example, enter `telnet` *`host_name`* `25` at a command prompt). If the telnet fails, this is the cause of the error message. The gateway will be unable to send any messages to that machine until a listening agent answers on port 25. If it does answer but takes a while, increase the timeout value of GWSMTPD (`/te-`*minutes*). The default value is two minutes.

If you can telnet to port 25 and something answers, but increasing the timeout value doesn't help, telnet to your DNS machine and execute nslookup. Make sure that the machine you are attempting to get to has everything defined correctly. Specifically, you are making sure that if there is an IN MX record it is correct. Ping and Telnet use an IN A query, GWSMTPD uses an IN MX query if available. If it's not available, the daemon uses the IN A record.

GWCORR.DB corrupt

In the <domain>\WPGATE\SMTP directory, rename the GWCORR.OLD file to GWCORR.DB. The correlation database sometimes becomes corrupt after a file server crash.

Summary

In this chapter, you learned how to set up Internet mail connectivity using the GroupWise SMTP/MIME gateway. We also went into some detail on configuration, message flow, and troubleshooting the SMTP/MIME gateway. By the way, once it is configured properly, this gateway is really pretty bulletproof, and should not require too much attention.

CHAPTER 21

GroupWise WebAccess

With GroupWise WebAccess, the GroupWise mailbox is implemented as a home page on the Internet or on your company's intranet. To access GroupWise, you simply enter the correct IP address, your mail ID, and your password from any HTML-based World Wide Web browser. Once in your Universal Mailbox, you have access to GroupWise functionality with the look and feel of the Internet browser you're using. GroupWise WebAccess puts your Universal Mailbox as close as the nearest Web browser.

Figure 21.1 shows the Web Access client view of a GroupWise 5 In Box viewed with Netscape Navigator.

FIGURE 21.1

Web Access Client In Box

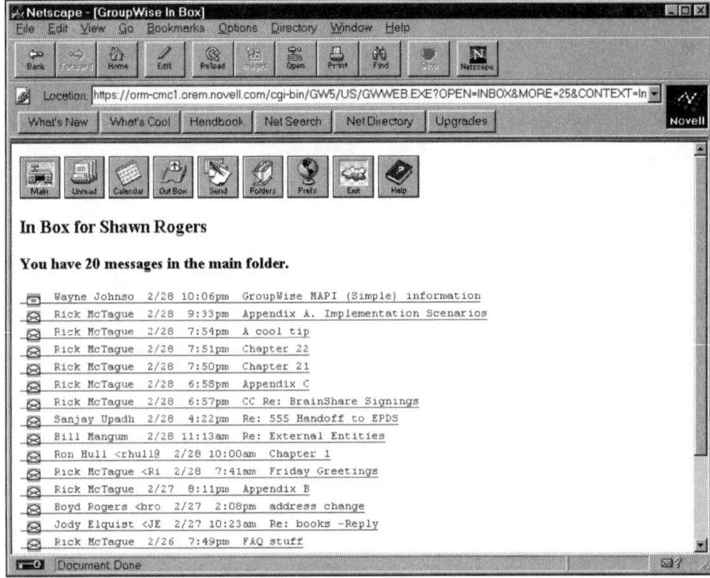

The WebAccess client is known as a "zero byte" client because you don't need any GroupWise software loaded on a user's workstation in order to allow them full access to their GroupWise mailbox. With WebAccess, users can perform all of the following tasks:

- Send and receive e-mail, Appointments, Tasks, Notes, voice messages, and personal messages
- View, send, and receive attachments

- Schedule group meetings
- View and act on Appointments, Notes, and Tasks in the Calendar
- Scroll the calendar view by multiple days, by week, or by month
- Perform busy search to check alternate calendar time/date availability
- Assign, track, and accept Tasks
- Search for and select users from GroupWise Address Books to include in the address list of any message type
- Status tracking (Tracks whether an outbound message has been opened, accepted, delegated, deleted, etc.)
- Convert e-mail messages to other message types, such as changing an e-mail message to an Appointment or Task

This chapter covers the basics of setting up a simple WebAccess solution on one NetWare server. More detailed information is available with the *WebAccess Setup Guide* that ships with the product.

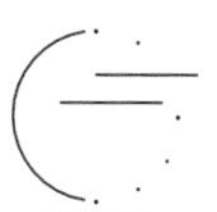
NOTE

WebAccess is also available for Windows NT and UNIX platforms.

This single-server solution requires the following components:

- NetWare 4.11
- NetWare Web Server 2.51 (Ships with NetWare 4.11)
- TCP/IP Protocol
- GroupWise WebAccess software

NOTE

This chapter describes the installation of Novell's Web Server 2.51, which ships with IntraNetWare 4.11 as of this writing. Future versions of Web Server will be JAVA-enabled and should enhance the appearance of WebAccess gateway interface dramatically.

The client requirements are very simple:

- A GroupWise account with a password
- An Internet or intranet connection
- A simple Web browser, such as Netscape Navigator or Internet Explorer

The GroupWise system requirements are as follows:

- A GroupWise MTA
- POAs must be enabled for client/server messaging (see Chapter 15)

Once these requirements have been met, three steps will set up a simple WebAccess server:

- Install and load NetWare Web Server 2.51
- Install and Load GroupWise WebAccess
- Load the Web browser and access the WebAccess server

Web Server Installation

To install and load NetWare Web Server 2.51, follow these steps:

1. Mount the NetWare 4.11 CD as a volume on the server. For more information, refer to the NetWare 4.11 Online Documentation CD that ships with NetWare 4.11.

2 • From the server prompt, type the following command: LOAD INSTALL.

3 • From the installation menu, choose Product Options.

4 • Select Choose an Item or Product Listed Above and highlight Web Server 2.51.

5 • Press Enter to install the Web Server software.

At this point, files are copied to a directory on the SYS volume called WEB. You will also see a note about the README.TXT file on the product floppy. Press the Esc key to continue, and answer No to the "Stop installation to read the readme file."

More files are copied to the following directories (and their subdirectories):

- SYS:NETBASIC
- SYS:PUBLIC
- SYS:SYSTEM
- SYS:WEB

6 • After the file copy is complete, the screen shown in Figure 21.2 will appear with instructions on the next step:

FIGURE 21.2

Web Server Final Installation Screen

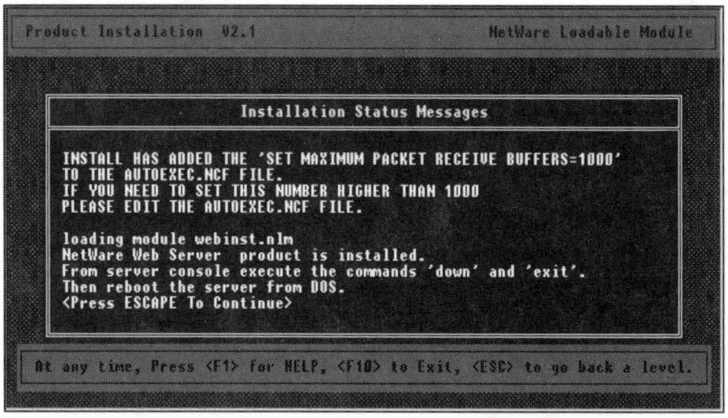

```
Product Installation  V2.1                              NetWare Loadable Module

                    Installation Status Messages

INSTALL HAS ADDED THE 'SET MAXIMUM PACKET RECEIVE BUFFERS=1000'
TO THE AUTOEXEC.NCF FILE.
IF YOU NEED TO SET THIS NUMBER HIGHER THAN 1000
PLEASE EDIT THE AUTOEXEC.NCF FILE.

loading module webinst.nlm
NetWare Web Server  product is installed.
From server console execute the commands 'down' and 'exit'.
Then reboot the server from DOS.
<Press ESCAPE To Continue>

At any time, Press <F1> for HELP, <F10> to Exit, <ESC> to go back a level.
```

7 • At this point, control is returned to the Install program. Press Esc twice and answer Yes when prompted to exit the Install program.

8 • After the server has been rebooted, the Web Server program will be loaded automatically.

The following two commands are useful when working with NetWare Web Server:

- `UNISTART` (Loads the Web Server software)
- `UNISTOP` (Unloads the Web Server software)

These commands are entered at the server console prompt.

The Web Server monitor screen displays information about the server's activity (see Figure 21.3:

FIGURE 21.3

Web Server Monitor

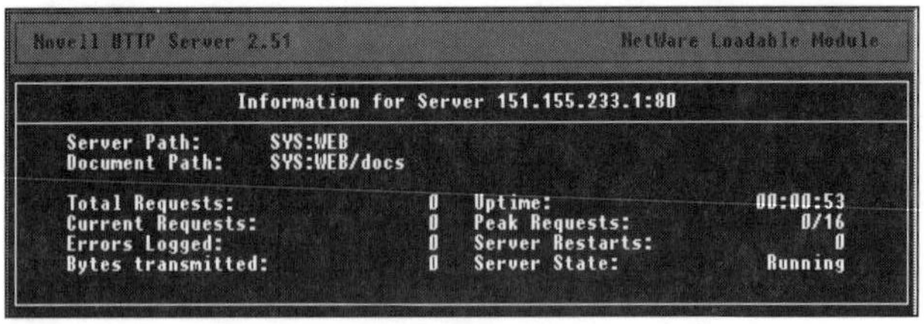

```
Novell HTTP Server 2.51                                NetWare Loadable Module

                    Information for Server 151.155.233.1:80

  Server Path:        SYS:WEB
  Document Path:      SYS:WEB/docs

  Total Requests:                   0   Uptime:                   00:00:53
  Current Requests:                 0   Peak Requests:                0/16
  Errors Logged:                    0   Server Restarts:                 0
  Bytes transmitted:                0   Server State:              Running
```

GroupWise WebAccess Installation

Once you have the WebAccess software and the Web Server is running, installation is relatively simple.

We have included GroupWise WebAccess 5.1 beta on the CD-ROM for your convenience and evaluation. Of course, this is beta software, and all agreements regarding beta software from Novell apply. Be sure to read the README.LCN file.

The README Envoy application that comes with the software is a very complete document that contains many more details on setup, configuration, and using the WebAccess gateway.

The beta version of WebAccess is a self-extracting file, and you will install from the directory the files are extracted into. We recommend extracting the files to a directory on the network.

Before you install the gateway, you need three pieces of information:

- The TCP/IP address of the server
- The NDS distinguished name and password of the GroupWise Access user. (This is required for a two-server solution, but it's a good idea to put into the configuration anyway.)
- The location of the domain directory where the gateway will be installed.

NOTE

As a precautionary measure, make a backup copy of the GWENN1.NLM file. From the SYS:SYSTEM directory, enter the following command: `COPY GWENN1.NLM GWENN1.OLD`

To install the WebAccess gateway, execute the following steps from a workstation logged in as Administrator or equivalent:

1. From the directory on which the WebAccess files were extracted, run the Install program. (This is done either at a command prompt or by using Start and then Run).
2. A welcome screen is displayed, telling you that the installation is in five parts. Press any key to continue.
3. Select Install NLM GW WebAccess Server and press Enter.
4. Select Install GW HTTP files and press Enter.
5. Press the Y key to answer yes to: "Are GroupWise WebAccess & HTTP Server on one box?"
6. Fill in the fields shown in Figure 21.4.

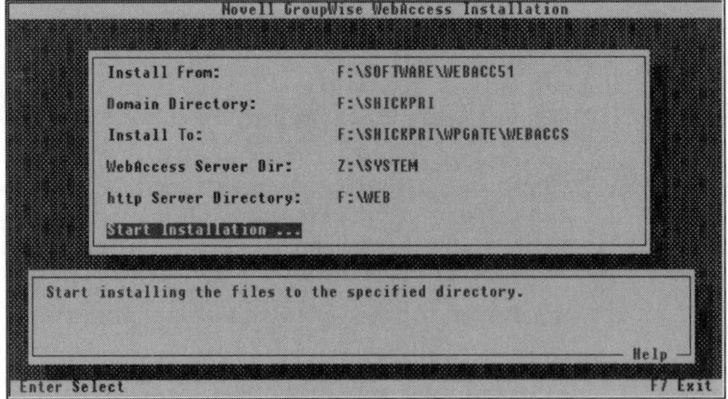

FIGURE 21.4
WebAccess Installation Options

- *Domain Directory.* NetWare path to the domain directory
- *Install To.* Press Enter to accept the default of <domain>\WPGATE\WEBACCS.
- *WebAccess Server Directory.* Press Enter to accept the default of Z:\SYSTEM.
- http Server Directory. Enter `SYS:WEB`.

7 • Highlight Start Installation and press Enter. Press the Y key if your server has enough disk space at the prompt. Files are then copied to the WPGATE\WEBACCS and SYS:SYSTEM directories. (Note: The GWENN1.NLM file that is copied to the SYS:SYSTEM directory may not be the most current version. Compare the dates with the GWENN1.OLD backup file you made, and make sure you are loading the most current GWENN1.NLM.)

8 • After the files are copied, you must configure some additional information, as shown in Figure 21.5.

FIGURE 21.5

WebAccess Volume Information

Novell GroupWise WebAccess Installation
Volume Name: SYS
Domain Server Name: shickfs1
Domain Volume Name: SYS
User ID: .gwaccess.grpwise.shick
User Password: chiefs
Start Installation ...
Modify the SRM.CFG for the GWWEB and build STARTWEB.NCF, STOPWEB.NCF unloads GWINTER and GWWEB.
Help
Enter Select
F7 Exit

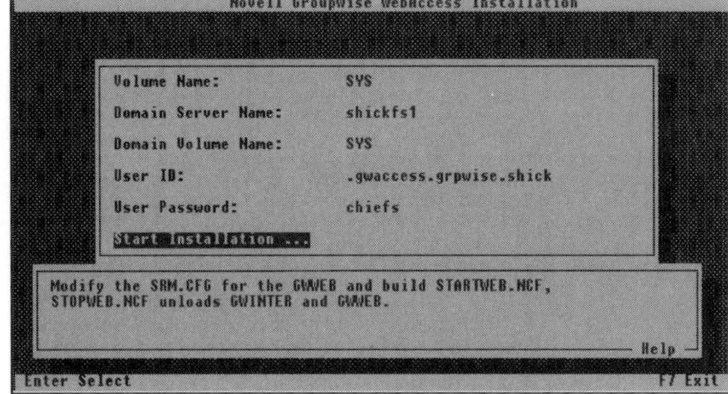

- *Volume Name.* Press Enter to accept SYS.
- *Domain Server Name.* The name of the NetWare server on which the gateway's GroupWise domain is located. Press Enter, type the name of the server, and press Enter again.
- *Domain Volume Name.* The volume on which the GroupWise domain is located. Press Enter and accept SYS (or your domain's volume).
- *User ID.* Enter the distinguished name of the GroupWise Access user (.GWACCESS.GRPWISE.SHICK for our system).
- *User Password.* Enter the case-sensitive password of the access user.

9 • Highlight Start Installation and press Enter to continue.

10 • The screen shown in Figure 21.6 will appear, giving you further instructions to complete the installation.

FIGURE 21.6

Installation Complete

Installation complete.
* Now go to Admin and create a gateway.
* For an NLM http server, unload and reload it so that the new RemoteScriptAlias line is read.
Check the srm.cfg & the STARTWEB.NCF, STOPWEB.NCF files.
* After creating the gateway, there should be a COMMGR.CFG in the CGI-BIN\GW5 subdirectory of the http server.
* There should be an INDEX.HTM in the DOCS dir.
Press any key to continue...

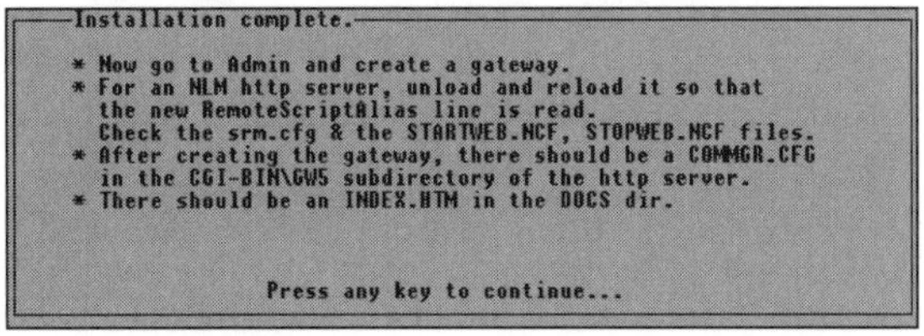

11 • Start NetWare Administrator, highlight the domain and press the right mouse button.

12 • Choose Create from the short menu and select GroupWise gateway.

13 • Create a gateway called WEBACCESS with the following properties defined. (Note: Creating a gateway is covered in Chapter 18.)

- *Name.* WEBACCESS
- *Gateway Type.* WebAccess
- *Gateway Platform.* NetWare Loadable Module
- *Database Version.* 5.X
- Gateway Alias. WEBACCESS

14 • Click on the Gateway Specific Setup property page. You'll see a note about a DLL not being installed. Click on the Launch button to launch the DOS-based setup program.

15 • Select the Configuration option by entering 1 (see Figure 21.7).

FIGURE 21.7

Configuration

WebAccess Configuration

1. Server IP Address: 151.155.233.1
(The IP address of the machine running
NGWINTER.EXE or NGWINTER.NLM.)

2. Server Port: 7201

3. Encryption Key: A8yE95n3ICpqZ78ek7Vgh753rTg

4. Max Threads: 12 ▲▼

OK Cancel

16 • Verify the correct IP address and port number. If you expect heavy use of the WebAccess gateway, and if the server is pretty much dedicated to GroupWise gateway traffic, you can increase the number of threads from the default of 12 to a higher number. You are limited by the processing power of your file server.

17 • Press OK to return to the main WebAccess Setup menu.

18 • Enter 2 to choose Access Rules. If you want all users in your system to be able to use this gateway to access their GroupWise mailbox, leave the defaults of All specified for the domain, post offices, and users. You can also specify certain domains, post offices, and users if you would like.

19 • Edit the Post Office paths by pressing the P key.

20 • Click on OK twice to return to the main WebAccess Setup menu. Choose Close to return to NetWare Administrator.

21 • After the WebAccess gateway is installed and configured, you can load the software. From the server prompt, enter the following commands:

- `UNISTOP` (Stops the Web Server software)
- `UNISTART` (Restarts the Web Server software)
- `STARTWEB` (Load the WebAccess gateway)

22 • To unload the gateway software, enter STOPWEB at the server prompt.

Figure 21.8 shows the WebAccess monitor screen, which displays the users who are accessing the WebAccess gateway, and the gateway's configuration.

FIGURE 21.8

WebAccess Monitor Screen

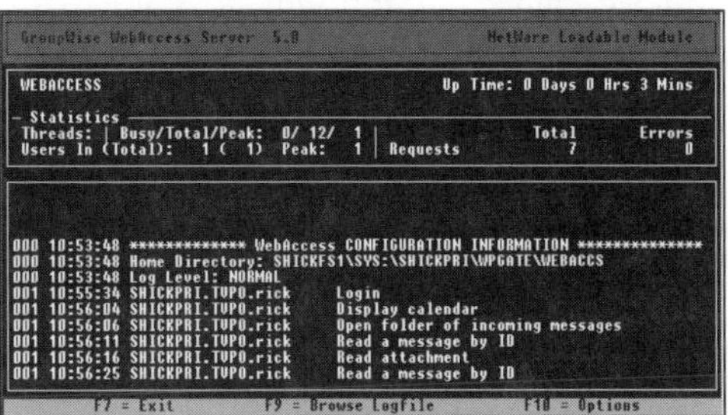

When you have completed the preceding steps, you will be ready to use WebAccess.

Using WebAccess

To use GroupWise WebAccess, follow these steps:

1 • Load your favorite Web Browser.

2 • Once it has started, enter the IP address of the Web Server in the URL location and press Enter. (Note: You may want to add this address to your browser's list of bookmarks or favorite locations.) You'll see the login screen shown in Figure 21.9.

FIGURE 21.9

WebAccess Login Screen

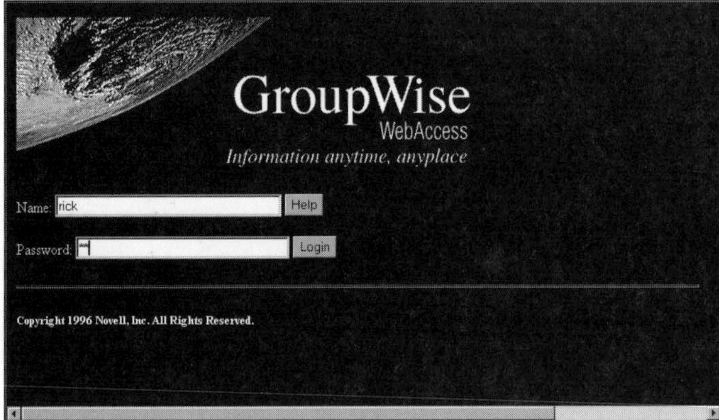

3 • Enter your mailbox ID and password in the appropriate fields and click on the Login button.

4 • Once you are logged in, you will see your mailbox, as shown in Figure 21.10.

You can use either the buttons or the desktop to access the different areas of your mailbox. Figure 21.11 shows a message being read with the WebAccess client.

FIGURE 21.10

WebAccess Mailbox View

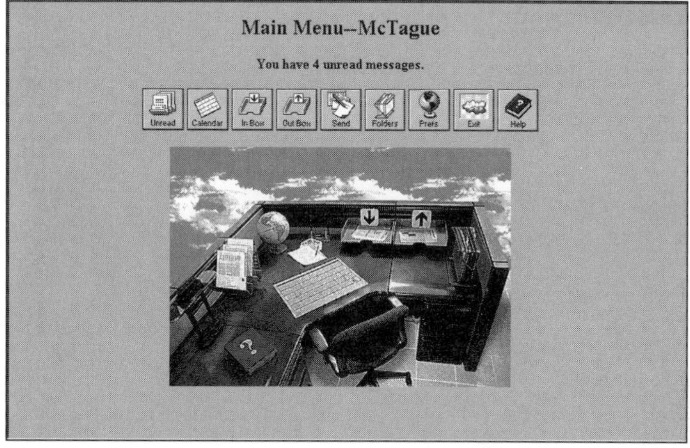

FIGURE 21.11

Reading a Message

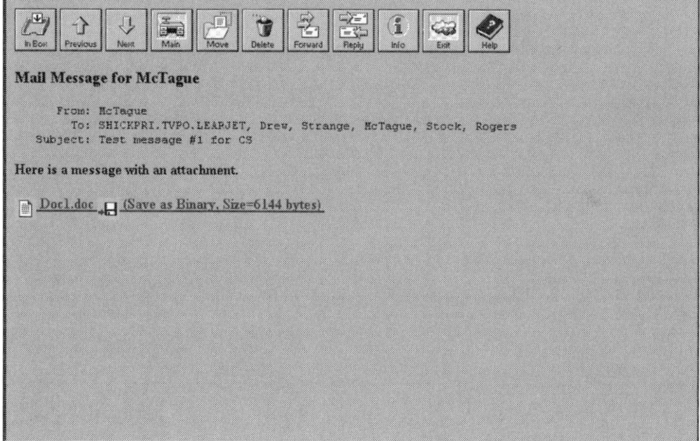

You can send messages with the WebAccess client and check the addresses against the Address Book by clicking on the Address Book. Figure 21.12 shows a new message being sent with WebAccess.

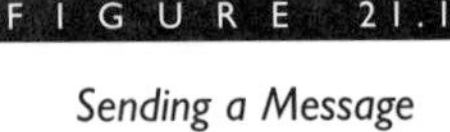

FIGURE 21.12

Sending a Message

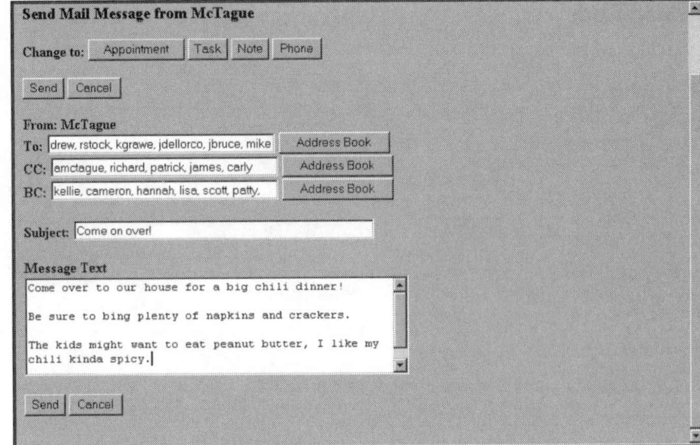

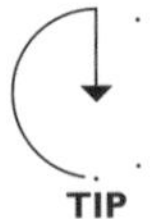

TIP

If you decide to change a message from an e-mail message to an Appointment, simply click on the Appointment button in the Change To: field of the new message screen.

Summary

In this chapter, you learned how to set up GroupWise WebAccess to provide your users with access to their GroupWise mailbox through a Web browser. WebAccess is key to the future of remote GroupWise computing. You will see future GroupWise products and releases take advantage of this "zero-byte" GroupWise client (called *zero-byte* because no GroupWise executable files are needed at workstations). We have included three documents on the CD-ROM that provide much more information about the capabilities of the WebAccess gateway: WEBPAPER.DOC, WEB51FAC.DOC, and WEBACCESS.DOC. In the next chapter, you'll learn more about WebAccess and get an overview of additional components you can implement to enhance your GroupWise system.

CHAPTER 22

Enhancements and Third-Party Products

This chapter will introduce you to the coolest enhancements you can imagine for GroupWise, enhancements developed by Novell and third parties.

The chapter is divided into the following sections:

- Novell enhancements
- The GroupWise application development environment
- Third-party development

Novell Enhancements

The products listed in this section are available in different states as of this writing. For example, GroupWise Imaging is available in beta.

These enhancements are in line with Novell's stated intention to make information available anyplace, anytime.

Future releases of GroupWise will both add new functionality to these enhancements as well as introduce new ones, so keep watching for announcements. (We could tell you some of them, but then we'd have to kill you.)

The following products are described here:

- Conversation Place
- PhoneAccess
- GroupWise Imaging
- GroupWise WorkFlow

Conversation Place

The Conversation Place within GroupWise brings you one step closer to a single solution for all forms of communication. The Conversation Place manages your telephone from the GroupWise desktop. It lets you answer your phone, place callers on hold, conference other callers, keep a log of calls, and even look up and dial phone numbers from the GroupWise Address Book. You can use Conversation Place while attached to the network or via a modem when you're on the road. Conversation Place is like having a hands-free front end for your telephone.

FIGURE 22.1

Conversation Place

The Conversation Place component adds telephony functionality to GroupWise, allowing telephone interactions to be controlled and tracked with the GroupWise system. Conversation Place utilizes either TSAPI servers (such as NetWare Telephony Services) or TAPI modems to provide its telephony features and does not require expensive telephone equipment. It will automatically detect which subsystem is in place and utilize those services. It also has the capability to replace the default Windows dialer program for more complete integration with the OS desktop and other applications.

The Conversation Place also fully integrates with the Address Book, taking advantage of the same Address Books and functionality that the client uses. This consistent integration allows users to very quickly become familiar with Conversation Place, greatly reducing training time.

The hardware and software necessary for Conversation Place depends on your phone system and how you want to use Conversation Place. If you want to use Conversation Place on a stand-alone PC with a modem, the TSAPI32.DLL Windows program is used to interface Conversation Place with your telephone.

The CPLACE.DOC document on this book's CD-ROM describes the installation requirements. For more information, see the documentation that comes with NetWare Telephony Services.

PhoneAccess

With GroupWise PhoneAccess, you can access your GroupWise Universal Mailbox from any touch-tone telephone worldwide when you don't have access to a computer. You simply call the PhoneAccess number, enter your user ID and password, and then follow the intuitive audio menu system. You can quickly browse message subjects and listen to the full text of any messages, including attachments, through the PhoneAccess text-to-speech technology.

You can also reply to any message (creating an audio message), forward any message, and even have GroupWise send text messages and documents to a nearby fax machine. With PhoneAccess you can also listen to, accept, and delegate, your appointments and tasks.

A particularly powerful feature of PhoneAccess is its ability to automatically forward a voice mail message, or any other type of GroupWise message, to any telephone number or pager. For example, you can specify that notification of incoming appointments be forwarded to a pager, or that any message from a specific person be forwarded to a cellular phone. You can use the telephone out-dialing capabilities of PhoneAccess for forwarding text messages and "reading" them to a list of people.

GroupWise PhoneAccess, when configured as a voice mail system, puts voice mail you receive directly into your Universal Mailbox. GroupWise will also support voice mail solutions from third-party vendors.

Figure 22.2 shows one possible configuration of the PhoneAccess gateway.

GroupWise PhoneAccess is an OS/2 gateway process that runs on an OS/2 2.1 or later workstation and needs a Dialogic board for digital-to-voice conversion.

NOTE

Dialogic information can be obtained directly from Dialogic Corporation at: `http://www.dialogic.com`**.**

For more information, see "Phone Access Configuration Guide," in the PACONFIG.DOC file on the CD-ROM that comes with this book.

FIGURE 22.2

TSAPI Implementation of PhoneAccess

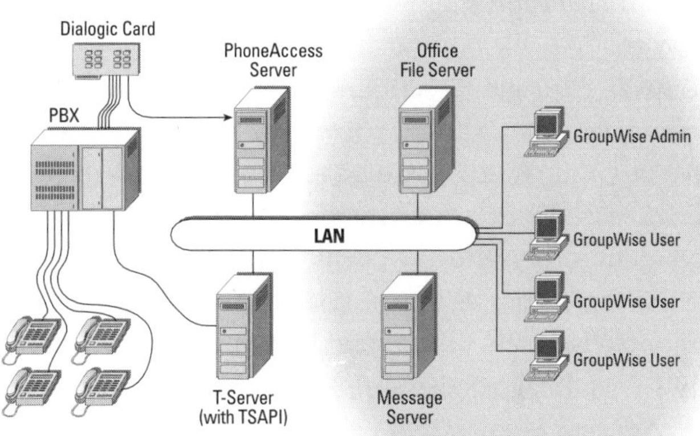

GroupWise Imaging

GroupWise Imaging merges the traditionally separate areas of desktop and production imaging and electronic publishing into a single collaborative imaging environment at a desktop price point. It allows users to view, store, edit, and route scanned document images across corporate networks and intranets via the GroupWise Universal Mail Box.

GroupWise Imaging represents a seamless integration of the following products:

- GroupWise 5
- Envoy portable document technology
- Xerox's PerfectScan image editing system
- Xerox's TextBridge Optical Character Recognition (OCR) software
- WhetStone's ViewWise image viewer and production imaging system

GroupWise Imaging comprises a set of image viewing and sharing capabilities for GroupWise 5 as well as the GroupWise Imaging Solutions Pack, a set of advanced image capturing, scanning, editing, and conversion features for users of GroupWise 5.

GroupWise Imaging offers fully integrated portable document and electronic publishing capabilities. The powerful document management and workflow features of GroupWise 5 enable users to view and manage image files from their Universal Mail Boxes just as they would text or e-mail. GroupWise Imaging can convert documents into Envoy file format; this allows image documents to be shared via the corporate e-mail system, like standard text documents, and allows non-GroupWise users to read and edit them as well.

GroupWise Imaging also supports the following advanced features:

- One-button image processing and enhancement capabilities through Xerox's PerfectScan technology for correcting resolution, alignment, and color of scanned documents with a single action
- Regional decomposition of scanned image documents, which lets users manipulate text and graphics from a single scanned image separately
- Full annotation and document image manipulation support gives users the ability to highlight, black out, rubber stamp or attach sticky notes to documents.
- Users can view images in black and white, grayscale, or color; and can shrink, magnify, and rotate them.
- Extended Image Capabilities: With Xerox's TextBridge OCR software and WhetStone's production imaging systems, GroupWise users can further enhance their scanning and imaging capabilities with industry-leading systems.

GroupWise Imaging supports the following industry standards:

- MAPI (Messaging Application Programming Interface)

- ODMA (Open Document Management API)
- ODMAWF (Open Document Management API for WorkFlow) Scanner standards, including TWAIN and ISIS, as well as support for the popular Visioneer PaperPort personal desktop scanner, give users a broad array of options for capturing documents as image files.

These standards allow e-mailed document images to be opened using popular office productivity suites from Corel, Lotus, and Microsoft. In addition, OLE (Object Linking and Embedding) Automation support enables the creation of images using industry-standard development tools and the GroupWise Object API

GroupWise Imaging supports a wide range of file formats, such as TIFF (Group 3 and 4), multipage TIFF 6, .BMP, .PCX, .JPG, .DCX, .GIF and .EVY. GroupWise Imaging also supports the Xerox XIF file format, which provides instant access to and interaction with all Xerox multifunction devices.

GroupWise Workflow

GroupWise WorkFlow builds on the infrastructure of the network and the GroupWise messaging system to automate everyday business processes, such as an approval process for expense reports, or the routing of a vacation request. GroupWise WorkFlow uses the Universal Mailbox as its interface. You can use GroupWise WorkFlow to create and participate in automated work processes.

Constructing Workflows

With its intuitive graphical user interface, GroupWise WorkFlow makes constructing a workflow process as simple as placing workflow step icons on the workflow canvas and drawing routing arrows to connect them. You use the GroupWise Address Book to assign people to each workflow step, and you can include detailed instructions for each participant. Once you send the workflow, you receive status messages that let you graphically track, using the workflow map, exactly who currently has the work and what's been done with it so far.

FIGURE 22.3

GroupWise Workflow

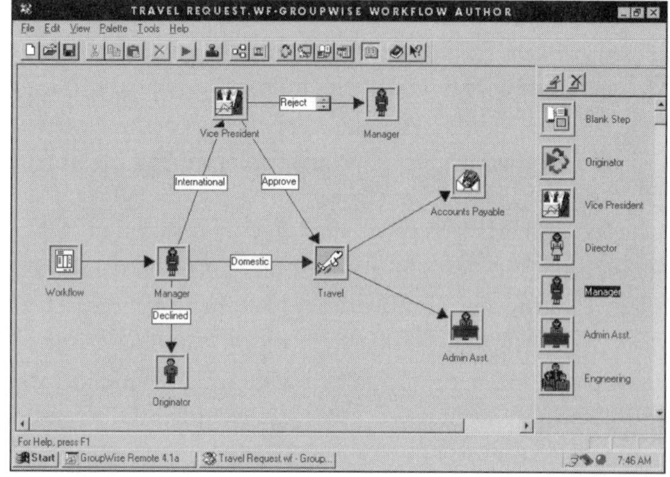

The GroupWise WorkFlow interface and workflow construction tools put the automation of workflow processes into the hands of front-line end users—those who really understand the business processes. By replacing a complex workflow programming language with a simple, intuitive, graphical user interface, GroupWise WorkFlow lets you concentrate more on structuring and refining your business processes and less on automation mechanics.

Participating in Workflows

With its tight integration with GroupWise, GroupWise WorkFlow makes participating in workflows as simple as using e-mail. If you're a workflow participant, you receive a workflow message in your Universal Mailbox when it's time for your step in the workflow. Opening the message displays your task in a simple dialog box with instructions for completing the task. You can respond to the workflow author, asking questions and making clarifications. And when you're finished with your part of the process, GroupWise WorkFlow automatically routes the message to the next participant.

System Requirements

Since GroupWise Workflow is integrated with the client program, and uses the GroupWise message transfer system and Address Book to route workflow messages, there are no additional system requirements. Of course, the introduction of new message types and the increased use of GroupWise place a higher demand on disk space, memory, and the processing power of the server.

The GroupWise Application Development Environment

GroupWise components make it easy for system administrators and software developers to integrate existing desktop and business applications with GroupWise, to extend GroupWise applications, and to create new GroupWise applications. In addition to supporting industry-standard APIs, such as MAPI 1.0, ODMA 1.0, ODMAWF 1.0, CMC 1.0, CSA 1.0., and SNMP, GroupWise provides its own Object API and custom third-party objects. Many third-party developers are using these tools to provide powerful solutions via GroupWise.

In this section, we briefly discuss the following topics:

- *Industry API Standards.* GroupWise 5 implements all of the aforementioned APIs, which provide developers with standards-based access to GroupWise.
- *GroupWise APIs.* In order to allow third-party developers to participate with and add value to Novell's core products, Novell has delivered an API set with the release of GroupWise 5.
- *The Novell GroupWise SDK.* The Novell GroupWise Software Development Kit (SDK) contains the GroupWise APIs; GroupWise Sticky Notes; and a sample application which demonstrates customization of the GroupWise client.

Through a combination of APIs, components, and interfaces, the GroupWise 5 product and its SDK form the basis of Novell's collaborative computing environment. GroupWise 5 is an environment that facilitates the development and deployment of collaborative applications.

Industry API Standards

All GroupWise 5 services are exposed through industry-standard APIs (MAPI, ODMA) where available; where industry APIs don't expose GroupWise services, GroupWise-specific API extensions are provided. These are discussed in the next section.

Table 22.1 contains a summary of the industry APIs supported by GroupWise 5.

TABLE 22.1

Industry APIs Supported by GroupWise

NAME	DESCRIPTION
MAPI 1.0	Windows-based e-mail API from Microsoft.
ODMA 1.0	Document management API from the ODMA committee of AIIM.
ODMAWF 1.0	WorkFlow API from the ODMA committee of AIIM.
CMC 1.0	E-mail API from XAPIA.
CSA 1.0	Calendaring and Scheduling API from XAPIA.
SNMP—MADMAN MIB	An administrative interface for server administration and monitoring.

MAPI 1.0

Microsoft's Messaging Application Programming Interface (MAPI) is a standard which enables developers to integrate applications with the e-mail functions of GroupWise (e.g., Address Books, e-mail transports, and e-mail stores). MAPI-enabled applications, such as Microsoft Word, can send mail through the GroupWise 5 system. Also, the Windows 95 In Box can automatically access the GroupWise 5 information store.

ODMA and ODMAWF

The Open Document Management API (ODMA) and the ODMA WorkFlow extensions (ODMAWF) come from the ODMA committee, sponsored by the Association for Information and Image Management (AIIM). Novell is a founding member of this committee and led the creation of the ODMA specification. ODMA describes the interaction between a productivity application (e.g., Microsoft Word) and a document management system.

Document management technology (from the SoftSolutions product) is an integral part of GroupWise 5. ODMA is used to provide integration with productivity applications. ODMAWF, which describes the interaction between productivity applications and workflow systems, is used by GroupWise 5 to provide integration into the GroupWise 5 WorkFlow system.

CMC and CSA

Common Message Calls (CMC) and Calendaring and Scheduling API (CSA) come from XAPIA. They provide standards-based access to an e-mail system and a calendar/scheduler system respectively. GroupWise 5 implements these APIs together on the server to provide server-side access to the GroupWise information store.

GroupWise APIs

The GroupWise 5 API set enables GroupWise and third-party applications to embrace a vastly improved replicated messaging model.

Table 22.2 summarizes the GroupWise 5 APIs.

TABLE 22.2

GroupWise 5 APIs

API	DESCRIPTION
Token Interfaces	The macro interface into Novell GroupWise 5 Client
GroupWise Object API	Allows access to the GroupWise 5 information store
C3PO Interfaces	GroupWise 5 Client extension interfaces
MTA Message Logging API	Allows access to information about the messages handled by the MTA
MTA Transport API	Allows the extension of MTA communication protocols
Address Book OCXs	Exposes the Address Book and the Name Completion Control interface into the Address Book

GroupWise Object API

The GroupWise Object API (GWOAPI) provides rich, data-level access to the GroupWise information store, so a developer can see, use, and manipulate the information store from outside GroupWise. The GWOAPI provides access to the Address Book and document management capabilities of GroupWise. You can access GWOAPI through OLE languages, such as Visual Basic and Delphi; and also from object-oriented languages, such as C++. The GWOAPI also supports OLE Automation—an industry standard for interfacing applications.

Unlike MAPI, which provides an e-mail centered view of data, the GroupWise Object API exposes all of the object types in the GroupWise information store, including e-mail, appointments, notes, tasks, phone messages, voice mail, and documents. Using the GroupWise Object API, developers can also extend the GroupWise information store to handle new object types.

From the GroupWise Object API's OLE Automation interface, a Visual Basic, Delphi, or other OLE Automation tool programmer can navigate a user's folders, messages, Address Books, document libraries, and documents. The C++ developer can use either the OLE Automation interface or COM interfaces. New folders, messages, documents, and other items can be created. Existing items can be both read and modified. The GWOAPI allows additional properties to be associated with both existing items and new items.

Custom Third-Party Objects

You can use *Custom Third-Party Objects* (C3POs) to extend the GroupWise environment—providing custom extensions to the GroupWise client. C3PO extensions take various forms, ranging from implementing custom data types and handlers in the GroupWise information store to modifying the toolbar functionality in the GroupWise interface. You can develop C3POs using C++, Delphi, or Visual Basic.

GroupWise 5's approach to C3PO is an excellent example of the extensibility and openness of GroupWise 5.

The C3PO interface provides developers with the ability to extend the GroupWise 5 client. Using this interface, developers can implement new objects with unique behavior in the GroupWise environment. This interface can also be used to extend or modify the behavior and properties of existing objects. The individual interfaces that comprise the C3PO interface are summarized in Table 22.3.

To manage these handlers, the C3PO manager component is also required. This component is registered with the client component and is started when the client is initiated. The component maintains a registry of C3PO handlers that have been defined and installed, and provides communication between the C3POs and the client.

TABLE 22.3

C3PO Interfaces

INTERFACE	DESCRIPTION
CmdCtx	Used to give C3POs an interface into Novell GroupWise 5 Client, which provides a user-interface context for the current operation.
Delivery	Called when associated data types are delivered to the GroupWise box.
DoCommand	Used to respond to commands invoked against the C3PO.
DropTarget	Allows a C3PO to support the drag/drop operation for custom data.
Icons	Used to retrieve icons that represent the state of C3PO data types.
Init	Required. Used to initialize the C3PO.
Ready	Called during the GroupWise 5 client initialization procedure.
SetupCommands	Used to define menu and toolbar changes.
SetupContainer	Used to notify a C3PO whenever a container for a data type is displayed.
Enum	Used to iterate among the C3PO servers in the system. Serves as the basis for navigating type hierarchy, installation lists, etc.
Man	This interface, along with ManCommand and ManMessage are interfaces into the C3PO manager. Together they provide access to C3PO functionality outside of the GroupWise 5 client.
ManCommand	The C3PO manager's command interface.
ManMessage	The aggregated C3PO Manager interface for the GW.APPLICATION.BROWSER-registered C3POs.

When the client performs certain actions, events are sent to the C3PO manager. This component then determines, based on C3PO registrations, which C3POs to pass the event to for further possible processing. The C3PO manager communicates with the C3POs using either COM or OCX mechanisms, depending on the type of C3PO that is registered.

Address Book User Interface

This component is fully based on Microsoft's Messaging Application Programming Interface (MAPI) and utilizes the MAPI subsystem provided by all Microsoft 32-bit operating systems. The Address Book User Interface (ABUI) component uses MAPI calls to communicate with the MAPI Address Book providers. This architecture allows the GroupWise Address Book user interface to use any MAPI-compliant provider, whether it is a GroupWise provider (described below) or a provider included with Windows 95 or Windows NT.

GroupWise 5 ships with two Address Book providers: the System Address Book provider and the Personal Address Book provider. These providers, which open up the GroupWise directory and enable lookup functionality, are fully MAPI-compliant and can be accessed by any MAPI-compliant application (such as Microsoft Exchange). The ABUI component exposes these services on behalf of the GroupWise 5 client.

Address Book providers are actual GroupWise 5 components, and as such use the services of the GroupWise component manager to ensure a single session and authentication framework. Both providers also use the GroupWise Engine component to communicate with the GroupWise messaging infrastructure and directory repositories.

The ABUI also extends the native OS by exposing a new Windows class that can be used by any other component or third-party application. This class allows other components or applications to easily integrate and communicate with the Address Book name-completion control so any component or application can provide a common look and feel for addressing and name lookup purposes. This same control is also exported as an OLE automation control (OCX).

Novell GroupWise SDK

The Novell GroupWise 5 SDK participates in Novell's Net2000 initiative. Net2000 is an effort to develop an open set of APIs to expose the rich functionality of network services to developers building distributed network applications. In particular, a primary Net2000 objective is to increase the value of Novell's network services to desktop component and object developers. The GroupWise 5 Object API, C3PO interfaces, and Address Book OCXs are among the first implementations of the Net2000 initiative.

Client Macros and Tokens

GroupWise 5 also provides the capability to script client behavior. In the past, GroupWise has shipped with a proprietary scripting language, PerfectScript. Following the mandate of openness, GroupWise 5 will not ship a proprietary scripting language, but will instead expose scriptable tokens via OLE automation to well-known tools such as Visual Basic and Delphi. The token set has been expanded to encompass the new capabilities of the GroupWise 5 client. This allows users to employ their favorite scripting tool to script GroupWise 5 client behavior. The Novell GroupWise 5 SDK describes this scripting environment.

Sticky Notes

The Sticky Notes component is a C3PO component that ships as part of the Novell GroupWise 5 SDK. This component provides annotation capabilities for all GroupWise messaging objects. It is initialized via the C3PO manager and uses the manager to communicate with the engine and client components. The Sticky Notes component uses the same interfaces that Novell exposes for third-parties to enhance and extend the GroupWise product. This ensures that the interfaces are fully featured and provide the capabilities needed by the development community.

Sample Application

As a sample of the applications that can be built in the GroupWise 5 environment, the Novell GroupWise 5 SDK contains a *Customer Tracking System* built with the C3PO interfaces and GroupWise Object APIs.

This sample application, complete with its source, creates three new data types: a Company object, a Contact object, and an Action object. Behaviors for these new objects (i.e., compose and open) are implemented via the C3PO DoCommands interface, with the GWOAPI used to read and write the data to the information store. Other behaviors, such as delete, are inherited from the GroupWise 5 client with no effort from the C3PO. The C3PO SetupCommands interface is used to extend the File → New menu to include Company, Contact, and Action as objects that can be created.

The Customer Tracking C3PO uses the Icons interface to associate appropriate icons with these new objects.

This application looks and feels like a native part of GroupWise 5. Because it is integrated directly into the user interface as well as the information store, the user is unable to tell where the GroupWise product code ends and the new application begins. Key subsystems of GroupWise 5 have been implemented as components:

- Address Book
- Conversation Place
- Note

These components, together with the GroupWise Object API, have all been implemented to run both independently of the GroupWise 5 client or in tight integration with it. This allows users to access key functionality (such as the Address Book) without having the client running. For developers, OCXs have been provided, which allow access to the Address Book and the Name Completion Control (an interface to the Address Book). This enables developers' applications to take advantage of these GroupWise 5 components.

Third-Party Products

Many third-party vendors have used and continue to use the tools mentioned above to provide GroupWise-based solutions and applications in the following areas: PDA and contact management integration, project management, voice messaging and telephony, systems monitoring, fax services, report writing, and imaging. You can leverage your GroupWise investment by implementing these third-party applications developed by companies you know and trust.

The development by third-party companies of technologies that hook into GroupWise is an ongoing process. The GroupWise development environment is open and based on standards. Novell publishes a list of the companies that are developing products that enhance GroupWise (called GroupWise Partners) on their Web site:

`http://www.novell.com/groupwise/partners/partners.html`

Table 22.4 lists some of these companies and their products.

TABLE 22.4

Third-Party Products

COMPANY	PRODUCT	DESCRIPTION
Active Voice	Message Integration Package	GroupWise e-mail messages, schedules, and tasks, as well as voice and fax messages controlled from a single mailbox that can be accessed by telephone or PC
ADVANSYS Pty Limited	LinkWise 1.1	Appointment synchronization among the Psion 3a, 3c, and Siena personal digital assistants
Applied Voice Technology	CallXpress3	Voice, fax, and telephone access to GroupWise
CallWare Technologies, Inc.	Voice and Call Processing Software	Voice mail integration with the GroupWise Universal Mailbox
Cheyenne Software	FAXserve Gateway	Inbound/outbound fax integration with the GroupWise Universal Mailbox
Decisive Technology Corporation	Decisive Survey for Windows	Surveys that can be sent through GroupWise to anyone with an Internet address
GroupLink	Contact Management	Interface of ACT!, GoldMine, Maximizer, and Sidekick with Novell GroupWise
	Human Resource Management	Employee data, routing, and image access via GroupWise
Information Builders	FOCUS Six GroupWise Reporting Interface	GroupWise administrative information reporting
Puma Technology	Intellisync for Pilot	Synchronization of US Robotics Pilot information with GroupWise contact, schedule, and "to do" information
Quarterdeck Corporation	RemoteMeeting	Document sharing with multiple parties in real time
Simplify	MailRoom	Document, image, and fax routing via GroupWise
St. Bernard Software	Open File Manager	Existing backup program access to open GroupWise, e-mail, database, and application files

(continued)

TABLE 22.4

Third-Party Products (continued)

COMPANY	PRODUCT	DESCRIPTION
Software Connections, Inc.	DIER—the UUCP Gateway for GroupWise	True dial-up capabilities for e-mail connectivity, eliminating the need for a dedicated connection to the Internet
Synaxis Corporation	AlertWare	Messaging environment monitoring with notification via pager, SNMP, Novell Send, and ManageWise
Time Line Solutions Corporation	Project Management Integrator	Project planning, implementation, and tracking using GroupWise
Visioneer	PaperPort	Capability to send paper quickly and easily
WhetStone Technologies	ViewWise 4.1	Image and text scanning and manipulation; automation of traditionally paper-based tasks, such as claims processing, inventory management, and financial record extraction

Summary

This chapter introduced you to the GroupWise 5 enhancements that Novell has provided to add functionality to GroupWise. You are also now familiar with the standards, tools, and environment that Novell provides for application developers who want to write their own enhancements, and some existing products by GroupWise Partners that add functionality to GroupWise.

In closing this book, we hope you have gained a thorough understanding of Novell's state-of-the-art messaging system, GroupWise 5. It was written to address the day-to-day problems faced by GroupWise administrators, and we kept this perspective in mind as we presented each topic.

For information on additional aspects of GroupWise administration, we invite you to thumb through the appendixes. They cover real-world implementation scenarios, planning worksheets, and sample e-mail policies. We also have a

Frequently Asked Questions appendix, which will answer many of your questions, and provide details of the directories and files that make up the GroupWise system.

The enclosed CD-ROM includes numerous white papers, utilities, and programs that should round out everything you need to be a successful GroupWise administrator. Appendix F covers the installation of these programs, and describes the documents found on the CD-ROM.

We sincerely hope this book serves as a valuable reference as you move forward with GroupWise.

APPENDIX A

Implementation Scenarios

This appendix describes three fictional companies' messaging environments and their respective GroupWise system designs.

In order to understand these scenarios, you need to be familiar with the concepts covered in this book, such as links, primary and secondary domains, and network protocols.

Each scenario addresses the business communication uses of GroupWise, the recommended servers, and a brief description of the GroupWise system.

Scenario #1: Small, Single-Site Company

This company has the following characteristics:

- It is located at a single site.
- The company is relatively small (15–100 employees).
- It has one or two production NetWare 3.12 file servers, used for file and print services.
- The users' workstations are running either Windows 3.1 or Windows 95.

Business Communication Uses of GroupWise

The company has the following communication needs:

- Internal messaging and scheduling
- The ability to send and receive Internet e-mail
- Document management and discussions
- Company-wide open calendar viewing

Recommended Solution

The company should upgrade one of the two existing NetWare 3.11 servers to NetWare 4.11 or IntranetWare, and upgrade the server's disk space and memory. If possible, the company should install a dedicated hard disk to serve as a MAIL volume.

The administrator should plan on around 40MB of disk space per user and configure archive settings so archived messages are stored on users' local hard drives.

The company should apply for an Internet domain name and obtain a connection to the Internet (ISDN).

GroupWise System Description

The administrator for this company should create a single-domain, single-post office GroupWise system. Installing the SMTP gateway will provide e-mail access to the Internet.

If the level of Internet messaging is low, this company should consider using an Internet hub service to handle Internet messaging. This configuration requires an Async gateway connection to the hub service, but eliminates the need for an Internet domain name and a connection to the Internet.

The administrator should have users access the client software from the software directory located on the server, which will minimize workstation-level administration.

For document management, the administrator should create a single GroupWise Library, and store library documents at the post office. The single POA can handle both message delivery and document indexing.

Figure A.1 shows the layout of the recommended GroupWise system.

FIGURE A.1

Small System Layout

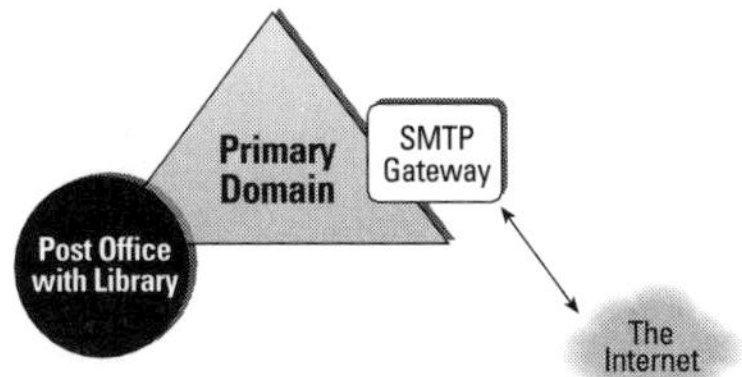

Scenario #2: Medium-Sized Company with Three Sites in One City

This company has the following characteristics:

- Three locations, connected with 56K WAN
- Medium size (100–500 employees)
- One NetWare 3.12 file server per site; used for file and print services
- One Windows NT server per site; used for application services
- Most users' workstations run Windows 95, but some are Windows NT workstations or Macintosh computers.

Business Communication Uses of GroupWise

The company has the following communication needs:

- Internal messaging, scheduling, fax routing, and Internet mail
- Document management and shared folders with discussions
- Proxy between all sites for managers and administrative assistants
- Remote access for 50+ mobile users

Recommended Solution

To prepare for the GroupWise system, this company needs a dedicated NetWare 4.11 server at the home office with adequate memory (256 MB) and disk space (6 GB) for the home office location (1–2 domains and 1 post office for 100–150 people). This server will also run the SMTP and Async gateway software.

At each site, either existing server (NetWare 3.12 or Windows NT) could be used for the post office, with a dedicated volume of 4GB on each server for GroupWise. The administrator needs to make sure the server has adequate memory for the additional volume and traffic, and they should also consider using a dedicated NetWare 4.11 server at each site for GroupWise, which would allow for growth.

The platform of the GroupWise POA (NLM or NT) should match the network operating system (NetWare or Windows NT) that is being used. On the NT servers that house post offices, the NT version of the POA should be used. On the NetWare 3.11 servers, the NLM version of the POA should be used.

The existing connections between all sites of 56K is adequate and should use the TCP/IP protocol.

They should plan on around 40MB per user, with archive files stored on the local hard drives.

An additional task to prepare for implementation is to apply for an Internet domain name and obtain a connection to the Internet (T1 would be best for performance and increased traffic).

GroupWise System Description

The administrator should create a single-domain GroupWise system, and locate the domain at the home office on a dedicated NetWare 4.11 server.

A post office at each site should be established, with TCP/IP links between them. The administrator should install an SMTP gateway and an Async gateway at the home office to provide connectivity to the Internet and support for GroupWise Remote access. This scenario should have users connect to their post offices via Client/Server access.

The administrator should create GroupWise libraries at each post office for sharing and storing personal documents, and a company library at the post office located at the home site. Write access to this library should be restricted. Because users are running in Client/Server mode, they will be able to use libraries throughout the system.

One SMTP gateway and one Async gateway (2 modems) at the home office would meet the Internet and remote messaging needs for this scenario. Cheyenne's Fax Server Solution, which is integrated with GroupWise, would meet the fax requirements for this company. NetWare Connect should be used for enabling users' remote access to the network, including their GroupWise mailboxes. For strictly GroupWise remote access traffic, users should dial into the GroupWise Async gateway. Figure A.2 shows the recommended GroupWise configuration.

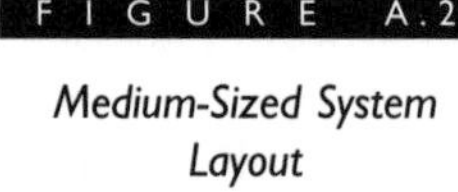
FIGURE A.2

Medium-Sized System Layout

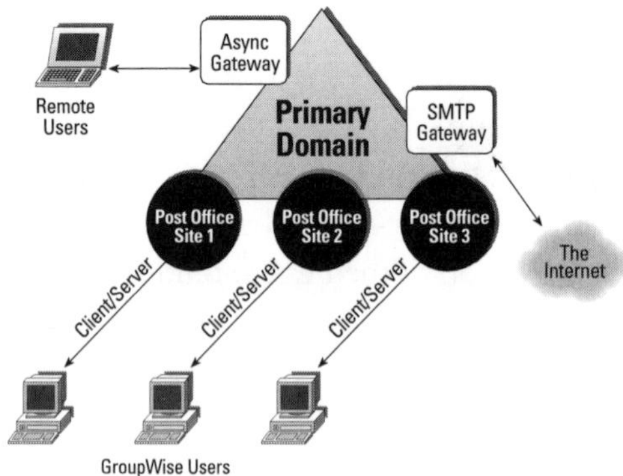

Scenario #3: Large Company with Sites in Several Geographical Regions

This company has the following characteristics:

- 10+ locations
- 1000–5000 employees total; 50–150 users at most sites; home office has 500 users
- 3+ NetWare 4.11 file servers per site, used for file and print services
- UNIX system at home office for time and billing system
- Workstations are a mixture of Windows 3.1, Windows 95, Windows NT, and Macintosh

Business Communication Uses of GroupWise

The company has the following messaging needs:

- Internal messaging, scheduling, fax routing, and Internet mail
- Voice-mail accessed through the Universal Mailbox

- Integration of GroupWise with UNIX time and billing system
- Proxy between users within a site
- Remote access needed for 500+ mobile users
- Access mailbox using Netscape browser on corporate intranet
- Communication with mainframe-based legacy e-mail system

Recommended Solution

This company first needs one server with the following features:

- NetWare 4.11 (or later)
- 512MB RAM
- 2GB disk space

This server will hold the primary domain, secondary domains for single-location post offices, and secondary domains for gateways. A DigiBoard (16 ports with modems) will be installed in this server for the Async gateway. The server should have SMP capability should WebAccess traffic increase. The TCP/IP protocol is also required on this server to enable TCP/IP links to all other domains and single-location post offices.

Second, the company needs another server with the following features:

- NetWare SFT 4.11
- 512MB RAM
- 16GB disk space

This server will hold a secondary domain and post office for the home office location. A four-port DigiBoard with modems will be installed in this server to handle the home office's remote requirements. This server should have SMP capability.

For the smaller sites (50–100 users), we recommend using the existing server for the post office, with a dedicated volume of 4GB on each server for GroupWise. The administrator at each site would need to make sure the server has adequate memory for the additional volume and traffic, and should consider using a dedicated NetWare 4.11 server at each site for GroupWise, which would allow for growth. These servers will need the TCP/IP protocol enabled in order to use TCP/IP post office links to the secondary domain (located on a server at home office).

For the larger sites (100–150 users), a dedicated, single processor NetWare 4.11 server with 6–8GB disk space and 184–256MB RAM will hold the secondary domain the location's post office. TCP/IP links should be used between post offices in the domain, and from the secondary domain back to the home office primary domain.

Smaller sites can be linked with at least 56K WAN connections; larger sites with T1 connections.

All sites will use the TCP/IP protocol back to the home office.

The administrator should plan on around 40MB per user, with archive files stored on the local hard drives; apply for an Internet domain name; and obtain a connection to the Internet (low-traffic T1).

The administrator should also plan on using the Novell GroupWise SDK and APIs to read calendar information (tasks, notes, and appointments) in GroupWise for use as input into the time and billing system.

GroupWise System Description

We recommend a primary domain, GWROUTE, and a secondary domain, GATEWAYS. The gateways that need to be used are as follows:

- SMTP gateway for all Internet mail; ASYNC gateway for company-wide Remote access; WebAccess gateway for access to mailboxes through corporate intranet
- API gateway for application integration with UNIX system
- SNADS gateway for access to mainframe e-mail system

For the home office, we recommend a secondary domain, HOME, with post offices for each location in the home office's city. It should also hold an Async gateway for the home office's remote users. Other secondary domains, CITY1 and CITY4, should be created with post offices for each location in the city, and an Async gateway for the city's remote users. Finally, secondary domains, CITY2 and CITY3, should be created; with post offices for each single-location city. Figure A.3 shows these GroupWise components.

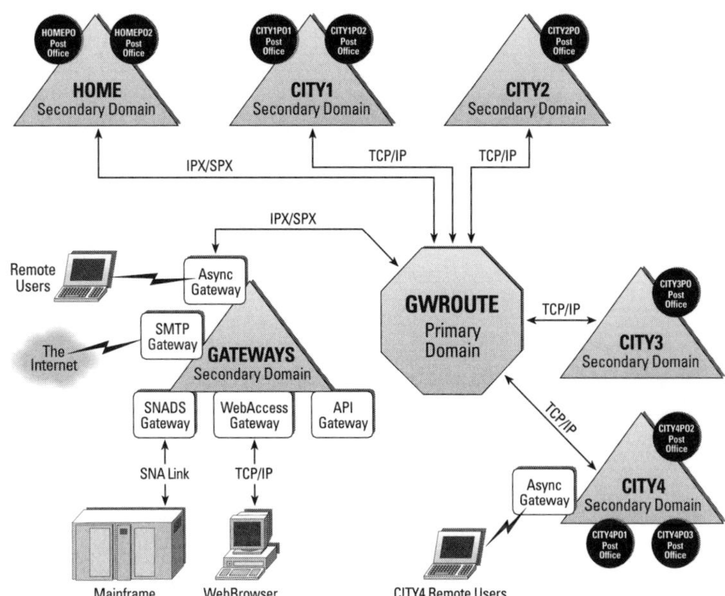

FIGURE A.3

Layout of Large GroupWise System

APPENDIX B

Planning Worksheets

These forms will help you plan, document, and implement your GroupWise system components.

Please feel free to copy them.

Primary Domain Planning Worksheet

Tree Name ______________________________
System Name ______________________________
Primary Domain ______________________________
\\Server\Volume\Path ______________________________
Context (OU.OU.O) ______________________________
Description ______________________________
Administrator ______________________________

MTA

TCP/IP Address : Port ____________________ : __________
Startup Filename ______________________________
/HOME- ______________________________
/User- ______________________________
/Password- ______________________________
Other switches ______________________________

ADA

Startup Filename ______________________________
/HOME- ______________________________
/User- ______________________________
/Password- ______________________________
Other switches ______________________________

Post Office Planning Worksheet

Post Office ______________________________
Domain ______________________________
\\Server\Volume\Directory ______________________________
Context (OU.OU.O) ______________________________
Description ______________________________
Users (Depts/Location/Contexts) ______________________________
____
____

Delivery Mode	Use App Thresholds	Agent Always	Client Delivers Locally
Access Mode	Direct Only	Client Server	Direct and Client Server

Software Directory ______________________________

POA

TCP/IP Address : Port ______________________ : ________
Startup Filename ______________________________
/HOME- ______________________________
Other switches ______________________________

Gateway Planning Worksheet

Domain ____________________
Gateway Name ____________________
Description ____________________
Home Directory: \\Server\Volume\ __________ \WPGATE\ __________
Time Zone ____________________
Type ____________________

Platform NLM OS/2 NT

Version 4.X 5.X

Alias Type ____________________
Foreign ID ____________________
Gateway Administrators ____________________

Secondary Domain Planning Worksheet

Secondary Domain ______________________________
\\Server\Volume\Path ______________________________
Context (OU.OU.O) ______________________________
Description ______________________________
Administrator ______________________________

Link to Primary Domain

Direct: UNC ______________________________
TCP/IP Address : Port ____________________ : __________
Indirect: via Domain: ______________________________
Gateway: ______________________________

MTA

TCP/IP Address : Port ____________________ : __________
Startup Filename ______________________________
/HOME- ______________________________
/User- ______________________________
/Password- ______________________________
Other switches ______________________________

ADA

Startup Filename ______________________________
/HOME- ______________________________
/User- ______________________________
/Password- ______________________________
Other switches ______________________________

Other GroupWise Components

GroupWise Access Account User Object

Distinguished Name ______________________________

Password ______________________________

R, W, C, E, F to Every Domain, Post Office, and Gateway Directory

Cleanup Options

Archive/Delete Mail and Phone Every _________ Days

Archive/Delete Appts., Tasks, and Notes Every _________ Days

Empty Trash Every _________ Days

External/Foreign Domain Planning Worksheet

External Domain Name ______________________________

Domain Type	External GroupWise	External Foreign
Database Version	4.X	5.X

Time Zone ______________________________
Description ______________________________

Link from Primary Domain

Direct: UNC \\ ______________________________
TCP/IP Address : Port ____________ : ____________
Indirect: via Domain: ______________________________
Gateway: ______________________________

External Post Office Information

Post Office Name ______________________________
External Domain ______________________________
Time Zone ______________________________
Description ______________________________

Distribution Lists

DISTRIBUTION LIST NAME	DOMAIN.PO	CONTEXT (OU.OU.O)	DESCRIPTION	MEMBERS

Resources

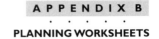

RESOURCE NAME	DOMAIN.PO	CONTEXT (OU.OU.O)	DESCRIPTION	OWNER

APPENDIX C

E-mail Policies

As you implement a GroupWise system, a solid e-mail policy will prevent problems that arise out of the misuse of the corporate messaging system. This appendix raises some of the issues associated with the use and administration of messaging systems.

Some of the issues you should consider are as follows:

Proprietary data. Companies should seriously consider making a statement or rule regarding the electronic sharing of proprietary data, including the penalties for violating such a rule.

Internet Material. One intriguing aspect of the Internet is the fact that it is unregulated and uncensored. Companies may wish to issue a statement regarding the use of the GroupWise system to transmit personal or offensive material.

E-mail Viruses. One of the most insidious activities in the world of computing is the generation of computer viruses. A new breed of viruses has surfaced, embedded into e-mail messages. Spread throughout the Internet, these viruses operate by playing macros (prerecorded programs) that harm recipients' machines.

The best defense GroupWise has against e-mail viruses is to disallow the automatic playing of macros in e-mail messages (see Chapter 7). You should set up the system to either prompt the recipient before playing a macro or completely disallow it.

Newsgroups. If a user subscribes to an Internet newsgroup, the information from the newsgroup can be viewed using a news viewer, such as Netscape Navigator. GroupWise cannot (at this point) receive news feeds.

If your news server has the ability to limit the newsgroups to which your users can subscribe, we recommend limiting news servers to business use only.

List Servers. List servers are global discussion groups based on a certain topic, such as GroupWise. Each subscriber to the list receives every message sent to the list. The number of messages these lists can generate can easily bog down your gateways and the GroupWise system. You can handle this in a couple of ways.

You can set up a mailbox to receive these messages in GroupWise, and create a rule that would forward all incoming messages to a shared folder for all interested users. The other option is to encourage subscribers to configure their list membership to receive the messages from the list in digest form. A list digest is one message containing a list of messages for that day, along with their message header information (sender, date, time, subject).

Archive Files. The archive files for GroupWise are very useful for managing the size of your message store (see Chapter 7). The problem with archive files is that they can be "hacked" by other GroupWise users because they are not stored in the post office. For example, if a user can access others' archive files, that user can copy and read those files, which may contain confidential information.

One way to avoid this security problem is to place the archive files in each user's "home" directory on the network, where no one but that user has rights.

Personal Messages. Messages that people send to one another are not always based on business topics. Your company needs to decide how it will handle offensive message content such as racial slurs, slander, accusations, and other negative communication.

Some companies choose to deal with this is in the same way they handle telephone communications. Basically, these companies tell their employees, "If you use company equipment for communication, you are liable for its content." Of course, there are First Amendment implications in all of this, but most people will adhere to a reasonable policy if it is communicated and enforced.

Encryption. GroupWise has its own built-in encryption because it is a closed, proprietary system. When you open communications up to the Internet, you lose this proprietary encryption. Therefore, we recommend using a product such as Pretty Good Privacy (PGP) for Internet messages.

The Electronic Messaging Association. The Electronic Messaging Association (`www.ema.org`) is an international association of vendors, consultants, and companies that base a large percentage of their business on e-mail communications. They are involved with setting standards and defining business requirements and solutions for e-mail communications. They also sponsor annual conferences where new products are displayed, and issues and solutions are addressed.

The association is a good resource for finding out how other companies handle issues related to e-mail policies. It is very likely that at least one member of the EMA has seen your particular problem and dealt with it. The EMA is not affiliated with any particular vendor.

APPENDIX D

Answers to Frequently Asked Questions

Administration

Why does GroupWise 5 require NetWare 4.1?

All GroupWise 5 administration is done in NetWare Administrator, and GroupWise information is stored in Novell Directory Services (NDS). GroupWise 5 does not have a stand-alone administration program.

When you install GroupWise 5, your NDS schema is extended to include new GroupWise objects. Existing NDS User objects also have additional GroupWise properties added to them.

Although GroupWise 5 requires one NetWare server, the domains and post offices can be located on other types of servers, such as Windows NT Server 4.0.

How well is GroupWise 5 integrated into a NetWare 3.x environment? What else is required?

GroupWise can run easily in a pure NetWare 3.x environment from the user's perspective. Messages will be located on the NetWare 3.x server. The administration of GroupWise must be done in NDS, using NetWare Administrator. Therefore, at least one NetWare 4.x server is required for GroupWise 5.

When I run NetWare Administrator, why do my GroupWise objects appear as question marks?

This indicates that either the GroupWise 5.1 snap-in component is not installed in NetWare Administrator or you are using an earlier version of NetWare Administrator that does not support GroupWise administration. This usually happens when you run NetWare Administrator from a computer that was not used for the installation of the GroupWise software.

To set up a Windows workstation NetWare Administrator to perform GroupWise 5 administration, run SETUPGW.EXE from the ADMIN directory on the CD-ROM or in the software directory you specified during installation.

What versions of NetWare Administrator are supported for GroupWise 5 administration?

The NetWare Administrator snap-in module for GroupWise 5 was written using the 16-bit NetWare Administrator snap-in architecture. Therefore, as of this writing, you can only use the 16-bit version of NetWare Administrator (NWADMN3X.EXE) to administer GroupWise 5.

(Three versions of NetWare Administrator currently run under Windows. The only version that can be used is NWADMN3X.EXE.)

NWADMN3X.EXE will run under Windows 95 and Windows NT. You should use Novell's Client32 for Windows 95 or Windows NT.

Support for 32-bit versions of NetWare Administrator is planned. Watch www.support.novell.com for further information about updated administration DLLs.

How do I determine which user is responsible for the largest amount of messages in my post office?

If you run Mailbox/Library Maintenance against the post office and set a box limit, the resulting log file will break out a separate listing for violators of the limit. The complete size (in both number and disk space) of each user's mailbox is listed also.

Should I run Novell Transaction Tracking System (TTS) on GroupWise 5 databases?

No. GroupWise databases have built-in transaction tracking and rollback.

Internet Issues

How does WebAccess work when a message in the In Box is a custom message, such as an electronic form?

The WebAccess gateway converts standard GroupWise message views into HTML documents. You can edit these HTML files and customize your own message forms to be displayed through the WebAccess gateway.

Our Internet user name convention is first.last@domain.com. How do I manage this in GroupWise?

Because the period is an invalid character for any GroupWise component, the Gateway Alias field for each user should be used to create the desired Internet mail name using the period (see Chapter 20), and a different GroupWise mailbox ID naming convention would need to be established.

Is Novell Web Server required to use the WebAccess gateway?

No, you can use any HTML page generator that is compatible with the WebAccess gateway. However, the Web Server is required for a single-server solution.

Windows NT

Which versions of Windows NT can run GroupWise?

The GroupWise 32-bit client will run on Microsoft Windows 95 or Windows NT 4.0. The GroupWise 16-bit client will run on Windows NT 3.51. Windows NT 3.51 does not fully support the APIs that the GroupWise 32-bit client needs to run successfully.

The GroupWise agents will run on Windows NT 3.51 or later.

Can GroupWise run on a Windows NT network without NetWare servers?

You must have at least one NetWare server (version 4.1 or later) running NDS for administration purposes. With that requirement met, GroupWise can function on Windows NT networks.

Client Issues

How does GroupWise 5.1 differ from GroupWise 5?

GroupWise 5.1 is functionally about the same as the original GroupWise 5 release. While some functional enhancements were made, the specific focus of the GroupWise 5.1 release was to improve overall performance, reliability, and scalability. The functional enhancements for GroupWise 5.1 include support for Lightweight Directory Access Protocol (LDAP) on the client, support for embedded URLs, and multiuser calendar printouts.

What is the significance of having LDAP support on the GroupWise 5.1 client?

LDAP is an industry-standard protocol for directory access. With the provided LDAP support, GroupWise users can look up user information via any LDAP-compliant directory service as easily as they can from their personal Address Books and the GroupWise system Address Book.

What is an embedded URL?

With the release of GroupWise 5, users were able to send World Wide Web uniform resource locators (URLs) to other GroupWise users. Now, with GroupWise 5.1, any URL included in the subject or message body of any GroupWise message is automatically detected and hyperlinked to the user's default browser. This allows the recipient of a message that references information on the WWW via an URL to immediately follow the reference to that information.

Where is the view designer in GroupWise 5?

The GroupWise 5 view designer is now part of the GroupWise 5 Software Developer's Kit (included on the accompanying CD-ROM).

In GroupWise 4.1, the View Designer shipped with the GroupWise 4.1 client for Windows.

When installing the 32-bit GroupWise client, why does it prompt me for the Windows 95 CD?

You will be prompted to insert the Windows 95 CD if the Windows 95 messaging system has not been installed.

GroupWise uses MAPI32 for several GroupWise Address Book components. MAPI32 is found on the Windows CD. If you have stored the Windows 95 *.CAB files somewhere on the network, you can enter the path in the dialog box that prompts you for the CD.

Users cannot proxy across post offices. What could be the problem?

If you are accessing your post office with Client/Server mode, and the target's post office agent (POA) has Client/Server enabled, you can proxy across post offices.

If the target of the proxy's POA does not have Client/Server access mode enabled, there will be no access to the target mailbox from other post offices.

If you access your post office with direct access and try to proxy a mailbox on another server, it *will* work if you have TCP/IP on your workstation and if the target's POA has Client/Server mode enabled, because it reads the IP address of the target POA from Novell Directory Services (NDS).

If both POAs are in Direct Only mode, you can only proxy users in the post office you are in.

What are some differences between GroupWise 4 and GroupWise 5 (16-bit and 32-bit?)

There are many new features in GroupWise 5. However, some existing GroupWise 4.1a features are not compatible with GroupWise 5 because they are either integrated with the product or they are no longer available. Table D.1 provides information on what to expect from certain features when migrating from GroupWise 4 to 5. It lists features that have experienced significant change as well as some of the new capabilities of GroupWise 5. It also shows some of the differences between the Windows 3.1 and Windows 95/NT clients for GroupWise 5.

TABLE D.1

Comparison of 16-Bit Clients and 32-Bit Clients

ITEM	GROUPWISE 5 16-BIT CLIENT	GROUPWISE 5 32-BIT CLIENT
Client/Server	Yes	Yes
Collabra Share	No	No, replaced by shared folders and document management
Conferencing	No	Yes
Conversation Place	No	Yes, where telephone system switch is TSAPI- or TAPI-compliant
Cross-PO Proxy	Yes, in client/server configuration	Yes, in client/server configuration
Custom Development via Object API	No	Yes
Custom Views	Yes, but some views created with the 4.1 view designer will have inverted graphics because of an SCC viewer bug	Yes, but some views created with the 4.1 view designer will have inverted graphics because of an SCC viewer bug
Document Management	No	Yes
InForms 4.1	Yes	No (Direct InForms integration for routing and custom message type has not been completed. Also, MAPI macro calls no longer function.)
Internet/URL integration	No	Yes
List Server	Yes, the GroupWise 5 user can participate in an existing ListServer group (However, the ListServer must be hosted by a GroupWise 4.1 client on a GroupWise 4.1 post office.)	Yes, the GroupWise 5 user can participate in an existing ListServer group (However, the ListServer must be hosted by a GroupWise 4.1 client on a GroupWise 4.1 post office. Also, replaced by shared folders and document management.)
New Universal Mailbox Interface	No, GroupWise 5 for Windows 3.1 has the same interface as GroupWise 4.1	Yes
Personal Groups	Yes, except those that contain external addresses	Yes, except those that contain external addresses

TABLE D.1

Comparison of 16-Bit Clients and 32-Bit Clients (continued)

ITEM	GROUPWISE 5 16-BIT CLIENT	GROUPWISE 5 32-BIT CLIENT
Personal Address Book	Yes; limited to supporting personal groups	Yes, full stand-alone MAPI Address Book application
QuickViewer	No	Yes
Remote Document Server	Yes, with limited functionality (Can process requests as a client, but not as a server. The RDS must be hosted by a GroupWise 4.1 client on a GroupWise 4.1 post office.)	Yes, with limited functionality (Can process requests as a client, but not as a server. The RDS must be hosted by a GroupWise 4.1 client on a GroupWise 4.1 post office. Also, replaced by shared folders and document management. Remote document servers can continue to function against SoftSolutions datasets.)
Resizable Views	Yes	Yes
Rules	Yes, but some will need to be recreated	Yes, but some will need to be recreated
Shared Folders	No	Yes
SoftSolutions	No (However, SoftSolutions 4.1 can still be run as a separate application.)	No (Document Management is integrated in GW5.)
Type-ahead addressing	No	Yes
WordPerfect Macros	Yes	No
Display name in address field	No	Yes

Where is the version information stored for the GroupWise client?

On the workstation, in the Registry, in HKEY_LOCAL_MACHINE\SOFTWARE\NOVELL\GROUPWISE, there is an entry called BuildNumber = 1100. In the software directory, a file called SOFTWARE\CLIENT\SOFTWARE.INF (SETUP.INF in previous versions of GroupWise 5) contains the Build Number 1100.

Can additions to the public Address Book be added to individual, private Address Books of users, without it needing to be done manually?

Yes, by creating an Address Book that the system administrator mails to users to import into their private Address Books.

What's next for GroupWise?

GroupWise will continue to be Novell's premier application for intranets and the Internet. In addition, Novell recently disclosed plans to provide a corporate solution for the creation and management of documents on the World Wide Web, as well as on corporate intranets. This technology, code-named the "Jefferson Project," will allow GroupWise users to leverage the full power of the Internet for sharing information, while providing the security, management, and administration features required to keep that information secure, up-to-date, and easily accessible.

GroupWise WorkFlow is in beta testing. A single product that supports the GroupWise 5.1 Windows 95/NT client, the GroupWise 5.1 Windows 3.1 client, and the GroupWise 4.1 Windows 3.1 client will soon be available.

The GroupWise Imaging client is in beta testing. It will also soon be added to the GroupWise 5 package.

Connectivity

What connectivity is available for sharing databases on other platforms via SQL or Microsoft Access databases, such as customer contact or vendor databases?

See the Additional GroupWise Technologies chapter for more information on the application development environment of GroupWise 5.

Can you get the same functionality in GroupWise by calling into a NetWare server across an analog line using NetWare Connect?

Absolutely. As long as the executable files are being launched on the remote computer, GroupWise supports IPX or TCP/IP connections to the mailbox on the server. If offline access is desired, GroupWise can be used in remote mode and a periodic update can utilize the NetWare connect session to update the remote mailbox.

Can you administer the entire GroupWise system from any domain or only from the primary domain?

As long as NetWare Administrator is connected to a GroupWise domain directory, the only additional requirement for administration is adequate NDS rights to the GroupWise objects. Most administrative activities create update messages for the ADA, and the GroupWise databases will be replicated automatically.

In addition, you can create post office-level administrators in much the same way.

APPENDIX E

Domain and Post Office Directories

This appendix describes the subdirectories and files in the domain and post office directories. Some of the directory names are specific to the example system we've referred to throughout the book, i.e., the ShickTools system. This is obvious where we've specified the name of the domain, post office, or gateway.

For additional information, see the online help information in NetWare Administrator.

Domain Directory SYS:SHICKPRI

GWDOM.DC	GroupWise 5 domain database template
GWPO.DC	GroupWise 5 post office database template
WPDOMAIN.DC	GroupWise 4 domain database template
WPHOST.DC	GroupWise 4 post office database template
WPDOMAIN.DB	Domain database
1120ADA.001	ADA log file for November 20
1120ADA.002	Second ADA log file for November 20
MSMONITR	Heartbeat file for primary/backup MTA
MTANAME	File for TCP/IP connections; same name as the domain
WPOFFICE	Directory for view files
NGWGUARD DC	Guardian database template file
OFVIEWS	GroupWise 4.1 Views platform directory
DOS	GroupWise 4.1 DOS client view files
WIN	GroupWise 4.1 Windows client view files
OFDOS40	GW 4.1 DOS client directory (for backward compatibility)
OFWIN40	GW 4.1 Windows client directory (for backward compatibility)
WPTOOLS	Directory for backward compatibility with GW 4.1
WPCS	Specified working directory for MTA
MSLOCAL	Default working directory for MTA
0218MTA.001	MTA log file for Feb. 18
0210IP.001	TCP/IP log file for Feb. 10

Directory	Description
MSHOLD	Holding queue directory
DOMAINMS	MTA internal processing directory
SAL907C	Sales post office holding directory
TVP8FDB	TVPO post office holding directory
SMT29C8	MTP gateway holding directory
SHI373A	SHICKSEC secondary domain holding directory
MCR7D28	MCROGUE external domain holding directory
MTACONV	Conversion directory for GroupWise 4.1 to 5
MSIBOUN	TCP/IP queue Directory
WPCSIN	MTA TCP/IP input queue directory
WPCSOUT	MTA TCP/IP output queue directory
TRANSMOD	Third-party transport modules directory
WPCSIN	MTA input queue for messages from other domains
0	Busy Search messages
1	Remote requests
2	High-priority messages; Administrative messages
3	High-priority status messages
4	Medium-priority messages
5	Medium-priority status messages
6	Low-priority messages
7	Low-priority status messages
WPGATE	Gateways directory
ASYNC	Async gateway directory
SMTP	SMTP gateway directory
WEBACCS	WebAccess gateway directory
WPCSOUT	MTA output queue for domain messages
PROBLEM	Corrupted messages
ADS	Input queue for ADA (domain)
CSS	MTA server queue for administrative messages
MTAALM	Address lookup directory
MTALOG	Directory for message logging databases

Post Office Directory SYS:TVPO

NGWGUARD.DC	Post office guardian database template
WPHOST.DB	Post office database
NGWGUARD.DB	Post office guardian database
MTANAME	File for TCP/IP connections; same name as the post office
WPCSIN	MTA input queue for messages leaving the post office
0	Busy Search messages
1	Remote requests
2	High-priority messages; Administrative messages
3	High-priority status messages
4	Medium-priority messages
5	Medium-priority status messages
6	Low-priority messages
7	Low-priority status messages
WPCSOUT	MTA output queue parent directory for messages entering the post office
OFS	MTA output queue for the POA
PROBLEM	Corrupted messages directory
ADS	MTA output queue for the ADA
CSS	Post office MTA queue for administrative messages
OFMSG	Message database directory
NGWDFR.DB	Deferred message database
MSG0.DB	Message database
MSG23.DB	Message database
MSG23.DBA	Backup message database created during a rebuild
OFUSER	User database directory
USER4O2.DB	User database (4O2 = FID)
USERM6K.DB	User database (M6K = FID)
PU020101.DB	"Prime" user database for folders shared from other post offices

USERM6K.DBA	Backup user database created during rebuild
OFWORK	GroupWise Remote parent working directory
OFDIRECT	GroupWise Remote request/response working directory
OFFILES	File attachments parent directory
FD0–FDF	GroupWise 4.X file attachments directories
FD0–FD7F	GroupWise 5.X file attachments directories
OFVIEWS	GroupWise 4.1 view files parent directory for incoming GroupWise 4.1 messages
DOS	GroupWise 4.1 DOS client view files directory
WIN	GroupWise 4.1 Windows client view files directory
GWDMS	GroupWise document management parent directory
DMSH.DB	GWDMS database
LIBxxxx	Library directory
DMDL*xxxx*.DB	Document activity logs
DMSD*xxxx*.DB	Library configuration information database
DMDD*xxxx*.DB	Document profile information
ARCHIVE	Document archive directory
DOCS	Document storage
MSLOCAL	Post office's MTA working directory
0210MTA.001	Post office's MTA log file for Feb. 10
0210IP.001	Post office's MTA IP log file for Feb. 10
MSHOLD	Post office's MTA holding directory
MSIBOUND	Holding directory for TCP/IP messages
TVP8FDB	Holding directory for messages to TVPO
SHI8FDA	Holding directory for messages to SHICKPRI domain
MSIBOUND	Post office's MTA TCP/IP transfer directory
WPCSIN	MTA TCP/IP input queue directory
WPCSOUT	MTA TCP/IP output queue directory
MTACONV	Post office's MTA conversion directory for GW4 to GW5 messages
TRANSMOD	Third-party transport modules directory
IP	Post office MTA TCP/IP working directory

Software Distribution Directory

Admin			Directory for enabling GroupWise administration
	SETUPGW.EXE		Program to set up additional administration workstations
Agents			
	INSTALL.EXE		Installation program for agents
	NLM		NLM agents
	NT		NT agents
PO			
	WPHOST.DC GW		4.1 post office database template
	NGWGUARD.DC		Template for GW5 guardian database
Domain			
	GWPO.DC		GroupWise 5 post office database template
	WPDOMAIN.DC		GroupWise 4.1 domain database template
	WPHOST.DC		GroupWise 4.1 post office database template
Client			
	UPDATE.EXE		Auto-update executable
	SOFTWARE.INF		Build number file
	Win32		GroupWise 32-bit client
		PPFORMS	GW5 calendar printing forms
	Win16		GroupWise 16-bit client
	OFVIEWS		
		WIN	GroupWise 5 Windows client view files
		MAC	GroupWise 5 Mac client view files

Miscellaneous Directories and Files

*.DBA	GroupWise database backup file
*.FBK	Guardian database backup file
*.RFL	Guardian database incremental roll-forward log
*.VEW	GroupWise view files
*.IDX	GroupWise index files for databases
*.BFP	Form description files
*.PRS	Print resource files
ROFDATA	GroupWise remote mailbox parent directory

APPENDIX F

What's on the CD-ROM?

The CD-ROM that accompanies this book contains the following components:

- GroupWise 5.1 Software Developer's Kit (SDK)
- GroupWise utilities and patches
- GroupWise 5.1 WebAccess gateway (beta)
- GroupWise white papers and technical documents

The software provided on the CD-ROM is not supported by Novell Technical Services. The GroupWise SDK and other Novell SDKs are available on the World Wide Web at `http://developer.novell.com`**.**

GroupWise 5.1 SDK

The GroupWise 5.1 SDK is not an installable program. Rather, it is a collection of resources for developers. The SDK is located on the CD-ROM in the GW5_SDK directory.

Of particular interest to GroupWise administrators is the GroupWise 5 View Designer utility. This utility is located in the GW5_SDK\VDESIGN directory.

GroupWise Utilities and Patches

The CD-ROM contains several GroupWise utilities, located in the UTILITY directory.

Novell Registry Editor

Follow these steps to install the Novell Registry Editor:

1. From a Windows 95 computer, click on Start.
2. Click on Run.

on Browse.

vse to the UTILITY directory on the CD-ROM.

uble-click on SETUPNRE.EXE.

llow the prompts.

Vise Support Center Utility

nese steps to install the GroupWise Support Center utility:

From a Windows 95 computer, click on Start.

Click on Run.

Click on Browse.

Browse to the UTILITY directory on the CD-ROM.

- Double-click on SETUPGSC.EXE
- Follow the prompts.

ne utility also runs in a Windows 3.1x environment.

MHS Mail Conversion Utility

The MHS Mail Conversion utility, MHSMCU.EXE, is a self-extracting zip file. ouble-click the file to unzip the files and use the utility. The last three self-xtracting executable files must be copied to a read-write directory before xecuting them.

MSMail Conversion Utility

The MSMail Conversion utility, MSMCU.EXE, is a self-extracting zip file. Double-click the file to unzip the files and use the utility.

SMTP/MIME 4.11 NLM Gateway Patch

The SMTP/MIME 4.11 NLM gateway patch, SMTP1.EXE, is a self-extracting zip file. Double-click the file to unzip the files and use the patch.

GroupWise 5.1 WebAccess Gateway (Beta)

The GroupWise 5.1 WebAccess gateway (beta) is contained in the WEBACCESS directory on the CD-ROM. This file, named WEB5B.EXE, is a self-extracting zip file that contains the gateway files and documentation.

GroupWise White Papers and Technical Documents

The TECHDOCS directory on the CD-ROM contains several white papers and technical documents relating to GroupWise. Most of these documents are in Microsoft Word for Windows 95 format (those that are not are self-extracting files). The documents are described in Table F.1.

TABLE F.1

Documents on CD-ROM

FILENAME	TITLE
PLANDMS.DOC	"Planning Your GroupWise 5 System with the Addition of GroupWise Document Management Services (DMS)"
DMSINDEX.DOC	"GroupWise 5 Library Indexing Process"
APP_INT.DOC	"Application Integrations"
GW51FACT.DOC	"GroupWise 5.1 Fact Sheet"
GW51BACK.DOC	"GroupWise Background Information"
X400GATE.DOC	"Tech Brief: X.400 Gateway"
X25GATE.DOC	"Instant Expert Guide: X.25 Gateway"
AS400DS.DOC	"Tech Tip: AS/400 Directory Shadowing"
SNADS.DOC	"Tech Brief: SNADS Gateway"
OVVMGATE.DOC	"Tech Brief: Office Vision —VM Gateway"

TABLE F.1
Documents on CD-ROM (continued)

FILENAME	TITLE
NOTES.DOC	"Tech Brief: Notes Gateway"
MHS.DOC	"Tech Brief: MHS Gateway"
CCMAIL.DOC	"Tech Brief: cc:Mail Gateway"
FAXPRINT.DOC	"Tech Brief: FAX/Print Gateway"
PAGER.DOC	"Tech Brief: Pager Gateway"
TAS.DOC	"Tech Brief: Telephone Access Server"
API.DOC	"Tech Brief: API Gateway"
IMAGING.DOC	"Fact Sheet — GroupWise Imaging"
SMTPGATE.DOC	"Tech Brief: SMTP Gateway"
PACONFIG.DOC	"Phone Access Configuration Guide"
WEBPAPER.DOC	"GroupWise WebAccess Position Paper"
WEB51FAC.DOC	"GroupWise WebAccess 5.1 Fact Sheet"
WEBACCESS.DOC	"GroupWise WebAccess"
JAVANEW.DOC	"Java-Enabled WebAccess"
GWDMS.DOC	"GroupWise DMS Press Release"
CPLACE.DOC	Technical Paper on Conversation Place
DIGIBD.DOC	"Tech Brief: Working with DigiBoards"
NGWIE.EXE	Novell GroupWise Instant Expert Guides (self-extracting to Envoy runtime)
NGOUSSMT.EXE	SMTP/MIME Envoy Documentation (self-extracting to Envoy runtime)
GWGATE.EXE	Novell GroupWise Gateways Professional Guides (self-extracting)
MIGRATE.EXE	Migration from Other E-Mail Systems Guide (self-extracting to Envoy runtime)

Index

(continued)

(continued)

E

(continued)

(continued)

N

(continued)

(continued)

(continued)

Q

R

S

T

IDG BOOKS WORLDWIDE
END-USER LICENSE AGREEMENT

READ THIS. You should carefully read these terms and conditions before opening the software packet(s) included with this book ("Book"). This is a license agreement ("Agreement") between you and IDG Books Worldwide, Inc. ("IDGB"). By opening the accompanying software packet(s), you acknowledge that you have read and accept the following terms and conditions. If you do not agree and do not want to be bound by such terms and conditions, promptly return the Book and the unopened software packet(s) to the place you obtained them for a full refund.

1. **License Grant.** IDGB grants to you (either an individual or entity) a nonexclusive license to use one copy of the enclosed software program(s) (collectively, the "Software") solely for your own personal or business purposes on a single computer (whether a standard computer or a workstation component of a multiuser network). The Software is in use on a computer when it is loaded into temporary memory (RAM) or installed into permanent memory (hard disk, CD-ROM, or other storage device). IDGB reserves all rights not expressly granted herein.

2. **Ownership.** IDGB is the owner of all right, title, and interest, including copyright, in and to the compilation of the Software recorded on the disk(s) or CD-ROM ("Software Media"). Copyright to the individual programs recorded on the Software Media is owned by the author or other authorized copyright owner of each program. Ownership of the Software and all proprietary rights relating thereto remain with IDGB and its licensers.

3. **Restrictions On Use and Transfer.**

   (a) You may only (i) make one copy of the Software for backup or archival purposes, or (ii) transfer the Software to a single hard disk, provided that you keep the original for backup or archival purposes. You may not (i) rent or lease the Software, (ii) copy or reproduce the Software through a LAN or other network system or through any computer subscriber system or bulletin-board system, or (iii) modify, adapt, or create derivative works based on the Software.

   (b) You may not reverse engineer, decompile, or disassemble the Software. You may transfer the Software and user documentation on a permanent basis, provided that the transferee agrees to accept the terms and conditions of this Agreement and you retain no copies. If the Software is an update or has been updated, any transfer must include the most recent update and all prior versions.

4. **Restrictions On Use of Individual Programs.** You must follow the individual requirements and restrictions detailed for each individual program in Appendix F, "What's on the CD-ROM?" of this Book. These limitations are also contained in the individual license agreements recorded on the Software Media. These limitations may include a requirement that after using the program for a specified period of time, the user must pay a registration fee or discontinue use. By opening the Software packet(s), you will be agreeing to abide by the licenses and restrictions for these individual programs that are detailed in Appendix F and on the Software Media. None of the material on this Software Media or listed in this Book may ever be redistributed, in original or modified form, for commercial purposes.

5. **Limited Warranty.**

   (a) IDGB warrants that the Software and Software Media are free from defects in materials and workmanship under normal use for a period of sixty (60) days from the date of purchase of this Book. If IDGB receives notification within the warranty period of defects in materials or workmanship, IDGB will replace the defective Software Media.

   (b) **IDGB AND THE AUTHORS OF THE BOOK DISCLAIM ALL OTHER WARRANTIES, EXPRESS OR IMPLIED, INCLUDING WITHOUT LIMITATION IMPLIED WARRANTIES OF MERCHANTABILITY AND FITNESS FOR A PARTICULAR PURPOSE, WITH RESPECT TO THE SOFTWARE, THE PROGRAMS, THE SOURCE CODE CONTAINED THEREIN, AND/OR THE TECHNIQUES DESCRIBED IN THIS BOOK. IDGB DOES NOT WARRANT THAT THE FUNCTIONS CONTAINED IN THE SOFTWARE WILL MEET YOUR REQUIREMENTS OR THAT THE OPERATION OF THE SOFTWARE WILL BE ERROR FREE.**

   (c) This limited warranty gives you specific legal rights, and you may have other rights that vary from jurisdiction to jurisdiction.

6. **Remedies.**

   (a) IDGB's entire liability and your exclusive remedy for defects in materials and workmanship shall be limited to replacement of the Software Media, which may be returned to IDGB with a copy of your receipt at the following address: Software Media Fulfillment Department, Attn.: *Novell's GroupWise 5 Administrator's Guide*, IDG Books Worldwide, Inc., 7260 Shadeland Station, Ste. 100, Indianapolis, IN 46256, or call 1-800-762-2974. Please allow three to four weeks for delivery. This Limited Warranty is void if failure of the Software Media has resulted from accident, abuse, or misapplication. Any replacement Software Media will be warranted for the remainder of the original warranty period or thirty (30) days, whichever is longer.

   (b) In no event shall IDGB or the authors be liable for any damages whatsoever (including without limitation damages for loss of business profits, business interruption, loss of business information, or any other pecuniary loss) arising from the use of or inability to use the Book or the Software, even if IDGB has been advised of the possibility of such damages.

   (c) Because some jurisdictions do not allow the exclusion or limitation of liability for consequential or incidental damages, the above limitation or exclusion may not apply to you.

7. **U.S. Government Restricted Rights.** Use, duplication, or disclosure of the Software by the U.S. Government is subject to restrictions stated in paragraph (c)(1)(ii) of the Rights in Technical Data and Computer Software clause of DFARS 252.227-7013, and in subparagraphs (a) through (d) of the Commercial Computer—Restricted Rights clause at FAR 52.227-19, and in similar clauses in the NASA FAR supplement, when applicable.

8. **General.** This Agreement constitutes the entire understanding of the parties and revokes and supersedes all prior agreements, oral or written, between them and may not be modified or amended except in a writing signed by both parties hereto that specifically refers to this Agreement. This Agreement shall take precedence over any other documents that may be in conflict herewith. If any one or more provisions contained in this Agreement are held by any court or tribunal to be invalid, illegal, or otherwise unenforceable, each and every other provision shall remain in full force and effect.

CD-ROM Installation Instructions

Insert the *Novell's GroupWise 5 Administrator's Guide* CD-ROM into a CD-ROM drive, such as drive D.

1 • In Windows 95, click on Start.

2 • Click on Run.

3 • Click on Browse.

4 • Browse to the CD-ROM root directory; for example, D:\.

5 • Double-click on the file README.TXT (or see Appendix F of this book) for complete instructions on how to use each of the components on the CD-ROM.

IDG BOOKS WORLDWIDE REGISTRATION CARD

RETURN THIS REGISTRATION CARD FOR FREE CATALOG

Title of this book: **Novell's Groupwise™ 5 Administrator Guide**

My overall rating of this book: ❑ Very good [1] ❑ Good [2] ❑ Satisfactory [3] ❑ Fair [4] ❑ Poor [5]

How I first heard about this book:

❑ Found in bookstore; name: [6] ❑ Book review: [7]

❑ Advertisement: [8] ❑ Catalog: [9]

❑ Word of mouth; heard about book from friend, co-worker, etc.: [10] ❑ Other: [11]

What I liked most about this book:

What I would change, add, delete, etc., in future editions of this book:

Other comments:

Number of computer books I purchase in a year: ❑ 1 [12] ❑ 2-5 [13] ❑ 6-10 [14] ❑ More than 10 [15]

I would characterize my computer skills as: ❑ Beginner [16] ❑ Intermediate [17] ❑ Advanced [18] ❑ Professional [19]

I use ❑ DOS [20] ❑ Windows [21] ❑ OS/2 [22] ❑ Unix [23] ❑ Macintosh [24] ❑ Other: [25]________________ (please specify)

I would be interested in new books on the following subjects:
(please check all that apply, and use the spaces provided to identify specific software)

❑ Word processing: [26] ❑ Spreadsheets: [27]

❑ Data bases: [28] ❑ Desktop publishing: [29]

❑ File Utilities: [30] ❑ Money management: [31]

❑ Networking: [32] ❑ Programming languages: [33]

❑ Other: [34]

I use a PC at (please check all that apply): ❑ home [35] ❑ work [36] ❑ school [37] ❑ other: [38] ________________

The disks I prefer to use are ❑ 5.25 [39] ❑ 3.5 [40] ❑ other: [41]________________

I have a CD ROM: ❑ yes [42] ❑ no [43]

I plan to buy or upgrade computer hardware this year: ❑ yes [44] ❑ no [45]

I plan to buy or upgrade computer software this year: ❑ yes [46] ❑ no [47]

Name: Business title: [48] Type of Business: [49]

Address (❑ home [50] ❑ work [51]/Company name:)

Street/Suite#

City [52]/State [53]/Zipcode [54]: Country [55]

❑ **I liked this book!** You may quote me by name in future IDG Books Worldwide promotional materials.

My daytime phone number is ________________

IDG BOOKS

THE WORLD OF COMPUTER KNOWLEDGE

YES!

Please keep me informed about IDG's World of Computer Knowledge. Send me the latest IDG Books catalog.

NO POSTAGE NECESSARY IF MAILED IN THE UNITED STATES

BUSINESS REPLY MAIL

FIRST CLASS MAIL PERMIT NO. 2605 FOSTER CITY, CALIFORNIA

IDG Books Worldwide
919 E Hillsdale Blvd, STE 400
Foster City, CA 94404-9691